Successful Nonverbal Communication

FOURTH EDITION

Successful Nonverbal Communication

Principles and Applications

Dale Leathers
Late of University of Georgia

Michael H. Eaves
Valdosta State University

Boston   New York   San Francisco
Mexico City   Montreal   Toronto   London   Madrid   Munich   Paris
Hong Kong   Singapore   Tokyo   Cape Town   Sydney

Series Editor: *Jeanne Zalesky*
Editorial Assistant: *Brian Mickelson*
Associate Development Editor: *Jenny Lupica*
Marketing Manager: *Suzan Czajkowski*
Senior Production Administrator: *Donna Simons*
Cover Administrator and Designer: *Joel Gendron*
Composition Buyer: *Linda Cox*
Manufacturing Buyer: *JoAnne Sweeney*
Editorial Production Service and Electronic Composition: *Elm Street Publishing Services*

For related titles and support materials, visit our online catalog at www.ablongman.com.

Between the time website information is gathered and then published, it is not unusual for some sites to have closed. Also, the transcription of URLs can result in typographical errors. The publisher would appreciate notification where these errors occur so that they may be corrected in subsequent editions.

Library of Congress Cataloging-in-Publication Data

Leathers, Dale G.
   Successful nonverbal communication: principles and applications / Dale
G. Leathers, Michael H. Eaves.—4th ed.
      p. cm.
   Includes bibliographical references and index.
   ISBN 978-0-205-61742-5 (alk. paper)
   1. Body language.   I. Eaves, Michael H. (Michael Howard), 1964–   II. Title.

   BF637.N66L43 2008
   153.6'9—dc22

                                                    2007037415

ISBN-13: 978-0-205-61742-5   ISBN-10: 0-205-61742-5

Photo Credits: p. 188: Michael Stravato/New York Times Agency; p. 192: Michael Nagle/New York Times Agency; p. 219: Doug Mills/New York Times Agency; p. 221: James Estrin/New York Times Agency; p. 226: Barton Silverman/New York Times Agency; p. 268: Patrick Watson/Pearson Education/PH College; p. 269: Larry Downing/Reuters/Corbis; p. 340: Corbis

Printed in the United States of America

10   9   8   7   6   5   4   3   2   1   RRD-VA   11   10   09   08   07

CONTENTS

PREFACE

The fourth edition of *Successful Nonverbal Communication: Principles and Applications* results from conversations with students and instructors who have described in detail the kind of book they would like to see written for introductory nonverbal communication. The success of the first three editions reinforced our conviction that there is a need for a book that directly responds to their concerns. The fourth edition has been substantially updated with new research and examples for students in the twenty-first century.

Serious students of nonverbal communication have long recognized that knowledge of the subject gives them the potential to become more effective communicators. However, most existing books on the topic focus exclusively on the *nature* of nonverbal communication. They describe and classify different types of nonverbal messages without demonstrating how knowledge of the informational potential of nonverbal cues can be used to communicate successfully in the real world. Continuing in the tradition of the first three editions, this fourth edition is designed specifically to meet that central need.

As with the earlier editions, we have endeavored to present the current research, theory, and terms of nonverbal communication in a style that introductory students can easily understand and even enjoy. We have used stories, quips, personal experiences, and quotes that both balance the technical material and translate it into simple and direct language. Many new photos have been added to this edition.

This fourth edition contains new material that students should find particularly useful. For example, Chapter 6, "Tactile Communication," contains expanded coverage of the functions of touch in the development of both romantic and sexual relationships. Similarly, Chapter 7, "Personal Appearance," includes the impact of physical attractiveness on the self-concept of adolescents, a treatment of contrasting views of physical attractiveness and its psychological consequences, and a section on cosmetics as a medium of communication. Chapter 9 is a combination of the previous edition's chapters on Impression Formation and Impression Management. Finally, Chapter 10, "Selling Yourself Nonverbally," contains a detailed analysis of the impact of nonverbal communication on the credibility of political debates in modern contexts. Several debates are examined: the 2004 Bush–Kerry presidential debates; the 2004 Cheney–Edwards vice presidential debate; the 2006 Hillary Clinton–Spencer New York senatorial debate; the 2004 Keyes–Obama Illinois senatorial debates; and the 2006 Purdue–Hayes–Taylor Georgia governor debate.

Chapter 5, "Proxemic Communication," has greatly expanded coverage of the concept of crowding and its communicative implications. Chapter 12, "Nonverbal Determinants of Successful Interviews," covers the interrelationship of preinterview impressions and first impressions on success in the job interview. Chapter 14, "Successful Intercultural Communication," addresses the subtle question of how individuals fine-tune their nonverbal communication style in order to be as effective as possible in intercultural contexts. Additionally, this revised chapter expands the notion of chronemics, or the study of time, and includes a new section on olfactics, or the study of odor.

New to the fourth edition, Chapter 15, "Special Nonverbal Contexts," includes an expanded discussion of medical places, the courtroom, built environments including nonverbal communication in restaurants, and a brand-new section on virtual places (such as nonverbal elements in computer-mediated communication, e-mail, Web pages, etc.).

The subtitle of this book, *Principles and Applications,* reflects our conviction that knowledge *about* nonverbal communication is not enough. We must also know *how to use* that knowledge to communicate successfully in applied settings. Thus, Part Three, "Successful Communication in Applied Settings," treats the subject of how to communicate nonverbally in important, real-world contexts in unprecedented depth and detail. Each of the chapters in this part—"Nonverbal Determinants of Successful Interviews," "Female–Male Interaction," "Successful Intercultural Communication," and "Special Nonverbal Contexts"—focuses on how to apply knowledge of nonverbal communication.

The fourth edition fully explores the central role that nonverbal cues frequently play in areas such as relational communication, shaping interpersonal perceptions, personal selling, and the development of a positive self-concept. Because of this focus, the book can be particularly valuable as one of the required textbooks in introductory courses on subjects such as interpersonal communication, personal selling, and business communication. The first three editions were widely adopted by every type of educational institution: public and private research universities, four-year colleges, junior colleges, and community colleges. The fourth edition was designed to appeal to the same broad spectrum.

We would like to thank the following reviewers who have made many useful comments and suggestions: Kathleen Czech, Point Loma Nazarene University; Donald B. Egolf, University of Pittsburgh; Kory Floyd, Arizona State University; Trudy L. Hanson, West Texas A&M University; Narissra Maria Punyanunt-Carter, Texas Tech University; George B. Ray, Cleveland State University; Daniel Schabot, William Carey College; Don W. Stacks, University of Miami; Jason Teven, California State University, Fullerton; and Mei Zhong, San Diego State University.

The *Instructor's Manual* that accompanies this textbook has been designed to maximize the textbook's value to instructors and their students. It features detailed directions for using the textbook for both semester and quarter courses. In-class and out-of-class exercises can be used to explore the theoretical and practical implications of the concepts discussed in the book. The *Instructor's Manual* also includes detailed sets of objective test items on each chapter that have been pretested on students taking the course. It also presents both long- and short-answer essay questions as well as chapter summaries with sets of key terms that are useful in reviewing for examinations.

Since the publication of the third edition in 1997, Dale Leathers has passed away. I felt that it was necessary to extend the work that Dale started and to push his vision past his untimely demise. As his student at the University of Georgia, I developed a passion for nonverbal communication. Later, Dale and I published our article "Context as Communication: McDonald's versus Burger King." In 2003, I did a follow-up to the original study, including two new restaurants, and found interesting results that are reported in the final chapter. Today, I am constantly looking for new nonverbal places that Dale had mentioned to me. This book is dedicated to Dale's legacy.

MHE

Successful Nonverbal Communication

PART ONE

Nonverbal Communication

1 The Nature of Nonverbal Communication

Human interaction is a quest for meaning. We look anxiously to others to determine whether we have communicated our intended meaning. We are concerned that we may have communicated unintended meanings that will negatively affect the image we wish to project. If we are skilled in the art of impression management, we may cultivate a certain look or sound that is designed to control the judgments that people make about us. Politicians in the 2008 presidential campaign turned to nonverbal consultants to make sure they have a positive voice and use of gestures in their speeches. Duke lacrosse players in their court battle maintained a conservatively dressed image to counter the serious nature of the charges filed against them. Oftentimes, George W. Bush has been seen on his Texas ranch wearing a cowboy hat to help him better seem to relate to common people.

The individuals with whom we communicate are also on guard. They look apprehensively at us to judge whether they have accurately perceived our intentions. Do our communicative behaviors accurately reflect our inner feelings, or do they represent a carefully controlled presentation of self? The quest for meaning often produces, or results in, anxiety, apprehension, and uncertainty. This is because interpersonal communication is so complex.

The ways we communicate meanings are varied, and the sources of error in interpersonal communication are multiple. A single error may make us uncomfortable in an important situation. Multiple errors may be catastrophic.

Consider the following situations. You and a female friend are at a fraternity party on your first date. As the evening progresses and the second keg of beer is tapped, you notice that your date's hand is resting lightly on your arm; you can detect a strong and rather rapid pulse. You make your judgments as to what your date is communicating to you. Later, you fidget on the doorsteps of the sorority house. Suddenly, you lean forward to kiss your date, but she turns her face away from you, recoils, and walks briskly into the sorority house. You are left alone to ponder the complexities of the evening's communication situation.

Four years later, you are about to be interviewed by the head of a major advertising firm. The job interview is vitally important to you. You realize that you must communicate effectively if you are to get the job offer. As you enter the interview room, you introduce yourself to the advertising executive and she offers you a seat on the other side of a small table. You feel that it is important to sustain eye contact, and you attempt to do so. The executive often looks away from you as she speaks, however. She frequently leans far back in her chair. You think you are doing well. As the interview concludes, you cannot help but notice that the advertising executive has her chin tilted up into the air and is looking down at you over her glasses. While looking at you, she remarks that she has found your résumé to be most unusual. You are then left alone to ponder the complexities of the afternoon's communication situation.

You could interpret these two situations in a number of different ways. Your goal is to determine what meanings you communicated and what meanings were communicated to you. To achieve such a goal you must recognize at least two facts. First, great differences often exist between what you think you communicated and what the other person actually perceived. Second, meanings may be communicated through a great variety of channels.

You may have interpreted your date's hand on your arm as an invitation to more intimate behavior later in the evening; the quickened pulse may have suggested a certain amount of arousal. Your date's perception of the situation may have been quite different. The hand on your arm could have been a sympathetic response to your nervous mannerisms. The quickened pulse may have been triggered by your date's apprehension as to what actions you would take on the dormitory steps. You needed more information and more time before attempting a thorough analysis of this situation.

The job interview is also difficult to interpret. You have more facts at your disposal, however. You wisely focused on important factors in this situation. You should not be disturbed by the fact that the interviewer looked away from you as she spoke; this is characteristic eye behavior in an interview situation. You should, however, be concerned about the interviewer's tendency to lean far back in the chair. Body lean is the best indicator of an individual's involvement in a situation. Your biggest problem is the ambiguous message your interviewer conveyed to you (her chin was perceptibly tilted in the air as she said, "I find your résumé to be most unusual"). The verbal and nonverbal cues convey conflicting meanings. Unhappily for you, the nonverbal cue—the upraised chin, in this case—is apt to be a much more accurate indicator of your interviewer's true feelings than the verbal cue.

Both situations emphasize what society has been slow to recognize: human beings do not communicate by words alone. Individuals have many sensory mechanisms that play a vital role in interpersonal communication. Undeniably, we speak and hear, but we also move, touch, and feel. As communicators, we have a multidimensional capacity.

Some publications have drawn attention to nonverbal communication. Books such as *New Dress for Success* by John T. Molloy (1988), *Here Comes Everybody* by William Schutz (1971), and *Body Language* by Julius Fast (1970) have served a useful purpose. Yet, some of them may have had some undesirable side effects. They may have helped to create the misleading notion that knowledge of nonverbal communication is chiefly useful to investigate and invigorate a communicator's sex life.

The functional importance of nonverbal communication is hardly limited to the semantics of sex. LaFrance and Mayo (1978) documented that nonverbal cues serve a wide variety of valuable functions in the development of social relationships. The determinants of successful communication in real-world contexts are frequently nonverbal. To disregard the functions served by nonverbal cues is to invite unflattering characterization as an insensitive and inept communicator.

Most of us spend a great deal of time attempting to persuade others, to be liked or loved by others, to control others, and to enhance our own self-image. Whatever our communicative goal, the nonverbal channels of communication frequently function very effectively to help us attain that goal. To persuade others, for example, you must usually convince them of your honesty, sincerity, and trustworthiness. Think back to the last congressional hearing you observed on television. Did you think the witness was honest, sincere, and trustworthy on the basis of what the person said, or on the basis of the witness's nonverbal behavior?

Consider your attempts to develop an intimate relationship with another person. Did you assess the level of intimacy of the relationship primarily on the basis of the words that were spoken, or on the basis of the implicit messages communicated by nonverbal cues? Did you attempt to communicate your own feelings primarily by words or by nonverbal cues?

In addition, think about those instances of face-to-face interaction when you tried to control the communicative behavior of another person. Among the primary means of control at your disposal were your gestures, your posture, and the way you used the small space that separated you.

Finally, ponder the great amount of time you spend trying to attain or to retain a positive self-image. To a very large degree, your self-image and social identity are shaped by your personal appearance. This image is controlled to a striking extent by nonverbal factors unrelated to the content of your speech.

The Functional Importance of Nonverbal Communication

When we write of the functional significance of nonverbal communication, the obvious question is what do we mean by *functional?* The answer is complex. Basically, the function of communication is the creation of meaning. The functional significance of nonverbal communication, therefore, is related to: (a) the *purposes* for which meanings are communicated (information, persuasion, and so on); (b) the *accuracy* with which meanings are communicated (facial communication has more potential than tactile communication, for example); and (c) the *efficiency* with which meanings are communicated (the time and effort required for the communication of meanings). In the next section of this chapter we will address the complex task of defining nonverbal communication.

Viewed from any of these perspectives, nonverbal communication has great functional significance in our society. In a great variety of situations, communicators can more easily achieve their communicative purpose by improving the accuracy and efficiency of their nonverbal communication.

More specifically, nonverbal communication has great functional significance for six major reasons. First, nonverbal, not verbal, factors are the major determinants of meaning in the interpersonal context. Birdwhistell (1970) asserted that "probably no more than 30 to 35 percent of the social meaning of a conversation or an interaction is carried by the words" (p. 158). Mehrabian (1968) went even further, estimating that 93 percent of the total impact of a message is the result of nonverbal factors. Although Mehrabian's estimate has been criticized not only on methodological grounds but also because of the obvious implausibility of the estimate, Birdwhistell's estimate has been supported by other nonverbal researchers. Thus, Philpott (1983) concluded, after doing a statistical analysis of 23 studies, that slightly over two-thirds of communicated meaning can be attributed to nonverbal messages.

Children, Army recruits, and dating couples often find themselves in communication situations that are similar in one respect: They must quickly and accurately determine the meanings of messages being transmitted to them. They typically rely on tone of voice, facial expression, and bodily movement to accomplish this purpose. Children soon learn that the tone and intensity of a parent's voice are their best guide to action. Army recruits do not determine the priority of directives from their drill sergeant by analyzing the manifest verbal content of those directives. They focus on the sense of physical involvement the sergeant conveys to them nonverbally through the notoriously rough and tough voice. When your boyfriend or girlfriend says no to your most artful advances, you do not stop and apply the semantic differential to the verbal response in order to measure his or her meaning. You rely on facial and bodily expressions as the primary determinants of intent.

Second, feelings and emotions are more accurately revealed by nonverbal than verbal means. Davitz (1969) has conducted an impressively detailed set of studies on emotional expression. He concludes that "it is the nonverbal, of the formal characteristics of one's environment . . . that primarily determine the emotional meaning of one's world" (p. 201). Expressions like "keep your chin up," "down in the mouth," and "walking on air" are much more than empty figures of speech. They have emotional referents that are rich in meaning and communicative significance. A recent study confirms Davitz's findings, but adds a new element. Sternglanz and DePaulo (2004) found that close friends were able to recognize nonverbal expressions of emotion, but had more trouble when it came to "concealed" sadness or anger. These studies both point to evidence that nonverbal cues are relied upon when making judgments about our friends' emotional states.

The rapid development of sensitivity training, encounter sessions, psychiatric services, and, more recently, sexual therapy clinics is eloquent testimony to society's need to understand which emotions are communicated, how they are communicated, and how they are received. Because there are very few emotion-laden behaviors that universally take the same form, our need to understand variability in emotional expression is evident.

Significantly, we now know not only that nonverbal communication is our richest source of knowledge about emotional states but also that nonverbal cues are reliable and stable indicators of the emotion that is being conveyed or received. Specifically, we now know that nonverbal communication can provide us with the following information about emotions: (a) how sensitive communicators are to emotional expressions, measured in terms of accuracy of identification; (b) the kinds of emotional expressions that can be correctly identified; (c) the specific nature of incorrect identification of emotions; and (d) the degree to which communicators attend to the emotional meaning of a total communication (Leathers & Emigh, 1980). Rothman and Nowicki (2004) found that children's emotions are often revealed in their vocal tones. Using the Diagnostic Analysis of Nonverbal Accuracy Child Paralanguage (DANVA2-CP), they found that the instrument was an effective tool for coding emotions in elementary-school-age children. The study found, further, that with increased age of the child, coders are able to decode those vocal cues of emotion with greater accuracy.

We know too that our "emotional memories" are largely nonverbal in nature. Researchers (Westman & Wautier, 1994; Westman & Westman, 1993) have found that 74 percent of our first memories are nonverbal while only 45 percent have been talked about; 92 percent of these first memories in turn involve an emotional event. Furthermore, results from this recent research challenge the popular misconception that individuals must verbalize their memories in order to retrieve them. Thompson, Aidinejad, and Ponte (2001) found similar results. In their investigation, facial cues and memories of faces were important in memory reconstructions of past events. A good example of this is "I do not recall their name, but I never forget a face."

Third, the nonverbal portion of communication conveys meanings and intentions that are relatively free of deception and distortion. Although verbal messages are frequently used with a high level of consciousness and intent (Newton & Burgoon, 1990), nonverbal cues such as gestures are rarely under the sustained, conscious control of the communicator. For this reason, communicators can rarely use nonverbal communication effectively for the purpose of dissembling. In contrast, the verbal dimension of communication seems to obfuscate the communicator's true intentions much more frequently.

In an age that places a high priority on trust, honesty, and candor in interpersonal relationships, nonverbal communication takes on added importance. Interpersonal relationships are built by using the most effective kinds of communication at our disposal. These are primarily nonverbal. Not only do nonverbal cues usually convey a communicator's real meaning and intent, but they also suggest, rather precisely, what the communicator thinks of us.

Even such nonverbal cues as gesture, posture, and facial expression may, of course, be under the conscious control of the communicator. For all but the consummate actor—and possibly the notorious used-car salesperson—such conscious control is a temporary phenomenon. In most cases, nonverbal cues are not consciously controlled for so long a period of time as verbal cues, nor do they serve as frequently to transmit deception, distortion, and confusion. Although nonverbal cues may be used to deceive, they are more likely to reveal deception than to conceal it.

Fourth, nonverbal cues serve a metacommunicative function that is indispensable in attaining high-quality communication. Often the communicator provides additional cues that clarify the intent and meaning of his or her message. Verbal expressions such as "now, seriously speaking" and "I'm only kidding" are metacommunicative. A comforting hand on the shoulder or a radiant smile may represent nonverbal ways of performing the same function. Although both verbal and nonverbal cues can function metacommunicatively, nonverbal cues seem to take precedence in the mind of the person receiving the message (Capella & Palmer, 1989).

But what does this mean? How do we know that nonverbal cues are so important metacommunicatively? Leathers designed an experiment to answer those specific questions. One hundred subjects were exposed to a set of messages in which the words conveyed one meaning and the facial expressions of the "planted" communicators conveyed a conflicting meaning.

Imagine yourself in a small group faced with the following situation: One of the discussants responds to a remark you have just made. As he responds, he scratches his head vigorously and gets a very confused expression on his face. Looking utterly confused, he says to you, "Yes, I understand. What you just said seems completely clear to me."

You are faced with a decision. To resolve the seeming contradiction in meaning, you must rely on either the verbal cues (words) or the nonverbal cues (facial expression). In the laboratory situation, the subject almost invariably relied on the facial expression as the true indicator of the communicator's meaning (Leathers, 1979a).

When the verbal and nonverbal portions of a message reinforce each other by conveying the same basic meaning, the metacommunicative value of the two types of cues is relatively unimportant. In contrast, when the verbal and nonverbal cues in a message convey conflicting meanings, the metacommunicative value of these cues becomes of primary importance. At that point the communicator, much like the subjects in the experiment, is faced with a serious problem. Should verbal or nonverbal cues be used to determine the meaning and intent of the message? In effect, the communicator must decide which type of cue has greatest metacommunicative value. Typically, people who face such a decision rely on nonverbal rather than verbal cues.

Mehrabian (1981) indicated that individuals employ a systematic and consistent approach to determine the meaning of conflicting cues. The impact of facial expression is of primary importance, tone of voice (or vocal expression) is next in importance, and words are the least important. In short, facial expressions have the greatest metacommunicative value. Words have the least value.

We can safely conclude, therefore, that nonverbal cues serve the primary metacommunicative function in interpersonal communication. Because the metacommunicative function is a crucial determinant of high-quality communication, the proper decoding of nonverbal cues is one of the most important factors in attaining high-quality communication (Leathers, 1972).

Fifth, nonverbal cues represent a much more efficient means of communicating than verbal cues. Time is a vital commodity in many communication situations. Corporations willingly pay communication consultants handsome fees to improve the communicative efficiency of their executives. These executives want to know how to communicate more—in less time.

This goal is not easily achieved in our highly verbal culture. Verbal discourse is by its nature a highly inefficient means of communication. Redundancy, repetition, ambiguity, and abstraction have become standard qualities of verbal discourse in the United States. Although their use is sometimes necessary, these qualities help to make communication inefficient.

Do qualities such as repetition and ambiguity represent inherent liabilities of verbal discourse, or do they simply reflect the ineptitude of the individual communicator? That question is probably debatable, but solid evidence indicates that verbal communication is intrinsically more inefficient than nonverbal communication. Reusch and Kees (1956) wrote that

> in practice, nonverbal communication must necessarily be dealt with analogically and this without delay. Although verbal communication permits a long interval between statements, certain action sequences and gestures necessitate an immediate reply. Then the reaction must be quick and reflexlike, with no time to ponder or to talk. And whenever such a situation occurs, the slower and exhaustive verbal codifications are out of the question for practical reasons and are clearly more time-consuming and inefficient than nonverbal reactions. (p. 14)

These authors went on to point out that the nature of our language is such that words typically deal with the time dimension in a very inefficient manner. In a limited time frame there are few, if any, sequences of events that cannot be described more quickly with gestures than with words.

The old axiom that a picture is worth a thousand words may lack precision, universal applicability, and empirical verification. The axiom, however, suggests an idea of great importance in interpersonal communication.

Sixth, nonverbal cues represent the most suitable vehicle for suggestion. The nature of a communication situation often indicates that ideas and emotions can be more effectively expressed indirectly than directly. Suggestion is an important means of indirect expression in our society. When it is employed, either the verbal or the nonverbal channels may be used. For tangible reasons, however, suggestion is more closely associated with nonverbal than verbal communication.

In spite of the immense personal satisfaction and control potential associated with interpersonal communication, it is a high-risk endeavor. One's ego, self-image, and even psychological equilibrium are intimately bound up in the communicative interaction with other people. Most of us are so acutely sensitive about our own image that we devote a significant proportion of our efforts to preserving or enhancing that image. Hence, the integrative function of communication is becoming increasingly important.

Because many of us are so concerned about our own image, we prefer to use communication that has a maximum potential for enhancing our image with a minimum risk of deflating it. Nonverbal suggestion is a particularly suitable vehicle for attaining these ends. Because the seeming intent of nonverbal cues can always be denied, many of the negative psychological consequences that may result from nonverbal suggestions can probably be avoided. After all, the man across the room can never be sure that a woman's sustained and seemingly suggestive eye contact is not an idiosyncrasy rather than an open invitation to sexual intimacy. In contrast, as any frustrated lover knows, the most subtle suggestions couched in verbal terms do not provide the same psychological safeguards. Hence, although nonverbal suggestion does not entail the same risks as verbal suggestion, it may be used for the same purpose. For that reason, nonverbal communication is increasingly associated with suggestion.

In review, the intent of this part of the chapter has been to emphasize the compelling need to examine and expand our knowledge of nonverbal communication. To satisfy that need, we must understand the specific functions served by nonverbal communication. However, nonverbal communication and verbal communication are not separate, or completely separable, entities. Indeed, the enlightened student of communication would be well advised not to study one to the exclusion of the other.

Definitional Perspective: Nonverbal and Verbal Communication

Definitional Issues

Defining nonverbal communication is not a simple matter. On the one hand, some students of nonverbal communication seek to exclude the important area(s) of the subconscious encoding and decoding of nonverbal cues by placing the emphasis on conscious encoding and decoding. Thus, Ekman and Friesen (1969) argued in their early, influential article that nonverbal communication is limited to those nonverbal behaviors that are *intended* to be communicative. On the other hand, there seems to be a natural tendency to make the definition so inclusive that virtually everything is defined as nonverbal communication, including bodily smells, flags, and music.

The second definitional perspective has been strongly affected by the influential book *Pragmatics of Human Communication* (1967) by Watzlawick, Beavin, and Jackson. They argued that the intent criterion for defining nonverbal communication is irrelevant. Any nonverbal behavior or cue is communicative if it is informative. In his insightful critique of various attempts to define nonverbal communication, Peter Bull (1987) wrote:

> According to this view non-verbal cues are significant not because they constitute a generalized system of communication, but as a source of valuable information which only a skilled perceiver can learn to understand through careful observation. The same kind of assumption can also be seen to underlie the popular literature on body language (e.g., 1970), which seeks to instruct people on the tell-tale signs, for example, of sexual availability. (p. 6)

The question of intent represents a central and persisting issue for those who seek to define nonverbal communication. If all nonverbal behaviors must be both encoded and decoded consciously and with intent, many nonverbal behaviors and cues that have traditionally been treated as communicative must be eliminated. In the 2008 presidential campaign, both Hillary Clinton and Barack Obama have distinct gestures that they use in their speeches. But do politicians use just a few gestures? Consciously encoded behaviors may be broad in nature. What of gestural adaptors, for example? Gestural adaptors consist of those nonverbal behaviors of the encoder that operate out of awareness and are unintentional. Gestural adaptors such as the hand-to-face gesture and the hand over the mouth are known to tell us that a person's confidence is dissipating rapidly, or even that the person is engaging in deception.

The definition that focuses on intent is too restrictive not only because it eliminates many important kinds of nonverbal behaviors and cues that are generally recognized as part of nonverbal communication; Burgoon (1985) recognized further problems when she wrote:

> One difficulty with this perspective is that it is very easy to deny intentionality for much of what goes on nonverbally. For example, a person who frowns when hearing something she doesn't like may later deny that she intended to frown. The question then becomes one of who arbitrates what was intentional and what was not—the source, an "objective" observer, or who. If all behaviors that the source is unaware of or declaims responsibility for are ruled out as communication, then the nonverbal domain may become overly narrow. (p. 349)

The second definitional perspective—which stresses that all informative nonverbal behaviors/cues are part of nonverbal communication—is also problematic. If we define nonverbal communication only from a decoder perspective, we place too much pressure on the decoder. We know, for example, that there are many cues that human lie detectors (decoders) perceive to be nonverbal behavioral indicators of deception that are not in fact reliable indicators (see Chapter 11). Thus, Bull (1987) wrote that a

> second possibility is that non-verbal cues are commonly perceived as conveying a meaning which they do not in fact possess (decoding errors) . . . so that the extent to which non-verbal cues operate as a communication system will vary substantially according to the perceptiveness of the decoder. (p. 6)

A third definitional perspective used to define nonverbal communication was developed by Wiener, Devoe, Robinson, and Geller (1972). They emphasized that nonverbal communication must involve encoders and decoders using a socially shared signal system or code with intent. *Nonverbal behaviors that do not include intentional actions by the encoders and decoders may inform but they do not communicate.*

In spite of the sophistication and intuitive appeal of this third definitional perspective, it is susceptible to at least three criticisms. First,

> this definition excludes from the domain of nonverbal communication any behavior that bears a direct, nonarbitrary relationship to that which it signifies. Potential candidates for exclusion are the facial, vocal, and bodily correlates of affective experiences, the various hesitation phenomena that appear to signify cognitive processing and at least certain aspects of proxemics. (Siegman & Feldstein, 1987, p. 3)

In short, nonverbal communication must include both symbols and signs.

Many signs do not bear an arbitrary relationship to their referents. They actually resemble that to which they refer. They are iconic in nature. For example, if anyone has ever thrust an upraised middle finger in your face, you knew that you were observing an iconic sign that bore an uncomfortable resemblance to the physiological activity to which it refers. Secondly, as we shall see in the next chapter, some theorists of facial expressions argue that a facial expression of anger, for example, *is* anger. Finally, when a person turns red in the face and shakes a finger at you, it can be argued that these nonverbal behaviors are not symbols representing anger but iconic signs that *are* anger.

This third definitional perspective can be subjected to two other criticisms. First, the requirement that both nonverbal encoding and decoding behaviors be both intentional and systematic excludes those unintentional nonverbal behaviors that many people believe are most informative in interpersonal interaction. Second, this third definitional perspective says nothing about the importance of *context*. Indeed, some communication theorists argue that context is communication (Eaves, 2003; Eaves & Leathers, 1991).

The preceding criticisms of existing definitional perspectives and the following discussion of the nature of the systems and subsystems of nonverbal communication support the following definition of *nonverbal communication:* the use of interacting sets of visual, vocal, and invisible communication systems and subsystems by communicators with the systematic encoding and decoding of nonverbal symbols and signs for the purpose(s) of exchanging consensual meanings in specific communicative contexts. This leads us to the question of what are the systems and subsystems that make up nonverbal communication?

Nonverbal Communication Systems and Subsystems

In 1976 Leathers was the author of the first book that treated nonverbal communication as a set of interacting systems and subsystems that in turn interact with the verbal communication system, *Nonverbal Communication Systems* (Leathers, 1976). Although we do not treat the various kinds of nonverbal communication as systems throughout this book, we believe the systems approach to classification remains particularly useful. Our current representation of interacting communication systems is presented in Figure 1.1.

Nonverbal communication comprises three major interacting systems: the *visual communication system,* the *auditory communication system,* and the *invisible communication system.* As subsequent chapters in this book will establish, the visual communication

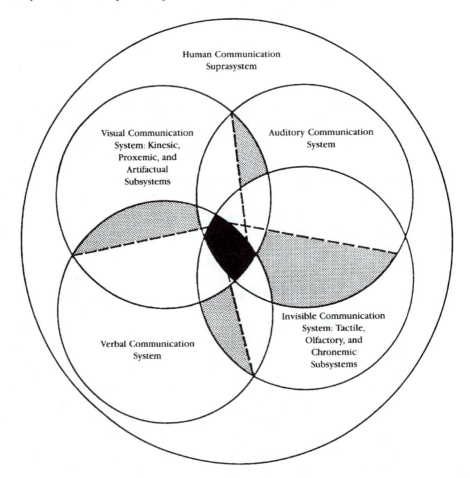

FIGURE 1.1   Verbal and Nonverbal Communication Systems Interacting in a Congruent State. (The dark gray color in the center suggests congruent interaction. When any part of the dark gray area becomes light gray, it suggests incongruent interaction between two or more of the systems. The areas colored light gray suggest the potential of each of the systems to interact with another system incongruently.)

system is the most important nonverbal communication system for at least two reasons. Visual communication is the major source of nonverbal meaning, and the visual communication system in turn is made up of extremely important subsystems: *kinesic, proxemic,* and *artifactual* communication.

Kinesic communication is defined by its own subsystems of facial expressions, eye behaviors, gestures, and posture. Proxemic communication is defined by the use of space, distance, and territory for purposes of communication. Artifactual communication starts with the appearance of our face and body and includes all of the options communicators may use to modify their appearance.

The auditory communication system is an important communication system in its own right. As we shall discover, nine different sound attributes, which are susceptible to our conscious control, combine to give communicators' vocal cues their distinctive quality: loudness, pitch, rate, duration, quality, regularity, articulation, pronunciation, and silence. Vocal cues in turn serve three important communicative functions: the *emotion function,* the *impression management function,* and the *regulatory function.*

The invisible communication system is different from the visual and auditory communication systems in several respects. First, the subsystems of tactile, olfactory, and chronemic communication are defined by their dissimilarity rather than by their similarity. Second, whereas we recognize that olfactory and chronemic communication (see Chapter 14) are defined by messages that are invisible, tactile messages can obviously be seen. Note, that tactile messages often communicate powerful meanings in the absence of any illumination and that the decoder of tactile messages relies on cutaneous receptors rather than eyesight to decode them.

Several qualifying comments about the invisible communication system are in order. First, a fairly convincing case can be made for the claims not only that individuals can communicate telepathically by extrasensory means but also that telepathic communication is an important subsystem that is part of the invisible communication system; this is a subject that was addressed elsewhere (Leathers, 1976). Second, although olfaction is frequently cited as a specific kind of nonverbal communication, it is such a limited and inflexible type of communication that we do not give it separate treatment in this book. Burgoon (1985) recognized the serious limitations of olfaction as a nonverbal communication subsystem when she wrote that "natural body odors, although potentially usable as a signal system (much as nonhuman species use them), do not meet the criteria of a coding system because they are not intentional, voluntarily, encoded signals, nor do they evoke a consistent interpretation from receivers" (p. 349).

Whereas some authorities assess the potential of given kinds of nonverbal communication by describing the properties of their "codes" (Burgoon, Buller, & Woodall, 1989), we compare and contrast the potential of nonverbal communication systems and their subsystems by rating the potential of the "channels" that are used to communicate messages. Nonverbal communication channels differ with regard to

1. the speed with which they can transmit signals
2. the ability of the channel to separate its own signals from those of other channels
3. how accurately meanings are communicated through the channel
4. the effectiveness with which the channel communicates emotional information
5. the effectiveness with which the channel communicates factual information

The channel capacities of the nonverbal communication systems (and subsystems) differ substantially with regard to the five important attributes just identified. To attempt to highlight these differences, Leathers previously rated the channel capacity for all of the nonverbal communication channels by using a five-point scale in which 5 = very good, 4 = good, 3 = average, 2 = poor, and 1 = very poor (1976). Although we need additional information for some channels to verify the accuracy of these ratings, they provide a useful profile for comparing the communicative potential of one nonverbal communicative channel with one or more others.

Let us take two examples to show how the ratings of the channel capacity of nonverbal communication systems and subsystems work. At present, we would rate channel capacity of facial expressions this way: speed = 5, channel separation = 5, accuracy = 4, emotional information = 5, and factual information = 2. The rated channel capacity of tactile communication is: speed = 1, channel separation = 2, accuracy = 3, emotional information = 4, and factual information = 1.

No other nonverbal communication system rivals facial expressions either for speed of transmitting meanings or for the communication of emotional information. Therefore, the face receives ratings of 5 on the channel characteristics of speed and the communication of emotional information. Although tactile communication serves important functions, touching others to communicate meanings is a slow means of communication. Furthermore, we cannot touch other people unless we are close enough to them. Finally, the close relationship between touch and hand gestures is obvious. Hence, the channel separation of touch is rated less than average because tactile messages are often not clearly separated from proxemic and gestural messages.

Interaction with Verbal Systems

We should recognize that nonverbal communication rarely occurs in the absence of verbal communication (see Figure 1.1). Indeed, the major nonverbal communication systems typically interact with the verbal communication system to determine the type and intensity of meaning(s) that are being communicated. Our perspective on the interaction of the nonverbal and verbal communication systems is grounded in several central assumptions that are rarely made explicit in books such as this. First, there are a number of situations in which the nonverbal communication systems serve important functions but verbal communication simply does not occur. Second, there are situations in which the nonverbal communication systems assume the dominant and central role while the verbal communication system necessarily assumes the secondary role.

American Sign Language (ASL) helps illustrate the complex interrelationships between nonverbal and verbal communication. People who are hard of hearing have developed a complex "nonverbal language" that uses the interacting nonverbal communication systems to serve functions ordinarily reserved for verbal communication, that is, the formulation and transmission of thoughts and ideas via appropriate grammatical structures.

One of the students in Leathers' undergraduate course in nonverbal communication, Lisa Wernick, wrote an insightful paper on sign language as a complex type of nonverbal communication. Wernick emphasized that ASL is a fascinating example of the use of nonverbal communication, particularly facial and bodily cues, to understand, represent, and transmit the meanings of complex sentences.

More specifically, ASL has been developed in such a way that it illustrates how nonverbal communication can be used effectively not only to communicate complex ideas but also to demarcate the syntactic structure of a text. For example, when facial expressions serve as grammatical markers, they have three basic functions: (a) marking specific syntactic structures, (b) representing adverbs that are used with various predicates, and (c) accompanying particular lexical items (Wernick, 1991).

Hemispheric Processing

The hemispheres of the brain serve decidedly different communicative functions, although the hemispheres do interact. Thus, neuropsychological research has clearly established that the right hemisphere of the brain (in right-handed persons) is primarily concerned with nonverbal functions of communication, whereas the left hemisphere focuses on verbal functions of communication. Research by Bowers, Bauer, and Heilman (1993) significantly expands our knowledge of the nonverbal communicative functions of the right hemisphere of the human brain. They found that the right hemisphere contains a "nonverbal affect lexicon" that uses separate sets of signals for facial expressions, vocal cues, and gestures. Moreover, the affect lexicon controlled by the right hemisphere of the brain is used to process and decode nonverbal messages of social importance that are exhibited by other individuals with whom we interact.

The intricate interrelationships between nonverbal and verbal communication are illustrated by the specialized role of the brain during communication. Don Stacks and Peter Andersen have been doing innovative research on *intrapersonal communication,* or the communication of the left and right hemispheres of the brain, for some time. In their provocatively titled article "The Modular Mind" in *The Southern Communication Journal* (1989), they write that the idea that the left hemisphere controls verbal communication and the right hemisphere controls nonverbal communication is both outmoded and overly simplistic.

For effective communication to occur, a communicator's left and right hemispheres must frequently "communicate" with each other through the connecting link of the corpus callosum—"interhemispheric cooperation" is vitally important. For example, Stacks and Andersen write that "research on split-brain indicates that when the left hemisphere must interpret a message without right hemisphere input (through a severing of the corpus callosum), that message is interpreted *literally* without an analysis of the underlying emotional content of imagery required for a total understanding of the message" (1989, p. 282).

In looking at "emotional intelligence," Goleman and colleagues have expanded our knowledge of the brain, especially with regard to how we form cognitions in emotional frameworks. Increasingly, the literature has welcomed more studies of the brain and communicative behavior, ever since the focus of the 1980s on B. F. Skinner's studies on behavior and determinism (Bryan, 2006; Emmerling & Goleman, 2003).

Jaffe (1987) demonstrated how complex the interrelationships of verbal and nonverbal communication are as reflected in the activities of the hemispheres of the brain. If you have a small brain or none at all, what goes in one ear may come out the other. For the average person, however, what goes in your right ear is processed by the left hemisphere of your brain, and what goes in your left ear is processed by the right hemisphere of your brain.

In general, information obtained from the right ear is used by the left hemisphere of the brain to decode and encode ideational information, whereas left-ear information is used by the right hemisphere of the brain to decode and encode nonverbal messages. Furthermore, it is not surprising that

> The speaker's right ear is primarily engaged in monitoring his own on-going speech; it would seem an efficient scheme to have the left ear turned to the procedural, paralinguistic interjections of the listener. The listener's right ear is engaged in selecting the proper linguistic syllables of the speaker for decoding; it would seem an efficient scheme to have his left ear turned to the intonational aspects of the message. (Jaffe, 1987, p. 30)

One recent study looked at how hemispheric processing operated during the presence or absence of gestures in a university lecture. Kelly and Goldsmith (2004) found that the presence of gestures in the lecture significantly affected both left brain (LB) and right brain (RB) processing, specifically that LB students found the lecture easier to understand when gestures were present than when they were not. However, there were no significant findings for RB students who processed the message, regardless of the presence of gestures in the lecture.

In another interesting study, Puccinelli, Tickle-Degnen, and Rosenthal (2004) wanted to see what effect the context of a subject's working on a puzzle had on a judge's perceived rapport (i.e., responsiveness, politeness, sympathy, etc.). Overall, the study found that the subject who sat on the judge's left received higher rapport scores than those of subjects who sat on the judge's right. These findings confirm the earlier hemispheric processing hypotheses laid out in Bowers et al. (1993) and Stacks and Andersen (1989). Specifically, then, the judge's favoring on the left side caused a specialization in right brain processing, or the hemisphere in the brain more concerned with nonverbal features such as rapport.

Interrelationships between Nonverbal and Verbal Communication

When communication systems are functioning in the congruent state (i.e., communicating essentially the same or supplemental meanings), communication is apt to be of high quality. It is when the systems begin to function incongruently that trouble begins. Communication systems in incongruent or inconsistent states are grist for the analyst's mill. Few phenomena have greater diagnostic significance for the communication consultant than verbal and nonverbal communication systems functioning in an incongruent state. The interrelationships between nonverbal and verbal communication systems in both congruent and incongruent states are of great importance.

In this book we will document a number of conclusions or generalizations about the relationship(s) between verbal and nonverbal communication. The following generalizations are representative of the ones we shall make: The most accurate communication occurs when the verbal and nonverbal systems transmit consistent meanings; the visual communication system conveys substantially more affective information than the verbal communication system or any of the other nonverbal communication systems; when different communication systems interact in the congruent state, nonverbal communication frequently represents the dominant source of meaning; the nonverbal systems of communication seem to be far more effective than the verbal in building empathy, respect, and a sense that the communicator is genuine; and when communication cues are transmitted simultaneously, the different channels acting together have a compensatory and additive effect.

Burgoon (1985) wrote that "verbal and nonverbal channels are inextricably intertwined in the communication of the total meaning of an interpersonal exchange" (p. 347). She documented the complex nature of the interrelationships between nonverbal and verbal communication by providing the following five propositions:

1. In general adults rely more heavily on nonverbal than verbal cues in determining "social meaning."
2. Conversely, children attach greater importance to verbal than nonverbal cues before they reach puberty.
3. Adults rely most heavily on nonverbal cues when the meanings communicated by the verbal and nonverbal communication systems are inconsistent or in conflict.
4. The function(s) of a given attempt to communicate tend(s) to determine whether the communicator will rely on one or more kinds of nonverbal communication or on verbal communication.
5. Individual communicators consistently exhibit a preference for either verbal or nonverbal communication as a source of information, although the situation or context determines the preference of some communicators.

The Functions of Nonverbal Cues

Nonverbal cues serve a number of communicatively significant functions (Burgoon, 1985; Harper, Wiens, & Matarazzo, 1978; Patterson, 1994). They not only function as powerful determinants of interpersonal perception but they also have a major impact on interpersonal relationships. Although nonverbal cues frequently reinforce or supplement information provided by the spoken word, they also provide specific kinds of information that cannot be obtained from speech communication.

A moment of reflection may help you confirm the central role nonverbal cues play in shaping interpersonal perceptions and behaviors. For example, the airplane passenger who conforms in appearance and mannerism to the highjacker profile is apt to be interrogated, at minimum; the highjacker profile is essentially nonverbal in nature. A prospective juror may be stricken from the jury if he or she does not conform to the profile the defense attorney or prosecutor wants or needs on the jury. The strike usually is based on information provided by nonverbal rather than verbal cues. Telephone callers seeking a first date run a high risk of rejection if their vocal cues suggest an undesirable personality profile.

To be more specific, what communicative functions are most directly associated with nonverbal cues? Authorities provide somewhat different answers to this question. Burgoon

(1980) identified the six functions as symbolic representation, expressive communication, structuring interaction, impression formation and management, metacommunication, and social influence. In her distinctive treatment of the symbolic functions of nonverbal cues, Burgoon noted that the predisposition to attack, to escape, and to form affiliative bonds may be communicated in the most socially acceptable ways by nonverbal means. In addition, she emphasized the symbolic importance of such nonverbal cues as flags, black armbands, picketing, marching, and music.

The most detailed classification of the functions of nonverbal cues, which is grounded in numerous empirical studies of those functions, was developed by Patterson (1982); he has subsequently refined and amplified his classification (1987, 1994). He concludes that the major communicative functions of nonverbal cues are providing information, regulating interaction, expressing intimacy, exercising social control, and facilitating service or task goals. Our own classification of the functions of nonverbal cues is based on this model, with three modifications. Although the expression of intimacy focuses on the communication of emotions, the communication of emotions does not necessarily involve the expression of intimacy. Second, nonverbal cues clearly serve one other important function not identified by Patterson—metacommunication. Finally, the impression formation and management function is so important that it is treated separately rather than as part of the social-control function.

Nonverbal cues can, therefore, be used to serve six major communicative functions:

1. providing information
2. regulating interaction
3. expressing emotions
4. allowing metacommunication
5. controlling social situations
6. forming and managing impressions

These communicative functions of nonverbal cues are not mutually exclusive because any single attempt to communicate nonverbally may serve a number of functions.

The informative function of nonverbal cues is the most basic because all nonverbal cues in any communicative situation are potentially informative to both the encoder and the decoder. Nonverbal cues are a potentially rich source of information because encoders frequently are unaware of their own nonverbal cues. When this is the case, they may inadvertently communicate a constellation of meanings that reveal much about their self-image, social identity, attitudes, and behavioral propensities. Note that in the past section the distinction was made between behaviors that inform but are not communicative and communicative behaviors that inform; informative behaviors do not constitute communication but communicative behaviors clearly can inform.

Leathers (1979b) suggests that nonverbal cues can provide certain distinctive kinds of information that cannot usually be obtained from the spoken word. The nonverbal behaviors of individuals reveal not only how they feel about themselves but how they feel about the individual with whom they are communicating. More specifically, nonverbal cues can be used to determine an individual's levels of *self-assurance* and *responsiveness*. The ability to determine those qualities at different points in time is indispensable to successful communication.

When the encoder's nonverbal cues are not consciously controlled and monitored by the encoder, the decoder derives from such cues the most valuable information. When the encoder's nonverbal cues are consciously controlled and monitored, the informational value of such cues is minimized for the decoder. This is so because the conscious control and monitoring of nonverbal cues frequently takes the form of impression formation and management. In this case, impression managers strive to provide only those kinds of information that will help them attain their own objectives.

The second function of nonverbal cues, regulating interaction, is an important one. We know, for example, that managing accessibility to "the floor" and managing "floor time" can have an immediate and significant impact on the development of interpersonal relationships (Palmer, 1989). Although they are frequently nonreflective, nonverbal cues represent the most efficient and least offensive means of regulating interaction in interpersonal situations. To say, "Shut up, John" may trigger a hostile and defensive reaction; to communicate the same message by eye behavior or hand movement is a more socially acceptable way of achieving the objective. The sensitive communicator will recognize that the turn-taking rules of a given culture are usually communicated nonverbally, and the cultural expectation is that such rules will not be violated.

The third function of nonverbal cues is to express emotions. As indicated previously, nonverbal communication represents the primary medium for the expression of emotions. If we believe that successful communication requires a sensitive reading of, and response to, the feelings, moods, and emotions of those with whom we communicate, the expressive potential of nonverbal communication becomes particularly important. In subsequent chapters, we will demonstrate that more detailed and precise information about the emotions of communicators can be obtained from their nonverbal cues than from any other source. We will also caution that some of that information may be counterfeit, because certain kinds of nonverbal cues can be consciously controlled for purposes of deception.

The fourth function of nonverbal cues, metacommunication, is a particularly distinctive one. In effect, metamessages, in the form of nonverbal cues, aid the communicator both in assessing the intent and motivation of the message sender and in determining the precise meaning(s) of verbal messages. Burgoon (1980) defines metacommunication as the use of nonverbal messages to qualify, complement, contradict, or expand verbal or other nonverbal messages. The importance of the metacommunicative function of nonverbal cues is particularly apparent when an individual is confronted with the task of decoding a multichannel message that seems to be communicating inconsistent meanings.

Social control is the fifth function of nonverbal cues. It is perhaps the most important function, in view of its relevance to a wide variety of socially significant communication contexts in the real world. *Social control* means that one individual attempts to influence or change the behavior of another individual.

Efforts to exercise social control frequently take the form of persuasion. Edinger and Patterson (1983) have convincingly demonstrated that the social-control function of nonverbal communication is also centrally involved in carefully calculated efforts to enhance one's status, power, and dominance; to provide selective feedback and reinforcement; and to deceive. They maintain that impression management is a social-control function so broad in scope as to embrace the more specific control functions. They have written that, in a way, "all of the topics considered so far involve impression management.

That is, in attempting to exert power, persuade others, provide feedback, or deceive, individuals are at least indirectly managing impressions" (p. 43).

Thus, impression formation and management constitutes the sixth function of nonverbal behaviors and cues. We will emphasize that this function is vitally important to a great range of people in an almost unlimited number of real-world situations. In the modern world it is almost imperative that the attorney, the physician, the politician, the teacher, and many other professionals have detailed knowledge of impression formation and management if they are to succeed. Because of the obvious importance of this function, separate chapters in this book are devoted to impression formation and to impression management.

In short, nonverbal cues serve a number of communicative functions that are vitally important to successful outcomes in the real world. The time has passed when nonverbal communication can be treated as a support system of secondary importance whose chief use is to help clarify the meaning of the spoken word.

Communicating Nonverbally in Specific Contexts

Although the different kinds of nonverbal communication have been treated in detailed and enlightening textbooks by several other authors, those texts, like their predecessors, are designed to tell us *about* nonverbal communication. For example, they define, identify, and describe different classes of visual cues such as facial expressions, gestures, and posture. What these books do not do, however, is demonstrate *how* we can successfully communicate in a nonverbal way.

In contrast, this book, *Successful Nonverbal Communication,* is designed to *demonstrate* how knowledge of nonverbal cues can be used to communicate more successfully in contexts of particular importance to the reader. As this chapter suggests, *detailed knowledge of nonverbal cues and their communicative functions can be used to communicate more successfully in a variety of real-world contexts.* Succeeding chapters provide concrete guidelines that indicate how knowledge of nonverbal cues should be used if we are to communicate successfully.

From a conceptual perspective, this book is a successor to the third edition of *Nonverbal Communication Systems* (Leathers, 1997). Part 1 describes the different classes of nonverbal cues, illustrating the various kinds of information they can provide and comparing and contrasting their communicative functions. Particular attention is given to the specific kinds of nonverbal cues that are desirable and undesirable in different communicative contexts.

This book departs most sharply from conventional practice in the content of Parts 2 and 3. These sections are designed to demonstrate how the knowledge presented in Part 1 can be used by individuals to manage the impressions they make, and to communicate more successfully in particular settings. The value of this emphasis on application should be apparent to any person who has contemplated the communicative intricacies of an upcoming job interview, considered the formidable barriers to effective intercultural communication, or pondered the complexities of communicating in a sensitive way with a member of the opposite sex.

Do you create a favorable first impression? Do others judge you to be less credible in certain situations than you would like them to? Are you easily manipulated and deceived? Are you usually seen as an insincere and untrustworthy individual? If your answers to these questions give you cause for concern, the contents of Part 2 should prove to be valuable. You may not know how to sell yourself nonverbally, to detect deception, and to communicate consistently; you may not know how impressions are managed. Each of these subjects is addressed in separate chapters in Part 2.

The chapters in Part 3 of this book focus on specific guidelines for using nonverbal cues to communicate successfully in applied contexts, which range from the selection interview to the classroom to the conference room to the office to the virtual community. Special attention is given to the distinctive contextual features of female–male interaction and to intercultural communication, as well as to the distinctive requirements for successful nonverbal communication in each of these contexts. Lastly, specific nonverbal contexts such as the medical field, the courtroom, the built environment, and virtual places are examined.

The central importance of nonverbal skills development to effective interpersonal communication has been clearly documented (Rosenthal, 1979). This book not only emphasizes the importance of developing both general and specific kinds of nonverbal skills but also provides specific empirically based guidelines for developing these skills.

Many measures have been developed to assess the current level of a person's nonverbal skills development. With several exceptions, however, such measures are too expensive, too complicated, and too time-consuming to be of much value to the reader of a book such as this. The PONS Test, which provides a profile of nonverbal sensitivity, is a good example of a test that is so expensive and complicated that it will only infrequently be used outside of the experimental laboratory (Rosenthal, Hall, DiMatteo, Rogers, & Archer, 1979).

Dane Archer was one of the developers of the PONS Test. He recognized the need for a straightforward and interesting measure of nonverbal skills. Archer along with Mark Costanzo devised a highly creative test of nonverbal skills that can be used both to measure and to develop such skills. The Interpersonal Perception Task (IPT) (1986) consists of 30 scenes of people interacting on videotape. The IPT is a measure of social intelligence that requires the "viewer" to test her or his skill in making five common types of social judgments: *intimacy, competition, deception, kinship,* and *status.* Social intelligence in turn is a concept developed by Archer that is defined as the ability to make accurate interpretations about people including their experiences, their individual characteristics, the nature of their relationships with others, and their emotions (1980).

The profile of nonverbal decoding skills associated with social intelligence is now beginning to emerge. Interestingly, one's early family experiences seem to have a marked impact on social intelligence. Thus, an easy child temperament, harmonious parental relationships, and moderate paternal strictness are associated with good adult nonverbal decoding skills (Hodgins & Koestner, 1993). Conversely, inefficient nonverbal decoders, when compared with efficient nonverbal decoders, use a more restricted repertoire as a source of information and are less sensitive to the meanings of the nonverbal cues they seek to decode.

Finally, particular contexts are emphasized in this book because of their social significance and because of the importance of nonverbal cues in these contexts. The job interview is a good case in point. Existing knowledge suggests that the interviewee's verbal communication may contribute less to the relative success or failure of a job interview than his or her nonverbal communication. To undertake a job interview with no knowledge of the potentially powerful communicative effects of one's nonverbal cues may be ill advised at best, and masochistic at worst.

In short, this book is designed for the reader who wishes to use knowledge of nonverbal cues to communicate more successfully. Such knowledge is neither simple nor easy to apply. The judicious use of nonverbal cues should help one to communicate more successfully, but it does not guarantee success.

Summary

Nonverbal communication functions in vitally important ways in our society. Frequently, communicators can achieve their purpose by using accurate and efficient nonverbal communication. They must begin, of course, with a clear understanding of what nonverbal communication is and what it is not.

The functional importance of nonverbal communication is obvious when we realize that (a) nonverbal communication is usually the dominant force in the exchange of meaning in the interpersonal context; (b) feelings and emotions are exchanged more accurately by nonverbal than by verbal means; (c) meanings exchanged nonverbally are relatively free of deception and distortion; (d) nonverbal cues serve a metacommunicative function, which is indispensable in attaining high-quality communication; (e) nonverbal cues represent a much more efficient means of communicating than verbal cues; and (f) nonverbal communication is a particularly suitable vehicle for using suggestion.

Major functions served by nonverbal cues include providing information, regulating interaction, expressing emotions, allowing metacommunication, exercising social control, and impression forming and managing. Of these six functions, the impression formation and management function is perhaps the most important in terms of its relevance to a wide variety of socially significant communicative contexts in the real world.

REFERENCES

Archer, D. (1980). *How to expand your social intelligence quotient.* New York: Evans.

Birdwhistell, R. L. (1970). *Kinesics and context.* Philadelphia: University of Pennsylvania Press.

Bowers, D., Bauer, R. M., & Heilman, K. M. (1993). The nonverbal affect lexicon: Theoretical perspectives from neuropsychological studies of affect perception. Special Section: Neuropsychological perspectives on components of emotional processing. *Neuropsychology, 7,* 433–444.

Bryan, S. P. (2006). Emotional intelligence and intrapersonal conversions. *Consortium for Research on Emotional Intelligence in Organizations.* Retrieved February 16, 2007, from http://www.eiconsortium.org

Bull, P. E. (1987). *Postures and gesture.* Oxford, England: Pergamon Press.

Burgoon, J. (1980). Nonverbal communication research in the 1970's: An overview. In D. Nimmo (Ed.), *ICA communication yearbook 4.* New Brunswick: Transaction Books.

Burgoon, J. K. (1985). Nonverbal signals. In M. L. Knapp & G. R. Miller (Eds.), *Handbook of interpersonal communication* (pp. 344–390). Beverly Hills, CA: Sage.

Burgoon, J. K., Buller, D. B., & Woodall, W. G. (1989). *Nonverbal communication: The unspoken dialogue.* New York: Harper & Row.

Capella, J. N., & Palmer, M. T. (1989). The structure and organization of verbal and nonverbal behavior: Data for models of reception. *Journal of Language and Social Psychology, 8,* 167–191.

Davitz, J. R. (1969). *The communication of emotional meaning.* New York: McGraw-Hill.

Eaves, M. H. (2003). McDonald's vs Burger King: *12 years later.* Paper presented at the annual convention of the National Communication Association, Miami, FL.

Eaves, M. H., & Leathers, D. G. (1991). Context as communication: McDonald's vs. Burger King. *Journal of Applied Communication Research, 19,* 263–289.

Edinger, J. A., & Patterson, M. L. (1983). Nonverbal involvement and social control. *Psychological Bulletin, 93,* 30–56.

Ekman, P., & Friesen, W. V. (1969). The repertoire of nonverbal behavior: Categories, origins, usage, and coding. *Semiotica, 1,* 49–98.

Emmerling, R. J., & Goleman, D. (2003). Emotional intelligence: Issues and common misunderstandings. *Consortium for Research on Emotional Intelligence in Organizations.* Retrieved February 16, 2007, from http://www.eiconsortium.org

Fast, J. (1970). *Body language.* New York: Evans.

Harper, R. G., Wiens, A. N., & Matarazzo, J. D. (1978). *Nonverbal communication: The state of the art.* New York: Wiley.

Hodgins, H. S., & Koestner, R. (1993). The origins of nonverbal sensitivity. *Personality and Social Psychology Bulletin, 19,* 466–473.

Jaffe, J. (1987). Parliamentary procedure and the brain. In A. W. Siegman & S. Feldstein (Eds.), *Nonverbal behavior and communication* (2nd ed., pp. 21–33). Hillsdale, NJ: Erlbaum.

Kelly, S. D., & Goldsmith, L. H. (2004). Gesture and right hemisphere involvement in evaluating lecture material. *Gesture, 4,* 25–42.

LaFrance, M., & Mayo, C. (1978). *Moving bodies: Nonverbal communication in social relationships.* Monterey, CA: Brooks/Cole.

Leathers, D. G. (1972). Quality of group communication as a determinant of group product. *Speech Monographs, 38,* 166–173.

Leathers, D. G. (1976, 1997). *Nonverbal communication systems.* Newton, MA: Allyn.

Leathers, D. G. (1979a). The impact of multichannel message inconsistency on verbal and nonverbal decoding behaviors. *Communication Monographs, 46,* 88–100.

Leathers, D. G. (1979b). The informational potential of the nonverbal and verbal components of feedback responses. *Southern Speech Communication Journal, 44,* 331–354.

Leathers, D. G., & Emigh, T. H. (1980). Decoding facial expressions: A new test with decoding norms. *Quarterly Journal of Speech, 66,* 418–436.

Mehrabian, A. (1968). Communication without words. *Psychology Today, 2,* 51–52.

Mehrabian, A. (1981). *Silent messages* (2nd ed.). Belmont, CA: Wadsworth.

Molloy, J. T. (1988). *New dress for success.* New York: Warner.

Newton, D. A., & Burgoon, J. K. (1990). The use and consequences of verbal influence strategies during interpersonal disagreements. *Human Communication Research, 16,* 477–518.

Palmer, M. T. (1989). Controlling conversations, turns, topics and interpersonal control. *Communication Monographs, 56,* 1–18.

Patterson, M. L. (1982). A sequential functional model of nonverbal exchange. *Psychological Bulletin, 89,* 231–249.

Patterson, M. L. (1987). Presentational and affect-management functions of nonverbal involvement. *Journal of Nonverbal Behavior, 11,* 110–122.

Patterson, M. L. (1994). Interaction behavior and person perceptions: An integrative approach. *Small Group Research, 25,* 172–188.

Philpott, J. S. (1983). *The relative contribution to meaning of verbal and nonverbal channels of communication . . . a metaanalysis.* Unpublished master's thesis, University of Nebraska.

Puccinelli, N. M., Tickle-Degnen, L., & Rosenthal, R. (2004). Effect of target position and target task on judge sensitivity to felt rapport. *Journal of Nonverbal Behavior, 28,* 211–220.

Reusch, J., & Kees, W. (1956). *Nonverbal communication.* Berkeley: University of California Press.

Rosenthal, R. (Ed.). (1979). *Skill in nonverbal communication: Individual differences.* Cambridge, MA: Oelgeschlager, Gunn & Hain.

Rosenthal, R., Hall, J. A., DiMatteo, M. R., Rogers, P. L., & Archer, D. (1979). *Sensitivity to nonverbal communication: The PONS test.* Baltimore: Johns Hopkins University Press.

Rothman, A. D., & Nowicki, S. (2004). A measure of the ability to identify emotion in children's tone of voice. *Journal of Nonverbal Behavior, 28,* 67–92.

Schutz, W. C. (1971). *Here comes everybody.* New York: Harper.

Siegman, A. W., & Feldstein, S. (Eds.). (1987). *Nonverbal behaviors and communication* (2nd ed.). Hillsdale, NJ: Erlbaum.

Stacks, D. W., & Andersen, P. A. (1989). The modular mind: Implications for intrapersonal communication. *The Southern Communication Journal, 44,* 273–293.

Sternglanz, R. W., & DePaulo, B. M. (2004). Reading nonverbal cues to emotions: The advantages and liabilities of relationship closeness. *Journal of Nonverbal Behavior, 28,* 245–266.

Thompson, L. A., Aidinejad, M. R., & Ponte, J. (2001). Aging and the effects of facial and prosodic cues on emotional intensity ratings and memory reconstructions. *Journal of Nonverbal Behavior, 25,* 101–125.

Watzlawick, P., Beavin, J. H., & Jackson, D. D. (1967). *Pragmatics of human communication: A study of interactional patterns, pathologies, and paradoxes.* New York: W. W. Norton.

Wernick, L. (1991, March). *The nonverbal communication of sign language.* Unpublished manuscript.

Westman, A. S., & Wautier, G. (1994). Early and autobiographical memories are mostly nonverbal and their development is more likely continuous than discrete. *Psychological Reports, 74,* 656–666.

Westman, A. S., & Westman, R. S. (1993). First memories are nonverbal and emotional, not necessarily talked about or part of a recurring pattern. *Psychological Reports, 73,* 328–330.

Wiener, M., Devoe, S., Robinson, S., & Geller, J. (1972). Nonverbal behaviors and nonverbal communication. *Psychological Review, 79,* 185–214.

CHAPTER

2 Facial Expressions

The face has long been a primary source of information in interpersonal communication. It is an instrument of great importance in the transmission of meaning. Within a matter of seconds, facial expressions can move us to the heights of ecstasy or the depths of despair. We study the faces of friends and associates for subtle changes and nuances in meaning, and they in turn study our faces.

In a real sense, our quest for meaning in this world begins and ends with facial expression. We study the faces of infants to determine their immediate needs, and they reciprocate by communicating many of their needs and emotional states through facial expressions. The elderly hospital patient studies the face of the surgeon to determine the chances of surviving the next operation, and the surgeon's facial expression often provides the definitive answer.

We know that the face may be used to complement or qualify the meaning of spoken messages and to replace spoken messages. We may also speculate that such facial features as a low forehead, thick lips, or oversized ears are all associated with undesirable personality characteristics, but such conclusions are speculative (Knapp & Hall, 2006). This speculation might of course be somewhat amusing for individuals who do not have low foreheads, thick lips, or oversized ears. Even if a connection between specific facial features and personality traits were firmly established, however, such a finding would tend to divert attention from the important communicative functions served by the human face.

We know too that facial expressions can serve many functions in their own right. The appearance of the face exerts a central and sometimes controlling impact on judgments of physical attractiveness (Alicke, Smith, & Klotz, 1986). The appearance of a person's face in turn strongly affects how dominant the person is judged to be (Berry, 1990; Keating, 1985). "Babyfacedness" defines faces with distinctive physical features and babyfaced males are perceived to be naive, honest, kind, and warm (Berry & McArthur, 1985).

Smiling is another important part of facial expression. Nonsmiling communicators with lowered brows, for example, appear more dominant than their smiling counterparts who raise their brows (Keating & Bal, 1986). We know too that the types of smiles (Ekman, Davidson, & Friesen, 1990) and onset and offset times for smiles can strongly affect the impressions a person makes. At an early age, infants develop smiling behavior (Messinger, Fogel, & Dickson, 2001). Their research found that infants develop three primary smiles that are effective in the communication process. They include cheek raise,

The faces of the women in this photo signal a message of caring, concern, and enjoyment.

open-mouth, and open-mouth/cheek raise combination. Each of these smiles is important to communication, and some smiles are more positive than others. For example, some infants will use an open-mouth smile if they want to make visual engagement with a parent, mostly the mother.

Furthermore, there are differences between felt and false smiles. Felt smiles are genuine and typically last for a few seconds. False smiles are either much shorter or much longer. The expectations of the decoder are either met or not met, and if they are violated, the smile is perceived as not genuine (Ekman & Friesen, 1982; Krumhuber & Kappas, 2005). Appropriate smiles enhance credibility while inappropriate smiles are often viewed as part of an ingratiating self-presentation strategy (Bugental, 1986).

The communicative functions of facial expressions already identified are important. Their potential to affect the impressions people make and the relationships they develop is undeniable. Some research supports the view that facial expressions signal the dominance of the sender. Tomkins (1962) in his early research found that the face is perhaps one of the most dominant features of our body, at birth and throughout our adulthood. Hess, Blairy, and Kleck (2000) provide evidence that there are cultural differences between facial displays of dominance. They found that sex and ethnicity (Japanese versus Caucasian, for example) of the encoder affected observers' ratings of perceived facial expressions of dominance. Furthermore, one study reports that a person's head tilt is associated with dominance. In fact, the study found that women who tilted their heads were more likely to be seen in a negative way as compared to men (Mignault & Chaudhuri, 2003).

The two most important functions of the human face are the communication of emotions and the identification of previously unidentified people. The preponderance of research has focused on the face as a medium of emotional communication, the function of overriding importance, to which we turn first.

The Face as the Most Important Source of Emotional Information

Successful communication places a premium not only on the ability to identify general emotional states of individuals with whom we communicate but also on the ability to differentiate among subtle emotional meanings that are constituents of the more general emotional states. The ability to identify fear is undeniably useful. However, the ability to distinguish special kinds of fear such as terror, anxiety, and apprehension is much more useful.

To obtain both general and specific emotional information, the communicator must develop the ability to decode facial expressions accurately because the human face is the most important source of emotional information. The face is the primary site for the communication of emotional states (Knapp & Hall, 2006), and one prominent researcher has gone so far as to assert that facial expressions *are* emotions (Tomkins, 1962). Tomkins' research is discussed in greater detail later in the chapter.

If the human face is unmatched in its ability to communicate emotions, we must begin with a fundamental question: What is emotion? Collier (1985) maintains that *emotion* is a complex but temporary psychological state involving physiological, experiential, and behavioral changes. Emotion theorists do not agree, however, on the precise nature of these changes or on the nature of the internal, neural phenomena that trigger them.

Levenson (1988) provided a particularly illuminating theoretical treatment of emotion and the vitally important role of the autonomic nervous system in controlling the emotion(s) experienced and displayed. He addresses such central questions as whether the categoric or dimensional models of emotion are most convincing, how many emotions there are, whether a baseline condition in a given person should be determined before studying autonomic nervous system (ANS) activity, how ANS activity is affected as the intensity of an emotion changes, how long an emotion lasts, and how verification procedures can be developed to establish what emotions individuals are feeling and when they are feeling them.

The theoretical study of emotion can be immensely helpful to the person who wants to make the most effective use of the human face as a medium of emotional communication. In order to derive practical dividends from theories of emotion, Collier (1985) maintained that the researcher must answer three questions satisfactorily:

1. How much *control* do communicators have over their own expressive behavior?
2. How *aware* are communicators of the internal changes taking place within them and of the emotions being displayed facially?
3. What is the *relationship* between the actual display of emotional expressions via facial expressions and the physiological and experiential aspects of emotion?

These questions in turn highlight issues that are of critical importance in understanding and developing skill in both the encoding and the decoding of facial expressions.

Encoders who are not aware of the kind of emotion they are displaying on their face, for example, do not have the capacity to modify that facial expression in desired ways. Similarly, decoders who may be subliminally aware of but are not attending to a given facial expression may have little chance of decoding it accurately.

The importance of facial expression in human communication is strong. This is so in large part because the complex and flexible set of muscles in the human face may be used to communicate a great variety of facial meanings. The Facial Action Coding System (FACS), for example, was developed for the purpose of classifying the units of facial expression that are anatomically separate and visually distinguishable. FACS distinguishes 44 "action units" (Ekman & Friesen, 1978; Ekman et al., 1982). Suzuki and Naitoh (2003) further support the FACS instrument. In their study, Japanese undergraduates were able to correctly identify facial expressions of disgust, anger, sadness, and fear. Do you recall watching your last horror film? The actors and actresses in the movie often reveal their state of emotion on their faces. As a viewer, it is easy to see who is about to scream, who fears what is around the corner, or who is running for his or her life in the inevitable chase scene.

Theorists and researchers disagree as to how the human face functions communicatively (Frank & Stennett, 2001; Oster, Daily, & Goldenthal, 1989). Two major approaches—the categoric and the dimensional perspectives—have been used by researchers in an attempt to describe or identify with some degree of precision the meanings communicated by facial expressions.

The Categoric Perspective

Proponents of the categoric perspective maintain that the human face, at any given moment, transmits one dominant type of meaning, often associated with such affective states as happiness or anger. The meaning transmitted facially is believed to have a single referent that will stand out in the mind of the decoder. Although any given facial expression may combine two or more classes of meaning in the form of a facial blend (Ekman et al., 1982), the decoder will use a single categoric label to describe the dominant facial meaning that is displayed.

Classes of Facial Meaning.   Not surprisingly, researchers who believe that the face functions categorically have attempted to identify and label all classes of meaning that they believe can be communicated accurately by facial expressions. Early attempts by researchers (Frois-Wittman, 1930; Woodworth, 1938) failed to provide specific classifications for the various facial displays of emotion.

Tomkins (1962) attempted to increase the precision with which facial expressions may be classified. He uses the following *sets* of labels to identify the eight classes of affective information that he contends can be communicated by facial expressions: (a) interest–excitement; (b) enjoyment–joy; (c) surprise–startle; (d) distress–anguish; (e) fear–terror; (f) shame–humiliation; (g) contempt–disgust; and (h) anger–rage. The first label in each pair represents a low-intensity manifestation of the given class of facial meaning, and the second represents a high-intensity counterpart. Tomkins says that in each of these facial expressions, it is our expectations of "fear" that produce a fearful face, or our expectations of "shame" that will cause our head to lower in anticipated failure.

In his influential book *The Face of Emotion* (1971), Izard used the same set of labels to develop a decoding test that measured the ability of nine different national–cultural groups to identify facial expressions. Surprisingly, decoders were not forced to differentiate between facial interest and excitement or facial distress and anguish. They were simply asked to determine the meaning of a given facial expression by placing it in one of the eight categories.

Ekman and his associates (1982) completed an exhaustive review, summary, and analysis of many of the major studies that treat the face as if it functions categorically. They concluded that the face is capable of communicating seven basic classes of meaning: (a) happiness, (b) surprise, (c) fear, (d) anger, (e) sadness, (f) disgust/ contempt; and (g) interest. Ekman continues to cite new findings that suggest that these basic classes of meaning are universal. They are universal, he claims, in that they are encoded and decoded at approximately the same levels of accuracy in a great variety of nations and cultures (Ekman, 1994). In a recent study, Frank and Ekman (2004) found that decoders generally agreed about "truthful" appearances in different contexts. For example, in their finding, they suggest that subjects appeared truthful in two separate high-stakes lie conditions. A modern understanding of this principle might be found in a presidential candidate's handling of a scam. George W. Bush's handling of his AWOL experience in the Air Force and John Kerry's awkward disposing of his Vietnam medal are examples of how politicians appear truthful during controversies in a political campaign. Both men were able to maintain positive facial expressions while being challenged on past military events.

In fact, Ekman maintained for at least 15 years that the facial displays of disgust and contempt represented categoric expressions that could not be reliably distinguished by American decoders; hence, he persisted in treating disgust/contempt as one category. Ekman and Friesen (1986) modified their position by maintaining that they had discovered a pancultural facial expression unique to contempt. Leathers and Emigh (1980) provided substantial support for their claim that contempt is a separate category of facial emotion that can be decoded at levels of accuracy that meet or exceed most of the other basic emotions. Recent research extends this claim through cultural lines (Matsumoto, 2005). In fact, Matsumoto claims that contempt is the newest universal nonverbal gesture. In his study, contempt was correctly identified in the following cultures: Estonian, Greek, Chinese, Japanese, Turkish, American, West German, Sumatran, Italian, Vietnamese, Polish, Hungarian, British (including Scotish), and Indian. This was an important finding in facial expression research, and contempt now represents the seventh universal facial expression across cultural variations.

A fairly extensive categoric explanation of the face was done by Leslie Zebrowitz (1997). In her influential book *Reading Faces: Window to the Soul?*, she argues that a babyface stereotype exists. Those individuals with large foreheads, short chins, and raised eyebrows typify a "babyface" stereotype. She suggests that these persons are generally seen as more naive, warm, weak, and submissive. Other trait perceptions that are often associated with babyfaces include less threatening, more lovable, but less sexy. In addition, she found that even when raters heard the voice on a videotape, they weighed the babyface stereotype more heavily in their overall evaluation of the person, regardless of the "mature or adult" nature of the voice.

Areas of the Face: Meaning Cues.   The categoric perspective is particularly useful for individuals who wish to determine how accurately they can distinguish among the basic classes of emotion that can be communicated by facial expressions. In fact, evidence now indicates that certain areas of the face provide meaning cues that are particularly useful in identifying specific kinds of emotions.

Although controversy still surrounds the defining features of facial contempt, the facial blueprint for disgust is rapidly being refined (Rozin, Lowery, & Ebert, 1994). The nose wrinkle characteristic of disgust, for example, is associated with irritating or offensive smells, and to a degree with bad tastes. Food that we find distasteful, as well as oral irritation, tends to elicit the gape and tongue extrusion form of facial disgust. Finally, the raised upper lip is most apt to be triggered by a wide variety of disgust elicitors, such as body boundary violations, inappropriate sex, poor hygiene, aversive interpersonal contacts, and certain types of moral offenses. In short, results from this research suggest support for a theory of disgust that focuses on bad tastes as elicitors of this category of facial emotion with the suggestion that disgust has evolved into a moral emotion. Have you ever watched the reality show *Fear Factor?* A contestant's disgusted face tells all when he or she is instructed to eat worms, drink a grasshopper shake, or sit in a bed with rats.

The Facial Affect Scoring Technique (FAST) breaks down the face into three areas: the brows and forehead; the eyes, lids, and bridge of the nose; and the lower face (Ekman, Friesen, & Tomkins, 1971). The upper portion of the face is apt to provide more useful cues for identifying anger than the lower part of the face, for example. Thus, when someone displays anger facially, the brows are lowered and drawn together, vertical lines appear between the brows, and both the upper and lower lids exhibit tension. A good example of this might be when a professor displays anger when a student walks into class during the middle of a classmate's speech. Have you had this happen to you recently? How did you feel?

In most cases the categoric approach features the use of posed facial expressions. You may find the use of spontaneous facial expressions more appealing. Intuitively, spontaneous facial expressions seem more realistic because they more closely approximate the way people display facial expressions in real-world contexts; facial expressions are rarely "frozen" as they are in photographs. In point of fact, spontaneous facial expressions have proved to have limited value in actual tests of facial decoding skills, however, because the levels of accuracy for decoders is extremely low. Thus, Wagner, MacDonald, and Manstead (1986) found that decoders were able to distinguish only three of seven types or categories of facial expressions at above chance levels: happiness, anger, and disgust. Even for these three emotions, decoders were 30 to 70 percent less accurate than decoders who identified posed facial expressions. Further research shows mixed results in coding accuracy (Alvarado & Jameson, 2002). In their study, participants strongly agreed about nuances in the coding of facial expressions of anger, but disagreed as to nuances' consequences or strength. This study supports the notion that while facial training for coding accuracy is successful, its parameters are limited. The success rate you may have later on in this chapter's FMST is a case in point.

The Dimensional Perspective

Few would deny that the face is capable of functioning to communicate given types or categories of emotional meaning in a given context. Students of facial communication believe, however, that the face usually functions to communicate a limited number of dimensions of meaning. The face conveys not one dominant meaning but a number of dimensions of meaning. Those who see the face as functioning as a multidimensional source of meaning have generally accepted the conceptual model developed by Osgood (1966) when he was attempting to identify and measure the dimensions of meaning that are conveyed by verbal means.

Dimensions of Facial Meaning.   Both Osgood's objective and his conceptual framework were as praiseworthy as they had been in his earlier research on verbal meaning, which led to the development of the *semantic differential*. Osgood's factor-analytic research suggests that facial communication includes the following factors: (a) pleasantness, (b) control (represented by such specific expressions as annoyance and disgust versus amazement and excitement), and (c) intensity (rage, scorn, and loathing versus boredom, quiet, and complacency). A fourth, though weaker, factor is labeled "interest."

Osgood's research is supported by Mehrabian, who has adopted Osgood's concept of semantic space as well as his multidimensional approach to facial communication. As with Osgood, Mehrabian (1970) contends that facial communication consists of three dimensions of meaning, which he labels (a) evaluation, (b) potency or status, and (c) responsiveness.

Because so many researchers have found three dimensions of facial meaning, one might conclude that they have all found the same dimensions. Such a conclusion is not necessarily warranted. Often investigators apply their own, idiosyncratic labels to dimensions of meaning, making direct comparisons difficult. In addition, there has probably been a natural tendency to conclude that facial meaning comprises the same three dimensions as those of verbal meaning.

Indeed, some of our most impressive research suggests that facial communication includes not three but at least six dimensions of meaning. In an early study, Frijda and Philipszoon (1963) found four dimensions of facial meaning, which they identified as (a) pleasant/unpleasant; (b) naturalness/submission; (c) intensity of expression/control of expression; and (d) attention/disinterest. The second expression, naturalness/submission, was considered to be new, not previously found by the "three dimensional" students of facial communication. In a follow-up study, Frijda (1969) identified the four original dimensions as well as two others. Dimension 5 is now labeled "understanding/amazed," and dimension 6 is "simple/complicated."

In their exhaustive review and evaluation of the dimensional approach, Oster and colleagues (1989) concluded that recent models designed to identify and illustrate the interrelated dimensions of facial meaning have serious flaws. They conclude that whether "identification of (and appropriate responses to) emotional expressions on the basis of abstract dimensions could be as rapid or as accurate as identification in terms of categories—discrete—or fuzzy—is a question that has not been empirically addressed" (p. 131).

In addition, controversy remains with regard to how many dimensions of meaning can be communicated by facial means. From a review of research to date, however, we can reach the following conclusions:

1. The face communicates evaluative judgments through either pleasant or unpleasant expressions that indicate whether the communicator sees the current object of his or her attentions as good or bad.
2. The face communicates interest or disinterest in other people or in the surrounding environment.
3. The face communicates intensity and, hence, the degree of involvement in a situation.
4. The face communicates the amount of control individuals have over their own expressions.
5. The face probably communicates the intellectual factor of understanding, or the lack of it.

Each of the foregoing five dimensions of facial meaning has both positive and negative qualities. For example, although the face may communicate pleasantness in one situation, it may communicate unpleasantness in the next. Similarly, the face may communicate interest or disinterest, involvement or uninvolvement, control of emotions or lack of control. In a recent study, Mendolia (2007) studied complete versus partial facial expressions. For the categoric perspective, both complete and partial facial expressions of emotion were decoded at accuracy levels greater than chance. The expression with the lowest accuracy was contempt. For the dimensional perspective, decoders were also successful in deciphering emotions from both partial and complete facial expressions. The emotion of surprise had the highest score.

Moreover, Mendolia found that while decoders strategically use the categorical perspective, they may, at the same time, be sensitive to the dimensional perspective in forming their final evaluation of the emotion. This study should have profound implications for future facial expression research in nonverbal communication.

Clearly, the face has the potential to produce communication of high quality in which the meanings transmitted and received are virtually identical. The preceding dimensional analysis of meaning in facial expressions establishes that the face is capable of conveying positive reinforcement, interest, involvement, a sense of control over oneself and the immediate environment, and an image of a thoughtful person deliberating on the facts. These meanings are of great importance in interpersonal communication and are necessary—singly and in various combinations—to produce high-quality communication. Facial communication is directly related to relational success, especially in courting behavior. Couples often rely on one another's facial expressions to cue them into disappointment, joy, sadness, and happiness in the relationship. The frequency and effectiveness of facial expressions in dating and courting seems to be positively correlated with relational satisfaction. One study suggests that this satisfaction in courtship is dependent on narrowcast nonverbal communication—that is, facial expressions and other forms of nonverbal communication that only the two in the relationship are aware of and that will be unknown to outsiders (Grammer, Honda, Juette, & Schmitt, 1999).

At the same time, it is now obvious that the face is capable of communicating negative reinforcement, disinterest, withdrawal, lack of control, and a visceral rather than a thoughtful reaction to various messages. More recently, the face has been associated with degrees of ambivalence (Heisel & Mongrain, 2004). Heisel and Mongrain found that highly ambivalent women were more likely to communicate negative facial expressions than less ambivalent women. Furthermore, they found that the degree of ambivalence had a damaging impact upon their interaction with a partner and their relational success. What was the recent reaction of your friend when you said that you wanted more time to decide because you had not yet made up your mind about where to go for spring break? Or to your significant other when you were unsure about which movie to go and see? The potentially disruptive effects of such meanings are often dependent on matters such as context. For example, your date last weekend may have indicated disinterest or withdrawal when you leaned forward to offer a good-night kiss.

Side of the Face: Meaning Cues. If you subscribe to the categoric approach to facial expression, you will study the human face to try to determine which basic class of emotion is being communicated. You might be able to make more accurate judgments by concentrating on certain areas of the face. If you believe that the face functions to communicate *dimensions of meaning,* you will be particularly concerned with determining the *intensity* of the emotion being communicated facially. You may be able to *more accurately* assess intensity of emotion by concentrating on the left side of the communicator's face.

There is increasing evidence that the intensity of emotions is more accurately communicated on one side of the face than the other. Two sets of researchers (Mandal, Asthana, Madan, & Pandey, 1992; Sackeim, Gur, & Saucy, 1978) have found that emotions are expressed more intensely on the left side of the face. This phenomenon of the primacy of the left side of the face—in terms of the intensity of emotions expressed—may well be an inherited phenomenon. Thus, we know that the left side of the face is as dominant in emotional expression for rhesus monkeys as it is for humans (Hauser, 1993). Although the results are typically complex and difficult to interpret, studies of individuals with brain damage also suggest that the right side of the brain and, consequently, the left side of the face provide the best cues to intensity of emotion (Borod, Koff, Lorch, & Nicholas, 1986). Although the evidence is far from conclusive at present, research done to date suggests that the left side of the face provides more accurate intensity cues than the right side. If true, this finding may be attributed to the fact that facial displays of emotion, as well as other kinds of nonverbal cues, are controlled by the right side of the brain.

As you look at the two photographs of the right and left sides of the face in Figure 2.1A and B, can you determine which emotion is being communicated and with what degree of intensity? Consider the face on the left side of the page first. Does the left side of the face communicate disgust and the right side happiness? Now consider the face on the right side of the page. Does the left side of the face communicate happiness and the right side disgust? Did the right or the left side of the faces provide the most useful intensity cues?

The categoric and dimensional perspectives that are used to describe facial expressions should not be thought of as mutually exclusive, however. There is some evidence that the meaning communicated by a given facial expression can be determined most accurately by first placing that facial expression in a descriptive category, and then rating it for intensity. Ekman, perhaps the foremost proponent of the categoric perspective, conducted research (Ekman, Friesen, & Ancoli, 1980) to determine whether facial expressions provide

(A)   (B)

FIGURE 2.1

reliable information with regard to both the *kind* of emotion the encoder is experiencing and the *intensity* with which the emotion is experienced. The study seemed to confirm that facial expressions are most accurately described by first classifying them and then rating them.

The Face as a Means of Identifying Individuals

A second important function of the human face has received almost no attention by communication scholars. Have you or a friend ever been in a police lineup? Have you ever been asked to describe a person who assaulted you or robbed you? Have you ever wondered how an infant is able to identify his or her parents? Have you ever recognized a classmate on MySpace or Facebook? Did you recognize Tom Cruise or Nicholas Cage in the *Academy Awards* show? Researchers say that identification of individuals is a common way that we recognize celebrities on television or in the newspaper (Macrae, Quinn, Mason, & Quadflieg, 2005).

If these questions interest you, then it may be important for you to know that the appearance of the human face is the most reliable nonverbal source of information used to identify previously unidentified persons. Indeed, Ellis and Young (1989) treated this function of facial communication in detail. They concluded that the face is the most important source of visual information that people use to identify other human beings. Moreover, they contended that the ability of the average person to discriminate between hundreds of faces represents the ultimate in perceptual classification skills.

Forensic applications of face memory skills to identify missing persons or criminal suspects represent the most important use of this function. Interestingly, forensics experts are now using computer programs such as CAPSTAR and FRAME to store large quantities of facial information about a criminal suspect. "By using the power of the computer to store large quantities of facial information which can then be analyzed and evaluated on the basis of information obtained from a witness, some of the problems of using large mugfiles effectively are addressed" (Laughery & Wogalter, 1989, p. 545). Often a witness's memory of the suspect's face is so strong that the size of the mugfile can quickly be reduced and the probability of correct identification increased markedly. The face functions so effectively for purposes of personal identification that experts now are concentrating on developing the best means of describing the structure of the human face (Bruce, 1989). More recently, scientists have developed what is called Facial Recognition Technology, or FRT for short. FRT use has increased especially since 9/11 in an attempt to better secure airport terminals from would-be terrorists. In addition, FRT is used in other high-risk areas such as banks, government buildings, and casinos. Did you know that your picture could be in a national database? This gives new meaning to "Big Brother."

The Deceptive Face: Some Considerations

Facial expressions are usually a reliable source of meaning, but in some situations they may be unreliable. In those situations, the enlightened communicator must know for which signs of facial deception to watch. It is when facial expressions are consciously controlled that they are most apt to be deceptive; the individual will make his or her facial expression conform to certain norms or *display rules.* It should be noted here that eye behavior, vocalics, and other nonverbal cues have been more characteristic of deceptive persons.

Facial display rules may be classified as *personal, situational,* and *cultural.* Personal display rules may dictate that we inhibit the harshest displays of facial expression when communicating with children or physically handicapped individuals, for example. Situational display rules may dictate that in certain business situations, for example, we modify or modulate genuine expressions of facial emotions, such as disgust, so as not to offend a client or colleague. Finally, cultural display rules may vary because cultural groups differ, not only in the intensity of their facial expressions but also in the specific kinds of facial expressions they are likely to exhibit in public. We do know that Anglo-Saxons are more likely than Latinos to consciously control their facial expressions. We also know that the Asian's repertoire of publicly displayed emotions is quite limited; and that certain kinds of specialized facial expressions are confined to certain parts of the world and even to certain regions of a given country.

The impact of display rules or the desire to deceive may make facial expressions misleading sources of information in some cases. Thus, LaFrance and Mayo (1978) distinguished between facial expressions that might be classified as *representational* and those that might be classified as *presentational.* Representational expression is associated with genuine facial expressions that accurately reflect the actual emotion that the communicator is experiencing.

Presentation, in contrast, is the consciously controlled use of the face for purposes of public consumption. One type of facial presentation is the "emotional put-on," in which there may be a marked disparity between the facial emotion displayed and the emotion actually experienced. LaFrance and Mayo (1978) captured the difference between truthful and deceptive facial communication when they wrote that "The presentation is a performance, an arrangement and appearance designed to be seen. Its connection is less to inner feelings than to outer effect. In contrast, the representation refers to the expression of inner feelings" (p. 32).

Whatever the reason for controlling facial expression, or, in some cases, "putting on a false face," the receiver should recognize that the sender is apt to use one of three techniques (Ekman & Friesen, 1984): (a) *qualifying,* (b) *modulating,* or (c) *falsifying.* The basic classes of facial meaning that might be communicated are qualified when you add another facial expression to the original in order to modify the impact. For example, the boss who gives the subordinate a look of anger, immediately followed by a look of bewilderment, may be trying to communicate to the subordinate that he or she is very upset by what the subordinate did, but does not want to believe that the subordinate really did it. Facial meaning is modulated when the intensity of the facial expression is changed to communicate stronger or weaker feelings than those actually being experienced. For example, you may communicate slight sadness, facially, when you feel abject grief.

Finally, facial falsification may take one of three forms. A person may: (a) *simulate,* by showing facial emotion when no emotion is felt; (b) *neutralize,* by showing no facial emotion although some emotion is felt; or (c) *mask,* by covering a felt emotion while displaying a facial emotion that is not really felt.

Whether facial deception is intentional or involuntary, deception complicates the task of the decoder and reduces the potential value of the face as a reliable source of emotional information. When facial deception is used, the question becomes how the receiver guards against being deceived by such facial expressions. Several recent findings show mixed support (Levine, Park, & McCornack, 1999; Park et al., 2002).

The best method of guarding against such deception is training to develop decoding skills. If the facial expression seems to lack spontaneity, to be poorly synchronized with the content of the words being uttered, or to involve seemingly calculated movement in the lower part of the face, beware. Finally, the receiver should be alert for involuntary micromomentary facial expressions. These facial expressions usually last for only a fraction of a second. When these fleeting facial expressions contradict the meaning of more sustained facial expressions, facial deception may be occurring. In the 2005 Carroll Arnold Distinguished Lecture Series, Judee Burgoon (2005) suggested that, through training, decoders can discover certain facial and other nonverbal cues that typify lying behaviors while terrorist suspects are being interrogated by government officials. Clearly, nonverbal training has influence not only for the academy but for homeland security as well.

Measuring Sensitivity to Facial Expressions

The face may be used to deceive; nevertheless, it has unsurpassed potential for the communication of emotional information. We know now that individuals vary markedly in their ability to use the informational potential of the human face. Until quite recently, however, attempts to measure an individual's ability to decode meanings from facial expressions lacked specificity and precision. This was so because decoding tests did not require that decoders make fine distinctions between facial expressions that were closely related in meaning (Leathers & Emigh, 1980). Decoders were usually asked to view facial expressions and place them in one of seven or eight categories of the primary emotions.

The Facial Meaning Sensitivity Test

The Facial Meaning Sensitivity Test (FMST) represents the most detailed and precise measure of the ability to decode facial expressions that has been developed to date. In 1982, O'Sullivan evaluated eight measures of the ability to recognize facial expressions, including the Brief Affect Recognition Task (BART), Communication of Affect Receiving Ability Test (CARAT), and the Profile of Nonverbal Sensitivity (PONS). Until the introduction of the FMST, eight emotions, at most, were used for any test in which posed facial expressions were the stimuli. However, none of these eight tests included the detailed and difficult discriminatory tasks that are part of the FMST.

The accuracy in meaning of the FMST's facial photographs has been established through application of the test to a national sample of decoders. The validation procedure established not only that decoders using the FMST accurately distinguish among 10 basic classes of emotion communicated by facial expressions, but that they accurately label the subtle and closely related facial meanings that are constituents of each of the 10 broad classes of facial meaning.

The FMST is composed of a set of photographs of different facial expressions; it is a three-part test. The photographs in the test are all of the same person. Lauren Tucker was chosen because she has an expressive and photogenic face.

STEP 1 Facial Meaning Sensitivity Test

Classes of Facial Meaning	Expression Number (From Figure 2.2)
Disgust	
Happiness	
Interest	_____
Sadness	_____
Bewilderment	_____
Contempt	_____
Surprise	_____
Anger	_____
Determination	_____
Fear	_____

Part I of the FMST (see Figure 2.2) contains 10 photographs that represent the 10 basic classes of facial meaning. Study them and place the photograph numbers in the appropriate blanks of the chart in Step 1.

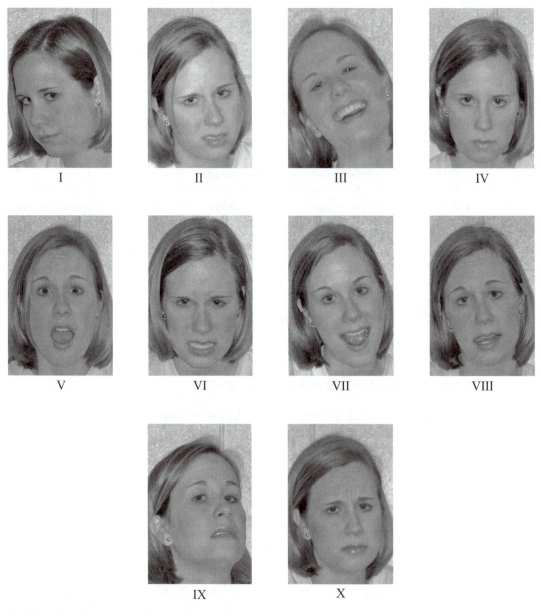

FIGURE 2.2 Facial Meaning Sensitivity Test, Part I

The correct answers for Step 1 of the FMST are

disgust	= I	contempt	= IX
happiness	= III	surprise	= VII
interest	= VIII	anger	= VI
sadness	= X	determination	= IV
bewilderment	= II	fear	= V

On the following pages you will see 30 more photographs of facial expressions (Figure 2.3 on pp. 40–41). Your task in Step 2 of the FMST is to group these facial expressions by class of meaning. Three of the photographs, for example, are intended to convey meanings that express a specific kind of disgust and, hence, should be perceived as part of that class of facial meaning. Among the 30 photos are three expressions that may be classified as specific kinds of happiness. Your task, then, is to select the three that you most closely associate with each of the 10 classes of facial meaning, using each photograph only once, and to place the photograph numbers in the appropriate blanks of the chart in Step 2.

STEP 2 Facial Meaning Sensitivity Test

Classes of Facial Meaning	Expressions That Are Part of Each Class (Expression Number from Figure 2.3)		
Disgust			
Happiness			
Interest			
Sadness			
Bewilderment			
Contempt			
Surprise			
Anger			
Determination			
Fear	_____	_____	_____

The correct choices for Step 2 of the FMST are

disgust	= 8, 12, 30	contempt	= 13, 24, 29
happiness	= 2, 9, 26	surprise	= 3, 16, 19
interest	= 6, 15, 23	anger	= 1, 20, 28
sadness	= 5, 7, 14	determination	= 11, 22, 25
bewilderment	= 4, 17, 18	fear	= 10, 21, 27

1

2

3

4

5

6

7

8

9

10

11

12

13

14

15

16

FIGURE 2.3   Facial Meaning Sensitivity Test, Part II

17

18

19

20

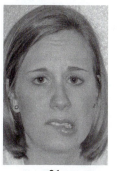
21

22

23

24

25

26

27

28

29

30

FIGURE 2.3 (Continued)

Results for each step of the FMST are scored separately because a weighted scoring system is used, with greater weight assigned to decoding decisions or answers that exhibited the highest degree of consensus. For Step 1, each correct answer (see Table 2.1) is worth 10 points, with a possible total of 100 points. The average score for the sample of decoders (n=268) for Step 1 was 90.9, with a standard deviation of 13.13.

In Step 3 of the FMST you have a discriminatory task of correctly identifying specific kinds of meaning. Consider the 30 photographs three at a time, and place the photograph number in the blank provided in the chart in Step 3. For example, you must decide whether picture 8, 12, or 30 communicates aversion. You must also identify repugnance and distaste in this series of three photographs.

TABLE 2.1   Accuracy of Identification for Basic Classes of Meaning Communicated by Facial Expression: Step 1 of the FMST

Class of Meaning	Photograph Number	Percentage of Correct Identification by Decoders	Type of Decoding Error	z-Value
Happiness	III	98.88	Surprise (0.75%) Interest (0.37%)	42.84
Sadness	X	96.64	Bewilderment (2.24%) Interest (0.37%)	48.47
Surprise	VII	95.90	Fear (2.99%) Interest (0.37%)	48.08
Anger	VI	92.91	Determination (6.34%) Disgust (0.37%)	45.91
Fear	V	91.41	Bewilderment (5.22%) Interest (1.40%)	37.83
Contempt	IX	89.18	Disgust (5.60%) Determination (2.61%)	43.93
Disgust	I	88.01	Contempt (4.49%)	42.84
Interest	VIII	87.31	Bewilderment (4.85%) Surprise (2.24%)	42.95
Determination	IV	86.94	Anger (5.97%) Contempt (4.48%)	43.54
Bewilderment	II	82.46	Fear (7.37%) Interest (3.86%)	39.29

All z-values are significant beyond the 0.0001 level. The two types of decoding errors that occurred most frequently for each class of meaning are reported in the Type of Decoding Error column.

STEP 3 **Facial Meaning Sensitivity Test**

Specific Kind of Facial Meaning			Photo Number: Choose from among the Following Expressions (Use Figure 2.3)
Aversion	Repugnance	Distaste	8, 12, 30
Amazement	Flabbergasted	Astonished	3, 16, 19
Rage	Hate	Annoyance	1, 20, 28
Confusion	Doubt	Stupidity	4, 17, 18
Terror	Anxiety	Apprehension	10, 21, 27
Disdain	Arrogance	Superiority	13, 24, 29
Laughter	Love	Amusement	2, 9, 26
Disappointment	Distress	Pensiveness	5, 7, 14
Attention	Anticipation	Excitement	6, 15, 23
Stubborn	Resolute	Belligerent	11, 22, 25

The correct choices for Step 3 of the FMST are:

30, 12, 8	24, 13, 29
16, 19, 3	9, 26, 2
28, 1, 20	14, 5, 7
18, 4, 17	23, 6, 15
10, 21, 27	11, 22, 25

National Decoding Norms. Results in Tables 2.1 to 2.3 provide decoding norms for each step of the FMST. The sample of decoders who produced these decoding norms were 118 engineers and corporate executives, 82 university students, and 68 members of fraternal and civic organizations; 201 decoders were males and 67 were females. To determine whether the level of skill reflected in your own attempts to decode the FMST's facial expressions was good, average, or poor, you need to follow a simple procedure.

Compute your decoding scores for each step of the FMST and compare your decoding performance with the decoding norms of the sample of decoders. For Step 1, scores of

TABLE 2.2   Accuracy of Classification of Facial Photographs into Classes of Meaning: Step 2 of the FMST

Class of Meaning	Photograph Number	Percentage of Decoders Correctly Classifying Each Photograph	Type of Decoding Error
Happiness	9	97.22	
	2	91.54	Interest (5.93)
	26	34.00	Interest (53.06)
	15	65.59	Happiness
Sadness	5	82.28	Fear (10.55)
	7	79.57	Bewilderment (7.18)
	14	70.17	Bewilderment (27.27)
Surprise	19	91.96	
	3	86.12	
	16	66.25	Fear (11.58); interest (12.36)
Anger	28	85.59	Fear (11.52)
	1	65.56	Determination (25.31); contempt (5.39)
	20	20.67	Disgust (48.56); contempt (11.54)
Fear	10	87.87	Determination (12.02)
	21	56.17	Bewilderment (21.70); sadness (16.60)
	27	62.98	Bewilderment (27.23); sadness (7.80)
Contempt	13	73.30	Determination (21.26)
	24	85.20	Disgust (5.00)
	29	75.57	Determination (14.47)
Disgust	8	72.93	Bewilderment (7.42); anger (6.11); contempt (5.48)
	30	56.67	Bewilderment (12.86); contempt (10.95); fear (10.00); anger (5.71)
Interest	6	91.95	
	23	81.86	Surprise (5.30)
	15	26.72	Happiness (65.59); surprise (6.48)
	26	53.06	Interest
Determination	11	71.49	Anger (27.00)
	25	69.70	Anger (17.31); contempt (8.66)
	22	51.91	Anger (29.36); interest (6.80); fear (5.10)
Bewilderment	18	77.12	Fear (6.78); sadness (6.36); disgust (5.93)
	17	56.52	Sadness (28.50); fear (5.80)
	4	18.69	Disgust (40.19); contempt (14.02) Anger (8.88); determination (7.94); interest (5.60)

TABLE 2.3   Accuracy of Identification of Specific Facial Expresions within Each Class of Meaning

Class of Meaning	Photograph Number (From Figure 2.3)	Percentage of Correct Identification	Type of Decoding Error	Percentage of Decoders Correctly Identifying All Facial Expressions within a Class
	28	Rage (95.74)	Hate (3.49) Annoyance (0)	
Anger	1	Hate (94.92)	Rage (3.49) Annoyance (1.94)	94.53
	20	Annoyance (98.96)	Rage (0.39) Hate (1.16)	
	9	Laughter (98.45)	Amusement (1.66) Love (0)	
Happiness	26	Love (91.09)	Amusement (8.53) Laughter (0)	90.27
	2	Amusement (90.31)	Love (8.14) Laughter (1.16)	
	18	Confusion (86.38)	Doubt (7.39) Stupidity (5.84)	
Bewilderment	4	Doubt (88.72)	Confusion (10.51) Stupidity (0.39)	85.66
	17	Stupidity (93.39)	Doubt (3.50) Confusion (2.72)	
	10	Terror (98.44)	Anxiety (9.78) Apprehension (0.30)	
Fear	21	Anxiety (77.43)	Apprehension (21.40) Terror (0.78)	76.74
	27	Apprehension (77.82)	Anxiety (21.40) Terror (0.39)	
	23	Attention (89.92)	Anticipation (6.98) Excitement (2.33)	
Interest	6	Anticipation (67.05)	Excitement (25.97) Attention (6.20)	66.16
	15	Excitement (71.32)	Anticipation (25.97) Attention (2.33)	
	14	Disappointment (56.59)	Pensiveness (25.19) Distress (17.44)	
Sadness	5	Distress (72.48)	Disappointment (21.71) Pensivenes (5.04)	53.91
	7	Pensiveness (86.61)	Disappointment (21.32) Distress (8.92)	

(continued)

TABLE 2.3 (Continued)

Class of Meaning	Photograph Number (From Figure 2.3)	Percentage of Correct Identification	Type of Decoding Error	Percentage of Decoders Correctly Identifying All Facial Expressions within a Class
Contempt	24	Disdain (55.25)	Arrogance (33.07) Superiority (11.28)	43.80
	13	Arrogance (47.47)	Disdain (35.41) Superiority (11.28)	
	29	Superiority (71.98)	Arrogance (19.07) Disdain (8.56)	
Disgust	30	Aversion (78.68)	Repugnance (9.69) Distaste (11.24)	42.25
	12	Repugnance (49.61)	Distaste (43.02) Aversion (7.36)	
	8	Distaste (43.35)	Repugnance (40.70) Aversion (13.95)	
Determination	11	Stubborn (51.55)	Belligerent (32.95) Resolute (14.73)	37.98
	22	Resolute (67.05)	Belligerent (22.09) Stubborn (10.47)	
	25	Belligerent (44.19)	Stubborn (37.60) Resolute (17.83)	
Surprise	16	Amazement (45.74)	Astonishment (32.95) Flabbergasted (20.93)	20.62
	19	Flabbergasted (35.66)	Astonishment (34.11) Amazement (29.35)	
	3	Astonishment (32.17)	Flabbergasted (42.25) Amazement (24.03)	

100 to 91 constitute good decoding, scores from 90 to 71 are average, and scores of 70 and below show poor performance. For Step 2, good, average, and poor decoding are determined, respectively, by the following range of scores: 100 to 83, 82 to 61, and 60 or below. For Step 3, 100 to 90 is good, 89 to 70 is average, and 60 and below is poor.

The Judgmental Process

You might profitably explore the judgmental processes that affect the encoding and decoding of facial expressions at this point. Intuitively you would probably assume that there would be a high correlation between the ability to encode and decode facial expressions.

If you made this assumption, your intuition failed you in this case. Correlations between measured levels of skill in encoding and decoding facial expressions have repeatedly been found to be low (Oster, Daily, & Goldenthal, 1989). Why?

No obvious or generally accepted explanation exists. Momentary thought might suggest, however, that the encoding of facial expressions is often preceded by careful contemplation. We recognize that the nature of the situation; our own age, ethnicity, gender, and social standing; the age, ethnicity, gender, and social standing of the person with whom we are communicating; the degree to which a facial emotion expressed is actually felt; and whether we work in a people-oriented job may all affect the type and intensity of the emotion(s) we choose to display on our face; these same factors may affect the decoder's judgment as to the type of emotion she or he sees displayed (Gosselin, Kirouac, & Dore, 1995; Morgado, Cangemi, Miller, & O'Connor, 1993; Nelson & Nugent, 1990).

The encoding of facial expression is clearly a skill that can be developed. We know that as you develop your ability to be emotionally expressive and your role-playing skills in a general sense, your ability to encode facial emotions is apt to increase (Tucker & Riggio, 1988). We know too that individuals who study the muscle involvements characteristic of certain facial emotions, and who practice expressing these emotions, will probably increase encoding skill (Leathers & Emigh, 1980).

While encoding facial expressions involves learned skills, some individuals are turning to surgical procedures to change and modify the way their face appears. For years, individuals have turned to makeup and plastic surgery to alter their facial appearance. More recently, some individuals have turned to face transplants to modify their facial features (Oakeshott, 2003). While surgeons insist in this British report that the surgeries will be performed only on patients with significant disfigurements and facial damage, this "bright line" remains to be seen, and undoubtedly, society will push for more vane, cosmetic reasons for the operation. While each of these cases involved personal injury or damage to the face, this still marks a societal shift away from "dealing with" the face that you were given. From a nonverbal communication perspective, face transplants could eventually involve more recreational or cosmetic improvements, not just for medical purposes. This could have a profound impact on nonverbal features and cues emitted from the face. Moreover, since the face is a significant nonverbal cue, this change could lead to significant success for the patient in his or her ability to communicate with spouses, family, friends, or co-workers. The communicative implications of this technological breakthrough are far-reaching.

At the same time, the facial expressions you choose to encode in public will probably be strongly affected by a variety of factors that have contributed to the distinctive social conditioning you have experienced within your own culture. Display rules, for example, dictate that certain emotions should and should not be expressed in certain cultures. The result frequently is that socially taboo emotions, when displayed facially within a given culture, are encoded at lower levels of accuracy. For example, if you work as a server in a restaurant and must appear polite even to rude customers, you would encode your facial expressions and mask what you really feel.

The decoding of facial expressions is fundamentally different from encoding in a number of respects. We recognize immediately that by encoding facial expressions, we run the risk of being labeled manipulative; the attempt to develop our decoding skills may, by contrast, be viewed as a sign of industriousness. Edwards and Bello (2001) looked at the impact of equivocation and face concerns. They found that while the decoders viewed equivocal speakers as more polite, decoders appeared more dishonest and less competent. For example, if you were a member of a Greek organization on campus and your face appeared to be polite or kind as you spoke in an equivocal tone, you might at the same time be perceived as more distrustful by other group members. These results have profound implications for how the face functions during conversation strategies and nonverbal impression management styles (see Chapter 9 for more information about impression management techniques). In addition, the factors that affect decoding accuracy are frequently outside of one's awareness and not consciously controlled by the decoder.

We know that generally, decoding accuracy is lower for men than it is for women; for the young and old than for the middle-aged; for persons decoding spontaneous as opposed to posed facial expressions; for individuals who have no situational or contextual cues; for persons decoding the facial expressions of strangers; and for learning disabled children, adolescents, emotionally disturbed children, juvenile delinquents, and psychiatric patients (Gepp & Hess, 1986; Oster, Daily, & Goldenthal, 1989; Rotter & Rotter, 1988; Tucker & Riggio, 1988). In most cases, we are not sure why the groups identified experience deficits in decoding accuracy.

Developing Sensitivity to Facial Expressions: Training Program

The fact that the decoding of facial expressions often takes place outside the decoder's conscious level of awareness does not mean that the decoder cannot become consciously aware of this activity. In fact, this is the first step in more accurately decoding facial expressions.

There can be little doubt that the ability to decode accurately the facial expressions of interactants in a variety of real-world situations is a vitally important communicative competency. *Such a competency, when fully developed, not only provides the interpreter of facial messages with a reliable means of detecting facial deceit, but it also provides a sound basis for identifying the emotions, moods, and feelings actually being experienced by the interactants.* That such information may be used to help achieve individual or organizational goals in given situations seems clear.

In particular, training programs should be designed for the express purpose of developing skill in decoding facial expressions. A detailed description of such a training program is the subject of another book. However, the following are some of the essential features and components of the training programs we have used for business groups.

One of the most useful training tools is videotape. Whenever possible, the facial expressions of interactants in communication situations should be videotaped and subjected to subsequent analysis. With the aid of the trainer, the interactants should study videotaped facial expressions in order to identify the use of display rules and techniques of facial management, to identify inconsistency in meaning between facial expression and words, and to identify the subtle nuances of emotional meaning that are being communicated by facial expression. This method is often used in the videotaping of police interrogations to help determine the falsehood of the arrestee's statements.

In addition to videotape, a training program should feature muscle-profile charts and facial blueprints. We now know which facial muscles are used to communicate such emotions as contempt and disgust, although this is a difficult distinction to make. Anyone who is fully familiar with the various facial muscles used to communicate facial disgust and contempt is not likely to make a decoding error when observing such facial expressions. In fact, decoding accuracy should be facilitated by familiarizing oneself with "families of facial expressions." Barrett (1993) argued incisively that emotions may properly be viewed as members of families of emotions. Thus, she claimed that "there are *intrinsic* but *not invariant* links between specific emotion families (e.g., fear, anger, shame/embarrassment)" (p. 154).

Finally, sets of facial blueprints should be used in combination with model photographs of particular facial emotions. The facial blueprints developed by Ekman and Friesen (1984) are especially useful because they break down the face into three areas. The trainee can learn that different emotions are more easily recognized by concentrating on certain areas of the face. For example, in facial sadness, the inner corners of the eyebrows are raised, the inner corners of the upper eyelids are drawn up, and the corners of the lips are drawn down.

In short, measuring and developing the ability to use facial expression as a reliable source of emotional information should be a central concern to any individual who wishes to be a socially sensitive communicator. With awareness, that concern could be reflected in widespread efforts to use the full communicative potential of the human face.

Summary

Facial expressions serve many functions. The impressions a communicator makes are often strongly affected by the appearance of the person's face or by the muscle involvements that define a given facial expression. Facial appearance often exerts a disproportionate influence in judgments of overall physical attractiveness, for example. The position of facial features such as eyebrows may shape judgments of dominance. To smile or not to smile is an important decision because different image qualities are attributed to the smiling and nonsmiling communicator.

The two most important functions of the human face are the communication of emotions and the identification of previously unidentified people. Because of its universal importance in human interaction, the communication of emotions is the primary function of facial expression.

A theoretical understanding of the nature of emotion, in turn, is a prerequisite to a complete understanding of the potential of the human face as a medium of emotional communication. Emotion is a complex but temporary psychological state involving physiological, experiential, and behavioral changes. The communicator's primary concerns should be the degree to which he or she is aware of facial emotions being communicated, the degree of control that the individual can exercise over such emotions, and the relationship between internal states of the body and the emotion being displayed on the face.

The two major approaches used to explain how the face functions communicatively are the categoric and the dimensional perspectives. Researchers who embrace the categoric perspective believe that the face functions to communicate a given type or category of meaning at any given point in time. Results from categoric research have established that the face is capable of communicating at least eight basic classes of meaning: happiness, surprise, fear, anger, sadness, disgust, contempt, and interest. By concentrating on the facial muscles used in different areas of the face, decoders can increase their ability to differentiate accurately among these eight general classes of facial meaning.

The dimensional perspective is based on the assumption that facial expressions are dimensional in nature. Consequently, they are best described by the dimensions of meaning that define them. Most dimensional researchers have found that facial expressions vary with regard to how pleasant and interested the communicator seems to be, and some evidence suggests that facial expressions reflect the communicator's degree of understanding. Recent research also suggests that emotions are displayed more intensely on the left as opposed to the right side of the face.

With the advent of computerized storage of information on the facial features of missing persons and criminal suspects, the face now also serves an important function as a means of identifying individuals. Forensic applications of face memory skills to identify missing persons or criminal suspects represent the most important use of this function.

Although facial expressions often accurately reflect the communicator's feelings, they may also be used to deceive. Genuine facial expressions are identified as representational, and deceptive facial expressions are known as presentational. In putting on a false face, communicators may use the techniques of qualifying, modulating, or falsifying.

Previous attempts to measure an individual's ability to decode meanings from facial expressions lacked specificity and precision. Most decoding tests lack precision because they do not require that decoders make the difficult discriminations between facial expressions that are closely related in meaning. Decoders can use the Facial Meaning Sensitivity Test (FMST) to measure their ability to make such difficult discriminations and compare their decoding accuracy against a set of decoding norms developed for the FMST. Readers who find their decoding skill to be deficient may wish to consider a training program designed to develop this important communicative skill.

REFERENCES

Alicke, M. D., Smith, R. H., & Klotz, M. L. (1986). Judgments of physical attractiveness: The role of faces and bodies. *Personality and Social Psychology Bulletin, 12,* 381–389.

Alvarado, N., & Jameson, K. A. (2002). Varieties of anger: The relation between emotion terms and components of anger expressions. *Motivation and Emotion, 26,* 153–182.

Barrett, K. C. (1993). The development of nonverbal communication of emotion: A functionalist perspective. *Journal of Nonverbal Behavior, 17,* 145–169.

Berry, D. S. (1990). What can a moving face tell us? *Journal of Personality and Social Psychology, 58,* 1004–1014.

Berry, D. S., & McArthur, L. Z. (1985). Some components and consequences of a babyface. *Journal of Personality and Social Psychology, 48,* 312–323.

Borod, J. C., Koff, E., Lorch, M. P., & Nicholas, M. (1986). Deficits in facial expression and movement as a function of brain damage. In J. Nespoulous, P. Perron, & A. R. Lecours (Eds.), *The biological foundations of gestures* (pp. 271–293). Hillsdale, NJ: Erlbaum.

Bruce, V. (1989). The structure of faces. In A. W. Young & W. D. Ellis (Eds.), *Handbook on research face processing* (pp. 101–104). Amsterdam: North-Holland.

Bugental, D. W. (1986). Unmasking the "polite smile": Situational and personal determinants of managed affect in adult-child interaction. *Personality and Social Psychology Bulletin, 12,* 7–16.

Burgoon, J. K. (2005). *Truth, lies, and virtual worlds.* Carroll C. Arnold Distinguished Lecture Series. Speech presented at the Annual Meeting of the National Communication Association.

Collier, G. (1985). *Emotional expression.* Hillsdale, NJ: Erlbaum.

Edwards, R., & Bello, R. (2001). Interpretations of messages: The influence of equivocation, face concerns, and ego-involvement. *Human Communication Research, 27,* 597–631.

Ekman, P. (1994). Strong evidence for universals in facial expressions: A reply to Russell's mistaken critique. *Psychological Bulletin, 115,* 268–287.

Ekman, P., Davidson, R. J., & Friesen, W. V. (1990). The Duchenne smile: Emotional expression and brain physiology. II. *Journal of Personality and Social Psychology, 58,* 342–353.

Ekman, P., & Friesen, W. V. (1978). *Manual for the facial action coding system.* Palo Alto, CA: Consulting Psychologists Press.

Ekman, P., & Friesen, W. V. (1982). Felt, false, and miserable smiles. *Journal of Nonverbal Behavior, 6,* 238–252.

Ekman, P., & Friesen, W. V. (1984). *Unmasking the face: A guide to recognizing emotions from facial expressions.* Englewood Cliffs, NJ: Prentice-Hall.

Ekman, P., & Friesen, W. V. (1986). A new pan-cultural facial expression of emotion. *Motivation and Emotion, 10,* 159–168.

Ekman, P., Friesen, W. V., & Ancoli, S. (1980). Facial signs of emotional experience. *Journal of Personality and Social Psychology, 39,* 1125–1134.

Ekman, P., Friesen, W. V., & Ellsworth, P. (1982). Research foundations. In P. Ekman (Ed.), *Emotion in the human face* (2nd ed., pp. 1–6). Cambridge: Cambridge University Press.

Ekman, P., Friesen, W. V., & Tomkins, S. S. (1971). Facial affect scoring technique: A first validity study. *Semiotica, 3,* 37–58.

Ellis, H. D., & Young, A. W. (1989). Are faces special? In A. W. Young & H. D. Ellis (Eds.), *Handbook of research on face processing* (pp. 1–26). Amsterdam: North-Holland.

Frank, M. G., & Ekman, P. (2004). Appearing truthful generalizes across different situations. *Journal of Personality and Social Psychology, 86,* 486–495.

Frank, M. G., & Stennett, J. (2001). The forced-choice paradigm and the perception of facial expressions of emotion. *Journal of Personality and Social Psychology, 80,* 75–85.

Frijda, N. H. (1969). Recognition of emotions. In L. Berkowitz (Ed.), *Advances in experimental and social psychology.* New York: Academic.

Frijda, N. H., & Philipszoon, E. (1963). Dimensions of recognition of expression. *Journal of Abnormal and Social Psychology, 66,* 45–51.

Frois-Wittmann, J. (1930). The judgment of facial expression. *Journal of Experimental Psychology, 13,* 113–151.

Gepp, J., & Hess, D. L. (1986). Children's understanding of verbal and facial display rules. *Developmental Psychology, 22,* 103–108.

Gosselin, P., Kirouac, G., & Dore, F. Y. (1995). Components and recognition of facial expression in the communication of emotion by actors. *Journal of Personality and Social Psychology, 68,* 83–96.

Grammer, K., Honda, M., Juette, A., & Schmitt, A. (1999). Fuzziness of nonverbal courtship communication unblurred by motion energy detection. *Journal of Personality and Social Psychology, 77,* 487–508.

Hauser, M. D. (1993). Right hemisphere dominance for the production of facial expression in monkeys. *Science, 26,* 475–477.

Heisel, M., & Mongrain, M. (2004). Facial expressions and ambivalence: Looking for conflict in all the right faces. *Journal of Nonverbal Behavior, 28,* 35–52.

Hess, U., Blairy, S., & Kleck, R. E. (2000). The influence of facial emotion displays, gender, and ethnicity on judgments of dominance and affiliation. *Journal of Nonverbal Behavior, 24,* 265–283.

Izard, C. E. (1971). *The face of emotion.* New York: Appleton.

Keating, C. F. (1985). Gender and physiognomy of dominance and attractiveness. *Social Psychology Quarterly, 48,* 61–70.

Keating, C. F., & Bal, D. L. (1986). Children's attributions of social dominance from facial cues. *Child Development, 57,* 1269–1276.

Knapp, M. L., & Hall, J. A. (2006). *Nonverbal communication in human interaction* (6th ed.). Belmont, CA: Thomson.

Krumhuber, E., & Kappas, A. (2005). Moving smiles: The role of dynamic components for the perception of the genuineness of smiles. *Journal of Nonverbal Behavior, 29,* 3–24.

LaFrance, M., & Mayo, C. (1978). *Moving bodies: Nonverbal communication in social relationships.* Monterey, CA: Brooks/Cole.

Laughery, K. R., & Wogalter, S. (1989). Forensic applications of facial memory research. In A. W. Young & H. D. Ellis (Eds.), *Handbook of research on face processing* (pp. 519–547). Amsterdam: North-Holland.

Leathers, D. G., & Emigh, T. H. (1980). Decoding facial expressions: A new test with decoding norms. *Quarterly Journal of Speech, 66,* 418–436.

Levenson, R. W. (1988). Emotions and the autonomic nervous system: A prospectus for research on autonomic specificity. In H. Wager (Ed.), *Social psychophysiology and emotion: Theory and clinical applications* (pp. 17–41). Chichester: Wiley.

Levine, T. R., Park, H. S., & McCornack, S. A. (1999). Accuracy in detecting truths and lies: Documenting the "veracity effect." *Communication Monographs, 66,* 125–144.

Macrae, C. N., Quinn, K. A., Mason, M. F., & Quadflieg, S. (2005). Understanding others: The face and person construal. *Journal of Personality and Social Psychology, 89,* 686–695.

Mandal, M. K., Asthana, H. S., Madan, S. K., & Pandey, R. (1992). Hemifacial display of emotion in the resting state. *Behavioural Neurology, 5,* 169–171.

Matsumoto, D. (2005). Scalar ratings of contempt expressions. *Journal of Nonverbal Behavior, 29,* 91–104.

Mehrabian, A. (1970). A semantic space for nonverbal behavior. *Journal of Consulting and Clinical Psychology, 35,* 248–249.

Mendolia, M. (2007). Explicit use of categorical and dimensional strategies to decode facial expressions of emotion. *Journal of Nonverbal Behavior, 31,* 57–75.

Messinger, D. S., Fogel, A., & Dickson, K. L. (2001). All smiles are positive, but some smiles are more positive than others. *Developmental Psychology, 37,* 642–653.

Mignault, A., & Chaudhuri, A. (2003). The many faces of a neutral face: Head tilt and perception of dominance and emotion. *Journal of Nonverbal Behavior, 27,* 111–132.

Morgado, I. A., Cangemi, J. P., Miller, R., & O'Connor, J. (1993). Accuracy of decoding facial expressions in those engaged in people oriented activities vs. those engaged in nonpeople oriented activities. *Studia Psychologica, 35,* 73–80.

Nelson, C. A., & Nugent, K. M. (1990). Recognition memory and resource allocation as revealed by children's event-related potential responses to happy and angry faces. *Developmental Psychology, 26,* 171–179.

Osgood, C. E. (1966). Dimensionality of the semantic space for communication via facial expressions. *Scandinavian Journal of Psychology, 7,* 1–30.

Oster, H., Daily, L., & Goldenthal, P. (1989). Processing facial affect. In W. W. Young & H. D. Ellis (Eds.), *Handbook of research on face processing* (pp. 107–161). Amsterdam: North-Holland.

O'Sullivan, M. (1982). Measuring the ability to recognize facial expressions. In P. Ekman (Ed.), *Emotion in the human face* (2nd ed. pp. 281–317). Cambridge: Cambridge University Press.

Oakeshott, I. (2003, November 10). Brits ready for face off. *Evening Standard,* pp. 1+.

Park, H. S., Levine, T. R., McCornack, S. A., Morrison, K., & Ferrara, M. (2002). How people really detect lies. *Communication Monographs, 69,* 144–157.

Rotter, N. G., & Rotter, G. S. (1988). Sex differences in the encoding and decoding of negative facial emotions. *Journal of Nonverbal Behavior, 12,* 139–148.

Rozin, P., Lowery, L., & Ebert, R. (1994). Varieties of disgust faces and the structure of disgust. *Journal of Personality and Social Psychology, 66,* 870–881.

Sackeim, H. A., Gur, R. C., & Saucy, M. C. (1978). Emotions are expressed more intensely on the left side of the face. *Science, 202,* 434–436.

Suzuki, K., & Naitoh, K. (2003). Brief report: Useful information for face perception is described with FACS. *Journal of Nonverbal Behavior, 27,* 43–55.

Tomkins, S. S. (1962). *Affect, imagery, consciousness, I.* New York: Springer-Verlag.

Tucker, J. S., & Riggio, R. E. (1988). The role of social skills in encoding posed and spontaneous facial expressions. *Journal of Nonverbal Behavior, 12,* 87–97.

Wagner, H. L., MacDonald, C. J., & Manstead, A. S. R. (1986). Communication of individual emotions by spontaneous facial expressions. *Journal of Personality and Social Psychology, 50,* 737–743.

Woodworth, R. S. (1938). *Experimental psychology.* New York: Holt

Zebrowitz, L. A. (1997). *Reading faces: Window to the soul?* Oxford, UK: Westview Press.

CHAPTER

3

Eye Behaviors

French philosopher Henri Louis Bergson once said, "The eye sees only what the mind is prepared to comprehend."

Eye behaviors clearly stand out as one of the primary nonverbal features in our human interaction. Oftentimes, eyes are the mirror of the soul, and can often reveal the true nature of the self.

Recently, Texas Hold'em poker has become a cultural phenomenon. Found on about every TV channel and on every neighborhood corner, individuals are becoming increasingly interested in playing this table game. One of the key strategies in the game of poker is being able to disguise one's true poker hand. This is usually done by the player who can successfully manage his or her eye behaviors. Often, poker professionals on TV will be seen wearing sunglasses while playing at the table. There is no doubt as to why this behavior is done—to hide their eye behaviors, which might reveal or "give away" their hand to their opponents.

In a nonverbal class at the university, Eaves's students played the game of Texas Hold'em poker as a class exercise. About one-half of the class played in groups of five as the other half observed the players' eye behaviors during the game. In addition, students were not allowed to wear sunglasses (and thus couldn't hide their eye movements). Those students who were the most successful were not necessarily the ones with the best hands. In fact, the observing class members found that those students who were able to disguise their eye behaviors and appear more stoic were the most successful at the poker table.

We have many beliefs about the symbolic significance of eye behaviors. These beliefs frequently take the form of stereotypes. The deceiver stereotype, for example, is based to a considerable extent on societal beliefs about the eye behaviors that deceivers characteristically exhibit. In fact, perceivers are much more likely to detect deception with greater accuracy by relying on the target's nonverbal, rather than verbal, cues (Anderson, DePaulo, Ansfield, Tickle, & Green, 1999). This stereotype suggests that honest and trustworthy individuals exhibit one type of eye behavior whereas devious and untrustworthy individuals exhibit another. Leathers and Hocking (1982) have done in-depth examinations of police interviewers' beliefs as to which nonverbal cues are the most useful indicators of the deception of a lying criminal suspect. The police interviewers are convinced that eye behaviors are the most reliable indicators of deception. In fact,

Our eyes communicate our interest to our friends.

one police interviewer for the Georgia Bureau of Investigation told Leathers that he had never observed a lying criminal suspect whose pupils did not dilate at the time of deception. In a related case, one local police officer told Eaves in a personal interview that the eye behaviors of arrestees are a key determinant of their deception during the police interrogation process. He went on to say that the interrogations are often videotaped, thus allowing the officers time to review key eye movements or behaviors that might reveal lying or fabrication of interview content.

The eyes serve an almost endless number of communicative functions and provide many different kinds of information. Have you ever encountered an individual whose eyes were hard, beady, sly, shifty, radiant, shining, dull, or sparkling? If so, you will probably admit that such eyes affected not only your perception of the person and your desire to interact with that person, but also your own behavior. In addition, human eyes have great communicative significance, as suggested by the numerous expressions used to describe eye behaviors; for example, a person is "shifty eyed" or "bug-eyed"; a person "gave me the eye" or "gave me the fish eye"; "see eye to eye," "have an eye to," "an eyesore," and "an eye-opener."

This chapter is designed to help you make the most effective use of the great communicative potential of your eye behaviors. To do so you must understand the types of eye behaviors that you may exhibit and know what modifications you should make if you are to overcome problems associated with dysfunctional eye behaviors.

The Language of the Eyes

There may well be a language of the eyes with its own syntax and grammar (Webbink, 1986). If so, we are years if not decades away from understanding that language in a structural sense.

Exhibited Eye Behaviors

Labels with definitions have been developed to describe the types of eye behaviors you can exhibit.

We need to define and explain the following eye behaviors and terms. The following descriptions and explanations are derived from earlier eye research (Cranach, 1971; Harper, Wiens, & Matarazzo, 1978; Kleinke, 1986).

Eye contact is a classic phrase used to describe when two people look at one another, but not necessarily eye to eye. This is often one of the most misunderstood and confusing terms used in eye communication research. Some researchers have described eye contact as the "one-sided look." Argyle and Dean (1965) provide some illumination on this subject. Eye contact becomes shorter the closer two people are standing to each other. In addition, when the eyes are shut, people are more likely to stand closer.

Face-gaze is when you are looking at someone else's face. For example, you may turn to look at your partner in a debate for help or gaze into the face of the cashier as you pay for your meal at the campus cafeteria.

Eye-gaze occurs when our gaze is focused directly upon a person's eyes. This is typically a more intense behavior than face-gaze. For example, a police interrogator is likely to eye-gaze into the arrestee's eyes to detect possible deception. In another example, your boyfriend or girlfriend might gaze into your eyes to assess the validity of your story about where you were the night before.

Looking and *gazing* are both general terms that refer to a person looking in the direction of another person's face. However, looking behavior can also refer to seeing an object. For example, a child may look for his mommy in the room or look for the ball that he dropped. Oftentimes, *looking* in the research is used interchangeably with *glancing*.

Mutual gaze is when two people gaze at each other's faces. Stronger than gazing alone, mutual gaze involves two people and thus has a stronger communicative impact. For example, mutual gaze would occur when a lawyer gazes at the witness on the stand and the witness returns the gesture to the attorney. In an interesting study, researchers found that when two people use mutual gaze, they are more likely to remember that person or specific things about the encounter that they would otherwise not know (Vuilleumier et al., 2005).

Mutual eye contact occurs when two people look into the eyes of each other. Mutual eye contact is a stronger eye behavior than mutual gazing, since gazing involves only the "region" of the eyes, not the eyes themselves. For instance, two honeymooners are often caught mutually gazing into one another's eyes for no apparent reason at all.

Gaze avoidance is defined as "intentional" avoidance of eye contact. For example, a child who is guilty of doing something wrong will often avoid eye contact with the parent who questions him or her. In one study, Kidwell (2003) found that children used gaze avoidance to resist the caregiver's intervention to punish the misconduct. This behavior happened whether they had bitten another child, pushed, stolen a toy, or taken something away from someone else.

Staring is defined as a persistent gaze or look that occurs regardless of the other person's reaction. For example, have you ever played the stare game and tried staring at your roommate for five minutes? Were you successful? Who was the first one to "crack"?

Gaze omission occurs when there is an unintentional failure to make eye contact with another person. This is not likely to happen in a speech class. The speaker may get nervous, but he or she chooses whether to look at the audience or not. For example, gaze omission might occur if you are in a hurry and you thank your neighbor or friend for getting your mail but forget to gaze at her or him. Also, some of your classmates may have difficulty looking at you when they speak to you. This is a habit—they are not doing this intentionally, but that does not make it any less frustrating on your part.

Gaze aversion is defined as movement of your eyes away from your interaction partner's eyes. For example, gaze aversion is likely to occur if you are embarrassed by one of your partner's comments or feel ashamed because of something you did to that person.

Eyeblinking is a nervous gesture that often has a negative association. Specifically, eyeblinking is defined as the number of times your eyelids close per unit of time. We will discuss this aspect of eye behaviors in more detail in Chapter 9 and 10 when we discuss the politician's ability to control his or her eye behaviors so as to send a positive message to his or her voting public.

Eye-flutter refers to the number of times your eyeballs exhibit slight but discernible horizontal and vertical movements per unit of time. This is sometimes associated with eye shifts. In the courtroom, for example, a lawyer will coach his or her client to avoid eye-flutters since they can be perceived by a jury as dishonest or untruthful.

Pupil size is defined as the average size of the diameter(s) of a person's pupils. For instance, a person with a startled look is likely to have larger pupils.

Gaze following occurs when someone looks where another person has just looked. Brooks and Meltzoff (2002) found that infants were more likely to look in the direction of an adult (probably a parent or guardian) when the infant had an unobstructed view of the target. This research refines earlier gaze research and tells us more about the early social learning of gaze techniques and gestures in infancy.

Measured Eye Behaviors

The language of the eyes is defined not only by the types of eye behaviors that you and one or more interaction partners exhibit but also by the types of eye behaviors that can be reliably measured. Exline and Fehr (1982) maintained that five types of gaze variables have been most frequently measured:

1. *Frequency:* the number of times that an individual looks at a conversational partner
2. *Total duration:* the number of seconds a communicator looks at a particular interaction partner
3. *Proportion of time:* the percentage of total interaction time that a communicator spends looking at or away from an interaction partner when engaging in a particular kind of communication, that is, speaking or listening
4. *Average duration:* mean or average duration of glances directed at an interaction partner
5. *Standard deviation of glances:* average duration of glances that provides information regarding variability in length of single glances

Although these eye behavior variables have been repeatedly and reliably measured, two measurement questions remain unanswered: Can glances directed at the interaction partner's eyes and face be reliably distinguished? Can we determine the degree to which individuals are consciously aware of different kinds of eye contact directed toward them?

The Functions of Eye Behaviors

The voluminous body of research on eye behaviors has clearly established what members of many cultures have believed through the ages: *Eye behaviors serve many vitally important communicative functions.* If for no other reason, eye behaviors would be functionally important because they are the primary center of visual attention. Janik, Wellens, Goldberg, and DeLosse (1978) established that more visual inspection time is spent looking in the region of the eyes than at any other part of the body. Attention is focused on the eyes 43.4 percent of the time; the second most important area of visual attention is the mouth, where attention is focused 12.6 percent of the time.

Because people do concentrate their attention on the eye region, it is reasonable to ask: Why do the eyes receive so much attention? The answer seems to be that people attend to the eyes because they serve a variety of important communicative functions. The eyes

1. indicate degrees of attentiveness, interest, and arousal
2. help initiate and sustain intimate relationships
3. influence attitude change and persuasion
4. regulate interaction
5. communicate emotions
6. define power and status relationships
7. assume a central role in impression management

The Attention Function

Eyes play an important role in the initiation of interpersonal communication because they signal a readiness to communicate. Argyle and Cook (1976) emphasized that mutual gaze "has the special meaning that two people are attending to each other. This is usually necessary for social interaction to begin or be sustained" (p. 170). Eye behaviors not only signal whether two people are attending to each other, however; they also reflect the *degree* of mutual interest.

The importance of our eyes in gaining attention is apparent if you reflect for a moment. Have you ever given someone you found attractive the eye? Have you tried to catch the eye of a waiter or a waitress in a restaurant while he or she in turn signaled readiness to serve or not to serve you by eye contact or avoidance?

Our eyes function effectively both to gain attention and to indicate our level of interest. Hess (1975) suggests that pupil size accurately reflects a person's level of interest. Pupils dilate as interest increases; they constrict when interest decreases. Hess stresses that the pupils of the eyes are a potentially rich source of information because "the pupil of the eye is intimately connected to all parts of the brain, and as a result, we have the anomalous situation of having a piece of the brain sticking out of the human body for all the world to see and to evaluate" (pp. 4–5). Metalis and Hess (1982a) have found that a person's pupil size reliably communicates two types of information about a communication: the attentiveness and interest of the listener and the pleasantness of the communicator's current object of attention.

In a general sense, Hess (1975) has established that pupil size accurately reflects the degree of a person's sexual arousal, whether a person is responding positively or negatively to the attitudes and values of another person, and the intensity of a person's feelings about another.

Research suggests that pupil size can provide even more specialized information. Pupil size increases as the cognitive difficulty of a reading task increases (Metalis & Hess, 1986; Suaste, Garcia, Rodriguez, & Zuniga, 2004), and subjects' pupils dilate (their interest level goes up) when observing pictures of main course meals but not snacks (Metalis & Hess, 1982b).

Pupillometrics defines that area of scientific research that focuses on the measurement of psychopupil response. *Pupillography* in turn consists of the actual photographing of the pupils of the eyes at different points in time. Because pupil size can be used to measure level of interest, attitude change, and cognitive processes, pupillometrics has potentially great value in the areas of marketing and advertising. One recent example of pupil size and marketing is found in Internet advertising. Pop-up ads are commonplace and perhaps one of the largest nuisances in Web shopping. Another good example of visual advertising is the large sign or banner on the passing NASCAR vehicle (e.g., the "Tide" car or the "Gatorade" car).

The Persuasive Function

The persuader who wishes to be perceived as credible must sustain eye contact while speaking and being spoken to by the persuadee. To avoid a marked decline in their credibility, persuasive communicators must not be shifty eyed, look down or away from the persuadee frequently, blink excessively, or exhibit eye-flutter. Petty and Cacioppo (1986) have advanced the ELM (Elaboration Likelihood Model) of persuasion. The model states that there are two routes to persuasion: central routes (i.e., when elaboration is high) and peripheral routes (i.e., when elaboration is low). It is in these peripheral routes of persuasion that nonverbal communication takes center stage.

Eye behaviors are a key peripheral variable in the persuasion process. For example, if a student were to focus on her professor's eye behaviors instead of on the content of the professor's lecture, the student would be processing the message peripherally. Another example occurs in politics. If one were to be swayed by Hillary Clinton's eye behavior and her strength in that area of public speaking, he would be persuaded along peripheral routes, or areas of low elaboration. Whenever we need a quick evaluation or an easy out, we often turn to peripheral routes to make a decision in a persuasive context. If the police officer who pulls you over asks you to take out your driver's license, you may be more compelled by the serious eye demeanor of the officer than by the message itself.

In his exhaustive review of eye behavior research, Kleinke (1986) documented the potentially powerful impact of eye behaviors on credibility and, ultimately, on persuasive effectiveness. He emphasized that a number of empirical studies support the stereotypic conviction that we tend to believe those individuals who look us directly in the eye, and we see individuals who do not as deceitful. Thus, witnesses in courtroom trials have been judged as more credible when they did not avert their gaze from the attorney who was questioning them. Similarly, airline travelers who avoided eye contact were judged as more suspicious and suitable for search by airport inspectors than airline travelers who maintained eye contact. Results from a recent study suggest once again that the persuasive effectiveness of persons who maintain eye contact with potential persuadees is greater than those who do not (Hornik, 1987).

For example, in the 2004 presidential campaign, George W. Bush suffered nonverbally in his early debate. His poor eye contact gave Senator John Kerry a decided advantage in the presidential race. After consultation, Bush improved significantly by his third debate against Kerry.

It should be noted, however, that while Kerry shined in the presidential debates, Bush was a more successful one-on-one communicator. Bush would often meet individuals and smile with warm eye contact. On the other hand, Kerry had difficulty when being asked impromptu questions by a voter or someone he met in the street. Oftentimes, Kerry's eye contact was inferior to Bush's eye behavior in these specialized contexts. Bush's strengths in eye behavior in those situations were persuasive and carried weight with the significant portion of the population that had not seen the debates.

There can be little doubt that eye behaviors are important determinants of credibility. Researchers (Burgoon, Coker, & Coker, 1986; Burgoon & Saine, 1978) have provided convincing documentation for their claim that direct eye contact in our society is interpreted as a sign of credibility. Direct eye contact is apt to have a beneficial impact on both the communicator's perceived competence and the communicator's trustworthiness. We generally assume that individuals who look directly at us know what they are talking about and are being honest with us. Conversely, when people avert their eyes before speaking to us or answering a question, we are likely to find them less trustworthy, less credible in terms of competence, and thus less persuasive.

Burgoon, Manusov, Mineo, and Hale (1985) found that gaze aversion significantly reduces one's chances of being hired in a job interview. Such a finding may be attributed in large part to the strong and decidedly negative impact of gaze aversion on the job interviewee's credibility. Burgoon and co-workers also found that individuals who maintain normal to high eye contact are judged to be much more credible than those who have eye contact of limited duration. More specifically, job interviewees with limited eye contact and gaze aversion were viewed as incompetent, lacking composure, unsociable, and passive. Secondly, they were judged to be unattractive—socially and physically—as task partners. Finally, the averted eyes were interpreted by the job interviewers as expressing dislike, detachment, disinterest, and tension. Furthermore, they concluded that individuals who have limited eye contact and who avert their gaze in an interview situation pay a stiff price in terms of their personal credibility. The researchers emphasized that "by virtue of negative meanings assigned to it as well as the detrimental evaluative and behavioral consequences, gaze aversion clearly qualifies as a negative type of violation" (p. 142).

The Intimacy Function

For centuries, our society has been fixated on the eyes and the role they play in the development of intimacy between persons (Grootenboer, 2006). Eye behaviors play a central role in establishing, maintaining, and terminating interpersonal relationships.

Gender differences in eye behavior can have a profound impact during intimacy formation. Typically, men vary more in their gaze behavior, because men break eye contact more often than do women. Women are more likely to interrupt men who look away during conversation than vice versa (Bente, Donaghy, & Suwelack, 1998). Clearly, this research illustrates the power of eye behavior and gaze upon relationship formation and maintenance. In addition, there are important gender differences about how eyes function during the intimacy phase of a relationship. In fact, one study found that men who looked down more than their counterparts were seen as less masculine and as a result less likely to be interested in a sexual encounter (Campbell, Wallace, & Benson, 1996).

Further, research discusses the role of eye behavior in developing and maintaining intimate relationships. Remland (2000) suggests that gazes and glances are part of the way that couples cue one another in times of maintenance, distress, joy, sadness, or happiness. One study suggests that looking at one another produces arousal and attraction in an encounter (Kampe, Frith, Dolan, & Frith, 2001). Indeed, one element is nonverbal echo. With regard to eye behavior, nonverbal echo occurs when one partner in a relationship returns a look, glance, gaze, or eye contact in a similar fashion. Research suggests that visual echo through the eyes is an important step in the process of relational satisfaction, maintenance, and development in couples (Eaves, 1997).

Predictably, dating couples spend more time gazing at one another than do pairs of unacquainted individuals (Iizuka, 1992c). Relatedly, we know that romantic attraction for a potential partner increases as the degree of mutual gazing between the potential partners increases. Even among previously unacquainted individuals under experimental conditions, pairs of individuals who were asked to exhibit a high degree of mutual gazing expressed a greater desire to be paired with the same partner in the future (Williams & Kleinke, 1993).

We should not be surprised to learn, therefore, that eye behaviors assume a central role in the development of the most intimate type of human relationship, love. Kellerman, Lewis, and Laird (1989) focused their research efforts specifically on this subject. They found that individuals who gazed at their partner's eyes and whose partner in turn gazed back at their eyes reported significantly higher feelings of affection than individuals experiencing any other kind of eye contact. They found too that individuals who engaged in sustained mutual eye gaze experienced a significant increase in their liking for each other and significant increases in their feelings of passionate and dispositional love for their partner.

The Regulatory Function

The regulatory function of the eyes is an important one. In particular, eye behaviors serve the regulatory function by alerting the decoder that encoding is occurring and continuing, by signaling the encoder whether listening and decoding are occurring, and by indicating when the listener is to speak (Ellsworth & Ludwig, 1971; Kalma, 1992).

There is growing evidence that the eyes in combination with gestures serve effectively to communicate the turn-maintaining, turn-yielding, turn-requesting, and turn-taking cues that are central to conversational management. Eyes can regulate communicative interaction effectively in part because eye behaviors represent a much more subtle and socially acceptable way of revealing one's turn predispositions than such verbal expressions as "Bob, don't interrupt me again" or "Shut up, Becky, I want to talk."

We cannot always predict how effective eye behaviors will be as conversational or behavioral regulators until we know more about the importance of factors such as race and culture, (Kleinke, 1986). In a recent study, researchers found that one's culture can have significant impacts on perceived managements in business contexts (Li & Karakowsky, 2001). While waiting in lines in America, generally shoppers are courteous and stay in lines. In other cultures, however, it is not uncommon for persons to break line to get to the front for quicker service. This phenomenon is more likely to happen in bigger cities than in smaller towns, American or otherwise.

Abele (1986) acknowledged the important regulatory function of the human eyes in social interaction in general. He maintained that eye behavior becomes even more important in regulating the interaction of intimates. If you believe that an equilibrium between approach and avoidance is important in intimate relationships, then gaze should function as an intimacy-regulating factor. For example, when the intimacy of a topic being discussed increases, there must be a compensatory decrease in gaze if equilibrium between intimates is to be maintained.

Finally, Kendon's classic study (1967) helped illuminate the regulatory function of eye behaviors through the extensive film recording of two-person conversations. The person attempting to communicate a message was identified as P, and the person to whom the message was directed was identified as Q. The time P spent looking at Q varied from 28 to 70 percent, depending on the individuals who were communicating. When P began addressing Q, 70 percent of the time P began by looking away from Q. Usually, P looked away from Q when P began talking; P typically looked at Q *when* P finished talking. In short, individuals usually look away from a person when they begin to talk, and while they are talking; and they are apt to look at you and pause if they wish you to respond.

There has been updated research on the regulatory function of the eyes. Cordell and McGahan (2004) studied the effect of mutual gaze upon the length of the conversation in male–female dyads. The researchers found that interactants looked at one another longer in the final two minutes than in the first two minutes of conversation. This suggests that the eyes can function to determine the length of the conversation, especially for lengthy conversation between male–female dyads.

The Affective Function

The eyes combine with the face to function as a powerful medium of emotional communication. Consider your reaction when you encounter persons whose eyes are cold, warm, hateful, passionate, or loving. You have probably recognized that the language of the eyes is the language of emotion. As Schlenker (1980) so graphically put it, "The eyes universally symbolize affect. The look in another's eyes can signal the start of a romance or the end of one. As the poet's mirror to the soul, the eyes express and intensify the affect present in a relationship" (p. 258).

When one individual wishes to determine whether another is experiencing a positive or negative emotion, and the intensity of the felt emotion, he or she can observe the pupils of the other's eyes. Pupils enlarge when individuals experience positive emotions such as happiness or joy, and contract when negative emotions such as sadness or sorrow are being experienced. Larger eyes, especially those on "babyfaced" adults, are generally seen as more honest, less deceitful, and more open in a relationship (Zebrowitz, 1997). These judgments are part of the babyface stereotype, and generally, more open eyes on those faces signify sincerity, trustworthiness, and frankness.

In short, the eyes can accurately reflect whether a person is experiencing a positive or negative emotion and reveal the intensity of the emotion. Thus, the individual who wishes to make an accurate judgment about the moods and emotions of another individual should rely on the information revealed in both the face and the eyes. We display the kind of emotion we are experiencing in our face and the intensity of the emotion in our eyes.

The Power Function

Are you reluctant to be hypnotized? Have you ever actively resisted the efforts of a friend or even a professional hypnotist to put you into a hypnotic trance? If so, you probably were fearful or at least apprehensive about the prospect of someone's exerting so much domination over you with his or her eyes that you would be forced to surrender conscious control of your actions to that person. Subconsciously, you may have dreaded the prospect of being "mesmerized" by the penetrating eyes of another person.

Interestingly, Franz Mesmer was an Austrian physician who developed a procedure for using his own eyes to cure the afflictions of his patients; Mesmer could induce trances by gazing into the eyes of his patients. Modern hypnosis relies on mesmerizing power to gain control over others and dominate them. Consequently, the "fear of being enveloped or devoured by someone's eyes, and a concomitant fear of having one's control surrendered to another, probably accounts for the reluctance of many people to be hypnotized" (Webbink, 1986, p. 40).

We have learned much about the central role of the eyes in establishing dominance and submissiveness among nonhuman primates. Monkeys and apes rely heavily on the stare to establish dominance; subordinate monkeys and apes respond with averted eyes. Many otherwise peaceful animals become so threatened by a stare from humans that they may attack. Animals also establish their place in a power hierarchy by their degree of visual attentiveness—the more visually attentive an animal is, the lower its place in the power hierarchy (Mitchell & Maple, 1985).

The eye behaviors of human beings also function as an effective and reliable index of the amount of power one individual possesses vis-à-vis another. People perceived as powerful usually *look* powerful. The license to stare at others for the purpose of domination is the exclusive prerogative of powerful people. Public speakers are often persuasive not because of the facts that they present, but because of their intense eye contact. In contrast, the averted and downward glance is universally recognized as a sign of weakness and submission. Individuals who are presumed to be afraid to look at others are judged to have minimal leadership capacity and are usually relegated to the perceptual category of low status.

Rasputin is a good case in point. Rasputin was born to modest circumstances in the nineteenth century in imperial Russia. He affected the image of a religious clairvoyant with a miraculous healing capacity. Finally, Rasputin rose to become the chief advisor to Tsar Nicholas and Empress Alexandra. Many high-level Russians who interacted directly with Rasputin attributed his great power to his remarkable eyes:

> The full expression of his [Rasputin's] personality, however, seemed concentrated in his eyes. They were pale blue, of exceptional brilliance, depth and attraction. His gaze was at once piercing and caressing, naive and cunning, far-off and intent. When he was in earnest conversation, his pupils seemed to radiate magnetism. . . . It was difficult to resist the power of Rasputin's steady gaze. (Massie, 1967, pp. 191–192)

Power, status, and personal dominance are all related to visual dominance behavior (Henley, 1977; Henley & Harmon, 1985).

The visual dominance ratio is now perhaps the best measure of the relative dominance and submissiveness of two individuals who are interacting. The *visual dominance ratio* is the ratio of the percentage of looking in two modes—the percentage of looking while speaking relative to the percentage of looking while listening (Dovidio, Ellyson, Keating, Heltman, & Brown, 1988). As your level of looking while speaking increases and your level of looking while listening decreases, your visual dominance ratio goes up. The perceived dominance of females has been found to increase as their visual dominance ratio increases (Iizuka, 1992a).

We now know that communicators who exhibit a high visual dominance ratio (55 percent looking while speaking versus 45 percent looking while listening) are perceived as significantly more powerful than communicators who exhibit a moderate visual dominance ratio (40 percent versus 60 percent) or a low visual dominance ratio (25 percent versus 75 percent). Not only do communicators who are relatively high in status, expertise power, and desire for interpersonal control display higher visual dominance ratios, visual dominance behavior is also reliably and accurately decoded by observers (Dovidio & Ellyson, 1985).

We know too that the more expert people are perceived to be, the more visual dominance they exhibit, and women generally have a lower visual dominance ratio than do men (Dovidio et al., 1988). In short, the eyes encode power and dominance powerfully. In general, communicators with high levels of eye contact are perceived to be more powerful or potent (Knackstedt & Kleinke, 1991).

In addition, there appears to be some evidence that power plays a key role in the use of dominant versus submissive eye behaviors. One study found that men and women equally use the eyes in dominant and submissive ways in same-sex relationships, suggesting that power differences, not gender differences, explain how they differ in mixed-sex relationships (Lamb, 1981). Moreover, Aguinis and Henle (2001) found that women who used eye behaviors in a dominant way were perceived to have "coercive" power, while their male counterparts who exhibited similar eye behaviors were perceived to have more positive types of power (e.g., expert or legitimate). These findings further confirm that there exists a male bias in our society with regard to eye behavior and power, especially in the workplace.

The Impression Management Function

Eye behaviors frequently assume a central role in the formation of impressions and in impression management. This subject is addressed in detail in separate chapters of this book. Communicators who wish to exercise conscious control over their communicative behaviors in order to make a desired impression would be well advised to begin by monitoring their eye behavior. In fact, eye behaviors do exercise a social-control function that is managed, intentional, and situational. Thus, eye behaviors have proven to be important in impression management efforts because they can be used to ingratiate, deceive, dominate, and avoid other human beings, as well as to suggest that one is extroverted (Iizuka, 1992b; Kleinke, 1986).

Public figures such as George W. Bush and Condoleezza Rice have been concerned about the impact of their eye behaviors on their public image. As an act of impression management, George W. Bush made modifications in his eye contact during the presidential debates in the 2004 campaign. Rice was careful to persuade with her eyes during the Iraq invasion hearings. Both recognize that impression management begins with the eyes.

Our self-concept and self-esteem are vitally important parts of impression management. Communicators with a negative self-concept and low self-esteem are obviously limited in the images they can credibly claim for themselves. Significantly, then, we now know that the longer we sustain eye contact with those with whom we interact, the greater self-esteem we are perceived to have (Droney & Brooks, 1993). In their study, an interviewee maintained eye contact with an interviewer for durations of 5, 30, and 50 seconds. Self-esteem scores of the interviewee increased significantly as her eye contact increased for each of the 10 scales that make up the Multidimensional Self-Esteem Inventory.

Eye behaviors have also been linked to compliance-gaining requests. A significant part of impression management, compliance seeking, is fundamental to our lives: at home, at work, at school, at church, or at other locations. In one simple study, Gueguen and Jacob (2002) investigated the effect of eye behavior upon compliance in busy sidewalks in a large metropolitan area. They found that those passersby who received direct eye contact were twice as likely (66 percent) to complete the compliance task than those who received an evasive glance (34 percent). This study illustrates the power of eye contact upon seeking compliance behavior.

Using the Communicative Potential of Eye Behaviors

Communicators should be aware of the potential value of eye behaviors as an aid in attaining rather specific communicative objectives. Successful communication requires a maximum amount of information about the perceptions of others, their feelings, and their expectations. We must recognize that eye behaviors have the potential to provide us with precisely these kinds of information.

Message senders should be sensitive to the fact that *much of the information communicated by their own eyes operates out of their own level of awareness and is, therefore, beyond their ability to consciously control* (pupil dilation is probably a case in point).

Because of this, our eyes may reveal highly personal information about us that we would not choose to reveal if we could consciously control all of our eye behaviors. Our eyes might show that we are uninterested in the message of a superior, or might reflect an attitude of indifference to an intimate, even when we are whispering words of love in the intimate's ear.

To avoid the constant transmission of inconsistent, unintended, and undesired meanings via our eyes, we may wish to exercise conscious control over selected eye behaviors that will help us make a desired impression. Such efforts are called *impression management.* For example, we could eliminate the downcast and shifty eye movements that are associated with ineffective persuasion. We could carefully monitor the eye behaviors of those with whom we communicate, in order to be sensitive to their turn-signaling prerogatives. We might seek to enhance our perceived power, status, and leadership potential by avoiding sustained visual attentiveness to individuals who compete with us for leadership. We recognize the paradox: The prize for sustaining visual attention is often to be unflatteringly characterized as a low-power and low-status individual

There are no absolute principles or truths you can rely on to make the most effective use of your eyes as a medium of communication. However, let us suggest several reasonable guidelines that seem to be soundly based on the eye behavior research we have just discussed.

First, beware of exhibiting eye behaviors that seem to confirm negative cultural stereotypes. Our society has well-developed eye behavior stereotypes both for the evasive and deceptive person and for the weak and submissive person. You might be the most truthful person in your neighborhood, but if you exhibit shifty eyes and gaze aversion when the truthfulness of your statements is at issue, your chances of being perceived as a liar are excellent. Similarly, you may be a person of great personal and moral courage, but if you characteristically exhibit a low visual dominance ratio when interacting with other persons, you run a very high risk of being seen as weak and submissive. This is a constant concern of the defense counsel when their client takes the witness stand.

Second, you should recognize that any given eye behavior you exhibit is susceptible to multiple interpretations. If most of those possible interpretations are negative, you might wish to suppress or eliminate those eye behaviors. Let us assume that you almost always look away from people when you are greeting them. The individuals with whom you interact may infer, as you hope they will, that you look away because you are so shy. Alternatively, your listeners may come up with other less favorable interpretations for your averted eyes, such as that you do not find them interesting or important enough to look at them, something else or someone else in the room is more important, or you simply do not care. In any event, your position is loosely analogous to that of the football coach who has just called a pass play. At best, one good thing can happen to you; at worst, a number of bad things are possible.

Finally, strive to conform to the rules of eye etiquette that are implicit in your social group(s), community, and culture. Keep in mind that if you are multilingual, the rules of eye etiquette may change as you move from one language to another. Some rules of eye etiquette are obvious. Do not stare at the erogenous body zones of a stranger unless you relish being branded as a deviant. Do not exhibit obvious visual inattentiveness in the presence of your boss unless you are overwhelmed with the desire to interview for a new job. To determine the rules of etiquette for a given group, you might observe the eye behaviors that members of that group characteristically exhibit. With regard to your own eye behaviors, we are almost tempted to say, "When in Rome do as the Romans do."

Message receivers should exhibit some of the same information-seeking concerns as message senders but, in addition, they must be concerned with the role of their own eye behaviors in providing visual feedback to the message sender. Abele (1986) maintained that monitoring another person's eye behaviors is more important than the message content of the eye behaviors itself. Thus, *feedback* in the form of eye behavior may be more valuable than *messages* sent via eye behaviors. Feedback is important in the game of table poker. The successful poker player must not only be a good decoder of other players' eye behaviors, but he or she must also be careful of the messages sent in return.

Message senders should recognize that their eyes might reveal more about their affective reaction to the message receiver and about their cognitive state than about anything else. Rasicot (1986) maintained, for example, that the direction of a person's eye gaze may reveal from what areas of the brain a person is gaining information. To look up and to the left is thought to indicate that a person is trying to figure out an appropriate response or answer—the part of the brain used in this instance is concerned with visual construction. To look up and to the left might also indicate deception; by contrast, a person who looks up and to the right is merely trying to recall factual information by accessing visual memory.

If perception is, literally and figuratively, in the eye of the beholder, individuals should recognize that their perceptual responses might be most accurately reflected in their own eyes. Their eyes may not mirror their souls, but they will probably mirror the depths and intensity of their innermost feelings.

Summary

The eyes have been a source of fascination for many centuries. Even today, the language of the eyes is a powerful form of communication. This language is defined in part by descriptive labels used to identify various types of eye behaviors: eye contact, face-gaze, eye-gaze, mutual gaze, mutual eye contact, gaze avoidance, gaze omission, eye shifts, staring, and blinking.

Because the eyes are the center of visual attention for the decoder, their importance as a source of information is enhanced. Empirical research has established that eye behaviors serve the following communicative functions: (a) the attention function, (b) the persuasive function, (c) the intimacy function, (d) the regulatory function, (e) the affective function, (f) the power function, and (g) the impression management function.

The eyes have great communicative potential. Message senders should be sensitive to the fact that much of the information communicated by their own eyes operates out of their level of awareness and is beyond their conscious ability to control. Thus, our eyes may reveal much highly personal information about us that we would not choose to reveal if we could consciously control all of our eye behaviors.

To make the most effective use of your eyes, you should consider several reasonable guidelines. You should beware of exhibiting eye behaviors that seem to confirm negative cultural stereotypes. You should recognize that any given eye behavior that you exhibit is susceptible to multiple interpretations. Finally, you should strive to conform to the implicit rules of eye etiquette that apply to you and those with whom you interact.

REFERENCES

Abele, A. (1986). Functions of gaze in social interaction: Communication and monitoring. *Journal of Nonverbal Behavior, 10,* 83–101.

Aguinis, H., & Henle, C. A (2001). Effects of nonverbal behavior on perceptions of a female employee's power bases. *The Journal of Social Psychology, 141,* 537–549.

Anderson, D. E., DePaulo, B. M., Ansfield, M. E., Tickle, J. J., & Green, E. (1999). Beliefs about cues to deception: Mindless stereotypes or untapped wisdom. *Journal of Nonverbal Behavior, 23,* 67–89.

Argyle, M., & Cook, M. (1976). *Gaze and mutual gaze.* Cambridge, MA: Cambridge University Press.

Argyle, M., & Dean, J. (1965). Eye-contact, distance, and affiliation. *Sociometry, 28,* 289–304.

Bente, G., Donaghy, W. C., & Suwelack, D. (1998). Sex differences in body movement and visual attention: An integrated analysis of movement and gaze in mixed-sex dyads. *Journal of Nonverbal Behavior, 22,* 31–58.

Brooks, R., & Meltzoff, A. N. (2002). The importance of eyes: How infants interpret adult looking behavior. *Developmental Psychology, 38,* 958–966.

Burgoon, J. K., Coker, D. A., & Coker, R. A. (1986). Communicative effects of gaze behavior: A test of two contrasting explanations. *Human Communication Research, 12,* 495–524.

Burgoon, J. K., Manusov, V., Mineo, P., & Hale, J. L. (1985). Effects of gaze on hiring, credibility, attraction, and relational message interpretation. *Journal of Nonverbal Behavior, 9,* 133–146.

Burgoon, J. K., & Saine, T. (1978). *The unspoken dialogue: An introduction to nonverbal communication.* Boston: Houghton.

Campbell, R., Wallace, S., & Benson, P. J. (1996). Real men don't look down: Direction of gaze affects sex decisions on faces. *Visual Cognition, 3,* 393–412.

Cordell, D. M., & McGahan, J. R. (2004). Mutual gaze duration as a function of length of conversation in male-female dyads. *Psychological Reports, 94,* 109–114.

Cranach, M. von (1971). The role of orienting behavior in human interaction. In A. H. Esser (Ed.), *Behavior and environment: The use of space by animals and men* (pp. 217–237). New York: Plenum Press.

Dovidio, J. F., & Ellyson, S. L. (1985). Patterns of visual dominance behavior in humans. In S. L. Ellyson & J. F. Dovidio (Eds.), *Power, dominance, and nonverbal behavior* (pp. 129–149). New York: Springer-Verlag.

Dovidio, J. F., Ellyson, S. L., Keating, C. F., Heltman, K., & Brown, C. E. (1988). The relationship of social power to visual displays of dominance between men and women. *Journal of Personality & Social Psychology, 54,* 233–242.

Droney, J. M., & Brooks, C. I. (1993). Attributions of self-esteem as a function of duration of eye contact. *Journal of Social Psychology, 133,* 715–722.

Eaves, M. H. (1997). *Nonverbal synchrony in dyads: Echoing nonverbal channels for relational maintenance.* Paper presented at the annual convention of the National Communication Association, Chicago, IL.

Ellsworth, P. C., & Ludwig, L. M. (1971). Visual behavior in social interaction. *Journal of Communication, 22,* 375–403.

Exline, R., & Fehr, B. J. (1982). The assessment of gaze and mutual gaze. In K. R. Scherer & P. Ekman (Eds.), *Handbook of methods in nonverbal behavior research* (pp. 91–135). Cambridge: Cambridge University Press.

Grootenboer, H. (2006). Treasuring the gaze: Eye miniature portraits and the intimacy of vision. *Art Bulletin, 88,* 496–507.

Gueguen, N., & Jacob, C. (2002). Direct look versus evasive glance and compliance with a request. *The Journal of Social Psychology, 142,* 393–396.

Harper, R. G., Wiens, A. N., & Matarazzo, J. D. (1978). *Nonverbal communication: The state of the art.* New York: Wiley.

Henley, N. M. (1977). *Body politics: Power, sex, and nonverbal communication.* Englewood Cliffs, NJ: Prentice-Hall.

Henley, N. M., & Harmon, S. (1985). The nonverbal semantics of power and gender: A perceptual study. In S. L. Ellyson & J. F. Dovidio (Eds.), *Power, dominance, and nonverbal behavior* (pp. 151–164). New York: Springer-Verlag.

Hess, E. H. (1975). *The tell-tale eye: How your eyes reveal hidden thoughts and emotions.* New York: Van Nostrand Reinhold.

Hornik, J. (1987). The effect of touch and gaze upon compliance and interest of interviewees. *Journal of Social Psychology, 12,* 681–683.

Iizuka, Y. (1992a). Evaluation of gaze pairs by female observers. *Japanese Journal of Experimental Social Psychology, 31,* 231–239.

Iizuka, Y. (1992b). Extraversion, introversion, and visual interaction. *Perceptual & Motor Skills, 74,* 43–50.

Iizuka, Y. (1992c). Eye contact in dating couples and unacquainted couples. *Perceptual & Motor Skills, 75,* 457–461.

Janik, S. W., Wellens, A. R., Goldberg, M. L., & DeLosse, L. F. (1978). Eyes as the center of focus in the visual examination of faces. *Perceptual and Motor Skills, 26,* 34–35.

Kalma, A. (1992). Gazing in triads—a powerful signal in floor apportionment. *British Journal of Social Psychology, 31,* 21–39.

Kampe, K. K. W., Frith, C. D., Dolan, R. J., & Frith, U. (2001). Reward value of attractiveness and gaze. *Nature, 413,* 589, 602.

Kellerman, J. L., Lewis, J., & Laird, J. D. (1989). Looking and loving: The effects of mutual gaze on feelings of romantic love. *Journal of Research in Personality, 23,* 145–161.

Kendon, A. (1967). Some functions of gaze direction in social interaction. *Acta Psychologica, 26,* 34–35.

Kidwell, M. (2003). *How very young children use gaze avoidance to resist caregiver interventions in their acts of misconduct.* Paper presented at the International Communication Association Convention, San Diego, CA.

Kleinke, C. L. (1986). Gaze and eye contact: A research review. *Psychological Bulletin, 100,* 78–100.

Knackstedt, G., & Kleinke, C. L. (1991). Eye contact, gender, and personality judgments. *Journal of Social Psychology, 131,* 303–304.

Lamb, T. A. (1981). Nonverbal and paraverbal control in dyads and triads: Sex or power differences. *Social Psychology Quarterly, 44,* 49–53.

Leathers, D. G., & Hocking, J. E. (1982, November). *An examination of police interviewer's beliefs about the utility and nature of nonverbal indicators of deception.* Paper presented at the convention of the Speech Communication Association, Louisville, KY.

Li, J., & Karakowsky, L. (2001). Do we see eye-to-eye? Implications of cultural differences for cross-cultural management research and practice. *The Journal of Psychology, 135,* 501–517.

Massie, R. K. (1967). *Nicholas and Alexandra.* New York: Laurel.

Metalis, S. A., & Hess, E. H. (1982a). Pupillary response/semantic differential scale relationship. *Journal of Research in Personality, 16,* 201–216.

Metalis, S. A., & Hess, E. H. (1982b). Pupillometric analysis of two theories of obesity. *Perceptual and Motor Skills, 55,* 87–92.

Metalis, S. A., & Hess, E. H. (1986). Pupillometric assessment of the readability of two video-screen fonts. *Perceptual and Motor Skills, 52,* 279–282.

Mitchell, G., & Maple, T. L. (1985). Dominance in nonhuman primates. In S. L. Ellyson & J. F. Dovidio (Eds.), *Power, dominance and nonverbal behavior* (pp. 49–66). New York: Springer-Verlag.

Petty, R. E., & Cacioppo, J. T. (1986). *Communication and persuasion: Central and peripheral routes to attitude change.* New York: Springer-Verlag.

Rasicot, J. (1986). *Silent Sales.* Minneapolis, MN: AP Publications.

Remland, M. S. (2000). *Nonverbal communication in everyday life.* Boston: Houghton Mifflin Company.

Schlenker, B. R. (1980). *Impression management.* Monterey, CA: Brooks/Cole.

Suaste, E., Garcia, N., Rodriguez, D., & Zuniga, A. (2004). *Dynamic visual acuity associated with eye movements and papillary responses.* Paper presented at the Medical Physics: Eighth Mexican Symposium on Medical Physics.

Vuilleumier, P., George, N., Lister, V., Armony, J., & Driver, J. (2005). Effects of perceived mutual gaze and gender on face processing and recognition memory. *Visual Cognition, 12,* 85–101.

Webbink, P. (1986). *The power of the eyes.* New York: Springer.

Williams, G. P., & Kleinke, C. L. (1993). Effects of mutual gaze and touch on attraction, mood, and cardiovascular reactivity. *Journal of Research in Personality, 27,* 170–183.

Zebrowitz, L. A. (1997). *Reading faces: Window to the soul?* Oxford, UK: Westview Press.

CHAPTER

4   Bodily Communication

Movement communicates meaning. Although human beings have accepted this general proposition through the ages, they have rarely examined its implications in detail. If movement communicates meaning, it follows that different movements serve different kinds of communicative functions by communicating different kinds of meanings. Some of the meanings communicated by bodily cues help us attain specific communicative objectives, and other movements communicate highly dysfunctional meanings.

Certain bodily movements do create lasting impressions. Think of the number of friends or acquaintances you remember because of the way they move or use movement to communicate. One college professor stands out because his incredibly deliberate gestures drew attention to pauses of remarkable length in his speech. The gestures and pauses convinced the students that he was terribly profound.

Musical artists have to build their images, oftentimes by their unique bodily movements. Shania Twain is known for her graceful walk and stroll, 50 Cent is known for his rap gestures and body movements, Britney Spears is known for her quick movement on stage, and Shakira is known for her fast dance twists. The same bodily movements by the same rock star may be perceived differently by fans and disinterested observers. Those who truly appreciate musicians and their body moves will notice the slightest alteration from a previous music video or concert performance. Were you surprised to see the latest music video of your favorite musical artist?

Whatever your personal response is to the various forms of bodily communication of musicians, you will probably agree that their bodily communication serves at a minimum to gain attention and at the most to signal an important message to the viewer. Bodily communication is attractive, attention-grabbing, and oftentimes seductive.

These examples focus attention on the functional importance of the gestures and postures that make up bodily communication. Bodily communication is important not only for musicians but also for public speakers. Thus, Collier (1985) wrote:

> These [bodily] cues provide information about the people speaking, their attitude toward what they are saying, and their relationship to those being addressed. When we meet people for the first time, we form an immediate impression about their character and their current emotional state. Without thinking, we take into account numerous minute details about how they stand, move, and position themselves. (p. 45)

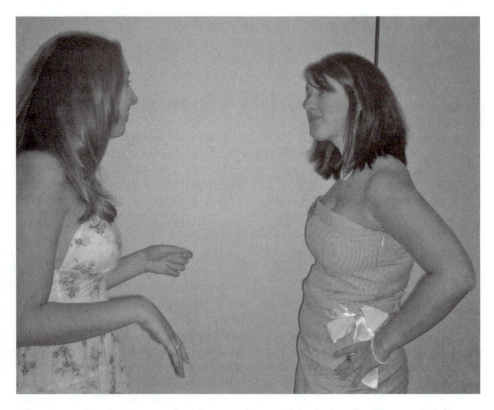

What message does the woman on the right communicate with her body to the woman on the left?

Gesture and speech communication are quite different in a number of respects (Marschark, 1994). First, gesture is a communicative medium that employs space and time, whereas speech uses only time. When the spatial dimension of communication is missing, misunderstanding often results. For example, look at the professor in the photo. In order to understand the real meaning of his hand gesture, one has to take into account not only the time of the gesture but also the space of the gesture. The professor uses this gesture while teaching his communication class in order to convey his thoughts on a relational concept in the book.

In addition, gestures are defined by the fact that they may describe action sequences more efficiently than words, and are a more discreet substitute for words in situations where words would be offensive (Kendon, 1986). If, for example, you told a friend that "you just got done using your Mitsubishi," the friend might not know whether you were referring to you car or to your big-screen TV; but by pretending to be driving a car with your hands, you would clarify your meaning immediately. Secondly, individuals such as dance instructors often use gestures rather than words to represent desired movement patterns more efficiently.

The gesture used by this professor signals the importance of the lecture to the class.

Hewes (1992) has argued that human language had its basis in hand and arm gestures rather than vice versa. Thus, bodily communication in the form of a preexisting gestural language seems to have provided the basis for the subsequent development of spoken languages.

We know that bodily movements assume important roles in successful interpersonal communication. They often are strong determinants of how likable, assertive, and powerful we are judged to be, for example. Nonetheless, most research efforts have been designed to identify bodily movements that are normative rather than specify which kinds of bodily cues can be used to attain specific communicative objectives. This chapter deviates from conventional practices. We shall specify not only how various bodily cues are typically used and what major communicative functions they serve, but also how bodily cues should be used. In the past, little effort has been devoted to sensitizing individuals to the functional and dysfunctional uses of bodily cues.

The contrast between nonverbal communication and written communication is striking. Students in writing classes spend many hours trying to improve their ability to transmit their meanings clearly. Similarly, law students spend hours trying to determine the exact meaning of laws or court decisions on terrorism, eminent domain, or privacy in order to increase their capacity to encode and decode written messages.

The following example should help make the point: We have studied communication by oral and written discourse intensively, and we assume that we will improve those communication skills by practice. In contrast, we have not expended comparable energy to distinguish between the functional and dysfunctional uses of bodily cues, or to develop our sensitivity to bodily cues.

The need to know more about bodily movements has resulted in a body of research called *kinesics*. Kinesics is the study of observable, isolable, and meaningful movement in interpersonal communication. Birdwhistell (1970) wrote that "kinesics is concerned with abstracting from the continuous muscular shifts which are characteristic of living physiological systems those groupings of movements which are of significance to the communication process and thus to the interactional systems of particular groups" (p. 192).

Movements that convey meaning are extensive. In the strictest anatomical sense, the sources of movement in the human body are almost unlimited. From a more practical perspective, Birdwhistell (1952) identifies eight sources of potentially significant bodily movement: (a) total head, (b) face, (c) neck, (d) trunk, (e) shoulder–arm–wrist, (f) hand, (g) hip joint–leg–ankle, and (h) foot.

Most basically, movement consists of the displacement of body parts in space and time. Rosenfeld (1982) provides useful descriptions of body part taxonomies, spatial frames of reference, and temporal frames of reference. As we shall see, some areas of the body have greater functional significance than others. Hand movements are more important than foot movements, for example, in part because of their visibility; the importance of hand movements is also accentuated by the fact that the relatively large area of the brain that is concerned with hand movements is much larger than the parts of the brain that are associated with other types of bodily movements. At the same time, we should recognize that hand movements may be a less reliable source of information than foot movements because they are more frequently subject to conscious control for purposes of deception.

In our society, the communicative significance of the hands is not confined to the ways we use them. "Handedness" is also important because assumptions commonly made about right-handers and left-handers are quite different. Lee and Charlton (1980) have developed an instructive but amusing test to determine what type of handedness is dominant for a given individual. Among the tasks they use to determine handedness are the following:

1. When you draw the profile of a dog or a horse, which way is it facing?
2. Imagine that you are locked in a room and tied with your hands behind you to a chair. Which foot will you use to try to pull the phone closer?
3. On which side do you chew your food?
4. When you applaud a performer, which hand is on top?

Left-handers will draw the profile of a dog or a horse with the head facing to the right; reach out for the phone with their left foot; chew on the left side of their mouth; and clap with their dominant left hand on top, into the palm of their right hand. Everything is reversed for right-handers.

Another component of body movements concerns "reaching." When one reaches for an object, he or she has to determine it if is within arm's length, whether or not one must lean to get the object, or if one has to physically move to reach the object (Mark et al., 1997). A great example of this occurs when you have to unlock a door for someone while you are seated inside a car, which happens when you are in a vehicle that does not have automatic door locks. One can also reach with one's foot for an object, but this is naturally rarer and more difficult than reaching with one's hand.

The Nature of Bodily Cues

Much like facial expressions, bodily cues have been conceptualized as both categorical and dimensional in nature. The categorical perspective is based on the assumption that bodily cues are best understood by classifying them with regard to: (a) the *level of awareness* and *intentionality* with which they are used; (b) the type of *coding* employed; and (c) the *communicative function* served. By contrast, the dimensional perspective is based on the assumption that bodily cues are best described by rating them on scales that represent the dimensions of meaning communicated by the bodily cues. The theory and research of Paul Ekman and associates best illustrate the categorical perspective, whereas the dimensional perspective is most closely associated with the work of Albert Mehrabian.

Classification of Bodily Cues

Ekman and Friesen (1969) developed what is probably the most frequently cited conceptual framework for classifying bodily cues. They emphasized that bodily cues vary not only with regard to their *usage* and the *code* employed but also with regard to the *functions* they serve.

The way a bodily cue is used is significant because it involves two questions of particular importance: (a) Was the communicator aware of exhibiting a specific kind of bodily cue? and (b) Was the bodily cue used with conscious intent to communicate a particular kind of information? Communicators who are aware that they are exhibiting certain bodily cues have the capacity to exert conscious control over those types of cues.

This capacity is a necessary, but not a sufficient, condition for individuals who wish to be successful as impression managers. Do you remember Saddam Hussein answering questions in his court trial? Do you recall Ken Lay's nervous mannerisms during the investigation as he recounted his actions at Enron? Impression management tactics such as these did not work well with the American television audience.

Similarly, the individual who does not wish to be perceived as deceiving and untrustworthy must take pains to eliminate or minimize the shifty eye behaviors, hand-to-face gestures, and nonfluencies that are part of the cultural stereotype of the deceiver. Determining whether bodily cues of the sender are used without awareness and intentionality is extremely important for message receivers. This is so because bodily cues of this type are apt to reveal much about the sender's attitudes, feelings, and level of self-esteem that he or she may not wish to reveal.

Bodily cues contain three basic codes. Each is important because each code signifies the impact or value of the body cue in the situation (Ekman & Friesen, 1969). The three codes are arbitrary codes, iconic codes, and intrinsic codes.

First, an arbitrary code is signaling rooted in symbolism that means something to the user, but is not fixed in time or space. For example, a hand raised to greet someone or signal good-bye is an arbitrary code because the raised hand is not directly related to what it signifies. How a student should dress in class might be based on the tradition of the school. Or, what you are to wear on your body to a funeral may be somewhat dictated by culture, religion, or place. Both of these forms of dress are arbitrary codes of bodily communication because their meaning is not fixed and changes with tradition, social mores, and cultural fluidity.

Second, an iconic code carries some clue about its meaning due to its appearance. There are many examples of iconic codes. For example, a woman's wearing high heels to appear taller or a gentleman's wearing a toupee to create the appearance that he has hair are both forms of iconic codes in bodily communication. The use of cosmetics and plastic surgery are modern examples of iconic codes. For years, men have shaved their faces and women have shaved their legs to shape their bodies to create different communicative messages.

Third, an intrinsic code is the natural system we inherit at birth rather than learn. For instance, recognizing someone by their facial features, hairstyle, body shape, etc., is a way that we use intrinsic codes to identify people in groups (Remland, 2000). The eyebrow is a good example of an intrinsic code. One scholar suggests that men have fuller eyebrows than do women because fuller eyebrows are seen as a masculine trait. Further, many women pluck their eyebrows to appear less aggressive and more feminine (Guthrie, 1976). The use of the babyface stereotype discussed in Chapter 2 is another example of an intrinsic code used in bodily communication.

Individuals who wish to refine their skill in decoding bodily cues must be sensitive to the type of code employed. Certain kinds of bodily cues frequently combine more than one type of coding. For example, confident individuals who are receptive to the ideas of those with whom they communicate frequently exhibit "open" gestures and postures, by way of uncrossed arms and legs. Such bodily cues combine elements of both arbitrary and iconic coding, which makes it easier to determine their meaning. Even those bodily cues that are coded exclusively via the arbitrary code are susceptible to accurate decoding when a *set* of bodily cues (such as downcast eyes and hand-to-face gestures) and an indirect bodily orientation is consistently associated with an inferred psychological state such as a decreasing level of self-confidence.

Bodily cues are perhaps most clearly defined and differentiated by the functions they serve. We will highlight all of the major communicative functions of bodily cues in a separate section of this chapter. The five categories of nonverbal behavior identified by Ekman and Friesen (1969) are particularly useful in describing the different kinds of bodily cues that provide different information and meanings: *emblems, illustrators, affect displays, regulators,* and *adaptors.*

Emblems.   Emblems are bodily cues that have a direct verbal translation consisting of a word or two, and that have a precise meaning that is known by most of the members of a given culture. They are used with the conscious intention of communicating a particular message. The receiver recognizes that the message was deliberately encoded, and the message sender takes direct responsibility for the message (Ekman & Friesen, 1972).

Most middle-class Americans have command of about a hundred gestural emblems. Gestural emblems are used to communicate interpersonal directions or commands ("Come here"), insults ("Shame on you"), and greetings and departures ("Good-bye" and "Hello"), among other things (Johnson, Ekman, & Friesen, 1975).

Emblems are used most frequently where speech communication is not possible because of noise or distance barriers. When a substantial number of emblems are organized in a form that might almost be called an emblematic language, we have a *gesture system.* Specialized gesture systems are used by grain merchants, individuals who work the floor of the stock exchange in New York City, airline employees who direct the big jets to their respective gates at airports, truck drivers, hitchhikers, directors of television shows, and baseball umpires (Argyle, 1988; Kendon, 1984).

The term *sign language* refers to highly developed gestural systems that include the primary sign languages of the deaf and alternate sign languages used by groups such as the Aborigines of Australia, the Trappist monks in Europe, and the women of Australia (Kendon, 1984). These examples of sign language systems draw attention to an important fact. Emblems serve as substitutes for words and are the most easily understood class of nonverbal cues. Perhaps because emblems are used so much more intentionally than other nonverbal behaviors, they are apt to provide little personal information about the person who uses them.

As we shall see when we discuss the cross-cultural aspects of nonverbal communication, many emblems carry culture-specific meaning. For example, the "chin flick" is a gestural emblem used in Italy, France, and other parts of Europe to indicate annoyance and a desire for the offending person to "bug off," but it has no generally recognized meaning in England and the United States (Lee & Charlton, 1980). The use of the middle finger is an American way to signal "bug off," or worse.

Illustrators. Illustrators are like emblems in that they are used with awareness and intentionality. Illustrator gestures may be used to augment what is being said and to reinforce or deintensify the perceived strength of emotions being experienced by the communicator.

Illustrators are typically used to increase the clarity of verbal expressions. The desire for clarity seems to be greater in face-to-face interaction. Thus, the initial portions of a narrative are accompanied by a higher rate of illustrator gestures; the objective here is to establish clarity of communication as one begins a narrative (Levy & McNeill, 1992). Similarly, Cohen (1977) found that subjects giving directions on how to get from one place to another used significantly more hand illustrators in a face-to-face situation than when giving directions over an intercom. Finally, Goldin-Meadow, Wein, and Chang (1992) reported that the reasoning of children who use illustrator gestures as a co-occurring phenomenon with their speech is easier to comprehend than the reasoning of children who do not use illustrator gestures.

Illustrators also can give emphasis to the message being communicated. Movements of the arms/hands and of the head are used most frequently to emphasize a message. Although no single type of gesture seems to be of overriding importance for giving emphasis, the outstretched arm with the pointing index finger and the double head nod are frequently used for purposes of emphasis (Bull & Connelly, 1985). In sports, a coach on the sidelines might signal to the quarterback by using a hand gesture. The hand gesture of circular motion tells the quarterback to use as much time as possible in the game to overcome the opponent.

Illustrators facilitate effective communication for a number of reasons. Visual information may logically be communicated most easily by visual means, some illustrator gestures are like representative pictures in that they at least partially represent the visual appearance of an object or even a person, and illustrators serve to punctuate conversation by providing intensity cues (Bull & Connelly, 1985).

Although illustrators are used with a fairly high level of awareness and intentionality, they can provide valuable information about a communicator's mood, self-confidence, and power in a given situation. A football coach can throw a flag onto the playing field to signal to the referee his disapproval with a call. Formally called "a coach's challenge," this act in sports is an excellent example of how an illustrator signals to the official that there is disagreement with the call made on the field. This act usually has more power than simply yelling, "Bad call."

We know that a drop in the number or rate of illustrator gestures exhibited by a communicator can be an indication of deception (Ekman, 1985).

Clearly, gestural illustrators serve a number of useful communicative functions. Their chief function, however, is probably to aid the listener in the comprehension of the spoken word. Rogers (1978) found that gestural illustrators can result in a significant increase in comprehension of the spoken word, even in the absence of facial cues. Gestural illustrators are increasingly useful as noise if introduced, and their value as aids to comprehending the meaning of the spoken word increases as the "ideal" content of the spoken message becomes more complex.

Affect Displays.   The communication of affect displays or emotions is much more closely linked with facial expressions than with bodily cues. As we have already indicated, the face is the primary site for the display of emotions. The communication receiver would be well advised, therefore, to *look to the face to determine the kind of emotion the communicator is experiencing and rely on bodily cues to determine the intensity of the emotion being experienced.*

Posture seems to be more important in communicating emotion than gestures. We know, for example, that a strong expression of contempt is associated with a clearly discernible head tilt. A stiff or even frozen bodily posture may be taken as a sign of fear, acute anxiety, or, if exhibited over long periods of time, as indicative of mental illness. The frequency or infrequency of bodily movements seems to be a much more reliable indicator of general emotional arousal (or lack of it) than an indicator that the communicator is experiencing a specific emotion (Collier, 1985). As we shall see, it is typically difficult and unrewarding to communicate with individuals who show a lack of affect or feeling.

Affect displays are used with less awareness and intentionality than either emblems or illustrators. As a result, they are apt to provide some personal information about the communicator that the individual would be reluctant to disclose voluntarily. Someone who watched Ken Lay in the Enron court trial would agree that the absence of his facial expression and body movement made determining his emotions very difficult.

Regulators. Regulators are bodily cues used by interactants to exercise a mutual influence over the initiation, length, and termination of spoken messages. Regulators usually seem to be used with a low level of awareness and intentionality. But it is vitally important that interactants be sensitive to each other's turn-taking prerogatives. A lack of sensitivity in the use of regulators is likely to be attributed to rudeness or unmannerliness (Ekman & Friesen, 1969).

Knapp and Hall (2006) have developed a particularly useful classification of turn-taking behaviors. They note that speakers use *turn-yielding* and *turn-maintaining* cues, and listeners use *turn-requesting* and *turn-denying* cues. Examples of turn-yielding cues are the cessation of illustrator gestures and a relaxed bodily posture. Turn-maintaining cues are manifested when we sustain our illustrator activity or touch the other person to indicate that we wish to continue. For the listener, an upraised index finger and rapid head nodding represent particularly effective turn-requesting cues. Finally, when we do not wish to make a comment, we may use such turn-denying cues as a relaxed listening pose, or we may stare at something in the surrounding environment.

Regulators assume more importance when we greet other individuals and bid them farewell because they are important determinants of successful interpersonal relationships. The individual who is successful in initiating and developing interpersonal interactions with others must rely heavily on the proper use of nonverbal cues.

Bull (1983) gave us a more detailed treatment of how bodily cues should be used in conversational management. He noted that effective conversational management requires appropriate use of and response to turn-yielding cues, attempt-suppressing signals, back channels, within-turn signals, and speaker-state signals. Back-channel cues such as "uh-huh," "yeah," "right," and head nods are certainly important in conversational management because they indicate to the speaker the level of the listener's attentiveness at any given point during the conversation.

A study by Krivonos and Knapp (1975) suggests that acknowledging the other person's presence with a head gesture, indicating a desire to initiate communication with mutual glances, and suggesting with a smile that you anticipate a pleasurable experience are the most important nonverbal cues used in successful greetings. In contrast, eyebrow flashes, a sweeping hand gesture in the form of a salute, an open mouth, and winking are nonverbal behaviors that should be avoided. These nonverbal cues are not used in the successful greeting; they deviate markedly from what has been found to be normative behavior in this kind of communicative situation. More recent research has confirmed the visual communication thesis of turn-taking and turn-ending cues (Rutter, 1984). In one study, visual communication was found to be instrumental to identifying turn-taking moments during and at the conclusion of the client-interviewing process (Reed, Patton, & Gold, 1993).

An insightful study by Knapp, Hart, and Friedrich (1973) established leave-taking norms that formed the basis for identifying nonverbal behaviors that were both "proper" and "improper" for guiding, controlling, or regulating departures in communication situations that were rather task oriented. The study suggested that (a) *breaking eye contact,* (b) *left-positioning* (pointing your legs or feet away from the person with whom you are communicating and toward the door), (c) *forward leaning,* and (d) *nodding behavior* all represent socially acceptable means of initiating the leave-taking step that is a central part of farewells. In contrast, the following were found to be inappropriate nonverbal means of initiating a farewell: (a) *leveraging* (placing hands on knees or legs in such a manner as to suggest a desire to rise from your chair); (b) *major trunk movements* (postural shifts in your chair, straightening up, and standing up); (c) *explosive hand contact* with some part of your body; and (d) a *handshake.*

Reflection on the nonverbal behaviors associated with successful, as opposed to unsuccessful, greetings and farewells suggests that subtlety and restraint in movement are particularly desirable. To consistently use such nonverbal behaviors in greetings and farewells is to invite the impression that you are rude and tactless.

Adaptors.   Adaptors are a potentially rich source of involuntary information about the psychological states of individuals who exhibit them. As a potential source of information about an individual's attitudes, anxiety level, and self-confidence, bodily cues in the form of adaptors are apt to be more useful than emblems, illustrators, affect displays, or regulators. Communicators who exhibit adaptors do not use them with the intent to communicate, and they are usually unaware that they are using them.

In their original form, adaptors were learned adaptive actions used to satisfy bodily needs. The itch was scratched, the unruly hair was groomed, or the tears were wiped away from the eyes (Ekman & Friesen, 1969). Through socialization, the form of many adaptors has been changed, and they have become more important.

Nespoulous and Lecours (1986) use the label "extracommunicative gestures" as a synonym for adaptor gestures. They include bodily movements reflective of degree of comfort/discomfort, autistic gestures (finger tapping, nail biting, etc.), and manipulations (smoking a cigarette or playing with it) as subcategories of extracommunicative gestures. The term *extracommunicative gestures* seems to be a singularly inappropriate label for adaptor gestures, however, because they communicate more valuable, personal information about interacting communicators than any other type of gesture.

The two most important kinds of adaptors are *self-adaptors* and *object-adaptors.* Self-adaptors that involve hand-to-face movements are the easiest to decode because of the symbolic significance of the face. For people in the United States, the face symbolizes the self. As a result, hand-to-face gestures are apt to provide reliable information about a person's current level of self-esteem and self-confidence. Ekman and Friesen (1969) wrote that when

> a person touches his face, the action can be conceived in terms of what the person has had done to him, what he wants done to him, or what he is doing to himself. Activities such as picking or scratching may be forms of attacking the self; holding may be giving nurture or support; rubbing or massaging may be caress or reassurance. (p. 87)

Object-adaptors, as the term implies, refer to the use of the hands to touch or hold objects in one's immediate environment. Clicking a pen is an example of an object-adaptor. One study (Sousa-Poza & Rohrberg, 1977) has suggested that object-adaptors are used less frequently to reflect uncertainty on the part of the encoder than are self-adaptors. As we shall see in our treatment of the use of nonverbal cues to detect deception, however, police interviewers report that, at the moment of deception, lying criminal suspects frequently play with objects in the interview room.

A later chapter of this book will examine the implications of gestural adaptors for impression management. We know that a variety of bodily messages are interpreted negatively by decoders (Manusov, 1990). More specifically, we know that many gestural adaptors (both self- and object-) are interpreted as signs of anxiety or discomfort. Interestingly, results from a study by Goldberg and Rosenthal (1986) indicated that job interviewees touch their hair and their upper torso/neck more than job interviewers and that female job interviewees exhibited more gestural adaptors of those types than male job interviewees. Females use more object-adaptors than do men for a variety of reasons. One reason is that females have more objects to play with—hair, earrings, purse, necklaces, bra straps, etc.

We now have one operational definition of gestural adaptor activity in the form of an instrument designed to measure fidgeting. Mehrabian and Friedman (1986) define fidgeting as "engaging in manipulations of one's own body parts or other objects with such actions being peripheral or nonessential to central or focal ongoing events or tasks" (p. 425).

Their 40-item fidgeting questionnaire asks respondents to choose a number on a 9-point scale, with numbers indicating response options from very strong agreement to very strong disagreement. Sample items include "I frequently rub my neck," "I hardly ever rub my scalp," "I don't fondle or play with my clothes," and "I don't tap or drum on things."

Factor analysis indicates that the fidgeting measure is composed of the two dimensions of localized self-stimulation, or self-manipulation and object manipulation. Importantly, a high level of fidgeting is suggestive of both anxiety and hyperactivity, and fidgeting seems to be an indicator of such psychological states as discomfort, tension, frustration, and irritation.

Dimensions of Meaning

In nonverbal or implicit communication, three metaphors are used to describe the distinct types of meaning represented by the dimensions of pleasure, arousal, and dominance: (a) the *approach metaphor,* (b) the *arousal-activity metaphor,* and (c) the *power metaphor.* Proponents of the dimensional perspective believe that these metaphors suggest the full range of meanings that can be communicated by nonverbal means.

Nonverbal researchers do not, however, use the metaphor terminology. Instead they have modified Mehrabian's (1981) language in such a way as to focus on the three dimensions of meaning communicated clearly and forcefully by bodily communication: (a) *like–dislike,* (b) *assertiveness–unassertiveness,* and (c) *power–powerlessness.*

In his fascinating treatment of this subject, Collier (1985) indicated that people who like each other communicate different types of bodily messages than do those who dislike each other. People approach, get more involved with, and exhibit more immediacy behaviors in the presence of individuals they like. Similarly, individuals who like each other stand closer together, assuming the most direct bodily orientation possible while making themselves accessible to the person with whom they are interacting.

Assertiveness behaviors tend to reflect via overt expression the intensity or strength of a communicator's feelings and attitudes and, perhaps more importantly, they frequently serve as accurate indicators of a communicator's current level of self-confidence. Confidence in turn is reflected in messages in which verbal and nonverbal components are consistent, the strength of feelings is communicated directly rather than masked, and attentiveness and interest are accurately expressed. For example, a firm handshake or forward lean toward another can be a good indicator of confidence during interaction.

Finally, communicators get high ratings on the power dimension if their bodies are relaxed, they are relatively uninhibited in their movements, and they exhibit postures that are both open and relatively expansive. For instance, a leader in a small group might communicate higher ratings of power when he or she has a more relaxed posture while sitting or standing. In fact, knowledge of the three major dimensions of meaning communicated by bodily communication—likability, assertiveness, and power—can help you make more effective use of this type of nonverbal communication.

Gestures versus Postures

In discussing the two perspectives used to describe nonverbal behaviors, we have not differentiated between gestures and postures. A number of definitional benchmarks can be used to differentiate between the two basic types of bodily cues. We may, of course, communicate with our entire body or with only some part of it. Thus, Lamb (1965) defined a gesture as an action confined to a part or parts of the body, and posture as an action involving a continuous adjustment of every part of the body, with consistency, in the process of variation.

The amount of bodily involvement in communication is not the only basis for distinguishing between gestures and posture, however. The amount of time used in communicating is also an important factor. Scheflen's penetrating research on bodily communication (1964) helps clarify the relationship between gesture and posture. He maintained that the three basic units of bodily movement are the *point,* the *position,* and the *presentation.* The point is the nonverbal equivalent of an individual's trying to make a point in discussion. While trying to make a point,

> an American speaker uses a series of distinctive sentences in a conversation, [and] he changes the position of his head and eyes every few sentences. He may turn his head right or left, tilt it, cock it to one side or the other, or flex or extend his neck so as to look toward the floor or ceiling. (p. 321)

Because one part of the body is usually involved for a short time, the point may be seen as a gesture. Recently, Bangerter and Oppenheimer (2006) found that while interpretation of a pointing gesture in conversation was commonplace, it is not the only variable used by the conversational partners to resolve issues of misunderstanding that may arise. Further, this research contests earlier claims about pointing gestures and perceived accuracy of joint attention (Bangerter, 2004), such as that accuracy is greater for perceived central targets than for peripheral targets in that attention process.

In contrast, when several points or gestures are combined, we have the position. The position is marked by a gross postural shift involving at least half the body. A typical position is assumed by the discussant who leans toward the person on the opposite side of the conference table. Finally, the presentation "consists of the totality of one person's positions in a given interaction. Presentations have a duration from several minutes to several hours, and the terminals are a complete change of location" (Scheflen, 1964, p. 323).

Kendon (1986) used the term *gesticulation* to refer to those situations where one or more of our bodily movements are interacting with our verbal utterances. Communication of maximum clarity and forcefulness requires a "synchrony" in the kinds and intensity of meanings communicated verbally, bodily, and vocally. In order to understand the role of gesture in synchronized communication, Kendon said that we must understand the meaning of a *gesture phrase* as a nucleus of movement having some definite form that is preceded by a preparatory movement and succeeded by a movement that either moves a limb back to a rest position or repositions it for the beginning of a new gesture phrase.

With regard to the synchrony of gestures, words, and vocal cues, Kendon (1986) wrote that "there is a close fit between the phrasal organization of gesticulation and the phrasal organization of the speech. . . . The association between Gesture Phrases and Tone Units arises because Gesture Phrases, like Tone Units, mark successive units of meaning" (p. 34). The implication for persons who wish to be successful communicators is clear: We must strive to synchronize the channels through which we communicate in terms of rhythm, phrasing, and, ultimately, meaning.

Iverson and Thal (1998) identify two main types of gestures: deictic and representational. Deictic gestures include holding an object to be seen by another or using your arm or finger to indicate a desired object. Representational gestures, on the other hand, carry not only a reference to an object but also fixed "semantic" content. Representational gestures include making a cup with your hand or nodding yes or no with your head.

Recently, research has suggested that children may acquire gestural development at an early age. Crais, Douglas, and Campbell (2004) found that infants were able to effectively use deictic and representational gestures at earlier ages than had been reported in earlier gesture studies.

Rather than three units of bodily communication, Ekman and Friesen (1967) identified two—*body acts* and *body positions.* Body acts are readily observable movements, with a definite beginning and end, that could occur in any part of the body or across multiple body parts simultaneously. Body positions are identified by a lack of movement for a discernible period of time—two seconds or more—with any body part. Scheflen (1964) and Ekman and Friesen (1967) defined the position as a fixed configuration of the parts of the body; therefore, the position might be properly identified as postural communication. Gestural communication is more properly associated with the point (Scheflen's term) and the body act (Ekman and Friesen's term), because both concepts involve movements of one or more parts of the body, with rapid changes to other movements.

Postures by definition represent a more limited medium of communication than gestures. Because they are more limited in number than gestures, postures are probably most effectively used to communicate such general attitudes as one's desire to increase, limit, or avoid interaction with another individual; a positive or negative reaction to someone; the current level of self-confidence; and the general presentation of self. In addition to their impact on perceptions of power, the number and kinds of postures accurately reflect a person's power and degree of responsiveness to another person, as well as the strength of a desire to establish a closer or more immediate relationship with another person. Some considerable evidence suggests that posture communicates a multitude of specific emotions varying from joy, happiness, sadness, and interest to shame, anger, and fear (Wallbott, 1998). In addition, posture has been found to indicate interest in conversations (Bickmore, 2004).

For example, a forward lean can indicate to a friend that you are ready for her or him to speak. This finding has also been seen in the doctor–patient setting. Patients reported higher satisfaction with doctors who used forward lean as a form of postural cue (Griffith, Wilson, Langer, & Haist, 2003). Nonverbal communication in the medical context is taken up in greater detail in the last chapter of this book.

The film *Glory Road* (2006) provides instructive examples of the communicative functions of postures. To watch Coach Don Haskins, a basketball coach, is to realize that his "command presence" and "command look" were communicated forcefully by his postures. His words served merely to reinforce the emotional intensity of his commands, which were communicated by his postures. Toward the end of the film, Haskins motivates his players by sitting with them in the bleachers. His posture is slumped and directed away from them to reinforce his attitude that the nation is not ready for an African-American basketball team.

Scheflen has provided a particularly satisfying answer to the most basic question that might be asked about postures: What meanings can be communicated by variation in posture, when communicators can choose freely from their postural repertoire? Scheflen (1964) identi-fied three basic types of postures, which convey distinctive meanings. In the Type 1 postural orientation, an individual communicates inclusiveness or noninclusiveness. When your body is placed in such a way as to exclude another person, you are clearly communicating your intent to limit or avoid interaction with that individual. In the Type 2 postural orientation, the individual may assume the vis-à-vis or parallel bodily orientation. The vis-à-vis orientation is associated with the exchange of rather intimate feelings, and the parallel bodily orientation conveys a desire to communicate with the entire group rather than with any individual in it. Finally, with the Type 3 postural orientation, the individual assumes a congruent or incongru-ent posture. When you assume a posture similar to that of the person with whom you are communicating, you are probably suggesting that you agree with the individual and that the person is your equal in status. Postural mirroring—that is, assuming the same posture as that of your interaction partner—also facilitates cooperation (LaFrance, 1985).

In the final section of this chapter, we will identify both functional and dysfunctional kinds of gestures and postures. The difficulty of this task is highlighted by Lee and Charl-ton's (1980) tongue-in-cheek guidelines specifying nonverbal behaviors that should not be exhibited in public. Among other things, they warn against sticking a finger or a hand into an orifice—especially someone else's. They stress that one should not diddle, fiddle, or twiddle in public. Flossing your teeth, pecking a forefinger on someone's shoulder, playing a drum solo on your teeth with a pencil, grooming your fingernails, or cracking your knuckles are also viewed as equally egregious types of nonverbal behavior that should not be displayed in public.

Major Communicative Functions of Bodily Cues

The chapter's emphasis to this point has been on defining the types of gestures and postures that are important in interpersonal communication. Although a good deal of information on the communicative functions of bodily cues has already been presented, these functions are so important that they deserve to be treated in a separate section of this chapter also.

Chapter 2 featured the face as the major medium for the communication of emotions. Chapter 3 stressed that the language of the eyes serves many communicative functions of which the attention, intimacy, and persuasive functions stand out. We would be speaking metaphorically if we said that the eyes are the windows of the soul. In contrast, we would be speaking literally if we said that our bodily cues—gestures and postures—serve as an accurate barometer to many of our internal, psychological states.

Bodily cues do of course serve many communicative functions. These functions include *framing* communicative interaction and helping synchronize it. Gestures in particular are integrally tied to the speech process; therefore, gestures function with speech to communicate ideas of great complexity. Finally, we know that our bodily communication may reveal how we feel about ourselves (Streeck, 1993; Wallbott, 1998). Although important, the functions of bodily communication just cited are of secondary importance.

Our bodily cues serve at least four major communicative functions. They communicate (a) attitudinal information; (b) highly personal information about a communicator's psychological state(s); (c) the intensity of emotions being experienced; and (d) relational information.

Gestures and postures surely help to reflect how we are predisposed to react to subjects and issues we encounter in our interpersonal interactions with others. These bodily cues typically reveal much more, however, about our attitude toward the person(s) with whom we interact and our attitudes toward self. The kinds of bodily cues that communicate particular attitudes have already been identified in this chapter. We should recognize too that certain gestures and postures may reflect how we feel about ourselves at a given point in time. Thus, communicators who exhibit closed postures experience an increase in unpleasant emotions (Rossberg-Gempton, 1993).

Undeniably, bodily cues provide rather precise information about our psychological states. They accurately indicate not only whether we are confident but also how confident we are. They often reveal whether and when we are being deceptive. Recently, Miller (2005) revealed the importance of how professors use body talk in the classroom by saying that poor body cues can diminish the lecture's overall effectiveness. Have you ever been distracted by something your professor did with his or her body during a lecture? For instance, a professor pacing across the front of the room or continuing to scratch his or her head while lecturing would distract just about any student.

The face most accurately communicates particular types of emotions, but it is our bodily cues that indicate what our general level of emotional arousal is and how intensely we feel the emotion we may be displaying facially. Needless to say, intensity cues are vitally important if we are to respond in an appropriate way to the emotions displayed by our interaction partners.

Finally, our bodily cues serve a major relational function. This point is obvious when we realize that our gestures and postures are central determinants of how likable, assertive, powerful, or dominant we are perceived to be. Thus, our chances of experiencing many unsatisfying interpersonal relationships are excellent unless we familiarize ourselves with the relational functions of our gestures and postures.

Functional and Dysfunctional Uses of Bodily Cues

Bodily cues can communicate meanings and information that are both functional and dysfunctional from the perspective of the communicator. Also, as just stated, such cues frequently play a central role in determining how likely another person is to perceive the communicator as confident, likable, assertive, or powerful. Although it is difficult to generalize about bodily cues, certain types of cues typically have a much more positive impact than other cues on the perceptions, attitudes, and behaviors of those with whom we communicate. In this section, we will identify bodily cues that have been found to be desirable in a variety of communicative situations, as well as those cues that are undesirable.

When considered from the perspective of the categoric approach to bodily communication, bodily cues that communicate a sense of *openness* and *confidence* have been found to be highly desirable. Communicating a sense of openness in interpersonal communication is very important. It signals to the other person(s) that you are making a sincere effort to convey your feelings honestly. *Gestures of openness frequently trigger reciprocal gestures of openness in others* (Nierenberg & Calero, 1973). In one sense, gestures that communicate openness are the nonverbal equivalent of words that are self-disclosing. Both forms of communication eliminate or diminish behavior that is calculated to withhold or distort personal information. More recently, Kimbara (2006) found that typically, gestures are mimicked in closer relationships. For example, a local real estate agent shared with Eaves that in order to better secure a sale, one should echo the posture or other bodily movements to make the customer feel more comfortable with the seller.

Wallbott (1998) found several specific emotions associated with certain body movements or positions. Stronger correlations were found among the following emotion conditions:

- cold anger—lateral hand, arm movements; arms stretched out
- hot anger—shoulders up, hands open, lateral arm movements
- shame—upper body collapsed
- sadness—upper body collapsed
- despair—shoulders forward, hands open
- fear—shoulders forward

Confidence gestures are typically found in the following body positions: chin thrust forward, leaning back with both hands supporting head, and feet on table (Nierenberg & Calero, 1973).

Openness and confidence gestures are generally desirable, but defensiveness and nervousness gestures are not. Defensiveness gestures take many forms, but often they suggest a literal attempt to block out unpleasant ideas or individuals. If you have seen a baseball umpire retreat from an infuriated manager, you will recognize that crossed arms are a traditional gesture of defensiveness. Downcast eyes, indirect bodily orientation, and closed bodily postures are among the most notable of defensiveness gestures.

In a recent study, Eaves and Magnasco (2005) found that the media portrayed athletes differently when it came to athletes' use of nonverbal gestures. Women more than men found the mediated nonverbal behaviors of defensiveness (e.g., slamming a ball down, shouting at a referee, or using inappropriate gestures and body language) more deplorable and felt that such behaviors should be sanctioned in their respective sports. Further, the findings in the study suggest that the media should take a more active role in de-emphasizing the coverage of such deviant nonverbal displays of anger and hostility.

Finally, nervousness gestures take many forms but usually are exhibited unintentionally. Nervousness gestures are usually manifested in the form of adaptors that are associated with an increasing level of anxiety. Twiddling, fiddling, and fidgeting all suggest that a person is becoming more nervous. Tugging at clothing and ears, as well as playing with objects in the room (object-adaptors), are among the many bodily movements that quite clearly suggest "I am nervous."

When considered from the dimensional perspective, bodily movement can be used to communicate meanings on three dimensions: liking–disliking, assertiveness–nonassertiveness, and power–powerlessness cues. We will concentrate on those kinds of bodily cues that represent the particularly strong manifestations of meaning associated with likability, assertiveness, and power. Other kinds of nonverbal cues associated with those dimensions of nonverbal meaning will be considered as well.

Nonverbal Indicators of Liking versus Disliking

Liking is not the only label to identify the types of nonverbal cues that communicate pleasantness. *Interpersonally attractive, immediacy, intimacy,* and *pleasantness* are all terms that have been used to describe clusters of nonverbal cues that communicate similar, but not precisely the same, kinds of information. To simplify matters, we have decided to use the inclusive terminology of liking–disliking cues.

Certainly, the desire to be liked is almost universal. To communicate your desire to be liked is not, of course, to ensure that you will be. Nor is an expression of liking for another person certain to produce a reciprocal response. Nonetheless, those desires are closely related because we tend to like those who like us.

To establish that you like another person, you must express your desire for *high immediacy* by exhibiting your interest in that person. Positive indicators of liking include, but are not limited to, the following nonverbal cues:

1. forward leaning during encounters
2. body and head orientations that directly face the other individual
3. open-body positions
4. affirmative head nods
5. moderate amounts of gesturing and animation
6. close interpersonal distances
7. moderate body relaxation
8. touching
9. initiating and maintaining eye contact
10. smiling
11. postural mirroring (exhibiting similar or congruent postures) (Kimbara, 2006; Maxwell & Cook, 1985; Mehrabian, 1981; Schlenker, 1980)

Nonverbal indicators of disliking are, of course, associated with a relative absence of positive indicators of liking, or they may take the reverse form. Nonverbal indicators of disliking include the following cues:

1. indirect bodily orientations
2. eye contact of short duration
3. averted eyes
4. unpleasant facial expressions
5. a relative absence of gestures
6. bodily rigidity
7. visual inattentativeness
8. closed bodily posture
9. incongruent postures
10. bodily tension

As we have already indicated, dislike—or its weaker manifestation, disinterest—may result when individuals violate social norms in their overzealous efforts to be liked. Individuals who use sweeping gestures, nod too much, smile too much, sit too close, stare, and use gross postural shifts may think that they are communicating liking cues. Actually, such unsubtle, manipulative efforts may have the unintended effect of promoting dislike.

Nonverbal Indicators of Assertiveness and Unassertiveness

Social sensitivity is absolutely necessary for the development of satisfying interpersonal relationships. If individuals are to be perceived as socially sensitive, they must take pains to communicate that they are standing up for their rights, but without violating the rights of others. To communicate in a socially sensitive way, a person must be assertive without being aggressive.

Individuals who wish to be perceived as assertive must take special care to monitor their nonverbal cues. Positive nonverbal indicators of assertiveness include the following cues:

1. nonverbal and verbal components of the message used consistently
2. relaxed gestures and postures, with a forward lean preferred
3. firm but not expansive gestures
4. sustained eye contact, although staring should be avoided
5. illustrator gestures and vocal inflection used to emphasize key words and phrases
6. an appropriately loud voice
7. touching used when appropriate

Nonverbal indicators of unassertiveness are more numerous, although some are simply the opposite of the indicators of assertiveness. To avoid the inference that you are unassertive, you should seek to eliminate the nonverbal cues that are indicators of unassertiveness:

1. nervous gestures such as hand-wringing and lip licking
2. clutching the other person as the assertive remark is made
3. out-of-context smiling
4. hunching the shoulders
5. covering the mouth with the hand
6. wooden posture (bodily rigidity)
7. frequent throat clearing
8. deferentially raised eyebrow
9. evasive eye contact
10. pauses that are filled with nonfluencies (Lange & Jakubowski, 1976)

Nonverbal Indicators of Power and Powerlessness

The desire to be perceived as powerful may not be as universal as the desire to be liked, but for many people it is compelling. Some people let their desire get out of control, of course. You may have seen politicians as well as personal acquaintances strutting around, using overly expansive gestures, and laying claim to your territory in the errant belief that they will be perceived as more powerful.

Sometimes those "power" messages are in the hands of the media, not the politician. Tiemens (1978) conducted a fascinating study about the perceived political power created by the media (particularly in their use of camera angles) in a televised debate. Gerald Ford was cast more negatively by the media. His poor use of eye contact and facial expressions led viewers to believe he was powerless. Tiemens found that style, not content, matters most. Televised shots of Jimmy Carter were closer-up than they were for Ford. This camera framing had a positive effect for Carter's image and hurt how Ford's body was portrayed to the voter. The vertical camera angle was higher for Carter than it was for Ford, thereby producing a view that required one to "look up at" Carter, but "look straight at" or "look down at" Ford. In sum, the way the camera portrayed the candidates produced a body image of Carter that was characterized as more *powerful*, while the image produced of Ford was associated with *powerlessness*.

A recent study provides similar support of mediated gestures and body language. Cienki (2004) studied the kinesic differences between Al Gore and George W. Bush in the 2000 presidential debates. In his study, he found that certain gestures were used by the candidates to complement or accent the language they used in their speeches. Cienki found that Bush used more metaphoric gestures when discussing an abstract idea than Gore did. For example, Bush would clinch his fist to signal strength or raise his hand in the air to signal that the "time has come for action." Cienki also found in his study that Bush used substantially more of these types of power gestures and was, as a result, a more effective debater than Gore.

Schlenker (1980) illustrated that efforts to obtain power can reach the point of absurdity. He recalls that in Charlie Chaplin's famous movie *The Great Dictator*, Hitler and Mussolini are trying to gain dominance over each other by finding some way to assert their superiority. In one scene, both dictators are seated in chairs in a barbershop while getting shaves. Because they are seated, the only way they can think of to elevate their status is to elevate their chairs. Predictably, both begin pumping up their chairs furiously. Their wild efforts to enhance their power stop only after they reach the ceiling and crash to the floor.

Nonverbal indicators of power, status, and dominance are not always clearly differentiated in the research literature, so we will identify them under the single label of *power* cues. The following nonverbal cues have proved to be positive indicators of perceived power:

1. relaxed posture
2. erect rather than slumped posture
3. dynamic and purposeful gestures
4. steady and direct gaze
5. variation in speaking rate and inflection
6. variation in postures
7. relative expansiveness in postures
8. the option to touch
9. the option to stare
10. the option to interrupt
11. the option to approach another person closely (Archer, 1980; Harper, 1985; Schlenker, 1980)

As Schlenker (1980) pointed out, cues that communicate a sense of powerlessness or submissiveness are not always dysfunctional. In many instances, we encounter individuals with superior power and status whose self-presentation of relative submissiveness is expected. Everyone is accountable to someone else. For example, the basketball coach who takes pride in cultivating the "command look" and the "command voice" is apt to think twice about asserting such prerogatives of power when in the presence of the university president. Using nonverbal cues that communicate power in the presence of a more powerful person is to risk confrontation and even reprimand.

In general, however, the desire to be perceived as powerless is not a strong one. A relative lack of power is associated with the following indicators of powerlessness:

1. body tension
2. excessive smiling
3. continuous visual attentiveness while others are speaking
4. not looking directly at others
5. looking down frequently
6. arriving early for parties
7. sitting in the 11 o'clock position at conference tables (power moves clockwise from 12 o'clock around to 11 o'clock)
8. exhibiting distracting foot movement
9. not exposing the soles of your shoes
10. assuming closed postures
11. elevating your eyebrows frequently
12. never touching another individual (Archer, 1980; Korda, 1975; Schlenker, 1980)

In retrospect, we should keep at least two facts in mind: First, although judgments of a person's likability, assertiveness, and power are strongly affected by his or her bodily communication, these judgments are affected by other types of nonverbal behaviors as well. Secondly, different cultures may attach different priorities to the importance of being perceived as likable, assertive, and powerful. Matsumoto and Kudoh (1987) found, for example, that the Japanese attach the highest priority to being perceived as powerful, whereas Americans attach the highest priority to being perceived as likable.

Summary

This chapter concentrated not only on how bodily cues are typically used but also on how they should be used. In pursuit of this objective, the two major perspectives for conceptualizing bodily cues were discussed, the major functions of bodily cues identified, and functional and dysfunctional uses of specific kinds of bodily cues illustrated.

Bodily cues have been conceptualized from both the categorical and the dimensional perspectives. The categoric perspective is based on the assumption that the informational potential of bodily cues is best understood by classifying them with regard to level of awareness and intentionality, code used, and functions served by the cues. The five types of nonverbal behavior identified by proponents of the categoric approach are emblems, illustrators, affect displays, regulators, and adaptors. Because communicators frequently use adaptors without awareness and intentionality, adaptors are a particularly valuable source of information about the communicator's attitudes, feelings, and self-confidence.

The dimensional perspective is based on the assumption that the meanings communicated by nonverbal cues are best described by three independent dimensions: pleasantness, arousal, and dominance. These dimensions of meaning are best understood by considering the communicative implications of the approach, arousal, and power metaphors. Our bodily cues serve four major communicative functions. They communicate attitudinal information, personal information about a communicator's psychological state, the intensity of emotions being experienced, and relational information. Bodily cues also serve other communicative functions of secondary importance.

To enhance communicative effectiveness, individuals should cultivate the use of gestures and postures of openness and confidence. On the other hand, bodily cues that communicate defensiveness and nervousness are dysfunctional. In order to gain more effective control over the meanings they communicate by bodily cues, individuals should carefully consider the nature of the nonverbal indicators of liking–disliking, assertiveness–nonassertiveness, and power–powerlessness.

R E F E R E N C E S

Archer, D. (1980). *How to expand your social intelligence quotient.* New York: Evans.

Argyle, M. (1988). *Bodily communication* (2nd ed.). London: Methuen.

Bangerter, A. (2004). Using pointing and describing to achieve joint focus of attention in dialogue. *Psychological Science, 15*, 415–419.

Bangerter, A., & Oppenheimer, D. M. (2006). Accuracy in detecting referents of pointing gestures unaccompanied by language. *Gesture, 6*, 85–102.

Bickmore, T. W. (2004). Unspoken rules of interaction. *Communications of the ACH, 47*, 38–44.

Birdwhistell, R. L. (1952). *Introduction to kinesics.* Louisville: University of Kentucky.

Birdwhistell, R. L. (1970). *Kinesics and context.* Philadelphia: University of Pennsylvania Press.

Bull, P. (1983). *Body movement and interpersonal communication.* New York: John Wiley.

Bull, P., & Connelly, G. (1985). Body movement and emphasis in speech. *Journal of Nonverbal Behavior, 9,* 169–187.

Cienki, A. (2004). Bush's and Gore's language and gestures in the 2000 US presidential debates. *Journal of Language and Politics, 3,* 409–440.

Cohen, A. A. (1977). The communication functions of hand illustrators. *Journal of Communication, 27,* 54–63.

Collier, G. (1985). *Emotional experience.* Hillsdale, NJ: Erlbaum.

Crais, E., Douglas, D. D., & Campbell, C. C. (2004). The intersection of the development of gestures and intentionality. *Journal of Speech, Language, and Hearing Research, 47,* 678–694.

Eaves, M., & Magnasco, J. (2005). *The effect of nonverbal negative roles in the mass media.* Paper presented at the SSCA Convention in the Popular Communication Division, Baton Rouge, LA.

Ekman, P. (1985). *Telling lies: Clues to deceit in the marketplace, politics, and marriage.* New York: Norton.

Ekman, P., & Friesen, W. V. (1967). Head and body cues in the judgment of emotion: A reformulation. *Perceptual and Motor Skills, 24,* 713–716.

Ekman, P., & Friesen, W. V. (1969). The repertoire of nonverbal behavior: Categories, origins, usage, and coding. *Semiotica, 69,* 49–97.

Ekman, P., & Friesen, W. V. (1972). Hand movements. *Journal of Communication, 22,* 353–374.

Goldberg, S., & Rosenthal, R. (1986). Self-touching behaviors in the job interview: Antecedents and consequences. *Journal of Nonverbal Behavior, 10,* 65–80.

Goldin-Meadow, S., Wein, D., & Chang, C. (1992). Assessing knowledge through gestures: Using children's hands to read their minds. *Cognition & Instruction, 9,* 201–209.

Griffith, C. H., Wilson, J. F., Langer, S., & Haist, S. A. (2003). House staff nonverbal communication skills and standardized patient satisfaction. *Journal of General Internal Medicine, 18,* 170–174.

Guthrie, R. D. (1976). *Body hot spots.* New York: Pocket Books.

Harper, R. G. (1985). Power, dominance, and nonverbal behavior: An overview. In S. L. Ellyson & J. F. Dovidio (Eds.), *Power, dominance and nonverbal behavior* (pp. 29–48). New York: Springer-Verlag.

Hewes, G. W. (1992). Primate communication and the gestural origin of language. *Current Anthropology, 33,* 65–84.

Iverson, J., & Thal, D. (1998). Communicative transitions: There's more to the hand than meets the eye. In A. Wetherby, S. Warren, & J. Reichle (Eds.), *Transitions in prelinguistic communication* (pp. 59–86). Baltimore: Paul H. Brookes.

Johnson, H. G., Ekman, P., & Friesen, W. V. (1975). Communicative body movements: American emblems. *Semiotica, 15,* 335–353.

Kendon, A. (1984). Did gesture have the happiness to escape the curse of the confusion of Babel? In A. Wolfgang (Ed.), *Nonverbal behavior* (pp. 75–114). Lewiston, NY: D. J. Hogrefe.

Kendon, A. (1986). Current issues in the study of gesture. In J. L. Nespoulous, P. Perron, & A. R. Lecours (Eds.), *The biological foundations of gestures* (pp. 24–45). Hillsdale, NJ: Erlbaum.

Kimbara, I. (2006). On gestural mimicry. *Gesture, 6,* 39–61.

Knapp, M. L., & Hall, J. A. (2006). *Nonverbal communication in human interaction* (6th ed.). New York: Holt.

Knapp, M. L., Hart, R. P., & Friedrich, G. W. (1973). Verbal and nonverbal correlates of human leave-taking. *Communication Monographs, 40,* 182–198.

Korda, M. (1975). *Power!: How to get it and how to use it.* New York: Random.

Krivonos, P. D., & Knapp, M. L. (1975). Initiating communication: What do you say when you say hello. *Central States Speech Journal, 26,* 115–125.

LaFrance, M. (1985). Postural mirroring and intergroup relations. *Personality and Social Psychology Bulletin, 11,* 207–217.

Lamb, W. (1965). *Posture and gesture.* London: Duckworth.

Lange, A. J., & Jakubowski, P. (1976). *Responsible assertive behavior.* Champaign, IL: Research Press.

Lee, L., & Charlton, J. (1980). *The handbook: Interpreting handshakes, gestures, power signals, and sexual signs.* Englewood Cliffs, NJ: Prentice-Hall.

Levy, E. T., & McNeill, D. (1992). Speech, gestures, and discourse. *Discourse Processes, 15,* 277–301.

Manusov, V. (1990). An application of attribution principles to nonverbal behavior in romantic dyads. *Communication Monographs, 57,* 104–118.

Mark, L. S., Nemeth, K., Gardner, D., Dainoff, M. J., Paasche, J., Duffy, M., & Grandt, K. (1997). Postural dynamics and the preferred critical boundary for visually guided reaching. *Journal of Experimental Psychology, 23,* 1365–1379.

Marschark, M. (1994). Gesture and sign. *Applied Psycholinguistics, 15,* 209–236.

Matsumoto, D., & Kudoh, T. (1987). Cultural similarities and differences in the semantic dimensions of body postures. *Journal of Nonverbal Behavior, 11,* 166–179.

Maxwell, G. M., & Cook, M. W. (1985). Postural congruence and judgements of liking, and perceived similarity. *New Zealand Journal of Psychology, 14,* 20–26.

Mehrabian, A. (1981). *Silent messages* (2nd ed.). Belmont, CA: Wadsworth.

Mehrabian, A., & Friedman, S. L. (1986). An analysis of fidgeting and associated individual differences. *Journal of Personality, 54,* 406–429.

Miller, P. (2005). Body language in the classroom. *Techniques, Nov./Dec.*, 28–30.

Nespoulous, J. L., & Lecours, A. R. (1986). Gestures: nature and function. In J. L. Nespoulous, P. Perron, & A. R. Lecours (Eds.), *The biological foundations of gestures* (pp, 49–61). Hillsdale, NJ: Erlbaum.

Nierenberg, G., & Calero, H. H. (1973). *How to read a person like a book.* New York: Pocket Books.

Reed, J., Patton, M., & Gold, P. (1993). Effects of turn-taking sequences in vocational test interpretation interviews. *Journal of Counseling Psychology, 40,* 144–155.

Remland, M. S. (2000). *Nonverbal communication in everyday life.* Boston: Houghton Mifflin Company.

Rogers, W. T. (1978). The contribution of kinesic illustrators toward the comprehension of verbal behavior within utterance. *Communication Research, 5,* 54–62.

Rosenfeld, H. M. (1982). Measurement of body motion and orientation. In K. R. Scherer & P. Ekman (Eds.), *Handbook of methods in nonverbal behavior research* (pp. 199–286). Cambridge: Cambridge University Press.

Rossberg-Gempton, I. (1993). The effect of open and closed postures on pleasant and unpleasant emotion. *Arts in Psychotherapy, 20,* 75–82.

Rutter, D. R. (1984). *Looking and seeing: The role of visual communication in social interaction.* Chichester, England: John Wiley.

Scheflen, A. E. (1964). The significance of posture in communication systems. *Psychiatry, 27,* 320–323.

Schlenker, B. R. (1980). *Impression management.* Monterey, CA: Brooks-Cole.

Sousa-Poza, J. F., & Rohrberg, R. (1977). Body movement in relation to type of information (person- and nonperson-oriented) and cognitive style (field independence). *Human Communication Research, 4,* 19–29.

Streeck, J. (1993). Gestures as Communication I: Its coordination with gaze and speech. *Communication Monographs, 60,* 275–299.

Tiemens, R. K. (1978). Television's portrayals of the 1976 presidential debates: An analysis of visual content. *Communication Monographs, 45,* 362–370.

Wallbott, H. G. (1998). Bodily expression of emotion. *European Journal of Social Psychology, 28,* 879–896.

5 Proxemic Communication

The way we use space clearly communicates meaning. Different meanings are communicated in many different ways throughout the world. The beliefs, the values, and the meaning of a culture are communicated by the way people handle space. German culture, for example, has long emphasized orderliness and clearly defined lines of authority. The need for privacy is strong and is manifested in the impulse to define and defend well-marked territories. Hence, Germans object to individuals who literally "get out of line" or those who disregard signs such as "Keep Out" and "Authorized Personnel Only" that are intended to stipulate the approved use of space (Hall, 1969).

Americans are inclined to think of space, and to react to it, as "empty." In contrast, in Japan it is space—not objects—that communicates meaning. The Japanese customarily assign specific meanings to specific types of spaces. For this reason, intersections, not streets, are given names in Japan. The particular space, with its functional characteristics, is the thing of importance in Japan. The space available in a single room serves a number of functions because the Japanese use movable walls and separators to create the kinds of spaces that serve specific functional objectives. In fact, the Japanese cope with the problem of limited available space by miniaturizing parts of their environment. The gardening practices that produce bonsai plants are a case in point (Altman, 1975).

Whereas Americans covet privacy by demanding their own offices and maintain their distance from others through the use of large and elevated desks, the Arabs know no such thing as privacy in public, and they are offended by anything less than intimacy of contact while carrying on a conversation. Such conversations characteristically feature "the piercing look of the eyes, the touch of the hands, and the mutual bathing in the warm moist breath during conversation [that] represent stepped up sensory inputs to a level which many Europeans find unbearably intense" (Hall, 1969, p. 158). In effect, the Arab's use of space and olfactory stimuli communicates two meanings. It invites and demands intense involvement in interpersonal communication, and it ensures the withdrawal of those who reject that method of relating.

Meanings communicated by the use of space are not confined to the sometimes gross differences among cultures. Differences within cultures are probably of more practical importance, and they abound. Spatial needs seem to vary dramatically among citizens of a nation, residents of a city, and even members of a family. To satisfy those needs, some people define and protect a set of spatial boundaries with a persistence and vigor that would put the family dog or cat to shame. The stone wall around one's property may be interpreted by some to be the narcissistic attempt of a socially alienated person to find privacy; others may interpret the wall as an enlightened response to the overcrowding of urban living. The fact that one person's spatial boundaries might intrude on another person's territory accounts for the distinctive type of communication problem that is associated with spatial needs and their frustrations.

In our use of space, we must remember that there is often a great disparity between the meanings we intend to communicate and the meanings we actually do communicate. We must recognize that our proxemic or spatial behavior seems to be most strongly affected by two competing needs, the need for affiliation and the need for privacy. In general, we signal our desire to have contact with people and develop closer relationships with them through closer physical proximity. Thus, physical proximity when combined with touching clearly serves a central communicative role in close interpersonal encounters. In contrast, we seek to satisfy our privacy needs by maintaining greater distance from others while often seeking by physical means to ensure our separation from them; we may, for example, use our elbows to keep individuals from getting too close to us. Burgoon (1988) wrote that "there are times when we wish to distance ourselves from the group, to achieve greater physical security, to escape stimulation and stress, to gain a greater sense of personal control, or to permit greater psychological freedom and self reflection" (p. 351).

One's personal space can be violated by an on looker. Observe the woman's negative eye contact directed toward the intruder, signaling her disapproval of his behavior.

The ways we use space can have a profound impact on the impression we make on others. The judgments people make about how friendly, likable, dominant, honest, and empathic we are may be strongly affected by the way we relate to people spatially. As we shall see in subsequent chapters, our success in the job interview, in the selling situation, and in cross-cultural communication can be affected in important and readily identifiable ways by our use of space. In short, the impression manager must carefully consider which proxemic behaviors should and should not be exhibited in various contexts because such behaviors are often important in impression management.

Edward T. Hall, the pioneer of proxemic research, coined the term **proxemics** because it suggests that proximity, or lack of it, is a vitally important factor in human interaction. In its broadest perspective, Hall defines proxemics as the study of how people structure and use microspace (1968). Proxemics focuses not only on the ways individuals orient themselves to other individuals and objects in their immediate physical environment, but also on the perceptual and behavioral impact of these spatial orientations. Burgoon, Buller, and Woodall (1989) defined proxemics as the perception, use, and structuring of space as communication. For our purposes, *proxemics* is defined as the study of how individuals use space to communicate.

The Proximate Environment

We use space to communicate. When we use the space that can be perceived directly, we are communicating within the proximate environment. The **proximate environment** includes everything that is physically present to the individual at a given moment. The proximate environment of a student in a classroom includes the student's desk, the other students, the teacher, the chalkboard, the windows, and the doorway. The student's proximate environment does not include the soccer team practicing outside or students in another classroom (Sommer, 1966).

No single concept adequately describes how we communicate in our proximate environment. Because terms such as *space, distance,* and *territory* are clearly related in a conceptual sense, there is a tendency to treat them as synonyms. They are not synonyms, however, and should not be treated as such. To understand what and how we communicate via our proxemic behavior, we must understand the meaning of five interrelated concepts: space, distance, territory, crowding, and privacy. This chapter is designed to illustrate the communicative uses of space, distance, territory, crowding, and privacy and to demonstrate why each concept is important, to identify the major communicative functions served by proxemic behavior, and to describe the effects and assess the implications of the violation of proxemic norms and expectations.

Space

The concept of visual space in nonverbal communication is analogous to the concept of silence in verbal communication. Though both are devoid of content, the ways we use them may be rich in communicative significance. Edward Hall, for example, contended that our culture places severe constraints on the ways we use space. In fact, he maintained that there are basically three types of space: *fixed-feature, semifixed-feature,* and *informal* space (1969). Rapoport (1982) amplified Hall's (1969) classifactory scheme and modified his terminology. Rapoport identified three major types of space that have communicative significance in our society: fixed-feature, semifixed-feature, and nonfixed-feature space.

Fixed-feature space refers to the characteristic arrangement of rooms by function. Within the home, for example, formal meals are rarely served in the bedroom and bookcases rarely line the walls of the bathroom. Ironically, the fixed features that define how space is to be used in the home are often quite dysfunctional. Hall (1969) cites the kitchen as a particular problem. He emphasizes that "the lack of congruence between the design elements, female stature and body build (women are not usually tall enough to reach things), and the activity to be performed, while not obvious at first, is often beyond belief" (p. 105).

The problem may not be as severe as it seems for the working woman in our society because it is important that she foster the perception that she spends little time in the kitchen. As Rapoport (1982) emphasized:

> In the case of the Puerto Rican culture, status is gained during a party through a hostess being seen to produce food, being seen in the kitchen, and "performing" in front of an audience of her peers; in Anglo culture, a woman is seen as a good hostess when she apparently does no work, yet food appears as though by magic. (p. 94)

Semifixed-feature space refers to the placement of objects in the home, office, conference room, and other proximate environments. The objects we use in these types of spaces may include furniture, plants, screens, paintings, plaques, and even birds and animals. The objects we choose—to demarcate the boundaries and to accent the meanings of the semifixed-feature spaces in which we interact—are important because often they are direct extension of our personality. Our choices of curtains, interior colors, shutters, mailboxes, and decorative planting may reveal more about us than our handwriting or our IRS file.

The semifixed objects we choose to use do more than shape perceptions of presumed personality characteristics. The choice of objects and their placement in semifixed-feature space can have a strong impact on the credibility of the occupant of a home or office. Important as those communicative functions are, perhaps the most important communicative function of semifixed-feature space is the degree to which it promotes **involvement** or **withdrawal** among the individuals who are using the space.

Nonfixed-feature space is a concept with which all of us should be rather familiar. This is the space, immediately surrounding our body, that each of us perceives to be ours. We use no physical objects to mark the boundaries of our "personal space" because these boundaries are invisible. The amount of personal space that we claim as ours may vary, depending on our size, current emotional state, status, and sex. Malandro and Barker (1983) also emphasized that people claim varying amounts of personal space to be theirs, both in front of and in back of them.

As we consider the communicative implications of the three major kinds of space, we should pay particular attention to semifixed-feature and nonfixed-feature space. We have little opportunity to modify the nature of most fixed-feature environments. In contrast, we can consciously consider the communicative implications of the objects we choose to place in semifixed-feature space, and we can contemplate the advantages and disadvantages of claiming and defending a personal space of a given size and dimension.

Semifixed- and nonfixed-feature space can be used in a variety of ways to transmit meanings. Although the uses vary widely, they frequently serve one of two communicative functions. Either they bring people together and stimulate involvement (in which case they are serving a **sociopetal** function) or they keep people apart and promote withdrawal (in which case they are serving a **sociofugal** function). The sociopetal use of space satisfies the affiliative needs of individuals by promoting interaction. By contrast, the sociofugal use of space is well suited to satisfy privacy needs.

Sommer, who has been a leader in research on the sociopetal and sociofugal uses of microspace, maintains that we transmit very different connotative meanings by the way we use space. He refers to the sociofugal function as "sociofugal space," and finds that sociofugal spatial arrangements or conditions suggest the following meanings: large, cold, impersonal, institutional, not owned by an individual, overconcentrated, without opportunity for shielded conversation, providing barriers without shelter, isolated without privacy, and concentrated without cohesion (1967, 1974). By contrast, the sociopetal use of space promotes involvement, communicative interaction, and a feeling of involvement.

Before you consider how you can and should use space to be a more effective communicator, you should recognize that perceptions and definitions of space tend to be culture-specific. Latino perceptions of what constitutes a "large" space may be affected by their strong need to conserve space.

Distance

At least in theory, space has no finite barriers and becomes a tangible concept only when people or objects occupy space and when individuals attempt to define its boundaries. In contrast, distance is a relational concept and is usually measured in terms of how far one individual is from another.

Once again, Hall (1968) has done pioneering work in attempting to identify and classify the distances people use to separate themselves from others in order to satisfy their various needs. Hall identified four types of informal distance:

1. intimate
2. personal
3. social
4. public

Intimate distance (0–18 in.) is easily distinguishable because of the number and intensity of sensory inputs, of which the communicators are intensely aware. Intimate distance is considered inappropriate in public by the typical middle-class American (Hall, 1969). For example, one may touch you for comfort or stand really close to you for added security.

Personal distance (1½–4 ft) is the distance that individuals customarily place between themselves and others. Communication used in close interpersonal relationships typically occurs at this distance. Personal distance is important for several reasons. The personal distance that we characteristically assume might be a reliable clue to our self-confidence as well as to our felt privacy needs. Successful communicators will be sensitive to the personal distances that others maintain when interacting with them.

Social distance (4–12 ft) is the distance that typically separates individuals engaged in a business transaction or consultation and is also appropriate for a range of social gatherings that are informal in nature. Actual separation for social distance will obviously depend on such important factors as whether you are standing or seated and whether you are communicating with one other person or with a group of persons.

Finally, the shift from social to **public distance** (12 ft or more) has tangible and important implications for interpersonal communication. At the close phase of public distance (12–25 ft), the types of nonverbal meanings that can be perceived vary rather dramatically. Alert communicators can give the appearance that they have received no message, or they can remove themselves physically from the situation. If individuals do communicate at this distance, they will find that the interaction is of a very formal nature.

The far phase of public distance (25 ft or more) can have a particularly disruptive impact on interpersonal communication. Beyond 25 ft, the voice loses much of its potential to transmit meanings accurately, and facial expressions and movements must be rather expansive in order to be recognized. As Hall (1969) emphasized, "much of the nonverbal part of communication shifts to gestures and body stance" (p. 125).

Hall's distance zones have been widely cited as the guidelines we should use to assume proper spatial orientations vis-à-vis other individuals, but Burgoon's research suggests that those distance zones should be subjected to more careful scrutiny. In fact, Burgoon and Jones (1976) argued convincingly that *distance zones or "expected distancing" are determined not only by the normative expectations of our culture but also by the idiosyncratic preferences of individual communicators.* They contend that "Expected distancing in a given context is a function of (1) the social norm and (2) the known idiosyncratic spacing patterns of the initiator" (p. 132). In a study conducted at the University of Georgia, Eaves (1988) found that students varied greatly on the amount of spatial distance they expected to be maintained during the delivery of a message. Further, the study revealed that in the cases of those times when an invasion took place, subjects reported that their "new" distance was uncomfortable during the interaction.

Researchers developed and subjected to a number of empirical tests a theoretical model of proxemic violations that is designed to predict the effects of violating the kinds of proxemic norms just discussed. Not surprisingly, Burgoon concluded that distance violations—violation of proxemic norms and expectations—are arousing and distracting, and they communicate messages. Her three most innovative and important conclusions are derived from empirical tests of her model:

1. The characteristics and behaviors of a person who violates proxemic norms can be interpersonally rewarding to the person who is the object of the proxemic violation.
2. High-reward "initiators" seem to achieve the most desirable communication outcomes when they violate distance norms rather than conform to them. For instance,

a high-reward initiator would be someone of high status who might follow the invasion with a compliment, praise, or reward.

3. Nonrewarding or low-reward initiators are more likely to achieve desirable communication outcomes by conforming to rather than violating distance norms (Burgoon, 1982; Burgoon & Hale, 1988).

Burgoon's proxemic violations model is unique because it suggests that the violation of distance norms, that is, norms that specify ranges for personal or social distance, can produce positive effects in some instances. If the response to a violation of proxemic norms is to be positive, it is important that the "violator" of proxemic norms be a high-reward source in terms of such characteristics as personal appearance and that the violation be followed by other positively valued actions such as compliments (Burgoon, 1982). In this way, Burgoon is critical of Hall's foundation of proxemics and adds the element of "expectation" to our understanding of how spatial violations function during an interaction.

Afifi and Metts (1998) have expanded the critique of Hall's original theory and have added to Burgoon's understanding of how proxemics operates. While it was once held that violations were always negative in nature, this new line of research sheds additional light on the theory. Depending on the situation and with whom you interact when expectancy violation occurs, there will be different outcomes in such violations. This is formally called the expectancy violation theory (EVT). The researchers suggest that EVT can be best understood by looking at its three separate parts: 1) violation valence, 2) violation expectedness, and 3) violation importance.

First, violation valence is the possible range of whether the behavior is seen as positive or negative. For example, a violation valence for a spatial invasion between friends at a movie might be positive, whereas an athlete who receives a high five for no known reason may be startled by the action. Touch is another good example (touch will be discussed in greater detail in the next chapter). Some touch is seen as positive, especially when you need the comfort of a friend. In contrast, a stranger's touch could be seen as aggressive or outright hostile.

Second, violation expectedness is the possible range of expected behaviors during the violation. For instance, the invader expects you to be intimidated (e.g., to withdraw, especially during a cross-gender interaction). This action triggers a fight-or-flight thesis when it is unanticipated. The fight-or-flight thesis basically suggests that you will welcome the invasion or withdraw from the invasion. The invadee begins to attribute motives about the action, whether it provides comfort, security, attraction, anxiety, fear, or disapproval. Research suggests that the fight-or-flight thesis is more often triggered by a male invader than by a female invader (Kaitz, Bar-Haim, Lehrer, & Grossman, 2004). On an elevator, we will typically withdraw if someone stands too close to us while we are waiting for the doors to open on the appropriate floor.

Third, violation importance is the magnitude or impact that the violation of expectancy has on the relationship. When a woman on a date perceives her space to be violated, this perception will be a significant detriment to the future of the relationship. A business executive might be uncomfortable with how closely his boss sits next to him and, as a result, will begin to withdraw from future interactions with that manager at the company.

Proxemic norms are influenced not only by the beliefs and values that define a particular culture but also by demographic variables or personal characteristics of the communicator that differentiate one person from another. These variables make up the "idiosyncratic" component of proxemic norms that helps explain why different individuals have different preferences with regard to the distance(s) they prefer to be separated from other individuals when interacting with them. Among the more important of such variables are gender, age, ethnicity or race, status, personality, degree of acquaintance, and area of residence.

Within our culture, females sit and stand closer to each other than do males. Men respond negatively to face-to-face invasion by strangers, whereas females respond negatively to side-by-side invasion by strangers. Although opposite-sex pairs in the United States consistently adopt closer interaction distances than male dyads, the available evidence does not conclusively establish that opposite-sex dyads usually interact at closer distances in public than female dyads, although that frequently seems to be the case (Burgoon et al., 1989).

The tendency for opposite-sex dyads in the United States to interact at close interpersonal distance could be a culture-specific proxemic practice. In some cultures, opposite-sex pairs maintain a greater interaction distance than any other gender combination. Thus, a female in Turkey characteristically maintains a greater distance when interacting with a male than when interacting with a female; separation distance in Turkey for opposite-sex pairs is also greater than the distance for two interacting males (Hortascu, Duzen, Arat, Atahan, & Uzer, 1990; Rustemli, 1986). We also know that feminine women experience the sensation of crowding significantly sooner than either androgynous men, androgynous women, or masculine men, and only feminine women—of the four groups— experience a decrease in their task performance when they feel crowded (Lombardo, 1986). Crowding also affects performance in younger audiences. For example, children in highly dense living quarters were found to have lower academic scores and more behavioral problems in school than their counterparts (Evans, Lepore, Shejwal, & Palsane, 1998).

Generally, people maintain greater distances from other people as they get older. This is true from preschool through middle age, although closer contact is characteristic of the very old and young. This is partly due to the facts that very young children have not yet fully learned norms associated with distance expectations, and that the very old have difficulty hearing in many instances. Indeed, one study found that children who grew up insecure and with one only parent had smaller personal bubbles and welcomed more intrusions into their personal space than children who were secure in infancy with both parents (Bar-Haim, Aviezer, Berson, & Sagi, 2002). Not surprisingly, we tend to maintain closer distances when interacting with people who are approximately our own age. Age interacts with status on occasion to dictate that greater interaction distances between people are appropriate. In addition, adolescents have been found to regulate spatial behavior as a result of infant intimacy (Bar-Haim, Aviezer, Berson, & Sagi, 2002) and peer acceptance (Stiles & Raney, 2004).

The contribution of race or ethnicity to distance norms has not been clearly determined. Baxter's (1970) observation of the proxemic behaviors of dyads in the Houston city zoo suggested that Mexican-Americans of all age and sex groupings interacted "most proximally"—were consistently closest together—while whites were intermediate, and African-Americans stood most distant. However, black women appear to interact at closer distances than either white females or white males. In a recent study, Evans, Lepore, and Allen (2000) found that there are some cultural differences in perceived crowding. Apparently, as density rises, African-American and Anglo-American populations experience greater levels of crowding than do Mexican-Americans and Vietnamese-Americans.

The impact of status on distance norms is clearer. Preferred separation distance increases as the status differential between two interactants increases. Lower-status persons seem to be particularly aware of the need to "keep their distance" from high-status persons, whereas an increase in people's status is usually associated with their desire to decrease the amount of distance that separates them from the people with whom they are interacting. For instance, high-status persons might have executive washrooms. In some university settings, faculty have their own restrooms, and in some university libraries, faculty or staff may reserve some space that students cannot use.

The personality profile of individuals also has an impact on the distance they prefer to maintain when interacting with intimates, friends, business associates, or casual acquaintances. We know, for example, that extroverts approach others more closely and maintain shorter communicating distances than do introverts. We know also that people with high apprehension and low self-confidence and self-esteem prefer to maintain greater separation when communicating than do their counterparts.

Predictably, we tend to stand closest to intimates and close friends, stand farther away from acquaintances, and maintain the greatest distance from strangers. Burgess (1983) found that we tend not only to stand closest to individuals we know best and who are closest to us in age, but we also tend to avoid or ignore strangers. Interestingly, some evidence suggests that we can generalize across cultures about the impact of degree of acquaintance on distance norms. For example, students at the University of Rajasthan, Jaipur, India, had the sensation of feeling "crowded" first when approached by strangers and last when approached by friends (Kamal & Mehta, 1987).

Finally, area or region of residence can clearly shape people's spatial preferences. Thus, Pedersen and Frances reported (1990) that persons from the mountain states (Utah) scored higher than those on the West Coast (Los Angeles) in their preferences for isolation, anonymity, and solitude. People from the Southeast were similar to those on the West Coast in their low preference for isolation but resembled people in the mountain states in their high preference for anonymity. The findings for the West Coast residents of Los Angeles can be explained in part by the fact that low preferences for isolation and solitude are necessary in Los Angeles in order to avoid the frustration of frequent violation of proxemic expectations. Both isolation and solitude are in short supply in an area of such high population density.

The culturally determined distancing zones identified by Hall do not necessarily represent comfortable interaction distances for all communicators. Thus, Hayduk (1981) found that subjects experienced extreme discomfort at an interaction distance of 11.7 in., moderate discomfort at 19.5 in., and only slight discomfort at 27.3 in. More importantly, Hayduk found that preferred interaction distances for individual communicators vary. Individuals who prefer greater interaction distances become uncomfortable much sooner as a stranger approaches them than do individuals who prefer shorter interaction distances. Of the former group, 50 percent became moderately uncomfortable at a distance of 4.4 ft. Of the latter group, 50 percent became moderately uncomfortable at a distance of 1.3 ft.

This university student feels her space has been violated by the stranger on the elevator.

We should therefore beware of encouraging communicators to assume normative separation distances in our society. Thus, an interaction distance can be comfortable for one communicator but agonizingly uncomfortable for another. The best criterion in judging the appropriateness of separation distance for two or more people seems to be how comfortable they are with a given spatial orientation (Burgoon, 1988).

In short, results from research designed to determine desirable separation distances "generally suggest that people seek an optimal range of distance for interaction, and departures from this range that leave either too large or too small distances result in discomfort and dissatisfaction" (Sundstrom & Altman, 1976, p. 54). If we know and like an individual, for example, we are apt to prefer an interaction distance that is closer than the culturally prescribed norm. When we interact with an individual we dislike, our preferred interaction distance is usually greater than that indicated by the cultural norm.

Territory

The concept of territory has vast implications for interpersonal communication, and many of these implications remain unexplored. Much of our knowledge of the concept comes from studies that illustrate how animals identify and defend clearly delineated territories by means of instinct. Territoriality in this sense is a basic concept in the study of animal behavior; it is defined as behavior by which an organism characteristically lays claim to an area and defends it against members of its own species and in so doing ensures the propagation of the species by regulating density (Hall, 1969).

Sommer (1966) recognized that the concept of territoriality now has great relevance for the study of human behavior, even if humans do not define their territories exclusively or even primarily by instinctual means. He saw **territory** as an area controlled by an individual, family, or other face-to-face collectivity, with the emphasis on physical possession, actual or potential, as well as defense.

The biggest and best territories since time immemorial have been controlled by the most powerful, the most influential, and often the wealthiest members of a society. The two sets of walls that surround Windsor Castle in England clearly demarcate this type of choice territory. William the Conqueror chose to build Windsor Castle on a large, steep hill that is directly above the Thames River. His motivation was straightforward. He built not a residence but a fortress. The result was an impregnable stronghold that could be used to monitor and control the activities of the hostile population that lived below the castle.

Sommer (1966) captures the essential nature of territoriality:

> Since human communication is based largely on symbols, territorial defense relies more on symbols such as name plates, fences, and personal possessions than on physical combat, or aggressive displays. . . . Salesmen have, and actively defend, individual territories. One criterion of territoriality is . . . the home team always wins . . . [and] an animal on its own territory will fight with more vigor. . . . [Hence] a male on its own territory is almost undefeatable against males of the species. (p. 61)

Territorial behavior, therefore, is defined by attempts to mark the boundaries of territories that are "owned" by individuals or groups. Through the use of personalized markers, we strive either to regulate social interaction within territories perceived as ours or to prevent unauthorized individuals from entering or using the territory.

Some markers might include leaving a book to save a seat while you leave the classroom, leaving a book at a library table to mark your territory while you search for another book, or at a ballet recital putting a sign on a row of seats in the auditorium to reserve the section for your friends.

Sometimes people get a bit carried away in their use of territorial markers. For example, the owner of an antique shop in Santa Monica, California, has posted a sign on his front door that says "No Browsing. Stay out unless you plan to make a purchase today." Some owners of souvenir shops near the Eiffel Tower in Paris will slap the hands of children who touch their merchandise. In an expensive store in Grindewald, Switzerland, stickers are attached to hand-carved music boxes that say "You drop it. You pay for it." Although the insensitive use of personal markers may have undesirable side effects, the more personal the markers used to delineate territorial boundaries, the more effective they are in controlling or preventing interaction (Altman, 1975).

If territories serve so central a function in regulating human interaction, the obvious question is: What types of territories are typically defined and defended? Writing from a broad perspective, Lyman and Scott (1967) observe that there are four kinds of territories: public, home, interactional, and body.

Public territories are areas individuals may enter freely. Great constraints are placed on human interaction within public territories, however, because of explicit laws and social traditions. The fact that individuals are often anonymous when they use certain public territories means that they might be treated in ways that are impersonal and even rude.

The young men who serve as the Swiss Guard at the Vatican in Rome, for example, vigorously enforce rules about what territories visitors may and may not enter and what may be done within different Vatican areas. They do so with an unseemly curtness that they might not exhibit if the visitors they encountered were not anonymous. Similarly, the struggles to desegregate buses, restaurants, and beaches suggest that the term public territory can have a very restricted connotation for some individuals who choose to enter and attempt to interact with others within the territory.

By contrast, **home territories** feature freedom of interaction by individuals who claim the territory. **Home territories** are defined in part by the distinctive markers used to assure boundary maintenance. Examples include reserved chairs, personalized drinking mugs, and even the cat's litter. Fraternities, private clubs, and gay bars constitute home territories. In each of them, distinctive territorial markers are used to limit usage by outsiders.

Interactional territories are areas where individuals congregate informally. A party, a local pool hall, and an informal meeting on campus are all interactional territories. Although every territory has boundaries that are maintained, interactional territories are unique in that they have movable boundaries.

Interactional territories might also include space in a faculty meeting, the dining area at the university cafeteria, or the lobby area where you wait for a bank teller or a hotel clerk to become available.

Finally, **body territories** consist of space that is marked as reserved for use by our bodies. Goffman developed and supported the provocative thesis that "eight territories of self" exist, and their changeable boundaries are a function of variability in both individual behavior and environmental conditions. These territories of self are (a) personal space, (b) stalls, (c) use-space, (d) turns, (e) sheaths, (f) possessional territory, (g) informational preserves, and (h) conversational preserves (Goffman, 1971).

Of the eight territories of self identified by Goffman, five seem particularly relevant and important for interpersonal communication. First, the *stall* is space with clear-cut boundaries that individuals claim exclusively for their own use. Telephone booths, public toilets, and parking places are obvious examples of stalls. Unlike personal space, stalls have highly visible and fixed boundaries that can easily be protected from intruders.

Whereas stalls identify themselves by their structure, use-space identifies itself by its function. **Use-space** is the space immediately surrounding us that we must have in order to perform personal functions such as lighting our cigarette or swinging at a golf ball. Have you been bowling lately in one of those university classes? All persons need use-space while bowling so that everyone has the room to properly execute a good roll while not hitting anyone else in the immediate area. Our claim to use-space is usually respected by others in close proximity to us because they realize that they would require similar space to perform similar functions.

The **turn** represents a territorial claim based on both structure and function. Expressions such as "Take your turn" and "Get in line, Bud" suggest the nature of this type of territorial behavior. There are cultural and subcultural differences with regard to turn-taking norms. Some lines, such as at the theater or grocery store, are rarely broken, but lines at more crowded environments such as concert halls or amusement parks often have more ambiguous turn-taking guidelines. We have been socially conditioned to expect that such territorial claims will be honored.

The **sheath,** which consists of both our skin and the clothes we wear, functions to afford us with the desired degree of privacy. Examples of the sheath may include our shirt, pants, jacket, or skirt. This territory is extremely private and is often not violated since the objects are on our person. Much like the sheath, **possession territory** is closely identified with the human body. Rather than skin or clothes, which cover the body, possessional territory consists of objects that we claim as our own and that we array around us wherever we are. Objects such as gloves and handbags often function as markers to delineate the boundaries of possessional territory. Only the most insensitive individual will attempt to move such territorial markers.

Crowding

Crowding is a concept of central importance to the study of proxemic communication. To begin, crowding should be clearly differentiated from density. **Density** is a concept that is defined strictly in physical terms. Density refers to the number of people per unit of space. **Crowding,** in contrast, is a psychological concept. Crowding is the condition that exists when an individual's attempts to achieve a desired level of privacy have been unsuccessful, in the sense that more social contact continues to occur than is desired (Altman, 1975).

Common sense seems to suggest that there is a strong relationship between objective measures of crowding and the subjective feeling of being crowded. However, the actual relationship between objective and subjective crowding is not strong (Edwards, Fuller, Sermsri, & Vorakitphokatorn, 1994). For example, objective measurement indicates that four individuals forced to share a single room in a household are crowded. These individuals may not all feel equally crowded. In this instance, the lower the level of a person's perceived control of space, the stronger the feeling of being crowded and of psychological distress (Lepore, Evans, & Schneider, 1992). Conversely, the sensation of feeling crowded can be greatly reduced by giving people exclusive control over the small amount of space in which they find themselves (Edwards et al., 1994). But what happens when we perceive more opportunity or greater control to reduce the perception or impact of crowding? For instance, one might be able to move a bed to create more space in a room. Sinha and Nayyar (2000) found that elderly people who feel they are in control and have social support are more likely to feel less threatened by or uncomfortable with perceptions of crowding. In essence, social support and personal control are both ways that the elderly use to reduce the impact of a negative environmental stressor. A good example of this is how some elderly persons are able to choose the furniture arrangement in their room at a nursing home.

A number of factors enhance the feeling of being crowded—for example, a collectivist orientation, membership in a noncontact culture, and high population density when combined with a high crime rate (Iwata, 1992). As we shall see, the sensation of being crowded is associated with some highly undesirable effects.

Jails constitute one environment in which both subjective and objective overcrowding are chronic and the control of the inmates over most of the space in the jail is minimal. Accordingly, the potential for serious problems is great. Predictably, a national sample of 189 sheriffs reported that every one of the 13 problems they viewed as most important increased significantly as the inmates' sensation of crowding increased (Kinkade, Leone, & Semond, 1995).

The sensation of being crowded is subjective in that it depends on *who else* is involved, *when* and *where* it occurs, and *why* and *how* it occurs. For example, a person who is on a crowded bus waiting for a stop may feel a great deal of discomfort, while an individual who is at a crowded concert may enjoy the music so much that the lack of space is not important. Regardless of the circumstances, when we experience the sensation of crowding, we usually find interpersonal communication to be less than satisfying. We may or may not have the opportunity to modify our own proxemic behavior (or the proxemic behavior of persons with whom we interact) in ways that will minimize or eliminate the sensation of crowding.

Crowding clearly makes many people uncomfortable. We can now document that crowding negatively affects both health and behavior. Evans and Lepore (1992) maintained that three major mechanisms account for these negative effects: behavioral constraint, diminished control, and stimulus overload/arousal. High temperatures are a good example of a type of stimulus overload that contributes to the perception of overcrowding. Interestingly, the negative effects of high temperatures are reduced when individuals feel that they have some control over the space in which they find themselves (Ruback & Pandev, 1992). For example, a person could pull down a window shade to reduce the temperature in a room or decrease the amount of stimuli. This control might help a person to reduce the effects of overcrowding.

The sensation of crowding is related to dysfunctional behaviors and health problems, whereas objective crowding is not (Fuller, Edwards, Vorakitphokatorn, & Sermsri, 1993). Household crowding has consequences that are selective and modest in North America and Europe but stronger in Southeast Asia. In Bangkok, Thailand, for example, crowded households are associated not only with martial instability, more arguments, and parent–child tensions but also with more frequent disciplining of children. The greater behavioral impact of crowding in Southeast Asia may be explained in part by the fact that people living in this part of the world often have limited control over the space that is available to them. For example in China, three or four generations of a family frequently "share" a small living area.

Individuals who feel crowded also report a higher incidence of health problems. Health problems in turn seem to result at least in part from increased psychological distress that results from crowding (Fuller, Edwards, Sermsri, & Vorakitphokatorn, 1993). Further research must be done before precise relationships between overcrowding and personal health are known.

The feeling of being crowded seems to have a negative impact on our ability to establish and maintain satisfying relationships with others. Not surprisingly, people tend to cope much more successfully with crowding when it occurs in the presence of friends rather than when it occurs among strangers (Kamal & Mehta, 1987).

Our ability to cope with crowding and develop satisfying interpersonal relationships is also affected by the nature and amount of space that is available to us. McCarthy and

Saegert (1978) compared the behaviors of individuals living in a 14-story apartment build-ing and in a 3-story walk-up; the residents of the high-rise building felt much more crowded than residents of the walk-up. Those who felt crowded had greater difficulty establishing relationships with their neighbors, were less socially active, felt more detached from their places of residence, belonged to fewer voluntary groups, and felt they had less power to exercise influence on the decisions made by the management of the apartments. In fact, Stokols, Ohlig, and Resnick (1978) found that crowded dorm residents did poorer in school than students in more spacious settings.

The potential for perceptions of crowding to negatively affect our feelings about, and our relationship with, other individuals should not be overemphasized, however. Although feelings of overcrowding do typically result in some elevation in anxiety and stress levels (Altman, 1975), there are at least some indications that the feeling of being crowded is cathartic in some situations and helps to free up inhibitions in others.

A person may not experience crowding when in a large group. Interestingly, many individuals seek out large crowds, such as those who attend football games, because of the intra-audience effects that they experience. Hocking (1982) maintained that the dynamics of crowd behavior tend to be distinctive and that the reactions that members of a large audience or crowd have to other members of the collectivity are "a major factor contribut-ing to the excitement, the arousal, and ultimately the entertainment value" that results when large numbers of people interact with one another (p. 101). At a music concert, fans may be worried less about crowding and more about how close they can get to the front to see their favorite band or artist. When was the last time you felt a need to get closer to the front row at a concert?

The crowding associated with a large gathering clearly has persuasive implications. This is particularly true of crowd dynamics as they affect the response to an evangelists's persuasive message at a televised religious rally. Leathers (1989) suggests that televangelist Jimmy Swaggart skillfully used intra-audience effects in large crowds to his own advantage. Presumably he recognized that his ability to draw large crowds and make mass appeals to the anonymous members of the crowd greatly increased the susceptibility of his religious audience to his persuasive message (Newton & Mann, 1989). Today, Joel Osteen seems to draw large crowds to his Houston congregation with similar results. Osteen has the congre-gation stand before each lesson begins. Each member holds a Bible in his or her hand and cites a brief slogan before Osteen begins to speak. This serves as a modern-day example of an intra-audience effect among a large crowd.

Privacy

Altman (1975) clearly connects the importance of privacy to an understanding of the com-municative implications of our proxemic behaviors. He wrote that

> the concept of privacy is central to understanding environment and behavior relation-ships; it provides a key link among the concepts of crowding, territorial behavior and personal space. Personal space and territorial behavior function in the service of privacy needs and, as such, are mechanisms used to achieve desired levels of "personal or group privacy." (p. 6)

He went on to emphasize that crowding results from ineffective or unsatisfactory use of space, distance, and territory, with the result that individuals achieve inadequate levels of privacy.

Privacy may be defined as selective control of access to one's self or to one's group (Altman, 1975). To a considerable degree, we control access to ourselves and to groups that are important to us by our use of space. Our needs for privacy must be balanced against our needs to be perceived as friendly and outgoing individuals who seek interaction with others. Neither the hermit nor the member of the commune has achieved the balance that is necessary for most of us to be effective communicators in the real world. A case in point: during helping situations, one study found that unwanted personal space violations create a violation of privacy and interfere with the desire of one to help (DeBeer-Keston, Mellon, & Solomon, 1986).

Some individuals place a high premium on privacy. Rare indeed is the individual who views the bathroom as the appropriate place for social interaction in the home. On the other hand, some individuals make a practice of walking around nude in their own homes. Privacy, therefore, is defined by the felt needs of those who assert specialized types of claims to it.

The most comprehensive effort to compare and contrast types of privacy has been done by Burgoon (1982). She properly uses the term dimensions of privacy rather than privacy categories in recognition of a simple fact: A person rarely experiences complete privacy or a complete lack of privacy, rather, people experience varying degrees of privacy.

The major dimensions of privacy with their contrasting definitions are as follows:

1. **Physical privacy:** a measure of the degree to which one person is physically inaccessible to others
2. **Social privacy:** both an individual and a group state in which the option to withdraw from social interaction with another person(s) exists
3. **Psychological privacy:** people's ability to exercise control over both thoughts and feelings that can be expressed by them and to them
4. **Information privacy:** people's capacity to prevent the gathering and dissemination of information about themselves, their group(s), or their organization(s) without their knowledge or permission

In one sense the experiences of crowding and privacy are polar opposites. Thus, Burgoon (1982) wrote that

> if personal space invasion or crowding can be seen as one end of a distancing continuum, then physical privacy is the opposite end, since it involves freedom from intrusion on one's self-defined "body buffer zone" and freedom from the discomfiture of too many people for the available space. (p. 211)

Significantly, privacy is one of the most powerful needs that human beings experience. Because crowding frustrates and often blocks efforts to achieve a desired level of privacy, the consequences of feeling crowded can be severe.

On the positive side, knowledge of other persons' privacy needs and preferences is vitally important. Such knowledge can greatly enhance our potential for successful communication. This is particularly true when we use this information to respond in sensitive and socially appropriate ways to the expressed or implied privacy needs of those with whom we interact.

We must recognize two things at minimum. The strength of the privacy needs experienced by different individuals and groups is often quite different. Individuals and groups also vary markedly in terms of the importance they attach to different types of privacy. Thus, the person who seeks absolute isolation from others places the highest priority on solitude. By contrast, the person who places the highest priority on anonymity might even savor contact with others as long as personal identity is concealed.

We do know that individuals are most apt to seek privacy when they are distressed (Newell, 1994). We know too that where we choose to sit in a room in public may make a statement about our privacy preferences. Thus students who choose to sit in the back of a classroom receive significantly higher scores on the Privacy Preference Scale (PPS) than students seated in other parts of the classroom. The students seated in the back also scored significantly higher on the "Not Neighboring" and "Seclusion" scales of the PPS in one study (Pedersen, 1994). Finally, we know that both adults and children have certain "places" they prefer when they seek privacy. The bedroom is the preferred place of privacy for adults because it is associated with activities that require peace and quiet (Oseland, 1993). Children ages 3 to 5 report that the places where they seek privacy in a day care center are a cubby, a chair, or a concealed space underneath a playhouse (Zeegers, Readdick, & Hansen-Gandy, 1994).

Finally, the relative importance of physical, social, psychological, and informational privacy is strongly affected by the nature of the activities we undertake at a given point in time. These privacies vary and become more or less important depending on the situation. In some situations, we may not mind if someone comes into our living room to sell us a vacuum or ice cream product. On the other hand, we may take great strides to protect our informational privacy in cases of medical records or social security number.

The Communicative Functions of Proxemics

The functional importance of proxemics is undeniable. In fact, Patterson and Edinger (1987) maintained that our proxemic behaviors have at least some impact on the communicative functions of providing information, regulating interaction, and expressing intimacy. They highlight the importance of proxemic behaviors in persuasion and impression management, which in turn serve the social-control function of communication.

Even though proxemics may have some impact on a number of communicative functions, proxemic behaviors are particularly important when individuals are concerned with the impression management, persuasion, affiliation, and privacy functions of communication. While serving those functions, proxemic behaviors serve as a sensitive barometer that reflects the relative strength of the competing tendencies to both seek and avoid closer interaction with other individuals.

The Impression Management Function

Impression managers are concerned with many of the defining features of the images they project to others. Two of the most important dimensions of those images—likability and dominance—can be strongly affected by our proxemic behaviors.

In general, the closer you move to another person, the more that person is apt to like you (Andersen, 1988). The relationship between close physical proximity and liking is a strong one. Consider the people you know and ask yourself this question: Do I like best the individuals who stand or sit closest to me when I am interacting with them?

Liking is not apt to increase if a person moves so close to you as to be threatening or if you see the person as physically unattractive, however. Because the majority of the people we encounter are neither physically unattractive nor do they attempt interaction at distances that are so close as to be unseemly, communicating at close distances with most of the people you encounter should involve little risk for you. Research already cited in this chapter supports the conclusion that people will probably like you more as you move closer to them, even if you are violating their distance preferences; the qualifier here is that the "violatee's" general perception of you as "violator" must be favorable.

Judgments of how dominant you are will also probably be affected by your proxemic behavior. Dominant people typically interact with other individuals at closer interaction distances and claim more personal territory than submissive individuals. The impact of proxemics on judgments of dominance is particularly strong in the small group (Andersen, 1988). In small-group contexts, dominant individuals typically choose to sit at the head of the table (Riess, 1982), and the greatest degree of dominance is attributed to the person seated highest, who sits in front of the interaction partner, or who stands (Schwartz, Tesser, & Powell, 1982).

The Persuasion Function

Proxemics also serves a valuable role in persuasion. Interpersonal distance is often perceived as favorable or unfavorable, and when favorable distances between people are maintained, likability for each other increases. Likability has a profound effect on the development of persuasion (Schultz, 1998).

There are some interesting gender differences as well. One study finds that female persuaders are more successful invaders of space than are men, primarily because individuals typically welcome a female invasion more so than a male invasion of space (Kaitz, Bar-Haim, Lehrer, & Grossman, 2004).

Proxemic violations can serve as a distraction for some in the persuasive process. In other words, the persuader, when violating the listener's space, can be more persuasive with the distraction than without. For instance, one study found that when a person's space was violated while hearing a counterattitudinal message to raise university tuition rates, he or she was more likely to agree to the tuition hike than the group of subjects whose space was not violated (Eaves, 1990).

The Affiliation Function

The need for closer affiliation with other human beings is a strong one. The term *closer* in turn suggests that we communicate the strengths of our affiliative needs via our physical proximity to other human beings. We do know that persons who move closer to others are often viewed as more friendly and extroverted, whereas they tend to be perceived more negatively as they move away (Patterson & Sechrest, 1970). Relatedly, if we assume a sociopetal spatial orientation, we signal our desire to develop closer interpersonal relationships with others. If we assume a sociofugal orientation, we signal our desire for greater separation in both a literal and a symbolic sense.

In some instances, individuals seem to experience strong needs for affiliation and privacy at the same time. A physically intimate couple, for example, might communicate in public in such a way as to make clear their wish to be maximally involved with each other whereas they want minimal contact with anyone else. Similarly, groups such as nudists might live in a remote, walled area in order to satisfy their need to affiliate with each other. At the same time, their need for privacy dictates that they exhibit a type of territorial behavior that ensures that they will be protected from intrusion by and affiliation with outsiders.

The Privacy Function

The privacy need is also a strong one for many people. As we have already indicated, our attempts to satisfy that need are apt to begin and end with the ways we use space, distance, and territory. Although definitions of privacy are culture-specific, the need for some degree of privacy seems to be a universal one.

We communicate the strength of our desire for privacy in many ways. They include the way we relate to others spatially, the placement of furniture in our offices, and the use of territorial markers inside and outside of our home. Although the strength of our needs for privacy may vary, we should recognize that our proxemic behavior represents an effective way of communicating and satisfying our needs for privacy.

The Effects of Violating Proxemic Norms and Expectations

Whether we are talking about the concept of space, distance, territory, crowding, or privacy, individuals have well-developed expectations. Those expectations specify what is acceptable proxemic behavior in a given situation. Because many of those expectations are sufficiently stable and enduring and are shared by so many people, they might be called *proxemic norms*. Although it is difficult to generalize about proxemic behavior, one generalization has been consistently supported in the past by empirical research. Simply put, *the violation of proxemic expectations, or norms, results in consistently disruptive effects on the communication between two or more people.*

Burgoon's (1988; Burgoon & Jones, 1976) development and test of a model of proxemic violations suggests that qualification of this generalization is now necessary. As we have indicated, the violation of proxemic norms might result in positive effects under certain conditions. At the same time, we must recognize that the negative consequences that are associated with the strong and sustained violations of proxemic norms are well documented.

So long as we maintain a distance perceived as "comfortable" or appropriate by persons with whom we interact, we know that close physical proximity is consistently associated with positive affect, friendship, and attraction. Close physical proximity that does not violate the interactants' notion of "comfortable interaction distance" serves to signal liking and is viewed as a sign of friendliness. However, both the violated and the violator become visibly uncomfortable when interaction is attempted at inappropriately close distances (Eaves, 1989; Sundstrom & Altman, 1976).

Individuals who perceive the violator as someone who is apt to provide them with negative rewards will react negatively when the violator moves closer to them than the proxemic norm dictates. Violators seen as possessing negative-reward power are judged to be threatening at much great distances than violators possessing positive-reward power. As a result, negatively rewarding individuals would be well advised to maintain a communicating distance greater than that specified by the proxemic norm.

Unfortunately, many of the studies of the effects of proxemic violations that have been undertaken were conducted in the somewhat antiseptic and unreal environment of classrooms, libraries, and mental hospitals. In the classroom and library studies, a "plant" is typically used and one or more unsuspecting subjects is approached. In one typical library study, in which a person trained by the experimenter violated the spatial expectations of library users, only 18 of 80 subjects actually left during the 10-minute period of the intrusion (Patterson, Mullens, & Romano, 1971). Although a relatively small number of individuals resorted to "flight" when their proxemic expectations were violated, many used elbows, knees, books, and personal artifacts as barriers to preserve further violations of their personal space.

The communicative impact of violating (or conforming) to spatial expectations has been measured largely in quantitative terms. The questions are straightforward. How many people will physically withdraw from a social situation if their spatial boundaries have been violated? How many people in rather close proximity to a person will that person tolerate? How much space do people require to separate themselves from others? At what point does the violation of proxemic norms lead to the sensation of crowding and resultant efforts to achieve greater privacy?

Distance between individuals seems to have its greatest impact on the development of interpersonal relationships. Individuals who use mutually preferred interaction distances facilitate the development of satisfying interpersonal relationships. Beware of increasing the distance between yourself and another individual as you interact. This practice will probably create a negative impression and could destroy interpersonal trust (Patterson & Sechrest, 1970).

As we have already pointed out, personal characteristics of the proxemic violator such as age, sex, and ethnicity help shape the way violatees react to a violation of their proxemic expectations and preferences. Two studies (Kmiecik, Mausar, & Banziger, 1979; Smith & Knowles, 1979) support the view that physically unattractive persons should attempt more distant communication than physically attractive persons. Subjects waiting at a stoplight to cross a street were "threatened" by the approach of pedestrian whom they considered to be physically unattractive; they crossed the street more quickly as the physically unattractive pedestrian approached.

The important point to remember is that the violation of proxemic norms is typically disruptive unless the violator has some highly desirable personal qualities or qualifications. In general, violation of proxemic norms is a sort of "noise," because it diverts the attention of the interactants from their communicative objectives. In fact, we know that the violation of proxemic norms is almost always uncomfortable for both the violator and the invadee. Violations are particularly discomforting and stressful when the invadee neither expects nor desires interaction with the invader (Sundstrom & Altman, 1976).

If the violations of preferred spatial orientations typically produce identifiably disruptive effects on interpersonal communication, then certain types of violations seem to be particularly disruptive. Having one's territory invaded, being crowded, and having one's right to privacy violated are uncomfortable at best and threatening at worst.

The boundaries of public, home, and interactional territories are clearly delineated by personal markers. Violations of territorial boundaries are disruptive. Fences, hedges, "Private Property" signs, and guards are all examples of markers used to identify the boundaries of home territories. Reaction to the violation of home territory is so strong that on numerous occasions violators have been shot. Violations of public and interactional territories are typically handled by more subtle means. Books and clothing are used to reserve spaces in public; hostile glances and unpleasant facial expressions are used to warn violators that they are not welcome; groups might resort to in-group jargon or in-group languages to signal intruders that they have violated territorial boundaries; and the ultimate response to territorial encroachment is aggression and fighting (Altman, 1975).

The sensation of overcrowding can produce many disruptive effects. Burgoon (1982) documents that the feeling of being crowded can produce anxiety, excessive stress, illness, feelings of helplessness, impaired cognitive functioning, loss of self-identity, and withdrawal. Indeed, people living in crowded conditions not only tend to withdraw socially from their housemates, but they tend also to be less supportive of them (Evans & Lepore, 1993). High-density environments tend to be associated with the sensation of crowding and negative effects. Thus, employees in a high-density environment in an "open office" feel more crowded than colleagues in a low-density "partitioned office," with the result that they feel a perceived lack of task and communication privacy and report lower "office satisfaction" (Oldham, 1988).

Finally, the violation of a person's privacy preferences can result in more intense social stimulation than a person desires. When the desired level of privacy exceeds the actual level of privacy, the sensation of crowding results. Baldassare (1978) emphasized that if "there is not enough room or privacy to conduct desired roles alone and with others, competition for space use may occur. Undoubtedly, the possibilities of incomplete role performances, intrusions, and the blocking of desired role enactments are heightened" (p. 47).

Resentment, conflict, and withdrawal frequently result when individuals' felt need for privacy is frustrated by the violation of their proxemic expectations. In our society, certain groups of individuals have difficulty maintaining desired levels of privacy. For example, the personal space of people who are short is much more frequently violated than the personal space of people who are tall. In one study (Caplan & Goldman, 1981), the personal space of short males (5 ft 5 in.) was invaded 69 percent of the time, and the space of tall males (6 ft 2 in.) was invaded only 31 percent of the time. Furthermore, women are at a disadvantage when they use space to try to achieve desired levels of privacy. This is true in part because the "private territory" claimed by males as their own is significantly larger than that claimed by females (Mercer & Benjamin, 1980). Recent research indicates that adolescent males may have more open-person space boundaries than do adolescent females (Stiles & Raney, 2004).

In short, our use of space represents an important communicative medium. When we conform to the proxemic expectations of those with whom we interact, we enhance our capacity to communicate successfully. When we violate proxemic expectations, we can anticipate resentment, resistance, and conflict in our interpersonal relationships. Successful communicators exhibit the capacity to interpret accurately the spatial expectations of other persons and to adjust their own proxemic behaviors so that they are compatible with those expectations.

Summary

Proxemics is defined as the study of how individuals use space to communicate. To understand the communicative effects and implications of our proxemic behaviors, we must understand the significance of space, distance, territory, crowding, and privacy. The three major types of space that have communicative significance are fixed-feature, semifixed-feature, and nonfixed-feature space. Because semifixed-feature and nonfixed-feature space can be controlled by the communicator, they are especially important. Those two types of space can be used to satisfy the sociopetal function of promoting communicative interaction or to satisfy the sociofugal function of inhibiting communicative interaction.

Normative distances have been established for intimate, personal, social-consultative, and public communication. Beyond respective cultural norms, comfortable distances for individual communicators vary. To determine comfortable interaction distances, we must take into account both cultural norms and the idiosyncratic preferences of persons with whom we communicate.

The boundaries of public, home, interactional, and body territories are delineated by personal markers. To disregard such markers is to risk being perceived as both insensitive and inept. Violations of body territory have a particularly disruptive impact on interpersonal communication.

Privacy is defined as selective control of access to one's self or to one's group. Because individuals desire various degrees of privacy, it is particularly important to understand the nature and uses of the four major dimensions of privacy: physical privacy, social privacy, psychological privacy, and informational privacy.

When proxemic expectations are violated, individuals frequently experience the sensation of crowding. One result might be that a person's needs for adequate privacy are frustrated. In general, the consequences of overcrowding are undesirable.

Our proxemic behaviors are relevant to and have an impact on a number of important functions of communication. However, the most important communicative functions of proxemics are the impression management function, the persuasion function, the affiliation function, and the privacy function.

Finally, the violation of proxemic norms and expectations is associated with a substantial number of undesirable effects. Thus, the person who violates proxemic norms and expectations often makes negative impressions, runs the risk of personal rejection, promotes conflict, and contributes to the deterioration of interpersonal relationships. On the other hand, the violation of proxemic norms can produce positive effects if the violator is a high-reward person who compensates for the proxemic violation with appropriate adjustments in other proxemic behaviors.

REFERENCES

Afifi, W. A., & Metts, S. (1998). Characteristics and consequences of expectation violations in close relationships. *Journal of Social and Personal Relationships, 15,* 365–392.

Altman, I. (1975). *The environment and social behavior.* Monterey, CA: Brooks/Cole.

Andersen, P. (1988). Nonverbal communication in the small group. In R. S. Cathcart & L. A. Samovar (Eds.), *Small group communication: A reader* (5th ed., pp. 333–350). Dubuque, IA: Wm. C. Brown.

Baldassare, M. (1978). Human spatial behavior. *Annual Review of Sociology, 4,* 29–56.

Bar-Haim, Y., Aviezer, O., Berson, Y., & Sagi, A. (2002). Attachment in infancy and personal space regulation in early adolescence. *Attachment & Human Development, 4,* 68–83.

Baxter, J. C. (1970). Interpersonal spacing in natural settings. *Sociometry, 33,* 449–454.

Burgess, J. W. (1983). Developmental trends in proxemic spacing behavior between surrounding companions and strangers in casual groups. *Journal of Nonverbal Behavior, 7,* 158–168.

Burgoon, J. K. (1982). Privacy and communication. In M. Burgoon (Ed.), *Communication yearbook, 6* (pp. 206–249). Beverly Hills, CA: Sage.

Burgoon, J. K. (1988). Spatial relationships in small groups. In R. S. Cathcart & L. A. Samovar (Eds.), *Small group communication: A reader* (5th ed., pp. 351–366). Dubuque, IA: Wm. C. Brown.

Burgoon, J. K., Buller, D. B., & Woodall, W. G. (1989). *Nonverbal communication: The unspoken dialogue.* New York: Harper & Row.

Burgoon, J. K., & Hale, J. L. (1988). Nonverbal expectancy violations: Model elaboration and application to ‚immediacy behaviors. *Communication Monographs, 55,* 58–79.

Burgoon, J. K., & Jones, S. B. (1976). Toward a theory of personal space expectations and their violations. *Human Communication Research, 2,* 131–146.

Caplan, M. E., & Goldman, M. (1981). Personal space violations as a function of height. *Journal of Social Psychology, 114,* 167–171.

DeBeer-Keston, K., Mellon, L., & Solomon, L. Z. (1986). Helping behavior as a function of personal space invasion. *Journal of Social Psychology, 126,* 407–409.

Eaves, M. H. (1989). *Proxemic violations and spatial expectations theory.* Paper presented at the annual convention of the Southern States Communication Association, Louisville, KY.

Eaves, M. H. (1990). *The effects of proxemic violations as distractors on persuasive message attempts.* Paper presented at the annual convention of the Southern States Communication Association, Birmingham, AL.

Edwards, J. N., Fuller, T. D., Sermsri, S., & Vorakitphokatorn, S. (1994). Why people feel crowded: An examination of objective and subjective crowding. *Population & Environment: A Journal of Interdisciplinary Studies, 16,* 149–173.

Evans, G. W., & Lepore, S. J. (1992). Conceptual and analytic issues in crowding research. *Journal of Environmental Psychology, 12,* 163–173.

Evans, G. W., & Lepore, S. J. (1993). Household crowding and social support: A quasiexperimental analysis. *Journal of Personality & Social Psychology, 65,* 308–316.

Evans, G. W., Lepore, S. J., & Allen, K. M. (2000). Cross-cultural differences in tolerance for crowding: Fact or fiction? *Journal of Personality and Social Psychology, 79,* 204–210.

Evans, G. W., Lepore, S. J., Shejwal, B. R., & Palsane, M. N. (1998). Chronic residential crowding and children's well-being: An ecological perspective. *Child Development, 69,* 1514–1523.

Fuller, T. D., Edwards, J. N., Sermsri, S., & Vorakitphokatorn, S. (1993). Housing, stress, and physical well-being: Evidence from Thailand. *Social Science & Medicine, 36,* 1417–1428.

Fuller, T. D., Edwards, J. N., Vorakitphokatorn, S., & Sermsri, S. (1993). Household crowding and family relations in Bangkok. *Social Problems, 40,* 410–430.

Goffman, E. (1971). *Relations in public.* New York: Harper.

Hall, E. T. (1968). Proxemics. *Current Anthropology, 9,* 83.

Hall, E. T. (1969). *The hidden dimension.* New York: Doubleday.

Hayduk, L. A. (1981). The permeability of personal space. *Canadian Journal of Behavioral Science, 13,* 272–287.

Hocking, J. E. (1982). Sports and spectators: Intra-audience effects. *Journal of Communication, 32,* 100–108.

Hortascu, N., Duzen, E., Arat, S., Atahan, D., & Uzer, B. (1990). Intrustion upon same-sex or different-sex dyads in a Turkish university dining hall. *International Journal of Psychology, 25,* 33–37.

Iwata, O. (1992). Crowding and behavior in Japanese public spaces: Some observations and speculations. *Social Behavior & Personality, 20,* 57–70.

Kamal, P., & Mehta, M. (1987). Social environment and feeling of crowding. *Indian Psychological Review, 32,* 25–29.

Kaitz, M., Bar-Haim, Y., Lehrer, M., & Grossman, E. (2004). Adult attachment style and interpersonal distance. *Attachment & Human Development, 6,* 285–304.

Kinkade, P., Leone, M., & Semond, S. (1995). The consequences of jail crowding. *Crime & Delinquency, 4,* 150–161.

Kmiecik, C., Mausar, P., & Banziger, G. (1979). Attractiveness and interpersonal space. *Journal of Social Psychology, 108,* 227–279.

Leathers, D. G. (1989). *Jimmy Swaggart: The histrionics of piety.* Paper presented at the convention of the Southern States Communication Association, Louisville, KY.

Lepore, S. J., Evans, G. W., & Schneider, M. L. (1992). Role of control and social support in explaining the stress of hassles and crowding. *Environment & Behavior, 24,* 795–811.

Lombardo, J. P. (1986). Interaction of sex and sex roles in response to violations of preferred seating arrangements. *Sex Roles, 15,* 173–183.

Lyman, S. M., & Scott, M. B. (1967). Territoriality: A neglected sociological dimension. *Social Problems, 15,* 237–241.

Malandro, L., & Barker, L. L. (1983). *Nonverbal communication.* Reading, MA: Addison-Wesley.

McCarthy, D., & Saegert, S. (1978). Residential density, social overload, and social withdrawal. *Human Ecology, 6,* 253–272.

Mercer, G. W., & Benjamin, J. L. (1980). Spatial behavior of university undergraduates in double-occupancy residence rooms: An inventory of effects. *Journal of Applied Social Psychology, 10,* 32–44.

Newell, P. B. (1994). A systems model of privacy. *Journal of Environmental Psychology, 14,* 65–78.

Newton, J. W., & Mann, L. (1980). Crowd size as a factor in the persuasion process. A study of religious crusade meetings. *Journal of Personality and Social Psychology, 39,* 874–883.

Oldham, G. R. (1988). Effects of changes in workspace partitions and spatial density on employee reactions: A quasi-experiment. *Journal of Applied Psychology, 73,* 253–258.

Oseland, N. (1993). The evaluation of space in homes: A facet study. *Journal of Environmental Psychology, 13,* 251–261.

Patterson, M. L., & Edinger, J. (1987). A functional analysis of space in social interaction. In A. W. Siegman & S. Feldstein (Eds.), *Nonverbal behavior and communication* (pp. 523–562). Hillsdale, NJ: Erlbaum.

Patterson, M. L., Mullens, S., & Romano, J. (1971). Compensatory reactions to spatial intrusion. *Sociometry, 34,* 116–120.

Patterson, M. L., & Sechrest, L. B. (1970). Interpersonal distance and impression formation. *Journal of Personality, 38,* 106.

Pedersen, D. M. (1994). Privacy preferences and classroom seat selection. *Social Behavior & Personality, 22,* 393–398.

Pedersen, D. M., & Frances, S. (1990). Regional differences in privacy preferences. *Psychological Reports, 66,* 731–736.

Rapoport, A. (1982). *The meaning of the built environment.* Beverly Hills, CA: Sage.

Riess, M. (1982). Seating preferences as impression management: A literature review and theoretical integration. *Communication, 11,* 85–113.

Ruback, R. B., & Pandev, J. (1992). Very hot and really crowded: Quasi-experimental investigations of Indian "tempos." *Environment & Behavior, 24,* 527–554.

Rustemli, A. (1986). Male and female personal space needs and escape reactions under intrusion: A Turkish sample. *International Journal of Psychology, 21,* 503–511.

Schultz, P. W. (1998). Changing behavior with normative feedback interventions: A field experiment on curbside recycling. *Basic and Applied Social Psychology, 21,* 25–36.

Schwartz, B., Tesser, A., & Powell, E. (1982). Dominance cues in nonverbal behavior. *Social Psychology Quarterly, 45,* 114–120.

Sinha, S. P., & Nayyar, P. (2000). Crowding effects of density and personal space requirements among older people: The impact of self-control and social support. *The Journal of Social Psychology, 140,* 721–728.

Smith, R. J., & Knowles, E. S. (1979). Affective and cognitive mediators of reactions to spatial invasions. *Journal of Experimental Social Psychology, 15,* 437–452.

Sommer, R. (1966). Man's proximate environment. *Journal of Social Issues, 22,* 60–61.

Sommer, R. (1967). Sociofugal space. *American Journal of Sociology, 72,* 65.

Sommer, R. (1974). *Tight spaces: Hard architecture and how to humanize it.* Englewood Cliffs, NJ: Prentice-Hall.

Stiles, A. S., & Raney, T. J. (2004). Relationships among personal space boundaries, peer acceptance, and peer reputation in adolesecents. *Journal of Child and Adolescent Psychiatric Nursing, 17,* 29–40.

Stokols, D., Ohlig, W., & Resnick, S. M. (1978). Perception of residential crowding, classroom experiences, and student health. *Human Ecology, 4,* 46–47.

Sundstrom, E., & Altman, I. (1976). Interpersonal relationships and personal space: Research review and theoretical model. *Human Ecology, 4,* 46–47.

Zeegers, S. K., Readdick, C. A., & Hansen-Gandy, S. (1994). Daycare children's establishment of territory to experience privacy. *Children's Environments, 11,* 265–271.

CHAPTER

6

Tactile Communication

Touch is the communicative medium of close encounters. The closest, most intimate encounters of all are sexual in nature. We are all acutely aware that we signal sexual interest in another person by touching them, we acknowledge our readiness for the sex act by specific kinds of touching, and we consummate a sexual relationship by limb-to-limb tactile contact. Encounters with other individuals that develop into close interpersonal relationships are hardly limited to intimate sexual contact. You will recognize without extended thought that touch plays a central role in your relational communication with such close contacts as your parents, your brothers and sisters, your good friends, and other acquaintances with whom you would like to develop close relationships. Therefore, Collier (1985) simply stressed what surely has already occurred to you when he wrote that "Touching is one of the most powerful means for establishing and maintaining social contact" (p. 27).

When you think about touch as a medium of communication, there are probably some things you know and some things you do not know. You probably do not know that a large part of your brain is devoted to receiving and interpreting messages communicated by the skin. Similarly you may not know that your skin accounts for 20 percent of your body weight, or that there are more than a half-million receptor sites on your skin that pick up tactile contact from others and transmit a signal to your brain as to the type of touch made.

If you are honest, you will probably admit that on more than one occasion you have encountered a person in a social context who instantly struck you as physically appealing. Stephen Thayer, professor of psychology at City College and the Graduate Center of the City University of New York, writes that "Other means of communication can take place at a distance, but touch is the language of physical intimacy. And because it is, touch is the most powerful of all communication channels—and the most carefully guarded and regulated" (1988, p. 31).

Therefore, tactile communication refers to all the ways our skin affects and reacts to other forms of bodily contact either from others or ourselves and signals a message that has at least one meaning.

Touch communicates many different meanings. Touch has substantial communicative potential, but this potential has not been fully explored. Our lack of knowledge about touch can be attributed to a number of factors. First, many individuals have accepted the misconception that touch is a primitive sense and, therefore, has limited value in the transmission and reception of meanings in interpersonal communication. Second, ironic as it may seem, ours is a society with strong inhibitions and taboos about touching others.

Touch signals this couple's great love for one another.

Finally, much less empirical research has been done on touch than on other types of nonverbal communication such as facial expressions and eye behaviors. Consequently, we lack a sufficiently precise and detailed terminology to describe the modalities used to touch others, to define the more particularized meanings communicated by touch, and to pinpoint the impact of a variety of personality and demographic variables on the quantity and quality of touching done in interpersonal contexts.

We should not underestimate the important impact of touch on successful interpersonal communication, however. Touch cannot communicate the highly specialized emotions that can be communicated by facial expressions or vocal cues, but this should not obscure the fact that touch often serves as the last medium available to the elderly and the critically ill to communicate feelings. As a means of communicating caring, comfort, affection, and reassurance, touch is the preeminent sense. As we shall see, touch can also serve important power and affiliative functions in interpersonal communication, functions that are not served at all, or frequently are not served as well, by any other nonverbal medium of communication.

The Nature of Touch

For years we have recognized the need for touch at an early age. The power of touch at an early age is critical to development (Honig, 2005). Other seminal studies have been done in touch, including the work of Field and Hertenstein. Field (2002) suggests that we are just beginning to discover how important touch is in the communication process. While there have been studies on infancy and touch, many of the studies neglect converging research operations. Several measurement issues need to be worked out in the field of tactile communication.

In addition, Hertenstein (2002) says that touch is a fundamental part of human development and has important communicative implications for the development of the infant and how she or he will communicate in the future. As we will learn later in the chapter, touch gains in importance for the adult and for the elderly as well.

The skin is such a sensitive organ because its surface area has a tremendous number of sensory receptors that receive stimuli of heat, cold, pressure, and pain (Collier, 1985). Montagu (1971) estimated that there are 50 receptors per 100 sq mm; that tactile points vary from 7 to 135 per sq cm; and that the number of sensory fibers that connect the skin with the spinal cord is well over half a million. The number and importance of sensory stimuli experienced through the skin is much greater than most people realize.

We have known for some time that baby monkeys do not develop properly without physical intimacy and that lack of caressing is positively associated with a high death rate among nursery babies (Young, 1973). Harlow (1958), in his famous experiments, exposed baby monkeys to two types of surrogate mothers. One "mother" was made of wire and provided milk and protection to the infant monkeys; the other "mother" was made of rubber and terry cloth but provided no milk or protection. The infant monkeys consistently chose the terry cloth "mother," so it seems obvious that the need to be touched was overriding. Harlow concluded that a monkey's access to physical contact is a crucial variable in the development of normal adult behavior—ensuring normal affectional responsivity and normal sexual behavior. Subsequent studies on other monkeys, rats, lambs, and other animals have supported the same central conclusion: Touching is a requirement for the healthy development of animals. The Harlow monkey study results were also supported in a puppy study with surrogate mothers (Igel & Calvin, 1960), with monkeys and pseudofamilies (Chamore, Rosenblum, & Harlow, 1973), and with mothers' influence during puberty in mice (Gubernick & Nordby, 1992). The findings in adult animal behavior are similar to findings in adult humans as well.

Adult human behavior is also markedly affected by one's tactile history. For example, Hollender (1970) found that in some women, the need to be held is so compelling that it resembles addiction. Those deprived of tactile stimulation earlier in their lives used both direct and indirect means (i.e., sexual enticement and seduction) to obtain the holding or cuddling desired. Not surprisingly, half of Hollender's sample was composed of female psychiatric patients. Their behavior supported his conclusion that the need or wish to be held is a relevant consideration in the treatment of several psychiatric disorders. Similarly, Hollender, Luborsky, and Scaramella (1969) studied the correlation between the intensity of the need to be held or cuddled and the frequency with which sexual intercourse is bartered for this satisfaction. They found that every high scorer on the body-contact scale (those with a great need to be touched) used sex in order to be held, whereas not a single low scorer did so.

The behavioral effects of quantitative and qualitative insufficiency of touch in childhood are numerous and generally accepted. The communicative potential of the skin remained a mystery until recently. Slowly, we have begun to recognize that the skin is not only our most sensitive organ, but also our first means of communication (Montagu 1971).

As a reader, you may remain skeptical. You may think that it is fine to talk of touch as a mode of communication, but can anything of importance really be communicated solely through the medium of touch? Using electrodes attached to the fingers to monitor the electrical messages that the skin transmits to the brain, Brown (1974) has demonstrated the remarkable capacity of the skin as a communication **sender.** In contrast, Geldhard (1968) has documented the skin's great value as a communication **receiver.** In so doing, he has established that the skin is capable of decoding a set of electrical impulses into specific symbols, words, and thoughts. He has developed a language of the skin.

The Skin as a Communication Sender

The mind boggles at the possibility that the skin may be capable of sending messages that convey rather specific information and meaning. Nevertheless, Barbara Brown notes:

> All that is necessary to listen to the skin's emotional talk is several small electrodes taped to the skin, and a proper recording instrument. Then you listen. The skin will tell you when there is emotion, how strong the emotion is, and even just how emotional a person you are. It also will very likely tell you when you are lying. (1974, p. 52)

Polygraphers and medical researchers have long recognized the potential of the human skin as a communication sender. The polygraph exam is based on the assumption that changes in a liar's internal states at the moment of deception will be reflected in machine-monitored changes in skin-conductance, in pulse, and in heart rate. Similarly, physicians and medical technicians monitor the condition of the heart, brain, and other bodily organs by decoding the electrical messages that are transmitted via the skin (Collier, 1985).

A series of experiments have been conducted that suggest that the skin will much more accurately than the eye signal the brain as to what events are being perceived in the environment. Because the skin operates at the subconscious level, it is not biased by group-conformity pressures and other external stimuli that might affect the accuracy with which our various senses perceive events and stimuli in our external environment.

The skin's sending capacity, when aided by machines, has perhaps best been demonstrated in the area of subliminal perception. In one experiment, "naughty" and "emotion-arousing" words were flashed on a screen so briefly that the subjects could not report what they had seen. Neutral words were mixed in with the arousing words. Although the subjects could neither see the words nor recognize them consciously, the skin reflected the difference in the emotional meanings of the words. There was an orienting response by the skin to every naughty word, but an absence of tactile response to neutral or bland words (Brown, 1974).

Such research and the results seem astounding. Nonetheless, Brown reports that simple electrodes attached to an individual's fingers will pick up the electricity of the skin and separate the slow from the fast activity. Slow activity is converted into a signal that represents the level of emotional response; fast activity reflects the type of emotional response. Obviously, this communicative capacity of the skin has many practical applications.

One seemingly trivial though not unprofitable application is a machine you will see in virtually any large food supermarket, the Stress Test. The large sign on the machine says that by simply attaching a small sensor to two of your fingertips, your current level of stress will be revealed, that is, the machine may indicate that you are calm, normal, or under stress. Psychotherapists make a far more important use of the machine-read messages of the human skin; they interpret the messages sent by the skin to pinpoint emotional difficulties. Obviously, many other applications are possible, including the determination of whether the communicator is lying. Also, the emotion of the skin indicates whether an individual is really experiencing the emotion he or she attempts to convey by some other means such as facial expressions.

In most real-world situations, we do not have the luxury of attaching machines to various parts of a person's body in order to decode the electrical messages being sent by the skin. Obviously, our potential for highly effective and efficient tactile communication would be greatly enhanced if we could accurately perceive—unaided by machine monitoring—the electrical messages sent to us by the touch of other individuals whom we encounter.

The potential of communication by electrical impulses or charges is limited at the moment for several reasons. First, the electrical charges transmitted by the skin are so weak, typically only a few millivolts, that they are far below a person's threshold or ability to perceive. Second, even if some supersensitive person could detect such weak electrical impulses, that person would most likely be confused since electrical messages are transmitted from almost every organ of the body (Collier, 1985).

The skin also communicates many unintentional messages that do not require machine reading for accurate interpretation. Most notably, the skin communicates important messages by its appearance, for example, skin color, skin temperature, and perspiration (Collier, 1985). Such "appearance" cues can be the source of much personalized information about a communicator because communicators are generally not aware of the tactile messages they communicate by the appearance of their skin; they cannot consciously control these unintentional but undeniable messages.

Think for a moment about the information communicated to you by the skin color of persons with whom you have communicated. Have you been in a situation in which you noticed that an individual suddenly became "pale as a ghost"? What was your response when you noted that your interaction partner's skin felt "cold" even as you wrapped your partner in a passionate embrace?

Collier (1985) has provided the most detailed and insightful analysis of the specific types of emotional information communicated by the appearance of the skin. Moreover, he spells out the practical value of this type of information for practitioners such as police interrogators and physicians.

Changes in skin temperature reflect the amount of blood flow to the skin. Thus, our skin is typically hot when we are emotionally aroused and cold when we are depressed. When we become angry, blood flow increases, skin temperature goes up, and we typically become red in the face. Blood flow decreases during fear and sadness with the result that skin temperature decreases. Interestingly, blood flow both alternately increases and decreases when we are embarrassed, and as a result a person may blush one moment and turn pale the next.

Muscular tension, in contrast, reveals less about the emotion a person is experiencing than about how hard a person is working to suppress or control certain emotions. Thus, Collier (1985) wrote:

> Anxious people tend to tense their muscles, rigidify their movements, and overelevate their shoulders in an attempt to block the expression, and in some cases the experience, of an unpleasant or threatening emotional state. In extreme cases, this defense may develop into an enduring pattern of muscular rigidity. (p. 36)

More specifically, such muscular tension has been found to be associated with the anxiety experienced when a person is lying.

Finally, sweat is associated with negative emotions such as fear and stress. Visible perspiration is, therefore, a particularly unwelcome sight for the communicator who wishes to be perceived as cool, calm, and confident. Sweat is also a regulatory function that can occur for other reasons as well. For example, sexual arousal may cause the body's temperature to rise, thus creating sweat. In addition, an athlete who has worked hard on the playing field may sweat because of all that physical activity. Unlike a number of other types of tactile messages, sweating is a phenomenon that cannot be consciously controlled or suppressed. The unfortunate fact for impression managers is that to sweat or not to sweat is not the question—sweating is simply not a conscious choice available to them.

The Skin as a Communication Receiver

Few people would argue that the skin has no communicative value as a receiver. Is there anyone who does not receive a message from the bite of an insect, from an angry jab in the ribs, or from a light touch on the thigh? We can and do recognize that the skin functions as a crude form of communication. Furthermore, as the examples suggest, most of us tend to think of the skin as a communication receiver. It is doubtful, however, that very many of us have thought of the skin as a sophisticated receiving instrument capable of deciphering complex ideas and emotions transmitted by an outside source.

Thanks to the research of Frank A. Geldhard, at Princeton's Cutaneous Communication Laboratory, we now know that the skin does have amazing communicative capabilities as well as potential. Geldhard (1960) emphasized that the skin is the body's only communication receiver that can handle both spatial and temporal distinctions fairly effectively; the skin

> can make both temporal and spatial discriminations, albeit not superlatively good ones in either case. It is a good "break-in" sense; cutaneous sensations, especially if aroused in unusual patterns, are highly attention-demanding. It is possible, therefore, that the simplest and most straightforward of all messages—warnings and alerts—should be delivered cutaneously. . . . If we add the clear superiority of touch (when vision and hearing are lacking or impaired) to the remaining modalities, the chemical senses, smell and taste, we have a formidable set of properties to utilize in cutaneous message processing—a list that ought to challenge us to find ways to capitalize on it. (pp. 1583–1584)

In order to make reasonably effective use of the skin's communicative potential, it soon became obvious to Geldhard and his associates that a means for sending electrical impulses to different parts of the body would be necessary. In effect, these electrical impulses would symbolize thoughts and emotions that the skin would have to decode by assigning meanings to groups of symbols. Given this means of message transmission, the central question became how many different ways could the electrical impulses be used to transmit messages? In a real sense, the problem was analogous to that faced by Morse as he contemplated telegraphic communication. Morse's deductions were simple but important. Variation in the length of time the telegraph key was held down and in the periods of time between keystrokes could be used to send messages by a code that was understandable on the other end of the line.

In one interesting study, researchers found that slow stroking touches of fabric revealed the most information when compared with moderate or fast strokes of touch (Breugnot et al., 2004). The ability of the mind and brain to process the texture or surface of objects often depends on the precise use of touch.

The variations of touch and the rapidity of touch seem quite compelling. Take the use of touch in video games. Popular video game consoles and handheld devices often involve precise and rapid touch maneuvers. The advent of the Game Boy allows users to carry the games from place to place. Oftentimes, people are found in waiting rooms at doctors' offices or other public places playing the games. Some users, notably young children, are especially adept at making many touch behaviors on the control buttons or joysticks to score points or move from room to room in the game. The Nintendo DS game unit, for example, has two screens: one for the eye and the other for a "touch-sensitive" control of the game (Taylor, 2004). Arcade rooms often contain a golf game in which players must drive the ball and make tough putts. The virtual golfer must feel the roller ball on the unit and push the ball at the proper speed to make the putt. The ability to play well is highly dependent on one's "touch" of the roller ball and how fast the player pushes the device to make the proper putt (Fery & Ponserre, 2001).

Touching Norms

Tactile and proxemic communication are similar in one important respect, and they are interrelated conceptually. Both tactile and proxemic behavior are governed by an implicit set of norms that specify what types of behavior are acceptable in our society. When we violate either touching or proxemic norms, we usually make those with whom we interact uncomfortable. The absence of touching by others may be taken as a sign that the untouched person is insignificant and unimportant. Paradoxically, one who is touched too much is apt to be labelled as a person of inferior status.

Proxemic and tactile behavior are obviously interrelated in the sense that people must be close enough to one another for touching to be possible. Obviously, two individuals must be no farther separated from each other than intimate distance (0 to $1\frac{1}{2}$ ft if touching is to occur comfortably). Touching and close proximity both signal a desire for closeness and immediacy, although the physical act of touching may require greater physical proximity than is appropriate in public. A number of professionals such as nurses, gynecologists, masseurs, and beauticians are allowed to communicate at a distance known as *intimate distance* because the kind of touch they employ is defined as nonsocial rather than personal.

Such professionals rely on touch in their jobs. A beautician, for example, has to touch the customer's hair, perhaps to move it, cut it, curl it, dry it, straighten it, etc. A nurse has to touch patients in order to take their blood pressure, take their pulse, take their temperature, or perform other hospital or clinic functions. These forms of touch are generally accepted without hesitation on the part of the customer or the patient. Doctors obviously have to touch their patients to care for them. Therapists have to touch muscles or body parts in order to get patients healthy. We all know that these touches are part of the professional's job. A line can be crossed, however. As we will see later in the chapter, some touch is unwelcome, aggressive, or outright violent. Just ask a victim of spousal abuse or an athlete who was punched in the face by an opposing player.

Ours is a noncontact society, where limited touching in public is the norm. Touching norms dictate that even friends and intimates refrain from anything beyond perfunctory touching in public; touching among strangers is deemed to be deviant. Walker (1975) demonstrated the strength of touching norms in our society by asking strangers to touch each other during encounter-group exercises. He found that strangers who were forced to touch each other perceived the tactile contact as difficult, stress producing, and psychologically disturbing.

Touching norms that have developed in our society have been most strongly influenced by two factors: the region of the body that is touched, and the demographic variables that differentiate one communicator from another (i.e., gender, race, age, status, and culture). Successful communicators will not only exhibit an awareness of what regions of the body may be touched in specific contexts but will also understand that the gender, race, age, status, and culture of the interactants dictate what type and how much touching is socially acceptable.

Jourard (1966) has divided the body into the 24 regions that may be touched. His research indicates that opposite-sex friends may touch nearly all body regions. Touching of the head, shoulders, and arms occurs most frequently, but touching in other regions of the body is also acceptable. In general, touching of same-sex friends should be confined to shoulders, arms, and hands. Touching norms for males and females differ, however, and this difference seems to be reflected in their tactile behavior. Walker (1975) found, for example, that the amount of nonreciprocal touching exhibited by female pairs in sensitivity groups increased as the groups continued to meet, but touching of male pairs decreased over time. Heterosexual males are reluctant to touch or to be touched by another male because their masculinity is threatened by the homosexual connotations of tactile contact.

Although touching norms dictate that intimates may touch "personal regions" of the body, nonintimates must confine touching to "impersonal regions" of the body. Communicators generally conform to this touching norm (Willis, Rinck, & Dean, 1978). Accordingly, touch among strangers should be confined primarily to the hand-to-hand contact associated with greetings and farewells. Touching norms that specify what regions of the body may be touched by whom seem to have remained relatively constant over time, although recent research suggests that opposite-sex friends are now engaging in an increasing amount of touching in the body areas between the chest and knees (Major, 1980).

A handshake between strangers may not always be appropriate. Some prefer hugs or having their knuckles meet, as often exhibited by friends in a celebratory mood. Howie Mandel, host of NBC's game show hit *Deal or No Deal,* tells contestants not to shake his hands. He simply extends his closed knuckles out to meet their closed knuckles. Mandel has obsessive-compulsive disorder and washes his hands 20 or more times per day ("The Real Deal with Howie," 2006). We need to recognize that some touching behaviors or lack thereof is not a sign of unfriendliness but of illness instead.

Appropriate tactile communication requires familiarity with the demographic variables that exert a major influence on touching norms. These touching norms dictate that the gender, race, age, and status of the interactants all be considered before we are in a position to exhibit socially appropriate tactile behavior

Gender is clearly an important variable. The normative expectation is that the most touching should occur among opposite-sex friends. In both intimate and professional relationships, men are expected to touch women much more frequently than they are touched by women, and this is usually the case. Two decades ago, Major and Williams (1981) found that male-to-female touch was the most frequent type of touch (females touched children of both sexes more frequently than did men). In same-sex interaction, touch among women has previously been found to be more frequent than it is among men. Whatever the sex of the interactants, however, the cultural norm dictates that the amount of touching be increased as their relationship becomes more personal (Major, 1980). An interesting study about touching norms in athletes was done by Kneidinger, Maple, and Tross (2001) in which they examined male and female differences on the sports field. In support of Major's research in the 1980s, they found that female athletes touched each other more often than male athletes did. Interestingly, females touched each other more at home games, while male athletes were more likely to touch one another in away games. Perhaps this is partly due to the stigma placed on male-male touch in our most immediate "known" environment. In general, women are far more likely to engage in same-sex touch than are men (Floyd, 2000).

Yet, in light of the research that indicates reluctance on the part of men to do same-sex touch, male athletes often touch one another more often than you might realize. Consider the following examples. Male athletes often exchange high fives with their hands extended in the air and firm slaps to indicate celebration or victory. In football and basketball, male athletes often do a body five, a maneuver where the two men jump up in the air and their chests meet.

Besides the celebratory function, there is a comfort function to touch for male athletes. If a kicker misses a field goal or a ballplayer strikes out, a teammate may pat him on the back or shake his hand. Generally, male athletes do not hug; that behavior is more likely to be seen in female sports teams than in male teams.

In a study on gender patterns in social touch, Major, Schmidlin, and Williams (1990) provided support for results from some earlier studies that had come under increasing challenge, and they greatly expanded our knowledge of the relative frequency with which men and women touch and are touched when interacting with members of their own gender and with each other. In particular, they found the following to be true:

1. Females are significantly more likely to be the recipients of touch than males.
2. Male-to-female touch is significantly more frequent than female-to-male touch.
3. Females have more positive attitudes toward same-sex touching than do males.

4. Touch between females, by far the most frequent type of touch, is more frequent than touch between males.
5. Cross-sex touch is more frequent than same-sex touch.
6. Females more frequently touch children than do males.

Clearly the attitudes of men and women toward touching and their actual tactile behavior vary substantially. Since interpersonal touch is very important in both opposite-sex and same-sex communication, gender differences deserve particular attention. We must recognize, for example, that women in the United States consistently report more positive attitudes to same-gender touch than do their male counterparts (Willis & Rawdon, 1994). In fact, men have a much more homophobic attitude toward same-gender touch than do women, which in turn seems to affect their touching behavior directly. Men touch their same-sex acquaintances less frequently than do women (Floyd, 2000; Roese, Olson, Borenstein, Martin, & Shores, 1992). The touching pattern that emerges reflects a gender asymmetry that confirms early findings that high-status individuals are more likely to touch low-status individuals than vice versa.

Henley (1977) maintained that the different touching norms for men and women perpetuate the idea that men have superior power and status. Women who touch men in professional settings must be aware that such touching is often interpreted as a sign of unseemly sexual advance. In contrast, the disproportionate amount of touching of women by men gives men the edge in asserting their dominance over women.

One study reports that sexual orientation affects perceptions of "appropriate" touching norms between same-sex and opposite-sex pairs. Indeed, heterosexual men and women were likely to condone touching between male-female and female-female pairs, but not male-male pairs. On the other hand, homosexual men and women saw no difference between male-male touching norms compared with those for other pairs of interactants. This study further confirms that much of our touching norms in society are culture-based (Derlega, Catanzaro, & Lewis, 2001).

Race is also a potentially important determinant of touching norms. There is some evidence to suggest that tactile contact is much more frequent among blacks than among whites. In one study of racial touching patterns (Smith, Willis, & Gier, 1980), blacks touched each other on average 29.03 times per hour and whites touched each other only 9.87 times per hour. Consistent with previous findings, white males touched each other less frequently than any other sex–race dyad. However, black males touched each other more frequently than any sex–race dyad. Black females touched each other almost twice as often as white females. The available evidence does seem to point to a discernible touching pattern. When interacting with each other, blacks prefer and exhibit more touching than whites. However, both blacks and whites touch members of their own race much more frequently than they touch members of the other race (Smith et al., 1980; Willis et al., 1978).

Age has also proved to be an important factor in the development of touching norms. Age-related touching norms specify that high rates of touching are most appropriate for the young and the old. As might be expected, rates of touching are high during the first five years of a child's life. Recent research suggests that infants depend on touch for important communication functions. They need to feel loved and cared for, and touch is instrumental to that end (Field, 2002; Herenstein, 2002). Furthermore, touch in the early years of life has been associated with children's developing self-confidence and self-esteem (Jones & Brown, 1996). Are you from a family of huggers? If so, chances are you feel more included and think more highly of yourself. Frequency of touching has been observed to decrease from kindergarten through junior high, however. This finding may be attributed in part to the fact that the identity crisis experienced by young people makes the initiation of tactile communication difficult. Because tactile communication is one of the most intimate forms of communication, the initiation of tactile contact may be doubly difficult. During the high school years, opposite-sex touch becomes more frequent, presumably because of the important functions of such touch in courtship and in sexual relationships. Finally, the amount of touching characteristically exhibited during the adult years seems to remain relatively constant until retirement age approaches. At that point, frequency of touching behavior increases markedly (Major, 1980). In one study, elderly patients in nursing homes were analyzed. Researchers found that elderly patients were touched much more often in nursing homes than by nurses in the community (Caris-Verhallen, Kerkstra, & Bensing, 1999). In addition, researchers have discovered that the elderly enjoy foot massages. The massaging touch helps to relieve the stress and anxiety often experienced by older patients (Jirayingmongkol, Chantein, Phengchomjan, & Bhanggananda, 2002).

Status also exerts a major influence on touching norms. High-status individuals touch low-status individuals much more frequently than they are touched by low-status individuals. Henley (1977) maintains that the "touching privilege" not only reliably identifies the high-status person but is reserved almost exclusively for their use.

The status of touchers seems to affect directly the amount of nonreciprocal touching they initiate. Watson (1975) studied the amount of touching of patients by staff members in a home for the elderly. He found that the higher the rank of the nursing staff member, the greater the amount of touching of the patients. Nurses touched patients much more frequently than aides, and aides touched patients much more frequently than orderlies. Low-status individuals seem intuitively to recognize that the touching norm specifies that the amount of touching they initiate should be limited. Thus, Watson (1975) concluded that "the frequent omissions of touching behavior by orderlies suggested a clear relation between low status in the nursing hierarchy and social constraint against touching" (p. 107).

Finally, the *culture* of communicators is an important determinant of the frequency of the various types of touching they exhibit and receive. Cultures are divided on the basis of those that are noncontact and those that are contact. Touching occurs more frequently in contact than in noncontact cultures. As one moves from north to south in Europe, for example, the amount of tactile contact increases. Whereas a young female from the United States might be shocked if she received a pinch on a buttock from a decorous British male her own age, she would probably anticipate this type of tactile contact from a same-aged Italian male. Touching is considerably more frequent in contact cultures that include Arabs, Latin Americans, and southern Europeans than in noncontact cultures such as northern Europeans and Americans (Collier, 1985).

More recent research has called into question the traditional norms of contact and noncontact cultures' impact upon tactile development and touching norms. Indeed, in their research, McDaniel and Anderson (1998) suggest that a variety of cultures (except in Asian nations) engage in a variety of touching norm ranges. In fact, the United States and northern

European nations have a significant number of touching behaviors (a statistic once reserved only for "contact" cultures). Dibiase and Gunnoe (2004) found that both Italians and Czechs touch more often than Americans, however. Their study revealed that Italian and Czech cultures use more hand touches and non-hand touches than do Americans. Indeed, the Czech culture engages twice as often in hand touches and almost three times as often in non-hand touches. Interestingly, men in the Czech culture hand-touch twice as often as do women, while women in that same culture non-hand-touch about twice as often as do men. There is almost no difference for American men and women in either category. In a similar study, Remland, Jones, and Brinkman (1995) found that touching norms are more visible in contact cultures (i.e., Arabs, Latin Americans, and southern Europeans) than in noncontact cultures (i.e., Asians—except Japanese and Singaporeans—North Americans, and northern Europeans).

Touching norms are in turn closely related to the concept of *touch avoidance.* Andersen, Andersen, and Lustig (1987) defined touch avoidance as a measure of a person's attitude toward touching, where being touched produces varying degrees of discomfort; "touch-avoidant individuals" touch when they are required to do so, but they find the touching to be an unpleasant experience. Their survey of the touch-avoidance practices of almost 4,000 subjects nationwide produced one finding of particular relevance to touching norms: Opposite-sex touch avoidance was higher for females than males. Thus, males appear to seek actively to touch females, whereas females exhibit a significantly greater tendency to avoid touch with males than vice versa.

Interestingly, the frequency with which we touch and are touched seems to affect our self-concept. Results from the touch-avoidance study just identified indicate that as people's predisposition to be touch-avoidant increases, their desire to communicate with others decreases, their communication style becomes less open, and, most importantly, they tend to have lower self-esteem. Fromme and colleagues (1989) supported and amplified those findings. Individuals who reported a high level of "touch comfort" were also found to be better socialized and less reticent and shy than their touch-avoidant counterparts. Touch comfort was found to be associated with effective interpersonal skills, assertiveness, an absence of negative affective states, and an effective style of self-presentation (Field, 2002; Fromme et al., 1989; Guerrero & Anderson, 1994; Jones & Brown, 1996; Stenzel & Rupert, 2004).

Normative touching practices and patterns within a given culture should not be equated with what is desirable. The distinction here is between what is and what ought to be. Until we expand our knowledge of tactile communication, a detailed set of guidelines that spell out desirable, culture-specific touching behaviors is probably not realistic. At the same time, a communicator who is thoroughly familiar with the touching norms in her or his society should be in a much better position to use tactile communication in a way that is both sensitive and socially appropriate.

The Semantics of Touch

The semantics of touch is not a simple matter. In a professional setting, for example, a man touching a woman can communicate a distinctively different meaning than would result from a woman touching a man. The meanings of touch are affected not only by who touches whom but by the type of touch. Nguyen, Heslin, and Nguyen (1975) identified four different types of touches: a *pat,* a *squeeze,* a *brush,* and a *stroke.* The squeeze and the brush seem to communicate meaning that varies with the context. In contrast, a pat is usually interpreted to mean that the toucher is playful and friendly, whereas the stroke signals affection and sexual desire.

Jones and Yarbrough (1985) found that touch communicates 12 distinct meanings that in turn can be classified into four major types of communicatively significant touch:

1. positive-affect touches
2. playful touches
3. control touches
4. ritualistic touches

Positive-affect touches include touches that communicate the meanings of support, appreciation, inclusion, sexual interest or attraction, and affection. **Playful touches** in turn communicate the meanings of playful affection and playful aggression. The kinds of meanings communicated by **control touches** are compliance, gaining attention, and announcing a response. Finally, **ritualistic touches** communicate the meanings associated with greeting and departure.

In addition to interactional touch, there is also self-touch. Self-touch includes those gestures that we use alone or while others are present. One of the best examples of self-touch used in front of others is the gesture to be silent or to whisper.

Some research has found that persons are amazingly accurate at perceiving and decoding self-touch behaviors, more so than with any other nonverbal behavior (Hall, Carter, & Horgan, 2001). The ability to detect frustration, excitement, confusion, and boredom, among other emotions, is oftentimes perceived in others' self-touch behaviors. Self-touch is often associated with anxiety and nervousness. For example, people who are anxious in a social setting might touch their heads, grab their arms, or conduct other forms of self-touch, thereby sending an unfavorable impression to the receiver.

One of the earliest and most profound studies of self-touch was conducted by Morris (1971) in his book *Intimate Behaviour.* Morris outlines four basic types of self-touch:

1. shielding actions
2. cleaning actions
3. specialized signals
4. self-intimacies

First, self-touch involves shielding actions. **Shielding actions** occur when the hand is brought to the head to reduce input to the senses. For example, one might put both hands over the ears at a fireworks show, or one could hold his or her nose when a foul odor is present.

Second, self-touch includes cleaning actions. **Cleaning actions** are those of the hand being brought to the head region to wipe, scratch, or pick something. For example, picking your nose (while socially taboo) is a form of cleaning action. Another example might be wiping crumbs from your face that were left from the apple pie you just finished.

Third, self-touch also produces specialized signals. **Specialized signals** occur when the hand is brought to the head region to perform a symbolic gesture. Putting your finger over your mouth to indicate to others that they need to be silent is a case in point. Another specialized signal might include cupping your hand over your ear to indicate that someone needs to speak up in order for you to hear him or her.

Finally, self-intimacies make up the fourth form of self-touch. **Self-intimacies** include bringing the hand to the head to echo or mimic interpersonal intimacy. For example, someone may embrace oneself to signal a romantic interest to someone else. Still another example is interlocking the hands together in the absence of a companion's hand. Crossing one's legs is a common form of self-touch. Clasping one's hand on the thigh is another self-intimacy, one done mostly by women.

Not only have Jones and Yarbrough (1985) greatly expanded our knowledge of the semantics of touch, but their research also identifies the frequency with which particular types of touch are used to communicate each of the 12 meanings. Also noteworthy is the fact that once we as users of touch understand the nature of the meanings that can be communicated, we can write with more precision and insight about the major communicative functions served by touch.

Observe the woman who touches her face because she is surprised by what she sees on the computer.

The Communicative Functions of Touch

Touch serves a number of communicative functions of considerable importance, such as the communication of affection, commitment, control, intimacy, and sexual interest (Guerrero & Anderson, 1994). In the broadest sense, touch functions to express interpersonal attitudes (Argyle, 1986). From the perspective of the toucher, attitudes expressed may range from a mother's tender love for her infant to the unseemly aggression of an angry person.

We know too that touch plays a role in persuasion. Studies have repeatedly shown that communicators who touch those persons they are trying to persuade are more successful than those who do not (Patterson, Powell, & Lenihan, 1986). Similarly, Willis and Hamm (1980) report that touching behavior is linked to persuasive effectiveness. Experimenters asked consumers at a shopping center in Kansas City to either complete a brief rating scale or to sign a petition; half of the shoppers were touched lightly on the upper arm and half were not touched. The shoppers who were touched complied with the requests significantly more often than those who were not touched. Touch also plays a role of compliance gaining in the persuasion process. Remland and Jones (1994) report that touch and vocal intensity were related to a requestor's success in compliance gaining. They confirmed earlier 1970s research that had found that a light touch on the arm can improve the likelihood that a person will comply. Vocal intensity does have some impact, and it was found that moderate levels of vocal intensity coupled with a light touch are the best combination of behaviors to improve compliance.

Interestingly, marketers in business are also using touch to sell products. Peck and Wiggins (2006) found that when customers lack complete information on a product, a salesperson's touch helps to motivate them to buy the product. Have you ever noticed the samples that paint stores have on their shelves? Eaves noticed when visiting a popular hardware store that the crackle- and plaster-type paints have raised edges and grooves in the sample. In this way, the customer can feel the product before it goes on the living room wall.

There are four main communicative functions of touch: support, power, affiliation, and aggression. Therefore, these functions deserve closer scrutiny.

The Support Function

Tactile communication assumes primary importance when we wish to emphasize feelings of warmth, reassurance, or comfort (Marx, Werner, & Cohen-Mansfield, 1989). Tactile messages have been found to be particularly effective in providing reassurance to those who need emotional support. Tactile messages seem to serve the therapeutic function better than any other means of communication. Jourard (1966) wrote with conviction that the therapeutic function of touch is the most important of all.

In their insightful book *Nonverbal Communication with Patients: Back to the Human Touch,* Blondis and Jackson (1977) made quite clear that in nursing, touch can serve a more important therapeutic role than any other kind of nonverbal communication. They emphasize that our "first comfort in life comes from touch—and usually our last, since touch may communicate with the comatose, dying patient when words have no way of breaking through" (p. 6). Patients who have lost all verbal capacity can ordinarily feel a gentle touch and be moved by the message of caring and reassurance that it represents. Some terminally ill patients lose the power to speak. When this is the case, a tactile code is sometimes worked out whereby the patient squeezes the nurse's hand once to mean yes and twice to mean no. In these instances, the tactile message represents the patient's sole surviving means of communicating with the outside world.

Whether working in pediatrics, geriatrics, or the emergency receiving room, the nurse and other members of the medical team recognize that touch is frequently their most effective medium of emotional communication. This is probably true because the trauma associated with birth and critical illness strongly reinforces the patient's insecurities and fears while placing a premium on the emphatic response that provides reassurance. Thus, a

> patient may reach out to grasp the nurse's hand, seeking comfort and reassurance through the sense of touch. The positive feelings of sympathy, reassurance, understanding, and compassion are transmitted through touch—just as are the negative feelings of anger, hostility, and fear. To be truly therapeutic, tactile communication must be used at the appropriate time and place. (Blondis & Jackson, 1977, p. 9)

Previous research has established that touching between individuals can play an important role in the maintenance of health. In reference to their research, Lewis and her colleagues (1995) wrote:

> One particular emphasis, however, has been on the impact of touch initiated by nurses and other health providers in influencing how well patients cope. Nurses may pat, hold, or shake a patient's hand as they seek to convey comfort, and they also touch patients as part of hospital procedures (while giving intravenous medications or monitoring a patient's blood pressures). The question then emerges about the circumstances when the use of touch by a health provider is perceived as appropriate. (p. 101)

The answer to that question is not simple. On the one hand, nurses are rated as more supportive and competent the more they exhibit touching when interacting with the patient. However, the sex of the patient clearly affects how the nurse's touching is perceived. Female patients, compared to males, perceive nurse-initiated touch more positively. This finding in turn may be linked at least in part to sex-role stereotyping. Stereotypically, females prefer supportiveness whereas males may "react less favorably to a nurse who uses touch because the touch implies vulnerability and dependency for the patient" (Lewis et al., 1995, pp. 110–111).

The role of touch in providing support and nurturance in parent–child relationships is well established. With increasing concern about child sexual abuse, more attention is being given to assessing the relative appropriateness of different kinds of intrafamily touching. Thus, Harrison-Speake and Willis (1995) discovered reasonably clear overall norms for parent–child touch. They found, for example, lower approval ratings for touching older as opposed to younger children; higher approval ratings for mothers than for fathers when applied to lap sitting, kissing, and bathing their children; and higher approval ratings for lap sitting and kissing when applied to girls as opposed to boys.

The need for touching that provides support continues to be strong for many adults. Supportive touch by other persons is important in attaining and maintaining good health both physically and psychologically.

Given the therapeutic power of touch, it is a sad fact that many individuals who most need touch are the least likely to receive it. Results from one study indicate that severely impaired patients are touched much less frequently by members of a medical team than are those with less severe impairments. Similarly, patients who have had a breast removed or who have undergone a sex-change operation are less likely to be touched than those who have received less drastic medical treatment (Watson, 1975). Indeed, there are many businesses, especially in the telemarketing area, where employees are encouraged to be supportive of or complimentary to co-workers who have just completed a successful sale with a client on the phone. Workers must be aware that their actions are perceived by all, especially any touching behavior. If touch is a necessary part of the "sales" experience, then it is better to be the receiver than the sender of a tactile form of communication. Managers and employers must also be careful about using touch.

The Power Function

Touch probably functions most effectively to delineate the relative power, dominance, and status of interacting individuals. Henley's fascinating research (1977) has established quite clearly that the frequency with which we touch and are touched by others is a reliable indicator of our perceived power. Results from her research show that

> people reported more likelihood of their touching subordinates and coworkers than bosses; of touching younger or same-age people than older ones; and of touching sales clerks than police officers. Likewise, their expectations of others' touching them also reflected their hierarchical relationship: for example, they reported more probability of boss and coworker touching them than of a subordinate doing so. (p. 104)

In short, the powerful person is apt to be the toucher and the powerless person the touched. Because of this relationship, the power of touch is a privilege reserved for the powerful. This relationship applies even to the "untouchable" castes of India. They are called untouchable because their low status dictates that they may not touch members of a higher caste.

Touch is so effective a medium for the communication of power cues that touchers are perceived to have more power and status than the touched, regardless of the gender of the toucher or the touched (Scroggs, 1980). To touch enhances one's perceived power; to be touched diminishes perceived power. Touchers have consistently been perceived as more dominant and assertive than nontouchers (Major, 1980). Finally, observers who have looked at photographs of male–female dyads, some who were touching and some who were not touching, rated the touchers as significantly more powerful, strong, superior, and dominant (Summerhayes & Suchner, 1978).

In her insightful summary of research on the meaning of touch, Major (1980) emphasized that touch strongly and reliably shapes perceptions of one's power. She wrote that empirical research strongly supports Henley's theory that

> touching implies power. Across experiments, the initiator of touch is seen as more powerful, dominant, and of higher status than the recipient. Furthermore, it appears that touch affects the balance of power in a relationship by simultaneously enhancing that of the toucher and diminishing that of the recipient. (p. 26)

Although aggression has been treated by one scholar as a separate function served by touch (Argyle, 1986), it surely represents an extreme effort by one person to dominate another person. Thus, pushing, kicking, and outright physical attack may be socially inappropriate forms of tactile communication, but they are undertaken with the objective of dominating another individual. Aggressive touch, therefore, serves the power function.

The Affiliation Function

We have already discussed the importance of human touch in forming close, interpersonal relationships with other people. In fact, the amount of reciprocal touching done by two people is usually a reliable indicator of how much they like each other (Collier, 1985).

Touch is important in the courtship behaviors that start with sexual interest and end, in some cases, with sexual intercourse (Pisano, Wall, & Foster, 1986). In our society, the courtship process consists of a sequence of touching steps, defined by the part of the body that is touched, that must be followed. Engaging in mouth-to-breast contact on a second date, for example, would probably be judged as "fast." Not advancing beyond hand-holding after a year, however, might be regarded as "slow." In an intimate relationship, the physical messages communicated by your partner's skin may be your best guide as to whether and when you should proceed with more intimate touching.

The person contemplating the use of touch for sexual purposes would be well advised to read *The Right Touch: Understanding and Using the Language of Physical Contact* (Jones, 1994). The author has identified the following types of sexual touches in the suggestively titled chapter "Touch and Sexuality: Attracting and Finding Pleasure With a Partner": *explicitly sexual touches (type #1 being the casual sexual touch and type #2 being the intense sexual touch), seduction touches, flirtation touches, and the "this one is mine" touch.* The author also has made clear that prudent individuals should exercise great care in using any type of touch that is intended to communicate sexual meanings or that may be so interpreted.

We should recognize that individuals who are romantically involved with each other may interpret their touches quite differently. Thus, females tend to associate progressively intimate touches with greater commitment, whereas males do not necessarily do so; a woman's association of touching with commitment seems to become stronger as the touching becomes highly intimate (Johnson & Edwards, 1991). Relatedly, men initiate touch significantly more often in casual romantic relationships and during courtship, whereas women initiate touch more frequently in married relationships (Guerrero & Anderson, 1994; Willis & Briggs, 1992). The authors suggest that social control may be more important for men in casual relationships, whereas intimacy may become more important than social control in a stable, long-term relationship.

The Aggression Function

The final function of touch is aggression. The aggressive touch, or what is sometimes called *abusive* or *violent* touch, is problematic and worrisome for the victims. Inappropriate touch has been significantly curbed in the corporate world. Managers and executives point to a marked improvement in both efficiency and interpersonal relations. Yet, there are still problems with multiple meanings of touch used in the business context, especially within cross-sex relationships. One study found that men were more likely than women to interpret corporate touch from the opposite gender in a sexual manner (Lee & Guerrero, 2001).

Similar trends exist in psychotherapy about the rarity of physicians touching their clients. In a recent survey of almost 500 psychologists, more than 90 percent reported that they preferred not to use touch as a therapeutic device. Other than the handshake as a way to introduce oneself or to signal that the session is over, touch was avoided and highly frowned upon in the professional community (Stenzel & Rupert, 2004). Some therapists want to use touch, especially when it is needed. However, the use of touch is the exception, not the rule. One area where touching is not often used is with victims of abuse. In fact, Glickauf-Hughes and Chance (1998) provide four recommendations for the therapist when using touch with these clients:

1. If the therapist has any reservation, she or he should avoid the use of touch.
2. Touch should be avoided at the beginning of therapy.
3. Initiation of touch should always come from the client.
4. Great discretion should be used when the touch is initiated by a sexual-abuse survivor.

We have seen that the aggressive function of touch is a concern and must be continually addressed by professionals, academics, and persons in daily interaction. This form of touch is dangerous and can be detrimental to users during interaction.

Finally, we recognize that the functional importance of touch is not confined solely to support, power, affiliation, and aggression. Argyle (1986) maintained that touch serves important functions as an interaction signal in greetings and farewells, in congratulations, and in ceremonies. Touch seems to assume a less important role here, however, because touch must interact with eye behaviors and gestures to determine the effectiveness of such specific kinds of communication as greetings.

Summary

Touch can and frequently does play a central role in our maturational development from cradle to grave. The sending and receiving capacity of the human skin, when accentuated with the use of machines, is remarkable. With the aid of electrodes attached to the skin, tactile messages reveal when a person is experiencing an emotion, how strong the emotion is, and even whether the person is lying. When aided by machines, the skin as a communication receiver is capable of decoding both ideational and emotional messages. Those messages can serve vitally important functions when other senses are impaired or inoperative.

Rather detailed touching norms have developed in our society, and those norms specify who may touch whom and in what context. Touch-avoidance data reveal how strongly predisposed members of different groups in society are to avoiding being touched by others. The nature of touching norms depends not only on the region of the body that is being touched, but also on the sex, race, age, status, and culture of the interactants.

Touching norms shaped by sex dictate that opposite-sex friends should touch the most, and males should touch each other the least. Men often use the touching privilege—which allows them to touch women more frequently than they are touched by women—to assert their dominance over women. Racial touching norms result in a higher rate of touching among blacks than whites but a lower rate of interracial touching. Touching norms based on age specify that it is appropriate for the young and old to engage in the most frequent tactile contact. Finally, status norms dictate that the high-status person is the toucher and the low-status person the touched.

Twelve different meanings can be communicated by touch: support, appreciation, inclusion, sexual interest or attraction, affection, playful affection, playful aggression, compliance, gaining attention, announcing a response, greeting, and departure. In a general sense, these tactile meanings are used to express interpersonal attitudes. More specifically, they are to be used singly or in combination to serve the four primary functions of touch: the support function, the power function, the affiliation function, and the aggression function.

REFERENCES

Andersen, J. F., Andersen, P. A., & Lustig, M. W. (1987). Opposite sex touch avoidance: A national replication and extension. *Journal of Nonverbal Behavior, 11*, 89–109.

Argyle, M. (1986). *Bodily communication* (2nd ed.). London: Methuen.

Blondis, M. N., & Jackson, B. E. (1977). *Nonverbal communication with patients: Back to the human touch.* New York: Wiley.

Breugnot, C., Bueno, M. A., Ribot-Ciscar, E., Aimonetti, J. M., Roll, J. P., & Renner, M. (2004). Fabric touch: Responses of mechanoreceptive afferent units and mechanical characterization. *Archives of Physiology & Biochemistry, Supplement, 45.*

Brown, B. (1974). Skin talk: A strange mirror of the mind. *Psychology Today, 8,* 52–74.

Caris-Verhallen, W., Kerkstra, A., & Bensing, J. M. (1999). Non-verbal behaviour in nurse-elderly patient communication. *Journal of Advanced Nursing, 29,* 808–818.

Chamore, A. S., Rosenblum, L. A., & Harlow, H. F. (1973). Monkeys raised only with peers: A pilot study. *Animal Behaviour, 21,* 316–325.

Collier, G. (1985). *Emotional experience.* Hillsdale, NJ: Erlbaum.

Derlega, V. J., Catanzaro, D., & Lewis, R. J. (2001). Perceptions about tactile intimacy in same-sex and opposite-sex pairs based on research participants' sexual orientation. *Psychology of Men & Masculinity, 2,* 124–132.

DiBiase, R., & Gunnoe, J. (2004). Gender and culture differences in touching behavior. *The Journal of Social Psychology, 144,* 49–62.

Fery, Y.-A., & Ponserre, S. (2001). Enhancing the control of force in putting by video game training. *Ergonomics, 44,* 1025–1037.

Field, T. (2002). Infants' need for touch. *Human Development, 45,* 100–103.

Floyd, K. (2000). Affectionate same-sex touch: The influence of homophobia on observers' perceptions. *Journal of Social Psychology, 140,* 774–788.

Fromme, D. K., Jaynes, W. E., Taylor, D. K., Hanold, E. G., Daniell, J., Rountree, J. R., & Fromme, M. A. (1989). Nonverbal behavior and attitudes toward touch. *Journal of Nonverbal Behavior, 13,* 3–16.

Geldhard, F. A. (1960). Some neglected possibilities of communication. *Science, 131,* 1583–1587.

Geldhard, F. A. (1968). Body English. *Psychology Today, 2,* 45.

Glickauf-Hughes, C., & Chance, S. (1998). An individualized and interactive object relations perspective on the use of touch in psychotherapy. In E. W. L. Smith, P. R. Chance, & S. Imes (Eds.), *Touch in psychotherapy.* New York: Guilford Press.

Gubernick, D., & Nordby, J. C. (1992). Parental influence on female puberty in the monogamous California mouse. *Animal Behaviour, 44,* 259–267.

Guerrero, L. K., & Anderson, P. A. (1994). Patterns of matching and initiation. Touch behavior and touch avoidance across romantic relationship stages. *Journal of Nonverbal Behavior, 18,* 137–153.

Hall, J. A., Carter, J. D., & Horgan, T. G. (2001). Status roles and recall of nonverbal cues. *Journal of Nonverbal Behavior, 25,* 79–100.

Harlow, B. F. (1958). The nature of love. *American Psychologist, 13,* 678–685.

Harrison-Speake, K., & Willis, F. N. (1995). Ratings of the appropriateness of touch among family members. *Journal of Nonverbal Behavior, 19,* 85–100.

Henley, N. M. (1977). *Body politics: Power, sex, and nonverbal communication.* Englewood Cliffs, NJ: Prentice-Hall.

Hertenstein, M. J. (2002). Touch: Its communicative functions in infancy. *Human Development, 45,* 70–94.

Hollender, M. H. (1970). The need or wish to be held. *Archives of General Psychiatry, 22,* 445–453.

Hollender, M. H., Luborsky, L., & Scaramella, T. J. (1969). Body contact and sexual enticement. *Archives of General Psychiatry, 20,* 188–191.

Honig, A. S. (2005). The power of touch. *Scholastic Early Childhood Today, 19,* 25.

Igel, G. J., & Calvin, A. D. (1960). The development of affectional responses in infant dogs. *Journal of Comparative and Physiological Psychology, 53,* 302–305.

Jirayingmongkol, P., Chantein, S., Phengchomjan, N., & Bhanggananda, N. (2002). The effect of foot massage with biofeedback: A pilot study to enhance health promotion. *Nursing and Health Sciences, 4,* A4.

Johnson, K. L., & Edwards, R. (1991). The effects of gender and type of romantic touch on perceptions of relational commitment. *Journal of Nonverbal Behavior, 15,* 43–55.

Jones, S. E. (1994). *The right touch: Understanding and using the language of physical contact.* Cress-kill, NJ: Hampton.

Jones, S. E., & Brown, B. C. (1996). Touch attitudes and behaviors, recollections of early childhood touch, and social self-confidence. *Journal of Nonverbal Behavior, 20,* 147–163.

Jones, S. E., & Yarbrough, A. E. (1985). A naturalistic study of the meanings of touch. *Communication Monographs, 52,* 19–56.

Jourard, S. M. (1966). An exploratory study of body-accessibility. *British Journal of Social and Clinical Psychology, 5,* 221–231.

Kneidinger, L. M., Maple, T. L., & Tross, S. A. (2001). Touching behavior in sport: Functional components, analysis of sex differences, and ethological considerations. *Journal of Nonverbal Behavior, 25,* 43–62.

Lee, J. W., & Guerrero, L. K. (2001). Types of touch in cross-sex relationships between coworkers: Perceptions of relational and emotional messages, inappropriateness, and sexual harassment. *Journal of Applied Communication Research, 29,* 197–220.

Lewis, R. J., Derlega, V. J., Nichols, B., Shankar, A., Drury, K. D., & Hawkins, L. (1995). Sex differences in observers' reactions to a nurse's use of touch. *Journal of Nonverbal Behavior, 19,* 101–113.

Major, B. (1980). Gender patterns in touching behavior. In C. Mayo & N. M. Henley (Eds.), *Gender and nonverbal behavior.* New York: Springer-Verlag.

Major, B., Schmidlin, A. M., & Williams, L. (1990). Gesture patterns in social touch: The impact of setting and age. *Journal of Personality and Social Psychology, 58,* 634–643.

Major, B., & Williams, L. (1981). *Frequency of touch by sex and race: A replication of touching observations.* Unpublished manuscript, State University of New York at Buffalo.

Marx, M. S., Werner, P., & Cohen-Mansfield, J. (1989). Agitation and touch in the nursing home. *Psychological Reports, 64,* 1019–1026.

McDaniel, E., & Anderson, P. A. (1998). International patterns of interpersonal tactile communication: A field study. *Journal of Nonverbal Behavior, 22,* 59–73.

Montagu, A. (1971). *Touching: The human significance of the skin.* New York: Perennial.

Morris, D. (1971). *Intimate behaviour.* New York: Random House.

Nguyen, T., Heslin, R., & Nguyen, M. L. (1975). The meanings of touch: Sex difference. *Journal of Communication, 25,* 92–103.

Patterson, M. L., Powell, J. L., & Lenihan, M. G. (1986). Touch, compliance, and interpersonal affect. *Journal of Nonverbal Behavior, 10,* 41–50.

Peck, J., & Wiggins, J. (2006). It just feels good: Customers' affective response to touch and its influence on persuasion. *Journal of Marketing, 70* (October), 56–69.

Pisano, M. D., Wall, S. M., & Foster, A. (1986). Perceptions of nonreciprocal touch in romantic relationships. *Journal of Nonverbal Behavior, 10,* 29–40.

The real deal with Howie. (2006, March 13). *People, 65*(10), 78.

Remland, M. S., & Jones, T. S. (1994). The influence of vocal intensity and touch on compliance gaining. *The Journal of Social Psychology, 134,* 89–97.

Remland, M. S., Jones, T. S., & Brinkman, H. (1995). Interpersonal distance, body orientation, and touch: Effects of culture, gender, and age. *The Journal of Social Psychology, 135,* 281–297.

Roese, N. J., Olson, J. M., Borenstein, M. N., Martin, A., & Shores, A. L. (1992). Same-sex touching behavior:

The moderating role of homophobic attitudes. *Journal of Nonverbal Behavior, 16,* 249–259.

Scroggs, G. F. (1980, April). *Sex, status, and solidarity: Attributions for nonmutual touch.* Paper presented at the meeting of the Eastern Psychological Association, Hartford, CT.

Smith, D. E., Willis, F. N., & Gier, J. A. (1980). Success and interpersonal touch in a competitive setting. *Journal of Nonverbal Behavior, 5,* 26–34.

Stenzel, C. L., & Rupert, P. A. (2004). Psychologists' use of touch in individual psychotherapy. *Psychotherapy: Theory, Research, Practice, Training, 41,* 332–345.

Summerhayes, D. L., & Suchner, R. W. (1978). Power implications of touch in male-female relationships. *Sex Roles, 4,* 103–110.

Taylor, C. (2004, May 24). Battle of the handhelds. *Science Now,* 78–79.

Thayer, S. (1988). Close encounters. *Psychology Today, 22,* 31–36.

Walker, D. N. (1975). A dyadic interaction model for nonverbal touching behavior in encounter groups. *Small Group Behavior, 6,* 308–324.

Watson, W. H. (1975). The meanings of touch: Geriatric nursing. *Journal of Communication, 25,* 104–112.

Willis, F. N., & Briggs, L. F. (1992). Relationship and touch in public settings. *Journal of Nonverbal Behavior, 16,* 55–63.

Willis, F. N., & Rawdon, V. A. (1994). Gender and national differences in attitudes toward same-gender touch. *Perceptual & Motor Skills, 78,* 1027–1034.

Willis, F. N., Rinck, C. M., & Dean, L. M. (1978). Interpersonal touch among adults in cafeteria lines. *Perceptual and Motor Skills, 47,* 1147–1152.

Willis, F. N., Jr., & Hamm, H. K. (1980). The use of interpersonal touch in securing compliance. *Journal of Nonverbal Behavior, 1,* 49–55.

Young, M. G. (1973). The human touch: Who needs it? *Bridges not walls.* Reading, MA: Addison-Wesley.

CHAPTER

7

Personal Appearance

Appearance communicates meaning. In an age when our society gives lip service to the cliché that beauty is only skin deep, one might surmise that personal appearance represents a secondary and superficial value, one to which few people devote attention or time. Exactly the reverse is true. Our personal appearance has a pervasive impact on our self-image and on the image we communicate to others. As such, it is a major factor in shaping our behavior and the behavior of those with whom we interact. Indeed, we seem not only to place a significant value upon personal appearance but also to do so with amazing consistency and across cultural perspectives (Langlois et al., 2000).

Bloch and Richins (1993) recognize that many advantages accrue to physically attractive individuals in our society. They write that "attractive individuals are better liked, get better jobs, have increased self-esteem, and have more social power as compared with unattractive persons" (p. 467). There are still modern studies that confirm the prevailing physical-attractiveness stereotype. Indeed, the stereotype extends to include professionals, college students, both genders equally, and various job contexts (Hosoda, Stone-Romero, & Coats, 2003). Physically attractive persons are more likely to do well in the interview process (Watkins & Johnston, 2000). Even attractive males and females in film are portrayed more favorably than their unattractive counterparts (Smith, McIntosh, & Bazzini, 1999).

Television shows have capitalized on the physical-attractiveness stereotype. Game show hosts, while often well spoken, do not have the physical appeal to viewers. Barker's beauties were a staple on *The Price Is Right* and Vanna White has always carried Pat Sajak on *Wheel of Fortune.* More recently, Howie Mandel's appeal is enhanced by his models holding cases of money on *Deal or No Deal.* These shows have high ratings, to a large degree, because each employs attractive models to make the show more appealing.

In *Orpheus Descending,* Tennessee Williams wrote that "we're all of us sentenced to solitary confinement inside our own skins for life." For many Americans, that can be a severe sentence. Our "skin," or overall appearance, does, in many cases, dictate that we cannot date or marry a person more attractive than we are. If our personal appearance is subnormal, our childhood peers ridicule and ostracize us. Our social and sexual successes are heavily dependent on our physical attractiveness. Moreover, personal appearance can be used to predict vocational success.

There is a well-developed physical-attractiveness stereotype in our society that is based on the assumption that beauty is good (Dion, Berscheid, & Walster, 1972; Patzer,

1985). Adams and Crossman (1978) captured the essence of the physical-attractiveness stereotype when they wrote that

> Enough information is available to support the existence of a wide ranging physical attractiveness stereotype. . . . The message is that beauty implies goodness, talent, and success. Therefore, attractive people should be able to walk with their heads held high since everyone sees them in a socially desirable way. Also, when they are perceived as failing, this is construed merely as a case of stumbling but not falling. (p. 17)

This stereotype is even stronger today, and the bias is not reserved for just adults. In a recent study, Griffin and Langlois (2006) found that both attractive adults and children are more likely to be viewed favorably than unattractive persons. Their study suggests that "beauty as bad" hurts people more than "beauty as good" helps people.

Certainly many members of the general public, and some academicians, are resistant to the idea that physical attractiveness is a major component of successful communication. This resistance in turn may be attributable to several factors. In the first place, beauty may be defined in many ways in addition to physical attractiveness, such as beauty as an aspect of nature or beauty as intuition. What is moral might also be considered beautiful, as well as what is useful (as in the design of a product). Secondly, Vacker & Key (1993) argued that conceptualizing beauty strictly in terms of physical attractiveness tends to decontextualize beauty:

> Because a younger or more youthful individual, all other things being equal, likely possesses more elements of purely physical beauty or health, an individual adhering to the purely physical attraction standard of beauty will then evaluate the younger or youthful individual as embodying the (physical) beauty ideal. . . . In other words, individuals older than those considered youthful are evaluated in beauty terms that are out of context with the span of their lives. One example of this is female fashion models at age 24 being considered, by some experts, too old for their profession. (p. 489)

Understandably, a voluminous body of research that strongly affirms the importance of personal appearance in our daily lives makes people uncomfortable. Patzer (1985) wrote insightfully that people who become defensive about physical-attractiveness research and claim that such research is unethical or improper, or ignore the strong and widespread effects of personal appearance, might be well advised to expose themselves to reality therapy. Patzer noted pointedly that the "problem with such reactions is that ignorance of the person's environment is promoted. Such ignorance does not make the physical attractiveness phenomena disappear, nor does such action minimize the impact of physical attractiveness on our lives and within our interpersonal relations. In fact it maximizes the impact" (p. 13).

A multibillion-dollar cosmetics industry demonstrates that millions of Americans recognize the importance of accentuating the attractive features of their personal appearance. In fact, the increasing prominence of plastic surgeons in our society highlights the importance of personal appearance. Kurt Wagner, a plastic surgeon, and Gould (1972) wrote that "it used to be the great truism that it was the inner qualities that counted and the outer ones were superficial—as in the old saying that beauty is only skin deep. But we know now that there is no such thing as separating the mind from the body" (p. 22). For example, TV shows such as *Extreme Makeover, The Swan*, and *What Not to Wear* have had great success in transforming the "ugly duckling" into the "beautiful swan." These reality shows have enjoyed high ratings because society places so much value on "how you look" versus "who you are."

Our visible self functions to communicate, in the eyes of others, a constellation of meanings that define who we are and what we are apt to become. In interpersonal communication, the appearance of the participants establishes their social identity. By our appearance cues, we often send messages designed to construct a social reality or social identity for ourselves that we could not and would not want to construct by verbal means (Kaiser, 1990). Thus, the judicious person will not say to another person, "I am trying to impress you" or "I am trying to dominate you," but the same person will routinely and repeatedly communicate such messages visually by the kinds of clothing he or she chooses to wear.

Our visible self plays a major role in shaping our social identity. Once established, our social identity—as perceived by others and by us—places identifiable limits on how, when, and where we are expected to engage in interpersonal communication. Our social identity carries with it the implicit responsibility to communicate in such a way as to meet the expectations of those for whom that identity has meaning. When we violate those expectations, our communication with others is apt to become ineffective and unsatisfying.

This chapter begins by identifying facial and bodily features that are almost universally recognized by our society as physically attractive. The perceptual and behavioral effects of personal appearance are then examined. These effects in turn are used to highlight the major communicative functions served by personal appearance. Finally, the study of personal appearance begins and ends, as does this chapter, with a recognition that body concept is a central determinant of self-concept.

Our society has a commonly accepted perspective that suggests that what is beautiful is talented, good, and socially desirable. We have little difficulty in judging objectively the level of physical attractiveness of those with whom we interact. Accurately assessing our own level of physical attractiveness is another matter, however. Why are our self-descriptions of our own bodies and the appearance of the physical features of our own bodies so frequently distorted?

We should probably begin with the fact that body concept strongly affects self-concept. Because we recognize that we are apt to suffer severe perceptual and behavioral penalties if our personal appearance is far from normal, we often distort our own image (our physical features) so that, in our mind, they approximate the cultural ideal.

Features of Physical Attractiveness

As we consider the defining features of physical attractiveness, three facts should be kept in mind. First, Americans have a much more detailed stereotype, or mental picture, of the physical features that define beauty for women than for men. Second, cross-cultural ratings as to what features constitute a beautiful female face are highly consistent (Cunningham, Roberts, Barbee, & Druen, 1995). Third, Americans are much more precise in identifying physical features associated with facial beauty than in identifying physical features associated with bodily attractiveness.

Facial Attractiveness

From an early age, infants learn to appreciate and prefer attractive faces over unattractive ones. In their four-part study, Rubenstein, Kalakanis, and Langlois (1999) found that 6-month-old infants consistently preferred attractive faces. The reliabilities, ranging from 0.91 to 0.95, suggest strong agreement for the hypothesis. The trend seems to exist throughout childhood and into the adult years as well. So, what is the ideal face?

Symmetry and Proportionality.   One of the key defining features in physical attractiveness is facial and body symmetry and proportionality. **Symmetry** refers to how much the left side of the face/body looks like the right side. **Proportionality** refers to parts of the body or face being in proportion to one another in a desirable way.

Much of the research points to symmetry and proportionality as defining features of the face. Research conducted by Grammer and Thornhill (1994) was the first study that confirmed the hypothesis that facial symmetry is positively correlated with facial attractiveness. While some studies point to attractive faces as "average," most of the research says that very attractive faces are "far from average." A long-term study of Jamaican children found greater body and facial asymmetries in females than in males, especially regarding elbows (Trivers, Manning, Thornhill, Singh, & McGuire, 1999).

Further research has also supported the Grammer and Thornhill findings about facial symmetry and physical attractiveness (Mealey, Bridgstock, & Townsend, 1999). In one finding, males were seen as more attractive when they had facial symmetry (Scheib, Gangestad, & Thornhill, 1999).

In addition, updated research has indicated that symmetry affects reproduction. In one study, sexual selection was affected by body symmetry, and the partnering process was a direct result of symmetrical matchups (Thornhill & Gangestad, 1994). Facial and body asymmetry has also been associated with mating failures (Moller & Thornhill, 1998). One recent finding suggests that disappointments with body image, especially in the middle-life years, leads to sexual functioning and interpersonal problems.

Additionally, maxillofacial surgeon Stephen Marquardt has recently developed a reconstructive surgery "beauty mask" for the ideal face. His contemporary research uses the phi ratio method. In essence, the ideal face is measured in terms of proportionality and symmetry. Marquardt's methods have been verified in follow-up studies. For example, Bashour (2006) comments about the success of the Marquardt method. In a sample of 37 male and 35 female faces, judges rated the physical attractiveness of the faces. The faces were measured against the phi mask model and results indicated that deviation from the phi mask indicated strong correlations with the variance in facial-attractiveness levels. This is one of the first methods to objectively measure facial attractiveness.

Proportionality is also important in determining facial attractiveness. The relative size of your facial features will in large part determine your perceived physical attractiveness. Larger features in the face relative to other parts of the body are typically unattractive. A fascinating study by Cunningham (1986) on the sociobiology of female facial beauty suggests that for facial features, the small-is-good-and-big-is-bad distinction may need qualification or at least amplification. For male subjects in this study, female facial beauty was defined by the "neonate" features of large eyes, small nose area, small chin, and widely spaced eyes. Female beauty was also defined by the "mature" facial features of wide cheek-bones and narrow cheeks and the "expressive" features of highly set eyebrows, wide pupils, and a large smile. This profile for female facial beauty is augmented by a more recent study that identifies three facial features as most central to facial attractiveness: widely separated eyes, a short nose, and high placement of features. When considered together, these features on a female's face were judged attractive even with low placement. With low placement, however, a narrow mouth is particularly undesirable (Mckelvie, 1993).

Interestingly, females whose faces met the definition of beautiful were consistently perceived by male subjects to have more desirable personal qualities than females whose faces were not beautiful. Thus, females with greater eye height, small nose area, greater cheekbone width, and a wider smile were seen as brighter, more sociable, and more assertive than females with less attractive faces (Cunningham, 1986). In short, in American society, females with attractive faces start with a definite advantage in terms of the impressions they might want to make and are capable of making on individuals with whom they interact.

Bodily Attractiveness

People have known for centuries that human bodies differ in appearance, but they made few systematic efforts to measure the differences.

Sheldon's research established the empirical practice of *somatyping*—classifying people as to body type. Sheldon's classification is now widely used. According to Sheldon (1954), there are three body types: (a) *endomorphic* (soft, fat, and so on), (b) *mesomorphic* (bony, athletic, and so on), and (c) *ectomorphic* (thin, fragile, and so on).

When we classify individuals by body type, it is easiest to conjure up simplistic images of someone such as football star Reggie Bush, who is clearly mesomorphic, or a *Vogue* fashion model, who is clearly ectomorphic. To accurately describe a person's body type, however, you need to assign them three numbers on a seven-point scale. The numbers refer to the degree of endomorphy, mesomorphy, or ectomorphy. Reggie Bush would probably get a rating of 1/7/1, and the skinny fashion model would be rated 1/1/7.

Sheldon theorized that there is a relationship between body type and temperament, or personality characteristics. In Sheldon's view, the person with the endomorphic body type will probably exhibit a *viscerotonic* temperament—a laid-back, relaxed, and even indolent personality. Mesomorphic body types are associated with a *somatotonic* temperament—a highly confident, task-oriented, aggressive person. Finally, the ectomorphic body type is associated with the *cerebrotonic* temperament—individuals who are tense, fussy, and critical of others (1954).

Although Sheldon's theory and his system for body typing have both been criticized, body typing (or somatyping) represents an undeniably useful way of describing a dominant set of physical features that differentiate one body from another. As we shall see, the impact of a person's body type on his or her self-perceptions and behaviors, as well as on the perceptions of those with whom he or she interacts, is substantial.

In our society, it is more important for a woman than for a man to have bodily features that are physically attractive (Patzer, 1985). Relatedly, Americans seem to have a more detailed notion of what constitutes bodily beauty for women than they do for men. For females, slenderness is a particularly important feature of bodily attractiveness, and waist width and hip width correlate negatively with perceptions of physical attractiveness (Horvath, 1979). The bigger a woman's waist and the wider her hips, the less attractive she is perceived to be. When considered either from the perspective of male or female perceivers, female physiques that emphasize great curvature (e.g., very large breasts and a very small or a very large waist) are seen as less physically attractive than breasts and waists of moderate size.

For women, waist-to-hip ratio (WHR) is critically important. In fact, Singh (1994) identifies body fat distribution as reflected in WHR as being the most important determinant of female bodily attractiveness. Normal-weight females with low WHR are judged most attractive. Significantly, females with low WHR have many desirable image qualities attributed to them. More recently, Singh (2004) found that those women with low WHR are more likely to flirt and engage in mating strategies to make others jealous than are those women with high WHR. These findings confirm earlier research that a prevailing physical-attractiveness stereotype exists. Not surprisingly, depressed women with high WHR report higher levels of dissatisfaction with their own bodies than depressed women with low WHR (Joiner, Schmidt, & Singh, 1994). This is especially true of women who are in diet programs (Hefferman, Harper, & McWilliam, 2002).

The ideal body type for men features reasonably broad shoulders and a muscular chest (Horvath, 1981). Ideally, men should be tall with an average body mass (Melamed, 1994). The feminine female places a high priority on such stereotypically masculine features as well-muscled upper arms and a tapering upper trunk. Androgynous females attach much less importance to muscle development. Both feminine and androgynous women agree, however, that males who have small chests and arms, an "unmasculine physique," are physically unattractive (Lavrakas, 1975).

In short, there is nothing ambiguous about the proportions of the face and body that distinguish the physically attractive from the unattractive person. The profile for physically attractive women is more complete than the profile for physically attractive men, and, partially as a result of this fact, women attach a higher priority to physical attractiveness than do men.

Body Image

Body image, or body concept, is the mental picture we have of our own body. This mental picture consists of our estimate of the size, shape, and appearance of each of the parts of our body as well as our body as a whole. Our body image is vitally important because it is a central component of self-concept and ultimately of the communicative behaviors that we exhibit.

As we shall see, the behaviors exhibited by individuals who have a positive body image are strikingly different from the behaviors of individuals with a negative body concept (Domzal & Kernan, 1993; Zahr, 1985). In his insightful book *Development and Structure of the Body Image* (1986), Fisher stresses that body image has been linked with a wide array of behaviors that include achievement, sexual arousal patterns, clothing choice, authoritarianism, tolerance for stress, sociability, hostility, delinquent behavior, drug usage, and drug addiction. As you might expect, it is a negative body image rather than a positive body image that is linked to such socially unacceptable behaviors as delinquency and drug usage.

Although our own body concept is often quite distorted, our body image is strongly affected by how physically attractive others judge us to be. Not surprisingly, the impact of body image on self-concept is most pronounced for individuals who are either extremely attractive or extremely unattractive and for individuals who have a high public self-consciousness. Adolescents, for example, have a high public self-consciousness about their personal appearance. They are, therefore, particularly susceptible to the striking deterioration in self-concept that often results as their body image becomes more negative (Patzer, 1985).

We do not all use the same *body image dimensions* to form a mental picture of our own body. However, the following body image dimensions are widely used by individuals to describe and evaluate their own body:

1. degree of overall awareness of one's body
2. body boundary articulation
3. distribution of attention to the major parts of the body
4. evaluation of the attractiveness of one's body and its parts
5. perception of the size of the overall body and its parts
6. perceived degree of masculinity/femininity of one's body
7. amount of anxiety experienced about one's overall body and its subdivisions. (Fisher, 1986)

The image dimensions that we use to form our body image are both descriptive and evaluative in nature. The evaluative judgments we make about our body tend to be disproportionately important because they reflect how satisfied or dissatisfied we are with our own body. *Body-cathexis* is the degree of feeling of satisfaction or dissatisfaction with the various parts or processes of our body (Secord & Jourard, 1953). Empirical research has confirmed the hypothesis that body-cathexis or image is integrally related to the self-concept.

Empirical researchers have repeatedly confirmed the existence of a strong positive relationship between a high level of body satisfaction and a high level of social self-esteem (McCaulay & Glenn, 1988). People with a negative body image are predisposed to be anxious; concerned with pain, disease, and bodily injury; and insecure (Secord & Jourard, 1953). By contrast, individuals with a positive body concept (based in part on their self-perceptions as mesomorphs) have a much more sophisticated conception of their own body (Sugerman & Haronian, 1964). From such findings, we might infer that individuals with a negative body image attempt to avoid the negative connotations of such an image by deliberately maintaining a fuzzy or incomplete image of their own body.

The image we have of our own body is often quite inaccurate. Our distorted body image might be attributed in part to the fact that we rarely carefully observe our own body and its features. People have had great difficulty when exposed to a distorted mirror image of themselves in adjusting the image to its true proportions. Finally, we know that individuals estimate their own heart rate highly inaccurately (Fisher, 1986).

We cannot be sure how often we intentionally distort our conception of our body. Authorities such as Fisher suggest that much of the distortion is intentional, however. He writes that "people are endlessly engaged in defensive strategies to cope with body experiences that are complex, threatening, confusing, and even alien. . . . When asked publicly to rate their body, people are more positive than negative—but numerous sources tell a different story" (1986, p. 626).

Persons with negative body images have understandable reasons for developing an inaccurate image of their own body. The practice of distorting one's physical features in one's own mind is known as *body distortion* (Malandro, Barker, & Barker, 1989). People with negative body concepts experience unusual difficulty in visualizing accurately the physical features of their personal appearance and often have unrealistic notions about their personal appearance.

Gender seems to play an important role in body distorting. To begin, we know that women are more likely to express dissatisfaction with their bodies than men (McCaulay & Glenn, 1988). We are not surprised by such a finding in view of the physical-attractiveness stereotype in our culture that stipulates that physical attractiveness is more important for women than for men.

Women are also more likely than men to engage in body distortion. Race does not seem to be an important variable here, however, since the body image concerns of black and white women seem to be quite similar (Thomas & James, 1988). When women do distort their descriptions of their own bodies, their distortions might not operate at the conscious level, because they are hardly self-promotional in nature. Past research has indicated that women were much more likely than men to experience eating disorders and to view their body image in a negative manner, especially among adolescents (McCaulay & Glenn, 1988). More recent studies seem to indicate that the gender gap is narrowing in this regard. For example, while boys still suffer from the problem less than girls do, a number of recent findings indicate that adolescent boys are increasingly struggling with negative body images (Baranowski et al., 2003). One study conducted by Furnham and Calnan (1998) found that many boys want the ideal body shape. Teenagers want to send a favorable impression, oftentimes to the opposite sex. In this way, adolescent boys have become increasingly interested in losing weight and having a trim waistline and "six-pack" abs. Furnham and Calnan studied 143 male students who were from secondary school (about the ages of 16–18). The researchers measured the students' eating disorders, reasons for exercise, and self-esteem. Significant correlations were found among the adolescent boys in the following areas: drive for thinness (0.46), bulimia (0.32), body dissatisfaction (0.49), and maturity fears (0.53).

A newer study has replicated these findings. Toro, Castro, Gila, and Pombo (2005) looked at possible anorexia nervosa in 240 adolescent boys. The findings revealed a strong correlation between the ideal body shape and eating disorders. Some of the most revealing questions and their results include (the first number is the nonanorexic group, the second number is the anorexic group):

When you're watching a film, do you pay special attention to whether the actors are thin or fat?	0.45 vs. 0.79
When you eat with other people, do you notice how much they eat?	0.48 vs. 0.97
Have you ever used exercise to slim down?	0.31 vs. 0.85

These results are startling and support the trend of young boys suffering from eating disorders once experienced primarily by young girls.

Interestingly, both women and men distorted their descriptions of their own body away from the ideal body concept. Thus, the women who were sampled wanted to weigh about 8.5 lbs less, whereas the men wanted to weigh about 3 lbs more. These findings once again are consistent with the physical-attractiveness stereotype, which suggests that physically attractive women should be slender and their male counterparts should be muscular. Then too, narcissistic males, but not narcissistic females, are more likely to overestimate their own physical attractiveness (Gabriel, Critelli, & Ee, 1994). Indeed, Stonebraker (1989) found that both women and men may become compulsive in their efforts to achieve an idealized body image but that they use different means to achieve their goals. Women diet to become slim, whereas men exercise to become muscular.

The impact of gender on body-cathexis and body distortion is reflected in two other findings of note. First, feminine females evaluate their physical appearance less favorably than androgynous females (Jackson, Sullivan, & Rostker, 1988). Second, body image dissatisfaction is more pronounced among single women than among married women (Thomas & James, 1988). In our society it would seem that both feminine females and single females would be inclined to attach a high priority to being perceived as physically attractive. Both groups might, therefore, be inclined to make harsh judgments about their self-perceived levels of physical attractiveness.

Obese individuals represent another group who do not have to search for reasons for engaging in body distortion. The obese person probably recognizes that "once the endomorphic phenotype is firmly established, stigmatization sets in and blocks the exit to normal acceptance in interpersonal relationships" (Cahnman, 1968, p. 297). If you realize that overweight persons are frequently characterized as uninteresting, lazy, and unsocial (Worsley, 1981), you might subconsciously engage in some body distortion in order to slim down your bodily proportions—at least in your own mind.

There is little disagreement as to what physically attractive females and males *should* look like; this is *ideal body image.* There is also a good deal of evidence to suggest that most persons can make accurate judgments about how physically attractive *other* individuals are. People seem to encounter the most difficulty in describing accurately how they appear in the eyes of others.

Body Image: Self, Other, and Reflective

The communicator must be prepared to deal with at least three types of body image. Each of us has an image of our own body that varies both with respect to our feelings about our personal appearance and with respect to how detailed that image is. As indicated, the more positive our feelings about our body image, the more detailed that image is apt to be. Moreover, our friends, associates, and others with whom we interact also have an image of our bodies. Finally, there is the *reflective* image. The reflective image represents a completely objective and accurate description of our facial and bodily features, as measured by instruments such as the profilometer and the X-ray.

Mike and Marvin Westmore recognize the importance of making individuals completely aware of the features of their reflective image. (The Westmore brothers are sought-after consultants to the Hollywood movie industry; they own and operate their own cosmetic studio.) In an interview with the Westmore brothers in their office, they emphasized that they begin a series of consultations with a client by describing in detail a client's reflective image. They do so because the reflective image reveals, in an objective and precise manner, the undistorted features of the individual's personal appearance. Mike Westmore said they "are interested in the impact of the reflective image on the self-image. And we are dealing with, we are working on a reflective image but the impact is on the self-image. And the self-image determines our place in society" (D. G. Leathers, personal interview, May 29, 1973).

Effective communication based on fact rather than fantasy puts a premium on our ability to perceive accurately the defining features of our personal appearance. We must recognize that our actual (or reflective) body image may be different in important respects from our own image of our body or the image our friends and associates have of our body. We must have an objective basis for comparing and contrasting those three images of our body before we decide whether to modify our appearance. Procedures for measuring these images already exist (Leathers, 1976).

More recent findings seem to suggest that view of self has a direct and profound effect upon evaluation of attractive persons. Horton (2003) found that those who rated self as attractive were more likely to find positive values in attractive targets. Moreover, those who rated themselves as unattractive were more likely to find positive values in unattractive targets. This study gives additional clarity to earlier attraction studies that failed to take into account the "view of self" when evaluating attractive targets.

The Matching Hypothesis

Success in the development of intimate relationships seems to be based, at least in part, on the ability to seek out individuals who match your own level of physical attractiveness. In fact, individuals who have a realistic image of their own body frequently seek to associate with others with similar levels of physical attractiveness. This is particularly true for dating relationships.

The *matching hypothesis* has been developed to explain the role of physical attractiveness in the selection of dating partners. This hypothesis is based on the assumption that individuals of similar levels of physical desirability seek each other out as dating partners and, eventually, as marriage partners (Adams & Crossman, 1978; Patzer, 1985). There is considerable empirical evidence to support the validity of the matching hypothesis. In fact, we can safely conclude that individuals are likely to be attracted to other individuals who are similar to them in body build or type, dress, facial and bodily features, and overall physical attractiveness (Archer, 1980).

Patzer (1985) concluded, after a detailed review of studies examining the physical attractiveness of long-term dating couples and marriage partners, that evidence supporting the matching hypothesis is conclusive. The matching hypothesis might seem counterintuitive in view of a physical-attractiveness stereotype that suggests that males should seek out females of maximum attractiveness. At the same time, males expect a much greater probability of rejection when they approach the most attractive females. In the real world, then, the dominant tendency is for the level of physical attractiveness of married couples to be similar. Kalick and Hamilton (1986) raised questions about the methods used in studies designed to test the matching hypothesis, but their own methods were, in turn, indicted as flawed (Aron, 1988).

The matching hypothesis may not apply when other factors prove to be more important than physical attractiveness. The physically attractive person may be drawn to the physically unattractive person who is wealthy, or who has a compensating virtue. There is evidence to suggest, however, that even among friends of the same sex, similarity in degree of physical

CHAPTER SEVEN / Personal Appearance

attractiveness exceeds chance expectations (Cash & Derlega, 1978). Furthermore, the matching hypothesis for same-sex friends seems stronger for men than for women (Feingold, 1990).

Do you have the ability to match up dating couples by assessing their level of physical attractiveness? Will the matching hypothesis be supported if we consider the physical attractiveness of dating couples at a major university? The Matching Test that follows is not intended to be a comprehensive and valid test of the matching hypothesis. It is intended, however, to increase your awareness of the matching hypothesis and its implications for the development of intimate relationships.

Your task is to determine which of the individuals in the photographs of Figure 7.1 on pages 150 and 151 are dating couples. Study the physical features of Female A and decide which of the males is her partner. In Table 7.1, put the appropriate number for the male you chose in the blank across from "Female A." Follow the same procedure as you consider Females B, C, and so on. Photographs of the couples are shown in the Appendix.

Do not look at the Appendix at this time. You may wish to provide yourself with a further test of your ability to classify individuals by level of physical attractiveness. Look at the males in Figure 7.1. Write down the numbers for the three males whom you consider to be most attractive, the three males you would classify at a lower level of physical attractiveness, and the three you would classify at the lowest level of physical attractiveness. Go through the same procedures for the females in Figure 7.1, but use letters rather than numbers. See how your classification matches up with others in the class.

Effects of Personal Appearance

When we consider the effects of personal appearance, we should recognize that a number of the studies done on physical attractiveness exhibit both conceptual and methodological problems. Although Morrow (1990) focused on research designed to examine the impact of physical attractiveness in employment selection, his critique included many of the common criticisms of physical-attractiveness research: Many studies of physical attractiveness have compared only extremely attractive and unattractive subjects; laboratory rather than field studies are the norm; the ratings of judges who assess levels of physical attractiveness

TABLE 7.1   The Matching Test

Female A	COUPLE #1	Male_____
Female B	COUPLE #2	Male_____
Female C	COUPLE #3	Male_____
Female D	COUPLE #4	Male_____
Female E	COUPLE #5	Male_____
Female F	COUPLE #6	Male_____
Female G	COUPLE #7	Male_____
Female H	COUPLE #8	Male_____
Female I	COUPLE # 9	Male_____

FIGURE 7.1

may be biased if they are aware of what is being studied; and physical attractiveness is often operationalized in a limited and unrealistic way (for example, facial photographs are used). The fact that studies of physical attractiveness can and should be improved does not negate the powerful and pervasive effects of physical attractiveness, however.

Personal appearance has repeatedly been found to exert a major influence on impression formation in a wide variety of social contexts (Patzer, 1985). Our personal appearance strongly affects the personality traits and personal qualities that are attributed to us. As a

A

B

C

D

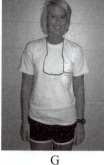

E

F

G

H

I

FIGURE 7.1 (Continued)

result, personal appearance is an influential determinant not only of the first impressions we make on others but also of more enduring impressions. Recent research reveals that appearance still biases how women are portrayed in print advertisements among three racial types: Caucasian, African-American, and East Asian. Sengupta (2006) found that East Asian women were more likely than Caucasian or African-American women to be portrayed in ads featuring technology products. This reinforces the belief that Asians are hard working and diligent. African-American women were found in most clothing ads of the three racial groups.

We know that personal appearance exerts a significant impact on perception and behavior in almost every setting in which its effects have been studied; physically attractive persons consistently receive preferential treatment. As we shall see, physically attractive persons seem to be discriminated against only when they take obvious advantage of their personal appearance.

Physical attractiveness clearly affects the expectations and perceptions of teachers and parents. In school settings, teachers seem to expect physically attractive children to be more successful, academically and socially. As a result of this expectation, a physically attractive child often becomes the "teacher's pet." In the family setting, too, parents' perceptions are often affected by their child's level of physical attractiveness. Thus, parents are inclined to attribute the misbehavior of unattractive children to personality flaws but dismiss the misbehavior of physically attractive children as a temporary aberration. Such parental behavior may reflect a general expectation: that physically attractive children will have better attitudes toward school and life in general and will be more popular (Adams & Crossman, 1978; Ritts, Patterson, & Tubbs, 1992).

In dating situations as well, physically attractive persons clearly have the advantage. They are usually better liked, seen as more desirable, and approached more often. In fact, Patzer (1985) emphasized the counterintuitive research finding that the impact of physical attractiveness on interpersonal attraction does not decline as time passes. In contrast to popular opinion, "physical attractiveness remains a major determinant of mutual romantic attraction regardless of the elapse of time, the number of meetings, and even competing negative information" (p. 82).

Even in the clinical setting, the physically attractive person is apt to receive preferential treatment. Thus, physically unattractive individuals are more likely than their physically attractive peers to be referred to a psychiatrist and are more likely to be diagnosed as extremely maladjusted.

Perceptual Effects

The perceptual impact of our level of physical attractiveness begins with our self-concept. As we have already stressed, there is a strong positive relationship between physical attractiveness and self-concept. In simple terms, the more physically attractive we are perceived to be, the more positive our self-concept is apt to be. The impact of physical attractiveness on self-concept is particularly pronounced for adolescents. In view of the rapid growth spurts and skin disturbances that are characteristic of the teenage years, it is not surprising that many teenagers become preoccupied with their personal appearance. However, mature college students and adults also find that self-concept is strongly affected by personal appearance.

Martin and Kennedy (1993) highlight that many young people are preoccupied with their self-concept and their belief that their level of physical attractiveness is perhaps the central determinant of their self-concept. This seems to be particularly true for young females. Martin and Kennedy's research findings support four conclusions of central importance: (a) the socialization period between the 4th and 12th grades is critical for female preadolescents and adolescents in terms of self-perceptions of their physical attractiveness; (b) the young female's perception of her own level of physical attractiveness tends to decrease during this time period; (c) the tendency of female preadolescents and adolescents to compare themselves to fashion models in ads not only increases with age but is greater for those with more negative self-perceptions of their physical attractiveness or lower self-esteem; (d) a single exposure to highly attractive advertising models raises the standards for physical attractiveness from the perspectives of female adolescents in the 8th through the 12th grades. In fact, a 15-year review of the literature revealed that the physical-attractiveness stereotype had a significant influence in the school system. Consistently, teachers rated physically attractive students from pre–K through 8th grade as being more intelligent and having greater academic potential and enhanced social skills (Ritts, Patterson, & Tubbs, 1992).

Physical attractiveness affects not only self-perceptions but the ways others perceive us. Dion, Berscheid, and Walster (1972) found, for example, that physically attractive individuals are more likely to be perceived as sexually warm and responsive, sensitive, strong, and sociable than are less attractive persons. Similarly, physically attractive counselors have been viewed as more intelligent, competent, trustworthy, assertive, and likable than less attractive counselors (Cash, Begley, McCown, & Weise, 1975).

Students in the university classroom often use the physical-attractiveness stereotype when evaluating their professors. Indeed, research suggests that attractive university professors receive student evaluations scores almost one full point higher on a 5-point scale than do their nonattractive counterparts (Riniola, Johnson, Sherman, & Misso, 2006).

The way we choose to dress clearly affects the way others perceive us. Thus, Behling and Williams (1991) found that dress affected both perception of intelligence and academic potential of students in secondary school settings. The greatest disparity in perceptions was for students who wore "the hood look" as opposed to "the dressy look." These styles were the most extreme and seemed to represent a good/bad dichotomy. The hood look was viewed as indicative of both lower intelligence and lower academic achievement. Even though suits are not a traditional type of attire worn in high school, male subjects who wore a suit and tie were perceived much more positively than those who did not.

Physical features over which a person can exert little if any control may strongly affect the way one is perceived. Height is a good example. Height is positively related to perceptions of dominance for both men and women and interpersonal attractiveness for men (Hensley, 1994). Children perceive taller males and females as stronger and more dominant than their shorter counterparts. Interestingly, taller females are judged to be stronger, more dominant, and smarter when they are seen in the presence of shorter males (Montepare, 1995).

A person's level of physical attractiveness also markedly affects the judgments that are made about the person's behavior. A number of studies have shown a relationship between an individual's personal appearance and the judgments made about the quality of work he or she produces. Landy and Sigall (1974) found, for example, that male readers of essays gave comparable grades to high-quality essays written by physically attractive and unattractive females. When the quality of the essay was inferior, however, unattractive females received significantly lower grades. Anderson and Nida (1978) found that physically attractive essay writers received the highest evaluations from members of the opposite sex, but individuals of moderate physical attractiveness received the highest ratings from members of their own sex.

Perhaps most importantly, essay writers with the lowest level of physical attractiveness received the lowest evaluations of all. Finally, attractive female essay writers have been judged, by male judges, to be significantly more "talented" than less attractive female essay writers (Kaplan, 1978). In short, the physically unattractive woman who does high-quality work may find that she receives relatively objective evaluations by men. When the physically unattractive woman produces work of marginal or low quality, however, she can expect much more negative evaluations by males than her more attractive female counterpart receives.

Physical attractiveness seems also to affect the dispensation of justice. This is particularly true when the plaintiff or defendant is a woman. Jurors, at least in a mock trial, who are exposed to an attractive plaintiff and an unattractive defendant more often find in favor of the plaintiff. They also award more money to the physically attractive as opposed to the physically unattractive plaintiff (Kulka & Kessler, 1978). Furthermore, attractive women are convicted less often for crimes they are accused of committing and in general receive more lenient sentences. Physically attractive female defendants seem to lose their edge in court only when they have taken advantage of their personal appearance to commit a crime. Thus, physically attractive females convicted of swindling receive stiffer sentences than their less attractive counterparts. If the conviction is for burglary, the unattractive female is apt to receive the harsher sentence (Adams, 1977).

Finally, there is some evidence to suggest that the morality of a person's behavior is affected by his or her level of physical attractiveness. In one interesting study, subjects were shown photographs of Barb and John. They were told that John invited Barb to his apartment and asked her to have sexual intercourse. Barb accepted the invitation. No matter what their attitude toward "casual sex," subjects judged the sexual behavior of the "highly attractive Barb" to be *less* moral than the behavior of the "quite unattractive" Barb. The study represents one of those rare instances in which physical attractiveness seems to be a disadvantage. Because the attractive female might be viewed as having more opportunities for socially acceptable sexual outlets than the unattractive female, she is apparently expected to set and meet higher standards of morality in her sexual conduct (Hocking, Walker, & Fink, 1982).

Behavioral Effects

Our level of physical attractiveness affects not only our own behavior but also the behavior of those with whom we interact. The impact of our level of physical attractiveness is perhaps manifested most strongly in its effect on our self-concept. As we have already indicated, the more physically attractive people are, the more positive their self-concept is likely to be. Adams (1977) has examined the physical attractiveness/self-concept relationship in detail, and has found that the behavioral profiles for physically attractive and physically unattractive persons do differ significantly in effectiveness of communication. For example, both physically attractive females and physically attractive males exhibit greater resistance to conformity pressure, more independence, and more self-disclosure than their less attractive peers.

Attractive facial features have a particularly pronounced effect on the behaviors of those who possess such features. Females with attractive facial features are more confident, experience little anxiety about having their own actions evaluated, and are less likely to be critical of self and others (Adams, 1977; Patzer, 1985). Moreover, physically attractive females are more popular than their less attractive counterparts (Adams & Roopnarine, 1994).

The potential of personal appearance to affect an individual's behavior is strikingly illustrated by the case of Rebecca Richardson. Becky Richardson came from a family with a history of congenital cleft palates. Her own condition was so bad that she had undergone 17 operations on her face to correct both articulatory and appearance problems associated with her cleft palate. After the final operation, she went to Mike and Marvin Westmore for professional cosmetic treatment of her face. When the Westmores began their cosmetic treatment, Becky Richardson's self-confidence was very low, she was withdrawn, and it was difficult to sustain communicative interaction with her. In the words of Mike Westmore (D. G. Leathers, personal interview, May 29, 1973), "She was twenty-two years old and obviously not getting her share of social intercourse with male members of society."

After she received a full set of aesthetic cosmetic treatments from the Westmore brothers, which produced a dramatic improvement in the attractiveness of her facial features, Becky Richardson's behavior changed dramatically. She who was once withdrawn and uncommunicative became a confident and sought-after young woman who assumed an active role in many social activities. She developed to the point where she actually became socially aggressive in some situations. In Becky Richardson's case, the change in her reflective image produced a significant, highly beneficial change in her self-image and, consequently, in her behavior. She became not only a much more effective communicator, but also a much more effective and satisfied human being.

The body's physical appearance also seems to have important behavioral implications. We expect people with given body types to behave in distinctive ways. For example, the stereotypical expectation is that mesomorphs will be more assertive, mature, and self-reliant than individuals with other kinds of body types. Endomorphs are stereotyped as relatively lazy, warm-hearted, sympathetic, good-natured, and dependent. Ectomorphs are viewed stereotypically as suspicious, tense, nervous, pessimistic, and reticent. Although not conclusive, there is evidence to support the view that persons with each of these body types do indeed behave in ways that conform to the stereotypes (Wells & Siegel, 1961).

The behavioral impact of body type may be stronger for children than for adults; we know that teenagers are particularly concerned about their personal appearance. In one study, Walker (1963), who had reliably classified children by body type, was able to confirm two-thirds of the predictions he made about the children's behavior, based solely on their body types. Girls' behaviors could be predicted from body type much more accurately than boys' behaviors. This finding is understandable in view of the fact that society attaches more importance to the physical attractiveness of females than males.

Parents' actual description of their children's behaviors indicated that endomorphic girls are eager to please, even-tempered, friendly, and relaxed. By contrast, ectomorphic girls are tense, jealous, unpredictable, moody, suspicious, worried, and afraid of failure. The behaviors of mesomorphic children could not be predicted with a high degree of accuracy (Walker, 1963). Subsequent research indicates, however, that adolescents with mesomorphic body builds have a much stronger achievement need than either endomorphs or ectomorphs (Cortes & Gatti, 1966, 1970).

In short, individuals who are perceived to be physically attractive do behave differently. In general, persons who are physically attractive have a more positive self-image than persons who are not. Their behavior is characterized by self-confident and assertive efforts to achieve demanding goals, by an independence of thought and action, and by an ability to resist the kinds of conformity pressure that would diminish their uniqueness as individuals.

Physically attractive persons of both sexes have more opportunities to interact with members of the opposite sex. They have more dates; they go to more parties; they spend more time conversing with members of the opposite sex; and they spend less time on nonsocial, task-oriented activities. Perhaps most importantly, both physically attractive females and physically attractive males report that they are more satisfied with their opposite-sex relationships over an extended period of time than are their less physically attractive peers (Reis, Nezlek, & Wheeler, 1980).

Physical attractiveness in turn is strongly affected by the ability to purchase socially appropriate clothing. Francis (1992) found that high school students who experienced "perceived clothing deprivation" (reflected in their inability to buy clothes or in clothing inadequacy relative to peers) suffered two negative consequences: They were perceived as less socially competent and experienced less social participation.

Whether an individual is a casual or a serious dater, the more physically attractive a person is, the greater the availability of opposite-sex partners. Also, attractive persons are less inclined to worry about the involvement of their partner with members of the opposite sex (White, 1980). In short, not only do physically attractive persons have more social interaction with members of the opposite sex, but the quality of that social interaction tends to be superior, from their perspective (Reis, Wheeler, Spiegel, & Kernis, 1982).

The physical-attractiveness stereotype emphasizes that physically attractive individuals are more socially desirable. As a result, many of us exhibit a desire to identify with, to associate with, and to be similar to physically attractive persons. The net result is that physically attractive persons receive preferential treatment in the initiation and development of interpersonal relationships.

We know, for example, that more positive personality characteristics are attributed to a female when she is associated with a physically attractive male (Strane & Warts, 1977). We are more self-disclosing when in the presence of a physically attractive person. We exhibit a greater willingness to reward physically attractive individuals monetarily (Mathes & Edwards, 1978). We are more willing to extend help to those who are physically attractive (Wilson, 1978). We view our attitudes as being more similar to physically attractive persons than to physically unattractive persons (Mashman, 1978).

Finally, we tend to judge the physically attractive as more credible and, ultimately, as more persuasive. Just because one is viewed as being physically attractive does not, of course, ensure that he or she will always be more persuasive than a less attractive person (Chaiken, 1979; Perlini & Hansen, 2001; Whaley, 1983), but it provides the physically attractive person with a decided advantage in a variety of communicative situations.

The Nature of Artifactual Communication

Personal appearance is clearly a powerful medium of communication. Appearance cues include not only a person's overall level of physical attractiveness, body type, size, shape, and weight, but also the clothing and other artifacts used to affect personal appearance. Indeed, many groups in our society rely almost exclusively on the visual medium of appearance cues to establish their social identity—for example, inner-city gangs, punks, skinheads, heavy metal rockers, and military units.

When we use the term *artifact,* we do not refer to the esoteric findings that came from an archaeological dig. We refer instead to those things that humans can wear on their body, do to their bodies, or use as extensions of their bodies for purposes of exercising conscious control over their personal appearance. Chief among such artifactual means are clothing, accent items, hairstyles (as well as hair care and treatment), eyeglasses, contact lenses, raincoats, and purses and briefcases.

Another modern form of artifactual communication is body mutilation, which includes body piercing, tattoos, Chinese foot binding, and nose and neck rings. Some of these markings and adornments are worn by special groups in our society to convey a special meaning to others. Oftentimes, tattoos are a form of initiation into a club or fraternity or sorority. Other tattoos may be a way for a gang member to represent his or her loyalty and allegiance to the group. Tribes in other countries may wear head, nose, or neck adornments as a sign of attraction or availability to other members of the group.

The distinctive features of artifactual communication as a specialized code were treated insightfully by Kaiser in the second edition of her book *The Social Psychology of Clothing: Symbolic Appearances in Context* (1990). She noted that the effectiveness of an artifactual message is determined by the degree to which it conforms to implicit aesthetic rules or standards; that is, the appropriateness of clothing choice at the present time is determined in large part by the degree to which the choice meets the dress expectations of the groups or individuals with whom we interact.

Appearance messages by their nature are nondiscursive, inflexible, and multidimensional in terms of the meanings they communicate. In contrast to verbal messages, appearance messages do not fade but tend to sustain their impact over time. At the same time, appearance messages are inflexible because they cannot be adapted to meet the changing demands of a given communicative context. Finally, the complex nature of appearance messages typically communicates multiple meanings:

> Seldom is only one meaning associated with an appearance message. More commonly, a range of possible meanings exist or meanings are layered on one another, almost creating a rainbow effect of meaning. Some meanings are derived from cultural experience, some are negotiated during social transactions, and some are conjured independently in the minds of participants. For two-way, meaningful communication to occur, the meaning intended by a programmed appearance should roughly coincide with that reviewed and interpreted by a perceiver. (Kaiser, 1990, p. 238)

Clothing as a Medium of Communication

Clothing represents a particularly important type of artifactual communication. The clothing choices we make frequently exert a strong impact on the impressions that we make on others. More specifically, the clothing we wear has been proven to be a strong determinant of four "image dimensions" that define the impressions that we make on others:

1. credibility
2. likability
3. interpersonal attractiveness
4. dominance (Molloy, 1988; Rasicot, 1983, 1986; Smith & Malandro, 1985)

Image dimensions are the components or defining features of the impression(s) we make on others.

Authorities seem to agree that the most potent effect of clothing is on how competent or authoritative we are judged to be. Molloy (1988) and Rasicot (1986) agreed that our clothing is a major determinant of not only how competent we are judged to be but also how likable we are in the eyes of those with whom we interact. Ironically, the clothing choices that have the effect of enhancing our perceived competence often have the effect of depressing our likability and vice versa. The big, tall person may gain authoritativeness because of size but actually be seen as so unapproachable as to lose likability. One way to cope with the problem is to sacrifice some authoritativeness by wearing less conservative, lighter-colored clothing in order to be seen as more approachable and likable.

Clothing also clearly communicates one's degree of power or powerlessness. This is particularly true of the uniform. Thus, there seems to be a proliferation of uniforms in countries and regions where a high priority is placed on differentiating groups of people on the basis of their power or status. In Rome, for example, the large number of different uniforms worn by different kinds of law enforcement officers is almost overwhelming. Disney corporation employees in the amusement parks wear uniforms that correspond to the part of the park where they work.

Nathan (1986) emphasized how clothing is used to control power judgments when he wrote that:

> A basic relationship read into clothing is that of power, or "who controls whom" in the realm of clothing. The powerful, or controllers, include the parent of the child, the master of the servant, or the husband of the well-dressed traditional wife. (pp. 39–40)

Finally, the impact of uniforms on impressions formed of the wearer is not confined to the impact on power judgments. Generally, people who wear uniforms seem to have more desirable personal qualities attributed to them. Hewitt and German (1987) found that a male Marine sergeant and a male Navy lieutenant were perceived as more attractive when in uniform than when dressed casually. Similarly, police officers were perceived as more competent, reliable, and intelligent when dressed in their uniforms (Singer & Singer, 1985). In contrast, Air Force enlisted personnel and officers viewed counselors in civilian attire as more expert, and they were more willing to cooperate with counselors when the counselors were dressed in civilian attire than when they were dressed in uniform (Huddleston & Engels, 1987). How would you account for the contrasting responses to individuals in uniform?

Cosmetics as a Medium of Communication

Cosmetics are clearly an important type of artifactual communication. They consist of things we put on our ourselves—particularly our face—that are intended primarily to serve the impression management function of nonverbal communication. Cosmetics include makeup, skin creams, perfume, aftershave lotion, and tattoos. Incidentally, the potential impact of tattoos on self-perceptions and interpersonal perceptions is often powerful and long-lasting. Tattoos, as we discussed in the section on artifactual communication, are a form of body message. These messages can be social meanings or ways to attract romantic interest. More and more, persons who would once not even consider getting a tattoo are getting them for mere entertainment or recreational reasons. Tattoos have surged in our society and it is not uncommon to see 5 to 10 tattoo stores in most towns these days. Regardless of their popularity, they still serve as a cosmetic message for the nonverbal perceiver.

Because makeup is used primarily to enhance the physical attractiveness of the female face, its use raises issues of profound psychological importance for many women (Cash, 1987). When considering whether and how to use makeup, the contemporary woman may have to resolve a number of issues: (a) Does the use of beauty-enhancing makeup help perpetuate sex-role stereotyping of women? (b) Is it appropriate to use makeup for identity construction or impression management? (c) How are women to deal with the paradoxical and oxymoronic overtones of using something that is artificial—makeup—to make them appear natural? (d) Can ideologically feminist women avoid wearing any makeup without appearing to be situationally inflexible (Fabricant & Gould, 1993)?

Questions such as these are addressed in some creative research. Respondents in this study suggested that the frequency with which women wear makeup, the amount of makeup used, and the kinds of makeup applied depend on the role a woman assumes at a given point in time. As Fabricant and Gould wrote:

> A woman's trajectory and predominant style of makeup use are tied in directly to her iden-
> tity construction and reflection. Makeup is a means by which women may construct aspects
> of their selves consistently over time, at least their visible self-images. It is also one very
> visible sign by which they may be seen to reflect who they are to other people or at least
> whom they want to be seen as. (1993, p. 538)

More specifically, the authors stress that the choices women make with regard to their use of makeup are affected by the time of day, the nature of the occasion, and the most central role being assumed. In constructing their desired identity through the use of makeup, women are aware of the differences between night versus day makeup, sexy versus nonsexy makeup, and makeup that emphasizes or de-emphasizes sex role and gender identity.

Other Artifacts as Communicative Messages

The choice of highly personalized artifacts, such as cosmetics, hairstyle, eyeglasses or con-tact lenses, and even orthodontal devices, clearly requires the aid of a professional image consultant. Molloy (1988) did not hesitate to provide guidelines for artifact choice. He did so at times with a sense of humor that is hardly self-deprecating. In his test of "Your Image I.Q.," he asked, "For which professionals are bow ties acceptable—and often preferred—attire?" Molloy's answer is waiters, clowns, college professors, and commentators.

Finally, plastic surgery is perhaps the most drastic means of modifying unattractive features. Plastic surgery is no longer undertaken exclusively for therapeutic purposes—reconstructing the face of the victim of an automobile crash or rebuilding the skin of a burn victim. Each year, millions of Americans now elect to have aesthetic plastic surgery because they are not satisfied with their physical image.

Almost without exception, individuals who seek plastic surgery have a negative image of their own body. They may be upset by the social stigma of ethnic facial features, excessive fatty tissue, or sagging skin. Their own sense of identification, or self-definition, is fuzzy at best and extremely self-deprecating at worst. Many of these individuals start with a negative personal sense of identification and seem to take conscious steps to make others aware of their feelings of inferiority. Thus, Dr. Kurt Wagner, who served part of his residency performing plastic surgery on inmates in a prison in Oklahoma, observed that "many inmates feel ugly, or they don't feel accepted or they have been made fools of. . . . With tattoos, they go out of their way to mark themselves and further isolate themselves" from society (Wagner & Gould, 1972).

The Communicative Functions of Personal Appearance

You will recall that different kinds of nonverbal communication serve different kinds of communicative functions. Eye behaviors, for example, serve no less than seven major communication functions: the attention, intimacy, persuasive, regulatory, affective, power, and impression management functions. Proxemic behaviors, by contrast, are particularly important whenever individuals are concerned with the impression management, persuasion, affiliation, and privacy functions of communication.

Personal appearance has an undeniable impact on a number of communicative functions. The importance of personal appearance in defining the societal role, occupation, class, gender, status, nationality, and age of the persons with whom we interact is undeniable. Moreover, personal appearance is also functionally important in the initiation and maintenance of romantic relationships. In fact, the sustained impact of personal appearance on romantic relationships is much greater than people might think. Patzer (1985) wrote that

> the research findings do not support the notion of subsiding effects and reveal instead enduring effects of surprising strength. Physical attractiveness remains a major determinant of mutual romantic attraction regardless of the elapse of time, the number of meetings, and even competing negative information. (p. 82)

In short, there are an almost unlimited number of communicative functions that are affected in some way by our personal appearance.

The two major communicative functions of personal appearance, however, are the *self-concept function* and the *impression management function.* Consider for a moment the integral and inseparable relationship of self-concept and body concept. As we have already demonstrated, numerous studies have confirmed the significant body image/self-concept/behavior linkage. When an investigator found that the academic performance of physically attractive schoolchildren in Lebanon was superior to that of their less physically attractive counterparts (Zahr, 1985), how did he interpret the results? Not surprisingly, the author cited the body image/self-concept/behavior linkage. He concluded that because they were physically attractive, one group of schoolchildren had a more positive body concept. Their more positive body concept contributed to a more positive self-concept that in turn resulted in superior grades.

The impact of body concept on self-concept and ultimately on behaviors has been illustrated in so many ways in this chapter that further amplification is hardly necessary. At minimum, we should remember that the impact of our body concept on our self-concept is manifested not only in our perception of self and others but also in the interpersonal perceptions and behaviors of those with whom we interact.

Finally, the impression management function of nonverbal communication begins and ends with personal appearance. You may wonder, for example, what clothing choices you should and should not make if your major concern is maximizing your own credibility. On the other hand, you might wish to know whether you should wear different kinds of clothes if you are putting a premium on being judged to be interpersonally attractive. Professionals such as doctors and attorneys now recognize the importance of such questions. Indeed, the importance they attach to the impression management function of appearance helps explain the rise of the well-paid image consultant.

Summary

In our society, a well-developed physical-attractiveness stereotype suggests that what is beautiful is talented, good, and socially desirable. Persons who deviate from the cultural ideal for physical attractiveness frequently suffer severe penalties in terms of self-concept, the undesirable personal traits attributed to them, and the relatively limited social rewards they are able to derive from interpersonal relationships.

The facial and bodily features that differentiate the physically attractive from the physically unattractive person are almost universally recognized in our society. Societal standards that are used to define beauty are more detailed for women than for men; and definitions for facial features are more detailed than those for bodily features. A precise profile exists that identifies the facial features that define facial attractiveness. In general, the smaller our facial features, the more attractive they are judged to be. Bodily attractiveness depends in part on whether one's body type is mesomorphic, ectomorphic, or endomorphic. For women, slenderness of body and body parts is an important feature of bodily attractiveness. For males, the physique that lacks muscles and muscle tone is viewed as particularly unattractive.

Body image, or the mental picture we have of our own body, is extremely important because body image strongly affects self-concept. Self-concept in turn has a powerful impact on our own perceptions and behaviors as well as on the way others perceive us and interact with us.

Body-cathexis is the concept that reflects how satisfied or dissatisfied we are with our own body. To the extent that we are unsatisfied with the appearance of our own body, or parts of it, we are apt to engage in body distortion. Body distortion is the distortion of our own estimates of the size of certain of our physical features, usually those that deviate from the cultural ideal.

The perceptual impact of personal appearance is perhaps strongest on self-concept; the more physically attractive we are perceived to be, the more positive our self-concept is apt to be. From a perceptual perspective, physical attractiveness also affects the kinds of persons we are perceived to be; it markedly affects judgments made about the quality of work we produce, and it affects the way we are treated by the judicial system.

The behavioral impact of personal appearance is also striking. Individuals who are viewed as physically attractive *do* behave differently. They are self-confident and assertive in their efforts to attain demanding goals; they exhibit independence in thought and action; and they exhibit an ability to resist conformity pressure, which is not characteristic of the physically unattractive person. When mingling with others, the physically attractive person has greater opportunities to interact with the opposite sex, and the nature of the interaction tends to be more satisfying.

Persons who do not meet the standards used to define acceptable personal appearance may wish to modify their personal appearance with artifacts. Artifacts are the things humans wear on their bodies, or do to their bodies, in order to modify their personal appearance. Clothing, cosmetics, hairstyle, eyeglasses and contact lenses, and plastic surgery are among the major artifactual means that can be used to exercise control over personal appearance.

Finally, personal appearance serves two major communicative functions—the self-concept function and the impression management function. These functions are integrally related. The impression management efforts we would like to undertake, and are capable of undertaking, are controlled to a considerable extent by how positive or negative our self-concept is.

REFERENCES

Adams, G. R. (1977). Physical attractiveness research: Toward a developmental social psychology of beauty. *Human Development, 20,* 217–239.

Adams, G. R., & Crossman, S. M. (1978). *Physical attractiveness: a cultural imperative.* Roselyn Heights, NY: Libra.

Adams, G. R., & Roopnarine, J. L. (1994). Physical attractiveness, social skills, and same-sex peer popularity. *Journal of Group Psychotherapy, Psychodrama & Sociometry, 47,* 15–35.

Anderson, R., & Nida, S. A. (1978). Effects of physical attractiveness on opposite- and same-sex evaluations. *Journal of Personality, 46,* 410–413.

Archer, D. (1980). *How to expand your social intelligence quotient.* New York: Evans.

Aron, A. (1988). The matching hypothesis reconsidered again: Comment on Kalick and Hamilton. *Journal of Personality and Social Psychology, 54,* 441–446.

Baranowski, M. J., Jorga, J., Djordjevic, I., Marinkovic, J., & Hetherington, M. M. (2003). Evaluation of adolescent body satisfaction and associated eating disorder in two communities. *European Eating Disorders Review, 11,* 478–495.

Bashour, M. (2006). An objective system for measuring facial attractiveness. *Plastic & Reconstructive Surgery, 118,* 757–774.

Behling, D. W., & Williams, E. A. (1991). Influence of dress on perception of intelligence and expectations of scholastic achievement. *Clothing and Textiles Research Journal, 9,* 1–7.

Bloch, P. H., & Richins, M. L. (1993). Attractiveness, adornments, and exchange. *Psychology & Marketing, 6,* 467–470.

Cahnman, W. J. (1968). The stigma of obesity. *Sociological Quarterly, 9,* 297.

Cash, T. F. (1987). The psychology of cosmetics: A review of the scientific literature. *Social and Behavioral Science Documents, 17,* 1–62.

Cash, T. F., Begley, P. J., McCown, D. A., & Weise, B. C. (1975). When counselors are heard but not seen: Initial impact of physical attractiveness. *Journal of Counseling Psychology, 22,* 237–239.

Cash, T. F., & Derlega, V. (1978). The matching hypothesis: Physical attractiveness among same-sexed friends. *Personality and Social Psychology Bulletin, 4,* 240–243.

Chaiken, S. (1979). Communicator physical attractiveness and persuasion. *Journal of Personality and Social Psychology, 37,* 1387.

Cortes, J. B., & Gatti, F. M. (1966). Physique and motivation. *Journal of Consulting Psychology, 30,* 408–414.

Cortes, J. B., & Gatti, F. M. (1970). Physique and propensity. *Psychology Today, 4,* 42.

Cunningham, M. R. (1986). Measuring the physical in physical attractiveness: Quasi-experiments on the sociobiology of female facial beauty. *Journal of Personality and Social Psychology, 59,* 925–935.

Cunningham, M. R., Roberts, A. R., Barbee, A. P., & Druen, P. B. (1995). "Their ideas of beauty are, on the whole, the same as ours": Consistency and variability in the cross-cultural perception of female physical attractiveness. *Journal of Personality & Social Psychology, 68,* 261–279.

Dion, E., Berscheid, E., & Walster, E. (1972). What is beautiful is good. *Journal of Personality and Social Psychology, 24,* 285–290.

Domzal, T. J., & Kernan, J. B. (1993). Variations on the pursuit of beauty: Toward a corporal theory of the body. *Psychology & Marketing, 10,* 495–511.

Fabricant, S. M., & Gould, S. J. (1993). Women's makeup careers: An interpretive study of color cosmetic use and "face value." *Psychology & Marketing, 10,* 531–548.

Feingold, A. (1990). Gender differences in effects of physical attractiveness on romantic attraction: A comparison across five research paradigms. *Journal of Personality and Social Psychology, 59,* 981–993.

Fisher, S. (1986). *Development and structure of the body image,* Vol. 2. Hillsdale, NJ: Erlbaum.

Francis, S. K. (1992). Effect of perceived clothing deprivation on high school students' social participation. *Clothing and Textiles Research Journal, 10,* 29–33.

Furnham, A., & Calhan, A. (1998). Eating disturbance, self-esteem, reasons for exercising and body weight dissatisfaction in adolescent males. *European Eating Disorders Review, 6,* 58–72.

Gabriel, M. T., Critelli, J. W., & Ee, J. S. (1994). Narcissistic illusions in self-evaluation of intelligence and attractiveness. *Journal of Personality, 62,* 143–155.

Grammer, K., & Thornhill, R. (1994). Human facial attractiveness and sexual selection: The role of symmetry and averageness. *Journal of Comparative Psychology, 108,* 233–242.

Griffin, A. M., & Langlois, J. H. (2006). Stereotype directionality and attractiveness stereotyping: Is beauty good or is ugly bad? *Social Cognition, 24,* 187–206.

Heffernan, D. D., Harper, S. M., & McWilliam, D. (2002). Women's perceptions of the outcome of weight loss diets: A signal detection approach. *International Journal of Eating Disorders, 31,* 339–343.

Hensley, W. E. (1994). Height as a basis for interpersonal attraction. *Adolescence, 29,* 469–474.

Hewitt, J., & German, K. (1987). Attire and attractiveness. *Perception & Motor Skills, 64,* 558.

Hocking, J. E., Walker, B. A., & Fink, E. L. (1982). Physical attractiveness and judgments of morality following an immoral act. *Psychological Reports, 51,* 111–116.

Horton, R. S. (2003). Similarity and attractiveness in social perception. *Self and Identity, 2,* 137–152.

Horvath, T. (1979). Correlates of physical beauty in men and women. *Social Behavior and Personality, 77,* 145–151.

Horvath, T. (1981). Physical attractiveness: The influence of selected torso parameters. *Archives of Sexual Behavior, 2.*

Hosoda, M., Stone-Romero, E. F., & Coats, G. (2003). The effects of physical attractiveness on job-related outcomes: A meta-analysis of experimental studies. *Personnel Psychology, 56,* 431–462.

Huddleston, J. E., & Engels, D. W. (1987). Influence of male military counselor attire on Air Force members' perceptions and preferences. *Military Medicine, 152,* 512–515.

Jackson, L. A., Sullivan, L. A., & Rostker, R. (1988). Gender, gender role, and body image. *Sex Roles, 19,* 429–443.

Joiner, T. E., Schmidt, N. B., & Singh, D. (1994). Waist-to-hip ratio and body dissatisfaction among college women and men: Moderating role of depressed symptoms and gender. *International Journal of Eating Disorders, 16,* 199–203.

Kaiser, S. (1990). *The social psychology of clothing: Symbolic appearances in context* (2nd ed.). New York: Macmillan.

Kalick, S. M., & Hamilton, T. E. (1986). The matching hypothesis re-examined. *Journal of Personality and Social Psychology, 51,* 673–682.

Kaplan, R. M. (1978). Is beauty talent? Sex interaction in the attractiveness halo effect. *Sex Roles, 4,* 195–204.

Kulka, R. A., & Kessler, J. B. (1978). Is justice really blind? The influence of litigant personal attractiveness on juridical judgment. *Journal of Applied Social Psychology, 88,* 366–381.

Landy, D., & Sigall, H. (1974). Beauty is talent: Task evaluation as a function of the performer's physical attractiveness. *Journal of Social Psychology, 29,* 299–304.

Langlois, J. H., Kalakanis, L., Rubenstein, A. J., Larson, A., Hallam, M., & Smoot, M. (2000). Maxims or myths of beauty? A meta-analytic and theoretical review. *Psychological Bulletin, 126,* 390–423.

Lavrakas, P. J. (1975). Female preferences for male physiques. *Journal of Research in Personality, 9,* 324–344.

Leathers, D. G. (1976). *Nonverbal communication systems.* Newton, MA: Allyn.

Malandro, L. A., Barker, L., & Barker, D. A. (1989). *Nonverbal communication* (2nd ed.). Reading, MA: Addison-Wesley.

Martin, M. C., & Kennedy, P. F. (1993). Advertising and social comparison: Consequences for female preadolescents and adolescents. *Psychology & Marketing, 10,* 513–530.

Mashman, R. C. (1978). Effect of physical attractiveness on the perception of attitude similarity. *Journal of Social Psychology, 106,* 103–110.

Mathes, E. W., & Edwards, L. L. (1978). Physical attractiveness as an input in social exchanges. *Journal of Psychology, 98,* 267–275.

McCaulay, M. M., & Glenn, A. A. (1988). Body image, self-esteem, and depression-proness: Closing the gender gap. *Sex Roles, 18,* 381–391.

Mckelvie, S. J. (1993). Effects of feature variation on attributions for schematic faces. *Psychological Reports, 73,* 275–288.

Mealey, L., Bridgstock, R., & Townsend, G. C. (1999). Symmetry and perceived facial attraciveness: A monozygotic co-twin comparison. *Journal of Personality and Social Psychology, 76,* 151–158.

Melamed, T. (1994). Correlates of physical features: Some gender differences. *Personality & Individual Differences, 17,* 689–691.

Moller, A. P., & Thornhill, R. (1998). Bilateral symmetry and sexual selection: A meta-analysis. *The American Naturalist, 151,* 174–192.

Molloy, J. T. (1988). *New dress for success.* New York: Warner.

Montepare, J. M. (1995). The impact of variations in height on young children's impressions of men and women. *Journal of Nonverbal Behavior, 19,* 35–47.

Morrow, P. C. (1990). Physical attractiveness and selection decision making. *Journal of Management, 16,* 45–60.

Nathan, J. (1986). *Uniforms and nonuniforms: Communication through clothing.* New York: Greenwood Press.

Patzer, G. L. (1985). *The physical attractiveness phenomena.* New York: Plenum.

Perlini, A. H., & Hansen, S. D. (2001). Moderating effects of need for cognition on attractiveness stereotyping. *Social Behavior and Personality, 29,* 313–322.

Rasicot, J. (1983). *Jury selection, body language and the visual trial.* Minneapolis: AB Publications.

Rasicot, J. (1986). *Silent sales.* Minneapolis: AB Publications.

Reis, H. T., Nezlek, J., & Wheeler, L. (1980). Physical attractiveness in social interaction. *Journal of Personality and Social Psychology, 38,* 604–617.

Reis, H. T., Wheeler, L., Spiegel, N., & Kernis, M. H. (1982). Physical attractiveness in social interaction: II. Why does appearance affect social experience? *Journal of Personality and Social Psychology, 43,* 979–996.

Riniola, T. C., Johnson, K. C., Sherman, T. R., & Misso, J. A. (2006). Hot or not: Do professors perceived as physically attractive receive higher student evaluations? *The Journal of General Psychology, 133,* 19–35.

Ritts, V., Patterson, M. L., & Tubbs, M. E. (1992). Expectations, impressions, and judgments of physically attractive students: A review. *Review of Educational Research, 62,* 413–426.

Rubenstein, A. J., Kalakanis, L., & Langlois, J. H. (1999). Infant preferences for attractive faces: A cognitive explanation. *Developmental Psychology, 35,* 848–855.

Scheib, J. E., Gangestad, S. W., & Thornhill, R. (1999). Facial attractiveness, symmetry and cues of good genes. *Proceedings of the Royal Society of London, Series B, 266,* 1913–1917.

Sengupta, R. (2006). Reading representations of black, east asian, and white women in magazines for adolescent girls. *Sex Roles, 54,* 799–808.

Secord, P. F., & Jourard, S. M. (1953). The appraisal of body-cathexis: Body-cathexis and self. *Journal of Consulting Psychology, 17,* 347.

Sheldon, W. H. (1954). *Atlas of man: A guide for somatyping the adult male at all ages.* New York: Harper.

Singer, M. S., & Singer, A. E. (1985). The effect of police uniform on interpersonal perception. *Journal of Psychology, 119,* 157–161.

Singh, D. (2004). Mating strategies of young women: Role of physical attractiveness. *The Journal of Sex Research, 41,* 43–54.

Singh, D. (1994). Is thin really beautiful and good? Relationship between waist-to-hip ratio (WHR) and female attractiveness. *Personality & Individual Differences, 16,* 123–132.

Smith, L. J., & Malandro, A. (1985). *Courtroom communication strategies.* New York: Kluwer Law Book.

Smith, S. M., McIntosh, W. D., & Bazzini, D. G. (1999). Are the beautiful good in Hollywood? An investigation of the beauty-and-goodness stereotype on film. *Basic and Applied Social Psychology, 21,* 69–80.

Stonebraker, P. M. (1989). Biocultural influences to male and females body images, eating, and activity behaviors (Doctoral dissertation, Howard University, Washington, DC). *Dissertation Abstracts International.*

Strane, K., & Warts, C. (1977). Females judged by attractiveness of partner. *Perceptual and Motor Skills, 45,* 225–226.

Sugerman, A. A., & Haronian, F. (1964). Body type and sophistication of body concept. *Journal of Personality, 32,* 393.

Thomas, V. G., & James, M. D. (1988). Body image, dieting tendencies, and sex role traits in urban black women. *Sex Roles, 18,* 523–529.

Thornhill, R., & Gangestad, S. W. (1994). Human fluctuating asymmetry and sexual behavior. *Psychological Science, 5,* 297–302.

Toro, J., Castro, J., Gila, A., & Pombo, C. (2005). Assessment of sociocultural influences on the body shape model in adolescent males with anorexia nervosa. *European Eating Disorders Review, 13,* 351–359.

Trivers, R., Manning, J. T., Thornhill, R., Singh, D., & McGuire, M. (1999). Jamaican symmetry project: Long-term study of fluctuating asymmetry in rural Jamaican children. *Human Biology, 71,* 417–430.

Vacker, B., & Key, W. R. (1993). Beauty and the beholder: The pursuit of beauty through commodities. *Psychology & Marketing, 10,* 471–494.

Wagner, K., & Gould, H. (1972). *How to win in the youth game: The magic of plastic surgery.* Englewood Cliffs, NJ: Prentice-Hall.

Walker, R. N. (1963). Body build and behavior in young children: II. Body build and parents' ratings. *Child Development, 34,* 20–23.

Watkins, L. M., & Johnston, L. (2000). Screening job applicants: The impact of physical attractiveness and application quality. *International Journal of Selection and Assessment, 8,* 76–84.

Wells, W. E., & Siegel, B. (1961). Stereotypes somatypes. *Psychological Review, 8,* 78.

Whaley, L. J. (1983). *The effects of physical attractiveness on persuasion.* Unpublished master's thesis, University of Georgia, Athens.

White, G. L. (1980). Physical attractiveness and courtship progress. *Journal of Personality and Social Psychology, 39,* 660–668.

Wilson, D. W. (1978). Helping behavior and physical attractiveness. *Journal of Social Psychology, 104,* 313–314.

Worsley, A. (1981). In the eye of the beholder: Social and personal characteristics of teenagers in their impressions of themselves and fat and slim people. *British Journal of Medical Psychology, 54,* 231–242.

Zahr, L. (1985). Physical attractiveness and Lebanese children's school performance. *Psychological Reports, 56,* 191–192.

CHAPTER
8

Vocalic Communication

Sounds communicate meaning. The meanings exchanged by sound are vitally important in communicating the emotional state, the perceived personality characteristics, and the impressions made by a communicator. If you doubt the truth of this assertion, listen to the audiotapes of President Franklin Roosevelt's Fireside Chats during World War II.

The expressed purpose of Roosevelt's extemporaneous speeches was to allay the fears of the nation, and FDR's consummate use of sound as a communication medium was highly instrumental in helping him achieve his purpose. Imagine for a moment the following situation: Roosevelt's voice comes over the radio; he is speaking in a high-pitched, quavering voice, at an extremely rapid rate. He stutters repeatedly and fills his frequent pauses with perceptible sighs. If this had been the case, the nation might have experienced a real panic. Americans might have been as fearful of an emotionally distraught president as they were of the Nazis.

In fact, Roosevelt recognized what many subsequent studies have verified. The voice can be a powerful instrument for transmitting the emotional state of the communicator. Perhaps more important to the person concerned with making a desired impression, the voice can be used as a major force in shaping the impressions other people form of a communicator. FDR used his voice to communicate the image of a vigorous, confident, and decisive leader who was completely in control of his emotions. Not so incidentally, he used his voice to mold a political personality that successfully withstood the critical scrutiny of four presidential campaigns. In fact, one recent study looked at the power of the presidential voice in 19 debates from 1960 to the 2000 debate between George W. Bush and Al Gore. Gregory and Gallagher (2002) found that in those 19 debates, candidates' voices were dominate and commanding and, furthermore, led them to victory at the polls. This study reinforces the notion that the voice is a powerful medium of communication, especially in political circles.

At least intuitively, most individuals recognize the role of the voice in shaping the impressions they make. Typically, students in public speaking class or forensics competitions will make concentrated efforts to reduce their nonfluencies, slow their speech rate, and lower their pitch to receive the best grade or ranking possible. Indeed, the voice, more than any other quality, tells the audience that the speaker is connecting with them (Genard, 2004).

Vocal cues can serve many functions. The sound of the voice can be used to signal extroversion or introversion, dominance or submission, and liking or disliking; to reveal turn-taking preferences; and to provide information on gender, age, and race (Scherer, 1982).

Moreover, the voice informs others about our interpersonal attitudes. We know that we use the sounds of the voices of those with whom we interact to determine their social class. In fact, our own dialect and accent strongly affect judgments of how much prestige we are perceived to have (Argyle, 1988). In addition, recent research reveals that when there is difficulty interpreting accented speech between native and nonnative speakers, persons who use nonverbal communication (e.g., gestures and facial expressions) are more likely to assess self-blame for problems in vocalized speech deliveries (Faux & Young, 2006). This study has profound implications for vocalic and intercultural communication.

Although vocal cues certainly have some impact on a number of functions of communication, they assume a vitally important role in serving three communicative functions:

1. the emotion function
2. the impression management function
3. the regulatory function

This chapter focuses on those primary functions of vocalic communication, and it begins with a consideration of the fundamental nature of vocalic communication.

The Semantics of Sound

The semantics of sound is not a simple matter. Siegman (1987) maintained that no generally accepted system exists that can be used to define and classify the vocal features of extralinguistic cues. We do know, that the vocal cues of communicators can be differentiated on the basis of attributes of sound uniquely associated with each communicator's vocal cues. Vocal cues consist of all the attributes of sound that can convey meanings and that have some measurable functions in interpersonal communication. The sound attributes that give any vocal cue its unique characteristics are (a) loudness, (b) pitch, (c) rate, (d) duration, (e) quality, (f) regularity, (g) articulation, (h) pronunciation, and (i) silence.

Loudness, or the power of the human voice, is perhaps the most basic attribute, because if a voice cannot be heard, none of its other attributes can be used to convey meaning. Loudness is defined in terms of *decibels,* a measure of the acoustic energy reaching the receiver at a given second. The terms *loudness* and *amplitude* may be used interchangeably (Argyle, 1988).

The quiet whisper, at 10 decibels, can be just as disruptive to interpersonal communication as the construction worker's hammer blows on steel plate, at 114 decibels. Very often, as individuals experience anxiety while they are delivering a speech or engaging in interpersonal communication, the power of their voice drops quickly and they begin talking in a whisper that is unintelligible to the individuals with whom they are trying to communicate. Research also indicates that whispering, in addition to problems with audibility, can intimidate those who are close to the encounter but not included in "the whisper" (Cirillo & Todt, 2005).

In spite of the fact that studies have been conducted on a great variety of conditions in big companies that use the assembly-line technique, few have focused on the damaging effects of excessive noise. The noise level in an average factory is 10 decibels above the noise level of a big-city street. This fact was dramatically emphasized for Eaves when one summer he worked in a golf club factory. The noise levels were excessive, making communication inaudible at times.

Anyone who has played a musical instrument is familiar with the concept of pitch. *Pitch* is the musical note that the voice produces. When you strike middle C on a piano, the C string is vibrating at the rate of 256 times per second. Likewise, a human voice that produces middle C is conveying the same pitch. Communicators have a *modal* pitch, that is, the one that occurs more frequently than any other pitch in their extemporaneous speech. You can easily identify your own modal pitch by recording a brief sample of your speech and matching the pitch of the sound that occurs most frequently with the appropriate note on a piano keyboard.

Your speaking or communicating *pitch range* is a measure of the musical interval (the number of notes) between the high and low pitches you use in speaking. Fisher notes that the ranges we employ in speaking depend on both our intent and the content of what we are attempting to communicate. Factual communication has a much more limited pitch range than emotional communication, and emotional communication is apt to be high-pitched because most of it falls above your modal speaking range. Apathetic and apparent monotone speech both have a narrow range (Fisher, 1975). Research in several places has demonstrated that a speaker who has a greater pitch range is perceived as having a more pleasant voice (Buller & Burgoon, 1986; Floyd & Ray, 2003).

Another study by Miyake and Zuckerman (1993) looked at positive qualities of the voice. Raters coded the vocalic and acoustic qualities of voices and concluded that the best-judged voices have high pitch range, low nasal sound, and infrequent monotone sound and are articulate. These speakers in turn were given more positive evaluations, and their voices were seen as more attractive.

Rate is the third sound attribute of vocal cues that may facilitate or disrupt the transfer of meaning. Rate refers to the number of sounds emitted during a given unit of time—usually 1 second. Of course, when the communicator uses sounds to produce speech, the speaking rate can have a vitally important impact on the quality of communication. Irregular rate may result in the communicator's combining words into units that are unconnected phrases rather than thought units.

Intelligibility and/or comprehension decline when the rate of utterance exceeds 275 to 300 words per minute, although individuals can learn through training in simple listening routines to comprehend material presented at faster rates (Orr, 1968). Although we recognize that the average individual's thought rate is considerably faster than his or her speech rate, an accelerated rate of utterance is not always desirable. People differ substantially as to the optimum rate of utterance that they as listeners prefer. One study found that younger (rather than older) audiences are better able to comprehend faster speech rates (Wingfield, Peelle, & Grossman, 2003). If the rate is too slow or the pauses too long, communicators will lose the attention of the persons with whom they are trying to communicate. In academic debate, speakers are often encouraged to speak at accelerated speech rates as a strategy to cover more arguments. As such, judges are expected to understand the arguments despite these speech rates.

Finally, rate is a variable of primary interest to the paralinguistic not only because it helps determine how fluent or dysfluent the communicator is and, hence, how effective the communicator is but also because speaking rate is positively related to the perceived intensity of a speaker's speech (Bond, Feldstein, & Simpson, 1988). In short, a person is typically seen as speaking with greater intensity as his or her speaking rate increases.

The attributes of rate and *duration* are integrally related because the length of time a communicator takes to emit a given sound or sounds is a major factor in determining the short-term, and often the long-term, rate at which sounds are emitted. Duration is sometimes treated as a component of rate, but it is treated separately here because duration is an identifiable attribute of sound and, as such, may either hinder or help the communicator in attempting to transmit distortion-free meanings.

Quality, the fifth attribute of sound, has a variety of connotations and is difficult to define precisely. Certainly the modal pitch and the loudness of a person's voice are important determinants of its quality (Argyle, 1988). In a broader sense, students of vocalic communication generally agree that voice quality refers to those dominant vocal characteristics that allow us to differentiate one person's voice from another.

Several authorities now maintain that an individual's voice qualities are so distinctive that an expert can identify a given individual's voice from a tape that includes the voices of many other individuals. In the past few years, *voiceprints* have been used increasingly in criminal trials in an attempt to provide positive identification of a suspect. More attention is now focused on the attempt to identify those sound attributes that are most helpful in facilitating "earwitness identification" (Read & Craik, 1995).

The dominant quality of a person's voice strongly affects the impression that person makes. Research indicates that individuals with flat voices are apt to be perceived as masculine, sluggish, cold, and withdrawn. The breathy female voice reinforces the stereotypical conception that females having such voice quality are superficial and shallow. The nasal voice makes a particularly bad impression because it is associated with a substantial number of socially undesirable personal qualities (Bloom, Zajac, & Titus, 1999; Pittam, 1987).

These vocal qualities and impressions have led some researchers, namely Zuckerman, to coin the phrase vocal attractiveness stereotype. The vocal attractiveness stereotype is apparent when someone with strong vocal qualities is preferred or favored over those persons with weak voices. Like facial attractiveness, vocal attractiveness leads to positive perceptions from others. In fact, those with vocally attractive qualities are generally seen as more likable, dominant, successful (Zuckerman & Driver, 1989), and personable (Zuckerman, Hodgins, & Miyake, 1990).

The sound attribute of *regularity* refers to whether your production of sound has a rhythmical, and possibly even a predictable, quality. If you have ever listened to newscaster Katie Couric, you know what is meant by *regularity of sound* and *sound pattern.* In contrast, comedian Dave Chappelle has made a sizable amount of money by emphasizing the arrhythmic or irregular nature of his sound production. Depending on the communicative situation, the sound attribute of regularity can be highly desirable or highly undesirable.

Articulation involves the use of movable parts at the top of the vocal tract such as the tongue, jaw, and lips to shape sounds and, in speech communication, to make transitions between individual sounds and words. Although primarily physiological, articulation represents an attribute of sound, much like loudness, that must be present in acceptable form, or communication virtually ceases to exist. If you remember saying, "Peter Piper picked a peck of pickled peppers" in your grade school days, you know that careful articulation was necessary or the listener would not be able to determine the exact nature of Peter's task.

Pronunciation is defined by specific vowel or consonant sounds in words and by the syllable that is emphasized. If you pronounce a word in a way that is inconsistent with general usage, or usage among the social groups with which you associate, it almost surely will result in confusion, at minimum. Perhaps more importantly, in terms of its long-range effect on the communicator, consistently mispronouncing words may impair a speaker's credibility and communicative effectiveness. For example, *irrelevant* is probably one of the most commonly mispronounced words in our society. Often *irrelevant* is pronounced "irrevelant." If such mispronunciation occurs frequently, this will markedly lower the quality of an individual's communication.

In the strictest technical sense, *silence* is not an attribute of vocal cues because silence ensures that none of the other eight defining attributes of vocal cues can be present. On the other hand, any sensitive observer of interpersonal communication recognizes that silence is a variable that is closely related to the other eight attributes of vocalic communication; therefore, silence serves important functions in interpersonal communication. We might give someone the "silent treatment" if we do not wish to acknowledge his or her presence; we sometimes become silent when we are unbearably anxious; or we may remain silent in order to exhibit emotions such as defiance or annoyance (DeVito, 1983). For example, a child may sit in silence at the dinner table to express distaste for the food, some form of rebellion, or conflict with a sibling or parent.

Many other important vocal variables cannot and should not be dissociated from the sound attributes just defined, such as vocal intensity, response latency, type of turn-maintaining or -relinquishing cue, turn duration, dialect, and accent (Street, 1984). Although these vocal variables are important individually and collectively, they are defined by the interaction of one or more of the sound attributes of vocal cues that were just discussed.

The Communicative Functions of Vocal Cues

The Emotion Function

Vocal cues represent an important medium of emotional communication (Frick, 1985; Fukushima & Aoyagi, 1994). Mehrabian (1981), for example, maintained that 38 percent of the emotional information transmitted by a given message can be attributed to vocal cues. Facial expressions, as the predominant medium of emotional communication, account for 55 percent of the total feeling in a message, and words account for only 7 percent.

In order to assess the potential of vocal cues as a medium of emotional communication, researchers have used a number of techniques to eliminate the effective impact of the words uttered. Subjects have been asked to read ambiguous passages from texts that have no readily identifiable meaning, to utter nonsense words and syllables, and to speak in a foreign language. Electronic "filters" have also been applied to speech samples, to eliminate the sounds of higher frequencies. This practice renders the verbal message unintelligible and leaves the vocal message relatively intact.

Fairbanks and Pronovost (1939) were among the earliest experimenters in speech communication who attempted to determine whether individuals could communicate

For instance, celebrities are known for taking voice and diction classes at universities and colleges in an effort to reduce "regionalism" in their accents, or to create an accent that may be missing from their vocal repertoire. In many cases, vocal training can reduce the "southern drawl" or create the realistic "British" accent that may be needed in casting for a role in a film or TV show.

Interest in the possible relationship between vocal cues and personality characteristics can be traced to the early days of radio, when massive national audiences were first attracted to that medium. Not surprisingly, many radio listeners became convinced that they could form accurate personality profiles of radio performers simply by listening to their voices. Other listeners were convinced that they could also accurately envision announcers' appearances by listening to them.

Stimulated by the intense curiosity of radio listeners, Pear (1931) analyzed the reaction of more than 4,000 radio listeners to nine trained radio voices and concluded that listeners consistently identified certain patterns of vocal cues with certain occupations such as clergymen and judges. Pear also found, however, that listeners consistently agreed that certain "vocal stereotypes" identified certain professions, although they made a number of errors in the application of such stereotypes.

In 1934, Allport and Cantril conducted the first major study specifically designed to examine whether, and to what extent, the natural voice is a valid indicator of personality. Their results strongly affirmed a positive relationship. The authors wrote that the voice definitely conveys "correct information concerning inner and outer characteristics." Specifically, they found that the sound attributes that comprise vocal cues are accurate indicators of the important personality dimensions of introversion–extroversion and ascendance–submission.

Although the pioneering study by Allport and Cantril did suggest a strong relationship between the nature of vocal cues and the dimensions of the speaker's personality, the authors were bothered by the apparent fact that a limited number of vocal cues seemed to create a stereotype of the speaker in the mind of the listeners. Initially, the tendency of listeners to deal in stereotypes suggested that the listeners took a limited number of vocal cues and erroneously concluded that a large group of people, who conveyed vocal cues with the same sound attributes, had the same personality characteristics.

The concern that "vocal stereotypes" might invalidate research that attempts to predict personality characteristics from vocal cues has persisted up to the present. Such concern seems unwarranted for a number of reasons: (a) Stereotypes, although sometimes inaccurate, are often accurate. (b) When the vocal stereotypes are inaccurate, the judges typically make the same error. Thus, Crystal (1969) wrote that

> such consistency in error may well be indicative of the existence of unformulated but none the less systematic voice-quality/trait correlations, or vocal stereotypes, as they are usually called in the literature, and is an important piece of evidence justifying the psychologists' optimism that a systematic basis for personality in vocal cues does exist. (p. 70)

(c) The accuracy of an audience's or individual's inferences about a speaker's real personality characteristics is not as important as an audience's agreement about a speaker's perceived personality characteristics.

As Pearce and Conklin (1971) wrote:

> it should be noted that the accuracy of audience inferences about a speaker is not particularly important in this context. Experienced public speakers develop characteristic manners of presentation that lead audiences to draw desired or undesired inferences about them which, whether accurate or not [author's italics], affect the continuation and effectiveness of the communication situation. If a speaker is perceived as effeminate, arrogant, unscrupulous, or incompetent because of vocal cues . . . his actual personality and credibility may be superfluous. (p. 237)

In spite of the great promise of the Allport and Cantril research, World War II, and perhaps the cyclical rhythms of researchers, resulted in a period of almost 25 years during which little effort was made to examine the relationship between vocal cues and perceived personality characteristics.

Another important distinction is the perception of masculinity and femininity in the voice. As indicated in the study above, this dichotomy is consistently found to be one of the most uniformly perceived personality characteristics. Lippa (1998) looked at how the voice differs between males and females and the degree to which nonverbal cues of masculinity and femininity are perceived in speakers' voices.

Lippa had 67 subjects (34 male and 33 female) read a mock TV spokesperson's script for various sales situations. Coders listened to subjects' voices and rated males and females and their perceived masculinity/femininity dimensions. The coders looked at inflected speech, high-pitched voice, harsh voice, soft voice, full voice, enunciation, and speech rate. Other nonverbal behaviors were also coded. Of a total of more than 20 nonverbal cues, each of the vocal cues was the most reliable measure, ranging from 0.81 to 0.40. Males in the study were perceived to have a voice similar to their occupational preference (fast-talker and loud voice), while females were perceived to have a vocal quality consistent with extroversion (loud voice, full voice, and fast-talker).

The study revealed the stereotypes that most "masculine"-sounding men are not articulate and that their voices sound deep. Stereotypes of the least "masculine"-sounding men are that their voices sound high at some points. Stereotypes of the most "feminine"-sounding women in the study are that they have cutesy, babydoll voices. The least feminine traits were mostly visual, not vocal. For instance, women who did not have their hair neatly combed or in a ponytail or who wore baggy clothes were perceived as least feminine.

Pitch, rate, and the distinctive overall quality of communicators' voices are attributes of vocal cues that determine which personality characteristics are attributed to the communicators. For both male and female speakers, those who use greater variety in *pitch* are thought to be dynamic and extroverted. Both male and female speakers who use variety in *rate* are thought to be extroverted; males are also seen as *animated,* but females are seen as high-strung, inartistic, and uncooperative. The voice, perhaps more than the face, can communicate specific emotions. There are many stereotypes associated with the voice and vocal attractiveness (Guerrero & Floyd, 2006). Typically, judges prefer younger voices to old voices. Research indicates that there is still a stereotype against the "old" voice (Hummert, Mazloff, & Henry, 1999).

Research has consistently confirmed the idea that the nature of vocalic communication materially affects the personality characteristics that listeners identify with the communicator (Miyake & Zuckerman, 1993). In addition, listeners consistently associate specific sound attributes—such as rate, pitch, or nasality—with the same specific personality traits. Further, research suggests that boys have "less nasal" qualities than girls, and thus favor better on socialization evaluations (Bloom, Moore-Schoenmakers, & Masataka, 1999).

When considered from a somewhat broader perspective, we know that "the attractive voice" is defined as sounding more articulate, lower in pitch, higher in pitch range, low in squeakiness, nonmonotonous, appropriately loud, and resonant (Zuckerman & Miyake, 1993). People with attractive voices in turn have greater power, competence, warmth, and honesty attributed to them than people with unattractive voices. Individuals with "babyish" vocal qualities are usually perceived to be less powerful and less competent but warmer and more honest than people with mature-sounding voices (Berry, 1992; Berry, Hansen, Landry-Pester, & Meier, 1994). We know too that vocal cues can have a significant impact on the most important image dimensions that define the impressions we make on other people: *competence, interpersonal attractiveness,* and *dominance.* As we shall see, different sound attributes affect each of these image dimensions in different ways.

Our society has a well-developed vocal stereotype that specifies how communicators must sound if they are to be viewed as *credible* (Thakerar & Giles, 1981). The dimension of credibility most apt to be affected by the sound of our voice is competence. We know, for example, that individuals who exhibit standard or prestigious accents, pause only briefly before responding, speak fluently, exhibit suitable variation in pitch and volume, and speak at a relatively fast rate are usually perceived as more competent than individuals who are associated with contrasting vocal cues (Street & Brady, 1982). Susan Berkley writes in her book *Speak to Influence: How to Unlock the Hidden Power of Your Voice* that we use our voices to captivate our listeners. She argues that pitch, tone, and inflection are key variables that establish the trust and competence we need in speech, especially in business contexts. Unsuccessful speech is phony, hostile, or boring, and will break any competence built up until that point (Berkley, 1999).

To speak with the "voice of competence," you must pay particular attention to those attributes of sound that are known to markedly affect judgments of credibility. Dialects and accents are known to be particularly important in affecting such judgments. Thus, communicators who speak with a general American dialect are viewed as more competent than those who do not. Standard dialects tend to enhance credibility in formal settings, whereas ethnic and in-group dialects are preferable in informal contexts such as homes and bars. Moreover, when the degree of accent is an important consideration for stereotyping and categorizing people, the more intense the accent, the more negative the impact on credibility (Street & Hopper, 1982). Specifically, the accent stereotype affects credibility for newscasters (Adams & Takakura, 1980).

Of note here is voice stress analysis, a method of measuring competence in one's voice. The voice stress analysis has been used with mixed results (we will take up deception in greater detail in Chapter 11). One study suggests that we normally produce 10 Hz cycles of microvibrations in our voice in normal conditions. With stress, those numbers go down (Panosh, 1996). However, a recent study compared a vocal and a nonvocal method of lie detection. The voice stress analysis was invalid while the GKT (Guilt Knowledge Test) was proven to be 90 percent accurate in detecting guilty knowledge (Gamer, Rill, & Godert, 2006). As we shall see in Chapter 11, other nonverbal codes must be examined besides vocal attributes in order to successfully detect deception. In addition, decoder training is a necessary, while often absent, step in lie detection research.

Finally, we know that competence seems to be enhanced by considerable variation in pitch and volume (Gregory & Gallagher, 2002; Sherer, London, & Wolf, 1973) and that competence increases as speaking rate increases. There obviously is a point at which speaking rate becomes so fast as to have a negative effect on competence, but there is no current consensus on what that rate is (Hecht & LaFrance, 1995; Siegman, 1987). We also know that short, purposeful pauses positively affect perceived competence but that both "hesitation pauses" and nonfluent speech depress perceived competence (Erickson, Lind, Johnson, & O'Barr, 1978).

In separate chapters on selling yourself nonverbally and impression management, we will identify in detail the sound attributes that you should and should not exhibit if you wish to speak with the voice of competence. In a variety of applied contexts, such as the sales and selection interviews, it is clear that the sound of your voice will go a long way to establish or destroy your personal credibility (Gray, 1982).

We have already indicated that vocal cues strongly influence judgments of *interpersonal attractiveness.* For example, communicators who sound alike, or whose speech "converges" in terms of similarity in dialect, speaking rate, and response latency, are apt to perceive each other as more interpersonally attractive (Street, 1984). Indeed, the person who wishes to be judged interpersonally attractive must speak with the "voice of social attractiveness." The socially attractive voice is one that simultaneously sounds confident and calm (Zuckerman, Hodgins, & Miyake, 1990).

The confident voice is defined by substantial but not excessive volume, a rather rapid speaking rate, expressiveness, and fluency. Cross-cultural research shows that appropriate loudness has a positive impact on perceptions of power in all groups studied (Peng, Zebrowitz, & Lee, 1993). Self-confidence and self-assurance are encoded in a clear and powerful manner by the confident voice (Kimble & Seidel, 1991). Communicators who exhibit a "confident" as opposed to a "doubtful" voice are perceived as significantly more *enthusiastic, forceful,* and *active* (Scherer, London, & Wolf, 1973). Eaves, as an assistant coach at a Florida university, found that his novice debaters did quite well, independent of their knowledge of the issues. Indeed, two students in particular, who were members of the football program, exuded a great deal of confidence in their voices when they spoke. While their physical statures were no doubt daunting to their opponents (as they are on the field), it was their vocal skills and commanding sound that combined to help them have a winning record at their first and only speech tournament.

Conversely, we attribute unacceptable levels of tension and anxiety to individuals who speak nonfluently. Nonfluencies include expressions such as "uh," sentence changes, word repetitions, stuttering (repeating the first syllable of a word), incomplete sentences, tongue slips, and intruding incoherent sounds, such as tongue clicks (Prentice, 1972). From a perceptual perspective, nonfluencies are, in the mind of the perceiver, strongly associated with high levels of anxiety (Jurich & Jurich, 1974). In class, a professor routinely hears two types of public speeches: one is characterized as polished, well rehearsed, and articulate; the other is identified as full of nonfluencies, vocalized pauses, or nervous hesitations that generally leave a poor impression on the audience. A good example of poor speech occurred in an episode of *The Apprentice* with Donald Trump. One of the show's contestants spoke so poorly in a business presentation that The Donald stopped him in midsentence, told the group that his speech was horrible, and told the contestant that he should not continue. While this reaction is obviously harsh, it still communicates the strong need for us to examine what impressions we convey through our vocal patterns and dialogue.

Finally, the voice assumes a central role in shaping judgments of how dominant an individual may be. Indeed, empirical research suggests that the voice is more important than the face in affecting judgments of dominance, whereas the face is more important than the voice in affecting judgments of liking (Zuckerman & Driver, 1989). More particularly, dominant individuals speak with a loud voice, whereas submissive individuals speak with a soft voice. Relatedly, dominant and powerful individuals exhibit speech that is relatively free from hesitations and hedges, whereas these vocal phenomena are characteristic of the speech of submissive and low-power people (Hosman, 1989).

A moderately fast rate, high volume, and full resonance all reinforce perceptions of power and status (Burgoon & Saine, 1978). Schlenker (1980) emphasized

> that an image of power can be communicated to an audience through paralanguage in several ways. When people are anxious and lacking in confidence, they speak with lower volume and exhibit more speech disturbances, such as stuttering, omitting portions of a word or sentence, failing to complete a sentence, and taking longer pauses between words and sentences—seeming to grope for the correct word but unable to find it. People who are self-confident do not display such awkward paralanguage. (p. 252)

Vocal cues clearly have the potential to play a major role in helping an individual make a desired impression. They are major determinants of first impressions (Kleinke, 1975), true in part because listeners intuitively distrust the calculated first impression that communicators try to project through the words that they utter. More importantly, lasting impressions can be strongly affected by our vocal cues.

The Regulatory Function

Vocal cues clearly serve a central role in regulating the communicative interaction that takes place in interpersonal communication. They interact with a number of kinesic behaviors, particularly gestures and eye behaviors, to signal the turn-taking desires of interacting individuals. In a definitional sense, Knapp and Hall (2006) put the matter clearly when they noted that speakers use turn-yielding and turn-maintaining cues whereas listeners use turn-requesting and turn-denying cues.

Cappella (1985) provided us with a particularly insightful treatment of the classes and kinds of vocal cues that are used to regulate conversational exchange between two people. The use of vocalic cues to manage conversations can take one of two general forms: first, the conscious control or alteration of sound attributes such as volume and pausing in order to impose turn-taking preferences on a conversation and, second, exploiting certain regularities in the sequencing of utterances that characterize the vocal component of conversation, for example, recognizing that your partner will generally increase her or his rate or mean duration of pauses to match your rate or mean duration of pauses (Cappella & Planalp, 1981).

How successful you are in the use of vocal cues to regulate or manage interaction depends on the criterion measure that you use. Because Coker and Burgoon (1987) attach a positive value to "involvement," they define "better interaction management" as the use of vocal cues that promote involvement, such as fewer silences/latencies and more coordinated speech. Recognize that in some instances the objective might be *not* to promote the involvement of one's interaction partner but to inhibit it.

If we wish to have favorable image traits attributed to us, we should modify our vocal cues so that we sound more like the individual with whom we are communicating. To reap the potential impression management benefits that "convergence" or "matching" may provide them, speakers often seek to make their vocal cues similar to the vocal cues of the person with whom they interact. Vocal cues that are particularly important in this regard include dialect choice, accent, and pausing. In general, the more we sound like the person with whom we interact, the more favorable the impression that we make (Street, 1982). A realtor was a guest speaker in one of Eaves's nonverbal classes. He suggested that he had to manage his vocal patterns and mimic those of the customer. He said that while he had to speak slowly for the rural farmer who was interested in land, the same strategy would fail for the city dweller. Indeed, he found that he had to speed up his speech rate markedly for a urban customer who was accustomed to faster speech delivery and was more time conscious. In this way, the salesperson was using "mirroring," a type of nonverbal act in which a person echoes or mirrors the nonverbal behaviors of others in order to maintain or improve the relationship.

Cappella (1985) recognized that the regulatory and impression management functions of vocalic communication are interrelated when he wrote that "the evidence is overwhelming in its support of the relationship between holding the floor and observers' rating of control and power (leadership, dominance, and so forth) and associativity (attraction, social evaluation, and so forth)" (p. 402). We know, for example, that courtroom attorneys use the loudness and cadence of their speech with the explicit intent of becoming the dominant figure in the proceedings. We also know that such attorneys seek to attain dominance in the courtroom not only for purposes of controlling conversation but also to define the impression they make in terms of high power.

At minimum, two people engaged in conversation must be concerned with three types of turns: within-turn interaction, simultaneous turns (when two people speak at the same time), and the management of turn taking when two individuals are sharing turns. The vocal behaviors of greatest importance in regulating interaction are duration of vocalization, pause duration, switching pauses, utterance length, latency (length of time taken to respond), and intensity or amplitude. The person who wants to maintain a turn, for example, will typically sustain vocalization, use short pauses, and maintain or increase loudness. It is interesting to note that when simultaneous turns occur—two people speaking at the same time—the person who speaks the loudest will typically win the floor (Cappella, 1985).

Individuals often speak with an unusually loud voice whenever they wish to command or order other persons to act in a certain way. The louder a person's voice, the more dominant that person is apt to be perceived (Siegman, 1987). Another study confirms the loudness–dominance connection. Tusing and Dillard (2000) looked at the perception of dominance through the voice in an interpersonal setting involving 760 subjects. They found that louder voices were perceived as more dominant than softer voices, and that loud male voices were perceived as more dominant than loud female voices. Interestingly, they found no correlation between speech rate and dominance. The findings are similar in animals too. In studying dominance in nonhuman species, Leinonen, Linnankoski, Laakso, and Aulanko (1991) found that 80 percent of subjects were able to detect dominance from the voice alone in monkeys. The "command voice" of the drill sergeant is legendary, and more than one parent has used it to regulate a child's behavior. For sheer stridency and volume, we have never heard anything that matches the vocal commands of the Beefeaters who guard the Queen's jewels, housed in a basement vault in the Tower of London. The Beefeaters, who are middle-aged men of some degree of distinction, are apparently charged with keeping the tourists moving. They cry out in almost unbelievably loud and aggressive tones, "Keep it moving. We can't let you stop. Other people want to see." The command voice seems to work in this instance, but it also seems to make a lot of tourists mad.

Developing the Ability to Encode and Decode Vocalic Messages

The ability to encode and decode vocalic messages represents an important nonverbal communication skill. As an encoder, you must develop this skill to an acceptable level if you are to make effective use of the great functional potential of vocalic communication. We have already established the functional importance of vocalic cues in conveying emotions, making first and long-term impressions, and regulating communicative interaction. Similarly, you must develop your skill in decoding vocalic messages to an acceptable level if you are to interpret accurately the important kinds of information that are being communicated to you.

The Vocalic Meaning Sensitivity Task (VMST) has been created both to test and to develop the accuracy with which individuals can communicate and perceive emotional meanings conveyed solely by vocal cues. The personal testimony of many classroom instructors who have used the VMST suggests that it is a useful training tool. Individuals who use the VMST almost always become very involved in the learning experience it provides. Many of those same individuals have emphasized that the VMST gives them a much better appreciation of the functions of vocalic communication, and with repeated use it significantly improves their encoding and decoding abilities.

To use the VMST in its simplest form you must do two things. First, have a friend or acquaintance attempt to communicate disgust, happiness, interest, sadness, bewilderment, contempt, surprise, anger, determination, and fear solely by using different vocal cues in reading the following sentences: "There is no other answer. You've asked me that question a thousand times, and my answer is always the same."

Your friend should repeat the two sentences 10 times, trying to communicate a different meaning each time by varying sound attributes such as pitch, loudness, and rate. Randomize the order in which attempts are made to communicate each class of vocalic meaning. For example, sadness could be the first meaning and determination the second.

To separate one reading from another, your friend should begin each reading by saying, "This is vocal message number 1," then, "This is vocal message number 2," and so on.

For communication of the highest possible quality, you might have your friend record the sentences on audiotape. Then, rather than listening to the communicator speaking in person, you can listen to the tape. When attempting to communicate vocally before a live audience, the communicators should sit with their chairs turned away from the audience. Ideally, communicators should sit behind a screen, to prevent the audience from seeing kinesic or other nonverbal cues.

Second, follow the directions for the VMST exactly, in order to produce accurate measurements. When you identify the vocal messages of others, your own decoding skill is being measured; when others attempt to identify your vocal messages, your own encoding skill is being measured.

The Vocalic Meaning Sensitivity Task (VSMT)

The communicator you are listening to—either live or on a tape recording—is attempting to communicate 10 different classes or kinds of meaning to you. Each attempt to communicate a class of meaning will begin with the words "This is vocal message number _____." You are to listen very carefully, then in Table 8.1 place the number of the vocal message in the blank across from the word, such as "Disgust" or "Happiness," that comes closest to representing the meaning just communicated to you vocally. Follow the same procedure for each of the 10 vocal messages.

TABLE 8.1   Vocalic Meaning Sensitivity Task (VMST)*

Class of Vocalic Meaning	Number of Vocal Message
Disgust	_____
Happiness	_____
Interest	_____
Sadness	_____
Bewilderment	_____
Contempt	_____
Surprise	_____
Anger	_____
Determination	_____
Fear	_____

*You may use an expanded form of the VMST if you desire. The 10 terms here were used for two reasons: They have previously been used in research on vocalic communication, and they are the same terms used in Step 1 of the FMST. Therefore, you can make direct comparisons between your ability to perceive and communicate meaning by facial and vocal means. Simply compare accuracy of identification scores for Step 1 of the FMST with scores on the VMST. If you want to make a more extended test of your ability to perceive and transmit meanings vocally, however, you should add the following 10 terms to the task. Which also are frequently used in tests of vocalic communication: *indifference, grief, anxiety, sympathy, pride, despair, impatience, amusement, satisfaction*, and *dislike*. By adding these terms to the VMST, you will have a more comprehensive and demanding measure of vocalic skills.

To test your ability to communicate meanings accurately as opposed to testing your ability to perceive meanings transmitted by vocal cues, you should attempt to communicate the 10 emotions that comprise the VMST by making a tape recording and then giving the test to a group of people of your own choice.

Students' ability to communicate the 10 emotions of the VMST vary dramatically (6 correct choices out of 10 is 60 percent accuracy of identification). The scores of the vocal communicators in our classes have ranged from 85 to 30 percent; the scores of the vocal perceivers have been in approximately the same range. As a rule of thumb, you can assume that a score of 70 percent or above is excellent; 69 to 50 percent is average; and below 50 percent is poor.

Repeated use of the VMST usually leads to marked improvement in both the ability to encode and the ability to decode messages conveyed by sound. You have the potential to improve your scores on the test by at least 20 percent. If you set realistic goals for yourself, the VMST can be a great help in attaining them.

The use of the VMST, or your own experiences in real-world contexts of importance to you, may indicate that you are vocally expressive or that you have specific problems. Let us assume, for example, that others perceive your voice to be unpleasantly nasal, harsh, or hoarse; that you exhibit a high nonfluency rate; or that you speak with a soft voice. Specific voice-training exercises have been developed to deal with such problems. You may wish to use such exercises on your own or to work with a voice-training coach (Linver, 1983).

Summary

Vocal cues consist of all the attributes of sound that can convey meanings and have some measurable functions in interpersonal communication. The sound attributes that differentiate one person's vocal cues from another's are loudness, pitch, rate, duration, quality, regularity, articulation, pronunciation, and silence.

Vocal cues serve many functions. They assume a particularly central and important role in serving three communication functions, however: the emotion function, the impression management function, and the regulatory function.

Vocal cues are an important medium of emotional communication. Their potential to provide specific information about a communicator's emotional state is exceeded only by facial expressions. We do know, however, that individuals' ability to encode and decode emotional information via vocal cues varies substantially.

Vocal cues serve the impression management function in two ways. First, the voice's sound is a major determinant of the personality traits that are ascribed to a person. Vocal cues strongly affect the specific kinds of personality characteristics and personal qualities that are attributed to the communicator. Pitch, rate, and the overall quality of a person's voice determine which personality characteristics are attributed to that person. Individuals who exhibit little variation in pitch and rate, for example, are typically viewed as introverts, lacking dynamism and assertiveness. Persons who exhibit a nasal quality are likely to have a wide array of undesirable personality characteristics attributed to them.

Second, vocal cues serve the impression management function by exerting a major impact on three image dimensions—credibility, interpersonal attractiveness, and dominance—that in turn define the impressions we make on others. Specific sound attributes are associated with "the voice of competence" and "the voice of social attractiveness." Also, the sound of our voice is very important in judgments people make about how dominant or submissive we are.

The regulatory function of vocalic communication has been receiving increasing attention recently. In order to engage in enlightened conversational management, we must understand how vocal variables such as duration of vocalization, pause duration, utterance length, latency of response, and amplitude can be used to regulate interaction. We typically will use not only vocal cues but also eye behaviors and gestures in our attempts to regulate communicative interactions.

Successful communication puts a premium on the development of important nonverbal communication skills. The Vocalic Meaning Sensitivity Task (VMST) presented in this chapter should be used both to test and to develop the accuracy with which individuals can communicate and perceive emotional meanings conveyed solely by vocal cues.

REFERENCES

Adams, R. C., & Takakura, S. (1980). A quasi-experimental study of some effects of accented speech on perceptions of credibility. *Communication, 9,* 24–32.

Allport, G. W., & Cantril, H. (1934). Judging personality through voice. *Journal of Social Psychology, 5,* 40–51.

Argyle, M. (1988). *Bodily communication* (2nd ed.). Methuen: London.

Berkley, S. (1999). *Speak to influence: How to unlock the hidden power of your voice.* Campbell Hall, NY: Campbell Hall Press.

Berry, D. S. (1992). Vocal types and stereotypes: Joint effects of vocal attractiveness and vocal maturity on person's perception. *Journal of Nonverbal Behavior, 16,* 41–53.

Berry, D. S., Hansen, J. S., Landry-Pester, J. C., & Meier, J. A. (1994). Vocal determinants of first impressions of young children. *Journal of Nonverbal Behavior, 18,* 187–197.

Bloom, K., Moore-Schoenmakers, K., & Masataka, N. (1999). Nasality of infant vocalizations determines gender bias in adult favorability ratings. *Journal of Nonverbal Behavior, 23,* 219–236.

Bloom, K., Zajac, D. J., & Titus, J. (1999). The influence of nasality of voice on sex-stereotyped perceptions. *Journal of Nonverbal Behavior, 23,* 271–281.

Bond, R. N., Feldstein, S., & Simpson, S. (1988). Relative and absolute judgments of speech rate from masked and content-standard stimuli: The influence of vocal frequency and intensity. *Human Communication Research, 14,* 548–568.

Buller, D. B., & Burgoon, J. K. (1986). The effects of vocalics and nonverbal sensitivity on compliance: A replication and extension. *Human Communication Research, 13,* 126–144.

Burgoon, J. K., & Saine, T. (1978). *The unspoken dialogue.* Boston: Houghton.

Cappella, J. N. (1985). The management of conversations. In M. L. Knapp & G. R. Miller (Eds.), *Handbook of interpersonal communication* (pp. 393–435). Beverly Hills, CA: Sage.

Cappella, J. N., & Planalp, S. (1981). Talk and silence sequences in informal conversations III: Interspeaker influence. *Human Communication Research, 7,* 117–132.

Cirillo, J., & Todt, D. (2005). Perception and judgement of whispered vocalizations. *Behaviour, 142,* 113–128.

Coker, D. A., & Burgoon, J. K. (1987). The nature of conversational involvement and nonverbal encoding patterns. *Human Communication Research, 13,* 463–494.

Crystal, D. (1969). *Prosoic systems and intonation in English.* Cambridge, MA: Cambridge University Press.

Davitz, J. R. (Ed.). (1964). *The communication of emotional meaning.* New York: McGraw-Hill.

Davitz, J. R., & Davitz, L. J. (1959). The communication of feelings by content-free speech. *Journal of Communication, 9,* 9.

DeVito, J. A. (1983). *The interpersonal communication book* (3rd ed.). New York: Harper.

Erickson, B., Lind, E. A., Johnson, B. C., & O'Barr, W. M. (1978). Speech styles and impression formation in a court setting: The effects of "powerful" and "powerless" speech. *Journal of Experimental Social Psychology, 14,* 266–279.

Fairbanks, G., & Pronovost, W. (1939). An experimental study of the durational characteristics of the voice during the expression of emotion. *Speech Monographs, 6,* 88–91.

Faux, W. B., & Young, R. (2006). *Misunderstandings in difficult conversations between native and non-native speakers of English: More than a language problem.* Paper presented at the International Listening Association Conference, Portland, OR.

Fisher, H. B. (1975). *Improving voice and articulation* (2nd ed.). Boston: Houghton.

Floyd, K., & Ray, G. B. (2003). Human affection exchange: IV. Vocalic predictors of perceived affection in initial interactions. *Western Journal of Communication, 67,* 56–73.

Frick, R. W. (1985). Communicating emotion: The role of prosoic features. *Psychological Bulletin, 97,* 412–429.

Fukushima, O., & Aoyagi, S. (1994). Learning to decode vocally encoded emotions. *Japanese Journal of Counseling Science, 27,* 37–45.

Gamer, M., Rill, H.-G., & Godert, H. W. (2006). Psychophysical and vocal measures in the detection of guilty knowledge. *International Journal of Psychophysiology, 60,* 76–87.

Genard, G. (2004). Leveraging the power of nonverbal communication. *Harvard Management Communication Letter* (pp. 3–4). Harvard Business School Publishing Corp.

Gray, J., Jr. (1982). *The winning image.* New York: AMACOM.

Gregory, S. W., & Gallagher, T. J. (2002). Spectral analysis of candidates' nonverbal vocal communication: Predicting U.S. presidential election outcomes. *Social Psychology Quarterly, 65,* 298–308.

Guerrero, L. K., & Floyd, K. (2006). *Nonverbal communication in close relationships.* Mahwah, NJ: Lawrence Erlbaum.

Harper, R. B., Wiens, A. N., & Matarazzo, J. D. (1978). *Nonverbal communication: The state of the art.* New York: Wiley.

Hecht, M. S., & LaFrance, M. (1995). How fast can I help you? Tone of voice and telephone operator efficiency in interactions. *Journal of Applied Social Psychology, 25,* 2086–2098.

Hosman, L. A. (1989). The evaluative consequences of hedges, hesitations, and intensifiers: Power and powerless speech styles. *Human Communication Research, 15,* 383–406.

Hummert, M. L., Mazloff, D., & Henry, C. (1999). Vocal characteristics of older adults and stereotyping. *Journal of Nonverbal Behavior, 23,* 111–132.

Jurich, A. P., & Jurich, J. A. (1974). Correlations among nonverbal expressions of anxiety. *Psychological Reports, 34,* 199–204.

Kimble, C. E., & Seidel, S. D. (1991). Vocal signs of confidence. *Journal of Nonverbal Behavior, 15,* 99–105.

Kleinke, C. L. (1975). *First impressions.* Englewood Cliffs, NJ: Prentice-Hall.

Knapp, M. L., & Hall, J. A. (2006). *Nonverbal communication in human interaction* (6th ed.). New York: Holt.

Leinonen, L., Linnankoski, I., Laakso, M. L., & Aulanko, R. (1991). Vocal communication between species: Man and macaque. *Language and Communication, 11,* 241–262.

Levy, P. K. (1964). The ability to express and perceive vocal communications of feeling. In J. R. Davitz (Ed.), *The communication of emotional meaning.* New York: McGraw-Hill.

Lippa, A. (1998). The nonverbal display and judgment of extraversion, masculinity, femininity, and gender diagnosticity: A lens model analysis. *Journal of Research in Personality, 32,* 80–107.

Linver, S. (1983). *Speak and get results.* New York: Summit.

Mehrabian, A. (1981). *Silent messages* (2nd ed.). Belmont, CA: Wadsworth.

Miyake, K., & Zuckerman, M. (1993). Beyond personality impressions: Effects of physical and vocal attractiveness on false consensus, social comparison, affiliation, and assumed and perceived similarity. *Journal of Personality, 61,* 411–437.

Orr, D. B. (1968). Time compressed speech—A perspective. *Journal of Communication, 18,* 288–291.

Panosh, R. (1996). Build a voice-stress analyzer. *Popular Electronics, 13,* 41–45.

Pear, T. H. (1931). *Voice and personality.* London: Chapman and Hall.

Pearce, W. B., & Conklin, F. (1971). Nonverbal vocalic communication and perception of a speaker. *Speech Monographs, 38,* 235–241.

Peng, Y., Zebrowitz, L. A., & Lee, H. K. (1993). The impact of cultural background and cross-cultural experience on impressions of American and Korean male speakers. *Journal of Cross-Cultural Psychology, 24,* 203–220.

Pittam, J. (1987). Listeners' evaluations of voice quality in Australian English speakers. *Language and Speech, 30,* 99–113.

Prentice, D. S. (1972). *The process effects of trust-destroying behavior on the quality of communication in the small group.* Doctoral dissertation, University of California at Los Angeles.

Read, D., & Craik, F. I. M. (1995). Earwitness identification: Some influences on voice recognition. *Journal of Experimental Psychology: Applied, 1,* 6–18.

Rothman, A. D., & Nowicki, S. (2004). A measure of the ability to identify emotion in children's tone of voice. *Journal of Nonverbal Behavior, 28,* 67–92.

Scherer, K. R. (1979). Nonlinguistic vocal indicators of emotion and psychopathology. In C. E. Izard (Ed.), *Emotions in personality and psychopathology.* New York: Plenum.

Scherer, K. R. (1982). Methods of research on vocal communication: Paradigms and parameters. In K. R. Scherer & P. Ekman (Eds.), *Handbook of methods in nonverbal behavior research.* Cambridge, MA: Cambridge University Press.

Scherer, K. R., London, H., & Wolf, J. J. (1973). The voice of confidence: Paralinguistic cues and audience evaluation. *Journal of Research in Personality, 7,* 31–44.

Scherer, K. R., & Oshinsky, J. S. (1977). Cue utilization in emotion attribution from auditory stimuli. *Motivation and emotion, 1,* 331–346.

Schlenker, B. R. (1980). *Impression management.* Monterey, CA: Brooks/Cole.

Siegman, A. W. (1987). The telltale voice: Nonverbal messages of verbal communication. In A. W. Siegman & S. Feldstein (Eds.), *Nonverbal behavior and communication* (2nd ed.). Hillsdale, NJ: Erlbaum.

Street, R. L. (1982). Evaluation of noncontent speech accommodation. *Language & Communication, 2,* 13–31.

Street, R. L. (1984). Speech convergence and speech evaluation in fact-finding interviews. *Human Communication Research, 11,* 139–169.

Street, R. L., & Hopper, R. (1982). A model of speech style evaluation. In E. B. Ryan & H. Giles (Eds.), *Attitudes towards language variations: Social and applied contexts* (pp. 175–188). London: Arnold.

Street, R. L., Jr., & Brady, R. M. (1982). Speech rate acceptance ranges as a function of evaluative domain, listener speech rate, and communication context. *Communication Monographs, 49,* 290–308.

Thakerar, J., & Giles, H. (1981). They are—So they spoke: Noncontent speech stereotypes. *Language and Communication, 1,* 255–261.

Tusing, K. J., & Dillard, J. P. (2000). The sounds of dominance: Vocal precursors of perceived dominance during interpersonal influence. *Human Communication Research, 26,* 148–171.

Wingfield, A., Peelle, J. E., & Grossman, M. (2003). Speech rate and syntactic complexity as multiplicative factors in speech comprehension by young and older adults. *Aging Neuropsychology and Cognition, 10,* 310–322.

Zuckerman, M., & Driver, R. E. (1989). What sounds beautiful is good: The vocal attractiveness stereotype. *Journal of Nonverbal Behavior, 13,* 67–82.

Zuckerman, M., Hodgins, H., & Miyake, K. (1990). The vocal attractiveness stereotype: Replication and elaboration. *Journal of Nonverbal Behavior, 14,* 97–112.

Zuckerman, M., & Miyake, K. (1993). The attractive voice: What makes it so? *Journal of Nonverbal Behavior, 17,* 119–135.

PART TWO

Developing the Successful Communicator

9

Impression Management

Impression management is a critical component of nonverbal communication. This process occurs in two main stages: (1) impression formation and (2) impression management.

Impression Formation

Do you recall the first time you asked someone out on a date? Have you served as a witness or a litigant in a courtroom? Do you remember your last job interview? In each of these situations, valuable impressions were formed by others who viewed your behavior. Generally, the importance of nonverbal impressions can be summarized into four main sections: (1) stereotypes, (2) the primacy effect (first impressions), (3) selective perceptions, and (4) the recency effect (last impressions).

Stereotypes. First, let us address the issue of stereotypes and how they taint impressions that others form about us. Celebrities are often targets of stereotyped evaluations. In the trial of Martha Stewart, the media were quick to label her as guilty since she was so wealthy; in the trial of Ken Lay, the media accused the corrupt Enron leader of providing misleading information about his company. Oftentimes, the physically attractive person will fall prey to a stereotype. As we discussed in Chapter 7 on personal appearance, the way we look and appear to others often guides their perceptions, both good and bad. One study has found that the facial stereotype can never be avoided in immediate impression formation (Olson & Marshuetz, 2005). Two good examples of this are a pleasant smile and a stoic expression on one's face.

Body size also leads to a common physical stereotype. Overweight women are often viewed less favorably than their thinner counterparts (Worsley, 1981).

The voice leads to another common stereotype. Individuals who use nonfluencies (e.g., "uh," "um," "ah," and "well") in their speech are much more likely to be harshly judged than their well-spoken counterparts (Johnson & Vinson, 1990). The voice can also be used to judge the likelihood of truth telling in the future. For example, if one appears nervous in his or her speech throughout an encounter, one may deduce that there is some untruthfulness to his or her testimony or credibility. In college debates, this seems to be the common impression made on judges about weak debaters.

Ken Lay trying to minimize the press during the Enron scandal.

The Primacy Effect (First Impressions).   Our image of others is strongly affected by the primacy effect, or first impressions. These impressions are often difficult to change later (Shaver, 1975). First impressions account for a disproportionate amount of all impressions formed later. One good example of the first impression is the handshake. Research suggests that there are different handshakes in different parts of the United States. On the East Coast, three to five short pumps are ideal, while in California one or two pumps will suffice. In Texas, however, three or four full pumps are necessary (Nazareno, 2004). One colleague shared with Eaves that in some Asian nations, a second hand must accompany the handshake in order to show respect for one's elders. In the United States, one would find that nonverbal behavior to be odd or bizarre.

Selective Perception.   Selective perception is the tendency to attend to and interpret only those stimuli or perceptual cues that are consistent with past experiences and concerns. In other words, individuals hear and see what they want, based on their beliefs, values, and attitudes. A good example of this is how we as voters perceive candidates who run for office. Oftentimes, we will filter out parts or most of a message that does not correspond with our philosophy or value system. Voters are notorious for casting ballots on the basis of misinformation or only "part" of the truth. The popularity of the sound bite in television campaign ads and messages taken out of context on a candidate's voting record are two good illustrations of this point.

Kim and Papacharissi (2003) found that there are striking differences in how Web pages are perceived. Oftentimes, our cultural background can inhibit our processing the complete message, and this seems to be the case in how we create and interpret Web material. Koreans, being from a collectivist culture, are more likely to use hyperlinks in their Web pages, whereas

Americans, being from a more individualistic nation, have fewer links in their Web pages. We should all be aware of the impact that our cultural background has on our perceptual processing of the world around us, especially in virtual communities.

The Recency Effect (Last Impression). The recency effect, or the last impression a person makes, can also be extremely important in impression formation. Perceptual distortion often seems to result from too much emphasis being placed on an individual's most recent action. We have all heard the phrase "What have you done for me lately?" This is an all-too-familiar phrase that often guides our perception process in evaluating others.

Politics serves as a good example of the recency effect. Recall Bill Clinton's term as president in 1993–2001. He will not be remembered for the good things that he did while in office, such as environmental reform, success with NAFTA, or the creation of the global village. Instead, many will remember Clinton for what he did last while in office: his infidelity with Monica Lewinsky.

More recently, George W. Bush will perhaps not be remembered for his economic or domestic reform, but for his failure to vacate Iraq in a timely fashion to suit not only Democrats but Republicans as well.

Impression Management

Edinger and Patterson (1983) maintained that "impression management may be seen as an actor's behavioral strategy designed to create some beneficial image of presentation for the individual" (p. 43). Ordinarily, the impression manager attempts to exercise conscious control over the impression he or she makes on the person with whom he or she is communicating. By contrast, the impression manager who exercises the presentational function is trying to make a given impression on a third party as a result of communication with the interaction partner.

> For example, a person may wish to be seen as a loving spouse, the considerate parent, or the patient and understanding friend. Under such circumstances, close attention to one's partner by holding gaze and maintaining a direct orientation . . . [could] contribute to creating the desired impression in a group of observers. (Patterson, 1987, p. 115)

The impression manager who exercises the affect management function consciously controls his or her emotional response to what someone else has done. When you encounter your married friend with someone else's spouse at a party, for example, you might decide to suppress a look of contempt because you think that would be a socially inappropriate expression. Instead you give your friend an embarrassed smile.

This chapter draws on the insights of Patterson (1994, 1995) and a number of other nonverbal and impression management researchers (DePaulo, 1992; Schlenker, Diugoleckie, & Doherty, 1994). Our own perspective is fundamentally different from Patterson's in several respects, however. He is concerned with how nonverbal communication affects impression management, which is narrowly conceived as serving a single function. Our broader concern is to identify the different impressions we may make, or the images we may claim, and to describe the particular kinds of nonverbal communicative behaviors and cues that are most useful in making a given impression.

To begin, *impression management* is defined as an individual's conscious attempt to exercise control over selected communicative behaviors and cues—particularly nonverbal cues—for purposes of making a desired impression. Look at the two photos of professors' offices. What is your impression of each office? How does the office's appearance affect your perceived judgments of the owner's credibility? We acknowledge that impression managers may affect some of the impressions they make on others without consciously intending to do so, but impression management that does not involve the conscious intent or awareness of the impression manager falls outside the scope of this chapter.

Impression formation and impression management are conceptually interrelated phenomena that cannot profitably be considered in isolation. The impression former generally assumes the role of the decoder whereas the impression manager assumes the role of the encoder, but those roles are interchanged often and instantaneously.

In order to make a desired impression, impression managers must carefully consider which impressions are consistent with their current reputation, known abilities, and attitudes. In short, the impression manager must consider not only which impressions can be emphasized and de-emphasized, but which impressions will be believable.

In seeking to make a desired impression by consciously controlling their nonverbal cues, communicators should be guided by the association principle: They must, through their communication, seek to associate themselves with desirable image traits while disclaiming association with undesirable image traits (Schlenker, 1980; Turnley & Bolino, 2001).

The principle of association can be illustrated by the actions of successful magicians. Successful magicians are by definition extremely skillful impression managers. They are masters of the art of misdirection; they draw our attention to movements that have no relevance to the performance of a certain trick while diverting our attention from those movements that are absolutely necessary to perform the trick.

Recently, one of the most popular magicians has been David Blaine. In a dangerous and lengthy stunt aired on ABC on May 8, 2006, he attempted to stay in a tank of water for one week (see the photo on page 192). He trained for six months, lost 50 lbs, and worked with the Navy Seals. While unsuccessful, he managed to stay in the tank of water for most of one week, and tried to hold his breath for almost nine minutes (the world record is 8 minutes and 58 seconds). He did hold his breath for over six minutes after being tied to 150 lbs of chains, but then was rescued by an emergency crew. He is a modern-day Houdini, mastering different escapes and dangers. His past stunts have included balancing on a beam for 35 hours, being buried alive in a see-through coffin for one week, and surviving inside a massive block of ice for 61 hours (Milton, 2006). In each of these ways, Blaine, like any magician, attempts to present an image of mystery by diverting his audience's attention and producing the "jaw-dropping" effect. In these ways, a magician is a successful impression manager.

The Nature of Impression Management

Although you might agree that knowledge of impression management can be valuable to you, a careful look at the impression management literature could cause you to become frustrated. You will discover that there has been no clear and comprehensive attempt to identify the

What impression do you form about this office?

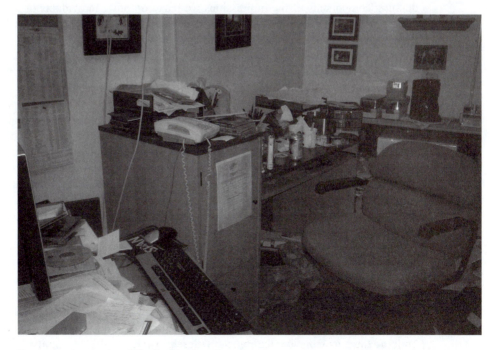

Does your impression differ in this photo?

David Blaine in a tank of water.

defining components of the impressions we make on other individuals or to determine whether we should exhibit different types of nonverbal communicative behaviors if we wish to make one type of impression as opposed to another. No one to date has developed a theoretical perspective that explains what motivates impression managers to claim specific images by exhibiting particular types of communicative behaviors and cues in certain contexts.

This section presents some of the essential parts of a new theoretical conceptualization that has been developed (Leathers & Ross, 1990). This conceptualization is designed to provide you with a fundamental understanding of the types of impressions you might wish to make and how you can most effectively use your own nonverbal communication to make one type of impression as opposed to another. Furthermore, more recent research expands the traditional approach to impression management studies. Schlenker and Britt (1999) expanded some of the traditional research that looked at impression management from a selfish or self-serving motive (e.g., pay raise, promotion, or better social standing).

They later found that empathy and friendship also affect beneficial impression management (Schlenker & Britt, 2001). These studies are important, namely because friends help to regulate information about their friends and what impressions are formed about them.

Schlenker (1980), in his innovative treatment of impression management, contends that impression managers are most directly concerned with claiming images that are useful to them in achieving their goals. Tedeschi and Riess (1981) amplified that position by maintaining that both impression formers and impression managers have been socially conditioned to believe that certain image dimensions are desirable and positively valued in our culture.

The Defining Components of an Impression: Image Dimensions

Impression is the broad and all-encompassing term that is made up of, or defined by, four image dimensions: credibility, likability, interpersonal attractiveness, and dominance (Ross, 1991). These image dimensions, which are part of an impression that you make on another person, are universal in at least one sense: Each one is important in almost any context that might be important to you. The context you are in will, of course, affect how you prioritize their importance. If you are going out on a date, likability or interpersonal attractiveness might be more important to you than credibility. On the other hand, if you are being interviewed by the admissions officer of a prestigious law school, you might feel that credibility is much more important than either likability or interpersonal attractiveness.

The image dimension of credibility has repeatedly been identified as centrally important to impression managers who attempt to control attributions about their believability in public. The work of Erving Goffman is noteworthy here. Goffman (1959) argued in his classic text that we present a certain self to be seen by others in everyday life. We continue to monitor the image we portray to others. Credibility includes what some have termed *goodwill* or *caring*. McCroskey and Teven (1999) found that goodwill is an integral part of source credibility. In looking at the context of teacher credibility, a number of studies have found that credibility impacted teacher ratings: caring impacted teacher trustworthiness (Teven & Hanson, 2004; Teven & McCroskey, 1996); immediacy influenced credibility (Thweatt & McCroskey, 1998); and the appearance of a faculty member's office affected students' perception of the teacher's credibility in the classroom (Teven & Comadena, 1996).

What happens when that credibility is threatened or questioned? A new study argues that denial serves as a form of impression management to defend one's reputation or credibility, especially in the workplace. Hippel et al. (2005) found that several conditions and groups exist that use denial as a form of impression management. They include:

1. Temporary employees are more likely to deny incompetence.
2. African-Americans are more likely to deny incompetence to a white interviewer, especially if they attended a predominantly black high school.
3. White students and their IQ scores are more likely to discount intelligence as important when compared with Asians' IQ scores.

This study is important because its sheds new light on how credibility operates in the impression management process.

Likability is the second image dimension that is a central, defining component of any given impression you make. You will probably agree that as an impression manager, you must be concerned with communicating in such a way that your interaction partner will judge you to be likable and that you must be concerned with being perceived as likable in a wide variety of contexts. Schlenker (1980) theorized that likability is one of the two most important image dimensions. DeMeuse (1987) came to a similar conclusion.

Interpersonal attractiveness is the third image dimension that is an important part of the impressions we make on others. When we make perceptual judgments about individuals seeking to make positive impressions in public, those judgments are almost invariably made on the dimension of interpersonal attractiveness (Albright, Kenny, & Malloy, 1988; Alicke, Smith, & Klotz, 1987). Although the evidence is far from conclusive at the moment, interpersonal attractiveness seems to be defined by three subdimensions: interestingness (Muehlenhard & Scardino, 1985); emotional expressivity (Riggio & Friedman, 1986); and sociability (Albright et al., 1988; Dion & Dion, 1987).

Finally, dominance is the fourth image dimension that is a defining component of the impression (DeMeuse, 1987; Ellyson & Dovidio, 1985; Henley & Harmon, 1985). Although a number of factors might be viewed as subdimensions or defining parts of the central image dimension of dominance, power and assertiveness seem to be the two most important.

In this theoretical conceptualization, positive labels have been used to identify each of the universal image dimensions—"credibility," "likability," "interpersonal attractiveness," and "dominance." However, negative labels might have been used to identify each of the universal image dimensions with equal accuracy—"noncredible," "unlikable," "interpersonally unattractive," and "submissive." The essential point is that the judgment made of impression managers by impression formers on each image dimension is not categorical but, rather, a judgment of degree; for example, a judgment is made about the degree to which an impression is or is not credible. One popular measure of degree is the Self-Monitoring Scale, a commonly mentioned instrument in the impression management literature (Gangestad & Synder, 2000, p. 541).

You must decide how you wish to prioritize these image dimensions. We would guess that an attorney might prioritize them from most to least important in the following way: credibility, dominance, interpersonal attractiveness, and likability. In comparison, a politician might prioritize the image dimensions differently: likability, interpersonal attractiveness, credibility, and dominance. The nonverbal communication that can have the strongest positive impact on your perceived credibility will be quite different from the nonverbal communication that will help you most in achieving your aim of being judged to be dominant in a given communicative context. Indeed, one study found that when context is ignored outright, the receiver is more likely to form a quick impression (Overwalle & Labiouse, 2004).

Major Motives of the Impression Manager

Impression management scholars have given little attention to the motives of the impression manager. Such an understanding is essential if we are to develop a sound explanation as to how and why impression managers decide on the relative importance to them of each of the four major image dimensions. Furthermore, understanding why impression managers are motivated to prioritize the four image dimensions from most to least important in a given interpersonal context greatly enhances the ability to predict what communicative behaviors or cues impression managers will actually exhibit in order to be positively perceived on one or more image dimensions. Significantly, Jones and Pittman (1982) contended that "We believe strongly that a theory of strategic self-presentation must be anchored in identifiable social motives. Self-presentation involves the actor's linkage of particular motives to his or her strategic resources" (p. 235).

Brembeck and Howell (1976) developed one of the most insightful treatments of the classes of social motives that can be used to explain the communicative behaviors individuals exhibit and predict how they will behave communicatively in the future. The classificatory framework presented in this chapter draws directly on their treatment of classes of motives.

The definitional relationship between *drives* and *motives* must be understood at the outset. Individuals experience drives when they are aroused and tense because they are suffering from a failure to satisfy one or more of their needs. Motives, in contrast, are socially conditioned drives. Both physiological motives and social motives combine to impel or compel an individual to behave in given ways. Thus, Brembeck and Howell (1976) viewed "some motives as *physiological motives* (those leading to the reduction of a drive based on a physiological need) and others as *social motives* which lead to the satisfaction of our socio-psychological needs" (p. 90).

An understanding of how an individual is motivated at a given point in time enhances our potential to predict how that individual will behave, because motives guide a person's behaviors in ways that he or she judged to be effective in reaching one or more goals. Motives serve not only a valuable predictive function but also a useful explanatory function, in part because the names of motives tend to identify the communicator's immediate goal, for example, the "hunger motive," the "social approval motive," and the "conformity motive."

Passing reference has been made in the impression management literature to such social motives as self-esteem, fear of failure, achievement, and approval (Tedeschi & Norman, 1985). McClelland's research (1987) on how categories of motives are measured and defined is brilliant. The major classes of motives he identified—the achievement, affiliation, avoidance, and power motives—are similar to the types of motives described here. However, McClelland and other researchers focusing on motives have not made systematic efforts to identify the major classes of social motives that shape the communicative behavior of impression managers. This book asserts that four major classes of motives are of overriding importance for the impression manager:

1. achievement motives
2. affiliation motives
3. social approval motives
4. mastery motives

The achievement motive is characterized by the felt need to meet high standards of excellence, to set and meet challenging goals, to be viewed as an achiever, and often to be viewed as an expert. Impression managers who are most strongly motivated by the achievement motives should ordinarily prioritize the image dimension of credibility as most important. Impression managers who are motivated by achievement will put a premium on competence. By exhibiting specific nonverbal behaviors/cues, impression managers can frequently exert a strong influence on the judgments others make about their competence. Some research suggests that impression management tactics can help produce achievement in the interview process, specifically for women (Kacmar & Carlson, 1994) and cross-cultural groups (Lopes & Fletcher, 2004).

The affiliation motive, the second major class of motives, is defined by an individual's felt need to develop relational ties and interpersonal bonds with other human beings, to form friendships, to trigger positive emotional responses from others, and above all else to be liked. Impression managers whose strongest motivation is affiliation will in all probability attach the highest priority to the image dimension of likability.

Social approval is the third major type or class of motive related to impression management. This is a broad-based motivation that is defined by people's need to be perceived positively rather than negatively, as the result of their actions and the kind of people they are judged to be. Perhaps more than the other major classes of motives, social approval is tied to societal rules, regulations, norms, and laws. Thus, both the person who meets the expectations of society and the individual with whom interaction occurs will be rewarded with social approval.

Although impression managers who are motivated most strongly by social approval might be concerned with more than one image dimension, most often they will attach the highest priority to being judged interpersonally attractive. Not surprisingly, interpersonally attractive individuals typically have beliefs, values, and attitudes that are similar to those of their interaction partners, and they are perceived to behave in ways that are compatible with the societal norms and the expectations of their interaction partners (Albada, Knapp, & Theune, 2002).

The final major class of motives that can be a driving force behind the actions of impression managers is mastery motives. By definition, persons who are motivated by a need to exhibit mastery over others want to lead, take charge, control, and in some cases order others around. Impression managers who are moved by the motivation to exhibit mastery over others will attach the highest priority to being positively perceived on the image dimension of dominance.

The Impression Management Process

In the past two decades, empirical knowledge of impression management has expanded rapidly. It is difficult to use, however, because such knowledge has not been synthesized and organized in a way that makes it easily usable by the impression manager. Self-monitoring is an invaluable part of the impression management process. The work of Synder and others is a major contribution to our understanding of how impression management operates. Basically, Snyder (1974) argues that people vary greatly on their ability to effectively control their outward appearance. Decades later he summarized much of the research in self-monitoring. Gangestad and Snyder (2000) did an extensive bibliographic review of the theory of self-monitoring to date. They proposed what is known as the Self-Monitoring Scale. The scale is divided into nine categories:

1. Expressive control—the ability to display expressions in contexts that normally do not elicit those reactions: for example, smiling when you feel sad. High self-monitors have greater expressive control than low self-monitors.
2. Nonverbal decoding skills—the ability to infer appropriate nonverbal perceptions of others: for example, being able to detect frustration in a friend. High self-monitors are better nonverbal decoders than are low self-monitors.

3. Attitude-behavior consistency—occurs when your attitudes match your behaviors. Unlike low self-monitors, high self-monitors have lower attitude-behavior consistency. For example, your high self-monitor friend may be less likely to be persuaded by you than your low self-monitor friend.

4. Behavioral responsiveness to external cues or others' expectations: for example, raising your hand before speaking. High self-monitors, more than low self-monitors, will behave according to others' expectations.

5. Behavioral variability across contexts and situations: for example, being able to adapt to more contexts in different situations. High self-monitors exhibit greater behavioral variability than low self-monitors.

6. Interpersonal orientations involved in friendships and relationships. High self-monitors are more willing to have friendships surrounding activities, instead of basing relationships on trust, and are more likely to engage in sex without commitment than are low self-monitors. For example, Jim may not be attached to Susan after sex since he is a high self-monitor. This has profound implications for relationships and communication.

7. Being impressed by physical attractiveness: for example, your friend's being more impressed than you are by the outfit you are wearing today. High self-monitors are more easily impressed by others' physical attractiveness than are low self-monitors.

8. Attention and responsiveness to others: for example, recognizing when a friend is upset. High self-monitors are generally more attentive and responsive to others than are low self-monitors.

9. Peer-self trait rating discrepancy. The correspondence made between self and peer ratings will be lower for high self-monitors than for low self-monitors. For example, your friend Jamie may not care about what you or others are saying about her. She rates herself high regardless of your views.

The following conceptualization was developed with its applicability to sales training in mind, but with minor modification it could also be useful for a wide variety of different groups of impression managers, including readers of this book, attorneys, doctors, diplomats, and politicians.

Impression management can be viewed as a process consisting of four interrelated stages. When used to train or educate individuals to become successful managers, the four stages in the process are treated as steps. The four-step description has proved to be particularly helpful in spelling out the sequence of actions necessary for corporate salespeople to become effective impression managers (Leathers, 1988). The following four stages make up the impression management process:

Stage 1: Familiarization with the communication of successful impression managers
Stage 2: Identification, selection, and application of the principles of impression formation and impression management
Stage 3: Measurement of the impressions made
Stage 4: Modification of undesirable communicative behaviors/cues to control the impressions made

Model Impression Managers

One source refers to politicians as "intuitive semioticians," or diplomats who use gestures and must be aware of the intentionality of their messages that are conveyed through signs and signals (Jonsson & Hall, 2003). Celebrities also have to be concerned with their image, both on and off the screen. A few examples of modern-day impression managers are George W. Bush, Condoleezza Rice, Donald Trump, and Oprah Winfrey.

George W. Bush as president of the United States is a good example of an impression manager. His style and communication were put to the test in his political debates with Al Gore and John Kerry (see Chapter 10 for more analysis about these debates). In addition, he strives to maintain a strong image in press conferences, when he visits world leaders for summits or meetings, and when reporters challenge him on the issue of the day.

Condoleezza Rice has been the secretary of state of the United States since 2006. She has a powerful position, one in which many are looking to her to be the voice of the president. She visits world diplomats, conducts important talks or negotiations, and generally represents Bush's ideals and philosophy when questioned on various topics.

Donald Trump is another good example of a successful impression manager. Known as the king of New York business, Trump has the best of everything: his suits, his plane, his penthouse, his yacht, his golf course, and his casino. Trump insists that image is everything and his approach is apparent if you have watched the NBC show *The Apprentice*. Potential employees look up to him as a business icon, and they want to emulate everything Trump does and what he stands for.

Finally, Oprah Winfrey is a long-lasting impression manager. Successful for years with her talk show, Oprah wants to portray a certain image to her viewing audience and to her skeptical public. She is often seen helping those less fortunate, such as having someone on her show who can help a viewer cope with divorce, stress, or depression. She has her own television channel, the Oxygen Network, which tries to reach a female audience with her message.

Principles of Impression Management

Step 2 in the impression management process requires that you identify, select, and apply relevant principles of impression management. The impression management principles in Figure 9.1 should prove to be useful to you. You will recognize that the four sets of impression management principles have been classified respectively under the four major image dimensions of credibility, likability, interpersonal attractiveness, and dominance.

The sets of impression management principles in Figure 9.1 draw on a substantial amount of the most recent empirical information on the subject. In addition, they are set up in such a way as to try to make them of maximum value. You might note three things before you begin to use the impression management principles in Figure 9.1: First, you may consistently view one of the image dimensions as particularly important to you; for example, likability. Second, the communicative contexts in which you communicate most often might make some principles more valuable than others. Third, you might want to concentrate on controlling or eliminating negative nonverbal communicative behaviors.

FIGURE 9.1   Impression Management Principles

Principles of Impression Management

Image Dimension I: Credibility
P1 Communicators who maintain a high level of eye contact with their interaction
    partner, but not continuous eye contact, are perceived as more competent
    (Kleinke, 1986; Webbink, 1986).
P2 Vocal cues such as relatively fast rate, substantial volume, and short, purposeful
    pauses are related to perceptions of increased competence (Street & Brady, 1982).
P3 Communicators who meet the personal appearance expectations of the person(s)
    with whom they interact will be judged to be more competent (Rosenberg,
    Bohan, McCafferty, & Harris, 1986).
P4 Communicators who speak the general American dialect with standard accent are
    viewed as more competent than those who do not (Burgoon & Saine, 1978;
    Street & Hooper, 1982).
P5 Competence is negatively affected by looking down before responding to a ques-
    tion, characteristically downcast eyes, and a low level of eye contact (Burgoon,
    Manusov, Mineo, & Hale, 1985; Kleinke, 1986).
P6 Communicators whose verbal and nonverbal messages are inconsistent are
    viewed as less trustworthy than communicators whose multichannel messages
    are consistent (Leathers, 1986; Mehrabian, 1981).
P7 Individuals who exhibit insincere smiles at inappropriate times will probably be
    viewed as less trustworthy than individuals who smile sincerely in context
    (Ekman, 1985; Ekman & Friesen, 1982).
P8 Communicators who exhibit behavioral "tension-leakage" cues in the form of non-
    fluencies, shifty eyes, and lip moistening will be judged to be less competent
    than those who do not (Exline, 1985).

Image Dimension II: Likability
P1 Communicators who exhibit immediacy behaviors in the form of close interaction
    distances, a direct bodily orientation, forward leans, socially appropriate touching,
    in-context and sincere smiling, bodily relaxation, and open body positions are con-
    sistently perceived as more likable than communicators who do not exhibit such
    immediacy behaviors (Anderson, 1985; Richmond, McCroskey, & Payne, 1987).
P2 Communicators who signal interest and attentiveness via direct body and head
    orientations, direct eye contact, and smiling are typically viewed as more likable
    than communicators who do not similarly signal interest and attentiveness
    (Schlenker, 1980).
P3 Communicators who dress in such a manner as to meet the dress expectations of
    those with whom they interact will be better liked (Leathers, 1988).
P4 The interaction of body type and clothing can have a major impact on judgments
    of likability; for example, big persons with endomorphic body types should wear
    softer, lighter shades of blue, gray, or beige in order to be perceived as likable.
P5 Impression managers should recognize that clothing that will make them appear to
    be likable (i.e., lighter-colored and informal clothing) may also make them appear
    to be less credible, and vice versa (Rasicot, 1983; Smith & Malandro, 1985).
P6 Sustained and direct eye contact, and the maintenance of mutual gaze with one's
    interaction partner, are strongly correlated with positive judgments of likability
    (Kleinke, 1986).
P7 Likability is positively associated with a speaking voice that is pleasant, relaxed,
    emotionally expressive, and friendly, and that sounds confident, dynamic,
    animated, and interested (Richmond et al., 1987).

(continued)

FIGURE 9.1   (Continued)

P8 Nonverbal indicators of disliking, which reinforce the perception that the person exhibiting such behavioral indicators is unlikable, are unpleasant facial expressions, a relative absence of gestures, visual inattentiveness, closed bodily posture, and an incongruent posture (Leathers, 1986).

Image Dimension III: Interpersonal Attractiveness

P1 Communicators whose nonverbal communicative behaviors seem to be spontaneous, disclosing, and uncensored are seen to be more interpersonally attractive (Sabatelli & Rubin, 1986).

P2 There is a strong positive intercorrelation between overall physical, facial, bodily, and interpersonal attractiveness (Alicke, Smith, & Klotz, 1987).

P3 Communicators who exhibit a high level of responsiveness via such nonverbal communicative behaviors as head nodding, positive vocal reinforcement (e.g., saying "uh-huh"), forward lean, direct body orientation, and direct eye contact with their interaction partner will be perceived as more interpersonally attractive than those who do not (Remland & Jones, 1989).

P4 Nonverbally expressive communicators are viewed as more interpersonally attractive (Friedman, Riggio, & Casella, 1988; Sabatelli & Rubin, 1986).

P5 Communicators can exhibit emotional expressivity via facial animation, appropriate vocal volume, vocal warmth, smiling and laughing, and gestural and bodily animation (Coker & Burgoon, 1987).

P6 Communicators who choose seating arrangements that provide for decreased interpersonal distance and increased capacity for visual contact with individuals with whom they interact are usually seen as more interpersonally attractive (Riess, 1982).

P7 Communicators who exhibit a low frequency of nonverbal communicative behaviors and cues will be judged to be less interpersonally attractive (Roll, Crowley, & Rappl, 1985).

P8 Communicators who exhibit a narrow pitch and volume range are often perceived to be uninteresting (Leathers, 1986).

Image Dimension IV: Dominance

P1 The eyes serve to define or reveal the distribution of power within social relationships (Webbink, 1986).

P2 Dominance is communicated strongly by staring and submissiveness by gaze avoidance—emotional states associated with gaze aversion include fear, guilt, shame, and social inferiority (Harper, 1985).

P3 Communicators are perceived as increasingly dominant as their amount of eye contact increases (Brooks, Church, & Fraser, 1986).

P4 Communicators become more dominant as their level of looking while speaking increases and their level of looking while listening decreases, that is, their visual dominance ratio goes up (Dovidio & Ellyson, 1985).

P5 Dominance is conveyed by controlling talk time, speaking in a loud voice, and frequently interrupting the interaction partner (Harper, 1985).

P6 Communicators who use hesitations and hedges are perceived as less powerful than those who do not (Hosman, 1989).

P7 Nonverbal indicators of submissiveness include constricted and closed body postures, a limited range of movement, hunched body, downward-turned head, and bodily tension (Harper, 1985).

P8 The soft voice with little volume communicates lack of assertiveness (Montepare & Zebrowitz-McArthur, 1987).

The principles of impression management would seem to require little explanation, but let us look briefly at the principles under the image dimension of dominance to illustrate how some of them might be used. These principles suggest that a person's eye behaviors and vocal cues have a particularly strong impact on judgments of dominance. Note, for example, that you will want to spend less time looking at interaction partners when they are speaking than the amount of time you spend looking at them while *you* are speaking—see Principle 4, which defines the visual dominance ratio. You must also avoid speaking with a soft voice, or a voice that lacks volume, because individuals who speak with a soft voice are typically judged to be unassertive.

Measurement of the Impressions Made

Impression managers who are equipped with the principles of impression management in Figure 9.1 clearly have the potential to make the desired changes in the impressions they are making. Before they become actively engaged in trying to modify the impressions they make on others (or the impressions formed of them by others), however, they must obtain rather detailed and objective information from business associates or significant others about how positive or negative their impressions are. Ken Cooper wrote perceptively in *Nonverbal Communication for Business Success* (1979) that the

> first step in building a successful image is to determine what your current image is. You may not be aware of your image or you may think others don't have an image of you. You are wrong! . . . The challenge is to develop an accurate picture of yourself as others perceive you. (p. 195)

In theory, at least, there are a number of ways to measure the impressions you are making; we will describe two ways. The first measure is a general one that gives you an overall picture of the positive and negative image traits that others are attributing to you. The second measure is set up to provide a precise quantitative reading of how positive or negative the impression you are making, based on each of the four image dimensions described previously.

The personality traits and personal qualities that others attribute to you are called *image traits*. The image traits identified in Figure 9.2 should be useful to the impression manager for at least two reasons. First, each of these traits has been repeatedly identified in empirical research as a trait that perceivers frequently use in forming their impressions of others. Second, specific nonverbal cues have been shown to be strongly linked, perceptually, to each of those image traits.

To obtain a complete description of your own image, ask individuals with whom you frequently interact in social or business situations to use Figure 9.2. They should place a check mark by each trait that they feel is clearly a defining feature of your image. Pay particular attention to the five positive and the five negative image traits that are checked most frequently. By simply tabulating the check marks, you will know what the dominant positive and negative features of your image actually are.

In order to get a more precise reading of how positive or negative the impressions you make are in regard to each of the four image dimensions, use Figure 9.3. In fact, you can simply run multiple copies of this figure and then ask individuals who have been the target of your impression management activities to fill out the form. When the evaluation forms are returned to you, compute a mean or average score for each of the 28 scales.

FIGURE 9.2   Image Traits

confident–anxious	honest–deceitful
friendly–unfriendly	expressive–unexpressive
sensitive–insensitive	mature–immature
spontaneous–unspontaneous	direct–evasive
active–passive	powerful–weak
forceful–tentative	relaxed–tense
wise–foolish	flexible–rigid
feminine–masculine	honest–dishonest
dominant–submissive	interesting–uninteresting
extroverted–introverted	uninhibited–inhibited
strong-willed–weak-willed	intelligent–unintelligent
happy–sad	patient–impatient
likable–unlikable	tactful–tactless
strong–weak	unaffected–affected
assertive–unassertive	comfortable–uncomfortable
considerate–inconsiderate	artistic–inartistic
sociable–unsociable	warm–cold
poised–flustered	agile–awkward
opinionated–unopinionated	competent–incompentent
modest–immodest	pleasant–unpleasant
vigorous–lazy	energetic–sluggish
tolerant–intolerant	sophisticated–naive
emotional–unemotional	gregarious–withdrawn
conventional–unconventional	selfish–unselfish
dependable–undependable	perceptive–dull

Let us assume that you receive the following mean ratings for the sets of scales in Figure 9.3:

Credibility
    Competence: 6.4, 6.2, 5.7, 5.8
    Trustworthiness: 2.3, 2.5, 2.1, 1.8
Likability: 1.3, 1.5, 2.2, 1.7
Interpersonal Attractiveness: 1.8, 1.6, 1.3, 2.1, 1.3, 1.2, 2.0, 1.9
Dominance: 5.8, 6.6, 6.8, 6.4, 5.9, 6.5, 6.7, 6.4.

You will quickly see that your credibility is defined in terms of high competence but low trustworthiness, that you are seen as quite unlikable and interpersonally unattractive, and that you are perceived to be highly dominant.

Making a Favorable Impression by Modifying Communication

You have discovered from the measurements you have undertaken that the impression you are making with regard to trustworthiness, liking, and interpersonal attractiveness is unacceptably negative. You must now decide what changes you can make in your

FIGURE 9.3

Impression Management Evaluation

Name of Impression Manager _____

Name of Evaluator _____

The communicative behaviors and cues that differentiate the impression(s) made by one person as opposed to another are often quite subtle. In order to determine how favorable or unfavorable an impression a given impression manager makes on each of the four image dimensions—credibility, likability, interpersonal attractiveness, and dominance—you will have to observe the impression manager's communicative behaviors live or on videotape. Then you will have to rate the impression manager on scales that define each of the image dimensions. The scales for each dimension and subdimension are listed below. Before you actually use these scales, you should reorder them randomly. Also, change the polarity on half the scales; for example, move the "Competent" label to the right end and the "Incompetent" label to the left end of Scale 1. Then assign a number between 7 and 1 to each scale as you observe the communicative behaviors of a given impression manager. If, for example, you believe the impression manager you are evaluating is extraordinarily competent, that person should receive a rating of 7 on Scale 1. When your ratings are complete, you will have a profile that indicates how favorable or unfavorable an impression the impression manager made on each of the four universal image dimensions.

Credibility

Competence
1. Competent/Incompetent
2. Qualified/Unqualified
3. Well informed/Poorly informed
4. Intelligent/Unintelligent

Trustworthiness:
1. Honest/Dishonest
2. Straightforward/Evasive
3. Trustworthy/Untrustworthy
4. Sincere/Insincere

Likability
1. Likable/Unlikable
2. Pleasant/Unpleasant
3. Agreeable/Disagreeable
4. Lovable/Hateful

Interpersonal Attractiveness
1. Interesting/Uninteresting
2. Desirable/Undesirable
3. Sociable/Unsociable
4. Attentive/Unattentive
5. Expressive/Unexpressive
6. Emotional/Unemotional
7. Social/Unsocial
8. Physically attractive/Physically unattractive

Dominance
1. Active/Passive
2. Assertive/Unassertive
3. Powerful/Powerless
4. Dominant/Submissive
5. Confident/Anxious
6. Relaxed/Tense
7. Direct/Evasive
8. Strong/Weak

---

communicative behaviors and cues so that the individuals with whom you interact will see you as more trustworthy, likable, and interpersonally attractive. You need to do two things at minimum: You must carefully assess the nonverbal communicative behaviors/cues you consistently exhibit to determine which ones reinforce the impression that you are untrustworthy, unlikable, and interpersonally unattractive. Then you should study the impression management principles in Figure 9.1 to determine which of them would be most useful in helping you deal with your impression management problem.

When we consider how we should modify our communicative behaviors and cues to make a more favorable impression, we should remember the importance of first impressions. Successful impression managers pay particular attention to first impressions. They do this because first impressions create images in the mind of the perceiver that are highly resistant to change.

The impression manager who wishes to make a favorable first impression must recognize at least two facts: (a) nonverbal cues are the major determinants of the kind of first impression that we make, and (b) personal appearance and vocal cues are known to have a strong impact on first impressions. By exercising conscious control over our visual and vocal images, we greatly enhance our chances of making a favorable first impression.

When considering the way you would like to look and sound, remember the importance of the physical-attractiveness stereotype and the vocal attractiveness stereotype. Because we also know that perceivers give more weight to negative rather than to positive information, the impression manager begins with an advantage. The message is clear: We should be less concerned with cultivating idealized visual and vocal images and more concerned with eliminating those undesirable features of our image that perceivers use to make unflattering attributions about us.

The importance of appearance cues and vocal cues is not, however, confined to first impressions. Both types of cues also are known to exert a major impact on the long-term impressions we make. The guidelines presented in Figures 9.4 and 9.5 are designed to help you become a more successful impression manager.

FIGURE 9.4   Personal Appearance Guidelines

    1. Strive to meet the dress expectations of the person (or group) with whom you interact by noting such factors as their age, education, class, gender, ethnicity, and region or specific area of residence. In general, it is important that your clothing and other appearance items such as jewelry not be markedly different in quality or level of sophistication from the same items worn by the person with whom you are communicating.
    2. Consider the way you have prioritized the image dimensions of credibility, likability, interpersonal attractiveness, and dominance. If the credibility dimension of competence or authoritativeness is of major concern to you, you should wear dark-colored, conservative clothing. If likability is most important, you may wish to sacrifice some perceived competence by choosing to wear the lighter-colored clothing that is known to enhance perceptions of likability and friendliness.
    3. Your body type should exert a major influence on your choice of clothing and other appearance items. If you are a large and tall person, you could intimidate individuals with whom you interact, due to your size. In order to be seen as less overpowering and more approachable, you would be well advised to choose softer, lighter shades of blue, gray, or beige. Conversely, you might wish to wear darker-colored clothing in order to seem more powerful and authoritative if you are a short and thin person.

FIGURE 9.4 (Continued)

4. Color choice strongly affects the overall impression we make on others. More specifically, color choice has been shown to affect how professional other persons judge us to be. Outer garments tend to be seen as reliable indicators of our status, whereas our accent items are used to make judgments about our personality traits. The color of our main items of clothing—for example, our suits—strongly affects judgments as to whether our clothing is sufficiently conservative for a given occasion; the color of our accent items—for example, ties and scarves—communicates information about our personality.

5. You should be sure that your clothing and other appearance items are sufficiently formal or conservative for your first meeting with another individual. In many business and social situations, a first meeting with another person or group requires that you have maximum credibility. Your appearance is one of the most important determinants of the first impression you will make, and you should recognize that although you can "dress down" when you meet a person for a second time in a business context, you cannot credibly "dress up."

6. You should avoid wearing glasses with heavily tinted or photosensitive lenses. Not only do such items limit the number of people who can identify with you, but also the eye-behavior stereotype dictates that people want to be able to see your eyes. If you are to be trusted, persons with whom you interact must be able to see your eyes.

7. Avoid designer clothing or accessories.

8. Avoid clothing choices that communicate inconsistent messages and, consequently, damage personal credibility—for example, a high-power suit with a low-power pair of shoes.

9. You should not wear any item (class ring, lapel pin, religious symbol, etc.) that serves to highlight your affiliation with a given civic, political, or religious organization. Such personalized accessories may, on occasion, be used to establish common ground with a person of similar background. However, they are more apt to trigger an emotional reaction that will make it more difficult for you to establish common ground with a person who notices that you have chosen to personalize your appearance in such a manner.

10. You should recognize that you will lose authority in the eyes of members of many professional groups if the length of your hair exceeds the norm for such groups. For males in particular, excessive facial hair is sometimes viewed as either expressing an unwillingness to conform to conventional societal standards or expressing a preoccupation with a machismo image.

From *The Professional Image* by S. Bixler, 1984, New York: Putnam; *The Social Psychology of Clothing* (2nd ed.) by S. B. Kaiser, 1990, New York: Macmillan; *New Dress for Success* by J. T. Molloy, 1988, New York: Warner; *Jury Selection, Body Language and the Visual Trial* by J. Rasicot, 1983, Minneapolis: AB Publications; *Silent Sales* by J. Rasicot, 1986, Minneapolis: AB Publications; and *Courtroom Communication Strategies* by L. J. Smith and L. A. Malandro, 1985, New York: Kluwer.

Personal Appearance Guidelines

Most communicators may exercise a number of options to modify, conceal, or eliminate negative features of their personal appearance. The obese individual can diet; the individual with a physical deformity can undergo plastic surgery; the individual with acne can use medicinal ointments; and the individual with crooked teeth can seek orthodontal treatment. In practice, however, those options might not be feasible, because they either are time-consuming and costly or will not correct the physical deformity.

FIGURE 9.5   Vocal Guidelines

Desirable Vocal Cues
1. Strive for a conversational speaking rate of 125 to 150 words per minute. If you are engaging in persuasive communication, then a moderately fast rate has been shown to be effective. Individuals who use a conversational speaking rate are viewed as more pleasant, likable, and friendly than those who do not.
2. Emphasize the most important points you are making with appropriate changes in volume and pitch; the monotone voice has been found to be very damaging to credibility.
3. The voice that is judged most credible is fluent, low-pitched. varied, moderately paced, and general American in dialect and accent.
4. Individuals with a narrow pitch range are viewed as unassertive, uninteresting, and lacking in confidence.
5. Speaking with appropriate variation in rate and pitch will make you appear more dynamic, animated, and extroverted.
6. Faulty or sloppy articulation and improper pronunciation are apt to have a highly negative impact on your perceived competence.
7. Inconsistent messages have a particularly damaging impact on the first impression you make. If you tell someone that you like them or their ideas, be sure to use your voice to reinforce the point you are making so that it sounds believable.
8. Deliberate pauses before the most important points you are making will make you seem more competent and will increase the likelihood that the point you are making will be remembered.

Undesirable Vocal Cues
1. To make a favorable first impression, try to eliminate nonfluencies such as "uh." incomplete words, and incomplete sentences. The nonfluent individual is usually perceived as underconfident, anxious, and less competent.
2. Avoid lengthy pauses before responding to a question. because such pauses raise questions about your competence and make you seem indecisive.
3. The excessively loud voice is associated with unseemly aggressiveness.
4. Seek to eliminate or minimize flatness, nasality, and tenseness in your voice. Those vocal qualities reinforce perceptions that an individual is nondynamic, uninteresting, and withdrawn.
5. Do not speak at a rate of over 200 words a minute, because an accelerated speaking rate is associated with an unacceptable level of anxiety.
6. Avoid interrupting others, because interruptions help to create the impression that you are socially insensitive.

   Clothing choice represents the most effective and efficient means of controlling your personal appearance (Damhorst, 1990). When you consider the implications of the association principle, you will realize that you must dress so as to concentrate attention on the most flattering features of your personal appearance, while diverting attention from the features that might be used to make negative attributions about your personal qualities (Francis, 1992).
   No one set of appearance guidelines will serve the impression management goals of all people in all situations all of the time (Gray, 1993). Nevertheless, there are basic guidelines that can be useful to many different people communicating in a wide variety of contexts (Roach-Higgins & Eicher, 1992). The guidelines in Figure 9.4 are drawn from some of the most valuable references on the subject.

These personal appearance guidelines may perhaps prove to be most useful in combatting or neutralizing features of personal appearance that are associated in a negative way with the physical-attractiveness stereotype. For example, what are the implications of the clothing guidelines for the big-busted woman with an endomorphic body type who is overweight? If she chooses to wear bright colors, she accentuates those physical features that have been linked perceptually with low self-confidence, below-average intelligence and competence, and submissiveness. Such a perceptual penalty could be avoided or minimized by the choice of neutral colors, which divert attention from bust size, body weight, and body type.

Consider also the importance of making choices that minimize the possibility that the perceiver will obtain other kinds of negative information from your personal appearance. Why should the salesperson who is a graduate of Southeastern Institute of Technology (SIT) not wear a class ring when making a sales call? The reason is obvious. The sales prospect might be a graduate of another university and have negative feelings about SIT. Moreover, the skillful impression manager should avoid wearing deeply tinted contact lenses or glasses. To hide or obscure your eyes is to perpetuate the part of the eye-behavior stereotype that suggests that untrustworthy individuals wear dark eyeglasses.

Your specific situation might require that you obtain much more specialized information on a subject such as the psychological impact of the color of clothing, the kinds of accent items you should wear, or the choice of a briefcase or an umbrella. The sources cited in Figure 9.4 provide highly specialized information and guidance on those appearance items.

Vocal Guidelines

Vocal cues play a central role in shaping the first impression that you make. Chapter 8 emphasized that the vocal cues of a communicator have been found to affect all three dimensions of credibility—competence, trustworthiness, and dynamism. Perhaps more importantly, we know that vocal cues are a major source of information that perceivers use to make judgments about the other three image dimensions that are the defining components of the impressions. For example, we know that vocal cues are major determinants of judgments made about how dominant or submissive you are.

Figure 9.5 provides specific guidelines, grounded in empirical research; see Chapter 8 for supporting references. By carefully considering the nature of desirable vocal cues, you increase the probability that others will assign a flattering personality profile to you. As the guidelines suggest, positive personality traits and personal qualities are associated with a conversational speaking style that features substantial but appropriate variations in rate, pitch, and volume.

Because perceivers attach more weight to negative than to positive information about a person, you should take pains to minimize or eliminate the use of undesirable vocal cues. If you place a high value on being perceived as confident, you must take pains to avoid nonfluencies and an excessive speaking rate. Both kinds of vocal cues have repeatedly been found to communicate the impression that the communicator has an unacceptably low level of self-confidence and an unacceptably high level of anxiety.

The guidelines in Figure 9.5 should help you to use your voice in such a way that you associate yourself with the flattering features of the vocal attractiveness stereotype and dissociate yourself from the unflattering features. When combined with the information contained in Chapter 10, these guidelines give you the potential to control the sound of your voice in ways advantageous to you. Indeed, Schlenker and Wowra (2003) found that being successful in one impression management context can spill over into future situations and lead to additional success.

Summary

This chapter begins by reviewing impression formation and its four main elements: stereotypes, first impressions, selective perception, and last impressions. Then, we emphasize the importance of impression management in a variety of real-world contexts. Impression management is defined as an individual's attempt to exercise conscious control over selected communicative behaviors and cues—particularly nonverbal cues—for purposes of making a desired impression.

Impressions are defined by four image dimensions: credibility, likability, interpersonal attractiveness, and dominance. How important each of these image dimensions is to you will depend on your motives, the context in which you communicate, your objectives, and a number of other factors. Impression managers typically prioritize these image dimensions in terms of their importance to them.

An understanding of how an individual is motivated in a particular situation enhances our ability to predict how that individual will behave, because motives serve to guide a person's behaviors in ways that person judges to be effective in reaching one or more goals. The major classes of motives of most importance to the impression manager are achievement motives, affiliation motives, social approval motives, and mastery motives.

This chapter develops an original conceptualization of the stages in the impression management process. Much of the chapter's second section concentrates on the guidelines that the impression manager can use to implement the stages or steps in that process.

R E F E R E N C E S

Albada, K. F., Knapp, M. L., & Theune, K. E. (2002). Interaction appearance theory: Changing perceptions of physical attractiveness through social interaction. *Communication Theory, 12,* 8–40.

Albright, L., Kenny, D. A., & Malloy, T. E. (1988). Consensus in personality judgments at zero acquaintance. *Journal of Personality and Social Psychology, 55,* 387–395.

Alicke, M. D., Smith, R. H., & Klotz, M. L. (1987). Judgments of physical attractiveness: The role of faces and bodies. *Personality and Social Psychology Bulletin, 12,* 381–389.

Andersen, P. A. (1985). Nonverbal immediacy in interpersonal communication. In A. W. Seigman & S. Feldstein (Eds.), *Multichannel integration of nonverbal behavior* (pp. 1–36). Hillsdale, NJ: Erlbaum.

Bixler, S. (1984). *The professional image: The total program for marketing yourself visually.* New York: Putnam.

Brembeck, W. L., & Howell, W. S. (1976). *Persuasion: A means of social influence.* Englewood Cliffs, NJ: Prentice-Hall.

Brooks, C. I., Church, M. A., & Fraser, L. (1986). Effects of duration of eye contact on judgments of personality characteristics. *The Journal of Social Psychology, 126,* 71–78.

Burgoon, J. K., Manusov, V., Mineo, P., & Hale, J. L. (1985). Effects of gaze on hiring, credibility, attraction and relational message interpretation. *Journal of Nonverbal Behavior, 9,* 133–146.

Burgoon, J. K., & Saine, T. (1978). *The unspoken dialogue: An introduction to nonverbal communication.* Boston: Houghton Mifflin.

Coker, D. A., & Burgoon, J. K. (1987). The nature of conversational involvement and nonverbal encoding patterns. *Human Communication Research, 13,* 463–494.

Cooper, K. (1979). *Nonverbal communication for business success.* New York: AMACOM.

Damhorst, M. L. (1990). In search of a common thread: Classification of information communicated through dress. *Clothing Textiles Research Journal, 8,* 1–12.

DeMeuse, K. P. (1987). A review of the effects of nonverbal cues in the performance appraisal process. *Journal of Occupational Psychology, 60,* 207–226.

DePaulo, B. M. (1992). Nonverbal behavior and self-presentation. *Psychological Bulletin, 111,* 151–161.

Dion, K. L., & Dion, K. K. (1987). Belief in a just world and physical attractiveness stereotyping. *Journal of Personality and Social Psychology, 52,* 775–780.

Dovidio, J. F., & Ellyson, S. L. (1985). Patterns of visual dominance behavior in humans. In S. L. Ellyson & J. F. Dovidio (Eds.), *Power, dominance, and nonverbal behavior* (pp. 129–149). New York: Springer-Verlag.

Edinger, J. A., & Patterson, M. L. (1983). Nonverbal involvement and social control. *Psychological Bulletin, 93,* 30–56.

Ekman, P. (1985). *Telling lies: Clues to deceit in the marketplace, politics, and marriage.* New York: W. W. Norton.

Ekman, P., & Friesen, W. V. (1982). Felt, false, and miserable smiles. *Journal of Nonverbal Behavior, 6,* 238–258.

Ellyson, S. L., & Dovidio, J. F. (1985). Dominance and nonverbal behaviors: Basic concepts and issues. In S. L. Ellyson & J. F. Dovidio (Eds.), *Power, dominance, and nonverbal behavior* (pp. 1–27). New York: Springer-Verlag.

Exline, R. V. (1985). Multichannel transmission of nonverbal behavior and the perception of powerful men: The presidential debates of 1976. In S. L. Ellyson & J. F. Dovidio (Eds.), *Power, dominance, and nonverbal behavior* (pp. 183–206). New York: Springer-Verlag.

Francis, S. K. (1992). Effects of perceived clothing deprivation on high school students' social participation. *Clothing and Textiles Research Journal, 10,* 29–33.

Friedman, H. S., Riggio, R. E., & Casella, D. F. (1988). Nonverbal skill, personal charisma, and initial attraction. *Personality and Social Psychology Bulletin, 14,* 203–211.

Gangestad, S. W., & Snyder, M. (2000). Self-monitoring: Appraisal and reappraisal. *Psychological Bulletin, 126,* 530–555.

Goffman, E. (1959). *The presentation of self in everyday life.* Garden City, NY: Doubleday.

Gray, J. (1993). *The winning image.* New York: American Management Association.

Harper, R. G. (1985). Power, dominance, and nonverbal behavior: An overview. In S. L. Ellyson & J. F. Dovidio (Eds.), *Power, dominance, and nonverbal behavior* (pp. 29–66). New York: Springer-Verlag.

Henley, N. M., & Harmon, S. (1985). The nonverbal semantics of power and gender: A perceptual study. In S. L. Ellyson & J. F. Dovidio (Eds.), *Power, dominance and nonverbal behavior* (pp. 151–164). New York: Springer-Verlag.

Hippel, W. V., Hippel, C. V., Conway, L., Preacher, K. J., Schooler, J. W., & Radvansky, G. A. (2005). Coping with stereotype threat: Denial as an impression management strategy. *Journal of Personality and Social Psychology, 89,* 22–35.

Hosman, L. A. (1989). The evaluative consequences of hedges, hesitations, and intensifiers: Powerful and powerless speech styles. *Human Communication Research, 15,* 383–406.

Johnson, C., & Vinson, L. (1990). Placement and frequency of powerless talk and impression formation. *Communication Quarterly, 38,* 325–333.

Jones, E. E., & Pittman, T. S. (1982). Toward a general theory of strategic self-presentation. In J. Suls (Ed.), *Psychological perspectives on the self* (Vol. 1, pp. 213–262). Hillsdale, NJ: Erlbaum.

Jonsson, C., & Hall, M. (2003). Communication: An essential aspect of diplomacy. *International Studies Perspectives, 4,* 195–210.

Kacmar, K. M., & Carlson, D. S. (1994). Using impression management in women's job search processes. *American Behavioral Scientist, 37,* 682–696.

Kaiser, S. B. (1990). *The social psychology of clothing: Symbolic appearances in context* (2nd ed.). New York: Macmillan.

Kim, H., & Papacharissi, Z. (2003). Cross-cultural differences in online self-presentation: A content analysis of personal Korean and U.S. home pages. *Asian Journal of Communication, 13,* 100–119.

Kleinke, C. L. (1986). Gaze and eye contact: A research review. *Psychological Bulletin, 100,* 78–100.

Leathers, D. G. (1986). *Successful nonverbal communication* (1st ed.). New York: Macmillan.

Leathers, D. G. (1988). Impression management training: Conceptualization and application to personal selling. *Journal of Applied Communication Research, 16,* 126–145.

Leathers, D. G., & Ross, C. S. (1990). *Theoretical conceptualization of the impression management functions of nonverbal communication.* Unpublished manuscript.

Lopes, J., & Fletcher, C. (2004). Fairness of impression management in employment interviews: A cross-country study of the role of equity and machiavellianism. *Social Behavior and Personality, 32,* 747–768.

McClelland, D. C. (1987). *Human motivation.* Cambridge: Cambridge University Press.

McCroskey, J. C., & Teven, J. J. (1999). Goodwill: A reexamination of the construct and its measurement. *Communication Monographs, 66,* 90–103.

Mehrabian, A. (1981). *Silent messages* (2nd ed.). Belmont, CA: Wadsworth.

Milton, P. (2006, May 1). *Magician spending week in water tank.* Associated Press.

Molloy, J. T. (1988). *New dress for success.* New York: Warner.

Montepare, J., & Zebrowitz-McArthur, L. (1987). Perceptions of adults with childlike voices in two cultures. *Journal of Experimental Social Psychology, 23,* 331–349.

Muehlenhard, C., & Scardino, T. (1985). What will he think? Men's impressions of women who initiate dates and achieve academically. *Journal of Counseling Psychology, 32,* 560–569.

Nazareno, A. (2004, July 3). Handshake, body language give powerful first impression in business world. *Knight Ridder Tribune Business News,* p. 1.

Olson, I. R., & Marshuetz, C. (2005). Facial attractiveness is appraised in a glance. *Emotion, 5,* 498–502.

Overwalle, F. V., & Labiouse, C. (2004). A recurrent connectionist model of person impression formation. *Personality and Social Psychology Review, 8,* 28–61.

Patterson, M. L. (1987). Presentational and affect-management functions of nonverbal involvement. *Journal of Nonverbal Behavior, 11,* 110–122.

Patterson, M. L. (1994). Interaction behavior and person perceptions: An integrative approach. *Small Group Research, 25,* 171–188.

Patterson, M. L. (1995). A parallel process model of nonverbal communication. *Journal of Nonverbal Behavior, 19,* 3–29.

Rasicot, J. (1983). *Jury selection, body language and the visual trial.* Minneapolis, MN: AB Publications.

Rasicot, J. (1986). *Silent sales.* Minneapolis, MN: AB Publications.

Remland, M. S., & Jones, T. S. (1989). The effects of nonverbal involvement and communication apprehension on state anxiety, interpersonal attraction, and speech duration. *Communication Quarterly, 37,* 170–183.

Richmond, V. P., McCroskey, J. C., & Payne, S. K. (1987). *Nonverbal behavior in interpersonal relations.* Englewood Cliffs, NJ: Prentice-Hall.

Riess, M. (1982). Seating preferences as impression management: A literature review and theoretical integration. *Communication, 11,* 85–113.

Riggio, R. E., & Friedman, H. S. (1986). Impression formation: The role of expressive behavior. *Journal of Personality and Social Psychology, 30,* 421–427.

Roach-Higgins, M. E., & Eicher, J. B. (1992). Dress and identity. *Clothing and Textiles Research Journal, 10,* 1–8.

Roll, S. A., Crowley, M. A., & Rappl, L. E. (1985). Client perceptions of counselors' nonverbal behavior: A reevaluation. *Counselor Education and Supervision, 24,* 234–243.

Rosenberg, S. W., Bohan, L., McCafferty, P., & Harris, K. (1986). The image and the vote: The effect of candidate presentation on voter preference. *American Journal of Political Science, 30,* 108–127.

Ross, C. S. (1991). *Image dimensions and impression managers' perception of nonverbal behavior.* Unpublished doctoral dissertation, University of Georgia, Athens.

Sabatelli, R., & Rubin, M. (1986). Nonverbal expressiveness and physical attractiveness as mediators of interpersonal perceptions. *Journal of Nonverbal Behavior, 10,* 120–133.

Schlenker, B. R. (1980). *Impression management.* Monterey, CA: Brooks/Cole.

Schlenker, B. R., & Britt, T. W. (1999). Beneficial impression management: Strategically controlling information to help friends. *Journal of Personality and Social Psychology, 76,* 559–573.

Schlenker, B. R., & Britt, T. W. (2001). Strategically controlling information to help friends: Effects of empathy and friendship strength on beneficial impression management. *Journal of Experimental Social Psychology, 37,* 357–372.

Schlenker, B. R., Diugoleckie, D. W., & Doherty, K. (1994). The impact of self-presentations on self-appraisals and behavior—The power of public commitment. *Personality and Social Psychology Bulletin, 7,* 79–100.

Schlenker, B. R., & Wowra, S. A. (2003). Carryover effects of feeling socially transparent or impenetrable on strategic self-presentation. *Journal of Personality and Social Psychology, 85,* 871–880.

Smith, L. J., & Malandro, L. A. (1985). *Courtroom communication strategies.* New York: Kluwer.

Snyder, M. (1974). Self-monitoring of expressive behavior. *Journal of Personality and Social Psychology, 30,* 526–537.

Street, R. L., Jr., & Brady, R. M. (1982). Speech rate acceptance ranges as a function of evaluative domain, listener speech rate, and communication context. *Communication Monographs, 49,* 290–308.

Street, R. L., Jr., & Hooper, R. (1982). A model of speech style evaluation. In E. B. Ryan & H. Giles (Eds.), *Attitudes toward language variation: Social and applied contexts* (pp. 175–188). London: Arnold.

Tedeschi, J. T., & Norman, W. (1985). Social power, self-presentation, and the self. In B. R. Schlenker (Ed.), *The self and social life* (pp. 293–322). New York: McGraw-Hill.

Tedeschi, J. T., & Riess, M. (1981). Identities, the phenomenal self, and laboratory research. In J. T. Tedeschi (Ed.), *Impression management theory and social psychological research* (pp. 3–22). New York: Academic Press.

Teven, J. J., & Comadena, M. E. (1996). The effects of office aesthetic quality on students' perceptions of teacher credibility and communicator style. *Communication Research Reports, 13,* 101–108.

Teven, J. J., & Hanson, T. L. (2004). The impact of teacher immediacy and perceived caring on teacher competence and trustworthiness. *Communication Quarterly, 52,* 39–53.

Teven, J. J., & McCroskey, J. C. (1996). The relationship of perceived teacher caring with student learning and teacher evaluation. *Communication Education, 46,* 1–9.

Thweatt, K. S., & McCroskey, J. C. (1998). The impact of teacher immediacy and misbehaviors on teacher credibility. *Communication Education, 47,* 348–358.

Turnley, W. H., & Bolino, M. C. (2001). Achieving desired images while avoiding undesired images: Exploring the role of self-monitoring in impression management. *Journal of Applied Psychology, 86,* 351–360.

Webbink, P. (1986). *The power of the eyes.* New York: Springer.

Worsley, A. (1981). In the eye of the beholder: Social and personal characteristics of teenagers and their impressions of themselves and fat and slim people. *British Journal of Medical Psychology, 54,* 231–242.

10 Selling Yourself Nonverbally: Politics and Sales

This chapter focuses on the role of nonverbal communication in the development of personal credibility. The nonverbal communication behaviors of political candidates and corporate sales representatives are used to illustrate the specific perceptual effects of such behaviors on credibility. Specific guidelines for developing credibility are presented, and the nonverbal profile of the credible communicator is highlighted.

Politicians live and die by their statements, their personal demeanor, and their nonverbal behavior. They are a 24/7 spectacle open to criticism. People are constantly watching them. They are easy targets of criticism and have to "sell themselves" every day while on the campaign trail and especially while in office. There are several good examples of this. Do you recall the words, "I never had sexual relations with that woman, Monica Lewinsky"? Those words from Bill Clinton were a sound bite years after he had said them. Or consider these words from George H. Bush: "Read my lips, no new taxes." That campaign promise was violated just years later. His son George W. Bush referred to terrorists as the "axis of evil." The problem was that his statement vilified a group of people in the process.

Politicians must also look at their nonverbal behavior. Perhaps as valuable if not more important than verbal communication, nonverbal messages can be more subtle and more difficult to control, but still have a lasting impact on the viewing populace. Later in the chapter we will look briefly at some historical presidential debates and then turn our attention to modern political debates in more detail.

Sales is another area where people are always on guard about nonverbal messages they might be sending to a potential customer. If you doubt the importance of credibility in personal selling, consider the case of the agritech salesperson in the Rio Grande Valley of Texas. The prospect is a vegetable farmer in the valley who has more than 50,000 acres in cultivation. The salesperson must try to persuade the farmer to purchase a liquid hormone that will be sprayed onto his vegetables and will allegedly increase his yield by up to 25 percent. Because the liquid hormone is a new product, results from field research are still limited. The farmer recognizes that a decision to use the salesperson's product on all of his vegetables will cost him many thousands of dollars. He does not want to make the wrong decision.

Salespeople in the Rio Grande Valley who actually find themselves in such a selling situation tell us that their personal credibility is frequently the critical issue. Their company's credibility might have been important in arranging the sales call, but it is their personal credibility that is of most concern to the farmers. Do the farmers find them to be knowledgeable and trustworthy enough to buy from them? One farmer told an agritech salesperson, "I can't buy from you. I give old Ned all of my business. He knows what he is doing. I trust him. I give Ned all of my business because he has never done me wrong."

The farmers found "old Ned" to be credible because to them he was believable. Credibility is a measure of how believable you are to those with whom you interact. The development of high credibility does not, of course, provide any assurance that you will achieve your objectives. Many other factors may also affect your persuasive effectiveness (Brembeck & Howell, 1976). Generally, however, the higher your credibility, the greater your chances for success as a persuader (Burgoon & Saine, 1978; Petty & Cacioppo, 1986). One study has found that high credibility of the speaker is more persuasive when the receiver is opposed to the message, and lower credibility of the speaker is more persuasive when the receiver already agrees with the message (Chebat et al., 1988). In addition, expertise and credibility seem to have a more positive impact on persuasion when the receiver believes that the message is more relevant to her or him (Kruglanski & Thompson, 1999).

A modern example of a salesperson who has regained lost credibility is Martha Stewart. Before having a business in her name, a line of products in Kmart stores, and several TV shows, Stewart had to regain lost credibility after her prison sentence a few years ago for insider stock information. Through her show, which airs daily, and her Web sites and magazine, Stewart has been able to reach her original audience and gain new interest. She is warm and friendly, smiles frequently, and just seems sincere with her audience. In light of her dishonest past, she has rekindled the relationship with her audience and regained the trust she'd lost.

Dimensions of Credibility

Credibility is a concept that has been studied extensively by communication scholars for at least four decades. These scholars have disagreed about how many dimensions define credibility and about the methodological procedures that should be used to discover such dimensions (Infante, Parker, Clarke, Wilson, & Nathu, 1983; Liska, 1978; Tucker, 1971). There does seem to be a consensus among credibility scholars with regard to two important definitional points, however: (1) the two most important dimensions of credibility are *competence* and *trustworthiness;* (2) *competence* is clearly the more important dimension of credibility.

Although *competence* and *trustworthiness* are clearly the two most important components of credibility, a third component, *dynamism,* is also frequently cited by speech communication scholars (Brembeck & Howell, 1976; Infante, 1980). Therefore, credibility is defined in this book by the three components just identified.

We should note that Infante (1980) argued that dynamism scales are evaluative scales that measure how "potent" a communicator's behavior is. He maintained that dynamism scales should, therefore, be included in the "general person perception set" that applies to impression formation, whereas competence and trustworthiness scales are properly used as measurements of a communication receiver's attitude toward the communication source.

McCroskey and Dunham's special report (1966) that identified two defining dimensions of credibility—competence or authoritativeness and trustworthiness or character— has proven to be a benchmark for credibility research. Not only did McCroskey and Dunham identify competence and trustworthiness as the two most important dimensions of credibility, but the figures they cite for the variance accounted for by the two factors also suggested that competence is almost twice as important as trustworthiness. Although as many as five dimensions of credibility have been identified in empirical research (Burgoon, 1976), the most common finding in subsequent studies has been that competence and trustworthiness are the two central defining dimensions of credibility (Beatty & Behnke, 1980; Lui & Standing, 1989; McCroskey & Young, 1981; Sternthal, Phillips, & Dholakia, 1978). The preponderance of impression management researchers also conclude that credibility is defined by the two dimensions of competence and trustworthiness. Because dynamism has also been identified as a third but much less important dimension than competence and trustworthiness, credibility will be treated as three dimensional in this chapter. As we learned in Chapter 9 on impression management, credibility also includes the issues of caring and goodwill (McCroskey & Teven, 1999; Teven & Hanson, 2004; Teven & McCroskey, 1996).

How competent, trustworthy, and dynamic a communicator is judged to be will vary, depending on such factors as personal reputation, organizational affiliation, personal appearance, and, most importantly, communicative behaviors. Although individuals have the potential to exercise considerable control over their perceived credibility, we should recognize that credibility is not defined by inherent qualities or characteristics of the source. On the contrary, credibility or believability is the receiver's perception of the message sender.

A person's perceived competence, trustworthiness, and dynamism can be positively or negatively affected in a given situation by the person's communication. For example, professors who provide inaccurate information in their lectures will lower their perceived competence. An individual's perceived competence, trustworthiness, and dynamism may vary from extremely high to extremely low in a given situation; therefore, those terms may be properly identified as *dimensions of credibility*.

Competence

Competence is an important dimension of credibility. Individuals who are recognized as experts on a given subject inspire confidence. Conversely, *incompetence* is a word with unflattering connotations. In our society, competence is associated with excellence. For example, universities that are widely recognized for their academic excellence receive such recognition in large part because their faculty members have been judged to be unusually competent.

As Table 10.1 suggests, an individual's perceived level of competence may be assessed by rating that individual on a set of scales that reflect how competent, qualified, well informed, and intelligent that individual is judged to be. When individuals exhibit communicative behaviors that raise serious doubts about their competence, their competence ratings usually drop sharply.

Until recently, competence was thought to be perceived almost solely according to the manifest content of a person's speech communication. The key questions were: (a) How

TABLE 10.1   Measuring Personal Credibility

Dimensions of Credibility	Initial Credibility	Terminal Credibility
Competence		
1. competent/incompetent	_____	_____
2. qualified/unqualified	_____	_____
3. well informed/poorly informed	_____	_____
4. intelligent/unintelligent	_____	_____
Trustworthiness		
1. honest/dishonest	_____	_____
2. straightforward/evasive	_____	_____
3. trustworthy/untrustworthy	_____	_____
4. sincere/insincere	_____	_____
Dynamism		
1. assertive/unassertive	_____	_____
2. bold/timid	_____	_____
3. forceful/meek	_____	_____
4. active/inactive	_____	_____

Communicator's Name _____

much relevant and useful information does an individual have on a given subject? (b) How familiar is the individual with that information? and (c) Does the individual use that information effectively to support carefully qualified generalizations? We now know, however, that our nonverbal communication often exerts a dramatic influence on how competent we are perceived to be.

One study found that perceived competence changes across racial lines. Black students were more likely to rate black professors as credible when they taught an ethnic class than white professors who were assigned the same class. Thus, ethnicity seems to impact, in some situations, perceptions of competence and expertise, given the subject and situation (Hendrix, 1995).

Competence has routinely been associated with expertise or expertness, and in some cases, affect for students (Myers & Bryant, 2004). In addition, these concerns are of paramount concern for the political candidate. A recent investigation found that credibility increases the chances of securing votes, even when the candidate resorted to negative political advertising (Yoon, Pinkleton, & Ko, 2005).

Trustworthiness

As a dimension of credibility, *trustworthiness* is a measure of our character as seen by those persons with whom we interact. Our presumed level of trustworthiness is based on an assessment of our personal qualities, intentions, and attitudes. The dominant sources of information that are used to determine how trustworthy people are may be nonverbal (McMahan, 1976), because individuals will not usually tell you how honest or sincere they actually are. Their actions are usually more important than their words. Indeed, research suggests that trustworthiness is more believable than expertness (Lui & Standing, 1989).

Recently, one study found that trustworthiness was related to attractiveness; thus more positive attributes of trust were formed when the subject was attractive (Zaidel, Bava, & Reis, 2003). Further, computer technicians are beginning to incorporate nonverbal communication into their models. In what are known as ECAs (embodied conversational agents), computer programmers are putting "trust" in the faces of their computer persons. As a way to engage the user and support interactive media, computer companies recognize the value of including "trust" in the computer face—whether real or virtual (Cassell & Bickmore, 2000).

As Table 10.1 indicates, you can assess a person's perceived level of trustworthiness by rating that individual on a set of scales that reveal how honest, straightforward, trustworthy, and sincere you judge that individual to be. Successful communicators almost invariably receive high ratings on this dimension of credibility.

Dynamism

The third dimension of credibility—*dynamism*—defines people's credibility or image in terms of the level of confidence they are perceived to have. The ability to project a feeling of confidence is important because it is apt to trigger a reciprocal feeling of confidence in those with whom we communicate. Further, the more dynamic we are perceived to be, the more credible we are apt to be. According to one authority, the "shy, introverted, soft-spoken individual is generally perceived as less credible than the assertive, extroverted, and forceful individual. The great leaders in history have generally been dynamic people. They were assertive and dynamic people" (DeVito, 1980).

Several studies have shown the negative impact nonfluencies have upon perceptions of credibility, thus reducing persuasion. Engstrom (1994) found that newscasters are perceived as less credibile when they use nonfluencies in their nightly newscasts, thus reducing perceptions of their expertise. In addition, research has pointed to reduced perceptions of competence when speakers use an excessive amount of nonfluencies in their delivery (Burgoon, Birk, & Pfau, 1990). These researchers found little effect of speech nonfluencies upon trustworthiness, however.

A communicator's level of dynamism can be accurately assessed by rating that individual on a set of scales that reflect how assertive, bold, forceful, and active he or she is judged to be. The meek may ultimately inherit the earth, but for the moment, at least, they have a serious credibility problem. Political satirists on *Saturday Night Live* have enjoyed high ratings by poking fun at political figures of the recent past. We remember the sketches of George H. Bush saying, "Not going to do it. Would not be prudent." Bill Clinton has been portrayed in many sketches. George W. Bush has been portrayed alongside "great speeches of the century." The sketch shows viewers a clip of Martin Luther King, Jr., saying, "I have a dream," John F. Kennedy saying, "Ask not what your country can do for you, but what you can do for your country," and then George W. Bush saying, "Uhh . . . uh, well . . . I . . . uh . . . [pause] . . . uh." Hillary Clinton has had a fanfare of caricatures drawn up of her as she has campaigned for president in 2007–2008.

The development of a communicator's credibility requires that individual dimensions of credibility be assessed at two points in time: *Initial credibility* is the credibility the communicator possesses *before* communication begins. *Terminal credibility* is the credibility that the communicator is seen to possess *after* communication occurs in a given situation. Terminal credibility is the product of the communicator's initial credibility and the credibility that was derived as a result of the individual's communicative behaviors (DeVito, 1980).

The scales in Table 10.1 should be used to make an accurate evaluation of a person's credibility. Write in the name of the communicator and rate the individual on the 12 scales measuring level of competence, trustworthiness, and dynamism. The initial set of ratings should be in the "Initial Credibility" column.

Imagine that the 12 sets of terms are on 12 separate bipolar scales. Use a 7-point scale to rate the person, with a 7 to identify the term on the left side of the scale and a 1 to identify the term on the right side of the scale. For example, if you judge an individual to be extremely competent before communication begins, you would put a 7 in the first blank in the "Initial Credibility" column. If you cannot decide whether the person is competent or incompetent, put a 4 in the same blank. A person perceived as extremely incompetent would receive a rating of 1. Any value from 7 through 1 may be used.

After the communication is completed, cover up the first column and rate the person again in the "Terminal Credibility" column. You should then have a before-and-after profile of the communicator's credibility.

Illustrating the Impact of Nonverbal Cues on Credibility

Presidential candidates engage in the type of personal selling that has generated widespread interest in this country. Millions of people study the candidates' efforts to sell themselves; those people then make their own judgments as to how the candidates' communication affected their credibility. Because of the high visibility of the candidates' communicative efforts, the presidential debates represent a useful vehicle for illustrating how nonverbal cues can affect credibility. (Gregory & Gallagher, 2002; Ladd, 2000; "Voters and the Internet," 2000).

Political Debates and Credibility

In this section of the chapter, we will briefly look at some important historical presidential debates and their key nonverbal elements. Next, we will look in great detail at modern debates. We will examine the 2004 Bush–Kerry presidential debates, the 2004 Cheney–Edwards vice presidential debates, and other recent significant political debates at the senatorial and governor level.

Historical Presidential Debates. There have been significant presidential debates in the recent past. The Ford–Carter debates of 1976 are noteworthy. Carter's strength was that his smile, eye behavior, and gestures were better after the first debate. His weaknesses included the nonfluencies in his speech and his rigid body behavior. In contrast, Ford's strengths were his effective use of powerful gestures and body language, as discussed in Chapter 4. One weakness was that he rarely smiled.

Another event of historical interest is the Clinton–Dole debate in 1996. Clinton was a superior communicator and debater. Dole perhaps identified best with veterans and common folk. Dole had shifty eye behavior, which lowered people's perception of his competence, while his kinesic behavior was more favorable. Leathers observed that Dole shifted his eyes as much as 160 times per minute. On the other hand, Clinton was successful in his campaign and debates. He was able to identify with younger audiences, especially college students, for example, when he used an MTV audience as a rallying effort to "rock the vote."

The 2000 Gore–Bush debates were also full of exciting moments. George W. Bush generally remained calm and collected. While Bush was resolved on key issues, he had several distracting mannerisms including nonfluencies, increasing use of self-adaptors (indicating nervousness), and hesitating before answering questions. While Gore was equally astute on issues, his nonverbal messages were also weak. Gore routinely interrupted Bush, to the extent that Bush benefited since the viewer was sympathetic with his situation. Gore also spoke with a flat and monotone voice on several occasions.

2004 Bush–Kerry Presidential Debates.   George W. Bush and John Kerry had a series of three presidential debates during the 2004 campaign. Although more successful in his later debates, Bush did poorly in his first debate with Kerry. In fact, the *Atlanta Journal & Constitution* asked Eaves and four other Georgia University debate coaches to assess the debate skills of the candidates during the election year. Eaves noticed that Bush had poor nonverbal skills although he excelled in the verbal skill area. With both nonverbal and verbal factors considered, the team of five critics scored the debate: Kerry received an A−, while Bush received a B+. In fact, Bush even admitted his first-round defeat to close colleagues. His defeat made the candidates closer in their chances and damaged some of Bush's predebate campaign image (DeFrank, 2004).

These debate scores are important because voters routinely gather their largest amount of information from televised debates, whether by watching them, reading reviews, or taking to friends. This has been the case in several presidential debates since the 1970s (Holbrook, 1999).

One reason for the negative perceptions of candidates' nonverbal communication today might be the way televised debates are formatted. Today's media technology allows the TV audience to see the nonverbal displays of candidates when they are not speaking. This is known as the *split-screen format*. One study found that when candidates' nonverbal disagreement is apparent through the split-screen format, viewers give those candidates lower ratings of credibility (Seiter & Weger, 2005). Eaves found in his analysis of Bush in the first debate that Bush's nonverbal gestures, which were apparent in the split-screen format, were generally poor. Such manifestations of nonverbal disagreement included facial disgust, nervous twitching, and numerous eye shifts.

There were a total of three debates between Bush and Kerry. As in any debate, the first one is more heavily watched and thus has more impact in the campaign than the remaining debates in the series (Benoit, Hansen, & Verser, 2003; Holbrook, 1999). In the Bush–Kerry debate series, viewership was strong throughout, the best since 1992. In fact, more people tuned in for the debates than watched the Yankees and Red Sox in the

Kerry and Bush greet the audience at their debate.

playoffs that year (Olson, 2005). Since Bush's team knew that his debating skills had been poor in the first debate, they consulted with a debating school in the Northeast to refine his style, especially his nonverbal elements. After consultating with the debating school, Bush was able to improve his skills and score much better in the second and third debates against Kerry. Bush's debate consulting and positive demeanor with voters on a personal level worked well, and he defeated Kerry for the presidency later that year.

While Kerry may have been a better debater, Bush sold himself in other ways. Bush, unlike Kerry, excelled in personal, one-on-one encounters with voters. Several sources indicated that Bush also interviewed better than Kerry. The Kerry campaign became really nervous when Kerry had to respond to impromptu questions. He did better than Bush only in prepared speeches (Nelson, 2004). Bush used his cowboy image and his southern accent to his advantage. He was able to approach the voters on the sidelines, while Kerry's demeanor was confusing or alienating at times for would-be voters.

Credibility was also won and lost in the advertising for Kerry and Bush. We now readily recognize the 2004 TV ads that started or ended this way: "I'm George Bush and I approve of this message . . ." or "I'm John Kerry and I approve of this message. . . ." We certainly tired of hearing those components of the attack ads—they were like a broken record. What effect did these TV ad strategies have on the viewers who were assessing the candidates' credibility? Were the independent or nonpartisan ads really nonaligned?

Let's review the controversy of these ads. Candidates would often have ads running under assumed names. For example, MoveOnPac.org ran several ads that were supported by John Kerry, but then other groups ran ads that attacked Kerry's Vietnam War record, and Bush denied ever having any involvement with or approval of the ads. One study looked at the ads that Bush and Kerry used in the 2004 election campaign. The study reveals that viewers were more likely to attribute higher credibility scores to the ads that were directly sponsored by the candidates than the ones sponsored by an independent group claiming responsibility for the ad's content (Simunich, 2005).

2004 Cheney–Edwards Vice Presidential Debates.   Unlike presidential debates, generally fewer people watch vice presidential debates (Airne & Benoit, 2005). On October 5, 2004, during the 2004 election campaign, Vice President Dick Cheney debated John Edwards. In the only vice presidential debate held at Case-Western University, these two men discussed issues about Iraq, terrorism, and Osama Bin Laden, among other social issues. Since the debate occurred somewhat recently and had an important social backdrop, this vice presidential debate is important to discuss. While only a vice presidential debate, it was still touted as a significant media event with over 1,000 media representatives in attendance. Also of note was the format of the debate. Both candidates sat on either side of a large round table. This was unusual since candidates normally stand behind a podium and can move freely about, much like the "town hall" format of the Bush–Kerry debates. Over 25 million people watched the debate, which was a lower number than watched the presidential debate, but it was still a significant audience where candidates had to "sell" themselves both on the issues and in their nonverbal communication style.

Eaves noticed several nonverbal differences between the candidates in the debate. First, let us compare and contrast the voices of the candidates. Cheney's voice was characterized as authoritative and stern. He did use many nonfluencies such as "uh" in his speech; Eaves counted over 20 nonfluencies. His vocal variety was good. In contrast, while Edwards had a flat and monotone voice, he used almost no nonfluencies in his speech.

Second, a look at gestures of the two debaters is in order. Cheney gripped his hands frequently and used other self-adaptors in a negative way. Edwards, on the other hand, tended to use gestures in a more meaningful way. Edwards seemed to be in control of his gestures, instead of his gestures' controlling him. Yet Edwards had a noticeable "babyface" image that made him appear immature and lacking leadership (recall the Zebrowitz discussion of the babyface in Chapter 2).

Third, eye contact was noticeably different in the two men. Cheney often looked down, especially when he first began to answer a question. Since much of the debate dealt with Iraq and questions of the administration's credibility, his poor eye behavior indicated areas of dishonesty or incompleteness in his message. Edwards spoke with much more confidence, especially in the use of his eyes. Edwards almost never looked down. This was especially true while he answered questions, a period when viewers are more likely to notice how a communicator is behaving.

Other Modern Political Debates.   Other modern debates that we will examine include the 2006 New York Hillary Clinton–John Spencer U.S. senatorial debate; the 2004 Illinois Alan Keyes–Barack Obama U.S. senatorial debate; and the 2006 Georgia Purdue–Taylor–Hayes governor debate.

2006 New York U.S. Senate Debate.   First, let us look at the recent 2006 U.S. senatorial debate between Hillary Clinton and John Spencer. The debate took place on Friday, October 20, 2006, at the University of Rochester in New York. Polls indicated that Hillary enjoyed a 2–1 lead with voters in the campaign; thus the debate may have had fewer implications for the outcome of the senate race, and more implications for her future presidential aspirations. There are main differences between each candidate in his or her vocal skills, use of gestures, and degree of eye contact with the audience.

First, some vocal differences, while slight in nature, were apparent. Spencer's voice was characterized as flat, monotone, and lacking in vocal variety. While he spoke with seriousness in his voice, he had difficulty capturing the attention of the audience away from the well-known Hillary Clinton. In contrast, Hillary spoke with zeal and enthusiasm. While she appeared tired and exhausted from travels during the campaign, she made up for it in her well-spoken vocal ability. Both Clinton and Spencer had only a handful of nonfluencies in their speeches.

Gestures were about dead-even. Both Spencer and Clinton used gestures effectively during the debate. Both used pointed gestures to give special emphasis where needed.

Strikingly, Spencer's eye contact was much stronger than Hillary's. Since neither of the candidates smiled much, their faces communicated very little in the way of positive nonverbal communication. Spencer, unlike Clinton, did look up and use better eye behavior that exuded confidence in his delivery. Clinton on several occasions looked down and appeared to be contemplating answers before she spoke. On the other hand, Spencer immediately spoke and rarely looked down before answering a question from the panel.

Hillary Clinton debates John Spencer in the 2006 New York senate race.

2004 Illinois U.S. Senate Debate.   Next, a close examination of the 2004 Illinois U.S. Senate debates between Alan Keyes and Barack Obama reveals several important differences between the candidates. Airne and Benoit (2005) conducted a study of the debate and looked at key elements of the discussion. They found that, like in presidential debates, the candidates focused on positive statements rather than on attacks or defenses. The acclaims in turn were reflected in their nonverbal style. Keyes was definitely more on the attack and Obama was on the defensive. We will examine the main nonverbal elements in the second and third debates: the voice, use of gestures, and amount of eye contact (the first debate was on the radio and was not recorded). The candidates were seated in the second debate, and in the third debate they stood at a podium.

The candidates had key vocal differences in the debate. Keyes spoke with a much higher pitch than did Obama. Keyes's speech rate was slightly faster than Obama's, which is indicative of higher credibility. Keyes used pauses effectively and used vocal emphasis on key words. Obama's voice had a deeper, more rotund quality. He had a more conversational vocal tone than did Keyes and was resolute and spoke with confidence. Both candidates had almost no nonfluencies.

There were several gestural differences between the candidates. Keyes had some head tilts when he spoke. He had a dynamic smile, especially when being introduced. Overall, his facial expressions were superior to Obama's. Obama had good gestures. He tended to accent his main points. He did have some distracting weight shifts in the last debate, however. These behaviors were absent from Keyes's body language.

Finally, there were observations made about the two men and their eye contact. Keyes used favorable eye contact. His eyes complemented his smile well. His best eye behavior seemed to be when he was confronted on an issue and used a forward lean. Obama's eye contact was equally strong. Perhaps the only real difference from Keyes's was that Obama's eye behavior was not complemented by other strong nonverbal cues such as a smile or pleasant facial expressions.

2006 Georgia Governor Debate.   Finally, the 2006 Georgia governor race is noteworthy. Some key elements of this three-party debate need to be examined. This was the first of several debates that featured Republican incumbent Sonny Perdue, Democratic challenger Mark Taylor, and Libertarian candidate Garrett Hayes. Eaves noticed several things about this debate. Taylor was quick to criticize Purdue in his land acquisitions, whereas Purdue defended his educational budget items and his fight against methane use by criminals.

Noticeably, Purdue smiled on many occasions when asked about his $40 million investment deals in Florida. The smile may have been meant to be a distraction since this was a serious allegation. In addition, on several occasions his nonverbal behavior contradicted his verbal comments, which were more serious in their tone. When he spoke about his plan on methane control, his facial expressions were serious and he generally had a commanding voice. Purdue was quick to lash out at Taylor, calling him Pinocchio. While he made these remarks, he used stern eye contact and had a sarcastic look on his face. In some ways, his mudslinging remarks was quite effective in the debate.

Like Purdue, Taylor had his own set of problems in the debate. When asked about his past financial deals, Taylor was more confrontational and appeared more "out of control" in his facial expressions and vocal patterns. Since Taylor did not appear relaxed when being confronted, he communicated a sense of dishonesty to the audience.

Taylor was also noticeably vague in his answers. While he was quick to pass judgment on Purdue for his answers, Taylor himself had difficulty responding in an effective manner. He made one cheap remark at Purdue by referring to him as "Greedy" in the seven dwarves.

As the Libertarian, Hayes repeated his message on numerous occasions: "Keep your money, don't let the government keep it." Unfortunately, the image he portrayed was one of a robot who had difficulty confronting the issues head-on. In essence, he committed the debater's worst sin: a tautology or mindless repetition. In addition, Hayes had trouble smiling or communicating favorably with his eyes or face. While he appeared to be serious throughout the debate, he was noticeably tense, not relaxed, and seemingly uncomfortable most of the debate. It is also worth noting that since he was in the middle of the other two candidates, he was pictured several times looking back and forth at them, the way a fan would watch a tennis match (back and forth, back and forth). This eye behavior was not only distracting but probably also became a negative influence since he was perceived as "not being included" in the debate.

The Selling of Corporate Sales Representatives

Nonverbal factors quite clearly play a central role in determining how successfully presidential candidates and others sell themselves nonverbally. Although most of you are not likely to be a presidential candidate, you may someday be in a situation in which the selling of your abilities is important. Most of us attach importance to success in the job interview, where the ability to sell oneself is pitted against the abilities of competing job applicants.

Modern corporations recognize that you must sell yourself to potential customers before they will buy from you. The sales training manual of one corporation, Burst Inc., identifies "Sell Yourself First" as a principle of overriding importance in sales training. Sales trainees are reminded to sell themselves first, even though some "people think it's an old worn-out cliche, but it's not worn out. It's absolutely essential for success in selling or any other occupation." The initial impression made by the seller often rests upon the proper use of nonverbal cues (Leigh & Summers, 2002).

Recently, a sales manager received a telephone call from a salesman who wanted to discuss an upcoming visit he was to make with a sales prospect. After talking to the salesman for five minutes, the sales manager realized he did not know to whom he was talking, so he asked, "Who is this?" The caller replied in a carefully modulated voice, which was free of stutters or nonfluencies, "Why, this is Omar Johnson. Don't you know who I am? I have worked for you for 10 years." The sales manager was amazed because Omar projected such a totally different image, by vocal means, that he was unrecognizable. "What have you done, Omar?" said the sales manager. "You have changed dramatically. You now seem to be confident and forceful." Omar explained that it "is the sales and communication program that I recently attended. I saw myself on the six-foot television screen for the first time, and I listened to myself. I looked and sounded like a fool. Since then, I've practiced my sales presentation on a tape recorder, and I'm a new man."

The sales manager subsequently accompanied Omar when he made a sales presentation to a prospect. Omar used his newly acquired communication skills to project an image of a much more competent, trustworthy, and dynamic salesperson. He persuaded the prospect to use a large quantity of the product that he was selling. Omar's sales manager was so impressed that he recommended that all of his company's salespeople be required to take a sales and communication training program. The company is currently implementing the sales manager's recommendation. The training program emphasizes the central role of nonverbal cues in developing the credibility of the corporate sales representative.

Although product salespeople and politicians must both sell themselves first, the selling situations they encounter are different in important respects. Politicians who attempt to sell themselves on television via a persuasive speech have control over many situational variables. Their captive audiences have no opportunity to provide immediate feedback; therefore the politician need not make any on-the-spot adjustments to a preplanned message. The well-known politician need not be concerned about exercising the listening skills associated with effective communicative interaction, because no direct interaction with another individual occurs. Recent evidence suggests, however, that political candidates are becoming increasingly attentive to online feedback during the campaign as a way to gauge voters' reception to their message (Ladd, 2000). In fact, one report says that a full one-third of voters get political information about their candidates online ("Voters and the Internet," 2000). This has important implications in nonverbal communication and suggests that political campaign managers and consultants should be proactive and sensitive to each and every message that is presented online to the potential voter via images, completeness, color choices, user-friendliness, and candidate's appearance in photo(s).

But corporate sales representatives engage in interpersonal rather than public communication. Because they interact directly with prospective customers, they cannot adhere rigidly to a preplanned text. They frequently encounter sales resistance that is both unanticipated and unwelcome or questions that directly challenge their credibility. To be successful, they must be able to adjust to the continually changing demands of distinctive kinds of communicative situations over which they can exercise only partial control.

Because of the distinctive situational demands of successful product selling, the development and maintenance of a corporate salesperson's personal credibility are particular challenges. To meet the constant threats to their credibility, less successful salespeople often communicate in ways that are either inappropriately aggressive or unassertive. The aggressive salesperson, for example, seems to take pride in cultivating an image of irreverence, toughness, and insensitivity, which ultimately limits sales.

The development of a salesperson's credibility places a premium on his or her ability to communicate in an assertive, as opposed to an unassertive or aggressive, manner. Judgments of a salesperson's level of assertiveness are strongly affected by the nature of his or her visual and vocal communication. When companies are promoting risky products, credibility in sales is placed at a premium. Indeed, research suggests that corporate image and trustworthiness are key variables to encouraging product purchasing in this situation (Gurhan-Canli & Batra, 2004).

The Nonverbal Unassertive Salesperson.   Many corporate sales representatives are so unassertive visually and vocally that they damage their credibility. Visually unassertive salespeople rarely look at the prospect during the greeting or the close of a sale, and they fail to sustain eye contact during the sales presentation. They tend to reveal their anxiety by means of hand-to-face gestures and other extraneous movements, and they use few gestures to emphasize the selling points they do make. Their rigid bodily posture makes them seem unresponsive to what the customer is saying. Nonverbally unassertive sales representatives frequently respond in inappropriate nonverbal ways when they encounter sales resistance or receive negative feedback from the customer. When encountering sales resistance, many salespeople become defensive; they cross their arms over their chest, smile nervously, and laugh at inappropriate times.

The nonverbally unassertive salesperson usually does not sound convincing. Imagine if you heard a salesman ask a client, "Can I send out five cases of our product, then?" in such a timid and unassertive tone of voice as to almost ensure noncompliance. If you do not sound convinced that you are selling a product with many tangible benefits, how can you expect the sales prospect to be convinced?

Vocally unassertive salespeople often try to let their products sell themselves. They tend to read the company literature to the prospective customer in an unexpressive voice that suggests a lack of enthusiasm about the product. Their speaking rate is too fast to allow purposeful pauses just before they make their most important selling points. Although they may not speak in a monotone, their pitch and volume ranges are narrow. Their anxiety is reflected not only in an excessive speaking rate but also in the nonfluencies they utter.

Consider the following sales critique:

> Avoid dropping the pitch of your voice at the end of sentences, since this practice makes you seem less enthusiastic about the product you are selling—and indecisive. Your fast speaking rate and many filled pauses will have the effect of eroding your perceived competence. When you asked the customer whether you could "send out five cases of our product?" you said it with a lack of conviction that might make it more likely that the customer would hesitate, or say no. Be sure to enunciate clearly and speak with vocal conviction. You must sound convinced that you are selling a superior product. Work for greater variation in pitch, rate, and volume. Practice your sales presentation with a tape recorder, in order to develop a persuasive voice.

The Nonverbally Aggressive Salesperson. Nonverbally aggressive salespeople have a different problem that threatens their perceived trustworthiness. They act and sound aggressive. Their apparent confidence borders on arrogance. Their visual and vocal images are such that customers can hardly avoid the feeling that they are being coerced rather than persuaded.

The aggressive salesperson frequently fixes the prospect with an unremitting stare, assumes a belligerent posture, and shakes a finger in the prospect's face in order to emphasize a selling point. Exaggerated gestures and postures are often combined with manipulative questions and judgmental statements such as: "Why ask me?"; "Don't you agree?"; "Isn't that right?"; and "That's a false economy, son." Unassertive salespeople become defensive when they encounter sales resistance, but the aggressive salesperson often becomes condescending. The stare becomes more pronounced, the tone of voice becomes sarcastic, and the volume becomes excessive. Nonverbal condescension is reinforced by statements such as, "It would be a serious mistake not to buy our product" or "Did you really buy that other company's product?"

In their zeal to sell their product, aggressive salespeople appear to be insensitive to the needs and feelings of the prospect. They not only dominate the prospect visually, vocally, and verbally, but they are also poor listeners. Unknowingly, they parody the hard-sell image of the used-car salesperson, who is commonly believed to have a credibility problem of gigantic proportions.

Nonverbal communication in sales also includes endorsements as a method of attracting customers. This occurs in two primary ways: celebrity and expert endorsements. First, celebrity endorsements are a powerful form of advertising. Oftentimes, companies use celebrities to market certain products in an effort to increase sales and profits. The celebrities reflect on the company's credibility and are powerful forms of persuading the customer.

Second, endorsements by experts in the field tend to make product purchase more likely. In addition, consumer endorsement and credibility are key variables to secure business when initial interest in the product is already established. For example, in one study, scholars found that online viewers were more likely to see a movie when viewing positive ratings from Yahoo!'s Web page, but were likely to focus more on customer or viewer ratings if they already had an interest in seeing the film (Wang, 2005).

Can you identify the product or service that the celebrity in the photo endorses? Why?

Developing Personal Credibility

The foregoing examples were designed to illustrate the impact of nonverbal cues on credibility. A careful reading of the previous section should give you a rather good idea of what you should and should not do if you wish to sell yourself nonverbally. Nonetheless, you might find it helpful to have a specific set of guidelines for developing your own credibility. Figure 10.1 presents such a set of guidelines. The guidelines focus on the four classes of nonverbal cues that are known to have the strongest potential for affecting personal credibility. Study the guidelines carefully, for they represent the nonverbal profile of the credible communicator.

FIGURE 10.1   Guidelines for Developing Your Nonverbal Credibility

---

Eye Behaviors

Eye behaviors represent particularly important cues that are used to make judgments about individuals' credibility. A well-developed cultural stereotype for Americans specifies the kinds of eye behaviors that will raise or lower a communicator's credibility.
Positive Eye Behaviors: Sustained eye contact while talking to others; sustained eye contact while others talk to you; and the maintenance of direct but not continuous eye contact with the individual(s) with whom you are communicating.
Negative Eye Behaviors: Looking down before responding to a question; exhibiting shifty eyes; looking away from the person with whom you are communicating; keeping your eyes down-cast; excessive blinking; and eye-flutter.

Gestures

Positive Gestures: Gestures should be used to add emphasis to the points you are making; gestures should appear spontaneous, unrehearsed, and relaxed; gestures should be used to signal whether you wish to continue talking or wish another individual to begin talking; hands and elbows should be kept away from the body; and gestures should be used to communicate the intensity of your feelings and emotions.
Negative Gestures: Gestures that suggest a communicator lacks confidence, is defensive, or is nervous should be avoided. Hand-to-face gestures, throat clearing, fidgeting, tugging at clothing, visible perspiration on face or body, lip licking, hand-wringing, finger tapping, extraneous head movements, out-of-context smiling and grimacing, and weak and tentative gestures should be avoided, as they are apt to undermine a communicator's credibility.

Postures

Posture is particularly important in communicating an individual's status or power; how responsive the communicator is; and how strongly a communicator desires to establish a warm rapport with interaction partners.
Positive Postures: Communicators who wish to be perceived as powerful spread their arms expansively in front of them, assume an open and relaxed posture, and walk confidently. Responsiveness is communicated by frequent and forceful postural shifts while communicating. Rapport is established in part by leaning forward and smiling (when appropriate) as you begin to answer a question.
Negative Postures: Communicators should avoid constricted postures that suggest that they are timid or lack assertiveness. Bodily rigidity, crossed arms and legs, arms and legs kept close to the body, and overall bodily tension are apt to impair a communicator's credibility.

(continued)

FIGURE 10.1   (Continued)

Voice

Communicators' vocal cues frequently play a major role in shaping their credibility. The personality characteristics communicators are presumed to have are often determined by the sound of their voices. Vocal qualities shape impressions about credibility, status, and power.

Positive Vocal Cues: A communicator should strive for a conversational speaking style while recognizing that a moderately fast rate will enhance perceived competence. Appropriate variation in pitch, rate, and volume is particularly important in projecting the image of a confident, competent, and dynamic person. Monotone delivery should be avoided. Sufficient volume has been found to be important for individuals who wish to be perceived as competent and dynamic.

Negative Vocal Cues: Communicators should avoid speaking in such a way that their voices sound flat, tense, or nasal. Nasality is a particularly undesirable vocal quality. Communicators should also avoid speaking at an excessive rate and should not use frequent, lengthy pauses, which suggest lack of confidence and sometimes a lack of competence. The following nonfluencies have been shown to have a markedly negative impact on credibility: "uhs," repeating words, interruptions or pauses in midsentence, omitting parts of words, and stuttering. Persons who wish to enhance their credibility should strive to eliminate the use of such nonfluencies.

You will recognize that the potentially powerful impact of nonverbal cues on perceived credibility is not confined to presidential candidates and corporate salespeople. The impact of individuals' communicative behaviors/cues has been proved to be greater than the impact of their verbal communication in many different interpersonal contexts. Significantly, the impact of nonverbal communication is most pronounced on the most important dimension of credibility, competence (Barak, Patkin, & Dell, 1982). You also should note that the impact of a person's nonverbal communicative behaviors/cues on perceived competence is greater during the early part of interaction with another person (Exline, 1985).

Eye behaviors are treated first because they play a central role in the development of personal credibility. We spend much more time monitoring the eye region of persons with whom we interact than any other part of their body; therefore, eye behaviors strongly affect judgments of credibility.

Chapter 3 discussed in detail some of the reasons our eye behaviors play such a central role in developing or damaging our personal credibility. Perhaps the most important reason is that our eye behaviors directly reflect the amount of self-confidence we are perceived to have. We know that communicators who exhibit behavioral "tension-leakage" cues in the form of nonfluencies, shifty eyes, and lip moistening will be judged to be less competent than those who do not (Exline, 1985). Jurich and Jurich (1974) found that failure to sustain eye contact correlated more highly with traditional measures of a communicator's level of anxiety than any other type of nonverbal cue. In short, failure to sustain eye contact is the most damaging thing you can do nonverbally if you are particularly concerned about being perceived as confident.

Eye behaviors are important determinants of credibility (Beebe, 1974; Burgoon, Coker, & Coker, 1986; Burgoon, Manusov, Mineo, & Hale, 1985; Burgoon & Saine, 1978; Edinger & Patterson, 1983; Harper, Wiens, & Matarazzo, 1978; Hemsley & Doob, 1978; Kleinke, 1975). They are important because we are simply not believable unless we exhibit certain types of eye behaviors (Webbink, 1986). Figure 10.1 specifies which eye behaviors should and should not be exhibited in developing personal credibility. As you study Figure 10.1 recall George W. Bush's eye behaviors in his first debate with John Kerry and how they affected his credibility. Think also of the visually unassertive and aggressive salespeople who damaged their credibility by exhibiting too few positive eye behaviors and too many negative eye behaviors.

Gestures and postures can also exert a strong impact on our credibility. Before considering Figure 10.2, you may want to return to Chapter 4. Think about the kinds of nonverbal cues that communicate liking versus disliking, assertiveness versus nonassertiveness, and power versus powerlessness. You will recognize that the development of your personal credibility depends to a considerable degree on how likable, assertive, and powerful others perceive you to be. As you become actively engaged in developing your own credibility by nonverbal means, you must seek to eliminate the gestures and postures that have the potential to negatively affect your perceived competence, trustworthiness, and dynamism.

FIGURE 10.2   Nonverbal Cue Evaluation

Communicator _____ **Evaluator** _____

Please monitor the communicator's nonverbal cues carefully to determine which cues had a positive or a negative impact on credibility. The communicator should use these evaluations to make the adjustments in persuasive communication that are necessary to develop personal credibility.

During the sales presentation, did the salesperson:

Eye Behaviors	**Yes**	**No**
(+)1. Sustain eye contact with the customer?	_____	_____
(+)2. Look directly at the customer?	_____	_____
(−)3. Look down or away before making a point?	_____	_____
(−)4. Exhibit shifty eyes?	_____	_____
(−)5. Blink excessively?	_____	_____

Gestures		
(+)1. Use hand and head gestures to emphasize points?	_____	_____
(+)2. Use gestures to signal a desire to continue talking?	_____	_____
(+)3. Keep hands and elbows out and away from the body?	_____	_____
(+)4. Avoid using distracting hand-to-face gestures?	_____	_____
(−)5. Exhibit any weak or tentative gestures?	_____	_____
(−)6. Clear throat?	_____	_____
(−)7. Smile out of context?	_____	_____
(−)8. Fidget?	_____	_____
(−)9. Put hand in pockets or on objects in the room?	_____	_____

Postures		
(+)1. Assume an open and relaxed posture?	_____	_____
(+)2. Use postural shifts to indicate interest?	_____	_____
(+)3. Lean forward while making a point?	_____	_____

(*continued*)

FIGURE 10.2   (Continued)

(+)4. Face the customer directly?   _____   _____

(−)5. Exhibit bodily tension?   _____   _____

(−)6. Appear rigid?   _____   _____

(−)7. Communicate with crossed arms and/or legs?   _____   _____

Vocal Cues

(+)1. Use a conversational speaking style?   _____   _____

(+)2. Emphasize important points with change in
      pitch and volume?   _____   _____

(+)3. Communicate with sufficient volume?   _____   _____

(+)4. Speak at an appropriate rate?   _____   _____

(−)5. Speak with a limited pitch rate?   _____   _____

(−)6. Sound flat, tense, or nasal?   _____   _____

(−)7. Pause at length before answering questions?   _____   _____

(−)8. Use nonfluencies such as "uh" and word repetitions?   _____   _____

(−)9. Interrupt the customer?   _____   _____

Write an evaluation of the persuasive communication. Begin by reviewing the assessments you made on page 1. Then identify each of the communicative cues that you felt had a positive or negative impact on credibility. Be sure to identify points not covered on the evaluation sheet.

Desirable Aspects of Communication:

Undesirable Aspects of Communication:

Suggestions for Improvement:

Finally, vocal cues are an important nonverbal determinant of credibility. As we indicated in Chapter 8, the sound of one's voice strongly affects the personality traits and personal qualities that person is presumed to have. Scherer, London, and Wolf (1973) emphasized that the "confident voice" exhibits considerable variation in pitch and volume, has high energy, and uses pauses of short duration infrequently. Communicators who use the "confident voice" are perceived as more competent, forceful, active, and enthusiastic than those who use the "doubtful voice." The development of personal credibility requires the development of a confident voice.

The "doubtful voice," which suggests a low level of self-confidence and a high level of anxiety, must be eliminated (Cooper, 1979; Erickson, Lind, Johnson, & Barr, 1978; Miller, Beaber, & Valone, 1976). Speech errors or nonfluencies in the form of stuttering, tongue slips, incoherent sounds, sentence changes, incompletions, and pauses filled with "uh," repetitions, and phrases such as "you know" are strong and reliable indicators of anxiety.

The individual who pauses and stutters before answering a question will probably be seen as less competent. The individual who pauses at length and uses many sentence fragments in trying to answer a question will probably be seen as untrustworthy, because such vocal cues are frequently associated with evasiveness. Finally, the individual who exhibits many nonfluencies will probably be seen as less than dynamic. Nonfluencies correlate highly with the perceived anxiety level of a nonfluent communicator (Jurich & Jurich, 1974).

Communicators' credibility can also be affected by whether they speak with an accent or dialect and by what kind of accent or dialect they exhibit. Regional accents have been rated in terms of their credibility; in general, the closer you come to speaking a standard Midwestern dialect, the more competent you will be judged. Although individuals who speak a regional accent may judge you to be more trustworthy if your own accent sounds like theirs, they will see you as less competent if that accent gets moderate to low marks on the competence dimension of credibility (Giles & Street, 1985).

Figure 10.1 spells out in detail what you should and should not do if you are to use the full potential of your voice to develop your own credibility. As we have seen, the cultivation of the persuasive voice is a major responsibility of individuals who wish to develop their personal credibility.

Monitoring the Communicator's Nonverbal Cues

In order to make full use of the potential of nonverbal cues in developing their personal credibility, individuals must be able to monitor the nonverbal cues they exhibit in specific persuasive situations. Figure 10.2 should be used to make a record of the nonverbal cues you actually exhibit.

The form provided in Figure 10.2 may be used to make a record of the nonverbal cues you exhibit in either a real or a simulated situation. You might try to sell a product to a potential customer in a real situation where other individuals can unobtrusively observe your persuasive effort, or you could make a sales presentation in a role-playing situation. In either case, it is easy enough to ask a third party to make a record of your nonverbal cues. Perhaps you could have the session videotaped. In that case, either you or another person could record your visual and auditory cues by placing check marks in the appropriate blanks while the videotape is being replayed.

Students and trainees who have used the monitoring and evaluation form provided in Figure 10.2 have found it to be valuable. The completed form provides a detailed profile of the nonverbal cues you actually have exhibited in a persuasive situation. The guidelines in Figure 10.1 identify the profile of nonverbal cues you should exhibit in order to be most credible. By comparing your actual profile with the desired profile, you should have a clear idea of the modifications you will have to make in your nonverbal communication if you wish to sell yourself more effectively.

Summary

Selling yourself is essential for successful persuasive communication. Selling yourself successfully requires the development of your personal credibility. Your credibility, in turn, is defined by how competent, trustworthy, and dynamic others judge you to be. Competence and trustworthiness are the most important dimensions of credibility; competence has repeatedly been found to be more important than trustworthiness.

Traditional treatments of credibility have been based on the assumption that our perceived competence, trustworthiness, and dynamism are controlled almost exclusively by the words we utter. This chapter provides information that challenges that assumption. In fact, we now know that nonverbal cues have the potential to exert a controlling influence on our personal credibility in many instances.

The persuasive efforts of political candidates and corporate sales representatives analyzed in this chapter illustrate how and why specific kinds of nonverbal cues affect our credibility. Eye behaviors, gestures, postures, and vocal cues are highlighted as the most important determinants of credibility.

In order to make maximum use of the image-building potential of nonverbal cues, careful attention should be given to the guidelines in Figure 10.1. The nonverbal profile presented in the figure spells out in detail what you should and should not do to develop personal credibility. Figure 10.2 provides you with a systematic means of identifying the nonverbal profile you actually exhibit. By carefully comparing the nonverbal cues you exhibit with the nonverbal cues you should exhibit, you can determine what changes you must make in your nonverbal communication in order to sell yourself successfully.

REFERENCES

Airne, D., & Benoit, W. L. (2005). 2004 Illinois U.S. senate debates. *The American Behavioral Scientist, 49,* 343–352.

Barak, A., Patkin, J., & Dell, D. M. (1982). Effects of certain counselor behaviors on perceived expertness and attractiveness. *Journal of Counseling Psychology, 29,* 261–267.

Beatty, M. J., & Behnke, R. R. (1980). Teacher credibility as a function of verbal content and paralinguistic cues. *Communication Quarterly, 28,* 55–59.

Beebe, S. A. (1974). Eye contact: A nonverbal determinant of speaker credibility. *Communication Education, 23,* 21–25.

Benoit, W. L., Hansen, G. J., & Verser, R. M. (2003). A meta-analysis of the effects of viewing U.S. presidential debates. *Communication Monographs, 70,* 335–350.

Brembeck, W. L., & Howell, W. S. (1976). *Persuasion: A means of social influence* (2nd ed.). Englewood Cliffs, NJ: Prentice-Hall.

Burgoon, J. K. (1976). The ideal source: A reexamination of source credibility measurement. *Central States Speech Journal, 27,* 200–206.

Burgoon, J. K., Birk, T., & Pfau, M. (1990). Nonverbal behaviors, persuasion, and credibility. *Human Communication Research, 17,* 140–169.

Burgoon, J. K., Coker, D. A., & Coker, R. A. (1986). Communicative effects of gaze behavior: A test of two contrasting explanations. *Human Communication Research, 12,* 495–524.

Burgoon, J. K., Manusov, V., Mineo, P., & Hale, J. L. (1985). Effects of gaze on hiring, credibility, attraction and relational message interpretation. *Journal of Nonverbal Behavior, 9,* 133–145.

Burgoon, J. K., & Saine, T. (1978). *The unspoken dialogue: An introduction to nonverbal communication.* Boston: Houghton Mifflin.

Cassell, J., & Bickmore, T. (2000). External manifestations of trustworthiness in the interface. *Association for Computing Machinery, 43,* 50–56.

Chebat, J.-C., Filiatrault, P., Laroche, M., & Watson, C. (1988). Compensatory effects of cognitive characteristics of the source, the message, and the receiver upon attitude change. *Journal of Psychology, 122,* 609–621.

Cooper, K. (1979). *Nonverbal communication for business success.* New York: AMACOM.

DeFrank, T. M. (2004, October 8). Bush privately fumes over his flop in first debate, hopes to improve tonight. *Knight Ridder Tribune Business News,* p. 1.

DeVito, J. A. (1980). *The interpersonal communication book* (2nd ed.). New York: Harper.

Edinger, J. A., & Patterson, M. L. (1983). Nonverbal involvement and social control. *Psychological Bulletin, 93,* 30–56.

Engstrom, E. (1994). Effects of nonfluencies on speaker's credibility in newscast settings. *Perceptual and Motor Skills, 78,* 739–743.

Erickson, B., Lind, E. A., Johnson, B. C., & Barr, W. M. (1978). Speech style and impression formation in a court setting: The effects of "powerful" and "powerless" speech. *Journal of Experimental Social Psychology, 14,* 266–279.

Exline, R. V. (1985). Multichannel transmission of nonverbal behavior and the perception of powerful men: The presidential debates of 1976. In S. L. Ellyson & J. F. Dovidio (Eds.), *Power, dominance, and nonverbal behavior* (pp. 183–206). New York: Springer-Verlag.

Giles, H., & Street, R. L., Jr. (1985). Communicator characteristics and behavior. In M. L. Knapp & G. R. Miller (Eds.), *Handbook of interpersonal communication* (pp. 205–261). Beverly Hills, CA: Sage.

Gregory, S. W., & Gallagher, T. J. (2002). Spectral analysis of candidates' nonverbal vocal communication: Predicting U.S. presidential election outcomes. *Social Psychology Quarterly, 65,* 298–308.

Gurhan-Canli, Z., & Batra, R. (2004). When corporate image affects product evaluations: The moderating role of perceived risk. *Journal of Marketing Research, 41,* 197–205.

Harper, R. G., Wiens, A. N., & Matarazzo, J. D. (1978). *Nonverbal communication: The state of the art.* New York: Wiley.

Hemsley, G. D., & Doob, A. N. (1978). The effect of looking behavior on perceptions of a communicator's credibility. *Journal of Applied Social Psychology, 8,* 136–144.

Hendrix, K. G. (1995). *Student perceptions of the influence of race on professor credibility.* Paper presented at the annual meeting of the Speech Communication Association, San Antonio, TX.

Holbrook, T. M. (1999). Political learning from presidential debates. *Political Behavior, 21,* 67–89.

Infante, D. (1980). The construct validity of semantic differential scales for the measurement of source credibility. *Communication Quarterly, 28,* 19–26.

Infante, D., Parker, K., Clarke, C., Wilson, L., & Nathu, I. (1983). A comparison of factor and functional approaches to source credibility. *Communication Quarterly, 31,* 43–48.

Jurich, A. P., & Jurich, J. A. (1974). Correlations among nonverbal expressions of anxiety. *Psychological Reports, 34,* 199–204.

Kleinke, C. L. (1975). *First impressions.* Englewood Cliffs, NJ: Prentice-Hall.

Kruglanski, A. W., & Thompson, E. P. (1999). Persuasion by a single route: A view from the unimodel. *Psychological Inquiry, 10,* 83–109.

Ladd, D. (2000, July 3). Credibility gaining over "dirty politics." *Interactive Week,* 66–67.

Leigh, T. W., & Summers, J. O. (2002). An initial evaluation of industrial buyers' impressions of salespersons' nonverbal cues. *The Journal of Personal Selling & Sales Management, 22,* 41–53.

Liska, J. (1978). Situational and topical variations in credibility criteria. *Communication Monographs, 45,* 85–92.

Lui, L., & Standing, L. (1989). Communicator credibility: Trustworthiness defeats expertness. *Social Behavior and Personality, 17,* 219–221.

McCroskey, J. C., & Dunham, R. E. (1966). Ethos: A confounding element in communication research. *Speech Monographs, 33,* 456–463.

McCroskey, J. C., & Teven, J. J. (1999). Goodwill: A reexamination of the construct and its measurement. *Communication Monographs, 66,* 90–103.

McCroskey, J. C., & Young, T. (1981). Ethos and credibility: The construct and its measurement after three decades. *Central States Speech Journal, 32,* 24–34.

McMahan, E. M. (1976). Nonverbal communication as a function of attribution in impression formation. *Communication Monographs, 43,* 287–294.

Miller, N., Beaber, R. J., & Valone, K. (1976). Speed of speech and persuasion. *Journal of Personality and Social Psychology, 34,* 615–624.

Myers, S. A., & Bryant, L. E. (2004). College students' perceptions of how instructors convey credibility. *Qualitative Research Reports in Communication, 5,* 22–27.

Nelson, F. (2004, August 25). The lethal weapon of Bush the bumbler. *The Scotsman,* p. 22.

Olson, K. M. (2005). Analyzing televised political debates in the 2004 election cycle. *Argumentation & Advocacy, 41,* 191–195.

Petty, R. E., & Cacioppo, J. T. (1986). The elaboration likelihood model of persuasion. In L. Berkowitz

(Ed.), *Advances in experimental social psychology*. New York: Academic Press.

Scherer, K. R., London, H., & Wolf, J. J. (1973). The voice of confidence: Paralinguistic cues and audience evaluation. *Journal of Research in Personality, 7,* 31–44.

Seiter, J. S., & Weger, H. (2005). Audience perceptions of candidates' appropriateness as a function of nonverbal behaviors displayed in televised political debates. *The Journal of Social Psychology, 145,* 225–235.

Simunich, B. (2005). *Investigating the effects of sponsorship of negative political advertisements on source credibility and candidate ratings.* Paper presented at the International Communication Association, New York.

Sternthal, B., Phillips, L. W., & Dholakia, R. (1978). The persuasive effect of source credibility: A situational analysis. *Public Opinion Quarterly, 42,* 285–314.

Teven, J. J., & Hanson, T. L. (2004). The impact of teacher immediacy and perceived caring on teacher competence and trustworthiness. *Communication Quarterly, 52,* 39–53.

Teven, J. J., & McCroskey, J. C. (1996). The relationship of perceived teacher caring with student learning and teacher evaluation. *Communication Education, 46,* 1–9.

Tucker, R. K. (1971). On the McCroskey scales for the measurement of ethos. *Central States Speech Journal, 22,* 127–129.

Voters and the Internet: Finding credibility. (2000, February). *Campaigns & Elections,* 9–10.

Wang, A. (2005, December). The effects on expert and consumer endorsements on audience response. *Journal of Advertising Research,* 402–412.

Webbink, P. (1986). *The power of the eyes.* New York: Springer.

Yoon, K., Pinkleton, B. E., & Ko, W. (2005). Effects of negative political advertising on voting intention: An exploration of the roles of involvement and source credibility in the development of voter cynicism. *Journal of Marketing Communications, 11,* 95–112.

Zaidel, D. W., Bava, S., & Reis, V. A. (2003). Relationship between facial asymmetry and judging trustworthiness in faces. *Laterality, 8,* 225–232.

CHAPTER

11 Detecting Deception

From the beginning of recorded history, society has placed a premium on the detection of deception. In part, the fascination with deception may be attributed to the fact that it occurs so often in so many forms. Thus, "white lies, cover-ups, bluffing, euphemisms, masks, pretenses, tall-tales, put-ons, hoaxes, and other forms of falsehoods, fabrications, and simulations have coexisted with truthfulness and honesty in human communication for centuries" (Knapp & Comadena, 1979, p. 270).

Some of the ancient methods used to detect deception seem humorous today, but they reflect societal determination to ferret out the liar. In King Solomon's day, a rather unusual method was used to resolve a dispute between two women who both claimed to be the mother of the same child. An order was given to cut the child in two by a sword. The woman who cried out against the order was presumed to be telling the truth and the woman who remained silent was presumed to be lying. The ancient Chinese also used a rather novel method to detect deception. A suspected deceiver was required to chew on rice powder while being questioned. If, after it was spit out, the rice powder was dry, the person was judged to be deceptive. The theory was that the anxiety associated with lying would block off the salivary glands, resulting in a dry mouth (Larson, 1969).

Law enforcement officials have been particularly concerned with refining methods and techniques for detecting deception. Their efforts have always been based on the same fundamental assumption: Deceivers will experience an elevated level of arousal or anxiety at the moment of deception, which will be reflected in changes in one or more of the internal states of the body.

A fascinating recent study sheds new light on deception cues for police officers. Typically, police officers are trained using the Inbau's manual, which is a collection of cues and behaviors that are stereotypically associated with liars. Mann, Vrij, and Bull (2004) had 99 police officers in the study look primarily at cues associated with those persons who were videotaped in a police interrogation. Such nonverbal cues included gaze aversion, frequent smiles, excessive blinking, fidgeting, head shakes/movements, and some form of self-touch (e.g., nail biting, hand to face or covering face, and legs/arms crossed). Those police officers, however, who focused on those cues were not extremely accurate in lie detection. While their lie detection rates were still better than chance, their inaccuracy addresses the need for improvement in police work. The good lie detectors said that they noticed fewer illustrators when detecting deceit. The bad lie detectors associated more gaze aversion and head movements with deception. This finding questions past research on lie detection and the amount of attention given to poor eye contact and deception.

In one study, Vrij and Semin (1996) looked at several groups and compared how each of them was able to detect deception. Surprisingly, prisoners had the highest success rate in detecting deception (32 percent)—followed by college students (25 percent), police detectives (22 percent), patrol police officers (24 percent), and prison guards (23 percent). Interestingly, college students vary greatly from prisoners in terms of what nonverbal behaviors they correlate with acts of deception. Such differences are striking: perceived gaze aversion was 0.78 for students and 0.33 for prisoners; perceived smiles were 0.28 for students and 0.06 for prisoners; perceived postural shifts were 0.63 for students and -0.17 for prisoners; and shoulder shrugs were -0.04 for students and 0.41 for prisoners. These findings are important since prisoners were best at detection rates and yet looked for different nonverbal cues compared to students and other lie detectors. (It should be noted that the professional lie detectors' correlations were similar to those of students.)

The polygraph was developed to monitor changes in heart rate, blood pressure, skin resistance, and other presumed physiological indicators of deception (Podlesny & Raskin, 1977). Israeli police use a device that measures palpitations of the stomach to detect deception of terrorist suspects whom they are interrogating. Some corporations now require that the Psychological Stress Evaluator be used when job prospects are being interviewed. This device is designed to pick up microtremors of the voice that indicate that deception is occurring (Goodwin, 1975). A recently developed neurological device has been found to be successful in detecting deception (Grezes, Frith, & Passingham, 2004; Mohamed et al., 2006). Some 14 areas of the frontal brain lobe are active when false information is given, whereas only 7 areas are active during truthful communication. Only time will tell whether this device is tested thoroughly and becomes widely used in society.

The fact that physiological measures indicate that an individual is aroused or anxious does not, of course, prove that the person is being deceptive. Proponents of voice stress analysis start with the fundamental assumption that the elevated level of anxiety that deceivers experience at the moment of deception will in turn be manifested in a measurably higher level of vocal stress. Those same proponents admit, however, that an elevated level of vocal stress has not proved to be a consistently accurate predictor or indicator of deception.

Researcher Dan O'Hair has led the effort to determine whether a person's level of vocal stress is a reliable indicator of deception. O'Hair, Cody, Wang, and Chao (1990) concluded that "vocal stress scores cannot be used to detect deception *in general*" (p. 159). They add that some evidence suggests that vocal stress can be used to detect prepared lies, as opposed to spontaneous lies. However, vocal stress can be used to detect this one, specialized type of deception only if the deceiver is prone to exhibit high levels of stress or arousal. In short, a high level of arousal might be a necessary condition for deception to take place but it is not a sufficient condition by itself to justify a judgment that someone is engaging in deception.

Although deceivers might always experience some degree of arousal when they lie, it is quite possible that other individuals experience comparable levels of arousal when they tell the truth. In one study, deTurck and Miller (1985) stimulated both truthful and deceitful communicators so that they experienced similar levels of arousal. They concluded that the "six cues (adapters, hand gestures, speech errors, pauses, response latency, and message duration) that distinguished deceivers from unaroused nondeceivers *also* differentiated deceivers from aroused nondeceivers" (p. 195). Thus, a heightened level of arousal or anxiety is not enough to explain the fact that deceivers and nondeceivers exhibit distinctively different types of behaviors. We are almost forced to conclude that deceivers experience a distinctive deception-induced type of arousal that truthful communicators do not experience. In fact, the most basic difference in arousal between deceptive and truthful communicators may be that deceptive communicators feel guilty whereas truthful communicators do not.

In a general sense, societal concern with deception has never been more evident. Our form of government requires that we trust our elected public officials to represent us in ways that are both straightforward and truthful. Such trust seems misplaced whenever we view such tawdry spectacles as government officials being forced out of office for allegedly soliciting the sexual favors of minors, laundering money from the drug syndicate in order to remain financially solvent, and peddling influence to foreign agents for no reason other than greed.

In the face of repeated acts of deception, it is not surprising that in a September 26, 2006, Gallup Poll, fewer than 50 percent of Americans reported having faith and trust in government, the lowest level in over a decade (Jones, 2006). Quite clearly, members of society must be able to determine if and when elected public officials are lying if they are to have a defensible basis for trusting those officials who are not lying.

Most of us, however, are most immediately concerned about possibly being deceived by the individuals with whom we interact on a personal and face-to-face basis. In order to make accurate assessments of the attitudes, feelings, and motivations of friends, business associates, and intimates, we must develop the capability to detect deception when it occurs. As we shall see, familiarity with the nonverbal profiles of deceivers provides us with the potential to develop that capacity.

One good example of detecting deception is in the game of poker. Players sit at a table and have to disguise their "true" cards by masking signs that give away a good hand or creating false signs, or what are known in poker as "tells." Tells are the act of creating a look that misleads another player. A good player is not only able to create false tells to deceive his or her opponents but is also able to detect the tells or nonverbal forms of deceptions in other players. In fact, it is well established that there are good liars and bad liars (Anolli & Ciceri, 1997). In their study, Anolli and Ciceri found that good liars are able to use vocal strategies that fool perceivers, whereas bad liars either overcontrol their voices or "leak" unintended behaviors.

Poker tournaments are known for having players who talk at the table. Some talk to agitate their opponents; some talk to confuse, bluff, or just flat out annoy the other players at the table. Some players will get other people to talk to figure out a tell on the opponents' hands. For example, a chip leader might ask an opponent who just raised, "How much do you have?" That means, the player is asking how much should I risk if I put you "all-in" here? The idea might be to truly find out how many chips the opponent has. But more often than not, that player wants to detect something in the opponent's voice: a nonfluency, nervousness, or another form of leakage cue that might indicate the strength of the opponent's hand. We should point out here that making a verbal response is not required,

Can you tell who has the best hand? What does their eye behavior say?

and some players will force the dealer to announce the chip amount. They may do this to insulate their voice from deception detection.

Nonverbal Indicators of Deception

Deception in interpersonal communication is difficult to detect. We know that untrained individuals can detect the deception of strangers at, or just above, an accuracy level that would be expected by chance (Knapp, Hart, & Dennis, 1974). The question of how accurate the accuracy figures actually are has been disputed by some investigators. Kalbfleisch (1990), for example, maintained that several of the accuracy figures that have been reported for human lie detectors might be somewhat inflated because of persisting measurement problems.

The finding that untrained individuals do little better than chance in their efforts to detect deceivers is hardly a damaging or counterintuitive finding, however. There is little reason to expect untrained persons to perform very well. We should focus our attention on a much more relevant and important question: How accurate are trained observers in their use of nonverbal indicators to detect deception?

A substantial body of literature indicates that trained lie detectors can detect deception above chance. In perhaps one of the most comprehensive reviews of 20 studies on lie detection, Frank and Feeley (2003) found that training does significantly raise lie detection rates. In addition, other findings have also supported the training–lie detection relationship in several contexts: during spontaneous deception (deTurck, 1991) and with vocal and visual training methods (deTurck, Feeley, & Roman, 1997). In addition, lie detection training specifically works when using baseline behavior (Feeley, deTurck, & Young, 1995; Vrij & Mann, 2004). Indeed, two recent studies suggest that much of the past research that found low accuracy in nonverbal detection of deception used only laypersons. When trained persons were looked at in other studies, those findings indicated marked increases in the accuracy of detecting deception (Frank & Feeley, 2003; Masip, Garrido, & Herrero, 2004).

The value of skills training for human lie detectors has been clearly established. For example, deTurck and Miller (1990) conclude that "people can be trained to use successfully a universal set of behavioral cues for detecting deception across a variety of communicators" (p. 617). Similarly, as deTurck, Harszlak, Bodhorn, and Texter (1990) emphasized:

> Results obtained in the current study clearly indicate that training social perceivers to detect deception enhances their accuracy in judging the veracity of communicators' messages. . . . Stated differently, the training enhanced social perceivers' ability to judge when communicators were lying and when they were telling the truth in a context that is highly arousing to deceivers. (pp. 196–197)

In the latter study, trained females were able to achieve an impressive detection accuracy of 77 percent. Other research also supports the notion that training improves the accuracy of detecting deception (deTurck, 1991; deTurck, Feeley, & Roman, 1997; Frank & Feeley, 2003).

We also know that a person's speech communication is not apt to reveal, in a consistent and reliable way, whether that person is engaging in deception. Nonverbal cues have primacy for human lie detectors. Thus, results from empirical research indicate that nonverbal communicative cues are the most important source of information that human lie detectors use in making veracity judgments. In addition, the established primacy of nonverbal cues in identifying deception has one other practical consequence. Human lie detectors rely primarily on nonverbal cues in making judgments of deception and veracity when the verbal and nonverbal portions of a communicator's message are inconsistent or contradictory (Hale & Stiff, 1990). As a result, analyses of communicators' verbal behavior for purposes of identifying indicators of deception are uncommon (Knapp & Comadena, 1979). One study found that verbal cues were more heavily relied upon when involvement was high. Thus, some nonverbal elements of deception are used primarily when involvement is low to medium, not high (Henningsen, Valde, & Davies, 2005). Still other research suggests that nonverbal elements in detecting deception may be the dominantly perceived mode of communication when the message is false, but that verbal cues are relied upon when the message is true (Anderson et al., 1999).

You should consider the relationship between deceptive and inconsistent messages carefully if you put a premium on increasing your ability to use a communicator's behavioral cues to detect deception. The multichannel messages communicated by all deceivers must be inconsistent to some degree or in some way if the human lie detector is to have the realistic hope of detecting deception when it occurs. By definition, liars must maintain, via their spoken words, that they are telling the truth. In rare instances, liars inadvertently reveal their deception by making verbal statements that are mutually contradictory. Unless they suddenly confess that they are lying or contradict themselves, however, their deception will be detectable only if the information they communicate through one or more of the nonverbal channels is inconsistent with, or seems to contradict, their claim that they are telling the truth. (Anolli & Ciceri, 1997).

The lie detector must decide which communication channel is the most useful source of information whenever inconsistent messages are being transmitted. Those channels that are most susceptible to conscious control by the deceiver are the least "leaky," whereas the channels least suspectible to conscious control are the most "leaky" (Ekman, 1985). The face, for example, leaks the least because it is the most susceptible to the conscious control of the communicator. "Since the face is more controllable, it is less likely to give away deception. Stated differently, the channel that is most informative when the communicator is truthful is most misleading when the communicator is deceptive" (Zuckerman, DePaulo, & Rosenthal, 1981, p. 5).

When you consider the relationship between deceptive and inconsistent messages, it is important to remember that the conscious intent of the liar is to deceive. By definition, deception is a type of communication that is intended to gain acceptance by another person of a belief or understanding that the deceiver recognizes consciously to be false (Zuckerman et al., 1981). Some recent evidence suggests that some people will deceive others to bolster the image of their friends. This provides a new reason some may choose to deceive (Schlenker & Britt, 2001). In the same way, we as lie detectors must be aware that not all deception is for personal gain, but may be used to help others instead. This finding has profound implications for the way deception operates in relational contexts. The deceptive message is only one type of inconsistent message. The intentions of individuals who communicate inconsistently are often multiple in nature and sometimes they are unknown. In short, all deceptive messages that are potentially detectable as deceptive are inconsistent to some degree, and they serve a wide variety of purposes in addition to deception.

Although deception is difficult to detect, the development of successful interpersonal relationships depends to a considerable extent on our ability to detect deception when it occurs. Rare indeed is the individual who would wish to develop a personal or business relationship that is not based on interpersonal trust. Interpersonal trust is, in turn, based on the anticipation that the individuals with whom we interact will be honest and straightforward in their dealings with us. In order to have a defensible basis for assessing an individual's level of trustworthiness, we must be able to determine whether and when that person chooses to be deceptive.

We now know that lying is apt to have disastrous consequences for interpersonal relationships. Results from one study (McCornack & Levine, 1990) show that

> more than two-thirds of the subjects who reported that their relationship had terminated since the time that the lie was discovered reported that the discovery of the lie played a direct role in their decision to end the relationship. Nearly all of these breakups were reported as being unilateral, initiated by the recipient of the lie. (p. 131)

Without question, the discovery that one of the partners in a relationship has been deceptive typically results in an emotional experience for those involved that is traumatic, intense, and negative.

Those with whom we interact must also be concerned about their ability to determine whether we are engaging in deception. We must recognize that even when we are being completely truthful, we might be perceived as being deceptive because there is a well-developed *deceiver stereotype* in our society that leads us to expect that deceivers will behave in certain ways. One survey suggests that the most striking feature of the deceiver stereotype is the belief that deceivers will exhibit more bodily movements than truthful communicators. Those surveyed believed that, on more than two-thirds of the 45 behavioral indicators that were identified, deceivers will exhibit more movements than their truthful counterparts (Hocking & Leathers, 1980). The implication is clear: If you do not wish to be perceived as a deceiver, you must make sure that your nonverbal behaviors do not conform to the defining features of the deceiver stereotype.

The human lie detector in turn must be aware of the fact that a number of the cues that are commonly *perceived* to be indicators of deception are not accurate indicators. In our society, for example, lie detectors have consistently expressed the *belief* that deceivers will sustain eye contact for shorter periods of time, smile less, speak more slowly, exhibit more postural shifts, take longer to respond to questions, speak with a higher pitch, hesitate more, and exhibit more speech errors than truthful communicators. Interestingly, the correlation between perceived and actual indicators of deception has been identified as around 0.50 (Zuckerman et al., 1981). Others claim that the correlations vary by cue and situation and can be lower, ranging from 0.16 to 0.39 (DePaulo et al., 2003). However, when training is included in detecting deception, the numbers are higher. One analysis of 20 studies showed that trained observers, as compared to untrained observers, are likely to detect deception at significantly higher correlations, ranging from 0.40 to 0.70 (Frank & Feeley, 2003). Professionals such as law enforcement officials and psychologists (with an emphasis in deception) are able to detect deception at fairly high rates: 74 percent and 56 percent, respectively (Ekman, O'Sullivan, & Frank, 1999).

Of course, no foolproof method exists for detecting deception. Even when time-tested machines such as the polygraph are used, the accuracy with which deception is detected may fall as low as 64 percent (Lykken, 1974). Furthermore, the use of machines (such as the polygraph, the Psychological Stress Evaluator, or the recent brain device) to detect deception is not feasible in the typical interpersonal communication situation. The use of such machines to detect deception may also be unethical and illegal in many situations.

Deception that occurs in interpersonal communication must be detected without the aid of machines. We can detect this sort of deception without the use of mechanical monitoring devices if we become thoroughly familiar with the nonverbal profiles that differentiate lying from truthful communicators. We now know that liars exhibit a number of identifiable nonverbal cues at the moment of deception that are distinctively different from the nonverbal cues exhibited by truthful communicators. Recent research on deception clearly documents that the guilt and the resultant anxiety associated with deception are reflected not only in changes in such internal physiological factors as the deceiver's heart and breathing rates. Deceivers also behave differently nonverbally because of an elevated level of anxiety that markedly affects their nonverbal communication. These external nonverbal indicators of deception have proved to be very valuable to the human lie detector.

Nonverbal Profile of the Deceptive Communicator—Low Stakes

The nonverbal behaviors of laboratory liars, who are asked to lie by an experimenter, have been examined in detail. Results from laboratory studies cannot, of course, be used to develop the nonverbal profile of all types of deceivers in the real world. These results are most useful in developing the nonverbal profile of the real-world deceiver who is exposed to conditions fundamentally similar to conditions experienced by laboratory liars.

Consider the following examples of "real" deception: You lie to the telephone caller about your real reason for not accepting a date. You lie to your boss's secretary when you call in to say you are sick. You lie to a job interviewer in order to pad your credentials. Each of these lies might be labeled "Low Stakes deception."

Low Stakes deception can be identified by three defining features. From the perspective of the deceiver, (a) the level of anxiety experienced at the moment of deception is typically fairly low; (b) the consequences of being detected as a deceiver are not severe; and (c) deception occurs for a short period of time. As we shall see, Low Stakes and High Stakes deceptions are quite different. In fact, High Stakes deceivers typically experience a high level of anxiety in their long-term efforts to deceive, because they recognize that the consequences of being detected may be catastrophic.

Low Stakes deceivers can consciously control at least some of the nonverbal cues that serve as telltale signs of their deception. Because their level of anxiety is relatively low, they have the opportunity to concentrate on their presentation of self without being overly distracted by their guilty feelings. Zuckerman and colleagues (1981) emphasized that "the extent to which deception fosters guilt, anxiety and/or duping delight varies according to the purposes of the deception, its social context, and the characteristics of the deceiver" (p. 9).

These liars are not ordinarily faced with the prospect of the gas chamber or a long jail sentence if their deception is detected. They can concentrate on what they perceive to be credible actions as they engage in impression management. In short, they are impression managers who are not distracted from their goal of monitoring the nonverbal cues that they believe will reveal their deception or from taking the necessary actions to suppress those cues that might reveal deception.

Finally, Low Stakes liars are usually required by an experimenter to lie for only a short period of time. Conventional wisdom suggests that deceivers may effectively control their presentation of self for limited periods of time, but lying convincingly for extended periods of time is much more difficult. The longer deception must be sustained, the greater the level of anxiety the deceiver is likely to experience. As we shall see, the nonverbal profiles for each type of deceiver differ in some important respects. The differences may be attributed to the contrasting conditions experienced by the two types of deceivers.

To develop the nonverbal profile for the Low Stakes deceiver, we have concentrated on those nonverbal cues that have most frequently and consistently been found to be indicative of deception. The cues identified in Table 11.1 have, therefore, been recognized as particularly reliable indicators of deception. No single cue will always be exhibited at the moment of deception, however. Nonetheless, the patterns of cues exhibited by Low Stakes deceivers are quite consistent.

You should be aware of the importance of baseline data, or of being familiar with the "truthful baseline," as you consider the information in Table 11.1. A number of researchers have found that lie detectors are much more accurate in identifying deceivers when they have

TABLE 11.1   Nonverbal Indicators of Deception: Low Stakes

| | **Deceivers Exhibit** | |
	More	*Less*

Vocal cues	Pausing
	    Pauses
	    Time before pausing
	    Lengthy pauses
	    Hesitations
	Nonfluencies
	    Sentence changes
	    Word repetitions
	    Intruding sounds
	Rapid speaking rate
	Overall vocal nervousness:
	    Voice sounds tense or stressed
		Lengthy answers

Gestures	Self-adaptors (touching face and body,
	    hand shrugs)
	Object-adaptors (touching or playing
	    with objects in room)
	Overall bodily nervousness
		Head movement
		Head nodding
		Foot movements
		Illustrators
		Leg movements

Eye Behaviors	Time spent looking away Averted gazes Pupil dilation Blinking	Eye contact duration
Smiling[a]	Masked smilies	Felt happy smiles

Note: Rather than concentrating on a single cue that might indicate deception, the lie detector should concentration on classes of indicators. When trying to determine whether an individual is engaging in some sort of low-risk deception, vocal cues are probably the most useful indicators, followed, in order of their potential value, by gestures, eye behaviors, postures, and facial expressions.

[a]In general, facial expressions do not reliably differentiate decietful from honest communicators.

had a chance to observe the same person engaging in truthful communication (Anolli & Ciceri, 1997). Without the truthful baseline for purposes of comparison, you might be misled by some stereotypical assumptions you have made about deceivers.

You also should recognize that we are focusing on micro-indicators of deception. A group of researchers (O'Hair, Cody, Goss, & Krayer, 1988) has been attempting to develop macro-assessments of honesty and deceit. So far, results lack specificity, but the approach does have considerable promise. Much additional research must be done, however, to determine the potential of the "macro" detection of deception.

To be successful in detecting deception, you must decide which type or class of nonverbal cue will receive your closest scrutiny. Vocal cues have proved to be a particularly rich source of deception cues. A number of studies have found that deceivers exhibit more speech errors than honest communicators (deTurck & Miller, 1985; Knapp et al., 1974; Mehrabian, 1971). Deceivers also consistently hesitate and pause more frequently and for longer periods of time than their truthful counterparts (Harrison, Hwalek, Raney, & Fritz, 1978; Kraut, 1978; O'Hair et al., 1990). Speech errors or nonfluencies associated with deception take the form of sentence changes, word repetition, and intruding sounds. The speaking rate of deceivers has been found to be both abnormally fast and abnormally slow, although a preponderance of studies have found that liars speak faster than truthful communicators (Hocking & Leathers, 1980; Zuckerman et al., 1981).

Finally, overall vocal nervousness has been identified as a particularly reliable indicator of deception (deTurck et al., 1990; Hocking & Leathers, 1980; Zuckerman et al., 1981). Because you are well advised to avoid relying on a single vocal cue in your efforts to detect deception, available evidence suggests that a stressed or tense voice could be a reliable warning that deception is taking place.

Gestures have also been found to be reliable indicators of Low Stakes deception. To make optimal use of gestural cues, you should be alert for any abnormality in the rate or frequency with which certain kinds of gestures are exhibited. *Self-adaptors*, in the form of hand-to-face gestures and hand shrugs, and *object-adaptors*, in the form of touching or playing with objects in the room, are exhibited with abnormal frequency by deceivers (Cody & O'Hair, 1983; Ekman & Friesen, 1972; O'Hair, Cody, & McLaughlin, 1981). Because gestural adaptors are known to reflect anxiety, we should not be surprised that even Low Stakes deceivers exhibit an abnormal number of adaptors. Low Stakes deceivers exhibit much less anxiety than High Stakes deceivers, but they are more anxious when lying than when telling the truth. The deceiver's adaptor rate is understandably accelerated because of the increased anxiety level.

Although deceivers exhibit more gestural adaptors, they exhibit fewer gestural illustrators. A number of studies have found that deceivers reduce the number of head movements, foot movements, and leg movements. Deceivers may seem abnormally unexpressive because of their reduced illustrator rate (Ekman & Friesen, 1972; Hocking & Leathers, 1980; Mehrabian, 1971; Zuckerman et al., 1981). One study found that deceivers are twice as likely not to use hand movements as truthful communicators (Vrij, Akehurst, & Morris, 1997).

Ekman (1985) agreed that illustrators decrease when deception occurs. He seems to stand alone, however, in his contention that "emblematic slips" may increase at the moment of deception. The most notorious emblematic slip is giving someone "the finger." We do not include emblematic slips in Table 11.1 for several reasons. First, emblematic slips have not been identified in multiple studies as reliable indicators of deception. Second, the term *emblematic "slip"* is almost a contradiction in terms because the individuals who use gestural emblems should be fully aware that they are using them and do so with conscious intent.

Postural indicators of deception are more limited in number. However, in several instances, deceivers have exhibited a preference for more distant seating, with little trunk swiveling, and an indirect bodily orientation. When the characteristic gestures and postures of Low Stakes deceivers are considered together, the image projected is one of unusual impassivity, immobility, and bodily rigidity.

The eye behaviors of Low Stakes liars have been found to vary in different studies (Matarazzo, Wiens, Jackson, & Manaugh, 1970; McClintock & Hunt, 1975). A number of studies have found, however, that the eye contact of deceivers is more limited than it is for truthful communicators (Exline, Thibaut, Hickey, & Gumpert, 1970; Hocking & Leathers, 1980). Exline's research in Machiavellianism and deception is an interesting note. Employers who are shrewd organizers have often used deception to manipulate employee reactions in the workplace. Averted gazes and substantial time spent looking away from the person with whom the deceiver is communicating might be indicative of deception (Druckman et al., 1982). Blinking and pupil dilation have also repeatedly been identified as reliable indicators of deception (O'Hair et al., 1990; Zuckerman et al., 1981).

Finally, the utility of facial expressions in identifying deception is open to serious question. For example, Ekman and Friesen (1969) theorized that facial expressions are apt to be less useful indicators of deception than bodily cues because facial cues are more susceptible to effective conscious control. Subsequent research by Ekman and Friesen (1974) did support the view that bodily cues are more accurate indicators of deception than facial expressions.

Hocking and Leathers (1980) theorized that facial expressions are less reliable indicators of deception than bodily cues, although their theoretical perspective is based on different assumptions than the ones Ekman and Friesen used to form their theory. In fact, evidence suggests that facial expressions of lying and honest communicators do not differ in ways that are consistently and reliably identifiable (Cody & O'Hair, 1983; Hocking & Leathers, 1980).

One type of facial message, smiling, has been cited as a reliable indicator of deception, however. We have already indicated that the stereotypical belief in our society is that deceivers smile less than their truthful counterparts. There is some evidence that deceivers actually do smile less than truth tellers, although the difference only approaches statistical significance (Zuckerman et al., 1981). Interestingly, deceivers smile significantly less than truthful communicators only when their motivation to lie successfully is low. Are we to conclude that highly motivated deceivers are so eager to please that they also throw in a smile?

The kind of smile rather than the frequency of smiling seems to be the important factor. Thus, Ekman, Friesen, and O'Sullivan (1988) reported that the types of smiles used by liars and truthful communicators can be used to differentiate between them. Liars more frequently use a "masking smile," whereas truthful individuals are more apt to display a "felt happy smile." When people use a masked smile, they do so to try to conceal the fact that they are experiencing strong, negative emotions such as fear or disgust. Deceivers are known to experience such emotions.

Ekman (1988) called the "felt smile" a Duchenne smile. Duchenne smiles in turn are strongly associated with honest as opposed to deceptive communication. Duchenne smiles "involve the muscle around the eye, in addition to the muscle which pulls the lip corners up" (p. 171). Masked smiles in contrast are reliable indicators of deception. Masking smiles,

> smiles in which there are muscular traces of disgust, anger, fear, sadness, or contempt in addition to the smile, as expected, occurred more often when the subjects were actually trying to conceal such negative feelings than when they were actually enjoying themselves. (p. 171)

The Duchenne and the masked smiles are, respectively, reliable indicators of honesty and deception. In one study, Ekman, O'Sullivan, Friesen, and Scherer (1991) used only three kinds of measures to differentiate between lying and truthful communicators: Duchenne smiles, masked smiles, and vocal pitch. Their overall accuracy, or "hit rate," was an extremely high 86 percent.

Both types of smiles should be identifiable by the untrained observer. The two most valuable clues to the masked smile associated with deception are traces of negative emotions on the face and the absence of crow's-feet around the eyes; crow's-feet are defining features of the felt happy smile. The two types of smiles can also be differentiated on the basis of how long it takes for them to appear, how long they remain on the face before fading, and how quickly they disappear.

To the human lie detector, the face should be considered primarily a source of noise, however. Concentrating on the suspected deceiver's facial expressions will divert attention from nonverbal cues that are known to be much more useful indicators of deception. When considered in the aggregate, vocal cues and bodily cues are the most useful nonverbal indicators of Low Stakes deception.

Finally, Burgoon and Buller's creative research on deception deserves attention since they focus on deception as an important type of impression management. Burgoon in particular has been a leader in assessing how the purposeful act of deception affects the interpersonal perceptions of those involved. Burgoon and Buller have identified four communication objectives that deception strategies are designed to achieve: impression management, relational communication, emotion management, and conversation management. They wrote:

> The twin functions of impression management and relational communication concern, respectively, the kinds of images people project for a general audience and the images or "messages" tailored to specific partners that have implications for defining the interpersonal relationship along such dimensions as trust, receptivity, and involvement. Emotion or affect management concerns how people regulate emotional experiences and expressions, including the appropriate revelation or suppression of emotional displays in social contexts. Conversation management concerns how interactants regulate conversational activities such as topic initiation and turn-taking. (Burgoon & Buller, 1994, pp. 157–158)

Using this perspective, Burgoon and her colleagues (Buller, Burgoon, Buslig, & Roiger, 1994; Burgoon & Buller, 1994) have compared deceptive and truthful communicators in terms of such collective and individual variables as nonverbal involvement, dominance, and formality cues. Whether using the perceptions that deceivers and their partners have of their own behaviors or direct observations of the deceivers' behaviors, certain results stand out. Deceivers, in contrast to truthful communicators, exhibit fewer immediacy behaviors and are more reticent, are more nervous particularly in the first part of the time period when deception occurs, leak some negative affect in that they are perceived as more unpleasant kinesically, and are less composed and more formal (Burgoon & Buller, 1994).

In order to use the nonverbal profile of the Low Stakes deceiver to develop our capacity to detect deception, we must understand why these deceivers behave as they do. Hocking and Leathers (1980) developed a theoretical perspective designed to explain the distinctive behaviors of Low Stakes deceivers. This perspective focuses exclusively on the behaviors of deceivers who are using prepared, as opposed to spontaneous, lies. We currently know little about the behavioral profile of the spontaneous liar. Because the spontaneous lie will probably induce less anxiety than the prepared lie, however, individuals engaging in the two types of lying might manifest somewhat different nonverbal behaviors (O'Hair et al., 1981).

The theoretical perspective is grounded in three explanatory propositions. Low Stakes deceivers are apt to (a) attempt to exercise conscious control over the nonverbal behaviors that they believe to be important defining features of the cultural stereotype for deceivers, (b) exercise conscious control over the nonverbal behaviors that can be most directly and easily monitored at the moment of deception, and (c) exercise effective conscious control over those behaviors that are most susceptible to conscious control.

As already indicated, the cultural stereotype of the deceiver fosters the expectation that deceivers will exhibit more bodily movements than will truthful communicators. For example, deceivers are expected to exhibit *more* defensiveness gestures, *more* extraneous movements suggestive of anxiety, and *greater* bodily nervousness. Clearly, skillful deceivers will not wish to be associated with the deceiver stereotype. Therefore, in order to avoid that association, they will presumably attempt to suppress the number of bodily movements they exhibit. The theoretical perspective developed by Hocking and Leathers (1980) predicts that Low Stakes deceivers will exhibit an abnormal lack of bodily movements. The perspective also provides a basis for understanding the facial expressions and vocal cues that Low Stakes deceivers exhibit.

The perspective focuses on the three classes of nonverbal cues that have most frequently been examined as potentially useful indicators of deception: bodily movements, facial expressions, and vocal cues. Bodily cues in the form of head, foot, and leg movements can be easily monitored and controlled by the deceiver. Vocal cues are most difficult to monitor and, therefore, are difficult to control consciously.

Two studies provide support for the explanatory value of this theoretical perspective. In fact, these two studies produced detailed information that can be used to develop fully the nonverbal behavioral profile of the Low Stakes deceiver. The first study (Hocking & Leathers, 1980) supports the conclusion that bodily movements and vocal cues are particularly useful indicators of deception and that facial expressions are not. Results from the second study (Cody & O'Hair, 1983) "support the Hocking and Leathers perspective" and provide additional information about the nonverbal profile of the Low Stakes deceiver.

If you wish to increase the accuracy with which you can detect Low Stakes deception, consider carefully the nonverbal indicators of deception identified in Table 11.1. Certain kinds of vocal cues are strongly indicative of deception. In contrast to truthful communicators, deceivers exhibit more hesitations, longer pauses, word repetitions, intruding sounds, and an accelerated speaking rate. Most importantly, deceivers are apt to *sound* nervous.

Bodily cues that may reveal deception require careful scrutiny. Low Stakes deceivers have been found consistently to exhibit fewer of the bodily movements that they can consciously control than do their truthful counterparts. Thus, deceivers, when compared with nondeceivers, exhibit less head movement, foot movement, leg movement, and illustrator activity. They also exhibit a less direct bodily orientation and do less trunk swiveling. Deceivers exhibit more self-adaptors and object-adaptors than truthful communicators. Most importantly, deceivers exhibit greater overall bodily nervousness.

Eye behaviors are less useful indicators of Low Stakes deception. This may be true because some eye behaviors are susceptible to effective conscious control and others are not. We do know that deceivers seem to have eye contact of relatively limited duration. Pupil dilation and blinking have been used to identify deceivers. In addition, deceivers exhibit a propensity to avert their gaze and more frequently look away from individuals with whom they are communicating than honest communicators.

Finally, facial expressions of deceitful and honest communicators do not seem to differ consistently. For this reason, human lie detectors would be well advised to pay little attention to a suspected deceiver's facial expressions and concentrate instead on vocal and bodily cues.

Nonverbal Profile of the Deceptive Communicator—High Stakes

The lying criminal suspect who is interviewed by the police interrogator is clearly a High Stakes deceiver. Most High Stakes deceivers do not of course experience a level of stress comparable to a person undergoing police interrogation. Nonetheless, the typical High Stakes deceiver is a highly anxious person. High Stakes deceivers experience a high level of anxiety for at least two reasons: The probable consequences of being detected as a deceiver are severe, and the deceivers must successfully sustain their deception for a considerable period of time.

A number of government officials such as Scooter Libby have been High Stakes deceivers. They face public disgrace, the loss of important positions, and jail sentences if their long-term efforts to deceive are detected. Additional examples of High Stakes deceivers abound. Consider the many married persons who have cheated on their spouses, the athletes who have been surreptitiously using hard drugs, employees who have been stealing from their employers, or alcoholics who struggle to conceal their affliction from friends and associates. Those individuals experience high levels of anxiety in their long-term efforts to deceive because the consequences of being detected are hardly trivial.

Do High Stakes deceivers exhibit an identifiable nonverbal behavioral profile that can be used as an aid in detecting their deception? There is now considerable evidence to suggest that they do. The evidence comes primarily from the reports of police interrogators who have interviewed lying criminal suspects. Because all High Stakes deceivers are apt to experience high levels of anxiety and fear the consequences of being detected as deceivers, there seems good reason to believe that different kinds of High Stakes deceivers will exhibit similar nonverbal behaviors at the time of deception.

Knowledge of the nonverbal behaviors of High Stakes deceivers comes primarily from law enforcement agencies. Law enforcement agencies continue to have extensive exposure to High Stakes deception. Those agencies are committed to detecting criminal deception when and where it occurs. Investigators receive highly specialized training that is designed to teach them to detect deception, and trained interviewers have many opportunities to study the behaviors of criminal suspects under the controlled conditions of the police interview.

The police interview is ideally suited to the study of High Stakes deception. If criminal suspects do exhibit identifiable nonverbal cues at the moment of deception, the probability of occurrence and of detection should be enhanced in this setting. In contrast to the low levels of guilt and anxiety typically experienced by the Low Stakes deceiver, guilt and anxiety levels for the lying criminal suspect should be exceptionally high.

Law enforcement agencies are increasingly relying on the nonverbal behaviors of arrestees as a method of detecting possible deception. As a reliable form of detecting deception, many interrogators use a baseline rating of the arrestee's behavior to determine the truth (Feeley, deTurck, & Young, 1995) or to provide their police officers with information about reliable nonverbal indicators of deception (Vrij, 1994). Indeed, Lieutenant Crow, of the Lowndes County Sheriff's Office, shared with Eaves in a March 17, 2007 interview about the ways he interrogates arrestees and how he looks for nonverbal deception cues. Oftentimes, these behaviors are termed *micro-expressions,* or behaviors that last for only a split second, a partial amount of the normal duration of deception. The local office gleans from much of the material discussed thus far in our text. The three main nonverbal areas are eye behavior, forehead behaviors, and facial expressions. The first area is eye behaviors:

- Blinking—an arrestee's frequent blinking may indicate high tension.
- Pupil dilation—people's eyes dilate when they are emotionally aroused.
- Tears—crying may be the result of fear, anger, or guilt. However, keep in mind that some individuals can cry at will.
- Asymmetry—facial expressions should match the emotion in the police interview. Emotions that are involuntary are symmetrical; those that are voluntary are usually asymmetrical. Therefore, if an arrestee communicates through asymmetrical means (i.e., the same reactions appear on both sides of the face), there is a good chance that deception is taking place.
- Surprise—facial cues should match other nonverbal behaviors. Genuine surprise should invoke facial, eye, and body behaviors.

The next area of possible detection in the police interview is the arrestee's forehead:

- Sadness, grief, and distress—the eyebrows are pinched together in the center of the forehead, creating an image similar to a triangle.

- Fear, worry, apprehension, and terror—the eyebrows are usually raised and pulled toward one another.
- Anger and surprise—the eyebrows are raised or lowered.

The final area of possible deception detection is the arrestee's face:

- Intensity of emotion is often revealed in the face.
- True felt emotional displays in the face should be involuntary.
- The common emotions that show distinctive facial expressions (as we discussed in Chapter 2 on the face) are anger, fear, sadness, disgust, distress, happiness, and surprise.

These areas are the principal ways of discovering the truth of the claims made in the police interrogation process. Videotapes are often made to review the behaviors.

Researcher Paul Ekman's (1985) creative conception of autonomic nervous system (ANS) clues may prove to be particularly useful in predicting which nonverbal behaviors High Stakes deceivers exhibit and in explaining why they exhibit them. Although Ekman did not distinguish between each type, his ANS clues are clearly more applicable to High Stakes deception because he assumed that the deceiver was highly aroused.

The ANS clues include noticeable changes in the pattern of breathing and in the frequency of swallowing, as well as blushing, blanching, and pupil dilation. Interestingly, Ekman believed that deceivers exhibit particular autonomic cues for different emotions. For example, Ekman noted that when his actors exhibited facial anger and fear, "different things happened to their skin temperature. Their skin became hot with anger and cold with fear" (p. 119).

The anxiety level of the High Stakes deceiver is so high that a substantial number of nonverbal cues are readily discernible to the trained observer. For example, during his many years as a police interrogator, Mike Smith (1979) said that he observed suspects who were undergoing interrogation do the following: (a) bite their lips until they bled; (b) foam at the mouth; (c) make clicking sounds while talking (because of a dry mouth); (d) bend their feet beneath their chair, at a painful angle; and (e) give a "weak, wet, and clammy" handshake. (These particular suspects were proved to have been lying.) Smith emphasized, however, that he relies on no single cue in making an inference of deception; instead, he is alert for *sets of cues*, in the form of eye behaviors, gestures, and vocal cues, all of which seem to support a judgment that deception is taking place.

To determine whether police interrogators agree on the defining features of the nonverbal profile for High Stakes deceivers, a survey was done of all active interrogators employed by the Georgia Bureau of Investigation (GBI). The survey was designed to accomplish two objectives. The researchers wanted to determine to what extent police interviewers rely on a suspect's nonverbal cues to detect deception. They also wanted to identify the nonverbal cues that are viewed as the most important in the nonverbal profile for the lying suspect (Leathers & Hocking, 1983).

Results from the survey indicate that the nonverbal cues of the lying criminal suspect represent a major source of information used by police interrogators to make a judgment of deception or truthfulness. Of the 86 police interrogators interviewed, 76.7 percent indicated that they either relied equally on both verbal and nonverbal behaviors to detect deception or relied more heavily on nonverbal than verbal behaviors to detect deception. When forced to rely solely on nonverbal cues, 64 percent of the agents indicated that their judgments would be proved "highly accurate."

Police interviewers in this study strongly endorsed the value of nonverbal cues as indicators of deception. They believe not only that these cues create that nonverbal cues are a valuable and accurate source of information about High Stakes deception, but also a nonverbal behavioral profile of the deceiving criminal suspect that is both detailed and internally consistent.

To begin, each GBI interrogator was asked to describe, in two or three words, each of the nonverbal behaviors that deceivers exhibit when lying in the police interview. Their responses were illuminating. Many of the nonverbal cues seem directly linked to the High Stakes deceiver's elevated level of anxiety (e.g., noticeable perspiration; fidgeting and twitching; pupil dilation; dry mouth, reflected in lip licking; unusual breathing; and abnormal swallowing).

Police interviewers clearly believe that eye behaviors and bodily movements are the two most important kinds of indicators of deception. Poor eye contact was identified as a distinctive and identifiable behavior of lying criminal suspects by a much higher percentage of police interviewers (82.6 percent) than the next most frequently identified variable, hand movement (50 percent). The importance of specific kinds of bodily movements as indicators of deception is reflected in part by the number of specific bodily movements identified. Of the 15 most frequently identified nonverbal cues, 11 involved some form of bodily movement, such as hand movements, foot movements, fidgeting, posture shifts, and object-adaptors.

The nonverbal profile for the High Stakes deceivers encountered by police interrogators is presented in Table 11.2. Results were obtained by asking police interrogators to rate 20 variables (identified in previous deception research as potential indicators of deception) on a 10-point scale as to their usefulness as indicators of deception (a rating of 10 indicated high usefulness, and a rating of 1 indicated very little usefulness). Directional ratings, using a 5-point scale, indicated whether police interrogators believed that lying criminal suspects exhibit more or less of a given nonverbal variable at the moment of deception. Interrogators reported that High Stakes deceivers exhibit eye contact of more limited duration (mean = 0.14) and more overall body nervousness (mean = 1.33) than their truthful counterparts.

Results in Table 11.2 indicate that the eye behaviors and bodily movements of High Stakes deceivers are the most useful kinds of specific nonverbal cues that indicate deception. High Stakes deceivers are thought to be identifiable in part by their limited eye contact and by their shifty eyes. In conversations with Leathers, almost all interrogators reported that the pupils of High Stakes deceivers dilate at the moment of deception.

High Stakes deceivers interviewed by police interrogators clearly exhibit an abnormal number of specific kinds of bodily movements. Whereas High Stakes deceivers exhibit more bodily movements than truthful communicators, Low Stakes deceivers exhibit fewer bodily movements than their truthful counterparts. The difference may be attributed to the fact that High Stakes deceivers cannot effectively suppress bodily movement at the time of deception because of the high level of anxiety they experience. In contrast, Low Stakes deceivers do suppress the number of bodily movements they exhibit in their attempts to escape detection. They have the opportunity to consciously control a number of the bodily movements they exhibit because of the relatively low level of anxiety they experience.

As you study the nonverbal profile for the High Stakes deceiver, you should recognize that any single nonverbal cue that seems indicative of deception could be misleading. Police interrogators repeatedly emphasized that they relied on their overall impression of the suspect's nonverbal behaviors rather than on a single cue. Thus, overall body nervousness, overall vocal nervousness, and overall facial nervousness were viewed as particularly useful indicators of deception.

The nonverbal profile presented in Table 11.2 may not, of course, apply to all High Stakes deceivers because it is a profile for one specific kind of deceiver. Opportunities for effective impression management are minimal in the high-stress conditions of the police interview. At the same time, there seems good reason to believe that the factors that exert a controlling impact on the nonverbal behaviors of High Stakes deceivers, both within and outside the context of the police interview, are fundamentally similar. For this reason, the nonverbal profile presented in Table 11.2 should certainly be helpful to you as you seek to identify High Stakes deception in the real world.

TABLE 11.2   Nonverbal Indicators of Deception: High Stakes

Variable	Usefulness (1 to 10)			Direction (-1 to $+2$)		
	Mean	Standard Deviation	Mode	Mean	Standard Deviation	Mode
Eye contact duration	8.12	1.70	10.0	-0.14	1.68	-2.0
Overall body nervousness	7.79	1.60	7.0	1.33	0.70	1.0
Eye movement	7.44	2.07	7.0	1.33	0.70	1.0
Defensiveness gestures	7.07	1.74	7.0	1.07	0.66	1.0
Overall vocal nervousness	6.89	1.84	7.0	1.04	0.70	1.0
Posture shift	6.94	1.86	8.0	1.08	0.73	1.0
Overall facial nervousness	6.89	1.84	7.0	1.04	0.70	1.0
Length of time pausing	6.82	2.09	7.0	1.04	0.70	1.0
Leg movement	6.75	1.93	7.0	1.01	0.69	1.0
Hand movement	6.55	1.78	8.0	0.92	0.59	1.0
Number of pauses	6.54	2.05	5.0	0.88	0.77	1.0
Hand-to-face-gestures	6.25	2.05	8.0	0.81	0.77	1.0
Foot movement	6.52	2.05	8.0	1.01	0.72	1.0
Head movement	6.20	2.09	5.0	0.77	0.74	1.0
Number of "uhs"	6.19	2.15	5.0	0.81	0.64	1.0
Number of stutters	6.04	1.85	5.0	0.69	0.72	1.0
Speaking rate	5.90	1.82	5.0	0.52	0.85	1.0
Illustrating gestures	5.53	2.15	5.0	0.65	0.73	1.0
Facial pleasantness	5.09	2.20	5.0	0.09	0.84	0.0
Number of smiles	4.94	2.30	5.0	0.10	0.85	0.0

The Deception Process

So far we have concentrated on the two major types of deception that occur and on the specific kinds and relative utility of the nonverbal behaviors that can be used to detect deception. As the title of this chapter suggests, the emphasis has been on detecting deception. We should recognize, however, that just as interpersonal communication is a process consisting of a set of interacting components, deception is a special type of communication consisting of those same components: the message sender (the deceiver), the message, the channel, the context, and the message receiver (the lie detector). In order to understand the nature of deception, it is important to know what variables affect each part of the process and how the parts of the process interact with each other. Let us look at how the deceiver functions in that process.

The Deceiver

Because lying is an activity we do not condone, our objective in this section is not to provide the deceiver with a blueprint for becoming a more effective deceiver. Instead we will simply attempt to identify some of the more important variables that positively and negatively affect the performance of the deceiver.

Planning and age might be thought to contribute in a positive way to a deceiver's success. However, being better prepared and becoming older hardly ensure success for a deceiver. In fact, if well-prepared liars are also highly motivated, the chances of being detected actually increase (Burgoon, Buller, & Woodall, 1989).

Similarly, the relationship between a deceiver's age and successful lying is so complicated as to almost defy precise generalization. Deception ability does seem to increase with age, but how much it increases depends on the sex of the deceiver, the channel of communication, and the type of lie (Zuckerman et al., 1981). Feldman, Tomasian, and Coats (1999) further argued that not only are older adolescents better liars than younger adolescents, but the social competence level seems to correlate highly with the ability to deceive. In the study, participants were told to lie about the pleasantness of a grape beverage. Judges thought the facial expressions of older participants were more genuine and less deceptive than the facial expressions of younger participants. The study illustrated that older adolescents were better at convincing the judges of their liking the drink.

Three factors can strongly affect a deceiver's performance in a positive way:

1. level of deceiving skill
2. honest demeanor bias
3. personality factors of high Machiavellianism and high self-monitoring

Let us consider each factor separately.

Level of Deceiving Skill. The deceiver's level of skill is very important. In particular, highly successful deceivers are differentiated from their less successful counterparts on the basis of their ability to identify and control the types of communicative behaviors that are most likely to reveal their deception. Control of, or suppression of, behaviors that are an important part of the deceiver stereotype is particularly important. "In fact, deceivers may hold to certain shared beliefs concerning the nonverbal cues that we stereotypically associate with deception and they may give particular attention to monitoring and controlling these 'known' cues of deception (i.e., controlling for lack of eye contact, or attempting to control nervous behaviors)" (Riggio, Tucker, & Widaman, 1987, p. 126). Poker players, as we mentioned before, are successful at deceiving their opponents, but that is a learned skill and often takes much practice. The successful poker player is often stoic, not revealing his or her hand. Some players wear sunglasses to disguise their eye behavior, so as not to give away their leakage cues in spontaneous or planned eye movements. A good example of this can be found on the TV poker tournaments. A recent amateur on the World Poker Tour won the 2007 Los Angeles Poker Classic by upsetting three professional players at the final table. Interestingly, the amateur wore sunglasses throughout the entire final table.

Honest Demeanor Bias.   Secondly, skillful deceivers will make *the honest demeanor bias* work to their advantage. They will recognize that certain types of nonverbal behaviors are typically perceived by potential lie detectors to be more believable than other kinds of behavior. For example, deceivers who exhibit fluent speech and sustained eye contact are making effective use of honest demeanor bias. However, deceivers may lose the advantage of the honest demeanor bias if they act in nonnormative ways that are perceived as "weird" or "fishy" (Bond et al., 1992).

A recent investigation by Frank and Ekman (2004) found that the honest demeanor bias works well in different situations, especially when there is a high-stakes lie as a condition. When low-stakes lies are used, less success is reported across multiple situations. In sum, there is greater consistency for skillful deceivers across situations when more is riding on their deception. This seems to be an intuitive finding consistent with the earlier sections in the chapter on Low Stakes and High Stakes deception.

High Machiavellianism and High Self-Monitoring.   Finally, a number of personality factors might affect the performance of the deceiver. However, the two personality variables that have consistently been found to have the most positive impact on deception efforts are high Machiavellianism and high self-monitoring (deTurck et al., 1990). The idea is simple: Individuals with these personality types not only tend to be more skilled at assessing the feedback they get from those they are attempting to deceive, but also can deceive with few, if any, telltale signs of guilt.

On the other hand, deceivers must recognize that a number of variables, including those that follow, can negatively affect their efforts to deceive others:

1. a high level of motivation to deceive successfully
2. the associated problems of the need to control certain behaviors—a heightened level of arousal, signs of guilt, and the cognitive complexity of lying
3. high public self-consciousness
4. emotionality

Counterintuitive though the finding may be, a high level of motivation has been found to negatively affect the efforts of individuals to deceive:

> As the pressure to perform well increases, performers pay closer attention to the processes of performance; however, if the components of the task that they are performing are not consciously known to them, then their efforts at deliberate control backfire, leading to a decrement rather than an increment in task performance. (DePaulo, Stone, & Lassister, 1985, p. 1201)

In short, the harder some deceivers try, the greater the likelihood that they will give themselves away. The breakdown of a highly motivated liar's performance is reflected partially in the findings that lies told to opposite-sex targets are easier to identify than lies told to same-sex targets, ingratiating lies are easier to detect than noningratiating lies, and senders addressing attractive targets are perceived as less sincere than those addressing unattractive targets (DePaulo et al., 1985). In short, deceivers do least well in trying to deceive the kinds of individuals they most want to deceive.

The effort to control certain behaviors can at times become a disadvantage because controlled behavior often appears to be premeditated, rehearsed, and unspontaneous. A high level of arousal and guilt are related problems in at least one sense. The more aroused a deceiver becomes, the greater the sense of guilt. The feeling of guilt, in turn, often causes a deceiver to lose the ability to control or suppress nervous behaviors that reveal deception. Finally, the more cognitively complex a lie is, the greater the level of concentration that is required; the result might be an increase in speech pauses or hesitations and increased pupil dilation, with the ultimate result being that the deception is detected (Zuckerman et al., 1981).

For reasons that are probably obvious, lying successfully in public is more difficult than lying successfully in private. In particular, deceivers who exhibit a high degree of "public self-consciousness" are less effective than liars who are less self-conscious. Have you ever seen a bowler who threw gutter balls when people were watching, but who bowled well when they were not watching? If so, you will probably understand how high public self-consciousness negatively affects a liar's performance (Riggio et al., 1987).

Finally, emotionality is negatively correlated with successful lying. The primary reason for this finding is that effective lying requires a carefully controlled presentation of self. Because we expect liars to be upset emotionally, we are more likely to judge them to be deceptive if they express a high level of emotionality. Furthermore, recent evidence suggests that the "presentation of self" is a skill that demands just as much work when telling the truth as when telling a lie (Schlenker, 2003). A good example of this craft is in the dating world. People now routinely lie about who they are, how much they earn, and what they look like in order to get a date (Rowatt, Cunningham, & Druen, 1999).

The popularity of the web site MySpace.com is a good example of how high school and college students create a version of self that is presentable, alluring, and, in many occasions, dishonest. Self-monitoring strategies (as we discussed in the previous chapter) would apply to this example. Students in MySpace and Facebook continually monitor contact lists, the image of their pages, and the "appearance" of the virtual space for the viewer.

The Channel

Because the chapter has focused in detail on the specific nonverbal characteristics that are associated with truthful and deceptive messages, let us turn briefly to the subject of channel. Knowledgeable deceivers will recognize that the nonverbal channels have primacy for most individuals who try to detect deception. For deceivers there are, therefore, at least two critically important questions: How believable is information transmitted by a deceiver over one nonverbal communication channel as opposed to one or more other nonverbal communication channels? How effectively can a deceiver exercise conscious control over one type of nonverbal communication channel as opposed to another?

For the lie detector, the channel variables of major importance are *deception accuracy* and *leakage accuracy* (Zuckerman et al., 1981). The lie detector who is most concerned with deception accuracy must focus on the communication channel of the deceiver that provides the most useful cues for determining whether deception is occurring. We have already established, for example, that the face provides the least reliable information about the occurrence of deception.

The lie detector who is concerned with determining what type of emotion the deceiver is experiencing must decide which nonverbal channel leaks the most information about the deceiver's emotions. For the lie detector concerned with accurately interpreting the deceiver's leakage cues, the choice of communication channel is critically important. Even if they choose the leakiest channel, untrained observers find it almost impossible to interpret a deceiver's leakage cues accurately unless they have access to the truthful baseline, that is, unless they have also seen the deceiver telling the truth.

The Context

The context is another important component of the deception process (Millar & Millar, 1995). In fact, the context in which the lying occurs is a vitally important difference between Low Stakes and High Stakes deception. Contextual features that maximize the deceiver's arousal, require that the lying be sustained for a long period of time, and involve serious consequences if the deception is detected (defining features of High Stakes deception) put a great strain on the deceiver. In such contexts it is more likely that deception will be detected. Finally, we have already established that successful lying in public is much more difficult than lying done in private.

The Receiver

The lie detector is the last component of the deception process. Because much of this chapter has focused on the lie detector, you might want to review what has already been said. In summary, at least four important factors have been shown to positively affect the performance of a lie detector:

1. basing deception judgments on information obtained from the deceiver's leakiest channel
2. familiarizing yourself with the deceiver's truthful baseline

3. starting with well-developed skills
4. using deception detection training to further develop skills

Successful lie detectors must deal with at least three negative factors. First, *the truthful judging bias* means that lie detectors are more likely to judge a person's communication as truthful than to judge it as deceptive. This is true because there seems to be "a general inclination toward trusting the information that others provide. It would be socially awkward to challenge the veracity of another's communication—we tend to give people 'the benefit of the doubt'" (Riggio et al., 1987). Levine, Park, and McCornack (1999) also shed new light on how the veracity bias works in the deception process. They found that the veracity of the message impacted the perceived honesty. Specifically, they observed that detection differs between truth detection and lie detection. In other words, detection success was higher than 50 percent for truths (73 to 87 percent) but lower than 50 percent for lies (22 to 37 percent). This finding rebuts earlier claims in Zuckerman's research that veracity of the message is either uninteresting or irrelevant. So then, as a receiver, do we trust everyone or doubt everyone? As a receiver, we need to be aware of the "veracity of the message" bias and seek out all possible explanations through various nonverbal channels in the evaluation of deception. As previously mentioned, this is why deception detection training is so valuable.

Second, the lie detector has to be wary of the *honest demeanor bias,* which is manifested in a tendency for lie detectors to see individuals with a certain demeanor as more believable, such as those who speak fluently and have direct eye contact. Several scholars address what the receiver needs to do to detect deception, especially among friends. Zebrowitz (1997) suggests that college friends or acquaintances may receive more "honest" scores from the receiver merely because of the relationship between them.

Finally, lie detectors must guard against relying too heavily on stereotypical cues of deception as opposed to cues that have been verified as accurate indicators. For example, the stereotype is that Low Stakes deceivers will exhibit more bodily movements than truthful people. In fact, the reverse is true.

Summary

The development of successful interpersonal relationships requires that individuals develop the ability to detect deception. Successful interpersonal relationships are built on mutual trust. In order to have a defensible basis for determining our level of trust for another person, we must be able to determine if and when that person chooses to be deceptive.

Nonverbal cues have proven to be useful indicators of deception in interpersonal communication. In order to make optimal use of the informational value of nonverbal indicators of deception, however, the human lie detector must be thoroughly familiar with the nonverbal profile for Low Stakes and High Stakes deceivers. Low Stakes and High Stakes deceivers differ with regard to the level of anxiety they experience, their fear of the consequences of being detected, and the length of time they are required to sustain their deception.

Nonverbal cues characteristically exhibited by Low Stakes deceivers seem to be controlled by three factors. Low Stakes deceivers attempt to (a) exercise conscious control over those nonverbal behaviors that they believe to be the defining features of the cultural stereotype for deceivers, (b) exercise conscious control over those nonverbal behaviors that can be most directly and easily monitored at the moment of deception, and (c) exercise effective conscious control over those behaviors that are susceptible to conscious control.

Low Stakes deceivers characteristically exhibit greater overall vocal nervousness, more nonfluencies, and more pauses, and they speak faster than their truthful counterparts. They also exhibit less overall bodily nervousness, and they use fewer of the bodily movements that they can control, such as head, foot, and leg movements. However, they exhibit more self-adaptors and object-adaptors, bodily movements that cannot be consciously controlled, than their truthful counterparts. Facial expressions do not provide a reliable basis for differentiating deceiving from truthful communicators.

High Stakes deceivers differ from Low Stakes deceivers in that they exhibit many more bodily movements than truthful individuals. Bodily movements and eye behaviors of High Stakes deceivers are particularly useful cues to their deception. However, we, as human lie detectors, should concentrate on collective measures, such as overall bodily nervousness and overall vocal nervousness, in order to maximize our chances of detecting High Stakes deception.

In order to understand the complexities of nonverbal deception, it is important to identify and define the components of the deception process: the deceiver, the message, the channel(s), the context, and the lie detector. Your understanding of the deception process will be based on your knowledge of those variables that positively and negatively affect each of the components of the process as those components interact with each other.

REFERENCES

Anderson, D. E., DePaulo, B. M., Ansfield, M. E., Tickle, J. J., & Green, E. (1999). *Journal of Nonverbal Behavior, 23,* 67–89.

Anolli, L., & Ciceri, R. (1997). The voice of deception: Vocal strategies of naïve and able liars. *Journal of Nonverbal Behavior, 21,* 259–284.

Bond, C. F., Jr., Omar, A., Pitre, U., Lashley, B. R., Skaggs, L. M., & C. T. Kirk, (1992). Fishy-looking liars: Deception judgment from expectancy violation. *Journal of Personality and Social Psychology, 63,* 969–977.

Buller, D. B., Burgoon, J. K., Buslig, A., & Roiger, J. F. (1994). Interpersonal deception: VIII. Further analysis of the nonverbal correlates of equivocation from the Bavelas et al. (1990) research. *Journal of Language & Social Psychology, 13,* 396–417.

Burgoon, J. K., & Buller, D. B. (1994). Interpersonal deception: III. Effects of deceit on perceived communication and nonverbal behavior dynamics. *Journal of Nonverbal Behavior, 18,* 155–183.

Burgoon, J. K., Buller, D. B., & Woodall, W. G. (1989). *Nonverbal communication: The unspoken dialogue.* New York: Harper & Row.

Cody, M. J., & O'Hair, H. D. (1983). Nonverbal communication and deception: Differences in deception cues due to gender and communicator dominance. *Communication Monographs, 50,* 175–192.

DePaulo, B. M., Lindsay, J. J., Malone, B. E., Muhlenbruck, L., Charlton, K., & Cooper, H. (2003). Cues to deception. *Psychological Bulletin, 129,* 74–118.

DePaulo, B. M., Stone, J. I., & Lassister, G. D. (1985). Telling ingratiating lies: Effects of target sex and target attractiveness on verbal and nonverbal deceptive success. *Journal of Personality and Social Psychology, 48,* 1191–1203.

deTurck, M. A. (1991). Training observers to detect spontaneous deception: Effects of gender. *Communication Reports, 4,* 81–89.

deTurck, M. A., Feeley, T. H., & Roman, L. A. (1997). Vocal and visual cue training in behavioral lie detection. *Communication Research Reports, 14,* 249–259.

deTurck, M. A., Harszlak, J. J., Bodhorn, D. J., & Texter, L. A. (1990). The effects of training social perceivers to detect deception from behavioral cues. *Communication Quarterly, 38,* 189–199.

deTurck, M. A., & Miller, G. R. (1985). Deception and arousal: Isolating the behavioral correlates of deception. *Human Communication Research, 12,* 181–201.

deTurck, M. A., & Miller, G. R. (1990). Training observers to detect deception: Effects of self-monitoring and rehearsal. *Human Communication Research, 16,* 603–620.

Druckman, D., Rozelle, R. M., & Baxter, J. C. (1982). *Nonverbal communication: Survey, theory, and research.* Beverly Hills: Sage.

Ekman, P. (1985). *Telling lies: Clues to deceit in the marketplace, politics, and marriage.* New York: Norton, 1985.

Ekman, P. (1988). Lying and nonverbal behavior: Theoretical issues and new findings. *Journal of Nonverbal Behavior, 12,* 163–175.

Ekman, P., & Friesen, W. (1969). Nonverbal leakage and clues to deception. *Psychiatry, 32,* 88–106.

Ekman, P., & Friesen, W. (1972). Hand movements. *Journal of Communication, 22,* 353–374.

Ekman, P., & Friesen, W. (1974). Detecting deception from the body and face. *Journal of Personality and Social Psychology, 29,* 288–298.

Ekman, P., Friesen, W. V., & O'Sullivan, M. O. (1988). Smiles when lying. *Journal of Personality and Social Psychology, 54,* 414–420.

Ekman, P., O'Sullivan, M., & Frank, M. G. (1999). A few can catch a liar. *Psychological Science, 10,* 263–266.

Ekman, P., O'Sullivan, M., Friesen, W. V., & Scherer, K. R. (1991). Invited article: Face, voice, and body in detecting deceit. *Journal of Nonverbal Behavior, 15,* 125–135.

Exline, R. V., Thibaut, J., Hickey, C. B., & Gumpert, P. (1970). Visual interaction in relation to Machiavellianism and an unethical act. In R. Christie & F. L. Geis (Eds.), *Studies in Machiavellianism* (pp. 53–75). New York: Academic.

Feeley, T. H., deTurck, M. A., & Young, M. J. (1995). Baseline familiarity in detecting deception. *Communication Research Reports, 12,* 160–169.

Feldman, R. S., Tomasian, J. C., & Coats, E. J. (1999). Nonverbal deception abilities and adolescent's social competence: Adolescents with higher social skills are better liars. *Journal of Nonverbal Behavior, 23,* 237–249.

Frank, M. G., & Ekman, P. (2004). Appearing truthful generalizes across different deception situations. *Journal of Personality and Social Psychology, 86,* 486–495.

Frank, M. G., & Feeley, T. H. (2003). To catch a liar: Challenges for research in lie detection training. *Journal of Applied Communication Research, 31,* 58–75.

Goodwin, G. L. (1975). PSE: New security tool. *Burroughs Clearing House, 59,* 29.

Grezes, J., Frith, C., & Passingham, R. E. (2004, June 16). Brain mechanisms for inferring deceit in the actions of others. *The Journal of Neuroscience, 24,* 5500–5505.

Hale, J. L., & Stiff, J. B. (1990). Nonverbal primacy in veracity judgments. *Communication Reports, 3,* 75–83.

Harrison, A. A., Hwalek, M., Raney, D. R., & Fritz, J. G. (1978). Cues to deception in an interview situation. *Social Psychology, 41,* 158–159.

Henningsen, D. D., Valde, K. S., & Davies, E. (2005). Exploring the effect of verbal and nonverbal cues on perceptions of deception. *Communication Quarterly, 53,* 359–375.

Hocking, J. E., & Leathers, D. G. (1980). Nonverbal indicators of deception: A new theoretical perspective. *Communication Monographs, 47,* 119–131.

Jones, J. M. (2006, September 26). *Trust in government declining, near lows for the past decade.* Gallup Poll. Retrieved October 23, 2006, from http://www.galluppoll.com

Kalbfleisch, P. J. (1990). Listening for deception: The effects of medium on accuracy of detection. In R. N. Bostrom (Ed.), *Listening behavior: Measurement and application* (pp. 155–177). New York: Guilford.

Knapp, M. L., & Comadena, M. E. (1979). Telling it like it isn't: A review of theory and research on deception communications. *Human Communication Research, 5,* 270–285.

Knapp, M. L., Hart, R. P., & Dennis, H. S. (1974). An exploration of deception as a communication construct. *Human Communication Research, 1,* 15–29.

Kraut, R. E. (1978). Verbal and nonverbal cues in the perception of lying. *Journal of Personality and Social Psychology, 36,* 380–391.

Larson, J. A. (1969). *Lying and its detection.* Montclair, NJ: Patterson Smith.

Leathers, D. G., & Hocking, J. E. (1983). *An examination of police interviewers' beliefs about the utility and nature of nonverbal indicators of deception.* Unpublished manuscript.

Levine, T. R., Park, H. S., & McCornack, S. A. (1999). Accuracy in detecting truths and lies: Documenting the "veracity effect." *Communication Monographs, 66,* 125–144.

Lykken, D. T. (1974). Psychology and the lie detector industry. *American Psychologist, 29,* 725–727.

Mann. S., Vrij, A., & Bull, R. (2004). Detecting true lies: Police officers' ability to detect suspects' lies. *Journal of Applied Psychology, 89,* 137–149.

Masip, J., Garrido, E., & Herrero, C. (2004). The nonverbal approach to the detection of deception: Judgemental accuracy. *Psychology in Spain, 8,* 48–59.

Matarazzo, J. D., Wiens, A. N., Jackson, R. H., & Manaugh, T. S. (1970). Interviewer speech behavior under conditions of endogenously-present and exogenously-induced motivational states. *Journal of Clinical Psychology, 26,* 148.

McClintock, C. C., & Hunt, R. G. (1975). Nonverbal indicators of affect and deception in an interview setting. *Journal of Applied Social Psychology, 5,* 62– 66.

McCornack, S. A., & Levine, T. R. (1990). When lies are uncovered: Emotional and relational outcomes of discovered deception. *Communication Monographs, 57,* 119–138.

Mehrabian, A. (1971). Nonverbal betrayal of feelings. *Journal of Experimental Research in Personality, 5,* 64–75.

Millar, M., & Millar, K. (1995). Detection of deception in familiar and unfamiliar persons: The effects of information restriction. *Journal of Nonverbal Behavior, 19,* 69–84.

Mohamed, F. B., Faro, S. H., Gordon, M. A., Platek, S. M., Ahmad, H., & Williams, J. M. (2006). Brain mapping of deception and truth telling about an ecologically valid situation: Functional MR imaging and polygraph investigation—initial experience. *Radiology, 238,* 679–688.

O'Hair, D., Cody, M. J., Goss, B., & Krayer, K. J. (1988). The effect of gender, deceit orientation and communicator style on macro-assessments of honesty. *Communication Quarterly, 36,* 77–93.

O'Hair, D., Cody, M. J., & McLaughlin, M. L. (1981). Prepared lies, spontaneous lies, Machiavellianism, and nonverbal communication. *Human Communication Research, 7,* 325–339.

O'Hair, D., Cody, M. J., Wang, X.-T., & Chao, E. Y. (1990). Vocal stress and deception detection among Chinese. *Communication Quarterly, 38,* 158–169.

Podlesny, J. A., & Raskin, D. C. (1977). Physiological measures and detection of deception. *Psychological Bulletin, 84,* 784–785.

Riggio, R. E., Tucker, J., & Widaman, K. F. (1987). Verbal and nonverbal cues as mediators of deception ability. *Journal of Nonverbal Behavior, 11,* 126–145.

Rowatt, W. C., Cunningham, M. R., & Druen, P. B. (1999). Lying to get a date: The effect of physical attractiveness on the willingness to deceive prospective dating partners. *Journal of Social and Personal Relationships, 16,* 209–223.

Schlenker, B. R. (2003). Self-presentation. In M. R. Leary & J. P. Tangney (Eds.), *Handbook of self and identity* (pp. 492–518). New York: Guilford.

Schlenker, B. R., & Britt, T. W. (2001). Strategically controlling information to help friends: Effects of empathy and friendship strength on beneficial impression management. *Journal of Experimental Social Psychology, 37,* 357–372.

Smith, M. (1979, May). Nonverbal indicators of deception: The lying suspect. Lecture given at the University of Georgia, Athens.

Vrij, A. (1994). The impact of information and setting on detection of deception by police detectives. *Journal of Nonverbal Behavior, 18,* 117–136.

Vrij, A., Akehurst, L., & Morris, P. (1997). Individual differences in hand movements during deception. *Journal of Nonverbal Behavior, 21,* 87–102.

Vrij, A., & Mann, S. (2004). Detecting deception: The benefit of looking at a combination of behavioral, auditory and speech content related cues in a systematic manner. *Group Decision and Negotiation, 13,* 61–79.

Vrij, A., & Semin, G. R. (1996). Lie experts' beliefs about nonverbal indicators of deception. *Journal of Nonverbal Behavior, 20,* 65–80.

Zebrowitz, L. (1997). *Reading faces.* Oxford, UK: Westview Press.

Zuckerman, M., DePaulo, B. M., & Rosenthal, R. (1981). Verbal and nonverbal communication of deception. In L. Berkowitz (Ed.), *Advances in experimental social psychology* (Vol. 14, pp. 1–60). New York: Academic.

PART THREE

Successful Communication in Applied Settings

CHAPTER

12 Nonverbal Determinants of Successful Interviews

You have no doubt heard the classic advice "Dress for success." Nowhere is this advice more applicable than the interview setting, especially a job interview. *Business Week* reported in a recent article that before the interview begins, one's body is sending countless messages to the interviewer (Gallo, 2007). Are you aware that most of the information conveyed in the interview is not with your *mouth,* but with your *body*? The married couple who bring the accumulated problems of a troubled marriage to a counseling interview can, or should, have a desire to resolve their problems.

In spite of the high aspirations we may bring to an interview, this kind of communication is often associated with a high level of anxiety. Such high anxiety can be attributed to at least two factors. Interviews have the potential to reveal much highly personal information about our self-definition, self-esteem, and self-confidence. In addition, interviews are a high-risk endeavor; unsuccessful interviews could have immediate and unpleasant consequences.

Consider the case of Mark Harrington, job applicant. Harrington is about to have a selection interview. He is being interviewed for a position as a sales representative for a major firm that manufactures and sells electrical appliances. As he contemplates the interview, he realizes that Equal Employment Opportunity legislation provides him with a measure of protection. He cannot be asked certain types of questions that might reflect negatively on the impression he creates. For example, he cannot legally be asked to provide a picture of himself, to describe what kind of discharge he received from the service, to reveal whether he is married or is living with someone, or to indicate what fraternity he belonged to in college (Stewart & Cash, 1997).

At the same time, Harrington realizes that he faces a paradoxical situation as a communicator. Professional interviewers have traditionally attached much importance to the interviewee's ability to communicate effectively. He must communicate in an assertive, self-confident, enthusiastic, and pleasant manner, one that serves to enhance the interviewer's perceptions of his intelligence, leadership potential, and sociability. He also recognizes that the pressures of the job interview have the potential to minimize the probability that he will communicate in such a manner. In fact, he fears that the interview may prove to be disastrous, in view of the fact that he stutters, is 40 lbs overweight, and has never been able to sustain direct eye contact. If you were Mark Harrington, what would you do to improve your chances for a successful interview?

Harrington would be well advised to familiarize himself with the nonverbal profile of successful job interviewees. There is much research to support the view that an interviewee's nonverbal cues frequently function as major determinants of success in the job interview. In Harrington's case, most of the communicative cues that he can effectively control in his upcoming job interview will probably be nonverbal in nature.

Harrington's communicative liabilities are likely more numerous and severe than yours. Nonetheless, the example may focus your attention on the critically important role that nonverbal cues frequently assume, not only in shaping an interviewer's perceptions, but also in affecting a decision to hire.

Nonverbal communication assumes added importance in the interview context because nonverbal cues can provide the kinds of highly personal information frequently sought by interviewers. Stewart and Cash (1997) suggest that the intimate nature of the interview requires both verbal and nonverbal successes. Nonverbal ingredients that are key to interview success include an appropriate handshake, strong eye contact, winks, a pat on the back, gestures, and good vocal skills.

There are many kinds of interviews in addition to selection and counseling interviews, of course. Exit interviews, informational interviews, performance-appraisal interviews, legal interviews, medical interviews, and sales interviews are all important in our society. This chapter will concentrate on only two types of interviews, however. Successful communication in the selection and the counseling interviews is probably important to the largest number of people because of the frequency with which those kinds of interviews occur in people's lives. Moreover, legal and medical interviews will be discussed in the last chapter.

The central objective of this chapter is to specify the kinds of nonverbal cues that are consistently associated with both successful and unsuccessful communication in selection and counseling interviews. By providing detailed nonverbal profiles of the successful job interviewee and the successful counselor, we do not mean to de-emphasize the importance of more traditional kinds of performance criteria. The following remain important: (a) express yourself verbally in a clear and logical manner, (b) adapt to the interests and concerns of the interviewer, and (c) demonstrate your mastery of relevant information. As the following sections will demonstrate, however, the cultivation of the foregoing is necessary but may not be sufficient to ensure success in an interview.

The Job Interview

Success in a job interview can be defined in various ways. Interviewees could consider an interview successful simply because they acquired interviewing experience or because they met or exceeded their own performance standards. They might even consider an interview successful if they resisted the temptation of accepting a position with dubious merits. The interviewer, on the other hand, may consider an interview successful if it elicited the information necessary to make a defensible decision.

Critical Interviewer Decisions

The most critical decision made by a selection interviewer is whether to accept or reject the job applicant; the interviewer can also place the interviewee in a "reserved" category, pending follow-up interviews (Kinicki & Lockwood, 1985). In addition, the interviewer must make critical decisions with regard to ratings of the applicant's qualifications, relative acceptability for a given position, and, perhaps, starting salary (Anderson, 1991; Anderson & Shackelton, 1990).

These critical decisions are in turn affected by the interviewer's judgments about the effectiveness of the interviewee's performance in the job interview. McGovern and Tinsley (1978) maintained that the following factors are critical in affecting a job interviewer's judgments about the interviewee:

1. ability to communicate
2. aggressiveness and initiative
3. self-confidence
4. enthusiasm and motivation
5. intelligence
6. leadership potential
7. maturity
8. persuasiveness
9. pleasant personality and sociability
10. positive attitude

Because most of those abilities and personal qualities are difficult to measure by objective means, interviewers must rely heavily on their own perceptions.

The prospective job interviewee would be justified in asking at least two questions at this point. First, are the interviewee's nonverbal cues likely to exert a major influence on the judgments the interviewer makes about specific abilities and personal characteristics such as ability to communicate, self-confidence, and sociability? Second, does the available evidence suggest that accept and reject decisions are affected in consistent and predictable ways by the nonverbal cues exhibited by the interviewee? As we shall see, the answers to both questions seem to be yes.

Nonverbal Profile of Successful Interviewees

McGovern and Tinsley (1978) provided solid support for the claim that an interviewee's nonverbal cues can be important determinants of success in the job interview. In their research, two groups of interviewees were labeled, respectively, "high nonverbal interviewees" and "low nonverbal interviewees," on the basis of the distinctive kinds of nonverbal cues they exhibited in a videotaped interview. The high nonverbal interviewees maintained steady eye contact; used varied voice modulations to express appropriate affect; demonstrated an appropriately high energy level by hand gestures, smiling, and general body movement; and responded to interviewer questions with fluidity and little hesitation. By contrast, the low nonverbal interviewees avoided eye contact; displayed little or no affect; had a low energy level; and spoke in a broken, nonfluent manner.

Fifty-two professional interviewers from business and industry rated the two groups of subjects on the 10 interviewee characteristics previously identified as particularly important to professional interviewers. They also classified interviewees on the basis of which ones they would invite for a second interview.

The results provide strong endorsement for the importance of nonverbal cues as determinants of successful interviews. Thus, the professional interviewers gave significantly higher ratings to the high as opposed to the low nonverbal interviewees on 39 of the 40 ratings they made of factors such as enthusiasm/motivation, confidence in self, persuasiveness, and pleasant personality. Moreover, the ratings of the interviewees' effectiveness were made after each of four 4-minute excerpts from the interview. The strong positive impact of the desirable nonverbal cues on the interviewers' perceptions remained constant during the full 16 minutes of the interview.

Finally, the nonverbal behaviors of the two groups of interviewees had a dramatic impact on the interviewers' decisions to invite interviewees for a second interview. Fully 89 percent of the interviewers who saw the high nonverbal interviewees would have invited them back for a second interview, but 100 percent of those who saw the low nonverbal interviewees would *not* have invited them for a second interview. The researchers noted that it would be hard to overstate the impact of nonverbal communication on the degree of success experienced in the job interview. They concluded that "it would be safe to say that the candidate who avoids eye contact, stutters and stammers, and is generally unemotional and flat will match a common stereotype of a 'reject' candidate" (p. 171). More recent research suggests that a candidate's perceived competence can have a marked effect on the hiring decision. The perception of competence is often a result of strongly displayed nonverbal skills (Ramsay, Gallois, & Callan, 1997).

A second study (Forbes & Jackson, 1980) is perhaps even more illuminating, in two respects. It focused on *real* as opposed to *simulated* job interviews, and examined the impact of desirable and undesirable interviewer nonverbal profiles on the reject and accept decisions of professional interviewers. In this instance, 101 recent engineering graduates were interviewed for real jobs by professional interviewers with extensive education and experience in engineering. The authors hypothesized that favorable decisions to employ would be associated with the interviewees who exhibited positive nonverbal styles, and reject decisions would be associated with the job candidates who exhibited unfavorable nonverbal styles.

The results strongly supported the hypothesis. Eye behavior seemed to be the most reliable nonverbal indicator of success or failure in those job interviews. Thus, direct eye contact occurred significantly more often in the accept interview than in the reserve or reject group; interviewees were either accepted or rejected for available jobs or placed in a reserve category, where follow-up interviews were possible. Gaze avoidance and eye wandering occurred much less frequently in the accept than in the reserve or reject group.

Although body position did not differentiate reliably between the three groups of interviewees, both smiling and frowning were important. Interviewees who were accepted for jobs had smiled much more frequently than those who were placed on reserve or were rejected; those who were rejected had frowned more than those who were accepted. Moreover, previous chapters have reported that individuals who smile "appropriately" are perceived as more credible (Bugental, 1986), and that individuals who exhibit "felt" smiles tend to be perceived as honest, whereas those who exhibit "masking" smiles that hide true feelings tend to be viewed as deceptive (Ekman, Friesen, & O'Sullivan, 1988).

Finally, interviewees who were accepted had exhibited more head movement (in the form of affirmative nodding) and less frequently had held their head in a static position than interviewees who were either rejected or placed on reserve. In short, eye behaviors, facial expressions, and head movements—both individually and collectively—proved to be good predictors of success or failure in the "real job" interview situation.

Eye behaviors, high-immediacy behaviors, and vocal cues have all been repeatedly identified as important determinants of success in the job interview. Silvester (1997) found that those candidates who practice effective self-presentational strategies through vocal adaptations are more successful in job interviews than those who do not conduct such a strategy. DeGroot and Motowidlo (1999) go one step further: these nonverbal adaptations in the interview accurately predict job performance. In sum, if you continually monitor images sent during the interview, you will have a much better chance of securing the job. For example, use nonverbal echo to mimic the interviewer's behaviors. Adjusting your speech rate or volume to mirror that of the interviewer's style are cases in point.

Eye behaviors clearly play a central role in the job interview. They are known to exert a significant impact on the perceived effectiveness of both the interviewee and the interviewer. Interviewees who sustain eye contact for the shortest amount of time have consistently been viewed as lowest in self-confidence (Tessler & Sushelsky, 1978). Similarly, interviewers who have received particularly unfavorable ratings from interviewees have been found to exhibit minimum amounts of eye contact (Kleinke, Staneski, & Berger, 1975). Conversely, individuals who sustain eye contact in a job interview are viewed as more persuasive (Hornik & Ellis, 1988). Interviewees who look directly at the interviewer not only are more likely to be hired, but also make a much more favorable impression, in that they are viewed as more assertive, confident, and as having more initiative (Arvey & Campion, 1984; Tullar, 1989). Use of impression management tactics by the interviewee, including proper eye behaviors, leads to improved interview success (Ellis, West, Ryan, & DeShon, 2002; Silvester, Anderson-Gough, Anderson, & Mohamed, 2002; Tay, Ang, & Dyne, 2006).

Exhibiting high-immediacy behaviors is also extremely important in the job interview. Interviewees who communicate *high immediacy* (via sustained eye contact, smiling, attentive posture, direct body orientation, illustrator gestures, and relatively close physical proximity to the interviewer), as opposed to low immediacy, seem to markedly increase their chances of being hired. Imada and Hakel (1977) found that 86 percent of the interviewees who exhibited high-immediacy behaviors were recommended by the interviewers for the jobs for which they applied, but only 19 percent of the interviewees who exhibited low-immediacy behaviors received a similar recommendation. Furthermore, research suggests that a premium is placed on face-to-face interaction with the interviewee. In sum, telephone interviews were viewed as negative and videoconference interviews were seen as less than favorable. Only the face-to-face interview was the preferred interview method (Chapman, Uggerslev, & Webster, 2003). This further supports the role that immediacy behaviors have in improving interview success.

One of the critical factors job interviewers use in assessing a job interviewee is level of self confidence. Adaptor gestures such as hand-wringing, hand-to-face gestures, and fidgeting all indicate nervousness, and, conversely, that the interviewee's level of self-confidence is eroding. Fidgeting is particularly undesirable because sometimes it is associated stereotypically in the interviewer's mind with the excessive movement that deceivers exhibit (Ruback & Hooper, 1986).

Notice the woman during a job interview. She exhibits immediacy behaviors such as strong eye contact, forward lean, and a pleasant facial expression.

The ability to speak fluently is an important nonverbal determinant of success in the job interview. Indeed, the use of nonfluencies is so damaging to job applicants that researchers advocate the use of training designed to decrease speech disturbances and to improve speech fluency. Excessive pausing and lack of expedient responses by the interviewee is not only unflattering but can also be a sign of deception to the interviewer. Some businesses are even using this as criteria to avoid "liars" from being hired and thus saving their company thousands of dollars (Walczyk, Roper, Seemann, & Humphrey, 2003; Walczyk et al., 2005). The best advice: Be well prepared and make some notes to avoid using pauses and nonfluencies. Composure, as communicated via nonverbal cues, is also very important.

One study suggests that there needs to be an effective balance between the vocal and visual cues sent by the interviewee in order to form a proper impression (DeGroot & Motowidlo, 1999). For instance, while in the interview, one does not need to be dominant in the voice but should have few gestures or facial expressions to accompany such cues. Others have emphasized that in order to detect deception, the interviewer must take into account not only the candidate's nonverbal behaviors but also the verbal message (Vrij & Mann, 2004). Messages that are consistent on the verbal-nonverbal channel are generally more reliable and truthful. For example, if a candidate is smiling when discussing a recent job layoff, this inconsistency may be of concern for the prospective employer. Another example of inconsistent messages is in computer-mediated communication. Since our e-mails and text messages often have little if any nonverbal clarity to them, those messages are often misunderstood and misinterpreted. (We will explore more about nonverbal communication in mediated contexts in the last chapter.)

Political interviews are also a good venue for misunderstood messages. Hillary Clinton and Barack Obama both claimed in 2006 that they had no presidential aspirations for 2008, but their facial expressions in their debates and televised interviews contradicted those statements. Another example of an inconsistent political message occurred during President George Bush's 2005 inauguration. In what he perceived to be an innocent hand gesture indicating that he was a Texas Longhorn fan, Bush was instead perceived to be a Satan worshipper by the Norwegians (see the photo). Douglas reports in January 23, 2005, that many misunderstood the longhorn sign. He further writes that some interpreted the longhorn sign in unique ways. For example, parts of Africa view the gesture as a way of putting a curse on someone and the Russians often use the sign to indicate the "New Russian," an arrogant and rich people. Other examples include: Making a circle with your index finger near your temple means "you're crazy" in the United States, but in Argentina it simply refers to the need for a telephone; the motion to wait indicated with a finger in the United States means "Stop" in India, and in Nigeria it indicates that you are putting a curse on someone; and the all-too-familiar thumbs-up, which is widely understood, means "Up yours" in Iraq, Iran, and Bangladesh. These examples, while culture-bound, show that nonverbal messages can be inconsistent with our true intent or verbal communication. When we know we have a diverse and varied cultural audience, we have to be keenly aware of the perceived inconsistency between our speech and our hand gestures.

In what he perceived to be an innocent hand gesture indicating that he was a Texas Longhorn fan, President Bush was instead perceived to be a Satan worshipper by the Norwegians.

More specifically, a premium is placed in the job interview on the ability to speak what is perceived to be standard English. Consider the study done by Atkins (1993). In her study, 65 employment recruiters who visited West Virginia University were to assume that they were interviewing job applicants who spoke either "Black English" (BE) or "Appalachian English" (AE). These job recruiters gave negative ratings to 93 percent of the job applicants speaking BE and to 58 percent speaking AE. Although individuals speaking both dialects were positively perceived in terms of some image qualities, they were also viewed as pessimistic, disreputable, dependent, and unintelligent. In a recent study, Edwards (2001) looked at Black English, or what has more recently been known as African-American Vernacular English (AAVE). Interestingly, he found age and gender variations for its use in interviews. In all, African-American men used more AAVE than did women—36 percent compared to 25.5 percent. In addition, older subjects used more AAVE than their younger counterparts—33.5 percent compared to 28 percent.

Physical attractiveness seems to be a less important determinant of success in the job interview than other kinds of nonverbal variables. In one study (Greenwald, 1981), social performance, previous experience, and qualifications were all found to be influential in affecting the interviewer's accept or reject decisions in a job interview. However, the study found no significant effect from the physical attractiveness of the interviewee. Results from this study should be interpreted with caution, however, because of the way physical attractiveness was manipulated—posed photographs from college yearbooks were used.

Heilman and Saruwatari (1979) found that the impact of physical attractiveness in the job interview depends on the sex of the applicants and the nature of the jobs they seek. Although physical attractiveness is advantageous for male applicants seeking white-collar organizational positions, it is useful for female applicants only when the position they sought is a nonmanagerial one. On the basis of the job interview, the physically attractive woman who applies for a managerial position is less likely to be hired than the physically unattractive woman. This finding has serious implications for the female interviewee with regard to the consequences of sex-role stereotyping.

We should keep in mind that the nonverbal behaviors that an interviewee exhibits are not necessarily accurate indicators of the interviewee's actual social skills. Some nonverbal behaviors seem to reflect more accurately the social skills of interviewees than others. One study showed that the interviewee's social skill was most accurately inferred from the amount of gesturing and talking and from the formality of dress. In each instance, more seemed to be better than less (Gifford, Ng, & Wilkinson, 1985).

There is some evidence to indicate that interviewers tend to discount some of the nonverbal behaviors of interviewees because the interviewees are victims of a social stigma or are being so manipulative as to damage their credibility. In the first instance, Cipolli, Sancini, Tuozzi, and Bolzani (1989) found that interviewees who were "anorexic" looked less frequently and more briefly toward the eyes of the interviewer than did control subjects, and mutual gazing was less frequent. Even if interviewees do not stigmatize themselves by their appearance, they could be stigmatized by exhibiting gender-inappropriate behaviors. Rachklowski and O'Grady (1988) found that female interviewees who exhibit male behaviors tend to be stigmatized. In addition, interviewers tend to discount nonverbal behaviors of interviewees whom they perceive to be manipulative. Baron (1986) found that male interviewers perceived a female interviewee who *both* exhibited positive nonverbal behaviors and used a clearly detectable perfume less favorably than a female interviewee who exhibited *only* positive nonverbal behaviors. When the interviewee's self-presentation goes so far as to be perceived as unappealing or manipulative, the interviewee makes a more negative impression.

The nonverbal profile that is associated with job applicants' success and failure in the selection interview is presented in Table 12.1. This profile is based entirely on results from empirical research. In view of the demonstrated importance of the interviewee's nonverbal cues as determinants of success in the job interview, this profile should be studied carefully by prospective job applicants.

TABLE 12.1   Nonverbal Profile of Successful Job Interviewees

Should Exhibit	Should Not Exhibit
High-immediacy behaviors: sustained eye contact; smiling; attentive posture; direct body orientation; illustrator gestures; close physical proximity	Low-immediacy behaviors: intermittent eye contact; frowning; inattentive posture; indirect body orientation; adaptor gestures; distant seating

Smiling

Appropriate smiling	Inappropriate smiling
Felt smiles	Masked insincere smiles

Vocal Cues

Voice modulation to express appropriate affect; suitable variation in pitch, rate, and volume	Monotone voice
Fluency	Nonfluencies—hesitation; stuttering, word repetition; sentence fragments; filled pauses (e.g., "uh")
Substantial volume	Soft voice—inadequate volume
No hesitation in responding to interviewer questions	

Eye Behaviors

Steady eye contact	Gaze avoidance
Sustained eye contact	Wandering eyes
Substantial amount of eye contact	Limited amount of eye contact
	Eye contact of short duration

Bodily Cues

Affirmative head nodding	Immobile head
Hand gestures communicating high energy levels	Hand gestures communicating low energy levels or anxiety
Responsive postural shifts	Rigid posture
Confidence gestures	Nervousness gestures
Open posture	Closed and defensive posture
	Hand-to-face gestures
	Extraneous bodily movements

The Counseling Interview

The counseling interview places a premium on the communicative skills of the interactants because counseling interviews are designed to solve problems. The problems addressed are not usually susceptible to resolution unless clients modify their attitudes and behaviors as a result of the confidence and trust they place in the counselor. In short, effective counselors must be able to promote self-disclosure and active problem-solving involvement on the part of clients. To achieve this objective, counselors must be perceived as unusually sensitive individuals who are highly credible, empathic, and trustworthy.

Counseling takes many forms. People seek counseling to deal with problems of emotional instability, physical health, marriage, morals, work performance, alcoholism, and child abuse, for example. Contrary to popular belief, many counseling interviews are conducted by individuals who are not professionally trained as counselors. Many counselors—doctors, teachers, supervisors, fellow workers, students, friends, and family members—may be "professionals" but most are not professionally trained counselors (Stewart & Cash, 1997).

The acquisition of effective counseling skills is important, because all of us will, at some time, assume the role of counselor, whether as a parent, friend, or co-worker. It is even likely that we will find ourselves in the role of client in a counseling interview. In either case, we are apt to put a premium on achieving success in the counseling interview. The degree of success achieved is often determined, to a striking degree, by the counselor's nonverbal behaviors.

Why should you familiarize yourself with the nonverbal profile of an effective counselor? Inevitably you will find yourself in contexts where your ability to be empathic will be valuable. In this regard, consider the empathic listening situations you frequently encounter with friends, co-workers, intimates, or family members. In those same situations, is it not very important that you also have the capacity to *behave nonverbally* in an emphatic and sensitive manner? If your answer is yes, pay careful attention to the following discussion and to Table 12.2.

Critical Objectives

The success of a counseling interview is much more difficult to measure than the success of a job interview. From the perspective of the job applicant, the success or failure of the employment interview can be assessed directly and immediately. Job applicants are either accepted or rejected for the position for which they apply, but the success of the counseling interview must be assessed in terms of both short-range and long-range objectives.

In most cases, the overriding short-term objective of the counselor is to inspire sufficient trust on the part of the client so that he or she will become actively involved in the problem-solving process. Well-trained counselors are probably sensitive to the fact that clients tend to form their basic impressions of them during the first four minutes of a counseling interview. This finding becomes even more important in view of the related finding that clients are better able to differentiate between the counselor's positive and negative nonverbal behaviors during the early part of the interview (Uhlemann, Lee, & Hasse, 1989).

The long-range objective usually focuses on the attempt to solve problems regarding alcoholism, drug abuse, marital discord, or sexual incompatibility. Because successful

TABLE 12.2   Nonverbal Profile of Successful Counseling Interviewers

Should Exhibit	Should Not Exhibit
High-Immediacy Behaviors	*Low-Immediacy Behaviors*
High level of eye contact; close physical proximity (sit within 3 ft of client); head and body oriented toward client	Low level of eye contact; distant seating; head and body oriented away from client
Responsive Behaviors	*Unresponsive Behaviors*
Open posture and gestures; head nodding; postural shifts; illustrator gestures; appropriate touching of client	Closed and defensive postures; gestures with arms crossed over chest and legs crossed at the ankles; immobile head and body; lack of touching
Consistent Messages	*Inconsistent Messages*
Vocal cues, gestures, postures, close distancing, and appropriate touching should be used to reinforce the meaning(s) of verbal messages that communicate liking, acceptance, empathy, warmth, and a genuine regard for the client's feelings, concerns, and problems	Vocal cues, gestures, postures, physical separation, and inappropriate touching, which contradict the meaning(s) of verbal messages, with the result that a lack of liking, acceptance, empathy, and warmth and an inauthentic regard for the client's feelings, concerns, and problems are communicated
Sets of nonverbal behaviors that enhance the counselor's perceived competence and trustworthiness	Sets of nonverbal behaviors that lower the counselor's perceived competence and trustworthiness

resolution of such problems can take months or even years, much of the research on counseling interviews has focused on how successfully the counselor attains short-range objectives.

The short-term goals of the counselor are to exhibit interpersonal skills and to develop sufficient credibility in the eyes of the client so as to inspire trust in the counselor's therapeutic actions and methods. To inspire this trust, counselors must be perceived as empathic, warm, and genuine (Lee, Uhlemann, & Haase, 1985; Sherer & Rogers, 1980). Imagine for a moment that you are about to have your initial counseling session with a psychiatrist. You suffer from depression. You have been so depressed for the last six months that you cannot sleep, you suffer from extreme fatigue, and you are convinced that you have a life-threatening heart disorder. As you enter the office of I. M. Cold, psychiatrist, you notice that she is talking on the telephone, with her back turned to you and her feet on the desk. She motions you to take a seat on the other side of the room and resumes her phone call. When, 10 minutes later, she finally finishes her phone conversation, she scowls, leans back in her chair, and thumbs casually through your medical records. She then says to you, "I am positive that your symptoms can be easily treated. You are a hypochondriac who feels sorry for herself. I have already written you a prescription for antidepressant pills. Take the pills for two months and call my secretary in the unlikely event that you still think you are depressed."

How would you react to such a counseling interview? Do you believe that her effectiveness as a psychiatrist will be measurably affected by the communicative behaviors she exhibited?

Nonverbal Profile of Successful Counselors

The level of expertness or competence attributed to the counselor by the client is perhaps the most important perceptual determinant of the counselor's effectiveness. Interestingly, Siegel (1980) found that a client's perception of the counselor's level of expertise was determined both by objective evidence of expertise and by the counselor's nonverbal behaviors. Counselors who displayed objective evidence of expertness (in the form of diplomas on the office wall) were judged as significantly more credible than those who did not. Less obvious but perhaps equally important is the finding that counselors who exhibited desirable nonverbal behaviors were judged more "expert" than counselors who did not exhibit such behaviors. Relatedly, Lee, McGill, and Uhlemann (1988) found that both counselors and clients rely more heavily on verbal cues in judging the others' competence but on nonverbal cues in judging attractiveness and trustworthiness. In still another study, clients (as opposed to trained judges) viewed counselors' nonverbal skills as important in assessing expertness, trustworthiness, and attractiveness (Lee, Uhlemann, & Haase, 1985).

Counselors' nonverbal behaviors have been found to have a strong impact not only on their perceived competence but also on their perceived trustworthiness. A study by Fretz, Corn, Tuemmler, and Bellet (1979) focused on three types of counselor nonverbal behaviors. One group of counselors maintained high levels of eye contact with the client, used a direct bodily orientation, and leaned forward while conversing. The other group of counselors exhibited an opposite set of nonverbal behaviors. Counselors in the first group were judged to be significantly more effective than those in the second group. Clients also judged them to be superior in terms of their level of regard for the clients and empathy.

The two kinds of nonverbal behaviors that seem to have the most positive impact on a counselor's perceived credibility and effectiveness are immediacy and responsiveness behaviors. Sherer and Rogers (1980) found that counselors who exhibited high-immediacy behaviors (i.e., sat within 36 inches of the client, maintained eye contact, and oriented the head toward the client 90 percent of the time) were judged to be much more effective than counselors who exhibited low-immediacy behaviors. In a recent study, Bedi (2006) found that clients identified three main nonverbal cues that gave them the assurance that the counselor cared for them: (1) the counselor nodded; (2) the counselor leaned forward; and (3) the counselor made eye contact with them.

A counselor's nonverbal responsivity is also important in clients' forming perceptions of expertness, trustworthiness, and attractiveness (Claiborn, 1979). Counselors who exhibit appropriate bodily movements are viewed as more responsive, warmer, and more empathic than those who do not. Arms crossed over the chest and crossed legs, with one leg resting on the other ankle, have been viewed by clients as particularly unresponsive forms of counselor behavior, and the counselor is typically viewed as cold and nonempathic (Smith-Hanen, 1977). In contrast, appropriate client touching by the counselor is viewed as a desirable form of responsive behavior (Alagna, Whitcher, Fisher, & Wicas, 1979). Indeed, touching is a powerful nonverbal tool that counselors employ to frame appropriate images. In one study, Suiter and Goodyear (1985) looked at 120 counselors (60 male and 60 female) and how they used touch in therapy sessions. Generally, clients had positive reactions to touching on a hand or shoulder, but less so when semi-embraced.

Overall, there were few differences between male and female counselors, but female counselors were seen as slightly more trustworthy and as possessing more expertise than male counselors.

Finally, counselors who wish to be perceived as effective must make sure that their messages are consistent. The counselor who tells the client how interested he or she is in the client's problems while exhibiting low-immediacy behaviors, for example, runs the risk of alienating the client. Clients have a much lower level of regard for counselors who use inconsistent as opposed to consistent messages and see them as less effective (Reade & Smouse, 1980).

The impact of the counselor's nonverbal behaviors on the client can be so powerful that they stimulate a self-fulfilling prophecy. In one study (Vrugt, 1990), therapists communicated their negative attitudes and expectancies toward the clients by exhibiting more "uh"-filled pauses, making more speech disturbances, and looking at the interviewees less. The clients reciprocated by increasing their pauses, adding speech disturbances, and averting the counselors' gaze. In short, the clients fulfilled the therapists' prophecy by exhibiting discomfort and acting less competent communicatively.

The nonverbal profile associated with successful and unsuccessful counselors is presented in Table 12.2. This profile is also based on results from empirical research. Counselors who wish to increase their effectiveness must, quite clearly, exhibit both high-immediacy and responsive behaviors, and they must exercise special care to ensure that their multichannel messages are consistent.

The Interviewer's Perspective

Biasing Factors

In the section on the job interview, we examined behavioral data from the interviewee's perspective. The reason is obvious. A much higher proportion of the individuals who read this book are apt to be job interviewees than job interviewers. At the same time, we should recognize that the job interview is a process in which interviewee and interviewer exert mutual influence on the behaviors they exhibit and, ultimately, on the results of the interview. Even if you never become a professional interviewer, you can become a more successful interviewee by learning something about the interviewer's perspective.

The interactive and interdependent relationship between interviewer and interviewee is illustrated by some research that focuses on the potential impact of the interviewer's preinterview impressions of the interviewee. First, research by Macan and Dipboye (1990) emphasized the strong positive relationship between a job interviewer's preinterview and postinterview impression. By definition this means that preinterview impressions are resistant to change. It also suggests that making a positive first impression in the job interview is vitally important for at least two reasons. A positive first impression is potentially advantageous for all of the reasons discussed in Chapter 9. Secondly, a positive first impression can be used to combat the tendency for an interviewers' preinterview impression and postinterview impression to remain essentially unchanged (Nordstrom, Hall, & Bartels, 1998).

The second, related type of research focuses attention on a fascinating finding. An interviewer's first impression of an interviewee tends to have a strong, predictable set of effects on the interviewer's behaviors throughout the job interview. Moreover, the interviewer's first impression of the interviewee may also affect the interviewee's behavior during the interview. Dougherty, Turban, and Callender (1994) indicate that job interviewers who form a positive impression of the job interviewee tend to act in positive ways during the actual interview such that their positive impression is "confirmed." Thus, job interviewers with a positive first impression of the interviewee exhibit "positive regard" toward the interviewee, actively "sell" their own company, give more information about the job and gather less information from the job applicant, and alter their communication style in an attempt to establish greater rapport. Relatedly, the multiple nonverbal signals from the interviewer that the interviewee made a favorable first impression have a reciprocal, positive impact on the nonverbal behavior of the interviewee; for instance, the interviewee's vocal style becomes more positive, the individual extends his or her available speaking time, the applicant's rapport with the interviewer increases, and so on.

No attempt will be made to build a separate nonverbal profile for the successful interviewer here. This subject is handled in a detailed and enlightening manner elsewhere (Gallois, Callan, & Palmer, 1992; Gorden, 1987; Harris, 1989). Although the desirable nonverbal behaviors for the interviewer and the interviewee are somewhat different, to compare them here would be an exercise in redundancy.

Instead, let us focus briefly on some of the perceptual biases that may affect the judgments that the interviewer makes of the interviewee. According to Arvey and Campion (1984), a number of factors strongly affect interviewers' judgments and may lead to biased judgments. Interviewers are influenced

1. by their own attitudes in interpreting the interviewee's responses
2. more strongly by unfavorable than by favorable information
3. by interaction that takes place early in the interview
4. by the stereotypes they bring to the interview
5. by "first-impression error"
6. by racial and gender biases

Of course, not all job interviewers are affected by the same biasing factors. Some may be relatively free from bias. Interviewers are prevented by legislation not only from exhibiting certain biases but also from posing insensitive questions. In any event, the objective here is not to impugn the integrity of professional job interviewers. Our experience suggests that most are highly ethical and skilled professionals who set high standards for themselves. The point to remember is that you give yourself an edge over your competitors if you are aware of the factors that have the potential to bias an interviewer's judgments.

Factors That Prevent Bias

Robert Half wrote an interesting book that he modestly titled *Robert Half on HIRING* (1985). Because he has devoted a lifetime to professional interviewing and finding jobs for people, his opinions carry some weight. In one chapter of his book—"On 'Reading' the

Candidate"—Half provides some guidance for job interviewers who want to guard against making biased judgments. Half stresses:

> Most personnel professionals will tell you that trying to get an accurate reading of a candidate's personality in one (or even two or three) interviews is all but impossible even for highly experienced interviewers. The problem, they point out, isn't only the limited amount of time you have to make the assessment. The personality that many candidates reveal during the interview may not be what you're likely to see once they're on the job. (p. 129)

In Half's view, job interviewers would be well advised to rely on general impressions of the interviewee rather than make highly specialized judgments. The interviewer should try to make judgments about no more than those two or three image qualities or personality traits that are most relevant to job performance and should rely heavily on the kinds of nonverbal behaviors exhibited by the interviewee that cannot be consciously controlled. He also stresses the importance of not being unduly influenced by first impressions and not being misled by prejudices. In fact, racial discrimination is a constant barrier to fair and equal interviewing. The interviewer must always check his or her racial biases (Frazer & Wiersma, 2001). In addition, sexual preference and identity also serve as potential forms of discrimination and should not be part of the job or counseling interview process (Moradi, van den Berg, & Epting, 2006).

In retrospect, you should recognize that most professional interviewers are well aware of the behavioral and perceptual factors that have the potential to bias their judgments of interviewees. They may not have seen it all, but they have seen enough to differentiate with relative ease between the skillful and the unskillful use of nonverbal behaviors to manage impressions in the job interview.

Summary

Nonverbal cues frequently are major determinants of success or failure in job and counseling interviews. The critically important role of nonverbal cues in the job interview has been clearly established. The interviewee's nonverbal cues are known to affect not only the interviewer's perceptions of the quality of the interviewee's performance, but also the critically important decision to hire the interviewee.

In the counseling interview, counselors must be perceived not only as credible but also as empathic if they are to be effective. The client's perception of the counselor's credibility and empathy are influenced to a striking degree by the counselor's nonverbal behaviors.

The nonverbal profile for job applicants, which is associated with success and failure in the selection interview, is presented in Table 12.1. Successful job interviewees typically exhibit high-immediacy behaviors, use voice modulation to express appropriate affect, maintain a high level of sustained eye contact, and use affirmative head nodding accompanied by responsive gestures and postures. In contrast, unsuccessful job interviewees frequently exhibit low-immediacy behaviors; speak in a broken and nonfluent manner; avoid eye contact; and are easily identifiable because of their lack of head movements, their rigid and defensive postures, and their nervousness gestures.

Table 12.2 provides the nonverbal profile of successful counseling interviewers. Successful counselors consistently exhibit specific kinds of high-immediacy and responsive behaviors while communicating consistent messages. Counselors who wish to enhance their perceived credibility and cultivate their interpersonal communication skills should study the nonverbal profile of successful counseling interviewers.

Finally, consideration of the interviewer's perspective is important, because the interview is a process in which the interviewee and the interviewer exert mutual influence on the behaviors they exhibit and on the outcomes of the interview. Interviewees should note that a number of factors may bias the judgments that interviewers make about them. At the same time, there are a number of guidelines that interviewers can follow to guard against making biased judgments.

REFERENCES

Alagna, F. J., Whitcher, S. J., Fisher, J. D., & Wicas, E. W. (1979). Evaluative reaction to interpersonal touch in a counseling interview. *Journal of Counseling Psychology, 26,* 465–472.

Anderson, N. R. (1991). Decision making in the graduate selection interview: An experimental investigation. *Human Relations, 44,* 403–417.

Anderson, N. R., & Shackleton, V. J. (1990). Decision making in the graduate selection interview: A field study. *Journal of Occupation Psychology, 63,* 63–76.

Arvey, R. D., & Campion, J. E. (1984). Person perception in the employment interview. In M. Cook (Ed.), *Issues in person perception* (pp. 202–241). New York: Methuen.

Atkins, C. P. (1993). Do employment recruiters discriminate on the basis of nonstandard dialect? *Journal of Employment Counseling, 30,* 108–118.

Baron, R. A. (1986). Self-presentation in job interviews: When there can be "too much of a good thing." *Journal of Applied Social Psychology, 16,* 16–28.

Bedi, R. P. (2006). Concept mapping the client's perspective on counseling alliance formation. *Journal of Counseling Psychology, 53,* 26–35.

Bugental, D. B. (1986). Unmasking the 'polite smile': Situational and personal determinants of managed affect in adult-child interaction. *Personality and Social Psychology Bulletin, 12,* 7–16.

Chapman, D. S., Uggerslev, K. L., & Webster, J. (2003). Applicant reactions to face-to-face and technology-mediated interviews: A field investigation. *Journal of Applied Psychology, 88,* 944–953.

Cippoli, C., Sancini, M., Tuozzi, G., & Bolzani, R. (1989). Gaze and eye-contact with anorexic adolescents.

British Journal of Medical Psychology, 62, 365–369.

Claiborn, D. D. (1979). Counselor verbal intervention, nonverbal behavior, and social power. *Journal of Counseling Psychology, 26,* 378–383.

DeGroot, T., & Motowidlo, S. J. (1999). Why visual and vocal interview cues can affect interviewers' judgments and predict job performance. *Journal of Applied Psychology, 84,* 986–993.

Dougherty, T. W., Turban, D. B., & Callender, J. C. (1994). Confirming first impressions in the employment interview: A field study of interviewer behavior. *Journal of Applied Psychology, 79,* 659–665.

Douglas, J. (2005, January 23). Some Norwegians thought Bush was saluting Satan. *Standard-Times,* pg. B3.

Edwards, W. (2001). Aspectual Den in African American Vernacular English in Detroit. *Journal of Sociolinguistics, 5,* 413–427.

Ekman, P., Friesen, W. V., & O'Sullivan, M. O. (1988). Smiles when lying. *Journal of Personality and Social Psychology, 54,* 414–420.

Ellis, A. P. J., West, B. J., Ryan, A. M., & DeShon, R. P. (2002). The use of impression management tactics in structured interviews: A function of question type? *Journal of Applied Psychology, 87,* 1200–1208.

Forbes, R. J., & Jackson, P. R. (1980). Non-verbal behavior and the outcome of selection interviews. *Journal of Occupational Psychology, 53,* 65–72.

Frazer, R. A., & Wiersma, U. J. (2001). Prejudice versus discrimination in the employment interview: We may hire equally, but our memories harbour prejudice. *Human Relations, 54,* 173–191.

Fretz, B. R., Corn, R., Tuemmler, J. M., & Bellet, W. (1979). Counselor nonverbal behaviors and client evaluations. *Journal of Counseling Psychology, 26,* 304–311.

Gallois, C., Callan, V. J., & Palmer, J-A. M. (1992). The influence of applicant communication style and interviewer characteristics on hiring decisions. *Journal of Applied Social Psychology, 22,* 1041–1060.

Gallo, C. (2007, February 8). *It's not your mouth that speaks volumes.* http://www.businessweek.com.

Gifford, R., Ng, C. F., & Wilkinson, M. (1985). Nonverbal cues in the employment interview: Links between applicant qualities and interviewer judgments. *Journal of Applied Psychology, 70,* 729–736.

Gorden, R. L. (1987). *Interviewing: Strategy, Techniques, and Tactics* (4th ed.). Chicago: Dorsey.

Greenwald, M. A. (1981). The effects of physical attractiveness, experience, and social performance on employer decision-making in job interviews. *Behavioral Counseling Quarterly, 1,* 275–287.

Half, R. (1985). *Robert Half on HIRING.* New York: Crown.

Harris, M. M. (1989). Reconsidering the employment interview: A review of recent literature and suggestions for future research. *Personnel Psychology, 42,* 691–726.

Heilman, M. E., & Saruwatari, L. R. (1979). When beauty is beastly: The effects of appearance and sex on evaluations of job applicants for managerial and non-managerial jobs. *Organizational behavior and human performance, 23,* 360–372.

Hornik, J., & Ellis, S. (1988). Strategies to secure compliance for a mail intercept interview. *Public Opinion Quarterly, 52,* 539–555.

Imada, A. S., & Hakel, M. D. (1977). Influence of nonverbal communication and rater proximity on impressions and decision in simulated employment interviews. *Journal of Applied Psychology, 62,* 295–300.

Kinicki, A. J., & Lockwood, C. A. (1985). The interview process: An examination of factors recruiters use in evaluating job applicants. *Journal of Vocational Behavior, 26,* 117–125.

Kleinke, C. L., Staneski, R. A., & Berger, D. E. (1975). Evaluations of an interviewer as a function of interviewer gaze, reinforcement of subject gaze, and interviewer's attractiveness. *Journal of Personality and Social Psychology, 31,* 115–122.

Lee, D. Y., McGill, M. E., & Uhlemann, M. R. (1988). Counsellor and client reliance on verbal and non-verbal cues in judging competency, trustworthiness, and attractiveness. *Journal of Counselling, 22,* 35–43.

Lee, D. Y., Uhlemann, M. R., & Haase, R. F. (1985). Counselor verbal and nonverbal responses and perceived expertness, trustworthiness, and attractiveness. *Journal of Counseling Psychology, 32,* 181–187.

Macan, T., & Dipboye, R. L. (1990). The relationship of interviewers' preinterview impressions to selection and recruitment outcomes. *Personnel Psychology, 43,* 745–768.

McGovern, T. V., & Tinsley, H. W. (1978). Interviewer evaluations of interviewee nonverbal behavior. *Journal of Vocational Behavior, 13,* 163–171.

Moradi, B., van den Berg, J. J., & Epting, F. R. (2006). Intrapersonal and interpersonal manifestations of antilesbian and gay prejudice: An application of personal construct theory. *Journal of Counseling Psychology, 53,* 57–66.

Nordstrom, C. R., Hall, R. J., & Bartels, L. K. (1998). First impressions versus good impressions: The effect of self-regulation on interview evaluations. *The Journal of Psychology, 132,* 477–491.

Rachkowski, R., & O'Grady, K. E. (1988). Client gender and sex-typed nonverbal behavior: Impact on impression formation. *Sex Roles, 19,* 771–783.

Ramsay, S., Gallois, C., & Callan, V. J. (1997). Social rules and attributions in the personnel selection interview. *Journal of Occupational and Organizational Psychology, 70,* 189–203.

Reade, M. N., & Smouse, A. D. (1980). Effect of inconsistent verbal-nonverbal communication and counselor response mode on client estimate of counselor regard and effectiveness. *Journal of Counseling Psychology, 27,* 546–553.

Ruback, R., & Hopper, C. H. (1986). Decision making by parole interviewers: The effect of case and interview factors. *Law and Human Behavior, 10,* 203–214.

Sherer, M., & Rogers, R. W. (1980). Effects of therapist's nonverbal communication on rated skill and effectiveness. *Journal of Clinical Psychology, 36,* 696–700.

Siegel, J. C. (1980). Effects of objective evidence of expertness, nonverbal behavior, and subject sex on client-perceived expertness. *Journal of Counseling Psychology, 27,* 117–121.

Silvester, J. (1997). Spoken attributions and candidate success in graduate recruitment interviews. *Journal of Occupational and Organizational Psychology, 70,* 61–73.

Silvester, J., Anderson-Gough, F. M., Anderson, N. R., & Mohamed, A. R. (2002). Locus of control, attributions and impression management in the selection interview. *Journal of Occupational and Organizational Psychology, 75,* 59–76.

Smith-Hanen, S. S. (1977). Effects of nonverbal behaviors on judged levels of counselor warmth and empathy. *Journal of Counseling Psychology, 24,* 87–91.

Stewart, C. J., & Cash, W. B., Jr. (1997). *Interviewing: Principles and practices* (8th ed.). Madison, WI: Brown & Benchmark.

Suiter, R. L., & Goodyear, R. K. (1985). Male and female counselor and client perceptions of four levels of counselor touch. *Journal of Counseling Psychology, 32,* 645–648.

Tay, C., Ang, S., & Dyne, L. V. (2006). Personality, biographical characteristics, and job interview success: A longitudinal study of the mediating effects of interviewing self-efficacy and the moderating effects of internal locus of causality. *Journal of Applied Psychology, 91,* 446–454.

Tessler, R., & Sushelsky, L. (1978). Effects of eye contact and social status on the perception of a job applicant in an employment interview situation. *Journal of Vocational Behavior, 13,* 338–347.

Tullar, W. L. (1989). Relational control in the employment interview. *Journal of Applied Psychology, 74,* 971–977.

Uhlemann, M. R., Lee, D., & Hasse, R. F. (1989). The effects of cognitive complexity and arousal on client perception of counselor nonverbal behavior. *Journal of Clinical Psychology, 45,* 661–665.

Vrij, A., & Mann, S. (2004). Detecting deception: The benefit of looking at a combination of behavioral, auditory and speech content related cues in a systematic manner. *Group Decision and Negotiation, 13,* 61–79.

Vrugt, A. (1990). Negative attitudes, nonverbal behavior and self-fulfilling prophecy in simulated therapy interviews. *Journal of Nonverbal Behavior 14,* 77–86.

Walczyk, J. J., Roper, K. S., Seemann, E., & Humphrey, A. M. (2003). Cognitive mechanisms underlying lying to questions: Response time as a cue to deception. *Applied Cognitive Psychology, 17,* 755–774.

Walczyk, J. J., Schwartz, J. P., Clifton, R., Adams, B., Wei, M., & Zha, P. (2005). Lying person-to-person about life events: A cognitive framework for lie detection. *Personnel Psychology, 58,* 141–170.

13 Female–Male Interaction

The communicative styles of men and women are distinctively different in our society. Our stereotypic conceptions of men and women are clearly and consistently reflected in their contrasting communicative styles. Men are stereotyped as active, dominant, aggressive, and insensitive persons who dominate communicative interaction by virtue of their superior status. By contrast, women are perceived stereotypically to be passive, submissive, supportive persons who are dominated as a result of their desire to adapt to men's needs, and to be accommodating. To a considerable degree, the stereotypes mirror the dominant characteristics of female–male interaction.

Sex-linked stereotypes are strongly reinforced by the use of sexist or exclusionary language, which relegates women to narrowly defined and dependent roles (Wood, 2007). The basic differences in male and female communication styles are revealed in implicit nonverbal messages rather than through the use of language, however.

Sex-Role Stereotyping

Strong and enduring sex-role stereotypes have developed in our society; similar sex-role stereotypes have also developed in nations with strikingly different governing systems. Men are expected to assume the *proactive* role. The cultural norm dictates that the proactive person will be active, independent, self-confident, and decisive. Individuals who assume the proactive role place a high priority on accomplishing the task at hand. Women are expected to assume the *reactive* role. Reactive individuals respond to the contributions made by others rather than initiate contributions; they are emotionally expressive and sensitive to the emotional needs of the initiator, and they are interpersonally supportive and accommodating (LaFrance & Mayo, 1978).

The sex-role stereotypes reflected in those roles are quite detailed. The stereotype for women, although more detailed than the stereotype for men, is less socially desirable. In spite of the fact that women tend to be stereotyped broadly as one large group, a woman's ethnicity may have an impact on the way that she is stereotyped. The stereotype for the black woman, for example, seems to be particularly detailed. The greater detail comes in part from the assumption that black women have suffered "double domination" from a white society and from males in general (Reid, 1989). The following descriptive labels are typically used to identify the more negative portion of the female stereotype: "submissive," "dependent," "touchy," "moody," "temperamental," "excitable," "frivolous," "talkative," and "timid." The more positive portion of the female stereotype is identified by these descriptive labels: "affectionate," "considerate," "cooperative," "supportive," and "sensitive."

While there has been some progress in society, female stereotypes have been fairly resistant to change (Wood, 2007). Indeed, television is a primary contributor to sex-role stereotyping; the more one consumes television, the more he or she believes in sex stereotypes (Zemach & Cohen, 1986). For example, let us briefly examine popular TV shows such as ABC's *The Bachelor*. On the show, two dozen or more single women vie for the attention of the "bachelor" to win him as a lifelong partner. Women are often portrayed accommodating the bachelor's every desire, including the magic question toward the end of the show. The bachelor asks the woman, "Will you share a night with me in the luxury suite?" If she says yes, she is more likely to get a rose at the end of the show. Since the show started in the early part of the twenty-first century, almost every woman has accepted the bachelor's offer.

Males are stereotyped in positive terms such as "task-oriented," "rational," and "active." More specifically, males are stereotyped by these positive adjectives: "logical," "industrious," "sharp-witted," "shrewd," "confident," "forceful," and "dominant." Descriptive labels typically used to identify the negative portion of the male stereotype are "boastful," "stubborn," "arrogant," "conceited," "hardheaded," and "opportunistic" (Eakins & Eakins, 1978; Heilbrum, 1976).

As we shall see, men and women frequently do behave in ways that are quite consistent with their stereotype. The obvious question is *why*? Biological differences seem to have a relatively limited impact on the contrasting communicative styles of women and men. Culture seems to have a powerful role in determining spatial preferences of men and women. American men are more likely to have a larger personal bubble than American women (Pearson, West, & Turner, 1995). Yet, this is not the case in Arabic cultures. Arabic men are more likely to hold hands, kiss each other on the cheek, etc., than are American men (Khuri, 2001). European men, like European women, prefer closer distances when standing near each other than do American men. Thus, the gender differences among proxemic behaviors in other cultures seem less pronounced than they are in America. Because women are generally smaller than men, their vocal cords tend to be shorter, and their shorter vocal cords may help explain why women's modal pitch is significantly higher than men's. However, Thorne and Henley (1975) maintained that the female's characteristically higher pitch is more a function of social learning than of anatomical differences.

The greatest difference between male and female communicative behaviors seems to be attributable to gender differences, as opposed to biologically determined sex differences. *Gender* is defined as the culturally established correlates of sex (Goffman, 1979). The fact that women and men do behave differently, then, might be largely a result of cultural norms that specify appropriate behavior. The characteristic domination of females by males is a socially learned behavior, reinforced by a man's gender rather than by his sex. A man's primary sexual characteristics do not usually dictate that he behave in a particular way, but his gender is associated with well-developed social norms that specify how he should behave.

Gender behavior is clearly learned. Boys and girls are expected to behave in ways that are consistent with their gender. They are expected to conform. If they do not do so, their behavior will be branded deviant. Thus, Wood (2007) writes that young girls are advised: "Don't be selfish—share with others," "Be careful—don't hurt yourself," and "Don't get messy." In contrast, young boys are told, "Don't be a sissy," "Go after what you want," and "Don't cry."

Goffman (1979) argued that the contrasting images of men and women have been strongly influenced by gender displays. *Gender displays* are conventionalized portrayals of those behaviors that society has defined as prototypically "masculine" and prototypically "feminine." The media have proved to be the strongest force in legitimizing and defining the gender displays that have become associated in the popular mind with so-called feminine and masculine behavior. In the popular reality TV show *Big Brother,* men and women compete in a house for 75 days, with the winner determined at the end. A recent study reveals that women use power on the show to compete, to deceive, to manipulate, and, ultimately, to win. Often in competitions and games, females exhibit forms of power to gain acceptance from and influence over housemates on the show. Once reserved for men only, distributive power as reflected in reality TV has changed the gender scenery in society (Eaves, 2007).

Umiker-Sebeok (1981) studied the ways gender displays are used to depict men and women in visual advertisements. She found that the image of women portrayed in magazine advertisements is one of "weak, childish, dependent, completely domestic, irrational, subordinate creatures, the producers of children and little else compared with men" (p. 211). In magazine advertisements, a young woman's high social status is frequently linked to her father's success, but a young man's success results from his own efforts; women are dependent and men are independent. The physical domination and subordination of the female is also frequently communicated clearly by the gender displays of the male. In the case of young lovers, it is the male who exhibits such stereotypic gestures as the "shoulder hold" and the "armlock"; it is the man who grasps the woman's upper arms, and it is the male who grasps the woman's hand, rather than vice versa.

Umiker-Sebeok (1981) indicated quite clearly that the advertising industry consistently portrays the male in the proactive role and the female in the reactive role. In the marriage ceremony, for example, the bride is "given away" and "carried over the threshold" of the couple's new home.

Sex-role stereotyping often forces women and men to make difficult decisions. Take the professional woman, for example. She is probably well aware that many of the personal traits that are associated with managerial success are also defining features of the male stereotype. The professional woman may, therefore, be caught on the horns of a dilemma. Should she exhibit some of the behaviors that are stereotypically associated with male leadership and sacrifice her femininity? Or should she emphasize behaviors stereotypically associated with femininity while disregarding the option of exhibiting selected masculine behaviors? No matter which choice she makes, she may not escape criticism.

Johnson, Crutsinger, and Workman (1994) noted that women have often been advised to adopt a masculine appearance in order to communicate credibility in an executive role. Their study focused on the question of whether a woman can appear too masculine and consequently negatively affect both her professional credibility and her chances for promotion. The female manager wearing either the necktie or the scarf was judged to possess significantly more managerial competence than the female wearing the open-collared shirt. The female executive wearing the necktie was judged as more likely to be determined than the one wearing the open-collared shirt. Importantly, the manager wearing the scarf was rated as significantly more likely to be promoted than the one wearing the necktie or the one wearing the open-collared shirt. Dress also affects physical attractiveness. Nicely dressed and attractive women who have achievement-related traits are given negative attributes, whereas nice-looking and attractive men are given positive attributes (Chia, Allred, Grossnickle, & Lee, 1998). Moreover, one study suggests that women have more to lose, compared to men, when they show a counterstereotypical impression management style in the workplace (Rudman, 1998).

Another study found interesting sex differences with regard to how men and women act during initial interaction. Lindsey and Zakahi (1998) found that women, not men, are more concerned about the other person's violating the traditional norms of their gender. Men do not care as long as it does not disrupt their perceived traditional role. In addition, the researchers found that women who talk more about themselves are seen as more competent.

Johnson and colleagues (1994) seem to suggest that the professional woman need neither dress like a man nor accentuate her femininity to succeed in a managerial position. The authors concluded that

> Preference for promotability may be given to females who wear adaptations or feminized versions of masculine symbols rather than the masculine symbol itself. One explanation of this finding may be that women are allowed to adopt some level of masculinity in appearance but not to the extent that their appearance is inconsistent with the gender role. When individuals adopt an aspect of dress that is inconsistent with gender role, they may violate expectations for appearance and question existing boundaries concerning what is masculine and what is feminine. (p. 30)

In any event, we continue to accumulate evidence that suggests that men and women do exhibit attitudes and behaviors that confirm the accuracy of at least part of their stereotypes. Thus, Townsend and Levy (1990) found that males are more willing than females to invest in a relationship simply because the heterosexual partner is attractive, and a man's willingness to become involved with a partner increases when the sexual potential of the relationship is emphasized. Women, in contrast to men, are more willing to make a high-level investment in a relationship and are less willing than men to enter a relationship that emphasizes the sexual component unless there is a high level of investment by the partner.

Differences in Nonverbal Communication of Women and Men

There are many distinctive differences in the nonverbal communication of men and women. In order to communicate more successfully with each other, men and women must become fully aware of the nature of those differences. They must also understand which nonverbal behaviors must be modified, and why they must be modified, if more successful communication is to result. Gender differences in nonverbal communication are manifested most clearly in contrasting communicative styles and in contrasting levels of encoding and decoding skills.

Nonverbal Profile of Female and Male Communicators

The vocalic communication of women and men is different in important respects. A woman's vocalic communication style is particularly important because it plays a central role in the way she is stereotyped (Kramarae, 1982). Contrary to the stereotype of women as *talkative,* men talk more than women (Mulac, 1989). Men's vocal dominance of women is not confined to the amount of talking they do, however. Men tend to dominate opposite-sex interactions because of the following: (a) the average duration of their talk-turns is longer, (b) the number and rate of their filled pauses is greater, and (c) they interrupt more frequently than women (Vrugt & Kerkstra, 1984).

Males' dominance of women in conversations is achieved in part by interruptions. The "interruption privilege" is one that men exercise frequently. LaFrance and Mayo (1979) emphasized that in same-sex conversations, interruptions, overlaps, and silences are almost evenly distributed between speakers. In male–female interaction, however, the following occur:

1. Women are frequently interrupted by men.
2. Women are often silent for long periods after being interrupted.
3. Women are often prevented from interrupting men by the exaggerated lengths of mens' "ums" and "hmms."
4. It is unusual for a woman to protest being interrupted by a man.

In contrast to men, women use reactive intonation patterns that may make them seem to be more emotionally expressive. Thus women, when surprised, characteristically use the "high-low down-glide" (as in "Oh, how awful!") and women often answer questions with declarative statements that end with a rising inflection. Those rising inflections can make women seem more emotional than men, but also more uncertain and indecisive.

Women do ask more questions than men and more frequently use justifiers, that is, they justify the statements they make by providing supportive evidence or reasons for their statements. The fact that women, in comparison to men, ask more questions, use more justifiers, more frequently employ intensive adverbs ("I *really* like him"), and more frequently begin sentences with adverbials ("Surprisingly . . .") suggests that women use vocal communication as a way of exercising social control by indirect means. In contrast, men use their voices so assertively that they try to exercise direct control over others via the sound of their voices (Mulac, Wiemann, Widenmann, & Gibson, 1988). More recently, Aries (1998) reports that sex differences in interruption rates are narrowing. Men tend to have interruption rates now ranging from ratios of 1.5:1 to 2:1 much lower than ratios of 3:1 or greater two decades ago. This can be attributed to situational and contextual factors, but more so from the improvements in women's equality and the increased role of women in the public sphere.

Hall (1984) summarized some of the more salient differences in the vocalic communication of women and men when she wrote:

> Females' voices are more fluent, softer, slower, higher pitched, and perhaps more variable in pitch; women also talk less in mixed groups, and interrupt less, overall, than men do. . . . It also seems to be the case that for the more sex-typed variables—such as loudness and rated dominance—men also receive more of the same kind of behavior that they themselves engage in. (pp. 139–140)

Women are also more nasal than men and are perceived to have more breathy voices. In two separate studies, the nasality of women's voices contributed to sex-stereotyped perceptions (Bloom, Moore-Schoenmakers, & Masataka, 1999; Bloom, Zajac, & Titus, 1999). Some modern-day examples are the characters in novels. One scholar indicates that male characters are typically afforded deep, loud, and husky voices, while female characters are given high-pitched, soft, and gentle voices (Talbot, 1998). Of course, many novels are made into movies, which in turn pass along sex stereotypes to the viewing audiences.

Finally, it is important to note that women laugh significantly more than men, both when speaking and listening; their total time spent laughing is almost twice that of men. Excessive laughter or out-of-context laughter is frequently interpreted in our society as a sign that a person lacks self-confidence (Frances, 1979; LaFrance & Mayo, 1979).

The visual communication of men and women also differs in important respects. Oscar Wilde reportedly said, "A man's face is his autobiography; a woman's face is her work of fiction." There is limited evidence to support the view that women are more likely than men to control their facial expressions consciously in order to avoid displeasing the person with whom they are communicating.

The fact that women smile almost twice as much as men, and that they smile more frequently when listening, seems to support the inference that female smiles are not always completely genuine. This finding may or may not be related to the fact that stereotypically, women are thought to smile more than men (Briton & Hall, 1995). Hall (1984) suggested that women smile more than men because women are conforming unconsciously to their sex-role stereotype. To explain the finding that women smile more than men, Vrugt and Kerkstra (1984) wrote that

> we may perhaps conclude that smiling in women has a different motivational basis from smiling in men. For men, smiling could be associated with feelings of friendliness, affiliation, and comfort. For women, it could also be an expression of feelings of uneasiness, socially desirable (stereotypical) behavior, and reconciliation. (p. 19)

Finally, Henley and LaFrance (1984) identified another function of smiling when they wrote that "ethologists have also suggested another function, and that is to signal appeasement and submissiveness. . . . In this sense, smiles are designed to ward off possible competition or assault by indicating that no threat is intended" (p. 364). More recent evidence supports the correlation between sex differences and smiling. Women typically smile more than men, while the impact smiling has on each perceived gender role may be somewhat different. In sum, smiling and other nonverbal forms of immediacy are crucial in gender-role development (Hall, 1998).

Women maintain eye contact with their partners for longer periods of time when listening than when speaking; low-status females sustain eye contact for significantly longer periods of time when listening than do high-status females (Ellyson, Dovidio, Corson, & Vinicur, 1980). In addition, women are consistently more facially reactive than are males (Thunberg & Dimberg, 2000). This phenomenon could explain part of the female sex stereotype of status inferiority. Yet it also illustrates the large role that immediacy plays in female interaction. Men, more often than not, either do not give proper facial reactions or fail to give any reaction at all.

In general, men exhibit more bodily movements, are more open, and appear to be more relaxed than women (Eakins & Eakins, 1978). Research also suggests that male gaze triggers body movement almost twice as often in females as female gaze provokes male movement. In addition, women stop body movement much faster when males look away than vice versa. However, this finding should be interpreted carefully because men generally move more than women, and when men are at rest, it is much more difficult for women to catch men's eyes. Finally, men are more likely to break contact with women than vice versa. Primarily, the reason for this is that women enjoy closer interactions more than men do. In addition, women are more likely to conduct respectful attentiveness to a partner, while men generally do not behave this way (Bente, Donaghy, & Suwelack, 1998).

Another area where gender differences are apparent is the communication of sadness. Men have always been told not to cry in public settings. In the film *A League of Their Own,* Tom Hanks tells his female baseball players, "There's no crying in baseball." This scene is a great example of a cultural idiom that has been passed down through the years. One study revealed that women are more likely to communicate sadness with their faces in social interactions (Plant, Kling, & Smith, 2004). This is another example of sex-stereotype differences that exist between men and women.

Men also use space as a means of asserting their dominance over women, as in the following:

1. They claim more personal space than women.
2. They more actively defend violations of their territories, which are usually much larger than the territories of women.
3. Under conditions of high density, they become more aggressive in their attempts to regain a desired measure of privacy.
4. Men more frequently walk in front of their female partner than vice versa.

The characteristic differences of men and women in their tactile behavior has already been treated in detail in Chapter 6. In general, the male is the toucher and the female the touched. Women touch others more frequently than men do only when women are interacting with children. This is not surprising, considering the stereotypical view that men are emotionally unexpressive individuals who have difficulty providing comfort and reassurance, but that women excel in this role.

The gender differences in the tactile behaviors of women and men are quite pronounced. Although males tend to take liberties in touching women, they seem inhibited when it comes to touching each other. Derlega, Lewis, Harrison, and Costanza (1989) have gone so far as to suggest that homophobia, the fear of appearing or being homosexual, accounts for the limited amount of touching among males. One area of male-male touching seems to be in sports when there is a touchdown or a winning field goal. Men might hug or do a body five on the field to show their excitement.

Other research still points to sex sterotypes in professional settings. Hall (1996) found that women are more likely to be touched by men at professional meetings when both have the same status than vice versa. Other research has suggested that younger people touch more often than older people (Hall & Veccia, 1990). More recently, Lee and Guerrero (2001) found that while women's use of touch is primarily seen as affectionate, trusting, and enjoyable, men's touch is often perceived to have sexual motivation.

When looking at culture, gender, and touch combined, there are striking differences (we will look at the role of culture and nonverbal communication in greater detail in the next chapter). For example, in their comprehensive study, Dibiase and Gunnoe (2004) compared men's and women's use of touch in three different cultures: American, Italian, and Czech. They looked at two different types of touch (hand touch and non-hand touch). Czech men use more hand touch than women do, compared to the other cultural groups; American men are second most likely to touch; and Italian men are hand-touched more by women. For non-hand touch, there are some differences. While the use of non-hand touch is almost the same for American men and women, men and women are quite different in Italian and Czech cultures. Once again, Italian women do more touching than Italian men, and Czech women do almost twice as much non-hand touching as Czech men. This study has profound research implications regarding touch in nonverbal communication, especially when considering cultural makeup.

Finally, another element of touch is violent touch or aggressive touch. Men typically get more violent physically with other men than do women with other women. A case in point: Look at the recent explosion in sports of benches clearing on both sides in football. Of course, this is commonplace in hockey, boxing, and karate. Sports venues are not the only places where violent touch is commonplace. Relational communication now involves some element of aggressive touch. One study found that college students who are courting enjoy playful aggressive touch, during both sexual and nonsexual encounters. However, men typically enjoy more physical touch and aggression during sex than do women (Ryan & Mohr, 2005).

Much of the nonverbal profiles for women and men focus on the relational dimension of dominance/submission. The other important relational dimension where the nonverbal profiles of women and men is of central importance is intimacy. In fact, many of the readers of this book may be particularly interested in which nonverbal behaviors of males and females are functional as opposed to dysfunctional in the initiation of a heterosexual relationship. A study by Simpson, Gangestad, and Biek (1993) addressed this topic in a stimulating way.

The authors maintained that *sociosexuality* is a concept of central importance. This construct concerns "the extent to which individuals require closeness, commitment, and strong emotional bonds prior to having sex" (p. 437). Individuals with an *unrestricted sociosexual orientation* require little closeness and commitment before engaging in sex and, hence, they enter relationships where sex and intimacy occur soon after the initiation of the relationship. In contrast, individuals with a *restricted sociosexual orientation* require more commitment and closeness prior to sex. In this type of relationship, emotional bonds must form before sex occurs.

This study produced nonverbal profiles that give some indication as to how men and women with unrestricted and restricted sociosexual orientations behave during initial heterosexual encounters. Males with an unrestricted sociosexual orientation smile more, laugh more, gaze downward less often, and display flirtatious glances more frequently compared to males with a restricted sociosexual orientation. Relatedly, men who are not unrestricted in sociosexuality but who are highly extroverted and self-monitoring are rated as more socially engaging, dominant, and phony. Unrestricted women are more likely to lean forward and tilt their head than restricted women.

These results are intriguing because individuals who share social and personality traits or qualities do behave nonverbally in ways that are consistent and predictable. Not surprisingly, the nonverbal behaviors exhibited by males and females with an unrestricted sociosexual orientation almost without exception communicate their "contact readiness." The interpretations of individual nonverbal behaviors such as head tilting by females is of course not always a simple matter. Interestingly, the authors (Simpson, Gangestad, & Biek, 1993) concluded that

> Forward lean also accentuates the impact of other nonverbal cues that emanate from the head and face (e.g., smiles, head cants) by drawing interactants closer together. It has been proposed that head canting may function as a flirtatious gesture designed to signal "coy" sexual interest without affect in heterosexual interaction. (p. 455)

Research has attempted to classify the kinds of nonverbal behaviors that are characteristically exhibited by men in contrast to women. Little attention has been given to how these characteristically "male" or "female" behaviors may be modified as a result of the reaction of the person with whom we are interacting. Weitz (1976) maintained that the sex of the message receiver and sender affects communicative behaviors in opposite-sex interactions.

Women seem to adapt their nonverbal behaviors to make them compatible with the personality traits and attitudes of their opposite-sex partners. Men tend to remain inflexibly committed to a proactive communicative style, but women do modify their nonverbal communicative behaviors. They adapt to meet their male partner's perceived needs, rather than to meet the distinctive requirements of a particular kind of communicative situation, however.

Weitz (1976) found that women are nonverbally adaptive when interacting with a dominant male partner, during the first phase of female–male interaction. Similarly, women exhibit less nonverbal warmth when interacting with a male partner who shows strong affiliative tendencies. In contrast, women who are interacting with other women (in the early stages of interpersonal interaction) do not seem to adapt their nonverbal behaviors in order to be compatible with the dominant personality traits of the female partner.

A similar pattern emerges in male–female interactions as they spend more time together. Women modify their nonverbal behaviors when interacting with a male partner to make their behaviors more compatible with the male's personality characteristics, but men do not make a complementary effort. Women's greater willingness to be accommodating to males may be attributable in part to the finding that individuals in general experience significantly more anxiety when interacting with a male than with a female.

Whether they are motivated by a desire to relieve their anxieties or by a desire to be accommodating, women do seem to adjust their nonverbal behaviors when they interact with a male. Females exhibit a higher focus of attention on their male partner and show significantly more sexual interest in him than vice versa. Moreover, career-oriented women communicate significantly more nonverbal warmth when interacting with a male than do family-oriented women. This adjustment in nonverbal behavior may involve an attempt to counteract the stereotypic conception that career-oriented women are colder and less emotionally expressive than their family-oriented counterparts (Weitz, 1976).

Gender Differences in Nonverbal Skills

We know little about the relative ability of women and men to encode nonverbal messages. However, some evidence suggests that women communicate the basic emotions more clearly via their facial expressions than do men. Whereas women seem to be better at encoding negative emotions such as dislike, men are better at communicating positive emotions such as happiness (Wagner, Buck, & Winterbotham, 1993). These differences in encoding performance could be related to the fact that women smile much more than men. Negative emotions are conveyed by facial expressions that are in striking contrast to the smile often displayed on a woman's face (LaFrance & Mayo, 1979). When men and women communicate more specialized kinds of emotional meaning, it appears that they exhibit comparable levels of encoding skill (Leathers & Emigh, 1980).

Women's decoding skills have consistently proved to be superior to men's, however. An exhaustive review of studies that compared the accuracy with which women and men decode nonverbal messages indicates quite clearly that women are superior decoders (McClure, 2000; Rosip & Hall, 2004). Women's advantage in decoding nonverbal cues is greater when the message contains both visual and auditory cues than when it contains visual cues alone (Hall, 1981). The superiority of women over men as decoders has also proved to be greater when they are decoding visual messages rather than vocal messages. Because women spend more time looking at men than vice versa, it is not surprising that they decode visual cues with particular skill. In fact, these decoding data support the view that women use the visual channel as their primary nonverbal source of information about others.

Women's decoding superiority is most pronounced whenever they are decoding messages that have been intentionally communicated by the message sender. Women are good at determining the meanings of messages they believe are intended for them. However, women seem reluctant, or unwilling, to determine the implicit meanings of messages that are not intended for them.

Rosenthal and DePaulo (1979) examined the comparative ability of women and men to decode messages that are communicated through channels that vary with regard to their "leakiness" (i.e., the probability that meanings are being communicated unintentionally). From the least to the most leaky, the channels used are facial expressions, bodily cues, tone of voice, and inconsistent messages (visual-auditory channels combined). Results indicated that women decoders lose their superiority over men when they are asked to decode messages transmitted over increasingly leaky channels. The diminution in decoding performance may be traced to a conscious decision on the part of women not to decode the meanings of messages transmitted through the leakier channels rather than to a relative lack of ability to decode such messages.

Subsequent research suggests that women recognize that it is not in their best interests to be too good at decoding the leaky, or unintended, nonverbal cues. They may simply not wish to know or to acknowledge that their male partner is deceiving them or is becoming unbearably anxious. Women might recognize intuitively that if they are to be supportive and interpersonally accommodating, they should refrain from decoding the meanings of messages that were not intended for them. In our society, the more accommodating a woman is nonverbally, the more likely she is to experience satisfactory interpersonal outcomes (Blanck, Rosenthal, Snodgrass, DePaulo, & Zuckerman, 1981). Indeed, one study reveals that women who use nonverbal cues to communicate power are generally less liked than men who use the same nonverbal cues for the same purpose (Carli, LaFleur, & Loeber, 1995). For example, women's actions that violate the personal space of others are seen as inappropriate, whereas men's proxemic violations are seen not only as appropriate but also as "part of the job." These stereotypes about women's nonverbal use of power are stronger than women's actual behaviors. In other words, society not only overestimates women's use of these nonverbal cues, but also exaggerates their potential negative impact in various contexts (Hall, Coats, & LeBeau, 2005). For instance, women (not men) are held at a higher standard when providing comfort (Holmstrom, Burleson, & Jones, 2005). These examples illustrate the sex stereotyping that occurs in different situations.

In short, when decoding messages are sent with a high level of awareness and intentionality by the message sender, women's superiority over men as decoders is quite striking. The fact that women exhibit no greater accuracy than men in decoding the meanings communicated through leaky channels should not be interpreted as evidence that women *cannot* decode such messages, and at high levels of accuracy. In these cases, the desire to be polite and accommodating seems to override the desire to utilize effectively their superior decoding skills.

Dysfunctional Male and Female Nonverbal Behaviors

A careful inspection of the nonverbal communicative behaviors that characterize male–female interaction reveals that many of those behaviors are dysfunctional. They are dysfunctional for the following reasons: (a) many link females and males directly to some of the most negative features of their respective stereotypes, (b) they are not consciously modified to meet the varying requirements for successful communication in different contexts, and (c) they often serve as barriers to satisfying interpersonal outcomes.

Men's nonverbal communicative behaviors seem to change little from one type of communication situation to another. Whether a man is trying to sell himself, to conduct an interview, or to run a business meeting, he exhibits a propensity to cultivate the proactive role. As we have seen, males talk more and for longer periods of time than females, and they inhibit immediate feedback by using long, filled pauses. By their visual inattentiveness, their exercise of the touching privilege, their familiar forms of address, and their bodily relaxation, men also indicate that they perceive themselves as superiors who can legitimately exercise the right to dominate heterosexual interaction. Even though men may not be aware of the implications of their nonverbal communication, their characteristic nonverbal behaviors serve to legitimate the gender-related image traits that are attributed to them (i.e., forcefulness, dominance, confidence, status, power, insensitivity, and inflexibility).

Women, in contrast, are nonverbally adaptive and supportive. Their adaptive and supportive behaviors are frequently dysfunctional, however, because they are misdirected. Rather than adapting their nonverbal behaviors to meet the distinctive requirements of specific communication contexts, women adapt to meet the perceived needs of their male partners. In their self-deprecating efforts to please, appease, and placate their male partners, they frequently lend credibility to the stereotypic terms that are used to describe their actions (i.e., *reactive, submissive, dependent,* and *inferior*).

The nonverbal behavioral profile of males is dysfunctional for three more specific reasons: (a) males become inflexibly committed to a single, unchanging communicative style; (b) males come to accept their unexpressive, nondisclosing, and insensitive communication as the norm; and (c) males cultivate a self-directed intrapersonal orientation that is incompatible with successful female–male interaction.

In one sense, the unchanging "male" style of nonverbal communication seems to have some desirable features in business situations. In a business world dominated by males, the unyielding attachment to the proactive role might seem to be desirable. This seems particularly true for leaders and those who aspire to leadership. Individuals who initiate most of the contributions, control communicative interactions, and enhance perceptions of dominance and status by their nonverbal cues might be thought to have the edge. However, this is also an age that values participative management and quality circles, and that puts a premium on a communicative style that encourages flexibility and interaction, minimizes status differences, and accents the uniqueness and intrinsic value of each individual. In the new business climate, the male who remains inflexibly committed to a single, domineering communicative style is at a severe disadvantage.

This is also an age that values the ability to express emotions openly and to read and respond with sensitivity to the feelings of those with whom we communicate. Although "women have been socialized to display their emotions, their thoughts, and ideas" (Thorne & Henley, 1975, p. 209), men continue to be verbally unexpressive, nondisclosing, and insensitive. Men's lack of expressiveness frequently means that their true feelings and emotions remain a mystery in female–male interaction. This inattentiveness seems to be linked directly to the fact that men are much less skillful decoders of nonverbal messages than women and thus have not developed the capacity to determine more precisely the nature of their female partners' emotional needs.

Finally, men's characteristic nonverbal communicative behaviors are dysfunctional because they perpetuate a preoccupation with self. Whereas women communicate their concern for others nonverbally, men exhibit a primary concern with self-assertion and self-protection; their preoccupation with short-term sexual relationships is a good example (Townsend & Levy, 1990). Men's nonverbal behaviors focus on a set of goals that are frequently important only to them, but women's nonverbal behaviors focus on their desire to facilitate interpersonal outcomes that are satisfying to *both* interactants.

In one sense, the nonverbal communicative behaviors that seem to be prototypically female are desirable. In a family setting, the emotionally sensitive and supportive woman has no peer in providing the comfort and emotional support that is so essential to the development of the cohesive family unit. The intrapersonally oriented father, in contrast, may be as likely to brood about his own concerns as to be concerned about the emotional needs of family members.

In contemporary society, however, women must function effectively in many contexts outside of the home. Whenever they do so, their nonverbal behavioral profile might be dysfunctional because (a) females frequently display nonverbal behaviors that invite the attribution of unflattering image traits, (b) females display adaptive nonverbal behaviors that raise questions about their motivations, and (c) females do not fully utilize their impressive nonverbal communication skills.

Skillful impression managers try to associate themselves with favorable images and dissociate themselves from unfavorable images. Women seem to associate themselves with unfavorable images due to some of the nonverbal behaviors they most frequently display. The fact that women smile and laugh twice as much as men may be seen to imply that their anxiety is high and their self-confidence is low. Women's polite forms of address, the small amount of personal space they claim as theirs, their visual attentiveness to men, the disproportionate amount of touching they receive, and their constricted and tense bodily postures almost ensure that they will be perceived as persons of inferior status and power (Henley, 1977).

Women's repeated efforts to be emotionally supportive and to adapt their behaviors to meet men's need to be made comfortable might in one sense seem desirable. But a woman's efforts to be interpersonally adaptive and supportive could raise questions about her motivations. How likely is it that a man will interpret a woman's smile as being genuine if it is displayed frequently? Excessive smiling, laughter, and eye contact seem to invite inferences that a person is insincere, manipulative, and deceptive. Because these nonverbal behaviors are such prominent features of the nonverbal profile for women, it is not surprising that these behaviors sometimes reinforce doubts about the wholesomeness of women's motivations in female–male interactions.

Finally, women do not fully and effectively exercise their ability to decode nonverbal messages. In order to be polite, supportive, and accommodating, women apparently choose not to decode the meanings of messages they believe their male partners did not wish to send. In view of the great informational potential of unintentional messages, women's disregard of such messages represents a serious sacrifice.

Nonverbal Differences among Genders in Families

Several elements of the family need to be addressed. Men and women communicate differently in their families. While men and women typically talk to their children about the same amount of time (Hart & Risley, 1995), their nonverbal behaviors are distinctively different. One area that deserves attention is *how* men and women communicate with their children. Miller-Day and Lee (2001) studied the different nonverbal strategies that parents employ with their sons and daughters. Specifically, how parents communicate disappointment varies. In a study of almost 400 undergraduate college students, subjects reported that their mothers used more nonverbal behaviors than their fathers in expressing disappointment. For example, when mothers were disappointed, they communicated their feelings through their body language. When fathers were disappointed, they also used body language, but not to the same degree as mothers. In addition, mothers were more likely to use nonverbal communication with their daughters than with their sons. Fathers were perceived as harsher and more critical to their sons than to their daughters.

One area of gender sameness in the family is the relationship between romantic partners, specifically the conversational interruptions husbands and wives use. As previously mentioned in the chapter, the gap between male and female interruption rates has narrowed from what earlier studies found. Robey, Canary, and Burggraf (1998) were able to confirm such a trend in the literature when they found similarities between husbands' and wives' rates of conversational interruptions. These results can be summarized in six ways:

1. Husbands and wives communicate about the same amount of time.
2. Husbands and wives take about an equal number of turns talking.
3. Contrary to earlier findings, husbands engage in more back channels (efforts at conversational maintenance).
4. Wives ask significantly more nonhostile questions than do husbands.
5. Wives and husbands ask very few hostile questions.
6. Interruption differences between husbands and wives are negligible.

Guidelines for Successful Female–Male Interaction

The messages communicated nonverbally through female and male gender displays are both powerful and resistant to change. These messages frequently serve as barriers to successful communicative interaction between males and females; therefore, the need for change is apparent. But the extent to which the dysfunctional features of female–male communication can be modified is debatable.

Potential for Modifying Nonverbal Cues.   In their penetrating essay on the potential of nonverbal communication as an agent for modifying the dysfunctional features of gender displays, Mayo and Henley (1981) argued that gender-defining nonverbal cues are resistant to change for these reasons: (a) nonverbal behaviors that are out of awareness obviously will not be changed, (b) nonverbal behaviors characteristic of gender displays are reinforced by powerful social forces such as the media, and (c) nonverbal behavior that is gender-deviant is frequently punished.

These arguments clearly have merit. Neither males nor females can modify their undesirable nonverbal communication behaviors unless they know that those behaviors *are* undesirable. At the same time, we must recognize that individuals can be trained to become aware of nonverbal behaviors that are demonstrably dysfunctional or undesirable. Evidence suggests that many dysfunctional, gender-linked nonverbal behaviors can be eliminated with appropriate training (Brown, Dovidio, & Ellyson, 1990). In fact, some sensitivity training is based on the proposition that individuals can learn to communicate more effectively by increasing sensitivity to their own behaviors. In fact, many college and university campuses offer, alongside a sexual harassment course, sensitivity training for males and females so that they can learn to recognize and become aware of their own messages that may be misinterpreted by their interactants. For example, while touch can signal comfort and support, overly used touch can raise the suspicion of sexual motivation (Lee & Guerrero, 2001).

Clearly, many of the nonverbal behaviors that we have come to accept as characteristic of each sex are learned behaviors. Sex-role stereotypes reflect deeply embedded cultural values that are reinforced by powerful communicative forces such as the media. Comprehensive changes in the nonverbal profile for males and females must be preceded by major changes in cultural values. Dysfunctional gender-related behaviors are learned; therefore they can become unlearned. The force of cultural norms is not so strong at present that dysfunctional "male" and "female" nonverbal behaviors cannot be modified (Wood, 2007). Individuals will attempt such modification, however, only when they become convinced that the advantages of change outweigh the disadvantages of inflexible attachment to fixed communication styles.

Gender-deviant behavior by a woman involves some degree of risk. Such behavior might be punished. Porter and Geis (1981) recognized the double bind that a woman may encounter when interacting with a male who assumes the traditional proactive role. They wrote that if

> a woman is ignored when she presents ordinary, moderate demand signals which are effective for men, she may attempt to secure recognition by increasing the intensity of the signal, and end up being recognized, not for achievement, but as overly emotional, arrogant and abrasive. Indeed, from the perceiver's point of view, the strong demand is uncalled for. (pp. 55–56)

Punishment and negative reinforcement are far from inevitable, however, if males recognize that such reactions on their part are counterproductive.

Although nonverbal behaviors characteristic of gender displays cannot be changed easily, there is an increasing amount of evidence that the most dysfunctional of those behaviors can be changed in specific situations. For example, the psychologically androgynous person has consistently exhibited the ability to add selective opposite-sex behaviors and eliminate the least desirable behaviors associated with his or her own sex (Mayo & Henley, 1981). Androgynous persons have a communicative flexibility not possessed by the person who conforms to the behavioral norms associated with traditional sex-role stereotypes. They have demonstrated the valuable ability of emphasizing or de-emphasizing the male and female traits they display, and thus experience more satisfying interpersonal outcomes than proactive males and reactive females (LaFrance & Carmen, 1980).

Sensitizing Communicators to Dysfunctional Gender Cues.

The first step in modifying, and ultimately eliminating, dysfunctional nonverbal cues that are characteristic of gender displays is making communicators *aware* of such cues. The success of conventional sensitivity training suggests that individuals can be made aware of behaviors that are dysfunctional. Individuals typically seek to change their own behaviors when they become fully aware that those behaviors serve neither their own ends nor the ends of successful interpersonal communication.

Nonverbal sensitivity training takes a variety of forms. For example, Leathers and a colleague conducted a sales and communication training program designed to sensitize salespeople to their communicative behaviors that serve as barriers to effective persuasive communication. In order to make the salespeople aware of their most dysfunctional behaviors, they were videotaped in both simulated and real sales situations. Their dysfunctional behaviors were then identified by their peers and by the trainers during a videotape replay. Similar formats are used by others to train police officers, politicians, and labor–management negotiators.

Modifying Gender-Stereotypic Nonverbal Behaviors.

Males and females, by virtue of their genders, tend to adopt inflexible communicative styles that limit their potential for successful communication. The reasons for trying to modify them are compelling. Helpful guidelines that can be used to modify stereotypic male and female dysfunctional nonverbal behaviors have been developed (Cannie, 1979; Eakins & Eakins, 1978; Hall, 1984; Thorne & Henley, 1975).

The following guidelines are not comprehensive, because our current level of knowledge about the nature of female–male interactions is still incomplete. They are, nonetheless, a basis for a beginning.

Both men and women should begin by examining their own styles of nonverbal communication for sex-stereotypical cues that are dysfunctional. They should recognize that they will probably have to modify some of their gender-related behaviors in order to have a marked impact on the image traits that are attributed to them. Porter and Geis (1981) found, for example, that a woman who sits at the head of a discussion table does not increase her chances of being perceived as the group's leader. The implication is that women must modify more than one nonverbal behavior if they are to enhance their prospects of being perceived as leaders. For a man to become a successful leader in a group that prefers democratic leadership, he must seek to suppress a number of the dominating and autocratic behaviors associated with the traditional male style of communication.

Men in particular must begin by developing a style of communication that features an interpersonal rather than an intrapersonal orientation. Through a modified communication style, men must demonstrate quite clearly that their attention is focused on the needs, concerns, and opinions of their opposite-sex partners. Men must become more physically and psychologically attentive. As Cannie (1979) put it, attending "is the basic nonverbal skill for valuing others. It is a process of showing people you are interested in them, you are listening, and what they say is important to you. This meets their self-esteem need and returns trust to you. Attending can be physical and it can be psychological" (p. 11).

In order to become a more flexible, sensitive, and attentive communicator, a man should do the following:

1. Minimize the use of dominance and power cues that characterize him as an insensitive and condescending person, one who relegates females to the defensive position of an inferior.
2. Develop his capacity to express clearly, and interpret accurately, a wide range of emotions, in the interest of facilitating emotionally appropriate and satisfying interpersonal communication.

3. Provide his opposite-sex partner with clear and complete feedback that can be used by the female to assess fully the nature of his communicative reactions.

Women should be guided by a different set of guidelines, including the following:

1. Suppress those nonverbal communicative behaviors that associate them with such undesirable traits as weakness, submissiveness, nonassertiveness, and powerlessness.
2. De-emphasize the display of nonverbal gender cues such as excessive smiling and laughing, which reinforce the impression that they are insincere, manipulative, and dishonest.
3. Fully exercise their impressive decoding skills, rather than interpreting only those male messages they believe are intended for them.

These guidelines, when used by both sexes, should help promote successful female–male interaction, which should result in mutually satisfying outcomes. Men and women must be able to adapt their communication styles not only to help satisfy mutual needs, but also to make them more responsive to the requirements of various communication situations.

Summary

Sex-role stereotyping has had a pervasive impact on female–male interaction in our culture. Men have been stereotyped as confident, dominant, and forceful individuals who, at the same time, are stubborn, arrogant, and inflexibly committed to the accomplishment of specific tasks. By contrast, women are viewed stereotypically as affectionate, supportive, and sensitive persons who are submissive, excitable, dependent, and timid. To a considerable degree, the communicative behaviors of men and women confirm the accuracy of their respective stereotypes.

Nonverbal cues seem to be the most powerful medium for communicating gender displays that feature prototypically "feminine" and "masculine" behaviors. The distinctive differences in the nonverbal communication of women and men are manifested most clearly in their contrasting nonverbal communicative styles and in the contrasting levels of their encoding and decoding skills.

The most dysfunctional features of the nonverbal communication styles of men and women are examined in detail in this chapter. Men's characteristic nonverbal communication style is dysfunctional because it is inflexible. It is emotionally nondisclosing and insensitive, and it reflects a preoccupation with self. In contrast, women's nonverbal communication style is dysfunctional because it features the display of nonverbal behaviors that invite the attribution of unflattering image traits. It helps create the impression that women are insincere and dishonest, and it prevents women from effectively utilizing their superior decoding skills.

Many of the dysfunctional features of female–male interaction can be modified. Such modification is not easy, however, because gender-defining cues are reflective of cultural values, which are resistant to change. Dysfunctional nonverbal cues must be raised to the individual communicator's conscious level of awareness before they can be successfully modified. When such modification is attempted, the guidelines presented in this chapter should prove to be useful.

REFERENCES

Aries, E. (1998). Gender differences in interaction: A reexamination. In D. J. Canary & K. Dindia (Eds.), *Sex differences and similarities in communication* (pp. 65–82). Mahwah, NJ: Lawrence Erlbaum Press.

Bente, G., Donaghy, W. C., & Suwelack, D. (1998). Sex differences in body movement and visual attention: An integrated analysis of movement and gaze in mixed-sex dyads. *Journal of Nonverbal Behavior, 22,* 31–58.

Blanck, P. D., Rosenthal, R., Snodgrass, S. E., DePaulo, B. M., & Zuckerman, M. (1981). Sex differences in eavesdropping on nonverbal cues: Developmental changes. *Journal of Personality and Social Psychology, 41,* 391–396.

Bloom, K., Moore-Schoenmakers, K., & Masataka, N. (1999) Nasality of infant vocalizations determines gender bias in adult favorability ratings. *Journal of Nonverbal Behavior, 23,* 219–236.

Bloom, K., Zajac, D. J., & Titus, J. (1999). The influence of nasality of voice on sex-stereotyped perceptions. *Journal of Nonverbal Behavior, 23,* 271–281.

Bohn-Robey, E. A., Canary, D. J., & Burggraf, C. S. (1998). Conversational maintenance behaviors of husbands and wives: An observational analysis. In D. J. Canary & K. Dindia (Eds.), *Sex differences and similarities in communication: Critical essays and empirical investigations of sex and gender in interaction.* Florence, KY: Lawrence Erlbaum Press.

Briton, N. J., & Hall, J. A. (1995). Gender-based expectancies and observer judgments of smiling. *Journal of Nonverbal Behavior, 19,* 49–65.

Brown, C. E., Dovidio, J. F., & Ellyson, S. L. (1990). Reducing sex differences in visual displays of dominance: Knowledge is power. *Personality and Social Psychology Bulletin, 16,* 358–368.

Cannie, J. K. (1979). *The woman's guide to management success: How to win power in the real organizational world.* Englewood Cliffs, NJ: Prentice-Hall.

Carli, L. L., LaFleur, S. J., & Loeber, C. C. (1995). Nonverbal behavior, gender, and influence. *Journal of Personality and Social Psychology, 68,* 1030–1041.

Chia, R. C., Allred, L. J., Grossnickle, W. F., & Lee, G. W. (1998). Effects of attractiveness and gender on the perception of achievement-related variables. *The Journal of Social Psychology, 138,* 471–477.

Derlega, V. J., Lewis, R. J., Harrison, S., & Costanza, R. (1989). Gender differences in the initiation and attribution of tactile intimacy. *Journal of Nonverbal Behavior, 13,* 83–96.

Dibiase, R., & Gunnoe, J. (2004). Gender and culture differences in touching behavior. *Journal of Social Psychology, 144,* 49–62.

Eakins, B. W., & Eakins, R. G. (1978). *Sex differences in human communication.* Boston: Houghton Mifflin.

Eaves, M. H. (2007). *Power as exhibited by females in reality TV: An examination of Big Brother 4 and 6.* Unpublished manuscript.

Ellyson, S., Dovidio, J. F., Corson, R. L., & Vinicur, D. L. (1980). Visual dominance behavior in female dyads and situational and personality factors. *Social Psychology Quarterly, 43,* 328–336.

Frances, S. J. (1979). Sex differences in nonverbal behavior. *Sex Roles, 5,* 519–535.

Goffman, E. (1979). *Gender advertisements.* Cambridge, MA: Harvard University Press.

Hall, J. A. (1981). Gender effects in decoding nonverbal cues. *Psychological Bulletin, 85,* 845–857.

Hall, J. A. (1984). *Nonverbal sex differences.* Baltimore: Johns Hopkins University Press.

Hall, J. A. (1996). Touch, status, and gender at professional meetings. *Journal of Nonverbal Behavior, 20,* 23–44.

Hall, J. A. (1998). How big are nonverbal sex differences? The case of smiling and sensitivity to nonverbal cues. In D. J. Canary & K. Dindia (Eds.), *Sex differences and similarities in communication* (pp. 155–178). Mahwah, NJ: Lawrence Erlbaum Press.

Hall, J. A., Coats, E. J., & LeBeau, L. S. (2005). Nonverbal behavior and the vertical dimension of social relations: A meta-analysis. *Psychological Bulletin, 131,* 898–924.

Hall, J. A., & Veccia, E. M. (1990). More touching observations: New insights on men, women, and interpersonal touch. *Journal of Personality and Social Psychology, 59,* 1155–1162.

Hart, B., & Risley, T. R. (1995). *Meaningful differences in the everyday experience of young American children.* Baltimore: Paul Brookes Press.

Heilbrum, A. B., Jr. (1976). Measurement of masculine and feminine sex role identities as independent dimensions. *Journal of Consulting and Clinical Psychology, 44,* 183–190.

Henley, N. M. (1977). *Body politics: Power, sex, and nonverbal communication.* Englewood Cliffs, NJ: Prentice-Hall.

Henley, N. M., & LaFrance, M. (1984). Gender as culture: Difference and dominance in nonverbal behavior. In A. W. Siegman (Ed.), *Nonverbal behavior* (pp. 315–317). Lewiston, NY: C. J. Hogrefe.

Holmstrom, A. J., Burleson, B. R., & Jones, S. M. (2005). Some consequences for helpers who deliver "cold comfort": Why it's worse for women than men to be inept when providing emotional support. *Sex Roles, 53,* 153–172.

Johnson, K. K. P., Crutsinger, C., & Workman, J. E. (1994). Can professional women appear too masculine? The case of the necktie. *Clothing and Textile Research Journal, 12,* 27–31.

Khuri, F. I. (2001). *The body in Islamic culture.* London: Saqi Books.

Kramarae, C. (1982). Gender: How she speaks. In E. B. Ryan & H. Giles (Eds.), *Attitudes towards language variations: Social and applied context* (pp. 175–188). London: Arnold.

LaFrance, M., & Carmen, B. (1980). The nonverbal display of psychological androgyny. *Journal of Personality and Social Psycology, 38,* 36–49.

LaFrance, M., & Mayo, C. (1978). *Moving bodies: Nonverbal communication in social relationships.* Monterey, CA: Brooks/Cole.

LaFrance, M., & Mayo, C. (1979). A review of nonverbal behaviors of women and men. *Western Journal of Speech Communication, 43,* 96–107.

Leathers, D. G., & Emigh, T. H. (1980). Decoding facial expressions: A new test with decoding norms. *Quarterly Journal of Speech, 66,* 418–436.

Lee, J. W., & Guerrero, L. K. (2001). Types of touch in cross-sex relationships between coworkers: Perceptions of relational and emotional messages, inappropriateness, and sexual harassment. *Journal of Applied Communication Research, 29,* 197–220.

Lindsey, A. E., & Zakahi, W. R. (1998). Perceptions of men and women departing from conversational sex role stereotypes during initial interaction. In D. J. Canary & K. Dindia (Eds.), *Sex differences and similarities in communication* (pp. 393–412). Mahwah, NJ: Lawrence Erlbaum Press.

Mayo, C., & Henley, N. M. (1981). Nonverbal behavior: Barrier or agent for sex role change? In C. Mayo & N. M. Henley (Eds.), *Gender and nonverbal behavior* (pp. 3–13). New York: Springer-Verlag.

McClure, E. B. (2000). A meta-analytic review of sex differences in facial expression processing and their development in infants, children, and adolescents. *Psychological Bulletin, 126,* 424–453.

Miller-Day, M., & Lee, J. W. (2001). Communicating disappointment: The viewpoint of sons and daughters. *Journal of Family Communication, 1,* 111–131.

Mulac, A. (1989). Men's and women's talk in same-gender and mixed-gender dyads: Power or polemic? *Journal of Language and Social Psychology, 8,* 249–270.

Mulac, A., Wiemann, J., Widenmann, S. J., & Gibson, T. W. (1988). Male/female language differences and effects in same-sex and mixed-sex dyads: The gender-linked language effect. *Communication Monographs, 55,* 315–335.

Pearson, J. L., West, R. L., & Turner, L. H. (1995). *Gender & communication* (3rd ed.). Madison, WI: Brown & Benchmark.

Plant, E. A., Kling, K. C., & Smith, G. L. (2004). The influence of gender and social role on the interpretation of facial expressions. *Sex Roles, 51,* 187–196.

Porter, N., & Geis, F. (1981) Women and nonverbal leadership cues. When seeing is not believing. In C. Mayo & N. M. Henley (Eds.), *Gender and nonverbal behavior* (pp. 39–61). New York: Springer-Verlag.

Reid, E. (1989). Black girls talking. *Gender and Education, 1,* 295–300.

Rosenthal, R., & DePaulo, B. M. (1979). Expectancies, discrepancies, and courtesies in nonverbal communication. *Western Journal of Speech Communication, 43,* 76–95.

Rosip, J. C., & Hall, J. A. (2004). Knowledge of nonverbal cues, gender, and nonverbal decoding accuracy. *Journal of Nonverbal Behavior, 28,* 267–286.

Rudman, L. A. (1998). Self-promotion as a risk factor for women: The costs and benefits of counter-stereotypical impression management. *Journal of Personality and Social Psychology, 74,* 629–645.

Ryan, K. M., & Mohr, S. (2005). Gender differences in playful aggression during courtship in college students. *Sex Roles, 53,* 591–601.

Simpson, J. A., Gangestad, S. W., & Biek, M. (1993). Personality and nonverbal social behavior: An ethological perspective of relationship initiation. *Journal of Experimental Social Psychology, 29,* 434–461.

Talbot, M. M. (1998). *Language and gender.* Cambridge, UK: Polity Press.

Thorne, B., & Henley, N. M. (1975). Womanspeak and manspeak: Sex differences and sexism in communication, verbal and nonverbal. In B. Thorne & N. M. Henley (Eds.), *Language and sex: Difference and dominance.* Rowley, MA: Newbury House.

Thunberg, M., & Dimberg, U. (2000). Gender differences in facial reactions to fear-relevant stimuli. *Journal of Nonverbal Behavior, 24,* 45–51.

Townsend, J. M., & Levy, G. D. (1990). Effects of potential partners' costume and physical attractiveness on sexuality and partner selection. *The Journal of Psychology, 124,* 371–398.

Umiker-Sebeok, J. (1981). The seven ages of woman: A view from American magazine advertisements. In C. Mayo & N. M. Henley (Eds.), *Gender and nonverbal behavior.* New York: Springer-Verlag.

Vrugt, A., & Kerkstra, A. (1984). Sex differences in nonverbal communication. *Semiotica, 50,* 1–41.

Wagner, H. L., Buck, R., & Winterbotham, M. (1993). Communication of specific emotions—Gender differences in sending accuracy and communication measures. *Journal of Nonverbal Behavior, 17,* 29–53.

Weitz, S. (1976). Sex differences in nonverbal communication. *Sex Roles, 2,* 175–184.

Wood, J. T. (2007). *Gendered lives: Communication, gender, and culture* (7th ed.). Belmont, CA: Thomson.

Zemach, T., & Cohen, A. A. (1986). Perception of gender and equality on television and in social reality. *Journal of Broadcasting and Electronic Media, 30,* 427–444.

CHAPTER

14 Successful Intercultural Communication

The communication styles of cultures are often distinctively different. To communicate successfully with members of another cultural group, we must be able to identify those behaviors that define the unique communication style. We must identify specific communicative behaviors, both those perceived as positive and those perceived as negative in a particular culture (Payrato, 1993). We should learn nonverbal communication not only to better adapt to a given culture, but also to become aware of our own ethnocentric views (Calloway-Thomas, Cooper, & Blake, 1999; Samovar, Porter, & McDaniel, 2007).

We know, for example, that individuals who communicate nonverbally in a manner that is consistent with the nonverbal communication style of a given culture will be perceived as more interpersonally attractive by members of that culture (Dew & Ward, 1993). Accomplished nonverbal communicators are held in high esteem in Japan, for example. In order to be viewed as an accomplished communicator in Japan, one's nonverbal behaviors must be consistent with the communication style for the Japanese culture. Indeed, conformity to the defining features of Japan's communication style is unusually important because Japanese culture is high context (McDaniel, 1993).

The nonverbal communication style of Native Americans is particularly distinctive. Their communicative style contains the following behaviors: (a) soft talk; (b) gentle handshakes; (c) minimal eye contact, especially with elders; (d) little facial display of emotion, with most facial movement around the eyes; and (e) varying expectations as to appropriate personal distances in different distance zones (Chiang, 1993). Careful study of this nonverbal communication style for Native Americans strongly reinforces the importance of communication style to help establish successful communication within a given culture.

A culture's communication style is strongly affected by its language. The potentially powerful impact of language on culture is perhaps most clearly and concisely described in the Sapir-Whorf hypothesis. This hypothesis stipulates that the language of a culture serves not only as a medium of communication but also as a major force in shaping the thought processes and perceptions of members of that culture (Condon & Yousef, 1975). Knowledge and command of the culture's language is not apt to be sufficient to ensure success in intercultural communication. In fact, Almaney and Alwan (1982) maintained that "cultural anthropologists consider nonverbal skills as far more important than verbal skills in determining communication success abroad" (p. 18). For reasons that will be emphasized in this chapter, the centrality of nonverbal message systems in successful intercultural communication has become widely recognized (Barnlund, 1989).

Nonverbal messages are particularly important in intercultural communication because they usually contain sets of implicit rules that specify what is and what is not acceptable behavior in a given culture. If outsiders are to become successful communicators in a culture other than their own, they must become thoroughly familiar with the socially learned display rules that make the communication style of the culture distinctive. Samovar, Porter, and McDaniel (2007) provide a good example of this when they discuss time in a culture (time will be discussed in greater detail later in this chapter). If you want to know how a culture operates, look at their "pace" to see how converbal communication function there. Notice the photo of two men from different cultures. As is the custom, the Asian-American scholar on the right greets his department head on the left with a two-handed handshake. He does this because it is disrespectful for one to address a person of higher status without using both hands.

Executives and employees of multinational corporations, exchange students, international travelers, and diplomats all need to communicate effectively in cultural contexts that are unfamiliar to them. This chapter is designed to be helpful to those individuals. To begin, cross-cultural similarities and differences in nonverbal communication are compared and contrasted. Next, an extensive analysis of time and odor across cultures is examined. Then, to demonstrate how a person becomes thoroughly familiar with the communication styles of contrasting cultures, the nonverbal communication styles of the Japanese and Arab cultures are examined in detail. A set of guidelines is included that can be used to identify with and adapt to the nonverbal communication style of the culture in which communicative interaction might occur.

As is the custom, the Asian-American scholar on the right greets his department head on the left with a two-handed handshake.

Cross-Cultural Similarities in Nonverbal Communication

Darwin (1872/1965) theorized that the "chief" facial expressions will be recognized universally by members of different cultures because the ability to communicate and identify the major classes of facial emotions is innately acquired. Ekman, Friesen, and Ellsworth (1972) conducted research that supports the view that six basic emotions—happiness, fear, surprise, anger, disgust–contempt, and sadness—are communicated via similar facial displays and are decoded at similar levels of accuracy by members of both literate cultures and preliterate cultures such as that of New Guinea.

Eibl-Eibesfeldt (1972) also maintained that members of different cultures use the same facial muscles to communicate emotions such as happiness and anger. For example, he observed the familiar eyebrow flash used in greetings by such diverse cultural groups as Europeans, Balinese, Papuans, Samoans, South American Indians, and Bushmen.

Like Ekman, Eibl-Eibesfeldt maintained that facial communication across cultures is similar in that members of different cultures use the same facial muscles to display basic emotions such as happiness or anger. Although different facial muscles are used to display happiness and anger, the looks of facial happiness and anger are quite similar in all cultures these researchers have examined. As a note of caution, however, Eibl-Eibesfeldt noted that even though members of all cultures may inherit a facial display that features an eyebrow flash to signal pleasure when greeting someone, the eyebrow flash is not a universal feature of greeting behavior. In Japan, the eyebrow flash is suppressed because it is considered indecent. Furthermore, Hess, Blairy, and Kleck (2000) found that Japanese individuals who communicate anger facially are more likely to be perceived as dominant compared to Caucasians who engage in the same nonverbal behavior. This study supports the notion that facially communicated anger is culture-bound and has different impacts in different societies.

More recent literature points to the universality of facial expressions across cultural contexts. Harvard scholars Elferbein and Ambady (2002) found that many emotions are now universally recognized above chance levels. Specifically, communicating emotion facially seems to contain great similarity across cultures. Haidt and Keltner (1999) conducted a study comparing U.S. and Indian participants. Results indicated that all subjects showed high levels of facial recognition. Some of the more significant findings of these cultural groups and their respected nonverbal codes are reported below:

Nonverbal Code	*U.S. Group*	*Indian Group*
Anger	82.5%	80%
Fear	55%	55%
Disgust	77.5%	82.5%
Embarrassment	40%	55%
Compassion	37.5%	40%
Amusement	40%	67.5%

Because shame is viewed as the most undesirable of emotions in Japanese culture (Sweeney, Cottle, & Kobayashi, 1980), we might infer that the reluctance to exhibit or acknowledge facial shame in Japan is a socially learned behavior.

The socialization experiences of the Japanese as opposed to Americans and Europeans differ greatly (Scherer, Wallbott, Matsumoto, & Kudoh, 1988). The cultural experiences of the Japanese shape the display rules that dictate which emotions should and should not be communicated nonverbally and ultimately affect the level of accuracy with which one or more emotions are encoded and decoded. (Display rules work similarly in cultures other than the Japanese culture.) Consider the fact that the Japanese experience great difficulty in decoding the facial expression of disgust (Ekman et al., 1987) and that in one study, Japanese subjects were able to identify disgust expressed by bodily movements only 2 out of 22 times. The problems that the Japanese experience in decoding and encoding disgust can be traced to a cultural display rule that says that disgust should not be communicated in public (Sogon & Masutani, 1989). Training apparently improves these numbers, however. Recent evidence points to the success of training Japanese and British subjects to accurately decode nonverbal cues from other cultural contexts (Nixon & Bull, 2005).

In short, there is evidence that a limited number of emotions are communicated by similar facial expressions across cultures. However, LaFrance and Mayo (1978b) noted that the pancultural element in facial communication seems to be limited to four or five basic emotions. They contend that emotional expression is subject to both cultural and biological influences. More specifically, "the innate elements link particular emotions with particular facial muscles while cultural elements adapt the facial signal to the environment in which it occurs" (p. 77). Thus, members of some cultures appear to experience and communicate sentiments and emotions that members of other cultures neither know nor recognize. For example, the facial blend that North Americans label "smug" is rarely named or recognized in any other culture. Similarly, the "wry smile" of the English, with one corner of the mouth up and the other corner down, may be unique to England.

Leathers and McGuire (1983) examined the skill of West German students in decoding facial expressions and suggested that people's cultural experiences can have a dramatic impact on their ability to identify the more subtle kinds of meanings that can be communicated by facial expressions. Using the Facial Meaning Sensitivity Test (FMST) described in Chapter 2, they compared the decoding performance of American and West German decoders. Consider the results reported in Table 14.1. Germans were significantly less accurate than Americans in identifying 13 of the 30 highly specific facial meanings in Step 3 of the FMST (pp. 305–306). Although Germans were more sensitive than Americans to such specific kinds of facial disgust as repugnance and distaste, they were much less sensitive to special kinds of facial sadness, bewilderment, and anger. We attribute the differences in ability to identify subtle nuances of facial meaning not to innately acquired skills but to culturally acquired attitudes about the emotions that are communicated by facial expressions.

The results for the German decoders (see Table 14.1) may be explained at least in part by two forces that may have helped shape German culture. Leathers and McGuire

TABLE 14.1   Accuracy of Identification of Specific Facial Expressions by German Decoders within Each Class of Meaning

Class of Meaning		Photo Number	Percentage of Correct Identification		Type of Decoding Error Made by German Decoders	Percentage of Decoders Correctly Identifying All Facial Expressions within a Class	
			American	*German*		*American*	*German*
Happiness	Laughter	9	98.45	94.37	Amusement (5.63) Love (0.00)	90.27	77.33
	Love	26	91.09	82.67	Amusement (10.67) Laughter (6.67)		
	Amusement	2	90.31	83.56	Love (12.33) Laughter (4.11)		
Fear	Terror	10	98.44	91.78	Anxiety (5.48) Apprehension (2.74)	76.74	68.00
	Anxiety	21	77.43	73.97	Apprehension (19.18) Terror (6.85)		
	Apprehension	27	77.82	76.06	Anxiety (23.94) Terror (0.00)		
Disgust	Aversion	30	78.68	77.46	Repugnance (21.13) Distaste (1.41)	42.25	56.00
	Repugnance	12	49.61	62.50	Aversion (19.44) Distaste (18.06)		
	Distaste	8	45.35	80.56	Repugnance (16.67) Aversion (2.78)		
Anger	Rage	28	95.74	61.11	Hate (23.61) Annoyance (15.28)	94.53	56.00
	Hate	1	94.92	67.12	Rage (28.77) Annoyance (4.11)		
	Annoyance	20	98.96	80.56	Hate (11.11) Rage (8.33)		
Interest	Attention	23	89.92	80.28	Excitement (14.08) Anticipation (5.63)	66.15	48.00
	Anticipation	6	67.05	60.27	Excitement (34.25) Attention (5.48)		
	Excitement	15	71.32	52.06	Anticipation (34.25) Attention (13.70)		

(*continued*)

TABLE 14.1   (Continued)

Class of Meaning		Photo Number	Percentage of Correct Identification		Type of Decoding Error Made by German Decoders	Percentage of Decoders Correctly Identifying All Facial Expressions within a Class	
			American	German		American	German
Bewilderment	Confusion	18	86.38	50.73	Doubt (34.78) Stupidity (14.49)	85.66	40.00
	Doubt	4	88.72	50.70	Confusion (43.67) Stupidity (5.63)		
	Stupidity	17	93.39	79.45	Doubt (13.70) Confusion (6.85)		
Contempt	Disdain	24	55.25	66.67	Arrogance (29.17) Superiority (4.17)	43.80	36.00
	Arrogance	13	47.47	41.10	Superiority (30.14) Disdain (28.77)		
	Superiority	29	71.98	65.28	Arrogance (30.56) Disdain (4.17)		
Determination	Stubborn	11	51.55	38.89	Resolute (36.11) Belligerent (25.00)	37.98	22.67
	Resolute	22	67.05	39.72	Belligerent (31.51) Stubborn (28.77)		
	Belligerent	25	44.19	43.84	Stubborn (31.51) Resolute (24.66)		
Surprise	Amazement	16	45.74	54.92	Astonishment (28.17) Flabbergasted (16.90)	20.62	16.00
	Flabbergasted	19	35.66	32.29	Astonishment (46.48) Amazement (21.13)		
	Astonishment	3	32.17	23.29	Flabbergasted (50.69) Amazement (26.03)		
Sadness	Disappointment	14	56.59	4.11	Distress (93.15) Pensiveness (2.74)	53.91	2.67
	Distress	5	72.48	5.48	Disappointment (39.73) Pensiveness (38.36)		
	Pensiveness	7	68.61	60.27	Disappointment (39.73) Distress (0.00)		

(1983) contended that the Germans' sense of superiority would seem to encourage the display of, and help to develop sensitivity to, those emotions that would reinforce or be consistent with a feeling of superiority. In addition, Germans' national sense of shame would seem to discourage the display of shame and prevent the development of sensitivity to those emotions that might be associated with a sense of shame.

Finally, the Germans' insensitivity to special kinds of facial bewilderment may be explained by an implicit cultural rule that discourages the public display of bewilderment. Certainly, the Germans' propensity to exercise self-control while cultivating a public image of superiority, or even arrogance, is not consistent with the frequent expression of bewilderment.

In short, the striking differences between the German and American decoders in their sensitivity to highly specialized kinds of facial emotions seem to be directly related to the impact of different display rules in the two cultures. *Cultural display rules* are a deeply ingrained set of implicit cultural conventions, learned early in life, that specify which emotions should and should not be expressed in public (Ekman & Friesen, 1975). During socialization, an individual learns not only whether the public display of emotions is positively or negatively rewarded, but also "which facial expressions are expected, preferred, or allowed in which circumstances and [communicators] learn to perform accordingly" (Kilbride & Yarczower, 1980, p. 282).

We know there are similarities across cultures with regard to infant development. At ages 9 months to 2 years, babies develop a sense of nonverbal awareness, codes, and ability to decipher caretaker emotions. One study found that among English-Canadian and Parisian-French babies, infants develop similar pointing gestures for requests, have similar facial expressions to communicate certain emotions, and are able to decipher, to a fairly reliable degree, the mood of the parent or caretaker (Blake, Vitale, Osborne, & Olshansky, 2005).

In the broadest perspective, the evidence supports the conclusion that individuals from a wide variety of cultures encode and decode a limited number of general classes of facial emotions at similar levels of accuracy. We know much less about the cross-cultural communication of vocal messages. Guidetti (1991) did a study on this unexplored field of research. Fifty French adults and 50 German adults were asked to take the vocal emotion recognition test designed by Scherer and Wallbott (1994). This test requires that the subject identify and differentiate among the emotions of fear, anger, joy, and sadness while the encoder relies strictly on vocal cues. The results indicated that German and French subjects decoded these vocally communicated emotions at similar levels of accuracy.

Rosenthal, Hall, DiMatteo, Rogers, and Archer (1979) took cross-cultural comparisons of nonverbal skills a step further by testing the relative sensitivity of different cultural groups to emotional and attitudinal information transmitted through 11 channels and combinations of channels. The Profile of Nonverbal Sensitivity (the "PONS" Test) has been administered by Rosenthal and his colleagues to such diverse cultural groups as Australians, Hawaiians, New Guineans, and Israelis.

The PONS Test is a 45-minute black-and-white film that contains 220 auditory and visual segments. Viewers are asked to respond to two-second excerpts from a scene portrayed by a female. Viewers must make judgments about dominance and submissiveness in five different scenes. The channels are as follows:

1. face alone, no voice
2. body from neck to knees, no voice
3. face and body down to thighs, no voice
4. electronic content-filtered voice, no picture
5. randomly spliced voice, no picture

The other six are mixed channels that use some combination of the first five channels. Interpreting their results, Rosenthal and co-workers wrote that the

> cultural universality hypothesis, which suggested that all cultures would do equally well due to the universality of nonverbal behavior, can also be considered disproved by the data. There was a wide variation among cross-cultural groups in their levels of accuracy in decoding the PONS film. (p. 211)

Interestingly, members of those cultures rated most similar to Americans had the highest PONS scores, and those rated least similar had the lowest PONS scores. Australian aborigines, Australian psychiatric patients, and Papua New Guinean Civil Service trainees received their the lowest ratings on their similarity to American culture scales and three of the four lowest scores on the PONS Test.

When considered in their broadest perspective, cross-cultural similarities in nonverbal communication seem to be primarily limited to affect displays. Similar facial expressions are used across cultures to communicate such broadly defined emotions as happiness and anger. The frequency with which such basic emotions are facially displayed varies from one culture to another, however, depending on how the emotion is valued in the culture. The more specialized the emotional meaning that is being communicated, the greater the cross-cultural differences in encoding and decoding accuracy. Those differences seem to be related directly to cultural display rules that specify which emotions should and should not be expressed.

While the vast majority of cross-cultural research showing similarities in nonverbal communication focuses on the face, one study looked at the use of touch. In a study of participants from Spain and the United States, subjects were able to decode various emotions of touch in similar ways. Both groups were able to decode, at similar levels, emotions of anger, fear, disgust, love, gratitude, and sympathy. In addition, both groups were able to successfully decode these emotions through touch in two situations: as the recipient of touch and as the viewer of others touching (App, Bulleit, & Jaskolka, 2006).

There also seem to be interesting similarities between cultures with regard to teachers, nonverbal styles in the classroom. Several studies vividly make the point that U.S. and Chinese students perceive teachers with similar nonverbal immediacy behaviors similarly (Zhang, 2005). For example, students respond equally well to "small-class" environment behaviors. Those nonverbal behaviors might include teacher–student interaction during question-and-answer periods, a teacher smiling at a great answer, a teacher leaning toward the student at the podium, or a teacher pointing to the student who gives good feedback in a discussion.

In another study of teacher immediacy, teachers who were most immediate were most successful and created better learning environments than those who were not. These findings included several cultures such as Australian, Finnish, Puerto Rican, and American. The findings were true regardless of whether the culture embraced high or low immediacy (McCroskey et al., 1996).

As we shall see, cross-cultural differences in nonverbal communication seem to become much more pronounced as we move from a consideration of affect displays to a consideration of emblems, illustrators, and regulators. Cross-cultural differences are also manifested clearly in the contrasting proxemic and tactile behaviors exhibited in different cultures. Chronemics, or the way a culture uses time, reflects and emphasizes cross-cultural differences in nonverbal communication. Finally, olfactics, or perception of odor, reflects individual and subcultural variations in nonverbal messages and interpretations.

Cross-Cultural Differences in Nonverbal Communication

Members of different cultures all experience the same biological drives that motivate them to satisfy their needs to be relieved of tensions associated with hunger, thirst, sexual desire, inadequate protection from the elements, and fatigue. In their attempts to satisfy those needs, members of different cultures all develop rules that are used in courtship, in marriage, in family relations, in division of labor, and in codes of ethics, for example.

Although our drives and needs are biologically determined, the ways in which we satisfy our needs are socially learned. For example, if you grew up in China, you would probably eat bird's nest soup, well-aged eggs, and rice. Members of other cultures eat snakes, grasshoppers, and lizards. From the perspective of intercultural communication, life would be much less complicated if all cultures developed identical behavioral responses to satisfy the same needs. We know that is far from the truth.

If one word best describes the communication that is characteristic of specific cultural groups, that word is *different*. This is particularly true when we consider cultures with dissimilar values and belief systems. In fact, one culture is differentiated from another on the basis of difference rather than similarity. A culture is defined as those values, beliefs, customs, rules, laws, and communicative behaviors that can be used to differentiate one societal group from another.

Cross-cultural differences in nonverbal communication are so numerous that they defy complete description. Suffice it to say that each "culture has its own distinct nonverbal communication system. Children learn this system before they master verbal skills and rely on it as their major vehicle of communication. As they grow up, nonverbal behavior becomes so deeply rooted in their psyche that they engage in it rather unconsciously" (Almaney & Alwan, 1982, p. 16). The nonverbal behaviors that are unique to human beings are wrapped up into sociocultural factors. A person can learn to control these behaviors to adapt to the culture or spontaneously suppress them to gain better outcomes (Buck, 2003). For example, a person might suppress a feeling of sadness in order to make a friend feel better or avoid scratching one's head to signal confusion to an onlooker.

Cross-cultural differences in nonverbal communication are manifested in many ways. Gestural emblems are perhaps the most important, and because this is true, gestural emblems are highly susceptible to misinterpretation. Similar gestural emblems have different meanings in different cultures, and different emblems are used in different cultures to communicate the same meaning. For instance, in the United States the head nod signals agreement, but in Japan it signals acknowledgment that the message has been received. In Italy, "up yours" is communicated by the forearm jerk; Americans use the upraised middle finger.

The diversity that is characteristic of cross-cultural gestural communication is documented in the detailed inventory of European gestures compiled by Morris, Collett, Marsh, and O'Shaughnessy (1979). They found not only that the same gestures have different meanings in different European cultures, but also that some cultures consistently use different gestures to communicate the same meaning. Furthermore, in some cases gestures used to communicate specialized meaning in one European culture are not used at all, or are not recognized, in another European culture.

Consider the case of the *hand-purse* gesture—the fingers and thumb of one hand are straightened and brought together in a point facing upward; held in that posture, the hand may be kept still or moved slightly. In Italy this gesture means "Please be more precise" or "What are you trying to say?"; in Spain the gesture means "Good"; in Tunisia the gesture means "Slow down"; in Malta the gesture means "You may seem good, but you are really bad." The hand-purse gesture interpreted as "Please be more precise" is widely understood throughout the Italian-speaking world, but only 3 percent of the persons surveyed in neighboring southern France knew its meaning.

Other cross-cultural differences abound. Chami-Sather and Kretschmer (2005) looked at the cultural variations developed early in life. Arabic youth solve problems differently than do American children. For example, Lebanese children are more likely to point, use gestures, and convey confrontation using nonverbal channels than are American children.

Interesting findings have also been discovered in relational and immediacy studies. Cutrone (2005) found cross-cultural differences in back-channel communication (i.e., listener responses) between Japanese and British dyads. Japanese persons use many more back-channel responses in relational communication than do their British counterparts. Hispanics reported that in a diverse working environment, they receive more immediate nonverbal feedback and social support from their Hispanic peers than from Anglo-Americans (Amason, Allen, & Holmes, 1999). In another study, Roach and colleagues (2005) found striking differences between American and French teachers' use of nonverbal immediacy behaviors while in the classroom—for example, American educators are more prone to using power gestures and affinity-seeking strategies in their teaching than are French teachers.

Cross-cultural differences occur also with regard to cross-cultural proxemic norms and behaviors. We know, for example, that Latin Americans prefer closer interaction distances than do North Americans. We also know that distance preferences vary among Latin Americans. Costa Ricans stand closer to those with whom they interact than do Panamanians or Colombians. Costa Ricans also touch others more frequently than Colombians or Panamanians (Shuter, 1976). When the proxemic behaviors of Italians, Germans, and U.S. citizens are compared, the finding is that Italians interact with others at the closest distances, Germans communicate at greater distances than Italians, and citizens of the United States are most distant in their interactions with others (Shuter, 1977).

Cross-cultural differences in nonverbal communication are not confined to differences in the visual, proxemic, and tactile behaviors that are exhibited in different cultures, however. Hall (1969) emphasized that different cultures place greater or lesser emphasis on certain sensory modalities that are used to encode and decode nonverbal messages. He stressed that Americans and Arabs live in different sensory worlds much of the time, and as a result they attach different priorities to certain kinds of nonverbal communication.

Thus, "Arabs make more use of olfaction and touch than Americans. They interpret their sensory data differently and combine them in different ways" (p. 3). Let us now look at two important nonverbal differences across cultures: chronemics (the study of time) and olfactics (the study of odor).

Chronemics (Time)

Chronemics is defined by the way members of a given culture define, experience, structure, and use time. From the perspective of a decoder, knowledge of time norms for a given culture can be valuable. Hickson and Stacks (1989) wrote:

> Culture begins to educate each of us at an early age as to the value of and the means by which we distinguish time. Each culture has its own particular time norms, which are unconsciously followed until violated. When such violations occur, however, they are perceived as intentional messages associated with that particular culture. In this regard each culture teaches its people what is appropriate or inappropriate with regard to time. (p. 186)

Chronemics is of much more limited value from the perspective of the encoder, however, because the cultural differences in the way time is defined, experienced, structured, and used remain relatively fixed over the years. As a result, the culture-bound messages a person may transmit about time norms will remain the same no matter what the nature of the communication situation.

One study found that the duration of an event is colored by routine. Anvi-Babad and Ritov (2003) found that those in a routine perceive the duration of a job to be shorter than those who are not in a routine, even when the job is of equal interest. A good example of this is that a frequent flyer might feel that the workweek is shorter than a person who flies only one or two weeks per year.

When we turn to international business, two types of time are used: *monochronic* and *polychronic* time (Hall & Hall, 1987). "Monochronic time (M-time) means paying attention to and doing only one thing at a time. Polychronic time (P-time) means being involved with many things at once. Like oil and water, the two systems do not mix" (p. 17).

Western cultures represented by such nations as the United States, Switzerland, Germany, and Scandinavia use M-time to conduct international business. M-time requires an allegiance to the clock and rather minimal involvement with the persons with whom one does business. P-time, in contrast, stresses maximum involvement with the parties to a business transaction, with recognition of the fact that many different personal and business activities might occur at the same time. A number of Latin American and southern European businesspersons operate on P-time.

In short, "Time talks. It speaks more plainly than words. The message it conveys comes through loud and clear. Because it is manipulated less consciously, it is subject to less distortion than the spoken language" (Hall, 1963, p. 15). Thus, sensitivity to culture-specific time norms and conceptions of time will reveal many intercultural differences (Hall & Hall, 1987). Cultures that share values similar to those of the United States expect rigid adherence to the deadlines and time limits associated with formal time. The past, present, and future are defined precisely, and an emphasis is put on time-bound planning.

In contrast, in the Navajo culture there is no conception of the future, so promises of future actions become meaningless. Latin American and similar cultures prefer an informal conception of time that places a premium on the leisurely development of interpersonal relationships. Finally, the Japanese culture seems to be able to combine the best features of formal and M-time with the best features of informal and P-time.

Perhaps one of the most extensive recent treatments of time and culture was conducted by Brislin and Kim (2003). In their research, they focused on nine key elements in the study of culture and time. Each element is listed below, followed by a paragraph on each.

1. clock and event time
2. punctuality
3. task and social time
4. P-time and M-time
5. work and leisure time
6. fast and slow paces of life
7. periods of silence
8. past, present, and future orientations
9. time as a symbol

Clock and event time is a strong adherence to the clock in which activities and events are planned around a certain time of the day. Such events might include the opening and closing of the stock market. North America, Western Europe, East Asia, Australia, and New Zealand all have strong adherences to clock time in their cultures. In contrast, work cultures in South America and South Asia do not strictly follow clock time since their economies are developing and business practices do not involve stock market dynamics.

Punctuality is the ability to be on time. North America is infatuated with its strict guideline of being on time. In fact, many colleges and universities have now placed atomic clocks in their hallways to ensure that students arrive "exactly" on time for their classes. If you show up late these days with no apology, you send a grave nonverbal message about yourself to the receiver (Samovar, Porter, & McDaniel, 2007). While it may be important to be "on time," especially at school or in the workplace, a flexible approach to "penciling you in today" also fosters an atmosphere of concern for the needs of the customer or client (Ballard & Seibold, 2003).

Task and social time is the simple ratio between time spent on work-oriented tasks while on the job versus time spent on social activities. Social activities include drinking coffee or planning a weekend getaway. Americans frequently say they spend 80 percent of their time at work on job-related tasks and only 20 percent on social activities, whereas workers in India, Nepal, Indonesia, and some Latin American countries divide their task and social time equally.

P-time and M-time have already been discussed. However, Brislin and Kim (2003) suggest that P-time and M-time have more meaning when one also looks at clock and event time. They suggest that two workers in the same M-time culture may approach time differently: one may feel more comfortable working with clock time while the other may not. P-time and M-time also function for us in nonbusiness contexts. One study found that we can perform what is called *role overload* in a P-time culture. Examples include eating while reading the newspaper or picking up dinner on the way home from school or work (Kaufman, Lane, & Lindquist, 1991).

Work and leisure time is the ratio of work to leisure in one's life; there are striking differences between cultures and their ratios of work to leisure. While the U.S. and Japanese cultures are known for demanding long hours from their employees, these cultures do not necessarily embrace the same standard of vacation time. The average American gets two weeks of vacation time in an average calendar year, while the average Japanese gets three weeks. While Americans are workaholics, not all work at the same pace. Brislin and Kim (2003) found that college-educated workers work more hours than high school graduates. But that does not mean you should think about dropping out of college! The researchers suggest that college graduates must work longer hours to afford the luxurious lifestyles that so many have grown accustomed to. In addition, Ackerman and Gross (2003) found that students are not upset when they have no "free time" but experience negative emotions when they feel "time pressure" or lack of time to complete assignments or papers.

Fast and slow paces of life are key ingredients to understanding how a culture approaches the value of time. Countries where the pace of life is faster (e.g., the United States, Switzerland, Ireland, and Germany) are much more productive economically than those cultures with slower paces of life (e.g., El Salvador, Brazil, and Mexico). Yet members of those fast-paced cultures who do well economically are much more likely to have heart disease and other health ailments. One study correlates P-time-culture workers with psychological strain and ill effects on well-being (Hecht & Allen, 2005).

Periods of silence is an important variable in understanding time across cultures. Historically, Americans and Europeans have been uncomfortable with silence. Yet Asian and Pacific Island cultures have no problem with silence. Has someone recently asked you to be quiet? Were you ever in a group when the teacher or leader said, "OK, let's all be quiet"? Did you succeed as a child when you played Quiet Mouse? Chances are, you probably didn't.

Past, present, and future orientation is also important in assessing time differences across cultures. Americans are obsessed with the here and now. Citizens of the United States are concerned with future events: what is going to happen next week, next month, or next year (Martin & Nakayama, 2007). Little attention is given to past events. But many cultures honor past activities, and some of their cultural values are linked to long traditional pasts. The Chinese look to tradition as a guide for behavior, and the Italian culture pays high regard to a long history of tradition in the arts. France is also a culture that places a premium on its history and the tradition in Paris.

Time as a symbol also varies from culture to culture. In fact, Doktor (1990) says that American and Asian CEOs are 95 percent the same and 5 percent different in all important ways. Doktor found that American CEOs tend to divide their time into small chunks, hold shorter meetings, and stay on schedule. Asian CEOs, however, tend to hold longer meetings with less structure in their schedules.

Culture-specific conceptions of time and time norms can operate very much like display rules. The sensitive observer of a foreign culture can learn what are and are not proper uses of time within that culture. As a result, many of the misunderstandings and misinterpretations associated with culture-bound notions of time could be eliminated or minimized (Bruneau, 1988). Let us now look at odor and its impact across cultures.

Olfactics (Odor)

Olfactics is the study of odor and how it communicates to the user. Strikingly, most differences in odor perception are subcultural. That is, few studies have addressed the effect of odor in international or cross-national contexts, but if we instead consider individual differences in buying behaviors according to regions and locales within the United States, we see that a few studies have addressed the impact of odor on human interaction. Recall Chapter 5 on proxemics, which addresses cultural variation between spatial needs, thereby influencing the impact of how odor is perceived and tolerated.

Odor or our sense of smell has a profound effect upon perception, especially in the built environment and during interaction with others. When was the last time you picked up a baby only to have her cry? The baby has a keen awareness not of "who" you are but of how "you" smell. Primates have long used olfaction as a way to communicate and interact with family and strangers in their environment. Some research suggests that odor plays a vital role in the family—in recognizing loved ones, mating, and in procreation (Filsinger & Fabes, 1985).

For humans, we are more complex and our use of odor is strategic, often used in marketing products in today's world. For years, companies have marketed aroma products by gender: men use Old Spice cologne and women use Secret deodorant. But in our androgynous culture, marketers are adapting their products to the unisex environment—from unisex bathrooms to personal fragrances. A recent report in *USA Weekend* says that there is now a unisex fragrance. This new smell, called "Unisex Bond No. 9's Bleecker Street," is making appeals to both genders. Famous New York Yankees ballplayer Derek Jeter and actress Julia Roberts are both using the aroma (Meyer, 2006). This product gives new meaning to odor and gender identity. Thus odor has subcultural implications that can be affected by gender.

Several studies have examined the impact of odor on behavior and mood. One study looked at the effects of odor on gambling behavior. Hirsch (1995) found that when pleasant odors were added to areas in a casino, slot machine use increased by almost 50 percent compared to areas in the casino that were not odorized. In addition, research has found that odor can affect mood and performance (Moss, Cook, Wesnes, & Duckett, 2003). In several studies, odor was found to affect one's ability to remember products or items associated with a certain scent or smell (Annett, 1996; Cain, 1979; Herz, 1997; White et al., 1998), or capture one's attention (Michael, Jacquot, Millot, & Brand, 2005). The smell of a neighbor's barbecue grill is a good example of odor's capturing a person's attention.

More substantial research has examined the effect of odor upon customers' buying behavior (see Turley & Milliman, 2000, for an extensive review). Spangenberg, Crowley, & Henderson (1996) also conducted a study about how olfactory cues impact customers' behaviors in stores. They found that scents can produce arousing atmospheres, or what Mehrabian calls *high-load environments* (see Chapter 15 on the built environment for more information about high- and low-load contexts). Interestingly, the researchers found that the "scented" condition caused customers to give more positive ratings in all 25 categories ranging from store image, environment, and product merchandise.

When was the last time you smelled a new car? Marketers realize the power of the "new" smell, and now a person can find the "new car" scent in stores where auto air fresheners are sold. Customers simply prefer the new smell to the old smell. Mitchell, Kahn, and Knasko (1995) found that odors congruent with a product are more likely to enhance customer decision making, prolong the time customers spend shopping, and increase the likelihood that customers will buy the product. Lindstrom (2005) found that customers rated a pair of shoes in a scented room to be worth $10 more than the same pair of shoes in an unscented room.

Other Issues in Cross-Cultural Differences

Belk, Garcia-Falconi, Hernandez-Sanchez, and Snell (1988) found that the nonverbal style of U.S. couples is assertive and confrontational when compared to Mexican couples. More particularly, Mexican women are much less likely to use nonverbal disapproval and voiced objections in dealing with an intimate than U.S. women are. Those differences in nonverbal communication style may be attributed in part to cultural differences. Masters and Sullivan (1989a, 1989b) have done research in that area with a somewhat different focus. In contrasting the nonverbal communication style of French and U.S. politicians, they found many similarities and differences. French citizens expect more authoritative and aggressive nonverbal behaviors from their political leaders and respond more favorably than U.S. citizens do. Although our knowledge in this area remains incomplete, we also know that many salient differences in the nonverbal communication systems of major cultures have been identified (LaFrance & Mayo, 1978a, 1978b).

In retrospect, we can conclude that when two or more cultures are compared, there are apt to be *both* cross-cultural similarities and differences in the ways they communicate nonverbally. For example, the Greek and U.S. cultures are quite different in many respects. One would expect, therefore, that there are many differences in the nonverbal communication style for Greeks and Americans. On the other hand, a study by Bernieri and Gillis (1995) found a high correlation between Greeks and Americans in terms of the nonverbal behaviors that they believe are most effective in communicating rapport, such as *extent* of gestures, supportive back-channel responses in the form of head nods and "hmms," close physical proximity, forward lean, and synchronized bodily movements.

Members of two strikingly different cultures may interpret the same nonverbal behaviors in ways that are both similar and dissimilar (Peng, Zebrowitz, & Lee, 1993). In a study by Montepare and Zebrowitz (1993), separate groups of Korean and American subjects were asked to observe the gaits of different people who were walking along. Interestingly, the different "patterns of gait" exhibited exerted a strong and highly similar impact on the social perceptions of both the Koreans and the Americans. Using "walker's gait" as their sole source of information, there was a high degree of intercultural agreement among Korean and American perceivers in terms of the perception of each walker's age and sex as well as rated happiness, physical strength, and sexiness.

Even though this study revealed many cross-cultural similarities in the way Koreans and Americans interpret a walker's gait, there was one important cross-cultural difference. Walkers with a "youthful gait" were perceived, by Americans but not by Koreans, as more dominant than those with an older gait. The authors suggested that youthfulness is positively valued in Western cultures, whereas in the Korean culture, senior citizens are treated deferentially and are seen as sources of enlightenment and strength.

Cross-cultural studies of nonverbal communication have focused in greatest detail on the functions of nonverbal cues in communicating emotions, greetings, status differences, and intimacy. Each of those functions assumes a central role in defining the distinctive nonverbal communication style of a given culture. In order to understand how knowledge of nonverbal communication styles of specific cultures can be used to facilitate more successful intercultural communication, we will compare and contrast the styles of two cultures of particular importance to U.S. citizens: the Japanese culture and the Arab culture.

Communicating Nonverbally with the Japanese and the Arabs

The dominant values of a culture reveal what is important to members of that culture (Shuter, 1983). Cultural values are reflected clearly in the nonverbal communication styles that differentiate one culture from another. Familiarity with a culture's communicative style is absolutely necessary if successful intercultural communication is to occur, because the implicit display rules that suggest how not to behave are an integral part of the nonverbal communication style of a culture.

A comparison and contrast of the nonverbal communication styles of the Japanese and Arab cultures should be useful for at least two reasons. In view of current political and economic realities, American contact with members of those cultures is increasing daily. In addition, we possess more in-depth knowledge of the nonverbal communication that is characteristic of those two cultures than of any other non-Western culture.

The previous statements about the potential utility of this section seem to have even greater force today than they did when the first edition of this book was completed in 1986. Indeed, you may have acquired much of your knowledge about the Arab culture during the first few days of the war between the U.S. coalition and Iraq. As you spent countless hours before your television set, you may have recognized that the American and Arab cultures are experiencing a type of forced and sustained contact that has never occurred before.

Because Japan is geographically isolated, there is a high degree of homogeneity and uniformity in Japanese values. The cultural values of the Japanese have been shaped by three religious faiths: Confucianism, Shintoism, and Buddhism (Barnlund, 1989). However, the impact of Zen Buddhism on the development of Japanese cultural values has been particularly pronounced. Zen Buddhism values introspection more than action. Partially as a result of that value orientation, the Japanese attach great importance to the value of silence. Nonobvious, subtle, and even indirect expression is also viewed as a cultural ideal. The inscrutable (expressionless) face of a Japanese is understandable in view of this value orientation.

The importance of maintaining self-control in public requires the conscious inhibition of those emotions that might reveal weakness. For example, to openly express an emotion that is as negatively valued as shame is to lose face in Japan. Disgust is also a negatively valued emotion in Japan and should not be displayed in public. Predictably, results from one study (Ekman et al., 1987) show that Japanese decoders identified facial disgust at a lower level of accuracy than they identified six other facial emotions. Furthermore, the decoders from the nine other countries in the study, including Greece, Italy, Turkey, and the United States, all identified facial disgust at a higher level of accuracy than the Japanese decoders. As Morsbach (1973) put it, "control of an outward show of pleasant emotions in public is also rarely relaxed in Japan. Women tend to cover their mouth while laughing, and males show true merriment (but also true anger) mainly after hours when their culture allows them greater freedom of behavior while drinking alcohol" (p. 269).

In Japan, it is extremely important to know your place (Lebra, 1976). Commitment and loyalty to the work group and family group are stressed, at the expense of developing the individual. Indeed "the family not only dominates; it is the prototypic model for society. All large organizations from the school to the corporation, even to the state itself, are modeled upon it" (Barnlund, 1989). A person's individual accomplishments are much less important than the accomplishments of the organization with which that person is affiliated (Ouchi, 1981). Interaction in Japan must conform to carefully prescribed "forms." The importance attached to the values of showing respect for superiors and being polite is manifested in cultural rituals that openly emphasize those two values (Barnlund, 1975b). Not surprisingly, the Japanese put a premium on the importance of achieving consensus and avoiding conflict (Barnlund, 1989). The recent success of the U.S. automaker Saturn Corportion is a result of building the company around the family model, which was specifically adopted from Japan (Sloop, 2005).

Because the Japanese value subtlety, restraint, indirectness in emotional expression, deference to authority, and politeness, it is not surprising that a rather detailed stereotype of the Japanese communicator has been developed. Japanese communicators are viewed by Americans, and by themselves, as silent, reserved, formal, cautious, serious, and evasive. Because of the strength of the stereotype, those stereotypic qualities have become an important part of the "public" communication style of the Japanese (Barnlund, 1975a).

In contrast, many of the values that are dominant in the Arab culture are quite different from Japanese values. Almaney and Alwan (1982) emphasize that hospitality, pride, honor, rivalry, and revenge are particularly important values to Arabs. Whereas the Japanese value a public presentation of self that is emotionally nondisclosing and unexpressive, polite, and withdrawn, Arabs attach great value to the uninhibited expression of emotions that exhibit maximum sensory experience and physical contact.

The Islamic faith is obviously an important cultural force in Arab countries. One of the direct effects of the faith is rather stringent prohibitions on what foreigners may not do in Arab countries. Saudi Arabia in particular has explicit rules that dictate what is and is not acceptable in public. This is true of how U.S. troops have behaved in the Gulf and Iraq Wars. Soldiers have to adapt to the local cultural norms, especially with regard to speech patterns, dress codes, etc.

The expansive hospitality of the Arabs has the effect of promoting social interaction rather than inhibiting it. A real or imagined insult to an Arab's well-developed sense of pride and dignity is apt to be met not with silence but with an immediate visceral reaction. The Arabs' preoccupation with honor, rivalry, and revenge means that the public display of emotions is the rule rather than the exception. Almaney and Alwan (1982) noted that Arabs "are plagued by excessive rivalry, bickering, and backbiting," and that "vengeance murder as a means of settling political disputes is still in evidence throughout the Arab world" (p. 96).

Whereas the Japanese covet privacy, Arabs place no value on privacy in public. Pushing and shoving, crowding, and high noise levels are the norm in Arab states. In fact, Arabs are offended by anything less than intimacy of contact while carrying on a conversation. Such conversations characteristically feature "the piercing look of the eyes, the touch of the hand, and the mutual bathing in the warm moist breath during conversation [that] represent stepped-up sensory inputs which many Europeans find unbearably intense" (Hall, 1969, p. 158).

The obvious question at this point is how do these contrasting values affect the nonverbal communication styles that are characteristic of the Japanese and Arab cultures? That question can perhaps best be answered by a cross-cultural comparison of the uses of nonverbal cues in communicating emotions, greetings, status differences, and intimacy.

Communicating Emotions

The nonverbal communication style of the Japanese is relatively expressionless. Implicit display rules seem to dictate that the impulse to show felt emotions via facial expressions should be inhibited and suppressed. Ekman and associates (1972) found that Japanese subjects who were asked to describe the stress-inducing films they had just watched displayed fewer negative expressions and more impassive expressions than their American counterparts.

Not only do the Japanese inhibit the expression of emotions, but they are also known to substitute the display of emotions they do *not* feel for those they *do* feel. They do so in order to avoid displaying such socially unacceptable expressions as shame or anger. This use of facial management has undoubtedly reinforced the popular view that the Japanese are evasive. Morsbach (1973) noted that although smiling is viewed universally as an indication of joy, it is used in Japan to hide pressure, anger, and sorrow.

In the Arab culture, in contrast, the open, direct, and uninhibited display of emotion is positively valued. Arabs slurp their coffee to show that they are enjoying it; belching after a meal is not uncommon—it indicates that the diner is full. The emotional richness of conversation with Arabs is also reinforced by their frequent use of gestures. Almaney and Alwan (1982) observe that to "tie an Arab's hands while he is speaking is tantamount to tying his tongue."

The importance that Arabs attach to a sensitive reading of, and response to, the emotions of the person with whom they are communicating is perhaps best revealed in their piercing and unremitting eye contact. Arabs carefully monitor dilation and contraction of the pupils of the eyes, because they believe that pupil dilation accurately reflects the level of interest, as well as information about the emotion being experienced. Japanese communicators, in contrast, do not directly monitor the eyes of the person with whom they are communicating; they look instead at the Adam's apple.

Greetings

In Japan, the "form" or "frame" of interpersonal relationships tends to be more important than the substance of communication. Thus, the *nakōdo,* or go-between, not only arranges marriages in Japan but also arranges meetings with a wide array of individuals ranging from government officials to corporation executives to political leaders. Other forms of communication or expression that are important in the Japanese culture include the tea ceremony (*cha-no-yu*), flower arrangements (*ikebana*), and calligraphic representation (*shodo*) (Barnlund, 1989).

For the Japanese, social interaction must begin with a bow. The complex set of rules that govern socially acceptable bowing seems to reflect the importance the Japanese attach to civility, politeness, status, and form in interpersonal communication. In Japan, torso angle is very important. Morsbach (1973) wrote that "reciprocal bowing is largely determined by rank: the social inferior bows more deeply and the superior decides when to stop bowing" (p. 268). Bowing is such an integral part of greeting behavior in Japan that animated bowing dolls with tape-recorded voices have been used to welcome customers to department stores.

When a Japanese businessperson and a foreigner greet each other, a combination of a bow and a handshake may be in order. Circumspection and restraint, with no mutual touching, is expected. Maximum distance should be maintained after the bow–handshake. Native Japanese prefer greater interaction distances than either Americans or Hawaiian Japanese (Engebretson & Fullmer, 1970). Conversation should be kept to a minimum, and business cards should be exchanged.

The nonverbal communication style employed to greet someone in the Arab culture is quite different. Effusive greetings are expected. Pleasantries are encouraged. Considerable verbalization, in the form of "How is the family?," "We pray that you are well," and "We are honored by your presence," is expected. Vigorous handshaking is used in conjunction with other nonverbal greeting behaviors to "size up" the person being greeted (Almaney & Alwan, 1982).

The Arab also likes to get close enough to the person being greeted to inhale his or her body aromas. We know that body scent frequently reveals emotional states; therefore this culture-specific greeting behavior certainly seems to be a useful way of obtaining highly personal information. The intimate and physically involving nature of Arab greeting behavior is reinforced by the lavish hospitality that is typically exhibited if an Arab is the host.

Status Differences

The hierarchical nature of both the Japanese and the Arab cultures means that both rank and status must be respected. Although both cultures profess to honor women, they treat women as status inferiors. Business is man's work and the family is woman's work. In Japan, a woman is expected to maintain a proper distance behind her spouse—usually two steps. In Arab countries, women are not permitted to drive or to work. Some Saudi Arabian women who recently tried to defy cultural custom by driving their own cars were rebuffed by the authorities. Women also are expected to keep their bodies covered, and when business associates visit the home, women are to be seen but not heard.

In Japan, status is perhaps reflected most clearly in the way people bow and in the artifacts they exhibit. Badges, costumes, and uniforms assume particular importance in status-conscious Japan because they quite clearly reveal status. There are, literally, specific costumes for hiking, biking, and striking. The uniform and costume serve a central role in establishing and maintaining status and in signaling the appropriate type of interaction between two people.

The business card, or *meishi,* also is used to signal rank. In view of the fact that the business organization is the single most important determinant of status in Japan, the name of the organization appears first on a business card, followed by the person's position in the organization, academic degree (if any), family name, first name, and address (Barnlund, 1989; Lebra, 1976; Morsbach, 1973).

Status distinctions are communicated in less formal and ritualistic ways in the Arab culture, where people's status is determined largely by the nature and magnitude of their possessions rather than by the rank of the organization with which they are affiliated. Arabs believe that it is better to give than to receive. As a result, the foreign visitor should be careful about expressing admiration of possessions in the home of an Arab. The Arab will feel duty-bound to give the possession to the visitor as a gift. Although formalized manifestations of status differences are relatively rare in Arab nations, the high status accorded to older people and persons of authority is reflected in a law that forbids smoking in their presence.

Intimacy

The nonverbal communication style of the Japanese clearly prohibits intimacy in public. The characteristic lack of expression, when combined with the Japanese sense of reserve, means that the Japanese expect communication in public to be formal and reserved. Of course, ritualized bowing, costumes that emphasize status differences, and the value placed on reserved and subtle expression all militate against the spontaneity that usually promotes intimate interaction in public.

Barnlund (1975a) emphasized that in Japan, physical intimacy communicated via touch drops off sharply after childhood. Physical inaccessibility due to maximum communicating distances and lack of touching reveal the negative value the Japanese place on intimate interaction in public. In fact, many "observers have noted the serious composure, lack of facial expression, and gestural restraint of the Japanese. Physical intimacies are avoided and even reinforcing gestures rarely accompany remarks" (p. 109).

In the Arab culture, in contrast, a lack of physical contact and involvement is considered aberrant. Arabs frequently communicate with strangers at distances as close as 2 ft. They encourage reciprocal touching, particularly in greetings, and they like to be breathed on, as well as to breathe on others. The late President Anwar Sadat of Egypt, for example, often placed a hand on the knee of the person with whom he was conversing. In addition, some eyebrows have apparently been raised at dinners for international diplomats by the propensity of representatives of Arab states to touch the persons with whom they are communicating.

Because Arabs do not value or practice privacy in public, it is not surprising that they are emotionally self-disclosing, physically expressive, and uninhibited. The public presentation of self in the Arab countries places a high value on two types of nonverbal communication that play a central role in the development of intimate relationships: touch and olfaction.

Guidelines for More Successful Intercultural Communication

Successful intercultural communication requires that we become thoroughly familiar with a communication style that may be quite different in important respects from the communication style that is dominant within our own culture. In his illuminating book *Counseling the Culturally Different* (1981), Sue emphasized that the culturally skilled counselor is one who moves from being unaware to being aware of and sensitive to his or her "own cultural baggage." This means that we must begin by rejecting the ethnocentric view that the communication style of our own culture is intrinsically superior.

The centrality of nonverbal behaviors and cues to successful intercultural communication becomes apparent when we recognize that "culture is primarily a nonverbal phenomenon because most aspects of one's culture are learned through observation and imitation rather than explicit verbal instruction or expression. The primary level of culture is communicated implicitly, without awareness, by primarily nonverbal means" (Andersen, 1988, p. 272).

Peter Andersen (1988) maintained that most of the important cultural differences in nonverbal behavior result from variations between cultures along five dimensions:

1. immediacy and expressiveness
2. individualism
3. masculinity
4. power distance
5. high and low context

When one culture has been differentiated from another along these five dimensions, the most important nonverbal behaviors and cues that make up the nonverbal communication style of that culture should be apparent. A closer look at Andersen's ideas emphasizes the importance of his five dimensions to successful intercultural communication.

Immediacy behaviors consist of acts or actions that signal a desire to establish closer contact with another person while exhibiting warmth, closeness, and availability. Importantly, cultures that exhibit a high level of immediacy behaviors are known as "contact cultures" because members of such cultures stand close to each other and touch frequently. Andersen (1988) maintained that contact cultures represented by countries such as Saudi Arabia, France, Greece, and Italy are typically located in "warm" climates. In contrast, "low-contact cultures," which include Scandinavia, Germany, England, the United States, and Japan, have "colder" climates. This is an important dimension because the socially sensitive visitor must know how much contact to exhibit within a given culture.

A second dimension that can be used to distinguish one culture from another is the degree of *individualism* versus *collectivism*. Western cultures are associated with individualism, whereas Eastern cultures are identified with collectivism. Countries with individualistic cultures include the United States, Canada, Belgium, and Denmark; countries with some of the least individualistic cultures include Colombia, Pakistan, Taiwan, and Hong Kong. There are a number of significant differences in the nonverbal behaviors of members of these two types of cultures. For example, members of individualistic cultures are rather distant proximally, but they are more nonverbally affiliative than people from collectivist cultures. Not surprisingly, bodily behaviors tend to be more predictable and more synchronized in collectivist cultures. "In individualistic countries like the United States, affiliativeness, dating, flirting, small-talk, and initial acquaintance are more important than they are in collectivist countries where the social network is more fixed and less reliant on individual initiative" (Andersen, 1988, p. 276).

Third, cultures are differentiated from one another along the dimension of *masculinity*. If you recall the masculine stereotype, you will not be surprised to know that masculine traits that define a masculine culture include assertiveness, competitiveness, and ambitiousness (whereas feminine traits include affection, compassion, and nurturance). If males and females are to be treated similarly within a given culture, androgynous behaviors—rather than masculine or feminine—must be a dominant part of the nonverbal communication style. The negative communicative implications for cultures that are high in either masculinity or femininity are obvious.

Fourth, *power distance* is another important dimension of intercultural communication. The power distance index (PDI) is used to measure the extent to which there is unequal distribution of power, prestige, and wealth within a culture. In effect, PDI measures the distance one group or member of a culture is separated from another in terms of power. The higher a culture's score on the PDI, the more authoritarian that culture is. Countries with the highest PDI include Mexico, Venezuela, Brazil, and Colombia. Note that all of these countries are highly stratified in terms of class distinctions. In contrast, class distinctions are relatively unimportant in countries such as Austria, Ireland, and Switzerland. If nonverbal cues encode power forcefully, then it is predictable that nonverbal behavioral indicators of both power and powerlessness will be exhibited more frequently in hierarchical than in egalitarian cultures.

Finally, *context* is an important dimension that can be used to differentiate cultures. *High context (HC)* messages are those in which much of the communicated information comes from the context or is not stated verbally. *Low context (LC)* messages, in contrast, contain most of the information in the particular language that is used. Cultures of particularly high context are found in the Far East. China, Japan, and Korea all have cultures of particularly high context. Significantly, members of low context cultures tend to view people with good verbal skills as particularly attractive, but "HC cultures are more reliant on and tuned into nonverbal communication than are LC cultures. LC cultures, and particularly the men in LC cultures, fail to perceive as much nonverbal communication as do members of HC cultures" (Andersen, 1988, p. 279).

If we are to succeed in our attempts to communicate with members of another culture, we must try to become aware of which communicative behaviors are, and which are not, acceptable in that culture. We can attain that level of awareness by becoming as familiar as possible with the distinctive features of the nonverbal style of the culture in which we seek to communicate.

Success in intercultural communication can be facilitated by training designed to develop intercultural communication competencies (Ben-Peretz & Halkes, 1987; Westwood & Borgen, 1988). Martin and Hammer (1989) provided a particularly useful profile of the nonverbal behaviors that must be exhibited in order to develop intercultural communication competence. They identified the nonverbal behaviors most strongly associated with intercultural competence when Americans are interacting with members of various cultures. The three nonverbal behaviors most strongly associated with intercultural competence in all of the cultures studied were direct eye contact, listening carefully, and smiling. Those three nonverbal behaviors were consistently found to be much more important than any other in making a favorable impression in any foreign culture.

Successful intercultural communication requires that we develop skills as impression managers. In a foreign culture, impression managers should seek to do at least two things: associate themselves with images that are positively valued and dissociate themselves from images that are negatively valued in the culture where communication occurs. Because more weight is usually given to negative than to positive information, it is particularly important to *avoid* behaving in ways that are considered inappropriate or deviant. One particularly valuable book that spells out in detail what one should and should not do nonverbally in countries and cultures in Europe, the Middle East, Africa, the Pacific and Asia, Central and South America, and the United States and Canada was published a few years ago (Axtell, 1993).

The following guidelines should prove useful to communicators who wish to exhibit appropriate nonverbal behaviors in cultures other than their own.

Guideline #1. Familiarize yourself with the facial expressions of the culture to determine whether the public display of emotions is encouraged or discouraged; determine which kinds of emotions are positively and negatively valued; and make the necessary adjustments in your own facial displays of emotion.

Guideline #2. Learn and follow the rules that govern proper form and interaction sequence for greeting behaviors, with an emphasis on the intricacies of cultural rituals.

Guideline #3. Become familiar with the types of status distinctions that must be acknowledged, and use culturally approved nonverbal behaviors for acknowledging such status distinctions.

Guideline #4. Determine the degree of physical contact, involvement, and accessibility that is expected in public, and act accordingly.

Guideline #5. Try to become sensitive to culture-specific touching, proxemic, eye-behavior, chronemic, and olfactic norms so that you will act in ways that are nonverbally appropriate.

Guideline #6. Become familiar with the nonverbal regulators that should and should not be used in culturally acceptable conversational management.

Guideline #7. Identify the most important nonverbal behaviors used in cultural ritual so that you can, if necessary, modify your own nonverbal behaviors as a way of identifying with important cultural values.

Guideline #8.   Systematically identify, itemize, and avoid the use of culture-specific emblems that communicate meanings that are apt to be interpreted as affronts or insults.

Guideline #9.   Determine the kinds of clothing and personal artifacts that are and are not compatible with cultural conventions.

Summary

Successful intercultural communication requires that a visitor to a foreign country acquire an in-depth familiarity with the nonverbal communication style of the culture of that country. This is necessary because the nonverbal communication style of a culture is defined by nonverbal behaviors that contain sets of implicit rules or commands. These implicit display rules, in turn, specify what kinds of communication are and are not appropriate.

Cross-cultural similarities in nonverbal communication are most evident in the use of facial expressions, which communicate a limited number of basic emotions. Cross-cultural differences abound. Those differences are strongly reflected in a great variety of gestural emblems that communicate culture-specific meanings and, as a result, are highly susceptible to misinterpretation by the foreigner. Proxemic, tactile, eye-behavior, chronemic, and olfactic as well as conceptions and uses of time and odor also tend to be distinctively different in cultures with dissimilar value orientations.

In order to demonstrate how knowledge of the nonverbal communication style of specific cultures can be used to facilitate more successful communication, the Japanese and Arab cultures are compared and contrasted in this chapter. The point is made that important differences in the nonverbal styles of the two cultures are manifested most clearly in the communication of emotions, greetings, status differences, and intimacy.

Finally, a set of nine guidelines is included that can be used to facilitate more successful intercultural communication. These guidelines can be used to increase our awareness of the specific kinds of communicative behaviors that are and are not acceptable in a foreign culture of importance to us. Such awareness is necessary if we are to engage in intercultural communication that reflects a knowledge of and a desire to adapt to the distinctive communication style of a particular culture.

REFERENCES

Ackerman, D. S., & Gross, B. L. (2003). Is time pressure all bad? Measuring the relationship between free time availability and student performance and perceptions. *Marketing Education Review, 13,* 21–32.

Almaney, A. J., & Alwan, A. J. (1982). *Communicating with the Arabs: A handbook for the business executive.* Prospect Heights, IL: Waveland Press.

Amason, P., Allen, M. W., & Holmes, S. A. (1999). Social support and acculturative stress in the multicultural workplace. *Journal of Applied Communication Research, 27,* 310–334.

Andersen, P. (1988). Explaining intercultural differences in nonverbal communication. In L. Samovar & R. E. Porter (Eds.), *Intercultural communication: A reader* (5th ed., pp. 272–282). Belmont, CA: Wadsworth.

Annett, J. M. (1996). Olfactory memory: A case study in cognitive psychology. *The Journal of Psychology, 130,* 309–319.

App, B., Bulleit, A., & Jaskolka, A. R. (2006). Touch communicates distinct emotions. *Emotion, 6,* 528–533.

Avni-Badad, D., & Ritov, I. (2003). Routine and the perception of time. *Journal of Experimental Psychology: General, 132,* 543–550.

Axtell, R. E. (1993). *Gestures: The do's and taboos of body language around the world* (2nd ed.). New York: John Wiley & Sons.

Ballard, D. I., & Seibold, D. R. (2003). Communicating and organizing in time. *Management Communication Quarterly, 16,* 380–415.

Barnlund, D. C. (1975a). Communicative styles in two cultures: Japan and the United States. In A. Kendon, R. M. Harris, & M. R. Keys (Eds.), *Organization of behavior in face-to-face interaction.* The Hague, The Netherlands: Mouton.

Barnlund, D. C. (1975b). *Public and private self in Japan and the United States: Communicative styles of two cultures.* Tokyo. The Simul Press.

Barnlund, D. C. (1989). *Communicative styles of Japanese and Americans: Images and realities.* Belmont, CA: Wadsworth.

Belk, S. S., Garcia-Falconi, R., Hernandez-Sanchez, J. E., & Snell, W. E. (1988). Avoidance strategy use in the intimate relationships of women and men from Mexico and the United States. *Psychology of Women Quarterly, 12,* 165–174.

Ben-Peretz, M., & Halkes, R. (1987). How teachers know their classrooms: A cross-cultural study of teachers' understanding of classroom situations. *Anthropology and Education Quarterly, 18,* 17–32.

Bernieri, F., & Gillis, J. S. (1995). The judgment of rapport: A cross-cultural comparison between Americans and Greeks. *Journal of Nonverbal Behavior, 19,* 115–129.

Blake, J., Vitale, G., Osborne, P., & Olshansky, E. (2005). A cross-cultural comparison of communicative gestures in human infants during the transition to language. *Gesture, 5,* 201–217.

Brislin, R. W., & Kim, E. S. (2003). Cultural diversity in people's understanding and uses of time. *Applied Psychology: An International Review, 52,* 363–382.

Buck, R. (2003). Emotional expression, suppression, and control: Nonverbal communication in cultural context. *Journal of Intercultural Communication Research, 32,* 47–65.

Cain, W. S. (1979). To know with the nose: Keys to odor identification. *Science, 203,* 467–470.

Calloway-Thomas, C., Cooper, P. J., & Blake, C. (1999). *Intercultural communication: Roots and routes.* Boston: Allyn and Bacon.

Chami-Sather, G., & Kretschmer, R. R. (2005). Lebanese/ Arabic and American children's discourse in group-solving situations. *Language and Education, 19,* 10–31.

Chiang, L. H. (1993, October). *Beyond the language: Native American's nonverbal communication.* (ERIC microfiche document No. ED368540).

Condon, J. C., & Yousef, F. (1975). *An introduction to intercultural communication.* Indianapolis, IN: Bobbs.

Cutrone, P. (2005). A case study examining backchannels in conversations between Japanese-British dyads. *Multilingua, 24,* 237–274.

Darwin, C. (1872). *The expression of emotion in man and animals.* London: J. Murray. (Reprinted in 1965, Chicago: University of Chicago Press).

Dew, A. M., & Ward, C. (1993). The effects of ethnicity and culturally congruent and incongruent nonverbal behaviors on interpersonal attraction. *Journal of Applied Social Psychology, 23,* 1376–1389.

Doktor, R. H. (1990). Asian and American CEOs: A comparative study. *Organizational Dynamics, 18,* 46–57.

Eibl-Eibesfeldt, I. (1972). Similarities and differences between cultures in expressive movements. In R. A. Hinde (Ed.), *Non-verbal communication.* Cambridge, MA: Cambridge University Press.

Ekman, P., & Friesen, W. V. (1975). *Unmasking the face.* Englewood Cliffs, NJ: Prentice-Hall.

Ekman, P., Friesen, W. V., & Ellsworth, P. (1972). *Emotion in the human face.* New York: Pergamon.

Ekman, P., Friesen, W. V., O'Sullivan, M., & Chan, A. (1987). Universals and cultural differences in the judgments of facial expressions of emotion. *Journal of Personality and Social Psychology, 53,* 712–717.

Elfenbein, H. A., & Ambady, N. (2002). On the universality and cultural specificity of emotion recognition: A meta-analysis. *Psychological Bulletin, 128,* 203–235.

Engebretson, D. E., & Fullmer, D. (1970). Cross-cultural differences in territoriality: Interaction distances of native Japanese, Hawaii Japanese, and American Caucasians. *Journal of Cross-Cultural Psychology, 1,* 261–269.

Filsinger, E. E., & Fabes, R. A. (1985). Odor communication, pheromones, and human families. *Journal of Marriage and the Family, 47,* 349–359.

Guidetti, M. (1991). Vocal expression of emotions—A cross-cultural and developmental approach. *Annee Psychologique, 9,* 383–396.

Haidt, J., & Keltner, D. (1999). Culture and facial expression: Open-ended methods find more expressions and a gradient of recognition. *Cognition and Emotion, 13,* 225–266.

Hall, E. T. (1963). *The silent language.* Greenwich, CT: Premier.

Hall, E. T. (1969). *The hidden dimension.* Garden City, NY: Anchor.

Hall, E. T., & Hall, M. R. (1987). *Hidden differences: Doing business with the Japanese.* Garden City, NY: Anchor.

Hecht, T. D., & Allen, N. J. (2005). Exploring links between polychronicity and well-being from the perspective of person-job fit: Does it matter if you prefer to do only one thing at a time? *Organizational Behavior and Human Decision Processes, 98,* 155–178.

Herz, R. S. (1997). Emotion experienced during encoding enhances odor retrieval cue effectiveness. *The American Journal of Psychology, 110,* 489–505.

Hess, U., Blairy, S., & Kleck, R. E. (2000). The influence of facial emotion displays, gender, and ethnicity on judgments of dominance and affiliation. *Journal of Nonverbal Behavior, 24,* 265–283.

Hickson, M. I., III, & Stacks, D. W. (1989). *Nonverbal communication: Studies and applications* (2nd ed.). Dubuque, IA: Wm. C. Brown.

Hirsch, A. R. (1995). Effects of ambient odors on slot-machine usage in a Las Vegas casino. *Psychology & Marketing, 12,* 585–594.

Kaufman, C. F., Lane, P. M., & Lindquist, J. D. (1991). Exploring more than 24 hours a day: A preliminary investigation of polychromic time use. *Journal of Consumer Research, 18,* 392–401.

Kilbride, J. E., & Yarczower, M. (1980). Recognition and imitation of facial expressions: A cross-cultural comparison between Zambia and the United States. *Journal of Cross-Cultural Psychology, 11,* 282.

LaFrance, M., & Mayo, C. (1978a). Cultural aspects of nonverbal communication. *International Journal of Intercultural Relations, 2,* 71–89.

LaFrance, M., & Mayo, C. (1978b). *Moving bodies: Nonverbal communication in social relationships.* Monterey, CA: Brooks/Cole.

Leathers, D. G., & McGuire, M. (1983, November). *Testing the comparative sensitivity of German and American decoders to specific kinds of facial meaning.* Paper presented on the program of the Commission on International and Intercultural Communication at the annual convention of the Speech Communication Association, Washington, DC.

Lebra, T. S. (1976). *Japanese patterns of behavior.* Honolulu: The University Press of Hawaii.

Lindstrom, M. (2005). Follow your nose to marketing evolution. *Advertising Age, 76,* 136.

Martin, J. N., & Hammer, M. R. (1989). Behavioral categories of intercultural communication competence: Everyday communicators' perceptions. *International Journal of Intercultural Relations, 13,* 303–332.

Martin, J. N., & Nakayama, T. K. (2007). *Intercultural communication in contexts.* New York: McGraw Hill.

Masters, R. D., & Sullivan, D. G. (1989a). Facial displays and political leadership in France. *Behavioral Processes, 19,* 1–30.

Masters, R. D., & Sullivan, D. G. (1989b). Nonverbal displays and political leadership in France and the United States. *Political Behavior, 11,* 123–156.

McCroskey, J., Fayer, J. M., Richmond, V. P., Sallinen, A., & Barraclough, R. A. (1996). A multi-cultural examination of the relationship between nonverbal immediacy and affective learning. *Communication Quarterly, 44,* 297–307.

McDaniel, E. R. (1993, November). *Japanese nonverbal communication: A review and critique of literature.* Conference paper presented at the 79th Annual Meeting of the Speech Communication Association, Miami Beach, FL.

Meyer, M. (2006, August 5). Unisex fragrances: Does his-and-hers make scents? *USA Weekend,* p. 27.

Michael, G. A., Jacquot, L., Millot, J.-L., & Brand, G. (2005). Ambient odors influence the amplitude and time course of visual distraction. *Behavioral Neuroscience, 119,* 708–715.

Mitchell, D. J., Kahn, B. E., & Knasko, S. C. (1995). There's something in the air: Effects of congruent and incongruent ambient odor on consumer decision making. *Journal of Consumer Research, 22,* 229–238.

Montepare, J. M., & Zebrowitz, L. A. (1993). A cross-cultural comparison of impressions created by age-related variation in gait. *Journal of Nonverbal Behavior, 17,* 55–67.

Morris, D., Collett, P., Marsh, P., & O'Shaughnessy, M. (1979). *Gestures: Their origins and distribution.* New York: Stein & Day.

Morsbach, H. (1973). Aspects of nonverbal communication in Japan. *The Journal of Nervous and Mental Disease, 157,* 262–277.

Moss, M., Cook, J., Wesnes, K., & Duckett, P. (2003). Aromas of rosemary and lavender essential oils differentially affect cognition and mood in healthy adults. *International Journal of Neuroscience, 113,* 15–38.

Nixon, Y., & Bull, P. (2005). The effects of cultural awareness on nonverbal perceptual accuracy: British and Japanese training programmes. *Journal of Intercultural Communication, 9,* 63–80.

Ouchi, W. (1981). *Theory Z: How American business can meet the Japanese challenge.* Reading, MA: Addison-Wesley.

Payrato, L. (1993). A pragmatic view on autonomous gestures: A first report on Cattalan emblems. *Journal of Pragmatics, 20,* 193–216.

Peng, Y., Zebrowitz, L. A., & Lee, H. L. (1993). The impact of cultural background and cross-cultural experience on impressions of American and Korean male speakers. *Journal of Cross-Cultural Psychology, 24,* 204–220.

Roach, K. D., Cornett-Devito, M. M., & Devito, R. (2005). A cross-cultural comparison of instructor communication in American and French classrooms. *Communication Quarterly, 53,* 87–107.

Rosenthal, R., Hall, J. A., DiMatteo, M. R., Rogers, P. L., & Archer, D. (1979). *Sensitivity to nonverbal communication: The PONS test.* Baltimore: The Johns Hopkins University Press.

Samovar, L. A., Porter, R. E., & McDaniel, E. R. (2007). *Communication between cultures.* Belmont, CA: Thomson.

Scherer, K. R., & Wallbott, H. G. (1994). Evidence for universality and cultural variation of differential emotion response patterning. *Journal of Personality and Social Psychology, 66,* 310–328.

Scherer, K. R., Wallbott, H. G., Matsumoto, D., & Kudoh, T. (1988). Emotional experience in cultural context: A comparison between Europe, Japan, and the United States. In K. R. Scherer (Ed.), *Facets of emotion—Recent research* (pp. 1–30). Hillsdale, NJ: Erlbaum.

Shuter, R. (1976). Proxemics and tactility in Latin America. *Journal of Communication, 26,* 46–52.

Shuter, R. (1977). A field study of nonverbal communication in Germany, Italy and the United States. *Communication Monographs, 44,* 298–305.

Shuter, R. (1983). *Values and communication: Seeing the forest through the trees.* Unpublished manuscript.

Sloop, J. (2005). *People shopping.* Paper presented at the annual convention of the Southern States Communication Association, Baton Rouge, LA.

Sogon, S., & Masutani, M. (1989). Identification of emotion from body movements: A cross-cultural study of Americans and Japanese. *Psychological Reports, 65,* 35–46.

Spangenberg, E. R., Crowley, A. E., & Henderson, P. W. (1996). Improving the store environment: Do olfactory cues affect evaluations and behaviors? *Journal of Marketing, 60,* 67–80.

Sue, D. W. (1981). *Counseling the culturally different.* New York: Wiley.

Sweeney, M. A., Cottle, W. C., & Kobayashi, M. J. (1980). Nonverbal communication: A cross-cultural comparison of American and Japanese counseling students. *Journal of Counseling Psychology, 27,* 154.

Turley, L. W., & Milliman, R. E. (2000). Atmospheric effects on shopping behavior: A review of the experimental evidence. *Journal of Business Research, 49,* 193–211.

Westwood, M. U., & Borgen, W. A. (1988). A culturally embedded model for effective intercultural communication. *International Journal for the Advancement of Counselling, 11,* 115–125.

White, T. L., Hornung, D. E., Kurtz, D. B., Treisman, M., & Sheehe, P. (1998). Phonological and perceptual components of short-term memory for odors. *The American Journal of Psychology, 111,* 411–434.

Zhang, Q. (2005). Teacher immediacy and classroom communication apprehension: A cross-cultural investigation. *Journal of Intercultural Communication Research, 34,* 50–64.

CHAPTER

15

Special Nonverbal Contexts

This chapter examines several specific nonverbal contexts of concern and is divided into four main contexts: medical contexts, legal settings, built environments, and virtual places.

Medical Contexts

We are in an age in which U.S. citizens are living longer. As a result, health care has become an increasingly important issue. The Clintons, especially Hillary as first lady and in her bid in 2008 to be president, have placed the health care concern as their centerpiece in their political platform. Thus, health care contexts are of great importance, especially to the nonverbal communication scholar.

In spite of the raging national debate, the average citizen might have trouble defining health care. At minimum it is important to identify the full range of professionals who are involved in providing health care. Kreps and Thornton (1992) maintained that "The health care delivery system is like a wagon wheel with many different spokes. . . . The hub of the wheel is the client's role" (p. 4). The spokes of the wheel represent each of the professional categories involved in providing health care: medicine, dentistry, medical administration, therapy, nursing, pharmacy, and social work. Similarly, Northouse and Northouse (1998) provided a somewhat more detailed identification of the health professionals who make up a "health team." They wrote that the following health care professionals all have the primary objective of focusing on patient care: physicians, nurses, social workers, dentists, psychologists, nutritionists, allied health workers, physical and occupational therapists, health scientists, and pharmacologists.

Our knowledge of communicative interaction in medical contexts includes the interactions patients have with their physicians, nurses, other members of the medical team, and family members. Northouse and Northouse (1998) identified a number of factors as potential barriers to effective physician–patient communication. Three seem particularly important: (a) *role uncertainty,* (b) *power differences,* and (c) *unshared meanings.*

First, role uncertainty may make the patient hesitant to raise legitimate health concerns with the physician or other health providers. The doctor may misinterpret the patient's relative silence as signaling a lack of concern, and this role uncertainty may result in physicians and patients dealing with each other in stereotypical ways. Role uncertainty often becomes a particular problem for the patient who is hospitalized. Patients frequently must give up, at least temporarily, the familiar roles of husband, wife, employer, employee, sports enthusiast, artist, and so forth. The patient's new role in an unfamiliar setting is vague at best, and the suitable accompanying behaviors are unclear.

Next, power differences represent a second potential communication problem. The physician–patient relationship is seen as asymmetrical because the physician is seen as powerful and the patient as powerless. Clearly, the physician may simply assume more power than warranted. A good example of this is the use of space. Physicians often choose close spaces to interact with patients. This close use of space and body orientation is a way that medical professionals exert power during the interaction (Preston, 2005b; Robinson, 1998).

Finally, unshared meanings often serve as a third barrier to effective doctor–patient communication. To deal with the problem of unshared meanings, physicians obviously need to work harder to understand how their patients perceive themselves, their world, and the physician (Stewart & Roter, 1989). Good ways that physicians can communicate include maintaining strong eye behavior (Lee, 2000) and using positive gestures and head nods with the patient (Preston, 2005a).

Nonverbal Communication in the Medical Context

Northouse and Northouse (1998) identify some of the major reasons nonverbal communication is functionally important from the patient's perspective: (a) a health care setting such as the medical interview generates a high level of fear and uncertainty among patients as well as family members—to lessen their uncertainty, patients often rely heavily on what they perceive to be the most reliable information available to them, which is often unintentionally communicated by a physician's nonverbal communication; (b) because patients frequently feel that doctors are being less than completely honest with them, or even lying to them, they tend to rely on the "leakage" cues in the doctor's nonverbal communication to determine the true meanings of the doctor's messages; (c) patients often rely on nonverbal communication as a source of "preinteraction" information; for example, they study the physician's face to determine how reassuring or threatening the results from recent tests are; and (d) patients often rely heavily on the physician's nonverbal communication as the primary source of information when the doctor is either too busy to communicate with them at any length verbally or is unapproachable.

From the physician's perspective, nonverbal communication has great functional importance for several reasons: (a) the patient's physical or psychological condition may make verbal communication impractical or impossible; (b) doctors may recognize that a patient's implicit or unstated messages are the best source of information with regard to the patient's moods, feelings, emotions, and attitudes; and (c) in moments of crisis, the physician's only way of communicating with the patient, or with other physicians, may be by nonverbal means, such as a touch on the hand of a comatose patient or a sharing of concerns among members of the medical team via eye behaviors and facial expressions while working to revive a patient who has suffered cardiac arrest (Northouse & Northouse, 1998). Several studies have found that patient satisfaction is associated with strong physician nonverbal communication skills (Conlee, Olvera, & Vagim, 1993; Griffith, Wilson, Langer, & Haist, 2003).

Functions of Nonverbal Communication in the Medical Context

Northouse and Northouse (1998) argued incisively that nonverbal communication serves five major functions in the medical context where physicians and patients interact: (a) expression of feelings and emotions; (b) regulation of the interaction; (c) validation of the verbal message; (d) maintenance of the self-image; and (e) maintenance of relationships.

Their emphasis on the use of nonverbal communication to maintain self-image and relationships seems particularly insightful. A patient's maintenance of an acceptably positive self-image is an objective that is not easily attained. We have already commented in this chapter, for example, that role uncertainty often becomes a major problem when the patient moves from the familiar territory of his or her own home or office to the unfamiliar territory of the physician's office or a hospital.

A patient's self-concept is surely threatened in a medical setting not only by the lack of privacy but also by repeated, intrusive invasions of privacy. When you enter a hospital, for example, you are literally stripped of the distinctive clothing or uniforms that have designated your achieved status in the real world. You are also stripped of your self-identity in the real world. You are given a medical nightshirt, which may open ominously at the rear with the alarming prospect that some or all of your private parts will be exposed involuntarily to strangers. To make matters worse, a nurse, nurse's attendant, or orderly may enter your room at any moment without your invitation or consent. He or she may then move briskly to insert a medical device in one of your private bodily orifices. Just when you begin to relax in your room, a medical attendant may tell you to roll on your side and give you an enema. In short, there is almost no indignity that you may not be forced to endure in your new role as patient.

The final function of nonverbal communication that these authors stress is the maintenance of relationships. Although there are a number of features that may define a relationship between a physician and a patient, the degree to which physicians and patients *share control* in a medical setting is perhaps most important. We know that nonverbal messages strongly communicate the degree to which we are dominant or submissive in a relationship with another person. As this book has already documented, the loudness of one's voice encodes power powerfully. Strong, dominant individuals tend to speak with a loud voice. Conversely, weak, submissive persons tend to speak with a soft voice. Then, too, eye behaviors are particularly important in signaling the degree of control two individuals have in their relationship.

Our discussion in Chapter 1 and in this chapter suggests that nonverbal behaviors or cues can, therefore, be used to serve five major communicative functions in the medical context where physicians and patients interact: (1) exchange of emotions, (2) metacommunication, (3) self-concept protection, (4) impression management, and (5) reassurance.

The sensitive exchange and interpretation of the meanings of emotions are perhaps the most important functions of nonverbal communication when physicians and patients interact. Repeatedly, the authorities cited in this chapter stress that physicians must abandon the traditional, clinical method that was used to train them in order to embrace a new method. That new method puts a premium on physicians' developing a set of skills that will enable them to give a sensitive reading of the feelings, moods, and emotions of their patients. The open exchange of emotions in the medical interview must therefore be given the highest priority. Carroll (2004) found that nonvocal patients prefer nursing care that shows individualized care. Of the 111 participants in the study, the vast majority felt misunderstood when nurses did not exhibit nonverbal behaviors indicating immediacy and interpersonal relationship building.

We have already documented in this book that the three most effective ways of communicating emotions are the face (by far the most important), vocal cues, and touching. Therefore, patients and physicians must work not only to develop their encoding and decoding skills when using these three types of nonverbal communication, but they must also be sensitive to cultural norms that pertain to each of them (such as what types of facial expressions should and should not be exhibited in a medical setting; what combination of sound attributes most effectively communicate such emotions as apprehension, distress, and fear; and what touching norms are operative in a given medical setting).

Metacommunication too is a vitally important communicative function in the medical setting that is served mainly and best by nonverbal behaviors and cues. The meanings of the verbal messages of physicians and patients are often unclear. The lack of clarity may of course be affected by many things: physicians may be rushed, they may be reluctant to share disturbing information with the patient, they may get mired down in their own jargon, and so on. The patient in turn may be reluctant to disclose information verbally to a physician who is acting in an imperious or dominant manner, may be quite reticent because of threats to her or his self-concept in the medical environment, or may feel that the doctor is lying to him or her. In all of these instances, the manifest content of a message (the words) might not be adequate to make the intended meaning clear. When this is the case, patients and physicians may have to turn to the second-level order of communicative cues known as metacommunication. The most informative metacommunicative cues tend to be nonverbal in nature. Metacommunicative cues may include an unintended grimace, shifty eyes, a strident voice, or adaptor gestures that express heightened tension.

Clearly, self-concept protection represents an important communication function that is served particularly well by nonverbal cues in the medical setting. The subtle, implicit messages communicated by such things as whether a patient is given reserved places in which to keep prized, personal possessions; whether the doctor cultivates the perception that patient and doctor are "partners" by communicating at eye level with the patient (rather than towering over the patient who is lying prostrate in a hospital bed); or the degree to which the patient is treated in a highly impersonal way may signal to patients whether their self-concept is being threatened or protected. Nonverbal communication variables clearly can play a central role in protecting the patient's self-concept.

Several nonverbal communicative behaviors and cues are particularly relevant to the self-concept protection function of nonverbal communication in the medical setting. Successful efforts by the physician to respect the patient's privacy needs, to avoid violating preferred separation distances, and to help the patient preserve the "territories of self" that patients perceive as their own are all important in helping the patient protect her or his self-concept. The use of eye behaviors and gestures that signal that the physician wishes to establish a partnership relationship with the patient rather than a superior–subordinate relationship is also important. Finally, physicians must be careful to avoid using the command voice so that the self-concept of the patient is not threatened.

The impression formation and management function of nonverbal communication in physician–patient interaction is surely important, because both physicians and patients are concerned with claiming images that are acceptable to them (see the photo). As we already know, the three image dimensions that define the impression made by a given individual are credibility, interpersonal attractiveness, and dominance.

The physician's credibility may influence a patient's choice of a particular physician or surgeon. In the interactive context of the medical interview, however, the other two image dimensions of interpersonal attractiveness and dominance may prove to be more important. We know, for example, that interpersonal attractiveness is defined by how likable, sociable, interesting, and emotionally expressive a person is judged to be. All of these image qualities are seen as highly desirable features of the nonverbal communication style of the physician who has adopted the new, interactive model of associating with the patient. Indeed, research shows that patients who perceive medical professionals (doctors, nurses, and staff members) as credible are more likely to believe that their medical records are kept confidential (Paulsel, Richmond, McCroskey, & Cayanus, 2005). In today's world, that is a precious value.

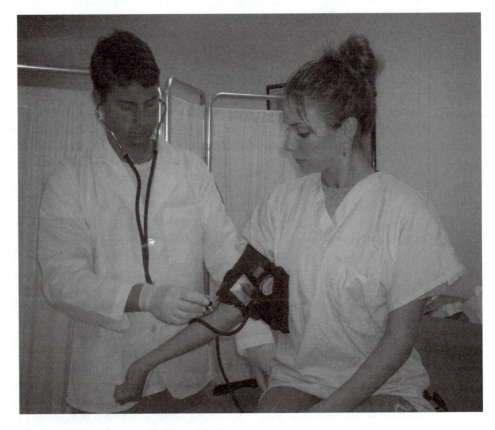

The doctor is seen here examining a patient.

We are already familiar with the nonverbal behaviors that most positively and negatively affect judgments of interpersonal attractiveness. Likewise, immediacy behaviors in the form of sustained eye contact, direct bodily orientation, forward lean, and appropriate touching have repeatedly been found to enhance interpersonal attractiveness in general and liking in particular.

The image dimension of dominance is obviously of great importance when considering the interaction of physician and patient. Indeed, previous discussion in this chapter has clearly documented that the single most important dimension along which physician and patient interaction may be evaluated is the degree of dominance or control exhibited by each of the interactants. Nonverbal communication is known to exert what is frequently a controlling influence over judgments of control, that is, relative dominance and submissiveness.

Nonverbal communicative behaviors and cues of particular importance in shaping impressions of dominance or submission are eye behaviors, vocal variables such as the sound of one's voice, and expansiveness of gestures and posture. In the medical interview, interactants may be faced with a difficult trade-off. Those nonverbal communicative behaviors and cues that enhance one's perceived dominance tend to depress one's perceived likability, and vice versa.

Finally, the patient's need for reassurance is undeniably stronger in the medical setting than in any other and the nonverbal means of reassuring the patient are unrivaled by other types of communication.

The Status Quo of Physician–Patient Nonverbal Communication

We should consider two facts at minimum before we describe the actual nonverbal communicative behaviors of physicians and patients. First, the milieu of the physician is dominated by male values, and medical training places a premium on the authoritativeness of the physician. At present, medical students, regardless of gender, continue to be exposed to male values (Hall, Roter, & Rand, 1994). Second, there has been much emphasis recently on the desirability of the physician being less controlling and instead sharing control with a patient to such an extent that a partnership results. Although there are good reasons for adopting this practice, we should recognize that it may not be without its liabilities. In a medical context, a high priority traditionally has been given to the physician's authoritativeness. Indeed, if the patient does not make a sufficiently positive assessment of the physician's expertise, the patient–physician relationship will be terminated. Furthermore, there is reason to believe that it is perhaps the norm for both physicians and patients to equate dominance with authoritativeness (Street & Buller, 1987).

What would your own reaction be if your physician communicated nonverbally in a way that reminded you of actors Owen Wilson or Adam Sandler? If you were about to undergo surgery, would you prefer that your surgeon in her or his conversations with you exhibit strong, decisive movements or timid, tentative gestures? In the medical context, a physician's communication of nonverbal messages of reassurance as a result of his or her self-assurance, authoritativeness, and being in command of the situation is not necessarily a bad thing.

In short, physicians are trained in a culture that embraces male values and attributes. This culture in turn is undoubtedly strongly influenced by the stereotype that suggests that males are active, dominant, aggressive, and insensitive persons who dominate communicative interaction by taking advantage of their superior status. By contrast, women are stereotypically perceived to be passive, submissive, and supportive persons who are dominated as a result of their desire to adapt to men's needs and to be accommodating. Our chapter on female–male interaction contrasted the defining features of the nonverbal communication styles of men and women. If all medical students are trained in a male-oriented culture, we would expect the nonverbal communication style of physicians in general to more closely resemble the male rather than the female nonverbal communication style. In their study of 44 English-speaking patients, Street and Buller (1987) confirmed that physicians dominate patients by their nonverbal communication. In this instance, physicians dominated patients by speaking for longer periods of time and exhibiting more social touch, which was not reciprocated by their patients. Significantly, Street's (1990) research suggests that as a dentist's level of control over the patient increases, the patient's degree of liking for the dentist decreases. Again, the training of physicians embraces the values of a macho culture; therefore it is not surprising that the nonverbal communication style of today's physicians rather closely resembles many of the defining features of the male nonverbal communication style.

The nonverbal communication style of today's physician should not, however, be treated as if it is unidimensional, that is, concerned exclusively with using the physician's communication to exercise the desired degree of control over a patient. Some evidence suggests that physicians may now be increasingly concerned with how interpersonally attractive they are perceived to be by their patients. Street and Buller (1987) found that the body orientations, gaze behaviors, gestures, and response latencies of physicians and patients are relatively congruent. This congruence or similarity in the nonverbal behaviors exhibited by patients and physicians as they are interacting suggests that their affiliative efforts are mutually acceptable. The researchers' findings also revealed a higher than expected level of expressiveness on the part of physicians. More recently, Caris-Verhallen et al. (1999) found a positive correlation with nurses who used positive nonverbal behaviors and good relations with patients. Such behaviors included maintenance of eye gaze, head nodding, and smiling toward the patient. Nurses in home elderly care were also likely to use touch as a supportive behavior.

Any attempt to characterize the nonverbal communication style of today's physician would be incomplete if the impact of gender is not taken into account, however. Thanks in large part to a study by Hall and her colleagues (1994), we now have definitive evidence that reveals how the nonverbal communication styles of female and male physicians differ.

The nonverbal communication style of the female physician differs from the style for male physicians in at least the following respects: Female MDs (a) elicit significantly more utterances from patients than do male MDs; (b) more evenly distribute the ratio of MD-to-patient speech than occurs when male physicians are interacting with patients; (c) exceed male MDs in "positive talk" (laughing, approving, and agreeing); (d) emit more backchannel responses than do male MDs ("mm-hmmm," "yeah," "ok," and "right"); (e) have a voice quality that is rated as more anxious than the voice quality of male MDs; (f) are rated as more submissive than male MDs; and (g) smile more than male MDs and smile more to male patients than do male MDs.

We should note, furthermore, that the gender of the patient and the gender of the physician have a marked impact on the nonverbal communicative interaction of these two parties. Female physicians communicate differently when in the presence of a male patient. When communicating with male patients, female physicians smile the most, are perceived as more dominant early in the visit (thus becoming more submissive as the interview continues), are less friendly later in the interview, and are more interested and anxious throughout the interaction.

The gender of the physician also affects the communicative responses of patients. Patients make more partnership statements to female as opposed to male doctors and provide more medical information to female MDs. The voices of male patients were rated as more bored-sounding when they were interacting with a female doctor, and the voices of female patients were rated as more anxious-sounding than the voices of male patients whether the physician was female or male.

Improvements Necessary in Medical Contexts

The sad fact is that medical schools in the United States and Great Britain rarely provide formal instruction in communication for physicians. Although medical students may receive some form of communication skills training, it is usually short term and relatively superficial (Frederikson & Bull, 1992). This is a particularly bothersome finding because the benefits of in-depth communication training for medical students and physicians have now been clearly established. In fact, Rowland-Morin, Burchard, Garb, and Coe (1991) found that surgery students who received even rudimentary training in nonverbal communication—that is, they were trained to exhibit direct eye contact and a moderate rate of response—perform significantly better on their oral examinations than surgery students who did not have such training. Interestingly, evidence now suggests that surgical specialists have a greater need for communication training than general practitioners. This may be due in part to the fact that surgeons get so preoccupied with the technical aspects of their work that they become insensitive to the requirements of effective communicative interaction with their patients (Roulidis & Schulman, 1994).

One study identifies eight attitudes that should be stressed in medical education. These attitudes are considered pivotal in developing a therapeutic relationship where physicians and patients treat each other as equals when interacting: (a) physicians and patients must exhibit unconditional positive regard for each other in order to foster a helping relationship; (b) the patient must show respect for the physician by visiting the physician only when there is a defensible reason for doing so, such as when the patient is experiencing substantial suffering; (c) the patient's actions and reactions must be reasonable and prudent; (d) the doctor must always feel that he or she has the capacity to help the patient in some way; (e) the doctor and patient must share the responsibility for "helping"; (f) both patient and physician must recognize that doctors have other agendas beyond patient care; (g) physicians must indicate explicitly how far they can go to help patients; (h) patients must recognize that physicians are human beings with emotions, feelings, and affectional needs (Wolfe, Ingelfinger, & Schmitz, 1994).

In seeking to modify their existing nonverbal communication style, physicians as well as patients should consider the type of relationship they seek to develop. The new, modified nonverbal communication style should stress the physician's and patient's ability to build rapport with each other, to share control of the medical interview, to be self-disclosing, to provide each other with needed confirmation, and to respond to each other in an empathic manner. Communication training that seeks to modify the nonverbal communicative interaction of physicians and patients cannot, of course, seek to do everything. Therefore, we believe that communication training at this moment should focus on the development of the nonverbal skills necessary for the physician and patient to build a rapport and to respond empathically to each other.

Significantly, individuals who are effective in building rapport have consistently been perceived as warm, enthusiastic, and interested. Heintzman, Leathers, Parrott, and Cairns (1993) indicated that the five types of nonverbal behaviors that are most effective in building rapport (when they are exhibited at appropriate times and with the proper degree of intensity) are smiling, touching, affirmative head nods, immediacy behaviors, and sustained eye contact.

The study by Heintzman and colleagues compared the effects on communicative interaction of a high- versus a low-rapport supervisor with his subordinates. Although there are differences between this type of relationship and the relationship of the physician and patient, some of the most important findings would seem to apply to the medical context where doctors and patients interact. First, the high-rapport supervisor was perceived by subordinates to be more interpersonally attractive than the low-rapport supervisor. Secondly, subordinates reported higher levels of satisfaction when working with the high- as opposed to the low-rapport supervisor. Finally, the rate of subordinates' compliance with requests from the high-rapport supervisor was significantly higher than their compliance with requests from the low-rapport supervisor.

Whereas rapport is a sender-oriented concept, empathy is a receiver-oriented concept. To begin, empathy must be distinguished from pity and sympathy. Pity is negative affect or sadness felt for another's misfortune. Pity connotes in some instances a feeling of sadness perhaps combined with smug superiority in that you are relieved that you have not experienced a similar misfortune. Sympathy in contrast is defined by an active, overt effort to show the person who has experienced the misfortune that you regret it and care for this person. Empathy goes beyond the efforts of the sympathetic person and provides solace and comfort. Empathy is a relational concept that becomes meaningful only at that point where our level of awareness becomes such that we are able to connect with and feel the inner experience of another person. We are able in effect to put ourselves in the place of another in terms of the other person's feeling states (Nadelson, 1994).

Because the positive relationship between a physician's empathy and the patient's satisfaction has clearly been established, additional justification for training physicians to communicate in an empathic manner nonverbally is hardly needed. Significantly, nonverbal communication has been found to be more than twice as important as verbal communication in responding in an empathic manner. Empathic communicators exhibit more sustained eye contact and a more direct bodily orientation than do nonempathic communicators. They also exhibit moderate forward lean and, most important of all, the nonverbal and verbal components of their messages communicate meanings that are congruent or consistent (Hasse & Tepper, 1972). Finally, one recent report says that doctors who display more inferior nonverbal traits (e.g., harsh voice, domineering gestures, etc.)

are more than twice as likely to be sued by patients than doctors who use favorable non-verbal skills (Rosenthal, 2002). This is food for thought, as we turn to our next nonverbal context: the legal setting.

Legal Settings

Millions of Americans now seem fascinated with legal settings, especially courtroom dynamics. Surely the nationally televised trials of William Kennedy Smith, Oliver North, Justice Clarence Thomas, and O. J. Simpson were fascinating spectacles. More recent trials such as those of Michael Jackson and Martha Stewart were not televised from the court-room. But televised trials turn countless Americans into self-appointed courtroom analysts. Americans now can give microscopic attention to every feature of courtroom interaction that they sense might have communicative significance. The courtroom has become a worldwide obsession. Moreover, the courtroom is a unique place, because ordinary nonverbal behaviors mean something special in the legal setting. The juror serves a key role in evaluating these nonverbal behaviors and becomes the ultimate decision maker of guilt or innocence in our judicial system (Hartje, 2005). Our analysis here will be confined to the trials that were covered in court by the media.

The eye of the television camera has revealed to the general public what has been apparent to attorneys for some time, which is that courtroom interaction is not shaped solely by the words of the participants—the attorneys, the judge, the accuser, the defendant, and the witnesses. The traditional, outmoded view is that court cases are typically won by the side that presents the best evidence. Leading courtroom attorneys have long recognized that the nonverbal communicative interaction that occurs in the courtroom may often be the most important force (Anthony & Vinson, 1987). In fact, lawyers are quick to point out a defendant's nonverbal inconsistencies in order to score points with the jury. It is this special place, the court, where microcommunication is observed in a *tight* context (Searcy, Duck, & Blanck, 2005). For example, the lawyer might point out to the jury that the defendant was looking down as he was questioned during the last cross-examination. This tell by the attorney could swing key juror votes at the end of the trial.

Rasicot (1985) drew attention to the functional importance of nonverbal communication in the courtroom. Rasicot emphasized that law schools have traditionally done a fine job in training courtroom attorneys in the technical aspects of legal work. However, they have done a very poor job of teaching communication skills. The seriousness of this training deficiency becomes apparent when we recognize two things at minimum: Communication is the most important part of the courtroom trial, and nonverbal communication is the most important part of that communication because over 60 percent of the messages exchanged in the courtroom are transmitted nonverbally (Rasicot, 1985).

The importance of managing impressions in the courtroom has been apparent to attorneys for some time. Three highly detailed books that are particularly rich sources of information on impression management in the courtroom were written by Aron, Fast, and Klein (1986); Bennett and Hirschhorn (1993); and Smith and Malandro (1985). Nonverbal communication in turn frequently assumes the central role in impression management efforts in the courtroom.

The legal profession leads the way in the use of image consultants. Not surprisingly, impression management has emerged as an important topic for legal scholars (LeVan, 1984; Pryor & Buchanan, 1984; Rieke & Stutman, 1990; Ryan & Syald, 1993; Varinsky & Nomikos, 1990; Wood, 1985). These publications focus directly on how members of legal teams and their clients seek to manage impressions and how jurors and judges form impressions. Witness preparation is a critical time for lawyers and consultants to review the positive nonverbal behaviors they wish their clients to demonstrate during the trial (Boccaccini, 2002).

Although publications on impression management in the courtroom cover a range of topics, two areas are receiving particular attention: (a) the functions of nonverbal behaviors and cues as attorneys seek to manage impressions formed by jury members, other members of their legal team, their clients, their witnesses, and themselves (Barge, Schlueter, & Pritchard, 1989; Bergin, 2006; Burke, Ames, Etherington, & Pietsch, 1990; Caldwell, Perrin, Gabriel, & Gross, 2001; Darby & Jeffers, 1988; deTurck & Goldhaber, 1988; Pettus, 1990; Sigal, Braden-Maguire, Hayden, & Mosley, 1985; Vinson, 1982; Wuensch, Castellow, & Moore, 1991); and (b) the monitoring of judges' nonverbal behaviors and cues to determine if they are revealing either positive or negative biases toward members of a legal team, clients, and witnesses, and, if so, how judicial bias is communicated and what its nature is (Bennett & Hirschhorn, 1993; Blanck, Rosenthal, & Cordell, 1985).

Jury and trial consultants work directly with attorneys by using the nonverbal profiles exhibited by potential jurors to make inferences about both personal qualities and attitudes. Once a trial begins, jury consultants often are seated in the courtroom a few feet from the jury so that they can study even the most subtle of the jurors' nonverbal behaviors in order to identify their emotional and attitudinal reactions to the given attorneys, witnesses, and clients (Aron, Fast, & Klein, 1986; Bennett & Hirschhorn, 1993).

Although many different kinds of nonverbal messages are undeniably important in the courtroom, four kinds are particularly important: (a) personal appearance, (b) kinesic behaviors, (c) the use of space, and (d) vocal cues. Let us first consider personal appearance guidelines. In general, conservative and traditional clothing enhances the credibility of the male attorney. Trendy or poor-quality suits as well as sports jackets should be avoided. Wool and wool blends are the preferred fabrics for the suits of male attorneys, whereas silk, ultra suede, and nontraditional fabrics are to be avoided. Male attorneys should wear a white shirt with a gray or navy suit. Eyeglasses are quite acceptable because they have been found to enhance credibility, but attorneys should avoid round, wire-rim frames (they make the eyes look small, beady, and untrustworthy), or any type of trendy frame. However, no type of tinted or photosensitive eyeglasses or contact lenses should be worn (anything that makes it difficult to have an unimpeded look at the male attorney's eyes is apt to depress the trustworthiness factor). A beard or mustache is acceptable if it is well trimmed and conservative (beards may enhance credibility in certain rather formal situations).

The personal appearance guidelines for approachability and friendliness for male attorneys contrast with the guidelines for credibility. Thus, male attorneys who wish to enhance the perception that they are approachable and friendly may decide to wear a sports jacket rather than a suit. If they do wear a suit, they should choose lighter colors such as tan or beige; acceptable fabrics for suits or sports coats in addition to wools include cashmere and wool blends. If eyeglasses are worn, they should be removed periodically to increase the perception of approachability. The approachable male attorney should be clean shaven.

Female attorneys who are dressing to enhance their personal credibility absolutely must avoid designer clothing and accessories—female attorneys who seem to be preoccupied with being fashionable and chic are not apt to inspire confidence in their credibility. In line with this perceptual point, female attorneys may wear limited jewelry but only up to five pieces—that is, a ring, a pin, earrings, and a necklace.

By contrast, female attorneys who wish to enhance their perceived approachability/likability may wear a contrasting skirt and jacket or even a tailored and conservative dress. They may of course wear a blouse with a bow or even with pleats, a slight ruffle, or a soft tie (though they should avoid a masculine-looking tie). Brighter blouse colors that include pastels such as blue, pink, rose, and green may be worn but they should avoid both bright-colored and white blouses. For cultivating the approachable look, the female attorney's hairstyle may be softened so that her hair is brought around her face in soft curls or waves. One startling investigation surveyed 58 female attorneys and found that one-third used their dress to what researchers describe as "sexualized advocacy," which includes short skirts or other inappropriate dress cuts (Bergin, 2006).

In a seminal study, Rasicot (1985) describes the communicative functions of clothing and artifacts in the courtroom in detail. However, his most original contribution may be his four general conclusions: (1) Although the visual image is always important throughout the trial, the first few minutes are of critical importance. First impressions are long-lasting and trigger emotions—particularly among members of the jury—that strongly influence subsequent attitudes and perceptions about a given individual. (2) In criminal cases the defendant should be dressed in such a manner that his or her appearance is inconsistent with the crime. The objective is to have the jury study the appearance of the defendant and conclude that linking the defendant to the crime is irrational. (3) In civil cases, the plaintiff should be dressed so that it looks like she or he not only needs the amount of money under consideration but also deserves it. Conversely, the defendant in a civil case should be dressed down to such an extent that it appears that he or she could not afford to pay any court-imposed settlement, no matter how small. (4) Both the social and professional dimensions of the client's image should be conservative in appearance.

Second, kinesic behaviors or human movements may be communicatively significant in the courtroom. Eye behaviors, gestures, and postures seem particularly important. The eyes represent a communicative medium of great importance in the courtroom. Jury and trial consultants have repeatedly emphasized the importance of looking at the jury and responding to their nonverbal behaviors (Bennett & Hirschhorn, 1993). Moreover, jurors are quick to notice the nonverbal mechanics of the room, even from judges themselves (Burnett & Badzinski, 2005). We know, for example, that the eyes indicate the level of attentiveness and interest not only of jury members but also of other principal players in a courtroom drama. In so doing, they serve a central impression management function in the courtroom.

In addition, gestures and postures are important in the courtroom. Adaptor gestures expressed with the hands may communicate valuable implicit messages. For example, jurors and witnesses who exhibit a closed fist are tense at best and angry at worst. All participants in a courtroom should avoid steepling their hands because those who steeple are frequently perceived to be lying or at least withholding part of the truth. Similarly, people who place their chin close to their neck may communicate either that they are trying to hide something or that they are trying to cover up something. Finally, a look at the jurors'

How is the young man using his eye behaviors in court? Are they positive or negative?

ankles and feet may be the best indicator of their relative level of comfort or discomfort. The feet are rarely if ever subject to conscious control by a communicator, so the messages they transmit should be almost completely free from deception.

Third, the use of space plays a central role in the courtroom in the sense that it is used by the attorneys to attain dominance or control. The primary way attorneys try to gain and maintain control in a courtroom is through the use of available space. Attorney and law professor Jeffrey Wolfe treated this subject in an enlightening way in his article entitled "Courtroom Choreography: Systematic Use of the Courtroom" (1985). Wolfe wrote that many factors contribute to the credibility of the case and of each courtroom participant (for example, voice level, order of presentation, questions asked, use of demonstrative evidence, and so on). He stressed that attorneys may be quite persuasive by the space they use in court.

There are some cultural differences in court space. For example, the Chinese courtroom is carefully constructed in favor of the state and against the defendant. Judges are placed at elevated desks and prosecutors sit behind desks. The desk serves as a nonverbal barrier indicating the inferiority of the accused in the trial (Chang, 2003). Also, the British venue seems somewhat different from American courtrooms. British judges laugh more often, and express more anger, which in turn can bias juror members (Collett & Kovera, 2003).

Fourth, the voice is a vitally important medium of communication in the courtroom. Because the voice encodes power (and its opposite—weakness or submissiveness) powerfully, attorneys may wish to speak with a soft voice, perhaps to dissociate themselves from an image of unseemly aggressiveness. Persons accused of aggressive crimes such as murder and rape may be especially concerned with distancing themselves from an image of aggressiveness. Blumenthal (1993) suggests that witnesses who lick their lips or hesitate in their speech are more likely to be perceived as deceptive, regardless of the truthfulness of their testimony.

Trial and jury consultants are particularly sensitive to the vocal cues of jurors as sources of perceptual information. Thus, a sudden increase in speaking rate may suggest increased nervousness or aggressiveness. A sudden change in the pitch of a person's voice may also be important. An individual who lowers her or his voice may want to hide something, or at least avoid discussing it. An increase in pitch may suggest an increase in the intensity level of the emotion being experienced. When a person blurts out something, the content is apt to be truthful. Inappropriate laughter is often a reliable sign of nervousness. Sustained crying also raises serious questions about a witness's credibility (Bennett & Hirschhorn, 1993). Since a great deal of the courtroom has a verbal component, the perceiver must take vocal cues into account when framing judgments. One study found that attorney questions that are overtly "leading" and accusatory in their tone can cause the defendant or witness to behave in an unbecoming way with the jury (Kassin, 2002).

Nonverbal Impression Management in the Courtroom

Few prototypes exist for the research we are about to present. One example stands out, however. Aron, Fast, and Klein (1987) conducted an in-depth analysis of the communication that occurred when Lt. Col. Oliver North took the stand at a congressional hearing during the famous Iran Contra Affair hearings. Consider the following example:

> There was one classic exchange when North projected this side of his personality. North said that he thought every penny of the remaining profits from the arms sale should go to the Nicaraguan resistance. When reminded that Albert Hakim was not so willing to turn over the money, North said, "Give me ten minutes with Mr. Hakim." When asked if after 10 minutes he could get Hakim to turn over the money, North responded, "If I can meet with anybody without a bunch of lawyers around, I reckon I could, sir!" and then he broke out into a big grin. (p. 21)

North used this brief exchange to claim four positive images for himself: he was a macho guy, he was a regular guy, he was a nice guy, and he was a truthful person who was up against lawyers who were trying to twist his words. Thus, North used the principle of association discussed in Chapter 9 on impression management. He was able to dissociate himself from a set of highly negative images claimed for him by his opponents while claiming a contrasting, positive set of images for himself via his own communicative behavior on the witness stand.

Finally, the even more central role of nonverbal factors in positively shaping North's image was evident since he wore a uniform, looking like the all-American boy exuding a great deal of patriotism for his country.

The Anita Hill–Clarence Thomas Senate Hearings. Nonverbal communication does not of course always assume the central role in impression management. Indeed, in the confrontation between Clarence Thomas and Anita Hill before the Senate Judiciary Committee, the content of the verbal exchanges was probably of primary importance.

Nonetheless, nonverbal communication played an important role in shaping the impressions that the protagonists made—particularly Judge Clarence Thomas.

Leathers (1996) examined the dynamics of impression management in this hearing. Clarence Thomas was George H. Bush's nominee to the U. S. Supreme Court. Anita Hill worked under Thomas' supervision at the U.S. Department of Education's Office for Civil Rights in 1981 and 1982 and at the Equal Employment Opportunity Commission (EEOC) from 1982 to 1983. Thomas had already undergone weeks of interrogation by the Senate Judiciary Committee before the fateful day of October 11, 1991. Witnesses by the score had appeared before the committee, and three volumes of more than 2,200 pages had already been devoted to the hearings.

The charges that triggered the confrontation between Hill and Thomas on Capitol Hill were both explicit and sensational in nature. Hill charged that on October 11, 1991, Thomas repeatedly talked to her about explicit sexual matters (Smolow, 1991). Finally, Hill claimed that after embarrassing and humiliating her with such references to sex, Thomas said to her at a dinner celebrating Hill's last day at the EEOC that "if I [Hill] ever told anyone of his behavior, that it would ruin his career" (Smolow, 1991, p. 39).

From the moment Anita Hill made these charges, the Republicans' impression management team moved quickly to try to destroy Anita Hill's credibility. In terms of political pragmatism, it was either destroy or be destroyed. Either Anita Hill's credibility had to be destroyed (or seriously damaged) or Clarence Thomas' own credibility would be destroyed. The latter would have been disastrous for the Republicans because the obvious result would have been that Clarence Thomas would have joined the ranks of such failed Supreme Court nominees as Robert Bork.

In their attempt to destroy Anita Hill's credibility, Republican members of the Senate Judiciary Committee claimed eight major negative images for her. They included the assertions that Anita Hill was a spurned woman; that Anita Hill was a prudish woman who experienced "sexual fantasies" as a result of a mental disorder known as erotomania; and that Anita Hill was a malevolently motivated, unfair person who was trying to force Clarence Thomas to bear the unbearable burden of the stereotype of the sexually promiscuous black man. The impression management confrontation that took place at the verbal level via a debate about the accuracy of these image claims was important.

The Republican impression managers also used nonverbal communication artfully to communicate implicit messages at the subconscious level. Their basic type of nonverbal persuasion was indirect suggestion. Recognizing that indirect suggestion requires the use of emotional rather than rational appeals, they focused on the controlled display of emotions, particularly by the two central players who proved to be most adept at nonverbal communication: Clarence Thomas and Senator Orrin Hatch.

The primary medium of nonverbal communication that Thomas and Hatch used, however, was their voice or vocal cues. We established in Chapter 8 that vocal cues may rival personal appearance in their impact on impressions made. Thomas and Hatch seemed to be acutely aware of the importance of vocalic communication in impression management.

More specifically, both Clarence Thomas and Senator Hatch proved adept at using their voices to communicate a given emotion or to make a desired impression. When Thomas used his face and hands to communicate a given emotion such as disgust, he also used the pitch, volume, and intensity of his voice to reinforce that emotion.

Interestingly, Thomas displayed a number of nonverbal behaviors that have previously proved to be indicators of deception when he responded to high-stress questions. During Thomas' answer to the question about the nature of his actions at Anita Hill's apartment, a number of his nonverbal behaviors accelerated markedly. The number of "ahs" exhibited per minute went from 5.56 on average to 21 per minute at this point in his Senate testimony. Thomas' eye shifts went from an average of 12.29 per minute to 15 per minute during this answer, and his blink rate increased from an average of 8.82 per minute to 12 per minute.

The most striking change in Thomas' nonverbal behavior during his answer to this particular question, however, was his speaking rate. His average speaking rate during his Senate testimony was 136.27 words per minute (in the baseline, Thomas spoke at the rather slow rate of 110 words per minute). While he was speaking about his actions at Anita Hill's apartment, his speaking rate rose to 176 words per minute or 60 percent faster than he had spoken in the baseline segments where his veracity was not at issue.

Now let us look at a other important court cases that received national attention in the last 20 years.

The William Kennedy Smith Rape Trial.   William Smith was virtually unknown to the general public in 1991 as he contemplated a trip to Palm Beach, Florida, to be with his close relatives over the Easter weekend. However, his anonymity was suddenly transformed into international celebrity as a result of events that transpired during the late evening of Good Friday and the early morning hours of Holy Saturday after he met a 29-year-old woman at a local bar. He invited her back to the mansion where he was staying. Subsequently, William Smith's female companion charged that he had raped her on the grounds of the mansion. He was indicted, charged with rape, and brought to trial.

William Smith and his multiple advisors instantly recognized that he faced an impression management problem of major proportions. He may have been charged and indicted for rape even if his name were simply William Smith. His name, however, was William *Kennedy* Smith. The fact that William Smith was a Kennedy meant that he would immediately be perceived to be authenticated by his bloodlines as a member of "America's first dysfunctional family."

In doing an impression management analysis of this trial, it is particularly useful to employ a problem-solution format. William Smith had, of course, multiple problems as his rape trial approached, but certainly one of his most serious problems was the highly negative images claimed for him by an important part of the print media—articles done on William Kennedy Smith and the Kennedy family by respected magazines such as *Esquire, Maclean's, Newsweek,* and *Time.*

As a member of the Kennedy family, Smith lost his personal identity and became part of a family that had repeatedly been associated with scandal. In the magazines that wrote articles on William Smith, the Kennedy family was referred to as a star-crossed dynasty, degenerates, and self-preoccupied hedonists who were "finished."

Newsmagazines claimed even more negative images for William Kennedy Smith because he was a Kennedy man, Senator Ted Kennedy was his uncle, and Smith was an accused rapist. Over and over the Kennedy men were labeled as sexual aggressors, exploiters of women, philanderers, and insensitive adventurers. Secondly, William Kennedy Smith was repeatedly linked with "Uncle" Ted Kennedy in a highly unflattering way. Ted Kennedy has been the object of some of the most highly negative labeling in terms of image qualities of any public figure in memory: woman chaser, selfish hedonist who was self-absorbed, "Joy Boy," drunk, self-destructive, reckless, and jaded. Finally, William Kennedy Smith's image was damaged by virtue of the fact that not only was he to stand trial for rape but also that unnamed women made additional charges of physical assault against him as he awaited trial. Specifically, William Smith's defense team would have to try to dissociate him from the labels that were repeatedly applied to him: aggressive, dominator, ferocious, animal, and power rapist.

Recognizing the multidimensional nature of his impression management problem, Black moved skillfully to rehabilitate not only the image of the Kennedy family but also the image of Uncle Ted Kennedy. Nonetheless, Black recognized that his biggest challenge was to reconstruct William Smith's own image.

William Smith's visual communication style while on the witness stand was ideal. Smith was visually unassertive almost to the point of immobility. He claimed virtually no personal space with his nonexpansive gestures. William Smith exhibited no hand gestures, few postural shifts, and little perceptible bodily movement of any kind. His repeated use of "Sir" as he responded to Black surely reinforced the impression of a polite and considerate young man whose manner was self-effacing.

Careful study of his performance on the stand suggests that William Smith's vocalic communication may have had the greatest impact on the impression he made. Surely Black recognized that vocalic communication is known to serve a central role in the formation and management of impressions. Thus, Zuckerman and Driver (1989) emphasized the importance of vocalic communication in impression management when they wrote that "there is a large literature showing that both voice cues (e.g., pitch, intensity, etc.) and speech cues (e.g., non-fluencies, speech rate, etc.) are rich sources of interpersonal impressions" (p. 68). We know that the sound of William Smith's voice was potentially very important because vocal cues powerfully encode impressions of aggression and power (or their opposites) (Berry, 1992).

William Smith spoke with a very soft voice and exhibited a number of qualities of what is known as powerless speech (Hosman, 1989). His soft voice clearly suggested that he was an unassertive if not a downright timid person. Relatedly, the fact that Smith often filled his frequent and long pauses with dysfluencies such as "uh" and "um" meant that he was exhibiting a vocal style that has been defined as "powerless." Powerless speech in turn tends to nurture the impression that a person is unassertive, hesitant, and perhaps even weak (Johnson & Vinson, 1990).

Finally, two other salient characteristics of William Smith's vocalic communication on the stand suggested that he was a highly unemotional and deliberative person: (a) he paused for long periods of time before he responded to Roy Black's questions (i.e., he had extended response latency), and (b) his pitch range was very narrow. The fact that Smith paused before responding to Black's questions clearly suggested that he was a disciplined person who kept himself under emotional control. The fact that Smith talked in a flat voice with almost no variation in his pitch clearly communicated the similar idea that Smith was an unemotional person—the greater the variation in a person's pitch range, the more emotional that person is generally perceived to be (Scherer, 1988).

In short, William Smith's vocalic communication on the stand was such as to deny the validity of the print media's image of him as an aggressive, ferocious animal who was known for his lack of emotional control. William Kennedy Smith claimed an image for himself on the stand via his nonverbal communication that contrasted strikingly with the print media's image: unassertive, unassuming, pleasant, courteous, thoughtful, and under emotional control.

Now let us turn our attention to one of the most-watched televised court cases perhaps of all time: The O. J. Simpson trial.

The O. J. Simpson Murder Trial. The O. J. Simpson murder trial surely fascinated millions of Americans. The preliminary hearing alone was watched by 25 to 30 million people (Kloer, 1994). The trial itself is widely recognized as the trial of the twentieth century. Impression management researchers will probably devote more attention to the defense than to the prosecution. This is because the defense made full use of image consultants. They did so from the time the jury was chosen until the final defense arguments were made to the jury. The credit lies with defense jury and trial consultant Jo-Ellan Dimitrius (Hutson, 2007). For reasons that are not entirely clear, the prosecution decided not to use the advice of a jury consultant. Moreover, no evidence suggests that the prosecution relied on one or more image analysts throughout any phase of the O. J. Simpson trial.

In its efforts to manage impressions in the courtroom, the defense team faced many problems and challenges. The following five seem worthy of attention: (a) How would the defense dissociate O. J. Simpson from the highly negative "private face" image that the prosecution had claimed for him? (b) How would the defense deal with the repeated prosecution claims that O. J. Simpson's guilt would be proved by overwhelming scientific evidence, much of it in the form of DNA test results? (c) How could the lead defense attorney, Johnnie Cochran, communicate nonverbally in such a manner as to be perceived as more credible than the prosecution attorneys?

The prosecution recognized that O. J. Simpson's highly positive public image would be difficult to attack effectively. They conceded that his public image as a sports hero, a pleasant pitchman for Hertz, a smiling sports commentator, and a good-natured sidekick for Leslie Nielsen in the *Naked Gun* movies gave the defense a great advantage.

As soon as O. J. Simpson was charged with double murders, however, his image came under sustained attack by the media. *Newsweek* led the attack on Simpson's image with an article titled "The Double Life of O. J." in its August 29, 1994, issue. This image attack was followed shortly by a feature article in *Esquire* titled "The Man Behind the Mask." The author, Teresa Carpenter, began by writing that "An accomplished liar fascinates me. So I am frankly in awe of O. J. Simpson" (Carpenter, 1994, p. 84). In this article, O. J. Simpson is described as a thug in a locker room, a phony jock, a world-class womanizer, a man with a drug problem, a narcissist, a brutal wife beater, and a stalker.

The most vitriolic attack on O. J. Simpson's image, however, was mounted by Faye Resnick in her book *Nicole Brown Simpson: The Private Diary of a Life Interrupted* (1994). Resnick claimed to be Nicole Brown Simpson's closest friend. The prosecutors relied heavily on claims Resnick made in this book to mount its attack on O. J. Simpson's image during their opening statement.

Resnick graphically describes Simpson as obsessively jealous of Nicole, a bully, a stalker, an animal, a wife beater, and ultimately Nicole Brown Simpson's killer. When

Nicole mentioned a former lover of hers while O. J. was present at a public gathering, Resnick wrote that

> O. J.'s face twitched uncontrollably. His body language was extremely aggressive. Horrified, I watched as sweat poured down his face. The veins in his neck bulged. His cheekbones bunched up, twitching beneath his skin. He ground his teeth in rage and hissed at me, "Why the . . . does she do this?" (1994, p. 9)

How did the defense team deal with the highly negative images claimed for O. J. Simpson? Cochran's first move was perhaps his most important one. If he did not expose the jury to subliminal perception, he came close to it. Cochran set a large photograph of O. J. Simpson and his daughter Sydney a few feet from the jury box so that it faced the jurors. He left it there for perhaps an hour during his opening statement. The photograph had been taken at Sydney's dance recital on the afternoon of June 12, 1994; the double murder of Nicole Brown Simpson and Ron Goldman occurred later that night. As the jurors studied that photograph, they must have been moved to question the credibility of some central prosecution claims. Christopher Darden had claimed in his opening statement that Simpson exhibited the appearance of a bitterly resentful, dazed, and zombie-like killer at daughter Sydney's dance recital. When the jurors looked at the photograph, they saw something different. The photograph showed a smiling and seemingly relaxed O. J. Simpson with his arm draped casually around his daughter. Daughter Sydney in turn had a big smile on her face.

Second, Johnnie Cochran knew that the jurors considered the wife-beating charge with its attendant negative images as irrelevant to the charges of murder. This information came to him from the mock juries assembled by trial consultant Jo-Ellan Dimitrius ("The Road to Panama City," 1995). Third, Cochran knew that the positive image that Simpson brought to court would be resistant to change in the minds of these jurors if Simpson's own nonverbal communicative behavior in court was inconsistent with the image of an emotionally undisciplined, obsessive, aggressive animal that the prosecution insisted he was. Finally, Cochran devoted one section of his opening defense statement to claiming a contrasting set of positive images for O. J. Simpson. Among other things Cochran claimed that Simpson was a benevolent man who provided money for the college education of several of Nicole's sisters, set up his father-in-law with a Hertz franchise, was an attentive and supportive father, and was a loving husband.

Cochran attacked the prosecution's "scientific" evidence in a highly original and effective way during his opening statement for the defense. He did it primarily with the use of graphic visual aids. Recognizing the power of visual stimuli, Cochran relied heavily on a set of visual aids that had highly desirable salient characteristics. They were attention-gaining, easily comprehensible, and memorable. Whereas the prosecution used visual aids and graphs that seemed to flood the jurors with information overload and deadly dull DNA detail, the visual aids used by Johnnie Cochran made the point concisely and graphically.

Cochran placed a large photograph before the jurors that showed a woman standing virtually on top of O. J. Simpson's Ford Bronco and peering into it; the Bronco was attached to a tow truck but obviously had not been towed from Simpson's estate. There was no police tape or ropes around the Bronco. After noting that two coffee stains were discovered on the hood of the Bronco, Cochran comments that the "Bronco was not secured. It wasn't secured so you cannot count on that evidence."

The Ford Bronco visual was followed by a second visual aid dealing with the integrity of the evidence—the words "Integrity of Evidence" appeared in red at the top of another 3-by-5-ft piece of plastic or thick cardboard that was placed near the jury. On the left side of this visual aid below the lettering "Integrity of Evidence" were a drawing of Nicole Brown Simpson's condominium, a drawing of Simpson's Rockingdale Estate with the Ford Bronco parked outside, and a drawing of a partially filled blood vial. Large arrows ran from the condominium, estate, and blood vial to a large box in the middle with the large letters "LAPD" in it. From the LAPD box, three arrows pointed, respectively, to an LAPD badge, a police station, and the LAPD laboratory. Each of these arrows had a large question mark running through it. Cochran began by saying, "Garbage in, garbage out." A person could be quite dense and still see why it was being suggested that they should dismiss the results from the DNA tests. The DNA evidence allegedly had no integrity because it had been contaminated, compromised, and corrupted by LAPD officers who were either conspiratorial, bumbling, or both.

The third question that will surely receive much attention by researchers is how, or whether, lead defense attorney Johnnie Cochran used his nonverbal communication so that he would be perceived as more credible than lead prosecuting attorneys Christopher Darden and Marcia Clark. Because the opening statements are frequently considered to be the most important part of the trial, let us consider the performances of Darden, Clark, and Cochran during their opening statements.

Darden and Clark clearly both used the lecture mode when they addressed the jury. They almost always looked down before they began to make a point; this practice has repeatedly been found to depress one's perceived competence. Moreover, they did not sustain eye contact with members of the jury and they frequently looked away from members of the jury.

In contrast, Johnnie Cochran began the defense's opening statement by saying, "Ladies and gentleman, good morning to you." Cochran looked directly at the jury before, during, and after uttering these words. Cochran went on to say that "If you have had occasion to go to the movies, you know what this [opening statement] is supposed to be." His eye contact with the jury was sustained and direct. Shortly thereafter, Cochran said, "Here we are now in this search for justice." He not only sustained eye contact with the jury, but his eyes moved slowly from one juror to another as if he were trying to communicate with each juror personally.

Next, let's look at a trial that received a significant amount of media attention in the twenty-first century.

The Scott Peterson Murder Trial.   This case was brought to trial in 2004 when Scott Peterson was charged and sentenced to death row for killing his wife, Laci Peterson, and their unborn baby. This trial was on Court TV and carried by countless newspapers and TV news channels for months. The guilty verdict was read on November 12, 2004, and was watched by 2.6 million TV viewers, the largest audience of a murder verdict since the O. J. Simpson verdict in the 1990s (Hartje, 2005; "News of the Market," 2004).

This trial is significant for several reasons. For our purposes here, we will focus on the nonverbal forms of communication that took place during the trial.

First, Scott was dressed nicely each day. His overall physical appearance seemed to have little effect on the verdict, however. His attire could have been inconsistent with his cold and clammy demeanor while in the courtroom. He looked stoic during most of the trial, appeared lifeless on several occasions, and even when he leaned over to discuss something with his lawyer, he seemed nonchalant about his behavior and his displayed emotions. He almost appeared as though he was at a shareholder's meeting, not on trial for the murder of his wife.

Second, the prosecution was quite successful with the visual aids they presented in the trial. Laci and the unborn baby's body were discovered on shore. The defense attorney had a model of a boat created and left it in a parking lot that he owned that was only a block from the courthouse. This nonverbal stunt was used in hopes of influencing the jury prior to the trial (Ryan, 2004). Instead of helping, this nonverbal stunt actually hurt the defense's credibility and the ethical integrity of the defense team. This nonverbal tragedy further complicated Scott Peterson's already troublesome defense.

Third, Scott's facial expressions during much of the trial appeared stoic, almost emotionless. During one phase of the trial during the judge's reading of his decision about a change of venue, Scott appeared still, motionless, almost worried. While he did not appear terrified, he did seem worried and concerned. At the end, Scott had no visible reaction when the verdict of guilty was read and he was sentenced to death row.

Fourth, Scott's body language during the trial is also noteworthy. His kinesics were still and he seemed not to provide the suitable nonverbal characteristics of someone experiencing a "loss" or remorse for any of his role in his wife's death. He was motionless throughout the trial, which made him seem almost like a statue at times. This nonverbal display was cold and "icy" as the jurors and viewing public saw him. These nonverbal behaviors signaled a ruthless and insensitive attitude to those looking at his courtroom demeanor.

In addition to Scott's behavior in the trial, we need to address the jury selection process in the trial. Jeffrey Frederick (2005) describes this important part of the trial in his book *Mastering Voir Dire and Jury Selection*. He says that nonverbal communication is an important element in the jury selection process. Image consultants are paid large sums of money to help trial attorneys look for those expressions that may tip off the legal team to move, keep, or strike the prospective juror.

In fact, nonverbal communication in the courtroom is often split-second, much like the micro-expressions that were previously discussed in our text. The savvy courtroom trial attorney looks for such micro-expressions and tries to discern meaning, significance, and impact on the "believability" or "viability" of the juror to the outcome of the trial. In the Peterson trial, one of the legal defense team members noticed a tattoo on one of the prospective jurors. When the attorney asked about the tattoo, the prospective juror tried to conceal a micro-expression on her face about the tattoo, but revealed enough rage, while short in duration, for the attorney to recognize her opinion about the case, which became a reason to keep her on the jury (Hutson, 2007).

We next turn to our third nonverbal context, the built environment.

Built Environments

Recently, social scientists have become increasingly interested in the impact of environments and their distinctive physical features on our perceptions, attitudes, and behaviors (Sommer, 1983). The macroenvironment and microenvironment both function as powerful mediums of communication. Urban planners have established that the affective tone of our perceptions is strongly influenced by such features of our macroenvironment as the physical dimensions of streets, paths, and districts (Lynch, 1960). We now know that such microenvironmental variables affect both land value and crime rate in Tokyo (Hanyu, 1993). Similarly, communication researchers have demonstrated that spatial relationships in the microenvironment may exert a controlling influence on both the quality and the quantity of communicative interaction (Burgoon, 1978; Sundstrom, 1989). Sommer (1969) emphasized the need to know more about the impact of microenvironments on individuals who engage in face-to-face interactions within their confines.

The environments within which we interact with others vary widely in scope from entire cities to small groups. The terms *microenvironment* and *proximate environment* are used interchangeably. The proximate environment of a student in a classroom includes the student's desk, the other students, the teacher, the chalkboard, the windows, and the doorway (Sommer, 1966). Frequently included as central, defining features of microenvironments are furniture, lighting, color choice, decorative items, and, most importantly, the amount of space available and the way that it is used (Sommer, 1969, 1974, 1983).

Designers of microenvironments such as the business office have been concerned almost exclusively with functional questions. Thus, Konar and Sundstrom (1986) wrote that "the symbolic qualities of those workspaces and offices have typically received far less attention in this context" (p. 203). Today that perspective is changing. Designers still are concerned with such practical questions as how many offices they can get into a building with so many square feet and with the most efficient way to light such a building, but they are concerned with more. Designers of corporate microenvironments are also highly concerned with the communicative significance of their decisions in terms of their impact on the corporate image, on customers and clients, and on the behaviors of employees.

Physical features of the office microenvironment can and frequently do serve important communicative functions. They can, for example, define or demarcate the status of the occupant of an office. *Status markers* that serve this communicative function include *furnishings, location, privacy, size,* and *personalization* (Konar & Sundstrom, 1986). Similarly, we also know that the presence or absence of aesthetic and professionally related objects can exert a significant effect on the credibility of the occupant of a faculty office (Miles & Leathers, 1984).

The *design* of the furniture placed in a microenvironment is also an important variable. Considerable research has already been done on the communicative impact of furniture design. Some scholars have concluded that furniture design can communicate specific meanings to users of that furniture (Knachstedt, 1980; Mehrabian & Diamond, 1971; Stacks & Burgoon, 1981); communicate information about an owner's attitude or personality (Argyle & Dean, 1965; Kleeman, 1981; Mehrabian, 1968, 1969; Pile, 1979; Yee & Gustafson, 1983); and contribute to individual differences in affiliative behavior, most notably during user interaction and conversation (Kleeman, 1981; Yee & Gustafson, 1983).

There are striking cultural differences in furniture arrangement. The Chinese may wish to sit around a table in a business meeting to be in harmony with the natural environment (Samovar, Porter, & McDaniel, 2007). In restaurant designs, Asians and Europeans are more likely to reject our notion of fast-food places since we de-emphasize the dining experience and see eating there, as a ritual, not a cultural reflection of importance. This point was vivid when major fast-food giants such as McDonald's had initial trouble in Asian nations because the décor flew in the face of what was considered culturally appropriate (Eaves & Leathers, 1991).

Finally, the *placement* of objects in the microenvironment is very important. For example, companies who own supermarkets know that there is a strong relationship between where a particular type of merchandise is displayed and how much of it is sold (Sommer, Wynes, & Brinkley, 1992). Even morticians take great care in where they display their caskets. Thus, expensive and inexpensive caskets are rarely displayed next to each other. Emling (1995) stressed that "in principle, a casket showroom is not unlike a new car showroom, or a furniture showroom. Funeral homes place the most expensive caskets near the front of the showroom, the cheap models to the rear" (p. E4). In fact, you may not even be able to find the most inexpensive caskets in some mortuaries if you are not accompanied by a private detective.

Context as Communication

In one sense, it is easy to embrace the old axiom that "Meaning is in people, not in things." The latest thinking and empirical research on the communicative significance of context suggest that this view is both narrow and misleading, however. In fact, Rapoport in his significant book *The Meaning of the Built Environment: A Nonverbal Communication Approach* (1982), argued that things both elicit and communicate meanings. He contended not only that the physical features of the built environment affect communication but also that context is communication. Rapoport (1982), Hall (1974), and Sommer (1983) provided impressive support for the thesis that environments, and more particularly the distinctive physical features of given environments, do communicate meaning. The argument is based on the assumption that individuals' communicative behaviors are directly affected by the "meanings" that environments have for them. These individuals, in turn, assume that the placement of furniture or the use of decorative items on a wall in a business office represents a conscious and purposive decision made by a human being. Such features of the microenvironment, therefore, serve a "latent" rather than a "manifest" communicative function. Thus, "by making the selection and placement of elements in a room *purposive* these environmental elements clearly become communicative" (Rapoport, 1982, p. 13).

In short, context, and the defining features of context, *is* a distinctive form of nonverbal communication. "The growing concern about *perceived* crowding, density, crime, or environment quality implies, even if it does not make explicit, the central role of subjective factors, many of which are based on the associations and meanings that particular aspects of environment have for people" (Rapoport, 1982, p. 26).

To the extent that we can exercise conscious control over the physical features of our microenvironments, we may be forced to choose between environments that are arousing or pleasant. Mehrabian (1976) maintained that *high-load environments* are emotionally arousing, because their physical features force individuals who work there to process much information or cope with many microenvironmental stimuli that are not directly relevant to the work assignment. For example, a business office that features an "open plan" having red wallpaper, no partitions to separate the desks of the occupants, high density, and excessive noise levels is a high-load environment.

In contrast, a private business office, with walls and a door, subdued wall colors and lighting, and carpeting to control or eliminate disruptive noises, is a *low-load environment*. Although the high-load environment is emotionally arousing and promotes communicative interaction, it can be unpleasant because the collective impact of the microenvironmental stimuli produces fatigue. In contrast, the low-load environment is often perceived as pleasant because its inhabitants do not have to cope with a multitude of arousing microenvironmental stimuli. Nevertheless, low-load environments might not be sufficiently arousing for individuals who work in them, because they do not facilitate either productivity or effective communicative interaction with colleagues.

As we shall see, the physical features of microenvironments such as the places where we work affect not only our own perceptions and behaviors but also the perceptions and behaviors of individuals we encounter in those environments (Sundstrom, 1989). This is particularly true in a workplace such as a private office. The size and use of work space can be major status determinants. Since we can control the type and placement of furniture in our office, we can influence impressions made about us. In fact, we now know that the decorative items we choose to put in our offices can affect the image we project to others. This is particularly true with regard to our personal credibility. In many applied settings, the communicative impact of microenvironmental variables is now receiving increasing attention. The primary focus of researchers has been on public settings, although some attention is now being given to private contexts such as families (Beeghley & Donnelly, 1989). Among the communicatively significant public settings that come to mind are the courtroom (Adelsward, Aronson, Jonsson, & Linell, 1987), the hospital with its various departments, the department store, and the funeral home (Leathers, 1990). Although we interact with other persons in various real-world contexts of importance to us, four kinds of contexts will receive close scrutiny in this text. The classroom, the conference room, the office, and the fast-food restaurant seem particularly important for us to investigate. We have the potential to markedly affect the appearance of these four kinds of microenvironments by the decisions we make.

The Classroom Environment.   To a considerable degree, administrators are committed to the development of a distraction-free classroom environment, one that minimizes student interaction and affective response while maximizing the potential to regulate and control students' behaviors. In contrast, students and teachers prefer a classroom environment that minimizes the use of control mechanisms while maximizing opportunities for uninhibited communicative interaction. Administrators who are committed to the traditional classroom environment prefer fixed, straight-row seating; high density; and drab, institutional colors. Experimental seating arrangements and emotionally arousing colors are thought to produce a level of stimulation for the students that is incompatible with effective discipline (Sommer, 1974).

Sommer and two colleagues returned to studying their original "soft classroom," so called because of the texture of the fabric used in the wall decorations, the covered seats, and the carpeted floor. Results showed that this humane classroom in contrast to the traditional classroom was viewed by students as more aesthetically pleasing, and it enhanced student participation (Wong, Sommer, & Cook, 1992).

The creation of a more humane classroom is not easily achieved. Administrators typically have almost complete control over such important microenvironmental variables as the size of the classroom, the size of the class, and the type of seating. There are increasing indications, however, that some administrators are beginning to work collaboratively with teachers and students to modify physical features of traditional classrooms that inhibit successful communication and learning. To be successful, such efforts must, at minimum, consider the perceptual and behavioral impact of room size, class size, seating arrangement and choice, teachers' spatial orientations, and the appearance of the classroom.

Classroom size is an important variable. Classroom size clearly determines the actual amount of space available for a given student. Students have well-developed preferences as to the amount of usable space that is designated as theirs. Expressed in square feet of space available to each student, ideal personal space in a lecture hall is 19 to 27 ft; in a study hall, 20 to 29 ft; in a library, 24 to 31 ft; and in a discussion group, 31 to 43 ft (Weldon, Loewy, Winer, & Elkin, 1981).

In a classroom, actual space is less important than perceived space, however. Inadequate space usually results in the feeling of being crowded. The further result, frequently, is that students have difficulty maintaining attention, task performance decreases, and aggressive behavior increases. In fact, a number of low-cost steps may be taken in the high-density classroom to moderate the students' perceptions that they are being crowded. Such steps include using room partitions, decreasing the number of entrances, choosing rectangular over square classroom designs, promoting acquaintance and mutual cooperation among students, and maintaining a comfortable room temperature (Weldon et al., 1981). Each of these steps is known to contribute to a good classroom environment, and has been highly correlated with enhanced student performance (Cheng, 1994).

A bigger classroom is not necessarily better. Indeed, an unlimited amount of classroom space may result in low levels of student arousal. Moderate density seems to represent a desirable compromise between conditions of either low-density or high-density seating. Moderate density seems to promote student arousal that results in striking improvement in reading speed and comprehension, with only a slight decrease in the ability to acquire and organize new material. High density is another matter. Under conditions of high density, students find it difficult to assimilate and organize new material, even though their reading speed and comprehension may increase (Weldon et al., 1981).

Class size has a pronounced impact on the amount of student participation. Sommer (1974) found that in a small class of 6 to 20 students, students participate more than twice as much as they do in a class of medium (21 to 50 students) or large (more than 50 students) size. Even in small classes, however, students participate only 12 percent of the time during a class hour. If student participation and involvement represent desired educational objectives, the peril of ever-increasing class sizes should be carefully considered.

The impact of varying *seating arrangements* on student–teacher interaction is not so well documented. In one experiment, Sommer (1974) actually had a colleague enter 25 classrooms and change chairs from straight-row seating to a circular arrangement. However, the attachment to the straight row was so strong that chairs had to be rearranged to straight-row seating in 20 of the 25 classrooms before the classes began; in many cases the students themselves returned the chairs to the straight-row arrangement.

Although students have come to expect straight-row seats that are bolted to the floor, they have a negative attitudinal response to this type of seating arrangement. For example, Rubin (1972) found that high-IQ students prefer circular and horseshoe seating arrangements, and low-IQ students prefer a flexible seating arrangement that allows the teacher to walk about in their midst. Students almost uniformly report a negative reaction to straight-row seating. They believe that this type of seating arrangement inhibits student participation and interaction with the teacher. Moreover, straight-row seating reinforces the unhealthy perception on the part of the students that the seating arrangement is being used primarily to enhance the teacher's ability to regulate and control their behavior.

Although students can rarely exercise control over such variables as room size, class size, or seating arrangement, they can usually decide where they will sit. A number of studies have consistently shown that students who sit closest to the teacher, and who have the greatest opportunity for eye contact with the teacher, participate most and receive the highest grades (Levine, O'Neal, Garwood, & McDonald, 1980; Sommer, 1974; Wulf, 1977). Arbitrary assignment to seating in front of the classroom does positively affect participation. Whether front and center seating is voluntary or involuntary, students participate more in those seating zones (Levine et al., 1980).

Aside from the control they exercise over the seating arrangement, teachers can exert a major impact on the classroom environment by the *spatial orientation* they assume vis-à-vis their students. Hesler (1972) examined the perceptual impact of six types of spatial orientations by teachers: (a) BL—teacher in front of blackboard or front wall of classroom; (b) DK—teacher sitting on, beside, or behind desk; (c) T—teacher in front of desk; (d) S—teacher positioned along the side seats or along a side wall; (e) BK—teacher in back of room; and (f) AM—teacher among students.

Teachers who sit on, beside, or in back of their desks are seen as isolated from the students and less warm, friendly, and effective than teachers who stand in front of their desks. So long as their proxemic behavior is deemed appropriate by the students, the teacher is consistently perceived as warmer as they move closer to them. This research supports the conventional wisdom that the teacher who wishes to cultivate an image of a warm, caring, and emotionally sensitive individual must seek to interact at the closest possible distance with students but should not violate their personal space or trigger the uncomfortable feeling of being crowded.

In his essay on classroom ecology, Doyle (1977) took a position that seems to be counterintuitive. He maintained that teachers who want "managerial success" must seek to exercise prudent control over the students' activities while including as many students as possible in classroom activity. Those objectives led him to the novel recommendation that teachers should actually *increase* the distance between themselves and the student with whom they interact. By increasing interaction distance with the individual student, a greater number of students are supposedly brought within the teacher's conscious level of awareness. In addition, Doyle advised that the teacher not maintain direct eye contact with the interacting student, but scan wider sections of the classroom in order to visually involve the greatest possible number of students.

Doyle (1977) highlighted the difficult choice the teacher must make in choosing a proximate or distant spatial orientation vis-à-vis students. He wrote that with "regard to distance and eye contact, at least, the affective and regulatory uses of nonverbal behavior appear incompatible" (p. 186). To literally maintain distance from the students enhances the teacher's ability to control them, but at a considerable sacrifice in terms of the type and intensity of students' emotional responses to the teacher.

The precise effects of modifying the *appearance* of classrooms are not presently known. We have little empirical evidence to bring to bear on this subject because administrators are generally resistant to modifying the appearance of classrooms, which would have to be done if the impact on students' attitudes, their communicative behaviors, and, ultimately, their learning were to be carefully measured. Uniformity in the appearance of classrooms is justified on two bases: It is democratic (pictures or unusual wall colors might offend some students), and a uniform and dull appearance enhances teachers' ability to control the behavior of the students (Sommer, 1974).

Sommer went on to point out that school administrators, such as principals, show no reluctance to decorate the walls of their own offices with pictures and art objects, but they fear the behavioral consequences of similar decorative objects in the classrooms. He actually did modify the appearance of one classroom and found that the impact was highly beneficial. Decorations included three abstract yarn designs on the back wall, two pictures hung on the side wall, and two posters on the front wall. The bulletin board was decorated with flower stickers, a jar of paper flowers was placed on the front table, and a blue fish mobile with three God's-eyes was attached to a wall above the windows. Reactions of students and faculty to the modified classroom were uniformly positive.

Mehrabian (1976) also maintained that there is a strong need to modify the appearance of the traditional classroom. Because they appear sterile and drab, classrooms typically represent a microenvironment that is both nonarousing and unpleasant to the student. Aside from cost considerations, Mehrabian contended that school administrators remain committed to the drab classroom because they fear that the introduction of arousing, pleasant stimuli is potentially dangerous. If contrasting wall colors, plants, and paintings were used, they might arouse and stimulate students to such a degree that teachers would no longer be able to exercise the control necessary for effective discipline. Finally, Mehrabian noted that the classroom must be adapted to the learning activity.

The Conference Room Environment.   A conference room represents a particularly important type of microenvironment. Many physical features of the conference room can affect the quality and quantity of communicative interaction, the participants' perceptions of each other, and the task performance of a given group. Variables such as room size, room decorations, room color, and even temperature regulation are potentially important and are treated elsewhere in the chapter. The three microenvironmental variables of greatest importance in the conference room are *seating choice, table configuration,* and *communication networks.*

Seating position at a conference table is sometimes determined by status considerations or by habit. When you have freedom of choice in seating position, the communicative implications should be carefully considered, however. The man who sits at the head of a rectangular table significantly increases his chances of being perceived as the leader.

The conference room is an important place for communication.

Because women are stereotyped as followers rather than leaders, they are not afforded this same perceptual advantage. Individuals who choose a seat along the sides of a table not only decrease their chances of being perceived as leaders, but also are apt to be perceived as individuals with lower status and less self-confidence.

Seating position affects not only perceptions of leadership potential but also actual leadership emergence in the small group (Sundstrom, 1989). Strodbeck and Hook (1961) found that a person who chooses to sit at the end of a rectangular table is elected jury foreman more often than jury members sitting in the other 10 positions. Because the jury foreman is selected before any communicative interaction occurs, the impact of seating choice on leadership emergence is clearly very strong.

Leadership emergence as a result of seating position seems to be determined by the two advantages central seating gives a person: controlling communicative interaction and maintaining direct visual accessibility to the greatest number of discussants. For example, Howells and Becker (1962) conducted an experiment in which five group members sat at a rectangular table, two on one side and three on the other. The leaders who emerged in the five-member groups (by a ratio of more than 2 to 1) were on the two-member side. The greater likelihood that those on the two-member side would emerge as leaders was attributed to the fact that they had visual access to a majority of the group (three), but that the people on the three-member side had visual access to only two. Because discussion members seated at the side of rectangular tables have visual access to a limited number of group members, it is not surprising that they emerge as leaders much less frequently than discussants seated at the ends of the table.

The *Steinzor effect,* which has received strong empirical support from the results of many studies, is based on the finding that being visible in a group increases interaction, "and since leadership is strongly related to participation, being in a visible position in the small group should increase an individual's chance of becoming the leader" (Baker, 1984, p. 160).

A field study by Heckel (1973) suggested that individuals who wish to emerge as leaders not only select the central seating position in the conference room but also do so at such nontask functions as meals. Persons who do not wish to be chosen as leaders characteristically sit at the side of the table when eating meals. In short, seating choice at a conference table determines to a large degree whether a person will be a dominant figure or a member of the supporting cast in discussions that ensue. Given the important impression management and control functions of eye behaviors, it is not surprising that individuals who have limited visual access to other group members are disproportionately relegated to a supporting role. The converse is also true: leaders are more likely to choose to sit at the head of the table (Sundstrom, 1989).

Seating position also has a strong impact on how powerful or influential one is judged to be by other group members. Korda (1975) maintained:

> In meetings where people are seated around a table, whatever its shape, the order of power is almost always clockwise, beginning with what would be the number "12" on a clock face, and with power diminishing as it moves around past positions at three o'clock, six o'clock, nine o'clock, etc. (p. 101)

If you accept Korda's theory, the most powerful person at a conference table sits at the 12 o'clock position and the least powerful person sits at the 11 o'clock position.

Not everyone agrees that power moves clockwise around a conference table by virtue of seating position. For example, one study (Green, 1975) shows that the amount of the discussants' participation time increases *both* when they choose a seat closer to the leader *and* when their angle of visual access to the chairperson's line of sight is narrower relative to other discussion members. According to Green's study, the important consideration is not whether one sits to the right or left of the centrally seated leader, but how immediate one's visual access is to that leader.

Table configuration or *shape* is also an important variable in the conference room. In 1959, for example, the United States, the Soviet Union, France, and Great Britain were meeting in Geneva to discuss the future of Berlin. Before the talks began, a dispute arose over table shape. The three Western powers wanted a square table, which would have given them a three-to-one advantage in negotiating posture, from a perceptual perspective. Not surprisingly, the Soviet Union proposed a round conference table, in an attempt to neutralize the three-to-one ratio (Sommer, 1969).

Lecuyer (1976) examined the differences between problem-solving groups seated at either round or rectangular tables and the tables' effect on leadership. He found that a randomly appointed leader was more successful when a rectangular table was used. The appointed leader at a circular table had more difficulty controlling the flow of the discussion; discussants seated around the circular table more tenaciously supported their own proposed

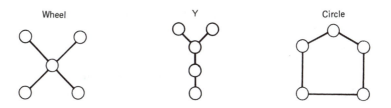

FIGURE 15.1   Communication Networks

solutions than those seated at the rectangular table. Because the leader at the circular table loses the potential for control and superiority of status that is associated with central seating at a rectangular table, the negative impact of the circular table seems predictable.

Patterson, Kelly, Kondracki, and Wulf (1979) compared the impact of circular versus L-shaped seating arrangements. Both quality and amount of communicative interaction deteriorated with L-shaped seating arrangements. Discussants were less involved and less comfortable; they exhibited longer pauses in their conversations, displayed more self-manipulative adaptor gestures, and fidgeted more by way of postural shifts. The negative impact of L-shaped seating on communicative interaction may be attributed in part to the fact that communication was made more difficult because discussants had much more limited visual access to each other than they had in the circular seating arrangement.

Communication networks consist of the actual paths or channels used by group members to transmit information to one another (see Figure 15.1). In practice, both seating choice and configuration of the conference table are apt to determine the kind of communication network used most frequently. Some discussants may, of course, choose not to participate, with a consequent impact on the types of communication networks that emerge.

Among the more common communication networks that have been experimentally manipulated in group research are the *wheel*, a *Y*, and a *circle*. The Y communication network is used to illustrate a highly centralized type of leadership in which one individual can communicate with other group members, who, in turn, are able to communicate only with that individual; the circle is associated with a highly decentralized type of leadership; the wheel combines the advantages and disadvantages of the circle and Y networks.

In his masterful summary of research on seating arrangements in small groups and the resultant communication networks that emerge from these seating arrangements, Shaw (1981) provided four generalizations of practical importance:

1. A leader is more likely to emerge in a centralized communication network than in a decentralized network.
2. Group members have higher morale in a decentralized than in a centralized communication network.
3. Decentralized communication networks are most efficient when groups must solve complex problems, but a centralized network is most efficient when the group must solve simple problems.
4. Centralized communication networks are more likely to result in a work overload for the leader than decentralized communication networks.

Similarly, Sundstrom (1989) provided a useful summary of the effects of small-group communication networks on performance, communication, leadership, decision making, and satisfaction.

From the perspective of communication networks, centralization is desirable for the person who wishes to emerge as leader and retain effective control. Centralization also is desirable when group tasks are relatively simple and when decisions must be made during moments of crisis. Whenever complex tasks are considered and a premium is placed on harmonious interpersonal relationships, the decentralized communication network is preferable.

The Office Environment.   With the possible exception of the family home, the office in which a person works is the most important microenvironment. The design and physical features of the office are known to strongly affect attitudes, the quality and quantity of communication with colleagues, and productivity. Entire books are now devoted to the behavioral impact of office design (Wineman, 1986). Many features of our offices are determined not by us but by our superiors and by designers who work for them. For example, the size of our office, furniture, carpeting, lighting, and noise control are all important variables that we may not be able to control directly (Cohen & Cohen, 1983; Sundstrom, Town, Rice, & Osborn, 1994).

In the past few years, the open-office plan has received much favorable publicity. *Open offices* contain no floor-to-ceiling walls. Panels that do not extend to the ceiling are used to define the macro-, midi-, and mini-environments in which people interact. Permanent walls and corridors are eliminated.

The open office has become quite controversial, in part because its proponents make broad-based claims about its alleged advantages that are not supported by existing research, while openly attacking the concept of the private office. Thus, proponents of the open office claim that such a spatial arrangement ensures the type of visual accessibility of occupants of the office that promotes face-to-face communication, that the sight of busy co-workers in an open office motivates others in the office to be more productive, and that an open office ensures that distinctions based on status are eliminated (Sundstrom, 1989).

The avowed objective of the open-office plan is to facilitate communication and interaction among employees while increasing employee satisfaction and motivation. Because the open-office plan de-emphasizes depersonalized contacts among employees, proponents of this plan maintain that it also promotes cooperation and friendship formation (Becker, 1981).

In practice, the behavioral impact of the open-office plan seems much less desirable than its supporters would have us believe. In part because employees feel that their privacy is being invaded and that they experience an uncomfortable sensation of crowding, open offices have been found to decrease employee satisfaction and motivation. In fact, a number of employees who use open offices have been so affected by perceived increases in noise level, visual distractions, and an accompanying loss of privacy that they report a loss in efficiency (Becker, 1981).

Mehrabian (1976) contended that a compromise embodying some of the physical features of the open and the closed office is the most desirable, in terms of its attitudinal and behavioral impact on the occupants of the office. An employee with a door to his or her office can enjoy privacy when needed by closing it and can have stimulation by leaving the door open. Even those who have their own enclosed offices might encounter frustrations, because they cannot control such factors as office location, size, and configuration. They may not even have the authority to decide on the colors of the walls. This would be an unfortunate restriction because the colors of walls are known to have a considerable impact on the moods of office occupants (Bellizzi, Crowley, & Hasty, 1983).

Many important intraoffice variables are subject to the effective conscious control of the occupant of a private office, however. Those intraoffice variables serve an important role in shaping the image projected by the office occupant and in affecting the nature of the communication that occurs in the private office. Of particular importance are seating and spatial arrangements, furniture arrangement, and decorative objects.

Seating and Spatial Arrangements. Where the occupant of an office chooses to sit will probably determine whether the occupant wishes to dominate a conversation or share control of it with other individuals. It may also indicate whether the office occupant is a superior. For example, J. Edgar Hoover sat at a large, elevated desk, and his visitors had to sit well below him at a small table to his right. Nelson Rockefeller went even further to try to ensure dominance and perceptions of high power in his office. At times, he ascended a ladder that folded out of a desk drawer and addressed office visitors from the top of his desk. In addition, Donald Trump has made his presence known with his chair behind the long table in the boardroom in the hit reality TV series, *The Apprentice.* Korda (1975) maintained that it is much more difficult to do business and communicate effectively with an office occupant who sits behind his or her desk. He advocates a variety of stratagems to lure a person out from behind a desk. He wrote that if you cannot get people to come out from behind their desks, you can put your hat or briefcase on the desk if you want to make them nervous. Note that people with old-fashioned desks that serve as barriers almost always leave them to say yes, and sit behind them to say no. Once they have taken refuge behind 500 lbs of mahogany, you can't argue with them.

If you wish to stimulate communication with others in your office, and to have them perceive themselves as your status equals, you must take pains to sit as close to them as proxemic norms allow. Sommer (1961, 1962) supports the conclusion that individuals prefer to sit where they have the greatest visual accessibility to those with whom they interact. Although individuals prefer to be able to face you when interacting with you in a business situation, they will often choose to sit at your side—perhaps on an available sofa—if face-to-face seating would require a separation of more than 5 ft.

Researchers have also established that where an individual sits has a measurable impact on the amount of communication that occurs and on how individuals perceive someone who selects a certain seat. Sitting around a table, as opposed to sitting in chairs along walls, has been found to increase interaction by almost 100 percent (Sommer & Ross, 1958). Finally, Pelligrini (1971) found that a person who elects to sit at the head of a table, as opposed to at other positions, will be perceived as significantly more talkative, persuasive, dominant, self-confident, and intelligent.

Furniture Arrangement. The business office has been the scene of a number of studies that examine the impact of furniture arrangement on the ways individuals perceive office occupants. Desk placement has been the variable most often manipulated. Results from one study (White, 1953) indicated that patients in a doctor's office are more "at ease" when no desk separates doctor and patient. An extension of this study (Widgery & Stackpole, 1972) found that high-anxiety subjects perceive a counselor to be more credible when there is no desk between them, and low-anxiety subjects perceive the counselor to be more credible when there is a desk between them. Joiner (1971) found that people in academic offices have their desks touching a wall significantly more often than people in either business or government and that higher-status office occupants are more likely to place their desks between themselves and the door rather than against a side or back wall.

Whether an office occupant chooses to sit behind a desk or at a table in the office can also have a considerable impact on the impression conveyed. Becker, Gield, and Froggatt (1983) found that professors who sit at tables in their offices, as opposed to sitting behind desks, are perceived as being significantly more fair, friendly, caring, helpful, and open-minded, and are also viewed as better listeners. When seated behind their desks, professors are perceived as more authoritative and aggressive.

Occupants of faculty offices, as opposed to occupants of business offices, are less concerned about their ability to control communicative interaction in their offices than they are about the impressions they make. Thus, Preston and Quesda (1974) found that occupants of business offices believe that the primary value of furniture arrangement is control of communicative interaction. Occupants of academic offices, in contrast, are relatively unconcerned about the control potential of objects in their office, but they attach considerable importance to such objects' potential impact on the image they project.

Aesthetic and Professionally Related Objects.   We know that the general appearance of an office can affect the perceptions of those who interact within its confines. In a classic study, Maslow and Mintz (1956) devised three "visually aesthetic" settings: a "beautiful," an "average," and an "ugly" room. Subjects were asked to rate a series of 10 pictures on two scales, fatigue–energy and displeasure–well-being. Although the same pictures were used in all three settings, subjects who viewed them in the "beautiful" room rated them significantly higher on energy and well-being than subjects in the other two settings.

Subsequent research has established that interviewees are more self-disclosing in a warm, intimate room as opposed to a cold, nonintimate room (Kasmar, Griffin, & Mauritzen, 1976). Hasse and Dimattia (1976) reported that counseling interviewees in a large room (13.9 sq m) make significantly more self-reference statements than interviewees in a small room (7.67 sq m). Finally, Bloom, Weigel, and Traut (1977) established that the appearance of an office can affect the credibility of the office occupant. Female counselors are judged to be more credible in a "traditional" office setting that features a desk between the counselor and the client, diplomas on the wall, and file cabinets. By contrast, male counselors are judged to be more credible in a "humanistic" setting that has no desk between the interactants, modern sculpture, and currently popular wall posters.

The Bloom et al. (1977) study did indicate that aesthetic objects such as wall posters and professionally related objects such as diplomas can affect the credibility of an office occupant when they are present in the office. What this study did not do, however, was

FIGURE 15.2

determine whether these two types of office décor had a different impact on the perceived credibility of the office occupant. Moreover, this study did not attempt to determine whether the individual dimensions of credibility—competence, trustworthiness, and dynamism—are affected in different ways by the two types of office décor.

Subjects who viewed photographs of the office with and without aesthetic and professionally related objects were asked to use sets of bipolar scales (representing the three dimensions of credibility) to measure the credibility of the office occupant, who was not present. Figure 15.2 shows some of the aesthetic objects in the office; Figure 15.3 shows some of the professionally related objects.

Results from this study indicate that aesthetic and professionally related objects had a marked impact on the credibility of the office occupant. The presence of aesthetic objects in the faculty office enhanced the perceived trustworthiness of the occupant. The presence of professionally related objects had a positive impact on both the occupant's perceived authoritativeness *and* the occupant's perceived trustworthiness.

Professionally related objects seem to be a particularly powerful medium of communication because their presence in a faculty office results in a significant increase in both the perceived authoritativeness and the perceived trustworthiness of the occupant of the office. Clearly, faculty members—and perhaps occupants of other types of offices as well—who wish to enhance their credibility should consider the potential benefits of displaying professionally related objects in their offices. Moreover, Teven and Comadena (1996) found that faculty who display professional objects in their offices are also judged as more credible during lectures in the classroom compared with faculty who have no objects placed in their offices.

FIGURE 15.3

Although both professionally related and aesthetic objects in the faculty office have a significant, positive impact on the perceived trustworthiness of the occupant of the faculty office, the impact of aesthetic objects is stronger. Such a finding may provide particular comfort to the individual who inspires little trust or to one who is widely mistrusted. In one sense, it serves to support the popular belief of image consultants that trustworthiness of a distrusted person may be more effectively enhanced by manipulating certain microenvironmental variables than by modifying the individual's communicative behaviors.

Past research has shown that source credibility may be a function of the source's appearance, reputation, organizational affiliation, or communicative behaviors. This research suggests that source credibility may also be affected by specific decorative objects placed in a person's office. Knowledge such as this should certainly be useful as we strive to communicate more successfully in applied settings.

The Fast-Food Restaurant Environment.   One distinctive microenvironment of undeniable importance to a large proportion of our population is the fast-food restaurant. Indeed, fast-food restaurants have become one of the most visible and pervasive social phenomena of our time. Nonetheless, the fast-food microenvironment has received little attention from communication scholars, a puzzling oversight for two reasons. First, design directors for the two major fast-food chains in the United States agree that the interior design of their restaurants is the major medium they use to communicate a desired corporate image to the public. Second, the physical features of the fast-food microenvironment are so distinctive that they should have a measurable impact on the communicative behaviors exhibited by customers.

In today's competitive restaurant industry, there is a continuous struggle to be number one in profit and sales. Although many types of restaurants still try to compete for business, the fast-food industry is now the dominant restaurant business in the United States. The fast-food industry, in turn, is dominated by McDonald's and Burger King.

Eaves and Leathers (1991) studied five suburban McDonald's and five suburban Burger King restaurants in the Atlanta area. We compared the customers observed in each of these two sets of five restaurants to determine whether there was a difference in their levels of *involvement* and *discomfort.* Behavioral indicators of involvement were smiling, amount of talking, head nodding, and leaning. Behavioral indicators of discomfort were fidgeting, extraneous foot movement, postural shifts, and side-to-side movement.

Our theoretical perspective led us to expect that McDonald's customers would be both more involved and more uncomfortable than Burger King customers. Our expectations were confirmed. McDonald's customers exhibited their greater involvement by smiling and talking significantly more than their counterparts at Burger King. Moreover, McDonald's customers exhibited their greater discomfort by fidgeting significantly more and by exhibiting a pattern of more extraneous foot movements, side-to-side movements, and postural shifts than Burger King customers. The obvious question is *why?* Our study indicates that one of the major determinants of the customers' behaviors was the distinctive but contrasting physical features of the microenvironments at McDonald's and at Burger King.

In terms of potential impact on customers' involvement and comfort levels, the most important design decisions seemed to be the size of the tables and chairs. This was so because the size of those furniture items in McDonald's and Burger King proved to be the most important factor influencing the spatial orientations of interacting customers. Certainly, the distance that separates two people can have a major impact on both their involvement and their comfort levels.

"Deucer" tables at McDonald's and Burger King are the same size: 21 in. by 24 in. The size and appearance of deucer seats are discernibly different, however. Burger King's deucer seat measures 18 1/2 in. wide by 17 in. long, whereas McDonald's deucer seat is 15 1/2 in. wide by 16 in. long. In Burger King's newest restaurants, the deucer seats are mounted to the floor via a steel arm, and they swivel both sideways and back and forth so that forward lean is facilitated. The deucer seats at Burger King sit well back from the table so that customers facing each other and sitting in upright positions will be separated (chest to chest) by a distance of 3 ft 5 in. In contrast, two people seated at a deucer at McDonald's with their feet under the table will be separated by no more than 2 ft 2 in.

The appearance of deucer table and chairs at the two fast-food restaurants is also notably different. Burger King uses wooden tables and chairs; McDonald's uses plastic in both. Because of their size and appearance, Burger King chairs and tables appear to be of higher quality and more comfortable. For example, a Burger King deucer chair has 11 supporting wooden spokes in the chair back; McDonald's deucer seats have five plastic spokes or strips for support in the chair back. Both authors experienced noticeable discomfort when seated at McDonald's deucer tables. The discomfort resulted because of the obviously small size of the seats and the inferior back support.

In addition to furniture, three other physical features of the microenvironments at McDonald's and Burger King seem to be particularly important: lighting, color choices, and mirrors and partitions. The contrast in lighting between McDonald's and Burger King is certainly an important feature of the microenvironment. Research on lighting in work spaces has shown that lighting is one of the most important factors contributing to the comfort of individuals who work there. In fact, studies of lighting in professional microenvironments indicate quite clearly that excessive illuminance may cause discomfort. Luminance is the apparent brightness of a surface and is the joint product of illuminance (light falling on the surface) and the surface reflectance (Ellis, 1986).

McDonald's, in contrast to Burger King, is intensely lighted on both the outside and the inside. During the observational phase of this study, a number of customers at McDonald's were observed complaining about the intense light that was attributable to numerous fluorescent lights and large windows, much larger than those at Burger King, and the lack of either shades or tinting; Burger King controls the intensity of lighting within their restaurants with both window shades and window tinting. McDonald's used fluorescent lighting in all the observed restaurants, whereas Burger King frequently used light bulbs with shades.

Color choices made by designers at McDonald's and Burger King are also quite different. McDonald's consistently opts for colors that are known to be stimulating and emotionally arousing (Smith & Malandro, 1985). On approach, a McDonald's restaurant stands out because of the "golden" (actually, yellow) arches that show McDonald's name displayed in white letters against a bright red background. In case this color combination is not enough to catch your attention, the American flag is conspicuously displayed in front. On the inside, McDonald's uses the same strong colors with eye-catching wallpaper hues of pure white and yellow. Burger King, in contrast, specializes in more subdued color combinations. Burger King frequently uses rustic colors in an apparent attempt to put customers at ease.

Both McDonald's and Burger King use mirrors and partitions. Mirrors are presumably used to create the illusion of greater space. McDonald's mirrors are often prominently placed in the main dining room or near the order-taking area. Mirrors are also used at Burger King, but less frequently and not usually in high-traffic areas.

Finally, both McDonald's and Burger King use some partitions. In McDonald's, partitions often seem to serve more of a symbolic than a functional purpose, in the sense that they might provide the customer with increased privacy. McDonald's uses wooden railings to separate one eating area from the other, but the railings are held up by see-through spokes that hardly serve as partitions. Thus, most of the customers in the main dining area have the opportunity to engage in direct visual inspection of most of the other customers. Furthermore, customers in McDonald's, in contrast to those in Burger King, can be directly and easily observed by passing motorists because McDonald's has large windows with no tinting or shades and the level of illumination inside is so high that little is concealed from the prying eye.

In a follow-up study, Eaves (2003) broadened the restaurant sample to include not only McDonald's and Burger King but also KFC and Taco Bell. Strikingly, the results indicated that Burger King customers were extremely similar to those customers at McDonald's: highly involved and most uncomfortable. Taco Bell customers also seemed to be behaving in a similar fashion, one characterized as a high-load environment. Interestingly, KFC customers exhibited the strongest comfort levels and this was an intuitive finding. KFC décor and interior design incorporate darker colors, use of more partitions and "private" space, and larger table tops for dining—all nonverbal factors a low-load environment one might expect to find in. Recent research suggests that ambient conditions can markedly influence customers in built environments. The use of color, music, and temperature can influence behaviors in these places and can positively affect the mood created by the space (Bitner, 1992). These fast-food chains use different colors and music to create certain moods for their dining customers, and therefore communicate a variety of messages.

Virtual Places

Of recent concern is the computer and Internet, or what we will call virtual places. Virtual places are Web pages, e-mail messages, chat rooms, or any place where online information or communication takes place. Eaves (2006) studied the dialogue that occurs in online poker tournaments, specifically on pokerstars.net. Many of the Web sites allow competitors to post photos of themselves to let others know what they look like. Even though some of the photos are clearly not the actual player, Eaves found that the nonverbal messages affected the game and often colored the type of dialogue that players were likely to use. In addition, other poker Web sites allow players to choose the type of avatar (such as fulltiltpoker.net), and depending on the result of the hand, players can make the avatar look happy, angry, confused, or calm. One poker Web site even allows players to see one another in three dimensions and choose from a myriad of nonverbal gestures, hand motions, and even "tells," or the specific nonverbal signals to indicate to other players the strength or weakness of your cards. Other research also points to the use of Web pages as a way to create identity for a virtual public.

Of the characters or players in the virtual community, one that is striking and has received attention in the literature is the energy creature. This person feeds off the negativity generated by other interactants—a person in a chat room, MySpace, or other virtual world who loves to use flaming rhetoric or vulgar speech. Some chat rooms have regulations about using vulgar speech and may sanction computer users who use improper language by restricting their chat prvileges (Rheingold, 2000). Of course, MySpace and Facebook can be just for networking and communicating with friends.

Another nonverbal expression in the virtual world is the representation of self through Web pages. Geocities, a Yahoo! community, is the largest provider of free Web hosting in the world with several million users who host using their server. Users are creative, with various links, photos, and expressions about themselves. Users are also unrestricted on the content or nonverbal displays of their Web material (Rheingold, 2000). Places on the Internet such as MySpace, Facebook, and the like, are ways that students can network with others. These pages are a way for students to express themselves, to show their creativity, and to create relationships with others (McKenna, Green, & Gleason, 2002).

One interesting feature of Web page development is the creation of an online identity. Stern (2004) suggests that there are significant gender differences between male and female Web pages. She notes that most of these differences are substantive in nature, not stylistic. In fact, Stern suggests that this form of media is an ideal way for teens to express themselves in both verbal and nonverbal ways. The photos and other artistic forms of public expressions are popular ways of communicating with others online. MySpace, Facebook, and Cyworld are all good examples of ways that college students are now expressing themselves in new ways to other students across the globe.

Other research points to other virtual networks that allow students to create identities and nonverbally express themselves. Use of creative e-mail systems, guest books, instant messaging, BlackBerrys, the iPhone and other technological vehicles allow students to network, form relationships, and create a tight community for sharing feelings, disclosing intimate details, and discussing general problems of life (Papacharissi, 2002). One study by Bortree (2005) examined teenage girls' use of Weblogs. She looked at the blogs of 40 teen girls: how they communicated and what self-presentation strategies they used to relate to their audience. Bortree found that Weblogs can represent a serious method of fostering interpersonal relations with others, especially for teen girls. Of special interest here is how these teen girls use self-presentational strategies online. Bortree noticed that many girls freely use advanced HTML and unique blog designs to create a nonverbal representation of themselves in cyberspace. Using graphics and visual enhancements helps to provide the identity of who they are and who they want to talk with in the virtual playground.

E-mail is another context where nonverbal elements or substitutes are being used to "humanize" this technically driven form of communication. Several recent studies have examined the impact of impression management strategies and quasi-nonverbal cues used in virtual contexts. Kimberly Carter (2003) writes in her article "Type Me How You Feel" that quasi-nonverbal cues are being used in chat rooms and e-mail communication to help users understand the feelings of the writer. She says that ambiguity is a common problem in all communication, including face-to-face interaction. The online communicator has to put forth special effort to reduce ambiguity and communicate one's true intentions with the online partner. In this way, since expectations are higher for the special context, nonverbal cues such as emoticons are often used, especially in e-mail, to communicate moods or feelings. In many chat rooms, photos or real-time pics can be used with the language so that users can see the writer's facial expressions at the time of the writing.

Virtual spaces and contexts are also being used in business to help market products and increase customer satisfaction. One recent study found that those businesses with e-scapes such as company Web sites improved overall customer satisfaction compared to companies who had no online services or poor online vehicles available to the customer. In addition, Web sites that have photos and pictures generally are preferred over Web sites that contain only information (Koernig, 2003). One good example of this is when hotel Web sites provide photo opportunities for customers to take a virtual tour to see the lobby, pool, room, lounge, restaurant, exercise room, or other amenities that are available.

Walther (1993) talks about impression development ideas in computer-mediated contexts. Such things as back channels during the conversation may contain emoticons that provide a rich listening atmosphere that is not always present in face-to-face communication. Furthermore, the use of "computer" handles, like in CB radio, provides a way for users to recognize or identify with the online communicator. As previously mentioned, MySpace and online poker tournaments are two good examples where users can be readily identified by their face or by their poker handle name.

In another study, Jacobson (1999) talks about impression management in virtual contexts. He says that online communication is all about inference making, and impression management is the ability to control those inferences that online users make about us. For example, you would want to have an attractive photo of yourself on Facebook to positively affect the impressions that people make about you. Jacobson also says that you can alter the capitalization of words to create a different impression. For instance, if you use all CAPS IN YOUR MESSAGE WITH SOMEONE ELSE, she or he might infer that you are yelling or screaming. A colleague of Eaves noticed that a staff member at our university communicates this way consistently. Whether intentional or not, that staff member may be perceived as a yeller and screamer to her faculty. Of course, there is the all-too-familiar smiley face that we can use at the end of e-mails, chats, and other online forms of communication. Many Web sites today offer countless facial expressions that you can use to communicate anger, sadness, joy, disappointment, anxiety, etc.

Summary

This chapter has looked at four nonverbal contexts: medical, legal, built, and virtual. The main theme behind each of these sections is that the context serves as communication—that there are unique nonverbal elements in each of these areas. It is important for the professional to realize his or her goal in creating the proper environmental effect upon the user, customer, client, or patient. As nonverbal scholars, we need to be able to identify elements in these contexts and discover ways to help the practitioner form the proper communication context for users of that space.

REFERENCES

Adelsward, V., Aronson, K., Jonsson, L., & Linell, P. (1987). The unequal distribution of interactional space: Dominance and control in courtroom interaction. *Text, 7,* 313–346.

Anthony, P. K., & Vinson, C. E. (1987). Nonverbal communication in the courtroom. You don't say? *Trial Diplomacy, 39,* 35–37.

Argyle, M., & Dean, J. (1965). Eye contact, distance, and affiliation. *Sociometry, 28,* 298–304.

Aron, R., Fast, J., & Klein, R. B. (1986). *Trial communication skills.* New York: McGraw-Hill.

Aron, R., Fast, J., & Klein, R. B. (1987 Supplement). *Trial communication skills.* New York: McGraw-Hill.

Baker, P. M. (1984). Seeing is behaving: Visibility and participation in small groups. *Environment and Behavior, 16,* 159–184.

Barge, J. K., Schlueter, D. W., & Pritchard, A. (1989). The effects of nonverbal communication and gender on impression formation in opening statements. *The Southern Communication Journal, 54,* 330–349.

Becker, F. D. (1981). *Workspace: Creating environments in organizations.* New York: Praeger.

Becker, F. D., Gield, B., & Froggatt, C. C. (1983). Seating position and impression management in an office setting. *Journal of Environmental Psychology, 3,* 253–261.

Beeghley, L., & Donnelly, D. (1989). The consequences of family crowding: A theoretical synthesis. *Lifestyles, 10,* 83–102.

Bellizzi, J. A., Crowley, A. E., & Hasty, R. W. (1983). The effects of color in store design. *Journal of Retailing, 59,* 21–45.

Bennett, C. E., & Hirschhorn, R. B. (1993). *Bennett's guide to jury selection and trial dynamics in civil and criminal litigation.* St. Paul, MN: West.

Bergin, K. A. (2006). Sex for sale: Sexualized advocacy: The ascendant backlash against female lawyers. *Yale Journal of Law and Feminism, 18,* 192–222.

Berry, D. (1992). Vocal types and stereotypes: Joint effect of vocal attractiveness and vocal maturity on person perception. *Journal of Nonverbal Behavior, 16,* 41–54.

Bitner, M. J. (1992). Servicescapes: The impact of physical surroundings on customers and employees. *Journal of Marketing, 56,* 57–71.

Blanck, P. D., Rosenthal, R., & Cordell, L. H. (1985). The appearance of justice: Judges' verbal and nonverbal behavior in criminal jury trials. *Stanford Law Review, 38,* 89–184.

Bloom, L. J., Weigel, R. G., & Traut, G. M. (1977). Therapeugenic factors in psychotherapy: Effects of office decor and subject–therapist sex pairing on perception of credibility. *Journal of Consulting and Clinical Psychology, 25,* 867–873.

Blumenthal, J. A. (1993). A lick of the lips: The validity of demeanor evidence in assessing witness credibility. *Nebraska Law Review, 72,* 1158–1204.

Boccaccini, M. T. (2002). What do we really know about witness preparation? *Behavioral Sciences and the Law, 20,* 161–189.

Bortree, D. S. (2005). Presenation of self on the web: An ethnographic study of teenage girls' weblogs. *Education, Communication & Information, 5,* 25–39.

Burgoon, J. K. (1978). A communication model of personal space violations: Explication and an initial test. *Human Communication Research, 4,* 129–142.

Burke, D. W., Ames, M. A., Etherington, R., & Pietsch, J. (1990). Effects of victim's and defendant's physical attractiveness on the perception of responsibility in an ambiguous domestic violence case. *Journal of Family Violence, 5,* 190–207.

Burnett, A., & Badzinski, D. M. (2005). Judge nonverbal communication on trial: Do mock trial jurors notice? *Journal of Communication, 55,* 209–224.

Caldwell, H. M., Perrin, L. T., Gabriel, R., & Gross, S. R. (2001). Primacy, recency, ethos, and pathos: Integrating principles of communication into the direct examination. *Notre Dame Law Review, 76,* 425–517.

Caris-Verhallen, W. M., Kerkstra, A., & Bensing, J. M. (1999). Non-verbal behaviour in nurse-elderly patient communication. *Journal of Advanced Nursing, 29,* 808–818.

Carpenter, T. (1994, November). The man behind the mask. *Esquire,* 84–100.

Carroll, S. M. (2004). Nonvocal ventilated patients' perceptions of being understood. *Western Journal of Nursing Research, 26,* 85–103.

Carter, K. (2003). Type me how you feel: Quasi-nonverbal cues in computer-mediated communication. *Etc., 60,* 29–39.

Chang, Y. (2003). *Who speaks next? Discourse structure as persuasion in Chinese criminal courts.* Paper presented at the annual meeting of the National Communication Association, Miami, FL.

Cheng, Y. C. (1994). Classroom environment and student affective performance: An effective profile. *Journal of Experimental Education, 62,* 221–239.

Cohen, E., & Cohen, A. (1983). *Planning the electric office.* New York: McGraw-Hill.

Collett, M. E., & Kovera, M. B. (2003). The effects of British and American trial procedures on the quality of juror decision-making. *Law and Human Behavior, 27,* 403–422.

Conlee, C. J., Olvera, J., & Vagim, N. N. (1993). The relationships among physician nonverbal immediacy and measures of patient satisfaction with physician care. *Communication Reports, 6,* 25–33.

Darby, B. W., & Jeffers, D. (1988). The effects of defendant and juror attractiveness on simulated

courtroom trial decisions. *Social Behavior and Personality, 16,* 39–50.

deTurck, M. A., & Goldhaber, G. M. (1988). Perjury and deceptive judgments: How the timing and modality of witness deception affects jurors' deceptive judgments. *Communication Quarterly, 36,* 276–289.

The double life of O. J. (1994, August 29). *Newsweek,* 43–49.

Doyle, W. (1977). The uses of nonverbal behavior: Toward an ecological model of classrooms. *Merrill-Palmer Quarterly, 23,* 179–192.

Eaves, M. H. (2003). *McDonald's versus Burger King: Twelve years later.* Paper presented at the annual convention of the National Communication Association, Miami, FL.

Eaves, M. H. (2006). *Online dialogue: An examination of communication in computer-mediated poker tournaments.* Paper presented at the annual convention of the Louisiana Communication Association, Lake Charles, LA.

Eaves, M. H., & Leathers, D. G. (1991). Context as communication: McDonald's vs. Burger King. *Journal of Applied Communication Research, 19,* 263–289.

Ellis, P. (1986). Functional, aesthetic, and symbolic aspects of office lighting. In J. D. Wineman (Ed.), *Behavioral issues in office design.* New York: Von Nostrand Reinhold.

Emling, S. (1995, August 27). Casket markups: 300%. *The Atlanta Journal/The Atlanta Constitution,* p. E4.

Enelow, A. J., & Swisher, S. N. (1986). *Interviewing and patient care* (3rd ed.). Oxford: Oxford University Press.

Frederick, J. T. (2005). *Mastering voir dire and jury selection.* (2nd ed.). New York: American Bar Association.

Frederikson, I., & Bull, P. (1992). An appraisal of the current status of communication skills training in British medical schools. *Social Science & Medicine, 34,* 515–522.

Green, C. S. (1975). The ecology of committees. *Environment and Behavior, 7,* 411–425.

Griffith, C. H., Wilson, J. F., Langer, S., & Haist, S. A. (2003). House staff nonverbal communication skills and standardized patient satisfaction. *Journal of General Internal Medicine, 18,* 170–174.

Hall, E. T. (1974). *Handbook for proxemic research.* Washington, DC: Society for Anthropology of Visual Communication.

Hall, J. A., Irish, J. T., Roter, D. L., Ehrlich, C. M., & Miller, L. H. (1994). Medical encounters: An analysis of physician and patient communication in a primary care setting. *Health Psychology, 13,* 384–392.

Hall, J. A., Roter, D. L., & Rand, C. S. (1981). Communication of affect between patient and physician. *Journal of Health and Social Behavior, 22,* 18–30.

Hanyu, K. (1993). The affective meaning of Tokyo: Verbal and non-verbal approaches. *Journal of Environmental Psychology, 13,* 161–172.

Hartje, R. (2005). A jury of your peers? How jury consulting may actually help trial lawyers resolve constitutional limitations imposed on the selection of juries. *California Western Law Review, 41,* 479–506.

Hasse, R. F., & DiMattia, D. J. (1976). Spatial environments and verbal conditioning in quasi-counseling interviews. *Journal of Counseling Psychology, 23,* 414–421.

Hasse, R. F., & Tepper, D. T., Jr. (1972). Nonverbal components of empathic communication. *Journal of Counseling Psychology, 19,* 417–424.

Heckel, R. V. (1973). Leadership and voluntary seating choice. *Psychological Reports, 32,* 141–142.

Heintzman, M., Leathers, D. G., Parrott, R. L., & Cairns, A. B., III. (1993). Nonverbal rapport-building behavior's effects on perceptions of a supervisor. *Management Communication Quarterly, 7,* 181–208.

Hestler, M. W. (1972). An investigation of instructor use of space. (Doctoral dissertation, Purdue University, 1972). *Dissertation Abstracts International, 33,* 3055A.

Hosman, L. (1989). The evaluative consequences of hedges, hesitations, and intensifiers: Power and powerless speech styles. *Human Communication Research, 15,* 383–406.

Howells, L. T., & Becker, S. W. (1962). Seating arrangement and leadership emergence. *Journal of Abnormal and Social Psychology, 64,* 148–149.

Hutson, M. (2007, April/March). Unnatural selection. *Psychology Today.* Retrieved from http://www.psychologytoday.com

Jacobson, D. (1999). Impression formation in cyberspace: Online expectations and offline experiences in text-based viutal communities. *Journal of Computer-Mediated Communication, 5,* 1–30.

Johnson, C., & Vinson, L. (1990). Placement and frequency of powerless talk and impression formation. *Communication Quarterly, 38,* 325–333.

Joiner, D. (1971). Office territory. *New Society, 7,* 660–663.

Kasmar, J. V., Griffin, W. F., & Mauritzen, J. H. (1976). The effects of environmental surroundings on out-patient's mood and perception of psychiatrists. *Journal of Consulting and Clinical Psychology, 32,* 223–226.

Kassin, S. M. (2002). Effective screening of truth telling: Is it possible? Human judges of truth, deception, credibility: Confident but erroneous. *Cardoza Law Review, 23,* 809–816.

Kleeman, W. B. (1981). The politics of office design. *Environment and Behavior, 20,* 537–549.

Kloer, P. (1994, July 2). 25 to 30 million watch TV hearing. *The Atlanta Journal/The Atlanta Constitution,* p. A12.

Knachstedt, M. V. (1980). *Interior design for profit.* New York: Kobro.

Koernig, S. K. (2003). E-scapes: The electronic physical environment and service tangibility. *Psychology & Marketing, 20,* 151–167.

Konar, E., & Sundstrom, E. (1986). Status demarcation and office design. In J. D. Wineman (Ed.), *Behavioral issues in office design* (pp. 203–233). New York: Von Nostrand Reinhold.

Korda, M. (1975). *Power! How to get it, how to use it.* New York: Random.

Kreps, G. L., & Thornton, B. C. (1992). *Health communication: Theory & practice.* Prospect Heights, IL: Waveland.

Leathers, D. G. (1990). The dynamics of impression management in the sales interview. In D. O'Hair & G. L. Kreps (Eds.), *Applied communication theory and research* (pp. 163–183). Hillsdale, NJ: Erlbaum.

Leathers, D. G. (1996). Impression management mismatch on Capitol Hill: The Anita Hill–Clarence Thomas confrontation. In S. Ragan, C. Beck, L. L. Kaid, & D. Bystrom (Eds.), *The lynching of language: Gender, politics, and power in the Hill–Thomas hearings* (pp. 84–110). Champaign: University of Illinois Press.

Lecuyer, R. (1976). Social organization and spatial organization. *Human Relations, 29,* 1045–1060.

Lee, J. (2000). 10 ways to communicate better with patients. *Review of Ophthamology, 7,* 38–42.

Levan, E. A. (1984). Nonverbal communication in the courtroom: Attorney beware. *Law and Psychology Review, 8,* 83–94.

Levine, D. W., O'Neal, E. C., Garwood, G. S., & McDonald, P. J. (1980). Classroom ecology: The effects of seating position and grades on participation. *Personality and Social Psychology Bulletin, 6,* 409–412.

Lynch, K. (1960). *The image of the city.* Cambridge, MA: Massachusetts Institute of Technology Press.

McKenna, K. Y. A., Green, A. S., & Gleason, M. E. J. (2002). Relationship formation on the Internet: What's the big attraction. *Journal of Social Issues, 58,* 9–31.

Maslow, A. H., & Mintz, N. W. (1956). Effects of aesthetic surroundings: I. Initial effects of three aesthetics conditions upon perceiving energy and well-being in faces. *Journal of Psychology, 41,* 247–254.

Mehrabian, A. (1968). Relationship of attitude to seated posture, orientation, and distance. *Journal of Personality and Social Psychology, 10,* 26–30.

Mehrabian, A. (1969). Some referents and measure of nonverbal behavior. *Behavior Research Methods and Instrumentation, 1,* 203–207.

Mehrabian, A. (1976). *Public places and private spaces.* New York: Basic.

Mehrabian, A., & Diamond, S. G. (1971). Effects of furniture arrangement, props, and personality on social interaction. *Journal of Personality and Social Psychology, 20,* 18–30.

Miles, E. W., & Leathers, D. G. (1984). The impact of aesthetic and professionally related objects on credibility in the office setting. *The Southern Speech Communication Journal, 49,* 361–379.

Nadelson, C. C. (1994). Health care: Is society empathic with women? *The empathic practitioner* (189–204). New Brunswick, NJ: Rutgers University Press.

News of the market. (2004, November 22). *MediaWeek, 14.*

Northouse, P. G., & Northouse, L. L. (1998). *Health communication: Strategies for health professionals* (3rd ed.). Upper Saddle River, NJ: Pearson Education.

Papacharissi, Z. (2002). The presentation of self in virtual life: Characteristics of personal home pages. *Journalism & Mass Communication Quarterly, 79,* 643–660.

Patterson, M. L., Kelly, C. W., Kondracki, B. A., & Wulf, L. J. (1979). Effects of seating arrangement on small group behavior. *Social Psychology Quarterly, 42,* 180–185.

Paulsel, M. L., Richmond, V. P., McCroskey, J. C., & Cayanus, J. L. (2005). The relationships of perceived health professionals' communication traits and credibility with perceived patient confidentiality. *Communication Research Reports, 22,* 129–142.

Pelligrini, R. J. (1971). Some effects of seating position on social perception. *Psychological Reports, 28,* 887–893.

Pettus, A. B. (1990). The verdict is in: A study of jury decision-making factors, moment of personal decision, and jury deliberations—from the juror's point of view. *Communication Quarterly, 38,* 83–97.

Pile, J. (1979). *Decorating your office for success.* New York: Harper & Row.

Preston, P. (2005a). Nonverbal communication: Do you really say what you mean? *Journal of Healthcare Management, 50,* 83–86.

Preston, P. (2005b). Proxemics in clinical and administrative settings. *Journal of Healthcare Management, 50,* 151–154.

Preston, P., & Quesda, A. (1974). What does your office say about you? *Supervisory Management, 19,* 28–34.

Pryor, B., & Buchanan, R. (1984). The effects of a defendant's demeanor on your perception of credibility and guilt. *Journal of Communication, 34,* 92–99.

Rapoport, A. (1982). *The meaning of the built environment: A nonverbal communication approach.* Beverly Hills, CA: Sage.

Rasicot, J. (1985). *Jury selection, body language & the visual trial.* Minneapolis, MN: AB Publications.

Resnick, F. D. (1994). *Nicole Brown Simpson: The private diary of a life interrupted.* Beverly Hills, CA: Dove.

Rheingold, H. (2000). *The virtual community.* Cambridge, MA: The MIT Press.

Rieke, R. D., & Stutman, R. (1990). *Communication in legal advocacy.* Columbia: University of South Carolina Press.

The road to Panama City: How a jury consultant got O. J. back on the first tee. (1995, October 30). *Newsweek.*

Robinson, J. D. (1998). Getting down to business: Talk, gaze, and body orientation during the openings of doctor-patient consultations. *Human Communication Research, 25,* 97–123.

Rosenthal, R. (2002). Covert communication in classrooms, clinics, courtrooms, and cubicles. *American Psychologist, 57,* 839–849.

Roulidis, Z. D., & Schulman, K. A. (1994). Physician communication in managed care organizations: Opinions of primary care physicians. *Journal of Family Practice, 39,* 446–451.

Rowland-Morin, P. A., Burchard, K. W., Garb, J. L., & Coe, N. P. (1991). Influence of effective communication by surgery students on their oral examination scores. *Academic Medicine, 66,* 169–171.

Rubin, G. N. (1972). A naturalistic study in proxemics: Seating arrangement and its effect on interaction, performance, and behavior (Doctoral dissertation, Bowling Green State University, 1972). *Dissertation Abstracts International, 33,* 3829A.

Ryan, H. (2004, November 17). As Peterson's lawyer prepares for penalty phase, he also faces ethics attack. *Court TV News.* Retrieved from http://www.courttvnews.com

Ryan, M. E., & Syald, D. (1993). Women in the courtroom: Increasing credibility through nonverbal behavior change. *Trial Diplomacy Journal, 16,* 253–258.

Samovar, L. A., Porter, R. E., & McDaniel, E. R. (2007). *Communication between cultures.* Belmont, CA: Thomson-Wadsworth.

Scherer, K. R. (1988). On the symbolic functions of vocal affect expression. *Journal of Language & Social Psychology, 7,* 79–100.

Searcy, M., Duck, S., & Blanck, P. (2005). Communication in the courtroom and the appearance of justice. In R. E. Riggio & R. S. Feldman (Eds.), *Applications of nonverbal communication* (pp. 41–61). Mahwah, NJ: Lawrence Erlbaum.

Shaw, M. E. (1981). *Group dynamics: The psychology of small group behavior* (3rd ed.). New York: McGraw-Hill.

Sigal, J., Braden-Maguire, J., Hayden, J., & Mosley, N. (1985). The effects of presentation style and sex of lawyer on jury decision-making behavior. *Psychology, 22,* 13–19.

Smith, L. J., & Malandro, L. A. (1985). *Courtroom communication strategies.* New York: Kluwer.

Smolow, J. (1991, October 21). She said, he said. *Time,* 36–40.

Sommer, R. (1961). Leadership and group geography. *Sociometry, 24,* 99–110.

Sommer, R. (1962). The distance for comfortable conversation. *Sociometry, 25,* 111–116.

Sommer, R. (1966). Man's proximate environment. *Journal of Social Issues, 22,* 59–70.

Sommer, R. (1969). *Personal space: The behavioral basis of design.* Englewood Cliffs, NJ: Prentice-Hall.

Sommer, R. (1974). *Tight spaces: Hard architecture and how to humanize it.* Englewood Cliffs, NJ: Prentice-Hall.

Sommer, R. (1983). *Social design: Creating buildings with people in mind.* Englewood Cliffs, NJ: Prentice-Hall.

Sommer, R., & Ross, H. (1958). Social interaction in a geriatrics ward. *International Journal of Social Psychiatry, 4,* 128–133.

Sommer, R., Wynes, M., & Brinkley, G. (1992). Social facilitation effects in shopping behavior. *Environment & Behavior, 24,* 285–297.

Stacks, E. W., & Burgoon, J. K. (1981). The role of nonverbal behaviors as distractors in resistance to persuasion in interpersonal contexts. *Central States Speech Journal, 32,* 61–73.

Stern, S. R. (2004). Expressions of identity online: Prominent features and gender differences in adolescents' world wide web home pages. *Journal of Broadcasting & Electronic Media, 48,* 218–243.

Stewart, M., & Roter, D. (1989). Introduction. In M. Stewart & D. Roter (Eds.), *Communicating with medical patients* (pp. 17–23). Newbury Park, CA: Sage.

Street, R. L. (1990). Dentist–patient communication: A review and commentary. In D. O'Hair & G. L. Kreps (Eds.), *Applied communication theory and research* (pp. 331–351). Hillsdale, NJ: Lawrence Erlbaum.

Street, R. L., & Buller, D. B. (1987). Nonverbal response patterns in physician–patient interactions: A functional analysis. *Journal of Nonverbal Behavior, 11,* 234–253.

Strodbeck, F. L., & Hook, L. H. (1961). The social dimensions of a twelve-man jury table. *Sociometry, 24,* 397–415.

Sundstrom, E. (1989). *Work places: The psychology of the physical environment in offices and factories.* Cambridge: Cambridge University Press.

Sundstrom, E., Town, J., Rice, R. W., & Osborn, D. P. (1994). Office noise, satisfaction, and performance. *Environment & Behavior, 26,* 195–222.

Teven, J. J., & Comadena, M. E. (1996). The effects of office aesthetic quality on students' perceptions of teacher credibility and communicator style. *Communication Research Reports, 13,* 101–108.

Varinsky, H., & Nomikos, L. (1990). Post-verdict interviews: Understanding jury decision making. *Trial, 26,* 64–66.

Vinson, D. E. (1982). Juries: Perception and the decision-making process. *Trial, 18,* 52–55.

Walther, J. B. (1993). Impression development in computer-mediated interaction. *Western Journal of Communication, 57,* 381–398.

Weldon, D. W., Loewy, J. H., Winer, J. I., & Elkin, D. J. (1981). Crowding and classroom learning. *Journal of Experimental Education, 49,* 160–176.

White, A. G. (1953). The patient sits down. *Psychosomatic Medicine, 15,* 256–257.

Widgery, R., & Stackpole, C. (1972). Desk position, interviewee anxiety, and interviewer credibility. *Journal of Counseling Psychology, 19,* 173–177.

Wineman, J. P. (Ed.). (1986). *Behavioral issues in office design.* New York: Van Nostrand Reinhold.

Wolfe, A. M. D., Ingelfinger, J. A., & Schmitz, S. (1994). Emphasizing attitudes toward the doctor–patient relationship in medical education. *Academic Medicine, 69,* 895–896.

Wolfe, J. S. (1985). Courtroom choreography: Systematic use of the courtroom. *Trial Diplomacy Journal,* 28–36.

Wong, C. Y., Sommer, R., & Cook, E. J. (1992). The soft classroom 17 years later. *Journal of Environmental Psychology, 12,* 337–343.

Wood, W. R. (1985). Preparation for voir dire. *Trial, 8,* 17–19.

Wuensch, K. L., Castellow, W. A., & Moore, C. H. (1991). Defendant attractiveness and type of crime on juridic judgment. *Journal of Social Behavior and Personality, 6,* 713–724.

Wulf, K. M. (1977). Relationship of assigned classroom seating area to achievement variables. *Educational Research Quarterly, 2,* 56–62.

Yee, R., & Gustafson, K. (1983). *Corporate design.* New York: Whitney Communications Corporation.

Zuckerman, M., & Driver, R. D. (1989). What sounds beautiful is good: The vocal attractiveness stereotype. *Journal of Nonverbal Behavior, 13,* 67–82.

Key to the Matching Test in Chapter 7

A–7

B–5

C–1

D–9

E–4

F–2

G–3

H–6

I–8

NAME INDEX

SUBJECT INDEX